# DEPRIVATION OF LI

Other titles available from Law Society Publishing:

**Elderly Client Handbook** (5th edn)
General editor: Caroline Bielanska

**Health and Social Care Handbook**
Caroline Bielanska with Fiona Scolding

**Lasting Powers of Attorney: A Practical Guide** (2nd edn)
Craig Ward

**Mental Capacity: A Guide to the New Law** (2nd edn)
Nicola Greaney, Fenella Morris and Beverley Taylor

Titles from Law Society Publishing can be ordered from all good bookshops or direct (telephone 0870 850 1422, email **lawsociety@prolog.uk.com** or visit our online shop at **www.lawsociety.org.uk/bookshop**).

# DEPRIVATION OF LIBERTY

## Collected Guidance

*The Law Society*

The Law Society

Appendix C5 is reproduced with the kind permission of the Association of Directors of Adult Social Services (© 2014).
Appendix C6 is reproduced with the kind permission of the Intensive Care Society (© 2014).
Appendix C13 is reproduced with the kind permission of the Care Quality Commission (© 2014).
Crown copyright material in Appendices C1–4 and C7–12 is reproduced with the permission of the Controller of Her Majesty's Stationery Office.

ISBN-13: 978-1-78446-043-3

Published in 2016 by the Law Society
113 Chancery Lane, London WC2A 1PL

Typeset by Columns Design XML Ltd, Reading
Printed by TJ International Ltd, Padstow, Cornwall

The paper used for the text pages of this book is FSC® certified. FSC (the Forest Stewardship Council®) is an international network to promote responsible management of the world's forests.

FSC
www.fsc.org
MIX
Paper from
responsible sources
FSC® C013056

# CONTENTS

# [A] IDENTIFYING A DEPRIVATION OF LIBERTY: A PRACTICAL GUIDE

*This guidance does not constitute legal advice, which must be sought – if necessary – on the facts of any specific individual case. While care has been taken to ensure the guidance is accurate, up to date and useful, no legal liability will be accepted in relation to it.*

## EXECUTIVE SUMMARY

There are many people in different settings who are deprived of their liberty by virtue of the type of care or treatment that they are receiving, or the level of restrictive practices that they are subject to, but they cannot consent to it because they lack the mental capacity to do so. In March 2014, the Supreme Court handed down judgment in two cases: *P v Cheshire West and Chester Council and P & Q v Surrey County Council* [2014] UKSC 19. That judgment, commonly known as *Cheshire West*, has led to a considerable increase in the numbers of people in England and Wales who are considered to be 'deprived' of their liberty for the purposes of receiving care and treatment. The judgment also emphasised the importance of identifying those who are deprived of their liberty so that their circumstances can be the subject of regular independent checks to ensure that decisions being made about them are actually being made in their best interests.

The Department of Health commissioned guidance to assist those professionals most directly concerned with commissioning, implementation and oversight of arrangements for the care and treatment of individuals who may lack the capacity to consent to such arrangements. Its purpose is to provide practical assistance in identifying whether they are deprived of their liberty, and hence to ensure that appropriate steps can be taken to secure their rights under Article 5 of the European Convention on Human Rights ('ECHR'). It serves – in some ways – as an informal update to Chapter 2 of the DOLS Code of Practice, although it does not have the same statutory status, and the views expressed in it are those of the authors rather than representing Department of Health policy. It does not constitute formal legal advice, which should always be sought where necessary on the facts of difficult cases.

This guidance is not a panacea for Article 5 ECHR: there are a number of important limitations. First, it relates only to those who lack the mental capacity to consent to their residential and care arrangements: it does not cover situations where those with capacity are objecting to the same. Second, those of any age could potentially be deprived of their liberty; however, this guidance focuses solely on those aged 16 and over because that is the minimum age at which the Court of Protection can authorise a deprivation of liberty. Third, its principal aim is to assist in identifying a deprivation: it does not address in detail how that deprivation ought to be authorised. Nor does the guidance consider the law regarding the challenging of a deprivation of liberty under Article 5(4) ECHR; resources addressing that question can be found in Chapter 11.

The guidance starts in Part I with an overview of the legal framework and of the key legal questions that must now be asked following the decision of the Supreme Court. Part II is the heart of the guidance, applying the legal principles across the following settings: the hospital setting, the psychiatric setting, the care home setting, supported living/shared lives/extra care, at home, and in relation to those aged 16 and 17. Where relevant, the guidance identifies particular sub-divisions within the care setting covered in the chapter (for instance, Accident and Emergency departments and Intensive Care Units within the hospital setting).

For each setting or sub-category, a list of potentially 'liberty-restricting' factors are given that may indicate that a deprivation of liberty is occurring; three scenarios are also given, one illustrating a deprivation of liberty, one a potential deprivation of liberty depending on the circumstances, and one a situation unlikely to amount to a deprivation of liberty. Each chapter then concludes with a list of questions that professionals may want to ask themselves whenever they are confronted with a situation which may amount to a deprivation of liberty. Each chapter can be downloaded separately, as can the list of questions for that chapter, so professionals need only have with them those parts of the guidance that are most relevant to the circumstances they are likely to encounter.

In Part III is to be found summaries of key cases (including those which must in light of *Cheshire West* be read with a health warning) and further information and resources for those needing to keep themselves abreast of developments. The law is stated as at the end of February 2015.

Given that there remain a significant number of areas in which the law has yet to be clarified by the courts, this guidance serves as much to provoke professionals to seek further specific advice in difficult cases as it does to give answers. It will, inevitably, be superseded in due course by further judgments of the court but will at least provide a starting point to assist professionals to ask the right questions.

## ABBREVIATIONS

We use the following abbreviations in this guidance:

| Abbreviation | Definition |
| --- | --- |
| A&E | Accident and Emergency |
| ATUs | Assessment and Treatment Units |
| CAMHS | Children and Adolescent Mental Health Services |
| CCG | Clinical Commissioning Group |
| *Cheshire West* | The judgment of the Supreme Court in *P v Cheshire West and Chester Council and P & Q v Surrey County Council* [2014] UKSC 19 |
| CPN | Community Psychiatrist Nurse |
| CQC | Care Quality Commission |
| CSSIW | Care and Social Services Inspectorate Wales |
| CTO | Community Treatment Order |
| DDA | Disability Discrimination Act 1995 |
| DOLS | The deprivation of liberty safeguards regime introduced by Schedule A1 to the MCA 2005 |
| DOLS Code | The Code of Practice accompanying Schedule A1 to the MCA 2005 |
| ECHR | European Convention on Human Rights |
| ECtHR | The European Court of Human Rights |
| IMA | Independent Mental Capacity Advocate |
| ICU | Intensive Care Unit |
| LPA | Lasting Power of Attorney |
| MCA 2005 | Mental Capacity Act 2005 |
| MHA 1983 | Mental Health Act 1983 |
| RPR | Relevant Person's Representative |

# I

# OVERVIEW

## 1 INTRODUCTION

**1.1** There are many people in different settings who are deprived of their liberty by virtue of the type of care or treatment that they are receiving, or the level of restrictive practices that they are subject to, but they cannot consent to it because they lack the mental capacity to do so. In most cases, the care and treatment is necessary and is being delivered in their best interests even though it amounts to a deprivation of liberty. The Deprivation of Liberty Safeguards ('DOLS') were brought into force in April 2009 to ensure that professionals applied checks and balances when they had to deprive people lacking capacity of their liberty.

**1.2** The State is under an obligation to make sure that where deprivation of liberty is delivered by social care or health care professionals, who are in law treated as 'State agents,' that there is lawful authority for that deprivation. Such authority is required to comply with Article 5(1) of the European Convention on Human Rights ('ECHR'), made part of English law by s.6 Human Rights Act 1998, which places strict limits upon the circumstances under which individuals can be deprived of their liberty.

**1.3** In March 2014, the Supreme Court handed down judgment in two cases: *P v Cheshire West and Chester Council and P & Q v Surrey County Council.*[1] That judgment, commonly known as *Cheshire West*, has led to a considerable increase in the numbers of people in England and Wales who are considered to be deprived of their liberty for the purposes of receiving care and treatment. The Supreme Court decided that when an individual lacking capacity was under continuous or complete supervision and control **and** was not free to leave, they were being deprived of their liberty. This is now commonly called the '**acid test**.'[2]

**1.4** Thus, after reviewing the restrictions on an individual, and if those restrictions amount to a deprivation of liberty, authority must be sought. Depending on the circumstances, that may be by way of a DOLS authorisation, under the Mental Health Act 1983, or by way of a court order.

**1.5** This guidance was commissioned by the Department of Health to assist those professionals most directly concerned with commissioning, implementation and oversight of arrangements for care and treatment of individuals who may lack the capacity to consent to such arrangement. Its purpose is to provide practical assistance in identifying whether they are deprived of their liberty, and hence to ensure that appropriate steps can be taken to secure their rights under Article 5 ECHR.

1.6    To that end, the guidance seeks to draw together the assistance that can be found from the case law decided to date and from the practical experience of the authors, who are all lawyers who (in different contexts) advise upon and act in cases involving questions of deprivation of the liberty. The authors particularly wish to thank the members of the formal practitioner group who provided detailed and helpful assistance at stages in its production, as well as a number of other individuals who provided ad hoc input.[3]

1.7    Whilst the guidance was commissioned by the Department of Health, it does not represent a statement of Department of Health policy, but rather the views of the authors.

## A    Audience for the guidance

1.8    Whilst we anticipate that some of those who will read the guidance will be legally qualified, the primary audience are frontline social and health professionals who need to be able to weigh up whether an individual they are concerned with may be deprived of their liberty and then to take appropriate action. To that end, its primary focus is upon the practical application of the legal principles in the most common care and treatment settings in which questions of deprivation of liberty are likely to arise.

1.9    This guidance can be seen as an informal update to Chapter 2 of the Code of Practice accompanying Schedule A1 to the MCA 2005 (often called the 'DOLS Code'[4]). However, this guidance (unlike the DOLS Code) does not have a statutory basis and professionals do not therefore have to have regard to it in the same way as they do the DOLS Code.[5]

## B    Outline of the guidance

1.10    The guidance is divided into chapters as follows:

**Part I: Overview**
Chapter 1: Introduction
Chapter 2: The law
Chapter 3: Key questions after *Cheshire West*

**Part II: Specific settings**
Chapter 4: The hospital setting
Chapter 5: The psychiatric setting

**1.11** Throughout the guidance, we provide hyperlinks to freely available transcripts of the case law to which we refer, as well as other relevant materials.


## C   How to use this guidance

**1.12** As discussed in more detail in Chapter 2, there is no statutory definition of a deprivation of liberty and so professionals must look to the DOLS Code of Practice, case law since the Code was introduced and this guidance as to what circumstances amount to a deprivation of liberty. Ultimately if professionals and their lawyers cannot agree upon whether a deprivation of liberty is occurring for a particular individual, it would be for a court to determine the matter. At the time of writing this guidance, however, the courts have not yet decided upon how the 'acid test' applies to all the contexts with which health or social care professionals may be concerned.[6]

**1.13** It is the gap between the decisions of the courts to date and the practical circumstances facing professionals on the ground which this guidance seeks to fill, but it is important that those referring to this guidance are clear as to how it is to be used.

**1.14** In Part II, we detail the most common settings in which a deprivation of liberty may occur. For each, we:

**1.14.1**   Identify a number of factors that may point towards there being a deprivation of liberty. After careful consideration, we have decided that it is not helpful to seek to break these down further to address specific elements of the 'acid test' identified in *Cheshire West*, (continuous or complete supervision and control and lack of freedom to leave) but there will be some which go more obviously to one or other limb of the test. We call these factors 'liberty-restricting measures'. They are practices that social workers or healthcare staff may or may not normally consider to be restrictive.

**1.14.2**   Suggest a scenario which we consider is very likely to amount to a deprivation of liberty; a scenario which we consider may amount to a deprivation of liberty; and a scenario (if they exist in any given setting) in which it is likely that the restrictions will not amount to a deprivation of the individual's liberty. We highlight after each the key factors underlining our thinking. Each scenario is fictitious, as are the names of the individuals used, although some of them are based upon actual cases decided by the courts (and where they are, we make this clear).

1.14.3    Pose a number of questions that professionals can ask to identify which side of the line a specific situation confronting them may fall.

1.15    It is important to emphasise that:

1.15.1    The test for considering whether to engage the DOLS process, the MHA 1983 or go to the Court of Protection is never whether the professional is **certain** that there is a deprivation of liberty, but rather there is a **risk** of a deprivation of liberty.[7] If there is such a risk, that should trigger further assessment.

1.15.2    Where a scenario is not based upon the facts of a particular case decided by the courts, it cannot be a substitute for a court decision upon similar facts.

1.15.3    It may well be that some of the scenarios that we outline provoke debate and discussion amongst frontline professionals – especially those we identify as being a potential deprivation of liberty. If nothing else, this means that if professionals come across similar facts they should stop and think very carefully about whether they are confident about whether they represent a deprivation of liberty or not (and, if necessary, seek legal advice).

1.15.4    The lists of factors that we identify in each chapter **are not** to be taken as a checklist to be applied mechanically. In some cases, the presence of one factor will be sufficient to indicate that the individual is likely to be deprived of their liberty. In others, several of the factors may be present but the individual may still only be subject to a restriction, rather than a deprivation of liberty, of their liberty. The factors – together with the questions we suggest – are set out to assist in the process of determining whether an individual is or is not deprived of their liberty, a process which ultimately relies upon the application of judgment by the professional(s) concerned.

## D    Limits of the guidance

1.16    In addition to the limitations set out immediately above, we make clear that:

1.16.1    The guidance does not provide detailed answers to the question of what should happen where a deprivation of liberty has been identified. A short answer is set out at paragraphs 2.41 to 2.43, but it is outside the scope of this guidance to provide detailed answers, which will depend upon the precise circumstances in which the deprivation of liberty has arisen. Professionals should note that the Law Commission is currently examining the question of how deprivation of liberty in the context of the delivery of care and treatment should best be regulated and authorised. It is anticipated that a consultation paper will be forthcoming in the summer of 2015 and a final report (and draft legislation) in the summer of 2017.[8]

1.16.2 This guidance is primarily addressed to the position in England and Wales: the considerations that arise in respect of Northern Ireland and Scotland, in particular in relation to the authorisation of deprivation of liberty,[9] are sufficiently different that space precludes consideration of these jurisdictions. It may nonetheless be useful for frontline professionals confronted with the same questions as their counterparts in England and Wales.

1.16.3 For the reasons discussed at the start of Chapter 9, this guidance is deliberately limited in respect of those under 18 to 16- and 17-year-olds lacking capacity to take the material decisions.

1.16.4 This guidance does not constitute legal advice, which must be sought – if necessary – on the facts of any specific individual case.

## E   The bigger picture

1.17   There are three crucial ways in which this guidance needs to be seen as part of the bigger picture.

### Why are we concerned about deprivation of liberty?

1.18   In order to understand why deprivation of liberty is only part of a bigger picture, it is important to stop and ask **why** we are concerned about whether a person is deprived of their liberty?

1.19   As important as the procedural steps required to authorise a deprivation of liberty are (including the right to challenge that deprivation of liberty),[10] it is almost more important in this context to remember that professionals are working with individuals who cannot take decisions about some of the most fundamental issues in their lives. Because such decisions are taken by others, these individuals are extremely vulnerable.[11] Therefore professionals must focus on whether the **whole care and/or treatment package** is in the best interests of the person who cannot consent to it because they lack the capacity to do so. In other words, the starting point must be a consideration of whether the arrangements made for them – their placement and the care and/or treatment plan around them – are in their best interests having regard to less restrictive alternatives. This represents – or should represent – no change to the normal approach adopted by health and social care professionals to the delivery of care and treatment of those without capacity.

1.20   In some circumstances that placement and those arrangements may amount to a deprivation of the person's liberty. If so, then professionals must seek authority for that deprivation. That they must do so – we emphasise – is not a reflection of anything 'wrong' being done by the professionals in terms of the delivery of care or treatment, but rather the proper operation of the law.

*Deprivation of liberty is not the only issue*

**1.21**    Many individuals whose situations may amount to a deprivation of liberty will also have decisions made for them by professionals about important aspects of their lives. Those decisions may or may not relate to steps amounting to a deprivation of liberty but are very likely to involve decisions that relate to the person's private and family life.

**1.22**    Respect for private and family life, one's home and correspondence, is a right guaranteed by Article 8 ECHR. Where the decisions do interfere with Article 8, (contact with family being the most obvious example), they can only be justified if they are necessary and proportionate and addressed to the individual's specific situation rather than – for instance – to assist the easier management of the placement.

**1.23**    Professionals must also appreciate that decisions as to whether to prevent or control a person's contact with others have a greater impact on that person when they are also deprived of their liberty. The European Court of Human Rights ('ECtHR') has emphasised how much more personal autonomy means for those who are the subject of 'authorised' deprivations of liberty.[12]

**1.24**    Further, professionals should always remember that authority to deprive someone of their liberty does not, itself, provide authority to provide care and treatment to them. If a person does not have capacity to consent to take decisions in this regard, then it will always be necessary to consider the basis upon which those decisions are being taken by others and their authority for doing so which, will, in general terms, be:

**1.24.1**    on the basis of the provisions of ss.5-6 MCA 2005,[13] in terms of the delivery of 'routine' care and treatment;

**1.24.2**    on the basis of a court order, where the care and treatment goes beyond the 'routine';

**1.24.3**    in some circumstances, on the basis of the provisions of Part IV of the Mental Health Act 1983 (but only ever in relation to the provision of medical treatment related to the individual's mental disorder).

**1.25**    In other words, no one should assume that just because the deprivation of liberty is authorised that this is the end of the story for that individual.

*The need for a plan*

**1.26**    As noted above, this guidance does not seek to answer the question of what individuals, organisations and public bodies are to do when there is a deprivation of liberty. However, we conclude this introductory chapter by emphasising the importance of organisations and public bodies having in place proper policies and procedures both to enable staff to identify when a deprivation of liberty may arise[14] and what they are meant to do if it does. Only if such policies are in place can frontline professionals get on with their primary task of making arrangements and caring for individuals, confident that they know what to do if those arrangements and that care amount to a deprivation of liberty.

## Endnotes

1   [2014] UKSC 19
2   Because Lady Hale, at paragraph 48 of the judgment, started her analysis by asking: '[s]o is there an acid test for the deprivation of liberty in these cases?'
3   Full details of the authors, the practitioner group and other acknowledgments can be found in the Appendix.
4   Available at **webarchive.nationalarchives.gov.uk/20130107105354/http://www.dh.gov.uk/ prod–consum–dh/groups/dh–digitalassets/@dh/@en/documents/digitalasset/dh–087309.pdf**
5   The status of Chapter 2 of the DOLS Code and the way in which it is to be read in light of subsequent developments is discussed in more detail at paragraphs 2.59 and 2.61.
6   The guidance is based upon the law as it stands in February 2015; at Chapter 11 we provide useful resources which can be used to keep up to date.
7   See *AM v. South London and Maudsley NHS Trust* [2013] UKUT 0365 (AAC): '... the DOLS regime ... applies when it appears that judged objectively there is a risk that cannot sensibly be ignored that the relevant circumstances amount to a deprivation of liberty' (para.59).
8   For more detail, see **lawcommission.justice.gov.uk/areas/capacity-and-detention.htm**.
9   For an overview in the context of proposals to amend the relevant legislation in Scotland, see **www.scotlawcom.gov.uk/law-reform-projects/ adults-with-incapacity**.
10  See further paragraph 2.10.
11  See paragraph 57 of the judgment in *Cheshire West*.
12  See *Munjaz v. United Kingdom* [2012] ECHR 1704 at paragraph 80, in the context of detention under the Mental Health Act 1983.
13  Which serve – in essence – to protect those delivering care and treatment from legal liability if they reasonably consider that the person in question lacks the capacity in relation to the relevant matter and that they are acting in the person's best interests.
14  Which may well include a specific indication as to what the particular organisation considers amounts to a 'non-negligible' period of time: see further paragraphs 3.29-3.32.

## 2   THE LAW

## A   Introduction

**2.1**   This chapter will be of use to professionals who need to have a detailed understanding of the legal framework that governs deprivation of liberty. It is likely to contain more detail than is required for professionals who need to decide on a day-to-day basis whether those to whom they are delivering (or arranging) care and treatment are deprived of their liberty; such professionals are likely to find it more useful to go straight to Chapter 3 which specifically addresses the 'acid test' identified in *Cheshire West* and its application.

**2.2**   In this chapter, we outline, first, the central principles of Article 5 ECHR; then summarise the key elements of the *Cheshire West* decision; outline (briefly) the authorisation of deprivation of liberty and the consequences of **not** getting appropriate authorisation; address the somewhat different legal issues that arise in the case of 'private' deprivations of liberty; and, finally, conclude with a short note on the status of the Code of Practice accompanying Schedule A1 to the MCA 2005 (often called the 'DOLS Code'[1]).

**2.3**    Since its amendment by the Mental Health Act 2007,[2] the MCA 2005 provides the primary vehicle through which the deprivation of liberty of those lacking capacity to consent to their care and treatment is authorised.[3] This is done primarily by the introduction of the Deprivation of Liberty Safeguards regime which is contained in Schedule A1 of the MCA 2005 as amended.[4]

**2.4**    At this juncture it is worth referring to ss.5-6 MCA 2005 with which professionals should be familiar. In almost every case, there will be a continuum from:

**2.4.1**    **'Routine' decisions or interventions in an individual's life to provide them with care and treatment**. These will be taken on the basis of a reasonable belief that the individual lacks capacity to take the material decision and that the professional is acting in the individual's best interests: these can be carried out safe in the knowledge that the professional is protected from liability under s.5 MCA 2005.
*Moving through to:*

**2.4.2**    **Interventions that constitute restraint**. Restraint does not merely mean the use of force, but can include the threat of the use of force or restriction of the individual's liberty, whether or not they resist.[5] By operation of s.6 MCA 2005, a professional restraining an individual will be protected from liability provided the restraint is proportionate to the risk of and likelihood of harm and is only used where the professional reasonably believes it to be necessary to prevent harm to the person.
*Moving through to:*

**2.4.3**    **Interventions that go beyond 'mere' restraint to a deprivation of liberty**. The professional at that point cannot rely upon the provisions of ss.5-6 MCA 2005, but authority will be required from one of the sources identified at paragraph 2.41 below.

**2.5**    It is identifying precisely where the measures lie on the continuum that can sometimes prove so difficult. This difficulty is not helped by the fact that the MCA 2005 does not contain a detailed statutory definition of what constitutes a deprivation of liberty. Rather, it provides in s.64(5) that '*[i]n this Act, references to deprivation of a person's liberty have the same meaning as in Article 5(1) of the Human Rights Convention.*' This means that when the courts are asked to decide whether a particular set of circumstances amounts to a deprivation of liberty, they have had to try to work out what the ECtHR – which has ultimate responsibility for interpreting the Convention – would say.

**2.6**    Authoritative guidance as to the broad approach to adopt has now been given by the Supreme Court in *P v Cheshire West and Chester Council; P & Q v Surrey County Council* [2014] UKSC 19, commonly known as '*Cheshire West.*' As set out in more detail at paragraphs 2.23 to 2.38 below, the court decided that a person lacking the relevant capacity met the 'acid test' of being deprived of their liberty in any setting where they were under continuous (or complete) supervision and control and not free to leave.

**2.7**   This chapter concentrates on Article 5 ECHR because it underpins both Schedule A1 to the MCA 2005 and it creates the requirement for applications to be made to the Court of Protection for judicial authorisation of deprivations of liberty in settings outside care homes and hospitals.[6]

**2.8**   However, as outlined in Chapter 1, it is important to remember that determining the care and treatment arrangements for someone lacking capacity to consent to them may give rise to the need to consider other ECHR rights, most obviously the Article 8 right to respect for private and family life. It may also, in some circumstances, require attention to other legal issues such as criminal liability or liability for false imprisonment. This chapter does not, and cannot, contain a detailed discussion of all the legal issues that might arise; for more reading, see the resources in Chapter 11.

## B    Article 5 ECHR

**2.9**   The most relevant parts of Article 5 ECHR are:

1.   Everyone has the right to liberty and security of person. No one shall be deprived of his liberty save in the following cases and in accordance with a procedure prescribed by law:

[ . . . ]

(e)    the lawful detention of persons for the prevention of the spreading of infectious diseases, of persons of unsound mind, alcoholics or drug addicts or vagrants[.]

**2.10**   Article 5 also carries with it an express procedural protection, set out in Article 5(4) which provides that:

Everyone who is deprived of his liberty by arrest or detention shall be entitled to take proceedings by which the lawfulness of his detention shall be decided speedily by a court and his release ordered if the detention is not lawful.

**2.11**   Alone amongst the provisions of the ECHR, Article 5 also provides a guarantee in Article 5(5) that those who have had their rights under this Article breached have an enforceable right to compensation. As discussed further at paragraph 2.46, this does not necessarily mean that they are entitled to money, but this guarantee emphasises the importance of the rights enshrined in Article 5.

**2.12**   As interpreted by the European Court of Human Rights and by the courts in this country, Article 5(1) has been identified as having three elements, all of which need to be satisfied before a particular set of circumstances will amount to a deprivation of liberty falling within the scope of the Article:

**2.12.1**    The **objective element**: i.e. that the person is confined to a particular restricted place for a non-negligible period of time.

**2.12.2**    The **subjective element**: i.e. that the person does not consent (or cannot, because they do not have the capacity to do so) to that confinement.

**2.12.3    State imputability**: i.e. that the deprivation of liberty can be said to be one for which the State is responsible.

**2.13**    Each of these will be examined briefly below, but it is always important to remember that there is a legal difference between a **restriction** upon a person's liberty and a **deprivation** of their liberty. Although the United Kingdom has not ratified Protocol 4 to the ECHR, which enshrines[7] the right to liberty of movement and freedom to choose one's residence, the ECtHR has made reference to this Protocol on several occasions in seeking to highlight the distinction between restriction and deprivation,[8] along with the points that:

**2.13.1**    the difference between deprivation of liberty and restrictions on liberty of movement is merely one of degree or intensity, and not one of nature or substance;[9] and

**2.13.2**    although the process of classification into whether it is a deprivation or a restriction will sometimes prove to be no easy task, in that some border-line cases are a matter of pure opinion, a decision[10] has to be taken as to which side of the line the circumstances fall.[11]

## C    The objective element

**2.14**    In deciding whether someone has been deprived of their liberty, the ECtHR has decided that the starting point must be their concrete situation and account must be taken of a range of criteria such as the type, duration, effects and manner of implementation of the restrictive measure in question.[12]

**2.15**    For a person to be deprived of their liberty for the purposes of Article 5 ECHR, it is clear from the ECtHR case law that they must be confined to a particular restricted place for a non-negligible period of time.[13] Exactly what will constitute a 'non-negligible' period of time appears from the case law to vary according to the particular circumstances under consideration. We discuss this in more detail at paragraphs 3.29–3.32.

**2.16**    The objective element (but not the time element) was considered in detail by the Supreme Court in the decision in *Cheshire West*, and is discussed further in Chapter 3 below.

## D    The subjective element

**2.17**    Even if a person is objectively confined, their circumstances will not fall within the scope of Article 5 ECHR if they have validly consented to the confinement.[14] A person can only give valid consent to being subject to circumstances amounting to a deprivation of their liberty if they have the mental capacity to do so.[15]

**2.18**    There have been very few decisions identifying what is required to have capacity to consent to what would otherwise be a deprivation of liberty. In *M* v. *Ukraine*,[16] a case concerning deprivation of liberty in a psychiatric facility, the ECtHR held that:

> 77. … [T]he Court takes the view that a person's consent to admission to a mental health facility for in-patient treatment can be regarded as valid for the purpose of the Convention only where there is sufficient and reliable evidence suggesting that the person's mental ability to consent and comprehend the consequences thereof has been objectively established in the course of a fair and proper procedure and that all the necessary information concerning placement and intended treatment has been adequately provided to him.[17]

**2.19**    In the English (and Welsh) setting, in *A PCT* v. *LDV & Ors*[18] – a case concerning deprivation of liberty in a psychiatric hospital – Baker J held that:

**2.19.1**    the relevant question to ask is that set out in the 'mental capacity requirement' in paragraph 15 of Schedule A1, i.e. 'whether or not he should be accommodated in the relevant hospital or care home for the purpose of being given relevant care or treatment;'[19] and

**2.19.2**    the information relevant to that question goes beyond simply the information relating to the placement to include information about the care and treatment and, broadly, the nature of the restrictions that will amount to an objective deprivation of their liberty.[20]

**2.20**    We suggest that the same broad approach will apply in other settings, i.e. that the material information will include the outlines – even if not the minute detail – of the circumstances (in many cases, the contents of the care plan) which give rise to the deprivation of liberty. Most obviously, the information will include the circumstances establishing that the person is under continuous supervision and control and not free to leave (addressed further below).

# E    Imputable to the State

**2.21**    The final requirement contained in Article 5 ECHR is that the deprivation of liberty must be imputable to the State. The ECtHR has held that this can arise in one of three ways,[21] two of which are relevant for present purposes:[22]

**2.21.1**    Direct involvement of public authorities in the individual's detention, which will be the case in the majority of the scenarios discussed in this guidance.

**2.21.2**    By violating the State's positive obligation under Article 5(1) to protect individuals against deprivation of their liberty carried out by private persons. This positive obligation is discussed further at paragraphs 2.50–2.58 below.

# F    *Cheshire West*

**2.22**    In March 2014, the Supreme Court handed down a judgment holding that three individuals, 'P', 'MIG' and 'MEG,' were deprived of their liberty in three different settings.[23] This case is more commonly known as the '*Cheshire West*' judgment. The general principles established by the majority of the Supreme Court[24] are ones that are of wide application in both the social and healthcare settings. Those principles are discussed in this section, after the background to the decision is summarised.

**2.23**    One preliminary point should be made: no one at any stage suggested that the arrangements for each of P, MIG and MEG were not in their best interests. The question was solely whether the arrangements amounted to a deprivation of their liberty. This emphasises the extent to which there is a difference between the **neutral** question of whether a person is deprived of their liberty and the **evaluative** question of whether those arrangements are in their best interests.

## Mr P

**2.24**    Mr P was an adult born with cerebral palsy and Down's syndrome who required 24-hour care. Until he was 37 he lived with his mother but when her health deteriorated the local social services authority obtained orders from the Court of Protection that it was in P's best interests to live in accommodation arranged by it. Since November 2009 he had lived in a staffed bungalow with two other residents near his mother's home, in which there were normally two members of staff on duty during the day and one 'waking' member of staff overnight. Mr P required prompting and help with all activities of daily living, getting about, eating, personal hygiene and continence. He sometimes required intervention when he exhibited challenging behaviour (including attempting to eat his continence pads), but was not prescribed any tranquilising medication. He was unable to go anywhere or do anything without one-to-one support; such one-to-one support was provided at such a level (98 hours a week) as to enable him to leave the home frequently for activities and visits.

**2.25**    Baker J held[25] that these arrangements did deprive him of his liberty but that it was in P's best interests for them to continue. On the Council's appeal, the Court of Appeal substituted a declaration that the arrangements did not involve a deprivation of liberty, after comparing his circumstances with another person of the same age and disabilities as P.[26] The Official Solicitor appealed to the Supreme Court.

## MIG (known also as 'P' before the Court of Appeal) and MEG (known as 'Q')

**2.26**    MIG was an 18-year-old girl with a moderate to severe learning disability and problems with her sight and hearing, who required assistance crossing the road because she was unaware of danger, and who was living with a foster mother whom she regarded as 'Mummy.' Her foster mother provided her with intensive support in most aspects of daily living. She was not on any medication. She had never attempted to leave the home by herself and showed no wish to do so, but if she did, her foster mother would restrain her. She attended a further education college daily during term time and was taken on trips and holidays by her foster mother.

**2.27** MIG's sister, MEG, was a 17-year-old with mild learning disabilities living with three others in an NHS residential home for learning disabled adolescents with complex needs. She had occasional outbursts of challenging behaviour towards the other three residents and sometimes required physical restraint. She was prescribed (and administered) tranquilising medication to control her anxiety. She had one-to-one and sometimes two-to-one support. Continuous supervision and control was exercised so as to meet her care needs. She was accompanied by staff whenever she left. She attended the same further education college as her sister daily during term time, and had a full social life. She showed no wish to go out on her own, and so there was no need to prevent her from doing so.

**2.28** When the care proceedings were transferred to the Court of Protection in 2009, Parker J held[27] that these living arrangements were in the sisters' best interests and did not amount to a deprivation of liberty. This finding was upheld by the Court of Appeal.[28] The Official Solicitor appealed to the Supreme Court.

## The decision of the Supreme Court[29]

**2.29** The Supreme Court held (unanimously) that Mr P was deprived of his liberty, and (by a majority of 4 to 3) that P and Q were also deprived of their liberty. Despite the unanimity of the decision[30] in relation to Mr P, the Supreme Court justices were also divided 4 to 3 as to the governing questions of principle.

**2.30** All the Supreme Court justices agreed that the ECtHR had never considered the precise combination of factors that arose in the context of the cases before them (and which prevail also in many cases involving the DOLS regime). The division between the minority and the majority was whether it was possible to distil a clear test from the principles in decided cases; the minority considered that it was not possible to derive a universal test, and that the approach had to be case-specific. Lady Hale, for the majority, held that there was an 'acid test' that could be applied, at least in the circumstances of the cases before them, namely to ask whether the individual in question was subject to continuous (or – elsewhere[31] – complete) supervision and control and was not free to leave.[32] In reaching this conclusion, Lady Hale cited the decision of the ECtHR in *HL* v. *United Kingdom* in which these same phrases had been used.[33]

**2.31** The majority also held that irrelevant to the determination of whether a person is deprived of their liberty is: (1) the person's compliance or lack of objection; (2) the relative normality of the placement (whatever the comparison made); and (3) the reason or purpose behind a particular placement.

**2.32** It was uncontroversial before the Supreme Court that, in order for a deprivation of liberty to fall within the scope of Article 5(1) ECHR, it will also be necessary for the person not to have given valid consent to the arrangements, and that the deprivation of liberty must be imputable to the State. As Lady Hale noted in respect of the latter, the positive obligation identified in Article 5(1) to protect the liberty of those within its jurisdiction may make the State on occasions *'accountable even for arrangements which it has not itself made'*.[34]

**2.33**    Lady Hale was also at pains to emphasise that the fact that the arrangements made for an individual who cannot consent to them may be the best that can be made for them is irrelevant in determining the question of whether they amount to a deprivation of their liberty: in other words *'a gilded cage is still a cage'*.[35]

**2.34**    Speaking extra-judicially in a speech in October 2014, Lady Hale summarised the judgment of the Supreme Court thus:[36]

> We all held that the man had been deprived of his liberty, but three members of the court held that the sisters had not been deprived of their liberty, while the majority held that they had. The acid test was whether they were under the complete control and supervision of the staff and not free to leave. Their situation had to be compared, not with the situation of someone with their disabilities, but with the situation of an ordinary, normal person of their age. This is because the right to liberty is the same for everyone. The whole point about human rights is their universal quality, based as they are upon the ringing declaration in article 1 of the Universal Declaration of Human Rights, that 'All human beings are born free and equal in dignity and rights'.

**2.35**    This statement does not, of course, represent a judicially endorsed summary of the decision, but it does represent a useful insight into the reasoning of the majority. As Lady Hale recognised in the next paragraph in her lecture:

> The decision has alarming practical consequences. It means that a great many elderly and mentally disabled people, wherever they are living, must have the benefit of safeguards and reviews, to ensure that their living arrangements are indeed in their best interests.

**2.36**    The practical consequences of the decision are outside the scope of this guidance, but it is important to note that in the lecture, as in the judgment itself,[37] that Lady Hale was concerned to emphasise that the **purpose** of the scrutiny is to ensure that the arrangements made for vulnerable individuals such as P, MIG and MEG are in their best interests.

**2.37**    It is important to note that the local authorities involved in the case could not appeal to the European Court of Human Rights. Until and unless either the Supreme Court holds that a deprivation of liberty in the context of Article 5(1)(e) ECHR means something different to that determined in *Cheshire West* or the European Court of Human Rights holds either expressly or implicitly that the Supreme Court was incorrect, the approach set down by the majority represents the current law of the land in England and Wales and must be respected by professionals and their legal advisers.[38]

**2.38**    We address the elements of the 'acid test' in more detail in Chapter 3.

# G    The need for authority to deprive a person of their liberty

**2.39**    If the three key elements of the Article 5(1) 'trinity' are met – i.e. the person is confined to a particular place for more than a non-negligible period of time, they cannot consent to that confinement, and the deprivation of liberty is imputable to the State – then it is necessary for authorisation to be obtained. The public body depriving the person of their liberty is otherwise acting unlawfully by virtue of s.6(1) Human Rights Act 1998, as they will be breaching their Article 5 ECHR rights.

**2.40**    It is beyond the scope of this guidance to outline the steps required to authorise the deprivation of liberty of a person unable to consent to the same.[39] In broad terms, the person will either have to be the subject of a DOLS authorisation issued under Schedule A1 to the MCA 2005 (if they are in a hospital or care home),[40] or detained under the Mental Health Act 1983,[41] or made the subject of a court order (most usually the Court of Protection, but in some circumstances potentially an order of the High Court under the inherent jurisdiction). Reference should be made to the Code of Practice accompanying Schedule A1 to the MCA 2005 (often called the 'DOLS Code'[42]), as well as the new Code of Practice accompanying the Mental Health Act 1983.[43] Where a person is deprived of their liberty other than in a care home or hospital and an order of the Court of Protection is required, reference should also be made to Practice Direction 10AA,[44] which provides more detail as to the steps that are required.[45]

# H    The effect of authorisation

**2.41**    It is important to understand that the grant of authority to deprive an individual of their liberty under the MCA 2005 (whether by way of a DOLS authorisation or an order of the Court of Protection) does not require the individual to be deprived of their liberty. In other words, it is not an order that the person must be detained. Rather, it means that a person or body can rely upon that authority to deprive the individual of their liberty secure in the knowledge that they are acting lawfully.

**2.42**    This means – for instance – that we consider that there is nothing wrong in having in place a standard authorisation to cover a regular deprivation of liberty in a respite placement[46] if the individual goes into that respite placement (say) for a week every month. It would not then be necessary for the managing authority of the respite placement to seek (and the relevant supervisory body to grant) a separate authorisation for each respite stay. As a matter of law, the authorisation would – in essence, cover those periods each month when the individual was a detained resident at the respite placement, and could be relied upon for those periods to provide authority to detain them (assuming that all the other conditions are met).

**2.43**    We should emphasise that we consider that this route[47] will be lawful only if the respite placement is a regular one because it would only be proper to construe the individual as being a 'detained resident' at the placement for purposes of paragraph 19(2) of Schedule A1[48] if there is such a degree of regularity.[49]

## I   Consequences of a failure to obtain an authorisation

**2.44**   As noted above, if a public body does not have authority to deprive an individual of their liberty, they will be acting unlawfully contrary to s.6 Human Rights Act 1998.[50] The individual in question will be entitled to a declaration that their rights have been breached. The question that is often asked, however, is whether they will be entitled to more – and, in particular, whether they will be entitled to financial compensation.

**2.45**   The question of when damages are payable for breaches of rights under Article 5 ECHR is a complicated one that lies outside the scope of this guidance to discuss in detail. However, we think it important to highlight the – limited – number of cases in which judges have considered damages awards in the Court of Protection:[51]

**2.45.1**    In *London Borough of Hillingdon v. Neary*[52], a period of a year's detention resulted in an award of £35,000 (no judgment being made public to accompany the consent order approved by the High Court).

**2.45.2**    In *A Local Authority v. Mr and Mrs D*,[53] District Judge Mainwaring-Taylor approved an award of £15,000 (plus costs) to Mrs D for a period of four months' unlawful detention (together with £12,500 to her husband and his costs). In *Mr and Mrs D*, District Judge Mainwaring-Taylor had noted that this was towards the lower end of the range if the award in the *Neary* case was taken as the bench mark.

**2.45.3**    In *Essex County Council v. RF*,[54] District Judge Mort noted the important difference between 'procedural' breaches, where the authority's failure to secure authorisation for the deprivation of liberty or provide a review of the detention would have made no difference to P's living or care arrangements and 'substantive' breaches occur where P would not have been detained if the authority had acted lawfully. As the judge noted, such breaches have more serious consequences for P. He further noted that two decisions above suggested that the level of damages for the substantive breaches of the right to liberty is between £3000 and £4000 per month. In the case before him, the judge was clear that the Council's practice was substandard – indeed that their conduct had been reprehensible, with '*very sad and disturbing consequences for P*'. The judge ultimately approved an award of £60,000 to reflect the unlawful deprivation of RF's liberty in a care home for a period of approximately 13 months.[55]

**2.46**   By contrast, in *A County Council v. MB, JB and a Residential Home*,[56] Charles J granted a declaration that a woman had been unlawfully deprived of her liberty at a care home from 29 March 2010 to 13 April 2010, but made no award of damages, noting – in his view correctly – that no such award had been sought. It is clear from the judgment in that case that this was a case where the breach was 'procedural' rather than 'substantive', and indeed that the local authority had made attempts to ensure that the appropriate authorisation was obtained, albeit unsuccessful.

**2.47**    The distinction between 'procedural' and 'substantive' breaches has also been highlighted – in the context of detention under the Mental Health Act 1983 – by the decision of the Court of Appeal in *Bostridge* v. *Oxleas Foundation NHS Trust*,[57] in which the Court of Appeal held that a person unlawfully deprived of their liberty cannot claim any more than nominal damages (usually £1) if they have suffered no loss in consequence.[58] In other words, if the public body could show[59] that they would have been detained in any event if they had followed the correct procedures (there, those provided for under the Mental Health Act 1983), the claimant could not claim more than nominal damages. We suggest that a similar approach is likely to be followed in cases involving unlawful deprivation of liberty in the context of the MCA 2005.

**2.48**    The cases discussed above therefore suggest that the courts will take a very different view as to whether damages should be awarded depending on whether:

**2.48.1**    the public authority in question has sought to comply with its statutory obligations and – above all – properly to direct themselves by reference to the best interests of the individual, in which case there is a good argument that only declarations and nominal damages should be awarded; or

**2.48.2**    the public authority has in its actions fallen below the standards expected of it, especially where it has failed to have appropriate regard to the impact of its actions upon the individual's best interests. It is clear in this latter regard that the courts are increasingly unwilling to accept ignorance of the MCA 2005 as an excuse given that the length of time since the Act came into force.

**2.49**    It should, finally, be noted that a failure to obtain an authorisation may expose the relevant body not only to a claim before the courts but also to sanction from regulators[60] and/or the relevant Ombudsman.[61] Regulatory sanctions will be much more likely to be imposed where the failures are systemic.

## J    'Private' deprivations of liberty and the positive obligation under Article 5(1) ECHR

**2.50**    As noted at paragraph 2.39 above, a deprivation of liberty only falls within the scope of Article 5(1) ECHR if it is 'imputable' to the State.

**2.51**    There has been a level of concern expressed following the *Cheshire West* judgment as to the extent to which the 'acid test' applies to 'private' deprivations of liberty – i.e. circumstances under which an individual lacking the relevant capacity is subject to continuous (or complete) supervision and control by a private individual (or body), they are not free to leave, but the arrangements are not made by the State.

**2.52**    As a starting point, we note that, whilst, strictly, those who are 'self-funding' in private care homes and hospitals (i.e. who have had arrangements made for them by family members and who are not reliant on State funding to pay for those arrangements) are outside the scope of Article 5(1) ECHR, they are to be treated as if they were within its scope, such that managing authorities of such institutions are required to apply for authorisations if they meet the acid test. The precise rationale for this is not explained in the DOLS Code[62] but we would suggest that it is because private care home and hospitals are institutions regulated by the State. As such, any notionally 'private' deprivations of liberty taking place in such institutions are – or should – be ones of which the State is aware. This, in turn, triggers the State's positive obligations to secure the Article 5 ECHR rights of the individuals concerned, which are discharged by operation of the authorisation procedure under Schedule A1.

**2.53**    Further, there will be many circumstances in which the person is cared for in their own home (or in some other living arrangement), where they are predominantly cared for privately, but where there is some State involvement. That State involvement can vary from – for instance – the payment of direct payments to an appropriate person on the individual's behalf for the purposes of arranging their care down to much more limited involvement, such as visits by a nurse on a monthly basis. The precise point on this spectrum at which the arrangements will cease to be the direct responsibility of the State and be a matter for which private individuals are responsible (and hence which trigger the positive, rather than negative obligations of the State bodies concerned) is something that has yet to be decided by the courts. It will tentatively be discussed in the different settings in which it arises in the relevant chapters below.

**2.54**    Where a deprivation of liberty can truly be said to arise out of arrangements that the State has had no part in making, the obligation on the State bodies is to take measures '*providing effective protection*' of the individual.[63] In *Re A and Re C*[64] Munby LJ held that:

> Where the State – here, a local authority – knows or ought to know that a vulnerable child or adult is subject to restrictions on their liberty by a private individual that arguably give rise to a deprivation of liberty, then its positive obligations under Article 5 will be triggered.
>
> (i)    These will include the duty to investigate, so as to determine whether there is, in fact, a deprivation of liberty. In this context the local authority will need to consider all the factors relevant to the objective and subjective elements [of the test for deprivation of liberty discussed above];
>
> (ii)   If, having carried out its investigation, the local authority is satisfied that the objective element is not present, so there is no deprivation of liberty, the local authority will have discharged its immediate obligations. However, its positive obligations may in an appropriate case require the local authority to continue to monitor the situation in the event that circumstances should change.
>
> (iii)  If, however, the local authority concludes that the measures imposed do or may constitute a deprivation of liberty, then it will be under a positive obligation, both under Article 5 alone and taken together with Article 14, to take reasonable and proportionate measures to bring that state of affairs to an end. What is

reasonable and proportionate in the circumstances will, of course, depend upon the context, but it might for example, Mr Bowen suggests, require the local authority to exercise its statutory powers and duties so as to provide support services for the carers that will enable inappropriate restrictions to be ended, or at least minimised.

(iv) If, however, there are no reasonable measures that the local authority can take to bring the deprivation of liberty to an end, or if the measures it proposes are objected to by the individual or his family, then it may be necessary for the local authority to seek the assistance of the court in determining whether there is, in fact, a deprivation of liberty and, if there is, obtaining authorisation for its continuance.

**2.55**    It is likely that the precise scope of the obligations on local authorities (and/or NHS bodies) who are – or should be – aware of 'private' deprivations of liberty will be the subject of further judicial scrutiny in due course, not least as certain of the Strasbourg cases on the subject have never been the subject of consideration by the English courts.[65]

**2.56**    It is perhaps important also to note that a private individual who is depriving an incapacitated individual of their liberty in a purely private setting may also, depending upon the context, be liable for false imprisonment. This is a common law tort (i.e. 'wrong'), the key elements of which are that the individual is imprisoned, and the person or body doing the imprisoning does not have authority to justify that imprisonment. A person who has been falsely imprisoned can seek damages from the responsible person or body. They do not need to show that they have suffered loss or damage (such as any form of injury) to be able to sue for damages, but if they cannot show that they have suffered any loss or damage they will not be entitled to more than nominal damages.[66] False imprisonment is also a common law criminal offence involving the unlawful and intentional or reckless detention of the victim.[67]

**2.57**    The interaction between false imprisonment and unlawful deprivation of liberty contrary to Article 5 ECHR is not straightforward,[68] in particular because issues arise as to whether the person/body doing the detaining can rely upon the defence of necessity to defend themselves against a claim or charge of false imprisonment (in a way that cannot be done in relation to a claim brought under Article 5 ECHR).[69] These are matters that lie outside the scope of this guidance.

**2.58**    It should, finally, be noted that, depending upon the circumstances, a private individual depriving an incapacitated individual in a purely private setting may also potentially guilty of an offence under s.44 MCA 2005 if the conditions under which the individual was kept amount to ill-treatment or wilful neglect by the person doing the detaining if they had care of them, or were an attorney under a lasting or enduring power of attorney or a court appointed deputy.

## K    The DOLS Code

**2.59**    The DOLS Code is a statutory one, to which all professionals providing care and treatment to individuals lacking capacity must have regard.[70] The Code itself provides that it must be read subject to subsequent legal developments[71] so it is absolutely clear that Chapter 2 – entitled '*What is deprivation of liberty?*' – must now be read subject to the judgments of the courts handed down since it was written in 2008.

**2.60**    This means that care must be taken when considering the factors outlined at paragraph 2.5 of the DOLS Code as potentially identifying whether steps taken involve more than restraint and amount to a deprivation of liberty. The factors identified there may well be valuable in indicating whether a particular person is under continuous (or complete) supervision and control and not free to leave, but they go no further than that. In particular, we would advise caution before a conclusion is drawn solely from the basis that a person's contact with others is restricted that they are deprived of their liberty. Imposing restrictions on contact with others is a significant interference with rights under Article 8 ECHR, but we suggest that they do not, in and of themselves, necessarily give rise to issues under Article 5 ECHR. It is further also extremely important to note that the DOLS regime (and also the procedure for judicial authorisation of deprivation of liberty) cannot be used to authorise restrictions on contact: if such are sought in the best interests of the individual concerned, it is likely that an application to the Court of Protection will be necessary.

**2.61**    We should emphasise that this guidance does not – and cannot – in any way intend to replace the DOLS Code insofar as it relates to the steps that must be taken if a person is deprived of their liberty.

### Endnotes

1    Available at webarchive.nationalarchives.gov.uk/20130107105354/http://www.dh.gov.uk/prod–consum–dh/groups/dh–digitalassets/@dh/@en/ documents/digitalasset/dh–087309.pdf.
2    To respond to the decision of the European Court of Human Rights in *HL v. United Kingdom* (2004) 40 EHRR 761 ('Bournewood case').
3    Save where that is for purposes of providing them with treatment for their mental disorder, in which case the Mental Health Act 1983 will be as – if not more – important.
4    Schedule 1A deals with the interface between the MCA DOLS regime and the Mental Health Act 1983.
5    Section 6(4) MCA 2005.
6    I.e. in settings for which it is not possible to seek authorisation under Schedule A1 to the MCA 2005.
7    In Article 2.
8    Perhaps the most relevant decision being *Stanev v. Bulgaria* [2012] 55 EHRR 22 at paragraph 115. Lady Hale in *Cheshire West* set out the key propositions from *Stanev* at paragraphs 19-25.
9    *Cheshire West* at paragraph 20 citing *Stanev* at paragraph 115.
10    Ultimately by the ECtHR.
11    *Cheshire West* at paragraph 20 citing *Stanev* at paragraph 115.
12    *Cheshire West* at paragraph 20 citing *Stanev* at paragraph 117.
13    *Cheshire West* at paragraph 20 citing *Stanev* at paragraph 117.
14    *Cheshire West* at paragraph 20 citing *Stanev* at paragraph 117.
15    *Cheshire West* at paragraph 23 citing *Stanev* at paragraph 118 and, in turn, *HL v. United Kingdom* [2004] 40 EHRR 761 at paragraph 90.
16    [2012] ECHR 732.
17    On the facts of the case, the Court held that there was no evidence suggesting that M's 'mental ability to consent was established, that the consequences of the consent were explained to her

or that the relevant information on placement and treatment was provided to her,' such that she could not be said to have given valid and lawful consent to what was objectively a deprivation of her liberty.

18   [2013] EWHC 272 (Fam).

19   See paragraph 29.

20   See paragraphs 39 and 40 which set out a list of factors that amounted to a deprivation of liberty in LDV's case.

21   *Storck* v. *Germany* [2006] 43 EHRR 6 at paragraph 89.

22   The third way that the ECtHR has held that a deprivation of liberty could be imputable to the State is where the courts have failed to interpret the law governing any claim for compensation for unlawful deprivation of liberty 'in the spirit of Art. 5' (*Storck* at paragraph 89).

23   Parts of this section draw (with permission) upon summaries produced by the 39 Essex Chambers Mental Capacity Law Newsletter editors, available at www.copcasesonline.com.

24   The lead judgment was given by Lady Hale, with whom Lord Sumption agreed. Lords Neuberger and Kerr expressly agreed with Lady Hale in their separate concurring judgments. Lords Carnwath and Hodge gave a joint dissenting judgment in the cases of P and Q.

25   [2011] EWHC 1330 (COP).

26   [2011] EWCA Civ 1257.

27   [2010] EWHC 785 (COP).

28   [2011] EWCA Civ 190.

29   The decision is discussed in more detail in the April 2014 edition of the 39 Essex Chambers Mental Capacity Law Newsletter.

30   Although the minority made it clear that it was a 'marginal' case, which, had they been considering the question for themselves, they might have concluded differently: paragraph 103.

31   Paragraph 53.

32   Paragraphs 48-49.

33   At paragraph 49, citing *HL* v. *United Kingdom* [2004] 40 EHRR 761 at paragraph 91.

34   Paragraph 26.

35   Paragraph 46.

36   'Psychiatry and the Law: An enduring interest for Lord Rodger': The Lord Rodger Memorial Lecture 2014, available at www.supremecourt.uk/ docs/speech-141031.pdf

37   At paragraph 57.

38   And, whilst not formally binding, is at a minimum highly influential in Scotland. Whilst this guidance does not purport to address the legal position in Scotland, we note the extensive reference to the decision in the Scottish Law Commission's report on Adults with Incapacity (setting out a draft statutory scheme to be the functional equivalent of Schedule A1 to the MCA 2005, available at www.scotlawcom.gov.uk/law-reform-projects/ adults-with-incapacity/).

39   If the person can consent (i.e. they have the capacity to do so) but does not do so, then there may be circumstances under which a deprivation of liberty will be lawful – most obviously where the person can be the subject of compulsory detention ('sectioning') under the Mental Health Act 1983. We do not discuss these situations in this guidance.

40   The process for doing so will differ whether the person is in England or in Wales because of the different arrangements made for supervisory bodies in the two areas.

41   Section 4B MCA 2005 also gives authority to deprive a person of their liberty if this is necessary to provide life-sustaining treatment or to prevent a serious deterioration in the person's condition pending determining of an application relating to that person by the Court of Protection.

42   Available at webarchive.nationalarchives.gov.uk/20130107105354/http://www.dh.gov.uk/ prod–consum–dh/groups/dh-digitalassets/@dh/@en/ documents/digitalasset/dh-087309.pdf

43   Available at www.gov.uk/government/uploads/system/uploads/attachment–data/file/396918/ Code–of–Practice.pdf: this will come into force in April 2015 subject to Parliamentary approval.

44   www.judiciary.gov.uk/publications/10aa-deprivation-of-liberty/

45   Following the decision of the President of the Court of Protection in *Re X & Ors (Deprivation of Liberty) (Nos 1 and 2)* [2014] EWCOP 25 and [2014] EWCOP 37. Note that the judgment of the Court of Appeal in appeals made against these decisions was awaited at the time of writing this guidance.

46   If it is a hospital or care home falling within the scope of Schedule A1.

47   Which we accept is not provided for expressly in either Schedule A1 or the DOLS Code, but which we consider is not inconsistent with either (and, most importantly, Schedule A1).

48    I.e. the first condition that must be satisfied for them to meet the best interests requirement under Schedule A1.

49    There is also a question mark as to whether it is necessary that the person be present at the placement at least once every 28 days, or whether the requirement in paragraph 24(2) of Schedule A1 that the person is 'likely – at some time within the next 28 days – to be a detained resident' only applies in relation to the initial deprivation of liberty. In the absence of any case law, we consider that it is legitimate to take the view that the requirement only applies to the initial deprivation of liberty, such that an authorisation can be granted even in the case of more infrequent (but still regular) periods of respite.

50    They may also be liable to a claim for false imprisonment: in other words, a claim at common law that they imprisoned the individual without lawful authority to justify such imprisonment. In practice, claims in this context are usually brought on the basis of the Human Rights Act 1998, in part because the legal framework relating to such claims is rather more straightforward.

51    It is perhaps important to note that none of these decisions actually stand formally as a precedent, the first because it was a consent order with no accompanying judgment, and the second and third because they are decisions of District Judges. They nonetheless stand as a useful guide to the approach that may be adopted.

52    [2011] EWCOP 1377.

53    [2013] EWCOP B34.

54    [2015] EWCOP 1.

55    The other elements of the compromise agreement he approved included: a declaration that the Council unlawfully deprived P of his liberty for period of approximately 13 months; the Council would waive any fees payable by P to the care home in which he was detained for the period of his detention (a sum of between £23,000 and £25,000); the Council to exclude P's damages award from means testing in relation to P being required to pay a contribution to his community care costs; the payment of all P's costs, to be assessed on the standard basis.

56    [2010] EWHC 2508 (COP).

57    [2015] EWCA Civ 79.

58    The case was also framed by reference to the common law tort of false imprisonment, but the Court of Appeal appeared to approach the question on the basis that the approach to the assessment of damages was identical.

59    It is for the public body to show this on the balance of probabilities: see, by analogy R(EO & Ors) v. SSHD [2013] EWHC 1236 (Admin) at paragraph 74.

60    The CQC now includes compliance with the MCA 2005 – including (where relevant) with provisions relating to deprivation of liberty – as one of its Key Lines of Enquiry; details of enforcement actions taken for failures to comply with the requirements of Schedule A1 in 2013/4 are discussed in its most recent report upon DOLS, available at www.cqc.org.uk/content/deprivation-liberty-safeguards-201314.

61    See for a recent example, the investigation of the Local Government Ombudsman into the case of Mr N, available at www.lgo.org.uk/downloads/ CO%20Adult%20social%20care/2014-2015/2111-13-016-935-Cambridgeshire-CC-20.1.2015.pdf, in which the Ombudsman was, in particular, critical of the failure of Cambridgeshire County Council properly to consider the question of Mr N's capacity and where his best interests lay in the decision-making process leading to his placement at a care home in circumstances that – it is clear – undoubtedly amounted to a deprivation of liberty but where no lawful authority was obtained.

62    Self-funders are – surprisingly – touched on only in passing in the DOLS Code at paragraph 5.23. That private care homes and hospitals fall within the scope of Schedule A1 is also supported by the confirmation in s.64(6) MCA 2005 that it does not matter for purposes of references to deprivation of liberty in the Act whether the person is deprived of his liberty by a public authority or not.

63    Stanev at paragraph 120.

64    [2010] EWHC 978 (Fam), at paragraph 95.

65    Most obviously Riera Blume v. Spain (2000) 32 EHRR 632 and Rantsev v. Cyprus and Russia (2010) 51 EHRR 1 and Rantsev v. Cyprus and Russia, as well as the more recent admissibility decision in Chosta v. Ukraine (Application no. 35807/05, decision of 14 January 2014).

66    See most recently Bostridge v. Oxleas Foundation NHS Trust [2015] EWCA Civ 79.

67    For a review of the complicated law in this area, see the Law Commission's project on simplification of the law relating to kidnapping and related offences: lawcommission.justice.gov.uk/areas/kidnapping.htm.

68   And a breach of Article 5 ECHR does not necessarily involve false imprisonment: see *Zenati* v.
     *(1) Cmr of the Police for the Metropolis; (2) CPS* [2015] EWCA 80 at paragraphs 49-55.
69   This was the clear conclusion of the ECtHR in the Bournewood case, but the same court did not
     have to decide whether necessity could still play any part in relation to the common law.
70   Section 42(4) MCA 2005.
71   Chapter 2, introduction.

## 3   KEY QUESTIONS AFTER *CHESHIRE WEST*

**3.1**   The formulation of the 'acid test' in the *Cheshire West* decision has led to an intense focus on the concepts of the practical meaning of '**continuous/complete supervision and control**' and '**freedom to leave**', as well as of what may be a '**non-negligible**' period of time.

**3.2**   The majority of the rest of this guidance represents an attempt to reflect what these concepts may mean in particular settings. In this chapter some initial and generally applicable observations are given. The obvious caution has to be given that these concepts may ultimately have to be given a judicial definition which will override anything within this guidance.

**3.3**   The approach taken by this guidance is also predicated upon the warning of Lady Hale that: '[b]ecause of the extreme vulnerability of people like P, MIG and MEG, [...] we should err on the side of caution in deciding what constitutes a deprivation of liberty in their case.'[1]

## A   Continuous/complete supervision and control – what is continuous/complete?

**3.4**   The phrase 'continuous supervision and control' was taken by Lady Hale from the European Court of Human Rights' judgment in *HL* v. *United Kingdom*.[2] This concept or variations of it has been used in the major ECtHR cases subsequently,[3] and in seeking to interpret the phrase, we consider that it is of use to have regard to the ECtHR case law.

**3.5**   The ECtHR case law indicates strongly that the requirement for continuous/complete supervision and control cannot and should not be interpreted as requiring 24-hour monitoring and/or that the person is to be physically accompanied over a continuous 24-hour period. In other words, if the individual is subject to such monitoring or such degree of accompaniment,[4] then the necessary degree of continuity or completeness will be satisfied. But it is capable of being satisfied even if the supervision and control is 'lighter touch'.

**3.6**   Perhaps the two most significant ECtHR cases here are:

**3.6.1**   *Ashingdane* v. *the United Kingdom*,[5] in which the ECtHR held that a person could be regarded as having been 'detained' even during a period when he was in an open hospital ward with regular unescorted access to the unsecured hospital grounds and the possibility of unescorted leave outside the hospital; and

3.6.2    *Stanev v. Bulgaria*,[6] in which Mr Stanev was able to leave the building where he resided and to go to the nearest village (and indeed had been encouraged to work in the restaurant in the village where his care home was located 'to the best of his abilities') and had also been on 'leaves of absence.' However, he needed to have permission to leave the care home, and his visits outside were subject to controls and restrictions; his leaves of absence were entirely at the discretion of the home's management, who kept his identity papers and administered his finances. When he did not return from a leave of absence, the home asked the police to search for and return him and he was returned to the home against his wishes. He was, in consequence, the Grand Chamber held, '*under constant supervision and was not free to leave the home whenever he wished* '[7] and was therefore deprived of his liberty.

3.7    These two cases suggest that the ECtHR would take a relatively broad-brush approach to deciding whether supervision and control was sufficiently 'continuous' or 'complete' to satisfy this element of the test.

3.8    A pragmatic way of answering the question is to ask whether the person(s) or body responsible for the individual have a plan in place which means that they need always broadly to know:

3.8.1    where the individual is; and
3.8.2    what they are doing at any one time.

3.9    If the answer to both questions is 'yes,' then we suggest that this is a strong pointer that the individual is under continuous/complete supervision and control. This is particularly so if the plan sets out what the person(s) or body responsible for the individual will do in the event that they are not satisfied that they know where the individual is and what they are up to.

3.10    We also suggest that it is clear that the test for completeness/continuity will also be met without **every** decision being taken for the individual. In other words, the individual may well be able to take quite a number of decisions as to their own activities (for instance what they would like to have for breakfast) but still be subject to complete or continuous supervision and control if the individual is in an overall structure in which aspects of decision-making are being allowed to them at the discretion of those in control of their care.

## B    Continuous/complete supervision and control – what is supervision and control?

3.11    What of 'supervision and control'? The terms are likely in due course to be the subject of further scrutiny by the courts. However, in our view, the ECtHR, if asked, would focus primarily on the fact that the arrangements have been made for an individual who lacks the capacity to consent to them. Even if these arrangements are conscientiously considered to be in their best interests, there is in all such situations a power imbalance between those providing the care and treatment and the person to whom it is being provided.

**3.12**    We suggest that caution must be exercised before concluding that arrangements amount to 'mere' care, support or enablement rather than shading into supervision and control. MIG's case makes this clear, because she was provided with what was described as *'intensive support'* by a woman she regarded as her mother, and was not subject to overtly controlling measures. She was nonetheless held by the majority in the Supreme Court to be under continuous supervision and control.

## C    Freedom to leave

**3.13**    It is vitally important not to conflate *'freedom to leave'* with *'ability to leave'* or *'attempts to leave.'* Doing so would lead to the reduction in the universality of the right to liberty upon which the Supreme Court placed such emphasis. As Lord Kerr noted, liberty is *'predominantly an objective state. It does not depend on one's disposition to exploit one's freedom.'* Reflecting this, it was clear that P, MIG or MEG would not – of their own accord – attempt to leave, but all of them were found not to be free to leave.[8]

**3.14**    In this context the focus should be upon the actions (or potential actions) of those around the individual, rather than the individual themselves. In other words, the question may well be a hypothetical one – if the person manifested a desire to leave (or a family member properly interested in their care sought to assist them to leave), what would happen?

**3.15**    If the answer is that steps would be taken to enable them to leave, then that points in one direction; if the answer is that steps would be taken to prevent them leaving that points in the other. Crucially, it would not matter in this regard if the steps to prevent the person leaving were said to be in their best interests.

**3.16**    Approaching matters on that basis helps make clear that, for example, whether not there are locks or keypads on the doors is not the answer.[9] It is what would be done by the staff with the ability to unlock the door if the individual were to seek to open that door that is important. It also helps make clear that compliance or lack of objection is irrelevant to the question of whether a person is deprived of their liberty,[10] and hence does not lead to the understandable but incorrect approach that questions of deprivation of liberty are only raised when the individual is continuously resisting personal care, subject to hands-on restraint or attempting to leave.

**3.17**    One important question that arises here is whether freedom to leave is:

3.17.1    'micro' – i.e. the freedom to come and go from the premises in question temporarily; or

3.17.2    'macro' – i.e. freedom to move from those premises to another one on a permanent basis (or simply to leave those premises permanently, even if they do not have a clear destination).[11]

3.18    As at the point of preparing this guidance, the answer to this question is not absolutely clear. Some have suggested that the focus should solely be on the 'macro' question, and that questions of whether or not the individual is temporarily able to come and go from the place in question are essentially not relevant.[12] However, we suggest that this is doubtful:

3.18.1    In the speech given by Lady Hale referred to at paragraph 2.35 above and in the course of discussing the situations of P, MIG and MEG, she noted that:

> they were under the complete control of the people looking after them and were certainly not free to go, *either for a short time* or to go and live somewhere else (emphasis added).

3.18.2    Even though Lady Hale was not speaking in a judicial capacity, this statement suggests that she does not consider that the majority of the court held that freedom to leave was only relevant in the 'macro' sense.

3.18.3    The Grand Chamber of the ECtHR placed considerable emphasis in *Stanev* on the fact that Mr Stanev was not able to leave the care home for such purposes as visiting the nearby village *'whenever he wished'* (i.e. not merely for purposes of permanent relocation) in finding that he was deprived of his liberty.[13]

3.19    Despite what has been said above, it may be that a higher court looking at the question of 'freedom to leave' might conclude that the question of whether a person is able to come and go as they like may more naturally fall to be considered when dealing with the question of whether they are under continuous/complete supervision and control. However, it would be unlikely if no account were to be taken of such restrictions being imposed. Taking a step back, and applying Lady Hale's approach from *Cheshire West*, it would appear clear that a person of unimpaired health and capacity who was prevented from being able to come and go as they see fit from a particular location would consider themselves to be deprived of an important right even if it was said that they would be able to relocate permanently whenever they wished. Indeed, it is not immediately obvious that there will be many situations in which a person will be prevented from coming and going as they wish but those in charge of the placement would be entirely happy for them simply to 'up sticks' and leave altogether.

3.20    Until and unless further clarification is given by the Court of Appeal (or Supreme Court), this guidance offers the following as a set of broad propositions:

3.20.1    If a person is not free to come and go as they wish (with or without help) from a placement or place of treatment save with the permission of the decision-makers around them, then this is, at a minimum, a pointer to the individual being subject to restrictions upon their liberty. This may – depending upon the other measures imposed upon them – amount to a deprivation of their liberty or it may be that they amount solely to a restriction upon their liberty and the body imposing the restrictions can rely upon the provisions of ss.5-6 MCA 2005.

3.20.2    A person will clearly not be 'free to leave' if they are able permanently to relocate from the place only with the permission of the person(s) or bodies responsible for their care and treatment; **and** if they do seek to leave that location permanently, and not to return, steps will be taken to locate and bring about their return if they do not do so of their own accord.

3.20.3    Both aspects of the test set out immediately above will need to be satisfied. If the reality is that **no steps at** all would be taken in the event that the person simply walked out one afternoon from a care home announcing their intention to move elsewhere – or simply to leave permanently – and did not come back, then they would clearly be free to leave.

3.21    Four further broad points should be made here:

3.21.1    There may well be circumstances in which a person is not to free to leave one specific place at the times when they are there, but they are not otherwise subject to restrictions. An obvious example of such a situation is a person who is cared for at home, but then receives regular respite care at a facility, from which they are not allowed to leave, but are not otherwise under similar restrictions when they are at home. It would, in such circumstances, be logically possible for the person to be deprived of their liberty whilst at the facility but not deprived of their liberty whilst at home. However, it is possible to produce absurd results by over-analysing such situations. We suggest that the better approach in such a case is to have regard to the individual's care plan and to identify whether – **taken as a whole** – it amounts to a plan in which their movements are sufficiently circumscribed and they are under a sufficient degree of supervision and control that it amounts to a deprivation of their liberty. We address the specific question of respite in Chapter 6 (and in relation to children, in Chapter 10).

3.21.2    If those who are making the decisions on the ground (especially if they are public bodies) would be content for the individual to live anywhere that they might be able to choose[14] other than one specific location, then this may indicate that they are not 'free to leave' for the purposes of the acid test.[15] It will, in any event, give rise to significant issues in relation to their rights under Article 8 ECHR[16] and would probably require an application to the Court of Protection so as to ensure that the necessity and proportionality of the actions could be subject to proper judicial scrutiny.

3.21.3    We reiterate that it is not necessary that a person has somewhere else to go for them to be deprived of their liberty: this is clear from the decision of the Grand Chamber in Mr Stanev's case: he had nowhere else to live (see paragraph 153 of the decision in his case) but this did not prevent him being held to be deprived of his liberty.

3.21.4    For the purposes of testing what steps professionals making decisions would take in the event that the person attempted to leave, it is appropriate to take into account that a person properly interested in their welfare[17] may request that they be allowed to leave. So, if a person is unable to express any wishes or feelings and would therefore be unable even to suggest leaving, it would be appropriate to consider what the decision makers would do if such a person (most obviously a family member) said that they wished to move them from the placement. Professionals should note *HL* v. *United Kingdom*, in which the European Court of Human Rights took note of the fact that Mr L would only be released from the hospital to his carers as and when those professionals considered it appropriate.[18] More broadly, taking this approach ensures that the proper distinction between 'freedom to leave' and 'ability to leave' is maintained in the case of those who are least able to exercise any freedom that would be afforded to those who did not have their level of disability.

## D    Both elements of the acid test must be satisfied

3.22    Lady Hale in *Cheshire West* was clear that it was necessary that both elements of the acid test needed to be satisfied. The Official Solicitor (on behalf of P, MIG and MEG) had argued that supervision and control was relevant only as it demonstrated that the person was not free to leave. Lady Hale was not prepared to go so far, and held that:

> A person might be under constant supervision and control but still be free to leave should he express the desire so to do. Conversely, it is possible to imagine situations in which a person is not free to leave but is not under such continuous supervision and control as to lead to the conclusion that he was deprived of his liberty.[19]

3.23    However, the second limb causes some difficulty in the case of a person who is locked in a room (or within a facility that is itself locked) but is not subject to continuous supervision and control. We suggest that this is not the situation that Lady Hale had in mind,[20] and it would be unwise to proceed on the basis that this kind of situation would not be capable of amounting to a deprivation of liberty. The situation that Lady Hale had in mind was much closer – we suggest – to the situation where a person is required to live in a particular place but is not subject to any additional controls upon them at that place.

3.24    Therefore, professionals should note that wherever a person is subject to a residence requirement imposed under the Mental Health Act 1983 ('MHA 1983'),[21] it should not be assumed that such requirement will, itself, give rise to a deprivation of that person's liberty. That is because: (1) it is strongly arguable that the power to impose such requirements do not, themselves, amount to power to prevent the person leaving; and (2) a requirement that a person does not leave a particular place does not, itself, amount to a deprivation of liberty unless the care and treatment package contains the necessary elements of supervision and control.[22]

## E     Irrelevant factors

**3.25**     In *Cheshire West*, Lady Hale acceded to the suggestion of the National Autistic Society and Mind to indicate certain factors that would not be relevant to the assessment of whether a person is objectively deprived of their liberty. These are:

**3.25.1**     the person's compliance or lack of objection;

**3.25.2**     the relative normality of the placement (whatever the comparison made); and

**3.25.3**     the reason or purpose behind a particular placement.[23]

**3.26**     In relation to the first of these factors, something of a working presumption had been established prior to the *Cheshire West* decision that it was only necessary to consider questions of deprivation of liberty where the individual was non-compliant (or their family were agitating for their departure from the facility). Whilst, as noted below, staff must be on alert if the person is non-compliant, the converse was not, and never has been true. In other words, the mere fact that the person was sitting quietly in the corner of the care home and apparently acquiescing to the arrangements made for them never meant that they could not be deprived of their liberty. Indeed, the irrelevance of compliance had long been acknowledged by the ECtHR.[24] A focus not just on the individual but upon the nature of the arrangements in place around them can assist in avoiding this trap.

**3.27**     However, whilst compliance is irrelevant, non-compliance, or resistance, is highly relevant. In particular, where a person strongly resists the arrangements (for instance an individual in a hospital setting has to be forcibly restrained to prevent them from absconding), this is highly significant. If they strongly resist, then it is clear that the measures will have a greater effect upon them. Further, the greater the resistance, the more intensive the measures will be. The more intense the measures, the shorter the period of time before the imposition of those measures will stop being 'merely' a restriction upon the person's liberty and become a deprivation of it. See further in this regard paragraphs 3.33–3.40 below.

**3.28**     The second of these factors is self-explanatory, and makes clear that the decisions of the Court of Appeal in (then) MIG and MEG and in *Cheshire West* were incorrect. If there is to be any comparison drawn, it is not between the nature of the setting but between the arrangements made for the individual in question and those that would be applied to an individual of unimpaired health and capacity.[25] In other words, and recognising the potentially (if inadvertently) pejorative nature of this exercise, if such a person would consider the arrangements in place to amount to a deprivation of their liberty, they will amount to a deprivation of liberty even for a person who, because of their disabilities, is unable either to recognise it as such or take advantage of the liberty of which they are deprived.[26]

## F    Non-negligible period of time

**3.29**    As noted at paragraph 2.15, in order for a person to be deprived of their liberty for the purposes of Article 5 ECHR, it is clear from the ECtHR case law that they must be confined to a particular restricted place for a non-negligible period of time.[27] Exactly what will constitute a 'non-negligible' period of time appears from the case law to vary according to the particular circumstances under consideration, including their nature and consequences.[28]

**3.30**    By way of two examples from English decisions (which consider ECtHR cases):

**3.30.1**    The total and '*intense*' restraint by police officers of a 16-year-old with autism for a period of 40 minutes was held to amount to a deprivation of his liberty.[29]

**3.30.2**    By contrast, it was held that in the 'ordinary case' it would be unlikely that a person required to remain in the s.136 MHA 1983 suite of a hospital during the processing of an application for admission under the MHA 1983 would be deprived of their liberty even if they are required to remain there for up to eight hours.[30]

**3.31**    In the absence of clear guidance from the courts as to the precise period of time that may constitute a non-negligible period, we suggest that it is open for individual public bodies to set down what they consider to be such a period for their own operational purposes where such may be necessary. An obvious example of this is in the hospital setting where a decision will have to be taken as to the length of time that – in general – a patient is in (say) an acute ward before they are considered to be deprived of their liberty. It would clearly make sense in such a setting for the relevant hospital Trust to have a policy as to the length of time considered to be 'non-negligible' for these purposes. That policy should allow for calibration to individual circumstances: in other words, to make clear that, the more intense the measures of control the person is subject to, and/or the more the person resents the control to which they are subject, the shorter the period of time that can be considered 'non-negligible'.

**3.32**    Because the period will vary from setting to setting, we have deliberately avoided in this guidance giving a period of time that can be considered 'safe'. Our clear view is that it is unlikely under any of the circumstances considered in this guidance to extend beyond a few (2-3) days and is likely to be substantially less in settings in which particularly intense measures of control are imposed. We would **strongly** suggest that it is not safe to use the rule of thumb that some public bodies have adopted that a deprivation of liberty is unlikely to arise where a person is confined for less than seven days. We understand that this may have been taken from a reading of certain paragraphs of the DOLS Code as to the circumstances under which it is appropriate to grant an urgent authorisation.[31] However, this is to conflate the question of **whether** there is a deprivation of liberty with the quite separate question of **how** such deprivation of liberty may be authorised.

## G    *Cheshire West*: a test of universal application?

3.33    It is clear that the Supreme Court was not expressly addressing the situation of all persons to whom the acid test might apply: for instance, those in hospices or intensive care units in hospitals.

3.34    Understandable concern has been expressed by many professionals and providers that applying the test in some of these contexts will lead to a diversion of clinical and social work professionals from their 'real' tasks in favour of the completion of DOLS paperwork that are perceived as serving no useful function for the protection of the rights of the individuals concerned.[32] Further concern has been expressed that the application of the test (for instance in the context of those in the last days or hours of their lives) leads to undue distress on the part of families and others concerned with the care and treatment of the individual.

3.35    It is proper to acknowledge these concerns. It is also proper to acknowledge the strong concern that many front line professionals feel that, although the Law Commission has been asked to review deprivation of liberty in the health and social care context,[33] the Commission will not produce draft legislation until the summer of 2017, and there is – at present – no plans for any legislative amendments in the meantime.

3.36    However, these wider concerns are beyond the scope of this guidance which focuses upon the question of **when** a deprivation of liberty may arise. Professionals must be careful not to let their concerns as to the consequences of the application of the acid test drive how the test is interpreted. Unless it is possible to identify a legal basis upon which the test does not apply in a particular set of circumstances, we suggest that it is necessary to proceed on the basis that it does. Even if Lord Neuberger's judgment in *Cheshire West* might be read as indicating that he considered that the test is not necessarily universal,[34] Lord Neuberger nonetheless indicated that it should be adopted '*unless there is good reason not to*'.[35]

3.37    This guidance highlights points at which it might properly be considered that there is good reason (founded upon the case law) to suggest that the acid test might not apply. Indeed, we highlight points where we consider it is very likely that a judge, asked to decide whether a particular individual was deprived of their liberty, would be very sympathetic to arguments that they were not.

3.38    It is perhaps helpful to highlight one overarching factor. Lady Hale's judgment can be read as suggesting that context is still a factor that may be of relevance –

in line with the decision of the Grand Chamber in *Austin* v. *United Kingdom*.[36] The judgment in *Austin* is a frustratingly ambiguous one, but suggests that it remains properly open to those on the ground to consider the context in which the deprivation of liberty is said to arise. The further away that any particular circumstances are from those of P, MIG and MEG, the more that it might be said that the court could properly find grounds upon which to apply the objective element of the Article 5 test in a different fashion to that set down in *Cheshire West*. In other words, the more likely we consider it is that the courts will find principled reasons for saying that the 'acid test' does not apply in exactly the same fashion as it did to P, MIG and MEG.

**3.39**   We emphasise, however, that the matters set out above are ultimately legal questions upon which only a court is capable of deciding.

**3.40**   Finally, we reiterate that, until the courts have considered the questions set out above (as well as others that will no doubt emerge), it is important that we should not abandon attempts to identify the dividing line between a restriction upon freedom of movement and a deprivation of liberty.[37] Throughout the 'setting-specific' chapters of this guidance, therefore, we outline situations in which we consider it can be properly said that the individuals in question are not deprived of their liberty but 'merely' subject to restrictions upon their freedom of movement.

## Endnotes

1    Paragraph 57.
2    [2004] ECHR 471 at paragraph 91.
3    In *Stanev*, the term was 'constant supervision' (paragraph 128).
4    As would be the case, for example, in a maternity unit where a woman lacking capacity (i.e. called P before the Court of Protection) to take decisions as to her own medical treatment is imminently to give birth, where 'It will commonly be the case that when at the acute hospital P: i) will have obstetric and midwifery staff constantly present throughout her labour and delivery; ii) will be under the continuous control of obstetric and midwifery staff who, because she lacks capacity to make decisions about her medical care, will take decisions on her behalf in her best interests' (*NHS Trust* v. *FG* [2014] EWCOP 30).
5    [1985] 7 EHRR 528.
6    [2012] 55 EHRR 22
7    *Stanev* at paragraph 128.
8    In the case of *Rochdale MBC* v. *KW* [2014] EWCOP 45, Mostyn J held that (in the context of a deprivation of liberty at home) a person who is not physically capable of leaving cannot be deprived of their liberty for the purposes of Article 5 ECHR. KW's appeal against the decision was allowed by consent by the Court of Appeal in February 2015 (without any accompanying judgment; see also Mostyn J's subsequent judgment [2015] EWCOP 13). We suggest that the decision is so clearly incompatible with the *Cheshire West* decision and with the Strasbourg case law that it should not be followed. We address this further below in Chapter 8.
9    Indeed, this is also clear from the Strasbourg case law: see *HL* at paragraph 92.
10   Paragraph 50. Their compliance/lack of objection is very relevant to the question of whether the deprivation of liberty can be said to be in their best interests.
11   It is not necessary that a person has somewhere else to go for them to be deprived of their liberty: Mr Stanev had nowhere else to live (see paragraph 153 of the decision in his case).
12   In *Rochdale MBC* v. *KW* [2014] EWCOP 45 Mostyn J held (at paragraph 20) that Lady Hale had in *Cheshire West* 'implicitly approved' this earlier finding, and that this was the 'required sense' of the second part of the acid test. The phrase quoted was the conclusion reached by Munby J (as he then was) in *JE* v. *DE & Ors* [2006] EWHC 3459 (Fam) (at paragraph 115). However, as noted above, KW's appeal was allowed by consent in February 2015.

13    Paragraph 128.

14    I.e. the place that they chose is actually available.

15    See *JE v. DE & Ors* [2006] EWHC 3459 (Fam) at paragraphs 115-117. Surrey County Council would also have moved MIG to a different foster placement had she wished, but this did not prevent her from being held to be deprived of her liberty.

16    See also in this regard the decision of Peter Jackson J in *Hillingdon LBC v. Neary* [2011] EWHC 1377 (COP) and that of Baker J in *AJ (Deprivation of Liberty Safeguards)* [2015] EWCOP 5.

17    We deliberately use this broad phrase, and intend it to encompass more than those who would have authority to take decisions regarding the individual's care and residence under the MCA 2005 (i.e. attorneys under a health and welfare Lasting Power of Attorney or health and welfare deputies).

18    Paragraph 91.

19    Paragraph 49.

20    This is clear from the fact that Lady Hale then explained in the next sentence that the possibility of someone not being free to leave but not being subject to sufficient control and supervision as to be deprived of their liberty 'could be the explanation for the doubts expressed in *Haidn v. Germany,*' (Application no 6587/04), where the court expressed 'serious doubts' whether instructing the applicant to live in an old people's home which he was not to leave without his custodian's permission amounted to a deprivation rather than a restriction of liberty. It is clear that this was not a case relating to physical steps being taken to prevent a person leaving a place.

21    E.g. by a guardian.

22    See the decision of the Upper Tribunal in *NL v. Hampshire County Council (Mental health: All)* [2014] UKUT 475 (AAC) at paragraphs 14-19. The Upper Tribunal held that, even if the power that could be exercised by the guardian could have the effect of meaning that Mr L was not free to leave the place where he was required to reside, he could not be considered to be deprived of his liberty because the requisite additional elements of continuous supervision and control were contained within the care plan. As the local authority was not imposing those elements of supervision and control upon Mr L, he was therefore not considered to be deprived of his liberty.

23    See paragraph 50.

24    Mr L was compliant, and never tried to leave Bournewood Hospital.

25    See Lady Hale in the speech quoted at paragraph 2.34 above.

26    See *Cheshire West* at paragraph 46.

27    *Cheshire West* at paragraph 20 citing *Stanev* at paragraph 117.

28    See, for instance, *Rantsev v. Cyprus and Russia* (App. No. 25965/04) [2010] ECHR 22: '*In all, the alleged detention lasted about two hours. Although of short duration, the Court emphasises the serious nature and consequences of the detention and recalls that where the facts indicate a deprivation of liberty within the meaning of Article 5(1), the relatively short duration of the detention does not affect this conclusion*' (paragraph 317, emphasis added).

29    *ZH v. Commissioner of the Police for the Metropolis* [2013] EWCA Civ 69 at paragraph 83.

30    *Sessay v. South London & Maudsley NHS Foundation Trust & The Commissioner of Police for the Metropolis* [2011] EWHC 2617 (QB).

31    Most obviously paragraphs 6.3 and 6.4.

32    Especially where there is no realistic prospect that the necessary assessments can be completed so as to allow, e.g. for a DOLS authorisation to be granted in an Intensive Care Unit prior to the patient's departure from that unit.

33    **lawcommission.justice.gov.uk/areas/capacity-and-detention.htm**. That review may give an opportunity to consider the philosophical objections to the test voiced by those who consider that the Supreme Court placed too much store on an abstract concept of physical liberty: see the judgment of Mostyn J in *Rochdale MBC v. KW* [2014] EWCOP 45.

34    At paragraph 61, he held that 'at least in principle, the approach proposed by Lady Hale appears to me to be attractive, and should be adopted unless there is good reason not to do so'. Whether this actually represents the view of the majority is questionable, given that Lord Sumption expressly agreed with Lady Hale, and Lord Kerr agreed with both Lady Hale and Lord Neuberger.

35    It is questionable whether Lord Neuberger was doing more than setting up his analysis of why the reasons advanced by Lords Carnwath and Hodge were not good reasons to adopt the approach. This point and that made in the footnote above will no doubt be the subject of legal argument in due course.

36    *Austin v. United Kingdom* (2012) 55 EHRR 14. See paragraph 44 of the judgment in *Cheshire*

*West* in particular, where Lady Hale expressly noted that it may be 'most helpful' to consider how the question before the Supreme Court 'has been approached in the particular context, *in this case the placement of mentally incapacitated people*, whose lawful detention in any setting designed for their care is always potentially justifiable under article 5(1)(e)' (emphasis added).

37    As Lady Hale noted in *Cheshire West*, the cases before the Supreme Court were 'not about the distinction between a restriction on freedom of movement and the deprivation of liberty. P, MIG and MEG are, for perfectly understandable reasons, not free to go anywhere without permission and close supervision'. Paragraph 48.

# II SPECIFIC SETTINGS

## 4 THE HOSPITAL SETTING

### A Introduction

4.1   This chapter focuses on deprivation of liberty of those lacking the capacity to consent to care, treatment and confinement in a hospital setting for purposes of treatment of physical disorders. This includes NHS hospitals and treatment by the independent sector/private hospitals, but also transfer to hospital in the first instance by ambulance, and care in the hospice setting. Questions relating to deprivation of liberty in the psychiatric setting are dealt with in Chapter 6. In line with the other chapters, it does not provide detailed answers to the questions of what should happen where a deprivation of liberty has been identified.

4.2   The majority of patients who lack capacity to make decisions about their care and treatment and admission to or discharge from hospital can be treated in their best interests under s.5 MCA 2005. Restraint may be used provided that the person using restraint reasonably believes that it is necessary to restrain the patient in order to prevent harm to the patient, and that the act is a proportionate response to the likelihood of the patient suffering harm, and the seriousness of the harm.[1] The difficult issue to identify is the point at which the level and intensity of the restraint used amounts to a deprivation of liberty.

4.3   As a starting point, we should emphasise that emergency life-sustaining interventions and the provision of emergency care to a patient lacking consent to such treatment **should always be given** as clinically required and **there should never be any delay** for prior deprivation of liberty authorisation to be sought. We acknowledge that this means that there may – in some cases – be situations in which the question of whether a person is deprived of their liberty (and if so, how that deprivation of liberty is to be authorised) cannot be resolved prior to the administration of such treatment.

4.4   As noted at paragraph 3.33 above, the acid test set out in the Supreme Court in *Cheshire West*, i.e. 'continuous (or complete) supervision and control' and 'lack of freedom to leave', did not address the situations of those in Accident and Emergency

('A&E') departments, hospices or intensive care units. There is no case law at the time of writing this guidance that deals specifically with deprivation of liberty in these settings,[2] and it is not absolutely clear how the courts will approach these questions.

4.5    However, in very broad terms, and although this has not been tested before the courts, we consider that:

4.5.1    it is likely that the immediate provision of life-sustaining treatment to an incapacitated patient in a true emergency situation will not be considered to be a deprivation of liberty (either in the ambulance or in the A&E setting);[3]
but that:

4.5.2    as the patient transitions from the initial emergency treatment to ongoing care the risk of deprivation of liberty increases with the increasing duration of such treatment (or other such treatment as identified as clinically necessary).

4.6    As soon as a deprivation of liberty has been identified, appropriate steps should be taken to obtain authorisation, either under Schedule A1 to the MCA 2005 (a 'DOLS authorisation'[4]), under the MHA 1983, or from the Court of Protection.[5] We should highlight here that, in the event that a person suffering from a mental disorder within the meaning of the MHA 1983 requires assessment and treatment for that disorder and wishes to leave the hospital before the assessment has been carried out, consideration should be given to the use of the powers of detention contained in the MHA 1983 to ensure that the person does not leave the hospital (see Chapter 5) before that assessment has been carried out.[6]

## B    The acid test and the hospital setting

4.7    When considering whether a patient is 'free to leave' for the purpose of the acid test the focus should not be on whether a patient is actually physically capable of leaving, but rather upon what actions hospital staff would take if for example family members, properly interested in their care, sought to remove them from the hospital.

4.8    In addressing the 'acid test' it is also particularly important in a hospital setting to consider the following:

4.8.1    whether the deprivation of liberty is likely to last for more than a negligible period of time;
4.8.2    whether the person is able to give consent to what amounts to the 'objective' deprivation of their liberty; and
4.8.3    whether the deprivation is imputable to the State.

4.9    The scenarios below attempt to distinguish those situations:

■    in which we consider the individuals in question to be deprived of their liberty;

- where there may be a potential deprivation of liberty; and
- where individuals are subject to restrictions in their freedom of movement not amounting to a deprivation of liberty.

4.10    Because, as set out above, the legal position regarding what amounts to a deprivation of liberty in hospital settings is unclear, it is essential that Trusts put in place policies which define for their purposes who they consider to be deprived of their liberty; and how they propose to authorise the same.

## C    'Imputable to the State'

4.11    A deprivation of liberty only falls within the scope of Article 5(1) ECHR if it is 'imputable' to the State. This will inevitably be satisfied in an NHS hospital setting. Care may also be arranged or commissioned by a Clinical Commissioning Group ('CCG') or Local Health Board to be provided by an independent healthcare provider[7] and in these circumstances, except for situations where the person is being cared for in the community, the Deprivation of Liberty Safeguards will also apply. There will also be circumstances where a patient is being cared for in a hospital and receiving treatment from a private provider and the arrangements are privately funded and not made by the State. The DOLS Code makes it clear that even though these situations are outside the scope of Article 5(1) ECHR, they are to be treated as if they were within its scope, such that managing authorities of such institutions are required to apply for an authorisation if the care and treatment of their patient meets the acid test.[8]

4.12    It is therefore necessary to consider whether the totality of the care and treatment arrangements amount to a deprivation of liberty, whether the person is being treated in an NHS hospital or by an independent healthcare provider and whether the care is arranged and commissioned by a CCG or privately.

## D    Conveyance by ambulance to or from hospital

4.13    Transporting a person who lacks capacity from their home, or another location to a hospital by ambulance in an emergency will not usually amount to a deprivation of liberty. In almost all cases, it is likely that a person can be lawfully taken to a hospital or care home by ambulance under the wider provisions of the Act, as long as it is considered that being in the hospital or care home will be in their best interests.[9]

4.14    The DOLS Code suggests[10] that there may be exceptional circumstances where taking a person to a hospital or a care home amounts to a deprivation of liberty. We suggest that the following situations which include, but go beyond those discussed in the Code, may give rise to the need to seek authorisation to ensure that the measures taken are lawful:

- where it is or may be necessary to arrange for the assistance of the police and/or other statutory services to gain entry into the person's home and assist in the removal of the person from their home and into the ambulance;

- where it is or may be necessary to do more than persuade or provide transient forcible physical restraint of the person during the transportation;
- where the person may have to be sedated for the purpose of transportation; or
- where the journey is exceptionally long.

**4.15**   Whilst we do not in general in this guidance address how authority is to be sought for deprivation of liberty in particular cases, we consider that we should make clear that, as the law stands, an authorisation under Schedule A1 cannot be used to authorise a deprivation of liberty on the way to the place where the patient will be treated.[11] If there is a real risk that cannot be sensibly ignored that the transport of the patient will amount to a deprivation of their liberty, it will be necessary to obtain an order from the Court of Protection.[12] It is less clear whether an authorisation granted in respect of one hospital can be used to authorise a deprivation of liberty that may arise in respect of a patient being transferred from that hospital to another,[13] and legal advice should be sought where it appears clear that there will be a deprivation of liberty in such a case. We would also emphasise that, in such a case, it will be necessary to ensure in advance that there is a standard authorisation in place in the second hospital (assuming that the circumstances in which the patient will be treated will also amount to a deprivation of liberty).[14]

## Transportation by ambulance: a deprivation of liberty

**4.16**   The measures in the following scenario are likely to amount to a deprivation of liberty:

Jane is 35 years old and lives alone in a rented property. Jane has moderate learning difficulties and can be uncooperative and violent. Jane has given birth to 2 children. They have both been taken into care shortly after birth. By chance Jane's social worker, Alice, meets Jane at the local shopping centre. Alice notices that Jane appears to be about 7 months pregnant. Alice is very concerned because Jane has not been engaging with social services, and has not to her knowledge received any antenatal care. Jane denies that she is pregnant and tells Alice that she is buying new clothes because she 'is getting fat', and that 'anyway they will take the baby away'. Jane had experienced difficulties with her last pregnancy that resulted in an emergency admission to hospital and the baby being delivered by caesarean section. Despite all attempts by the statutory services, Jane refuses to engage and does not attend appointments aimed at monitoring the pregnancy and providing obstetric care. Both social services, and the acute trust that will provide obstetric care to Jane and deliver her child, wish to make arrangements for Jane to be brought into hospital for an ante-natal assessment, blood tests and placental location ultrasound scan and to plan the delivery of her child. The Trust has taken advice and if Jane is not compliant a plan has been devised that provides for the police to assist in gaining entry to Jane's property and for Jane to be transferred from home by ambulance accompanied by professionals employed by the Trust and an anaesthetist. In the event that Jane cannot be persuaded to get into the ambulance she will be given mild sedation and taken from her home using physical restraint. The journey to hospital will take over an hour and during this time both physical and chemical restraint (as appropriate) may be used.

---

Key factors pointing towards a deprivation of liberty:

- the potential involvement of the police and that Jane may be taken to hospital against her will;
- the potential use of sedation and physical restraint to get Jane into the ambulance; and
- the potential use of physical and chemical restraint for a period lasting potentially over an hour.

---

## Transportation by ambulance: potential deprivation of liberty

**4.17**    We suggest that the measures in the following scenario may give rise to a deprivation of liberty:

Ahmed has a serious head injury caused by a road traffic accident. He has been assessed as lacking capacity to make decisions about his care and treatment. He has been admitted to a local Trauma Unit for stabilisation but then requires transfer to the regional Trauma Centre at a hospital 100 miles away. Ahmed is heavily sedated, intubated and ventilated. Because of poor visibility it is not possible for Ahmed to be airlifted to the Trauma Centre. The journey will therefore have to be undertaken by ambulance which will have to travel slowly because of the severity of Ahmed's head injuries and may take up to 5 hours to complete the journey. Ahmed will require continuous care, monitoring and supervision during the course of the journey.

---

Key factors pointing to a potential deprivation of liberty:

- the length of the ambulance journey (which is significantly longer than usual for such a transfer); and
- the degree of monitoring and supervision required.

---

Note: we accept that this scenario is one that may provoke discussion amongst practitioners, and have deliberately included it so that specific consideration can be given by Trusts in the formulation of policies as to the potential for a deprivation of liberty to arise in such cases.

## Transportation by ambulance: not a deprivation of liberty

**4.18**    We suggest that the following scenario is unlikely to amount to a deprivation of liberty:

Trisha lives at home with support. She suffers from dementia which has recently become worse. While making a cup of tea she knocks over a kettle of boiling water that scalds her leg. The care team do their best to treat her leg but it is quite clear that the burn will require medical attention. An ambulance is called by her care worker.

Trisha is in a great deal of pain and is reluctant to get into the ambulance. After some coaxing she gets into the ambulance. The ambulance crew with the assistance of her care worker persuade her to take some medication to ease the pain while she is transported to a nearby hospital Accident and Emergency Department. Trisha becomes agitated during the journey and the ambulance crew have to restrain her briefly during the short journey to avoid her injuring herself further.

Key factor pointing away from deprivation of liberty:

■    the short length of the journey and the short duration of the restraint.

## E    Accident and Emergency ('A&E')

**4.19**    It is of paramount importance that clinicians and hospital staff act in the best interests of their incapacitated patient and that the patient concerned receives appropriate and timely care and treatment.

**4.20**    As set out at paragraph 4.2 above the majority of people who lack capacity to make decisions about their care, treatment and admission to or discharge from hospital can be treated in their best interests under s.5 MCA 2005.

**4.21**    Although most people's stay in A&E is of short duration, as the scenarios below show, this does not of itself mean that a deprivation of liberty cannot occur during such a stay.[15] The more intensive the restraint upon the person (whether physical or chemical) and the more the person is able to perceive what is happening and become distressed or resistant, the shorter will be the period of time before liberty-restricting measures taken in relation to the patient amount to a deprivation of liberty.

**4.22**    There may be circumstances in which staff consider that there may be a deprivation of liberty but that there is, in fact, nothing that can be done about it by way of obtaining authorisation within a sufficiently short period of time. We note in this regard that caution should be adopted in relation to paragraph 6.4 of the Deprivation of Liberty Safeguards Code of Practice which suggests that an urgent deprivation of liberty authorisation should not be granted if a person is in A&E '*and it is anticipated that within a matter of a few hours or a few days the person will no longer be within that environment*'. As set out in paragraphs 3.29-3.32, there may well be cases in which a person is in fact deprived of their liberty within that period of time.

**4.23**    We recognise that the situation set out above is not a happy state of affairs. It is particularly important that Trusts put in place policies that address such situations so that staff are not distracted from the delivery of care to patients but can instead have a clear indication of what they should be doing, parallel to the delivery of that care, to obtain authorisation where such is properly possible.

**4.24**    The following are examples of potentially liberty-restricting measures that may be found in an A&E Department:

- physical restraint and the duration of any restraint;
- the use of sedation;
- the use of catheters and/or intravenous drips;
- the observation and monitoring levels;
- the requirement for a person to remain in a certain area of the A&E department and restricting the person to that area; and
- the requirement that the person does not leave the A&E department pending further tests or transfer.

## A&E: a deprivation of liberty

**4.25**    The measures in the following scenario are likely to amount to a deprivation of liberty:

Dan is brought into the A&E department having taken an overdose of paracetamol. Dan is vomiting, confused and very anxious. He resists attempts by staff to take a blood test and start N-acetylcysteine treatment. He has to be restrained and sedated by members of the hospital staff in order for treatment to be carried out. The treatment will take 24 hours to complete. He tells staff that at the earliest opportunity he will leave the hospital to complete his suicide. Dan is placed in a side room watched by a member of staff while his treatment is carried out and he is forcibly restrained and prevented from leaving during the 24-hour period.

---

Key factors pointing to a deprivation of liberty:

- the monitoring of Dan whilst in the A&E department (in his clinical interests);
- the use of restraint and sedation to carry out the treatment;
- the use of forcible restraint to prevent him leaving; and
- that Dan is aware of and is resistant to the measures being carried out upon him which will, in combination with the use of forcible restraint, compress the relevant time-frame for a deprivation of liberty to occur.

---

**Note:** this situation is one in which consideration should undoubtedly be given to admitting Dan for admission for assessment under the provisions of the MHA 1983.

## A&E: potential deprivation of liberty

**4.26**    We suggest that the measures in the following scenario may give rise to a deprivation of liberty:

John is a 19-year-old, who has gone out with his friends on a Friday night. At 3am, his parents find him showering fully dressed singing at the top of his voice. He has a large bruise and laceration to the left side of his head. His parents take him to hospital. In the A&E Department, John is initially willing to have a skull X-ray and some blood tests. These show a very elevated blood alcohol level and a fracture of the left temporal region of his skull. John then starts getting very argumentative and tells everyone that he is leaving to take a train to the beach. He cannot explain why he has to go to the beach. Clinically, he should have a CT of his brain and probable transfer to a neuro-sciences unit. John is assessed as lacking capacity to make decisions about his care and treatment. The team plans to sedate and ventilate him in order to carry out the transfer. It will take a number of hours for the CT scan to be carried out and thereafter for John to be transferred to the neuro-sciences unit. During this time, John has on one occasion forcibly to be restrained to prevent him assaulting a nurse, he is then administered sedatives and, whilst continuing to be argumentative, he has to be verbally dissuaded from leaving the ward.

---

Key factors pointing to a potential deprivation of liberty:

- the monitoring of John whilst in the A&E department (in his clinical interests); and
- the use of physical restraint and sedation.
- The key factors in determining whether this is a restriction or a deprivation of John's liberty will be the length of time that they are imposed for and the frequency and intensity of the restrictions.

---

## A&E – not a deprivation of liberty

**4.27**    The following scenario is unlikely to amount to a deprivation of liberty:

Olga lives in a rented flat. She has learning difficulties. Her care worker, Sarah, visits her twice daily to support her. On arriving in the morning she finds Olga sitting dazed on the kitchen floor. It appears that she has fallen and knocked her head on the kitchen unit. Sarah asks Olga what happened, but Olga cannot remember. Sarah calls an ambulance and Olga is taken to the A&E Department of the local general hospital. Once at the hospital Olga becomes very agitated because she does not know where she is and she vomits on the floor. She tells Sarah that she wants to go home now. A casualty doctor examines Olga and carries out a basic neurological examination. She explains to Sarah that she would like to keep Olga under observation for a couple of hours in the A&E Department before deciding whether further tests are necessary or sending her back home. Olga does not have capacity to consent to remain in the A&E Department. Sarah and the nursing staff explain to Olga that she needs to stay in hospital for a little longer and that Sarah will stay with her. Olga is pleased that Sarah will stay with her. After two hours she is sent home without any further assessments or treatment being necessary.

---

Key factors pointing away from deprivation of liberty:

- the short length of the stay in the A&E Department; and
- the absence of physical restraint or the use of medication used to manage or modify her behaviour.

## F   Intensive Care Units ('ICU')

**4.28**   The majority of patients in ICU lack capacity to make decisions about their care and treatment during some or all of their stay in ICU, due to the nature of their injuries, or disease, or level of sedation. Physical, mechanical or chemical restraint is often used to facilitate the care of patients in ICU and their care is closely monitored. The circumstances of patients lacking capacity who are in ICU for more than a negligible period of time may meet the 'acid test' criteria, although further judicial consideration is likely to be required in due course.[16]

**4.29**   We suggest that patients who have capacity to consent to their intensive care arrangements before being admitted to intensive care or whilst on the unit and prior to losing capacity are not considered to be deprived of their liberty because they do not satisfy the subjective element of Article 5(1) of the ECHR.[17] We should emphasise that this will only be the case so long as the circumstances in which they are treated and the length of their stay remain as anticipated at the point at which the patient gave their consent.

**4.30**   It is also important to bear in mind in this care setting that aside from mental incapacity, a patient's deprivation of liberty can only be authorised if they are also 'of unsound mind'.[18] For the purposes of seeking authorisation under Schedule A1 to the MCA 2005, this requires the patient to have a mental disorder within the meaning of the MHA 1983, that is, 'any disorder or disability of the mind'.

**4.31**   The state of unconsciousness, caused by a variety of disorders and injuries, presents a particular problem in the context of deprivation of liberty. The Department of Health has recently advised that it does not consider a state of unconsciousness in itself as being a mental disorder for purposes of Schedule A1 to the MCA 2005.[19]

**4.32**   It may be that a patient who is unconscious, but is not otherwise suffering from a mental disorder within the meaning of the MHA 1983, can be the subject of an application to the Court of Protection for an order authorising the deprivation of their liberty,[20] but legal advice will be required in such cases and/or Trusts will have to set out a policy (on the basis of such advice) as to how they intend to proceed in relation to such patients.

**4.33**   This is a difficult area and we anticipate that there is likely to be case law clarifying the position in due course. **However, we reiterate that any questions that may arise in this context of deprivation of liberty should not prevent the delivery of such immediately necessary life-sustaining treatment as continues to be required (and we reiterate again that those delivering such care and treatment will be protected from liability by s.5 MCA 2005 in relation to the delivery of treatment if they reasonably believe that the patient lacks capacity to consent, and that they are acting in the patient's best interests).**

**4.34**   Factors that are likely to be taken into account when considering whether a deprivation of liberty is taking place include:

- continuous monitoring (almost a certainty in ICU);
- length of time sedated and/ or ventilated and/or intubated;
- the use of restraint to bring about admission;
- the use of restraint/medication being used forcibly during admission;
- staff taking decisions on a person's behalf regarding treatments and contact with visitors;
- duration of the restrictions
- the patient not being free to leave the ICU;
- the amount of time it is likely to take for the patient to recover capacity once they are extubated/taken off ventilation/sedation;
- the amount of time the patient is likely to remain in the ICU before moving from the ICU to a an acute ward, or a rehabilitation ward; and
- the package of care taken as a whole.

## ICU: a deprivation of liberty

**4.35**    The measures in the following scenario are likely to amount to a deprivation of liberty:

Mr Smith is a 45-year-old man, who had no significant past medical history. While out jogging, he collapsed in front of an off duty nurse. She called for help and started basic life support until the ambulance arrived. The paramedics found that he was in VF and he was shocked back into sinus rhythm. The total downtime was around 12 minutes. On arrival in the Emergency Department his GCS was 3/15. Primary coronary intervention (PCI) demonstrated a lesion of his circumflex artery, which was stented. Following PCI, he has a CT scan of his brain was reported as normal. Following this, he is admitted to ICU and intubated and ventilated for temperature management. After 24 hours, his temperature is allowed to normalise, and he is ventilated for a further 48 hours (72 in total), after which time it is noted that he had a flexion response to pain, but that he did not localise. The ICU team in consultation with his family decide to perform a tracheostomy to allow early weaning from ventilation and accurate assessment of his neurological function. Following the tracheostomy, his neurology has not changed, but the longer-term prognosis is unclear. A repeat CT does not show any evidence of significant brain injury. A neurological opinion is that there could be significant, possibly complete, recovery, however, any recovery will occur over weeks to months. In the meantime he will have to stay in a hospital environment to optimise his rehabilitation. Mr Smith's family are unhappy that he has to remain in hospital and would like him to return home as soon as possible where they will care for him.

Key factors pointing to deprivation of liberty:

- the degree of monitoring of Mr Smith's condition;
- the length of the potential stay in hospital; and
- that Mr Smith's family would like him to return home in circumstances where the hospital team consider it necessary that he stay in hospital (if

the hospital team, in fact, agreed that he could return home, then there would be no deprivation of liberty).

## ICU: Potential deprivation of liberty

**4.36** We suggest that the measures in the following scenario may give rise to a deprivation of liberty:

Tony is 56 years old. He is in an acute ward recovering from the removal of a large meningioma that has left him with some persistent but minor cognitive impairment. While there he suffers a pulmonary embolism and is brought to ICU for monitoring. He wants to leave the ward to have a cigarette and when advised he will have to stay for his own safety, declares he wants to discharge himself. It is anticipated that he will require some form of sedative medication to ensure his compliance with treatment over the next few days.

Key factors pointing to a deprivation of liberty:

- the degree of supervision and monitoring;
- that Tony may not be free to leave the ICU: the key question will be what staff will do if he does, in fact, seek to discharge himself; and
- the potential use of sedation.

**Note** – it is (deliberately) not clear from this scenario whether Tony's decision-making capacity is impaired (and, if so, how): if the circumstances amount to an objective deprivation of his liberty, an assessment of this will be crucial

## ICU: not a deprivation of liberty:

**4.37** The following scenario is unlikely to amount to a deprivation of liberty:

Mr Dillett is a 55-year-old man, who has been diagnosed with oesophageal cancer. He is suitable for an oesophagectomy and receives adjuvant chemotherapy prior to his operation. He attends a pre-operative clinic and receives information about the operative procedure and his peri-operative management. Included in the information provided are details about the 2-3 days he is expected to stay on ICU post-operatively. On admission he signs the consent form for the operation. The operation goes well, and post-operatively he is sedated and ventilated on ICU and his treatment is going according to plan. The consultant expects Mr Dillett to be extubated in a day or two.

Key factors pointing away from a deprivation of liberty:

- Mr Dillett gave consent to the operation which, by extension, included consent to the consequential treatment plan; and
- the circumstances have not gone beyond those under contemplation at the time of Mr Dillett's consent.

## G    Acute ward

**4.38**    The following are examples of potentially liberty-restricting measures that may be found in an acute ward:

- physical restraint;
- baffle-locks on ward doors;
- mittens, or forms of restraint used to prevent a patient removing or interfering with a nasogastric feeding tube, or intravenous drip;
- raised bedrails;
- catheter bag attached to bed;
- a patient being placed in a chair and being unable to move from the chair without assistance;
- frequency and intensity of observation and monitoring levels;
- the requirement for a patient to remain in a certain area of the ward; and
- the requirement that a patient does not leave the ward, accompanied by a plan that, if he does he will be returned to the ward.

### *Acute ward: a deprivation of liberty*

**4.39**    The measures in the following scenarios are likely to amount to a deprivation of liberty:

Mrs Jones is an 80-year-old lady, who lives on her own in a semi-detached house. One evening her neighbours notice the smell of burning. Not finding anything in their house, they go next door. They find Mrs Jones slumped in her kitchen with the toaster on and a piece of burned charcoal in the toaster. Mrs Jones is admitted to hospital with a diagnosis of severe community acquired pneumonia. She responds well to antibiotics and after a week tells the treating team that she wants to go home. She has been assessed during her admission by the physiotherapy and occupational therapy team, who feel that she has significant problems with her activities of daily living. Their professional opinion is that it would be unsafe for her to return home. The doctors treating her note that she is slightly confused, and she scores 8/10 repeatedly on a mini-mental test. Mrs Jones is adamant that she will not consider anything other than returning home. Her neighbours, who have visited her daily in hospital, are very concerned about her returning home. The treating team considers that she should stay in hospital for further assessment and thereafter a suitable care home should be found for her. She will have to remain on the acute ward until then, and there is no immediate prospect of her returning home.

> Key factors pointing towards a deprivation of liberty:
>
> - the monitoring and supervision of Mrs Jones on the ward;
> - the decision of the treating team not to let her leave to return home; and
> - the potential that Mrs Jones will have to remain on the ward for a significant period of time.

## Acute Ward: potential deprivation of liberty

**4.40**   We suggest that the measures in the following scenario may give rise to a deprivation of liberty:

Alex suffered a serious cerebrovascular accident several years ago. He has been diagnosed as being in a minimally conscious state with little chance of recovering any further function. Although he vocalises and can track with his right eye he is inconsistent in his responses but shows some awareness. He is unable to carry out any activities for himself, he receives CANH via a PEG feeding tube. He required 24-hour nursing care and his care and treatment are constantly monitored. Alex is looked after in a long stay ward of a hospital that specialises in neuro-rehabilitation. He receives excellent care and his wife, Rose and children visit him regularly. Rose recalls Alex telling her before his accident that if at any time in the future he was unable to look after himself, he would want to be looked after at home. Rose has informed those treating Alex that she would like to make arrangements for Alex to be cared for at home. Rose has recently been told that such a move would not be in Alex's best interests and is due to have a further meeting with the treating team to discuss his future.

> Key factors pointing towards a potential deprivation of liberty:
>
> - the monitoring of Alex on the ward and the length of his stay;
> - whether he is free to leave will depend upon whether hospital would, in fact, prevent Rose taking him to care for him at home which will depend upon the outcome of the discussions with the treating team.

## Acute Ward: not a deprivation of liberty

**4.41**   The following scenario is unlikely to amount to a deprivation of liberty:

Cheryl brings her brother Daryl into A&E at 2 o'clock in the morning. Daryl is 19 years old and has mild learning difficulties. He has been involved in a fight with a bouncer at a local club. He is examined by the casualty doctor and sent for an X-Ray. He has a broken jaw and a number of broken teeth. Daryl is referred to a maxillofacial surgeon. He needs to operate on him as soon as possible. The operation will take three or four hours and during that time Daryl will be anaesthetised. After the operation his face will be very sore and his jaw will be held in place by bands in such a way that he will not be able to eat solid food for up to a week after the operation. He will not be able to go home for at least two days during which time he will be kept under observation. Daryl is admitted to a surgical ward. The surgeon assesses Daryl as having capacity to make decisions about his medical treatment and care. Daryl gives his consent to the operation. The operation goes as planned and Daryl goes home two days after the operation.

Key factors pointing away from deprivation of liberty:

■   that Daryl had capacity to give consent to the operation and the consequential treatment arrangements, including the requirement to stay in
hospital for up to two days post-operation.
■   If, however, Daryl did not have capacity to give consent to the operation
and the consequential treatment arrangements, the facts of this scenario
may point to a potential deprivation of liberty.

## H    Hospices

**4.42**   Hospice or palliative care is available in a range of settings, for example as a
hospital in-patient, as a hospice in-patient, as a patient attending a hospice daily or
at home. This part of the guidance concentrates on care provided in a hospice to a
person as an in-patient for a terminal illness.

**4.43**   Provided the proposed treatment and treatment plan is explained to the
person on admission and the person consents to the treatment plan when admitted
to the hospice then we consider that the subjective element of Article 5(1) ECHR
may not be met and the circumstances will not amount to a deprivation of liberty
falling within the scope of the Article 5(1).[21] This, however, must be kept under
review during the person's stay at the hospice and consideration given as to whether
the care and treatment provided to the patient differs from the agreed treatment
plan (because of changes to the patient's condition) to such an extent that the
consent given on admission is no longer valid and the person is deprived of their
liberty.[22]

**4.44**   If the person lacked capacity to make decisions about his care and treatment
at the time they were admitted then staff will need to look closely at the factual
situation to see if the person's circumstances objectively amount to a deprivation of
their liberty.

**4.45**   Most people suffering from a terminal illness are usually only admitted to a
hospice for periods of respite or towards the end of their life. Therefore the length of
time that a person is subject to constraint is likely to be a factor in whether or not the
person is deprived of their liberty within the meaning of Article 5(1) ECHR.
Hospices work together with the patient and the family to provide palliative care
and do not usually admit people who are resisting admission. A hospice is also
unlikely to insist on a person remaining in the hospice if the family wanted him to
return home with care provided for the person at home.

**4.46**   There may, still, however, be circumstances that will meet the 'acid test'.

**4.47**   Factors that are likely to be taken into account when considering whether a
deprivation of liberty is taking place include:

- that the circumstances are no longer covered by a consent given on admission;
- administering sedatives to decrease anxiety and agitation;
- chemical restraint;
- constant supervision in case of terminal agitation; and
- restricting movement of patients who are mobile, so that they are not free to leave the hospice grounds because they may be a danger to themselves.

**4.48**   Because we consider that, in very many cases, whether a person is deprived of their liberty will turn on (1) whether, in fact they are free to leave; and (2) whether they have given consent in advance, we offer here only one scenario that amounts to a deprivation of liberty and one that we suggest does not amount to such a deprivation.

## Hospice: a deprivation of liberty

**4.49**   The measures in the following scenarios are likely to amount to a deprivation of liberty:

Mariam is 34 years old. She has a 4-year-old daughter and 2-year-old son. She has an inoperable primary brain tumour. Some time before admission she had discussed her end of life plan in a general way with her GP, family and staff of the Hope Hospice. She chose Hope Hospice because of its location near to her family home and beautiful gardens. She has agreed with her partner that she will spend weekdays at the hospice and weekends at home. She had been receiving care at home so that she could spend as much time as possible with her young children, but she has deteriorated more rapidly than had been anticipated. She is now very confused, has become doubly incontinent and suffers from acute headaches that require constant pain relief. In accordance with her previously known wishes she is brought to the hospice by her partner and is admitted to the hospice. At the point of admission she is assessed as lacking capacity to consent to her admission and the proposed treatment plan. Although confused she is still mobile. She requires constant supervision because she wanders out of the hospice into the road where she is at risk of injury. At times she becomes very agitated and wishes to go home to be with her children and has to be restrained by staff to ensure that she remains at the hospice to receive care. Mariam's partner has told hospice staff that he is unable to cope with Mariam's care at home during the weekends as well as looking after their children. The hospice does not consider it in Mariam's best interests to go home. Mariam is in receipt of palliative care and she is likely to remain at the hospice until her death, which may be some weeks away.

> Key factors pointing towards a deprivation of liberty:
>
> - Mariam is under constant supervision; she is not free to leave (and, additionally, must be restrained to prevent her acting upon her desire to leave).
> - Mariam is likely to remain at the hospice for a number of weeks.

## *Hospice: not a deprivation of liberty*

**4.50**    The following scenario is unlikely to amount to a deprivation of liberty:

Mandeep has stage 4 ovarian cancer which has reached a terminal phase. During most of her illness she has been cared for at home by her mother and sister. Once she became aware that her illness was terminal she visited her local hospice with her sister and agreed that she would go there for care within the next week or two. While there she discussed and agreed an advance care plan that detailed her end of life care wishes and preferences. This plan includes pain relief and the use of sedative medication to manage the symptoms of the terminal phase of her illness and the use of a nurse call system that will activate if she starts to wander. She was told that her family could visit her at any time. When she was admitted to the hospice she gave her agreement to a care package which reflected the terms of the advance care plan. Not long after Mandeep is admitted she loses capacity to make care and treatment decisions. The hospice continues to care and treat her in accordance with the agreed care package.

---

Key factors pointing away from a deprivation of liberty:

■    Mandeep gave advanced consent to the care and treatment arrangements that are now in place.

---

## I    Questions for frontline practitioners

**4.51**    These questions may help establish whether an individual is deprived of their liberty in this context:

■    What liberty-restricting measures are being taken?
■    When are they required?
■    For what period will they endure?
■    What are the effects of any restraint or restrictions?
■    What are the views of the person, their family or carers?
■    How are any restraints or restrictions to be applied?
■    Are there less restrictive options available?
■    Is force or restraint (including sedation) being used to admit the patient to a hospital to which the person is resisting admission?
■    Is force being used to prevent a patient leaving the hospital, hospice, or ambulance where the person is persistently trying to leave?
■    Is the patient prevented from leaving by distraction locked doors, restraint, or because they are led to believe that they would be prevented from leaving if they tried?
■    Is access to the patient by relatives or carers being severely restricted?
■    Is the decision to admit the patient being opposed by relatives or carers who live with the patient?
■    Has a relative or carer asked for the person to be discharged to their care and is the request opposed or has it been denied?

- Are the patient's movements restricted within the care setting?
- Are family, friends or carers, prevented from moving the patient to another care setting or prevented from taking them out at all?
- Is the patient prevented from going outside the hospital or hospice (escorted or otherwise)?
- Is the patient's behaviour and movements being controlled through the regular use of medication or, for example, seating from which the patient cannot get up, or by raised bed rails that prevent the patient leaving their bed?
- Does staff exercise complete control over the care and movement of the person for a significant period?
- Is the patient constantly monitored and observed throughout the day and night?

## Endnotes

1   Sections 6(1)-(3) MCA 2005.
2   Although the case of *NHS Trust & Ors* v. *FG* [2014] EWCOP 30 suggests that the 'acid test' may well be satisfied in the context of the delivery of obstetric care to a person incapable of consenting to it.
3   For a fuller discussion on this see M. Crews et al, *Deprivation of Liberty in Intensive Care*, Journal of the Intensive Care Society, October 2014.
4   Most likely an urgent authorisation in the first instance, although note that an urgent authorisations should only be granted if the situation giving rise to the deprivation of liberty could not have been anticipated in sufficient time to enable a standard authorisation to be sought: see *NHS Trust & Ors* v. *FG*, footnote 2 above, at paragraph 101.
5   For further discussion, see the paper entitled: *Deprivation of Liberty in a Hospital Setting* by Alex Ruck Keene and Catherine Dobson: **www.39essex.com/docs/articles/ deprivation-of-liberty-in-the-hospital-settingv3.pdf.**
6   See ss.136, 5(2) and 5(4) of MHA 1983. Section 5 of the MHA 1983 only applies to patients who have been admitted to hospital. The Accident and Emergency Department waiting area of a hospital is considered a public place for the purpose of section 136 MHA 1983 – *R (Sessay)* v. *(1) South London & Maudsley NHS Foundation Trust (2) The Commissioner of Police for the Metropolis* [2011] EWHC 2617 (QB) at paragraph 39.
7   See paragraph 2.50. Independent healthcare providers are private, voluntary or non-profit individuals or organisations that are not owned or managed by the NHS. Their services may be contracted by the NHS, may be paid for by and individual or funded through healthcare insurance schemes. Some providers deliver services both privately and for the NHS. Independent providers deliver a wide range of services to both adults and children. There are 276 independent acute hospital and 47 independent treatment centres registered with the Care Quality Commission. The Care Quality Commission does not currently oversee the regulation of the independent healthcare services that deliver secondary and tertiary care, but proposes to begin doing so in 2015.
8   Paragraph 1.21 of the DOLS Code, available at **webarchive.nationalarchives.gov.uk/ 20130107105354/http:/www.dh.gov.uk/prod-consum-dh/groups/dh-digitalassets/@dh/@en/ documents/digitalasset/dh-087309.pdf.**
9   Paragraph 2.14 of the DOLS Code.
10   Paragraph 2.15.
11   *GJ* v. *The Foundation Trust* [2009] EWHC 2972 (Fam) at paragraph 9: 'The new provisions in the MCA [i.e. in Schedule A1] do not cover taking a person to a care home or a hospital. But they can be given before the relevant person arrives there so that they take effect on arrival (see for example paragraph 52 of Schedule A1 to the MCA).'
12   Court of Protection judges are available, in suitably urgent cases, to hear cases 24 hours a day 365 days a year. The guidance at paragraph 23(a) of the Annex to the judgment in *NHS Trust & Ors* v. *FG* [2014] EWCOP 30 contains details of as to matters to be considered when arranging ambulance transfers, relevant beyond the context with which that case is concerned.
13   The question is as to the point at which it can properly be said that the patient ceases to be a 'detained resident' in the first hospital. Up until that point, it appears that an authorisation

granted in respect of that first hospital may provide authority to deprive the patient whilst they are on 'leave' from the hospital: *Re P (Scope of Schedule A1)* (30 June 2010) (Unreported) (Mostyn J). Once the patient ceases to be a detained resident, the first standard authorisation must lapse. The standard authorisation that would authorise the deprivation of liberty in the second hospital could not take effect until the patient arrived at the hospital.

14    See *NHS Trust & Ors v. FG* [2014] EWCOP 30 at paragraph 101.

15    The legal reasons why this is so are set out at paragraphs 3.29-3.32.

16    See also here M. Crews et al *Deprivation of Liberty in Intensive Care*, Journal of the Intensive Care Society, October 2014.

17    The subjective element is discussed at paragraphs 2.27-2.20.

18    The requirement imposed by Article 5(1)(e) ECHR.

19    Department of Health Letter to DOLS Leads, 14 January 2015 at: www.mentalcapacitylawandpolicy.org.uk/wp-content/uploads/2014/04/DH-Letter-to-MCA-DoLS-Leads-14-January-2015-FINAL.pdf.

20    Because the Court of Protection does not have to apply the requirement that the individual suffers a mental disorder within the meaning of the MHA 1983, but instead may be able to take a broader approach to the meaning of the phrase 'of unsound mind'.

21    The subjective element is discussed further at paragraphs 2.17-2.19.

22    See also the Department of Health letter to MCA DOLS leads, 14 January 2015, available at www.mentalcapacitylawandpolicy.org.uk/wp-content/uploads/2014/04/DH-Letter-to-MCA-DoLS-Leads-14-January-2015-FINAL.pdf.

# 5    THE PSYCHIATRIC SETTING

## A    Introduction

**5.1**    This chapter considers how to identify deprivation of liberty in psychiatric hospitals. These vary greatly depending on the level of security and the client group.

**5.2**    Please also see Chapters 6 and 7 which consider two different types of community settings where residents may be subject to powers under the MHA 1983, such as conditional discharges, Community Treatment Orders (CTOs) and Guardianship.

## B    Hospitals

**5.3**    A 'hospital' is defined in s.275 National Health Service Act 2006 as:

(a)    any institution for the reception and treatment of persons suffering from illness,
(b)    any maternity home, and
(c)    any institution for the reception and treatment of persons during convalescence or persons requiring medical rehabilitation,

and includes clinics, dispensaries and out-patient departments maintained in connection with any such home or institution, and 'hospital accommodation' must be construed accordingly.

**5.4**    The same definition appears in s.206 National Health Service (Wales) Act 2006. This is also the definition used by the MHA 1983.

**5.5**    Within this broad definition, there is a huge range of hospitals for the care and treatment of people with mental disorders which we will refer to as 'psychiatric hospitals'. Secure Mental Health Services comprise the three High Secure Hospitals (Broadmoor, Rampton and Ashworth), medium secure services and low secure services. These are not considered further in this chapter as those cared for in such secure settings will always be liable to detention under the MHA 1983, which provides authority to deprive the patient of his or her liberty for assessment and psychiatric treatment. We consider that the nature of secure settings is such that they will almost inevitably involve a deprivation of liberty.

5.6    Identification of deprivation of liberty, or of a risk that cannot be ignored that a particular patient may be deprived of his or her liberty, will be important in settings where the MHA 1983 may or may not be used. These will include:

5.6.1    acute wards;

5.6.2    rehabilitation wards or 'stepdown' placements;

5.6.3    CAMHS (Children and Adolescent Mental Health Services) wards;

5.6.4    assessment and Treatment Units (ATUs); and

5.6.5    dementia specialist units.

5.7    These settings are provided both by the NHS and the independent sector. In the great majority of cases the patient's care will have been commissioned by the relevant Clinical Commissioning Group ('CCG').[1] In all these settings patients may be treated for their mental disorder informally (where the patient is described as an 'informal' or 'voluntary' patient), provided (1) the care and treatment regime does not amount to a deprivation of liberty; or (2) if it does, they can consent to the restrictions amounting to a deprivation of their liberty.[2]

5.8    If the patient either cannot or does not consent to their admission, assessment and/or treatment for mental disorder in the psychiatric setting, and that admission, assessment and/ or treatment will involve a deprivation of their liberty, then authority will be required under one of four routes:

5.8.1    the provisions of the MHA 1983;

5.8.2    DOLS, i.e. the provisions of Schedule A1 Mental Capacity Act 2005 ('DOLS');

5.8.3    (unusually) by way of an order made under the inherent jurisdiction of the High Court; or

5.8.4    (unusually) by way of an order made by the Court of Protection.

5.9    The decision as to which legal framework to use is outside the scope of this document but will first require an assessment of:

5.9.1    whether the arrangements made for the patient's care and treatment deprives them of their liberty, or whether there is 'a possibility that cannot sensibly be ignored'[3] that they may do so; and

5.9.2    if so, whether the patient can, and does, consent to those arrangements.

5.10    In addition to the availability of legal frameworks to authorise deprivation of liberty, practitioners must apply the provisions of the MHA Code of Practice (the

'MHA Code'), whether or not the compulsory powers of the MHA 1983 are being used. This is because – in addition to giving guidance about the use of the MHA 1983 – the Code provides guidance for 'medical practitioners and members of other professions in relation to the medical treatment of patients suffering from mental disorder.'[4] This also includes treatment in the community.

**5.11**    This guidance looks at the settings set out in paragraph 5.6 and considers how a deprivation of liberty can be identified in each setting. It is worth remembering that all hospitals – whether treating physical or mental disorder – need to run on the basis of a structured timetable. Anyone who has received in-patient treatment in a busy surgical ward will know this can involve surrendering control over many aspects of life, in ways that may not have been anticipated before the admission begins. We stress that the fact that we identify measures that restrict liberty is not a criticism of the care provided: some restrictions are unavoidable. Similarly, where we identify risks that a particular scenario involves a deprivation of a patient's liberty, this simply means that the patient is entitled to the legal safeguards, in the form of independent checks, required by Article 5. Lady Hale summed this up in the Supreme Court judgment in *Cheshire West*: thus '[n]or should we regard the need for such checks as in any way stigmatising of them or of their carers. Rather, they are a recognition of their equal dignity and status as human beings like the rest of us' (paragraph 57).

**5.12**    It should be noted that the Care Quality Commission ('CQC') which inspects mental health services and monitors the use of the MHA has expressed the view that any incapacitated patient who requires psychiatric admission is likely to satisfy the 'acid test' for deprivation of liberty.[5]

## C    Psychiatric hospitals generally: measures which restrict liberty

**5.13**    The following are examples of potentially liberty-restricting measures that apply in psychiatric hospitals generally:

- Wards are busy places where there may be a high turnover of patients and significant pressure on staff time. This can result in blanket restrictions. These include: limited access to bedrooms during the day; restrictions on access to parts of the ward such as kitchen areas.
- Setting of observation and monitoring levels.
- Requirements for patients to be escorted in certain parts of the ward or site.
- The physical environment (e.g. wards not on ground level) may limit patients' access to the outdoors.
- The prescription and administration of medication to a patient who lacks capacity to consent to it, in particular medication to sedate and/or to control the behaviour of the patient.
- The extent to which the patient is required to adhere to a timetable.
- Locked doors, or use of 'baffle locks', unless patients have the code and are able to come and go as they please.[6]

- The concept of 'protected time' is a valuable means of ensuring that patients have quiet periods during the day but also represents control over the activities of patients.
- Limited visiting time.
- Lack of easy access to telephones, internet, equipment for hobbies and interests such as art or music materials, possibly on safety or availability grounds.
- Use of seclusion[7], especially where such seclusion is regular and/or prolonged.
- Use of physical restraint, especially where such restraint is regular.
- Sanctions, such as time out, for behaviour that causes concern.
- Restriction of access to finances.

## D   An Acute Ward

5.14   Many patients admitted to psychiatric hospitals will be treated in acute wards. These wards can be very busy depending on the pressure on admissions at the time. Acute wards are not usually intended to be long-stay settings and as such the make-up of the client group will change and may at times be volatile, with patients presenting with a range of different disorders, at an early stage in their recovery.

### Acute Ward: a deprivation of liberty

5.15   The measures in the following scenarios are likely to amount to a deprivation of liberty:

Miss Sara Wong, aged 59, has had mental health issues for many years and has a diagnosis of schizophrenia. She lives on her own now that she has retired and neglects her personal care and her diabetes is not well managed. She is non-compliant with diet guidance and does not like taking her anti-psychotic medication. It is winter and her central heating boiler is no longer working. She is reluctant to spend money on a new boiler.

Due to her increased paranoia, and threats to neighbours who she accuses of spying on her, a decision is made to admit her to hospital under s.2 MHA 1983 for assessment. She is admitted to the acute ward of the local psychiatric hospital. She becomes cooperative with taking medication and after some weeks, as she agrees to stay on the ward, she is not made the subject of an application under s.3 MHA 1983 at the end of the 28-day period of her initial section, but remains on as an informal patient.

Miss Wong thinks that she is on the ward for treatment of her diabetes and her bad foot. She has agreed to stay on until her foot is better and states that when the doctors tell her she is ready for discharge, she will return home. A formal capacity assessment as to whether she can consent to informal admission has been conducted and Miss Wong is considered to lack such capacity.

A discharge planning meeting takes place attended by the hospital's social worker. The psychiatrist is concerned about Miss Wong's ability to cope on her own, and suggests that she may also have dementia but is awaiting scan results. The psychiatrist recommends that Miss Wong be placed in residential care. No relatives in England have been identified.. The social worker agrees with the psychiatrist that Miss Wong lacks capacity to make a residence decision as she cannot weigh up the risks of returning home and it is feared that once home, she will revert to her habits of not letting the district nurses visit to check her foot and diabetes and also that she will not allow the CPN to check that she is taking her medication. She has also refused a key safe, as she fears that it will include a spy camera and that neighbours will use it to enter her home.

Miss Wong has not asked to go out. However, the hospital is on a very busy road and staff consider it would not be safe for her to go out without staff. She could go out with family but no family have been found. If Miss Wong wanders into the male ward, she is redirected to her own ward. There is a keypad on the door and no one can leave, even visitors, without staff entering the code.

> Key factors pointing to a deprivation of liberty:
>
> ■ the level of supervision and control on the ward; and
> ■ that Miss Wong is not free to leave temporarily without staff present or to go home.

## Acute Ward: potential deprivation of liberty

**5.16** We suggest the measures in the following scenario may give rise to a deprivation of liberty:

Mr Nicholas James has treatment resistant schizophrenia with co-morbid physical problems. He is to be started on clozapine (a drug that needs considerable physical monitoring).

Although this can be done in the community, the team consider it would be preferable and more efficient to do this in hospital, because of concern that Mr James will not attend appointments for monitoring on time. Mr James lacks capacity to consent to treatment as he believes the treatment offered is for an alien infection not a mental disorder. He is happy to come into hospital as an in-patient and receive tablets as this is, he thinks, appropriate treatment for an infection. He thinks it irrelevant that this is a psychiatric hospital as he states that as there are doctors and nurses there who can help him. When on the ward, the staff would be concerned were he to seek to leave while the treatment gets under way and would have to consider invoking s.5 MHA 1983 to prevent him leaving pending assessment for admission under the Act.

> Key factors pointing to a potential deprivation of liberty:
>
> ■ the level of supervision and control on the ward;
> ■ the level of monitoring required in relation to clozapine and the need for staff to consider invoking s.5 MHA 1983; and
> ■ that Mr James may be on the acute ward for a number of days.

- Whether Mr James would in fact be deprived of his liberty would depend in large part upon exactly what plan the staff would have if he sought to leave and the planned length of his admission.

## Acute Ward: not a deprivation of liberty

**5.17** We suggest that the following scenario is unlikely to amount to a deprivation of liberty:

Ms Razia Ahmed has sought help for feelings of depression and hopelessness. She has capacity to consent to admission to hospital for assessment and treatment and has and continues to consent. The consent includes an understanding and agreement that there will inevitably be some restrictions on her movements and that she will be asked to follow the advice of staff about when to leave the ward, and for how long. Ms Ahmed recognises that meals and visits are at set times. She is aware that she may be offered medication, as well as other treatment such as talking therapies, but is not obliged to accept it.

Key factors pointing away from a deprivation of liberty:

- Ms Ahmed has capacity to consent to the admission and the attendant restrictions upon her liberty.

## E   A rehabilitation or 'step down' ward

**5.18** This setting will share some of the features of the acute ward, and many of the measures outlined at paragraph 5.13 are likely to be present. The nature of such placements is that for therapeutic reasons a very structured timetable may be present, which patients are expected to adhere to. Patients are likely to move to these placements at a relatively advanced stage in their recovery and the client base will be more stable as patients are likely to remain for longer.

## Rehabilitation ward: a deprivation of liberty

**5.19** We suggest the measures in the following scenario are likely to amount to a deprivation of liberty:

Mr Alfred Smith has a long history of mental illness. He has a diagnosis of schizophrenia. He has been detained many times under section 3 MHA and has relapsed between admissions. He has held a tenancy in supported living but has neglected himself and his flat is a health hazard. He uses drugs and this is said to compound his problems. He is very pleasant when well but when ill can be aggressive and unpredictable. He has a number of negative symptoms and although it is suspected that his cognitive functioning is impaired. A referral has been made for neuropsychological testing. He always holds residual delusional beliefs and lacks capacity to make decisions about where to live and his care arrangements. He was moved to a locked rehabilitation unit as he has lost many of the skills relating to Activities of Daily Living. He is complying with the timetable but has not yet got escorted leave.

Alfred was detained under s.3 MHA 1983 and applied to the Tribunal. Somewhat to the surprise of the clinical team the Tribunal discharged him on the basis that he would remain informally and he has in fact continued on the ward with the current care plan, which involves a significant degree of oversight over his activities because he is not safe to carry out many Activities of Daily Living unaccompanied. Staff are aware they may need to review this in view of the lifting of the section.

Key factors pointing to a deprivation of liberty:

■    Alfred is not free to leave the locked ward (and when he gets leave, it will be under escort); and
■    Alfred is under supervision and control on the ward, particularly whilst carrying out activities of daily life.

## Rehabilitation or 'step down' ward: potential deprivation of liberty

5.20    We suggest that the measures in the following scenario may give rise to a deprivation of liberty:

Ms Mary Smith is in her 60s with chronic schizophrenia and has been in a cycle of admissions and relapses for many years. She has lived a chaotic life in the community and is street-homeless. She has been in hospital for the past 12 months and has recently moved from an acute ward to a rehabilitation ward. Her psychotic symptoms are controlled by medication but she has significant negative symptoms. Her consultant thinks she may additionally have some cognitive defects. She has lost many of the skills related to the Activities of Daily Living. The aim of the placement is to help her rebuild these and the plan – which she supports – is for her to move into supported accommodation for those with severe and enduring mental health problems. She is compliant with medication which is administered partly orally and partly via depot. However, she needs to be prompted as she would forget otherwise. The ward has a structured timetable: Ms Smith is expected to get up at 8am and is prompted to attend to her personal hygiene which she tends otherwise to neglect. She is encouraged to choose healthy options for breakfast which she helps to prepare and tidy up. She is then encouraged to tidy her bedroom, do her laundry and attend a community meeting with other patients. Each weekday she has a timetable which could involve going to a day centre, attending a cooking class, doing some shopping, or attending a keep fit class. At the end of the day she is encouraged to go to bed no later than midnight. There are limited facilities on the ward for cooking but she is expected to prepare simple meals and snacks. She is discouraged from reliance on takeaways but there is a weekly pizza or curry evening for everyone. There are also organised activities such as trips to the cinema with other patients. The majority of the time Ms Smith accepts and appears to welcome the structured timetable on the ward as part her rehabilitation. Ms Smith would not be allowed to leave the ward unaccompanied without the permission of the clinical team, but can go out with permission when the staff know where she is going.

Key factors pointing to a potential deprivation of liberty:

- Ms Smith is not free to leave and there is a degree of supervision and control over her on the ward and when she leaves the ward.
- A key factor will be the extent to which it can be said that this represents 'support' as opposed to supervision and control. In light of MIG's case (discussed further at paragraph 2.26), we suggest that caution would need to be exercised before such a conclusion is reached.

## Rehabilitation ward: not a deprivation of liberty

5.21   The following scenario is unlikely to amount to a deprivation of liberty:

Ms Naomi Archer is 66 and has schizophrenia. She has a history of alcohol abuse. She has been detained under s.3 MHA 1983 for the last year. Prior to her admission to hospital she had been living in a hostel but was evicted as a result of her behaviour when drinking. Her mental health had deteriorated and she was thought-disordered, aggressive and delusional when she was admitted.

Ms Archer spent six months on an acute ward and her section was renewed. She has made good progress and her psychotic symptoms have receded significantly. She has managed to remain abstinent from alcohol. She continues to hold a number of delusional beliefs including that she has been abducted and an impostor put in her place. She does not believe that the hospital is a real hospital. When she was admitted to hospital she found these beliefs frightening and distressing but now can tolerate them. She has been assessed as lacking capacity to decide where to live. She has been on the rehabilitation ward for the last six months. The plan is for Naomi to move to highly supported accommodation when she leaves hospital and she is on the waiting list for a particular place she has visited and liked very much. The clinical team have made plans for Naomi to be discharged from the hospital as soon as a place is available. If she were to insist on leaving her care coordinator would make an urgent referral to the local authority's homelessness team to secure bed and breakfast for Naomi until her care home place comes up and would arrange support in the community for her until then.

Naomi takes part in the ward programme and at one stage had four hours' unescorted leave a day which she used to visit the library, or spend time with her cousin who lives nearby. She appealed to the Tribunal and at the hearing said she was willing to stay in 'this place, whatever it is' until she was allocated a room at the new placement. The Tribunal discharged her on the basis of her agreement to remain. Naomi's responsible clinician has made it clear to her that she can come and go from the ward as she pleases and is no longer restricted to four hours' unescorted leave. She appears to enjoy taking part in ward activities and rarely spends more than four hours off the ward.

Key factors pointing away from a deprivation of liberty:

■  Naomi is free to leave.
■  Careful examination of whether the arrangements on the ward amount to continuous supervision and control will be necessary to reach a decision.

## F    A CAMHS ward

**5.22**    The Child and Adolescent Mental Health Services ('CAMHS') setting will share some of the features of the acute ward, and many of the measures outlined at paragraph 5.13 are likely to be present. However, the environment should be suitable for their age which allows for their personal, social and educational development and with access to age appropriate leisure activities and facilities for visits from family and carers.[8]

**5.23**    Where a 16- or 17-year-old with capacity refuses admission, consent from those with parental responsibility cannot be relied upon: s.131(4) MHA 1983. Nor can such consent be relied upon where someone under 18 lacks capacity or competence to consent or refuse care arrangements which amount to a deprivation of liberty: *RK v. BCC, YB and AK*.[9] For further details regarding the 'nuanced' acid test for those under 18, see Chapter 9.

## *A CAMHS ward: a deprivation of liberty*

**5.24**    The measures in the following scenario are likely to amount to a deprivation of liberty:

Anna is 16 years old and suffers with severe anorexia. She is admitted to a locked CAMHS ward with a very low body mass index and is refusing food. As she lacks capacity to make dietary decisions or her care and treatment arrangements more generally, given the risk of damage to her organs it is decided with her parents that she will require nasogastric feeding or PEG feeding through her stomach wall which, it is anticipated, she is likely to resist. Physical or chemical sedation will therefore be required to minimise risk of harm and she will not be able to leave her hospital bed for a number of weeks during the re-feeding process.

Key factors pointing to a deprivation of liberty:

■  the use of physical/chemical sedation during the course of her stay on the ward; and
■  her lack of freedom to leave.
■  It is important to also note that if Anna is deprived of her liberty, this falls outside the scope of parental responsibility: see further paragraph 9.5. The use of the MHA 1983 will be required to authorise her detention and psychiatric treatment.

## A CAMHS ward: potential deprivation of liberty

**5.25**   We suggest that the measures in the following scenario may give rise to a deprivation of liberty:

Jon is 16 years old and his concerned mother organised his admission to the locked ward. He suffers from a nervous condition and a chronically neurotic state of mind. The conditions on the ward are as similar as possible to a real home and, whilst there he is regularly observed by staff. He needs permission from staff to use his phone, receives no medication but is engaged in talking and environmental therapies. He is allowed to leave the ward with staff permission, for example to attend the hospital library. He also goes outside to playgrounds and museums with other children, always accompanied by staff. He is able to visit his parents and school friends regularly and, towards the end of his 5-month hospital stay, starts going to school during the day. On one occasion he absconded and was returned by the police. The restrictions are being relaxed as his treatment progresses.

---

Key factors pointing to a potential deprivation of liberty:

■ The degree of control over his activities exercised by the staff on the ward and the extent to which they control his ability to leave the ward.

■ As discussed further in Chapter 9, a key factor will be the extent to which it can be said that the conditions imposed upon Jon are akin to those which would be imposed upon any 16-year-old young person admitted to hospital.

---

**Note:** this case is based upon the facts of the case in *Nielsen* v. *Denmark*,[10] although the child in question in that case was 12 years old. The ECtHR considered that the circumstances did not amount to a deprivation of liberty because any restrictions upon the liberty of the child arose out of the proper exercise of parental responsibility. We suggest that the logic of this case, which has been criticised, is not necessarily applicable to a young person of 16.

## A CAMHS ward: not a deprivation of liberty

**5.26**   The following scenario is unlikely to amount to a deprivation of liberty:

Debbie is 16 years old and lacking the relevant capacity was admitted in her best interests with obsessive compulsive traits concerning keeping herself and her environment immaculately clean. She has a skin rash from scrubbing herself so hard and her hand have become itchy as a result. Every morning her mother attends the ward to collect her for school and returns her in the afternoon. If the family decide to have dinner at home it is expected that she will come back before 8pm. Often her mother returns her at 4pm. Sometimes Debbie will spend the night with her parents, about which the hospital will be informed. Debbie enjoys school greatly and has excellent grades. She engages with psychological therapy at weekends and staff are available during the weekday evenings to learn to tolerate the idea of germs and also to the risks to her physical and mental health arising from her obsessive compulsive traits. Debbie rarely chooses to go out alone and does not wish to go out without her mother or father.

> Key factors pointing away from a deprivation of liberty:
>
> ■ Debbie's age and maturity and the involvement of her parents, and the reality that the hospital does not have the degree of control to require her to be on the ward: see further Chapter 9 for the application of the 'nuanced' acid test in relation to relatively young children.

## G    An Assessment and Treatment Unit (ATU)

5.27    ATUs are specialist in-patient settings for patients with learning disabilities. The level of security of such settings varies. In addition to the features set out at paragraph 5.13 above, some or all of which may be present in ATUs, the CQC has found evidence of a number of restrictive practices in learning disability services.[11] These include:

■ physical restraint;
■ seclusion (often described in misleading terms, not recognized as such and thus not reviewed in accordance with the MHA 1983 Code of Practice);
■ blanket rules which were rarely justified by the needs of the individual patient. This can be exacerbated by pressure on staff through low numbers; and
■ routine and clear boundaries, which can be beneficial and a source of reassurance, but can also entail assuming control over what the individual does with their time.

5.28    It is difficult to identify scenarios in this setting that would not give rise to a real risk of deprivation of liberty (where the individual lacks the material capacity to consent to the restrictions imposed upon them).

### ATU: a deprivation of liberty

5.29    The measures in the following scenario are likely to amount to a deprivation of liberty:

Mr Jaswant Singh has epilepsy, severe autism and learning disabilities and has a history of failed placements. He is twenty years old. He can display challenging behaviour and this can involve self-harm in the form of banging his head against walls, assaulting others, and causing serious damage to property. A community placement broke down 18 months ago and he was admitted to an ATU informally in the absence of any other available alternative. It has however proved very difficult to arrange an alternative placement partly due to a dispute as to who is responsible for funding his care and partly due to the complexity of his needs. He therefore remains in hospital. He has been classified as a delayed discharge for the past year. He lacks capacity to consent to admission or treatment.

Mr Singh finds it hard to tolerate others. He is able to live in a small self-contained bungalow on the hospital site. This is usually occupied by two people but is currently used for Mr Singh alone. Some adaptations have been made, for example handles have been removed from cupboard doors and there are no pictures or ornaments on the walls because Mr Singh would pull them down.

Mr Singh's treatment consists of medication for epilepsy and nursing care. He is encouraged to wear a helmet because of the risk of injury due to head-banging. Otherwise, staff attempt to engage him in a programme of activities inside and outside the ward. His day is very structured and tends to follow a very similar pattern as he finds this easy to cope with Mr Singh is not allowed out of the unit without staff support.

> Key factors pointing towards a deprivation of liberty:
>
> ■ the degree of supervision and control over Mr Singh's day-to-day activities at the ATU;
> ■ the lack of freedom to leave; and
> ■ the indefinite nature of the placement

## H    A dementia specialist unit

5.30    Many of the liberty-restricting measures identified above will be present in such settings. In addition the following features may be present:

■ the need for restraint and other physical interventions, in the patient's best interests, to deliver personal care; and
■ blanket restrictions to avoid risks such as falls.

5.31    As such, we consider it highly unlikely that a patient in this setting who lacks capacity to consent to admission will not be considered to be deprived of his or her liberty. A typical example of an incapacitated compliant patient, who is receiving appropriate care and treatment in his best interests but who satisfies the 'acid test' is set out below.

Mr James Henry has severe dementia and does not understand why he is in hospital, does not know he is in hospital and is calm and settled following treatment with an antidepressant which has reduced his irritability and resistance to care. He does not try to leave and walks with assistance, though his key risk when walking is that he may fall over. Therefore he is often (though not always) accompanied when he walks.

Personal care is provided by nurses so that he can enjoy cleanliness and comfort. At times he resists them and sometimes this is dealt with by the staff leaving and coming back half an hour later. At other times, care is occasionally imposed by using mild restraint so as to assure his cleanliness.

Mr Henry does not try to leave the ward, accepts care and support and accepts food and drink. If he did try to leave he would be stopped, but in fact he is not trying to leave. If he refused medication and his behaviours and distress returned, he would be treated but he is willingly taking medication although he does not understand the purpose.

Mr James regularly has visitors. His wife holds a health and welfare LPA for him; she regularly attends ward rounds and is fully supportive of his care and treatment.

> Key factors pointing to a deprivation of liberty:
>
> ■   Mr Henry is not free to leave in that if he attempted to do so, he would not be allowed to do so (in fact he has not made such attempts); and
> ■   the level of intervention needed to provide safe care for him.

## I   Summary of questions for frontline staff

**5.32**   These questions may help establish whether an individual is deprived of their liberty in this context:

■   Is the door to the ward or unit locked? Does the patient either know the code or have a swipe, and is he or she able to make use of it to come and go as he or she pleases?

■   Can the patient leave the ward at any time or are there any conditions the person is required to adhere to?

■   How easy is it for the patient to go outside and get access to fresh air?

■   What if any steps would be taken by staff if the patient were to announce their intention to leave the ward a) temporarily or b) permanently?

■   Is the patient able to access all areas of the ward when they wish to?

■   Can the patient prepare any refreshments for themselves?

■   Is the patient able to access items for leisure activities when they wish, such as: games consoles, books, means of listening to music, art, craft or writing equipment, the internet?

■   What observation levels is the patient on and how are they monitored?

■   Is the patient prescribed medication? If so, can they consent to such medication, and what is its purpose? Is it to control their behaviour?

■   To what extent is the patient required to adhere to a timetable?

■   Does the ward have a period of 'protected time' when visitors cannot come onto the ward?

■   How easy is it for the patient to use the phone in private?

■   What are the visiting hours?

■   Is the patient ever nursed alone and if so in what circumstances?

■   Is the patient ever secluded? If so, why and for how long on each occasion? Is seclusion regularly used?

■   Is restraint ever used and in what circumstances? How often is it used?

■   Are there any sanctions used if the patient's behaviour is cause for concern? If so what are they and why?

■   Does the patient manage his or her own finances? If not, who does, why, and under what authority?

■   Could any of the liberty-restricting measures be dispensed with and if so how?

## Endnotes

1    There will be a few occasions where the State is not involved in the patient's admission, care or treatment but we do not deal with these in the balance of this guidance, largely because any private hospital would still have to seek authorisation for the deprivation of the patient's liberty under Schedule A1 to the MCA 2005. See further paragraph 2.49.

2    A patient can only be an 'informal' or 'voluntary' patient in such circumstances if they have capacity to consent to their admission and treatment and to the restrictions inherent in that admission and treatment, and give that consent freely: see *A PCT v. LDV* [2013] EWHC 272 (Fam) and paragraph 2.19.

3    *AM v. South London and Maudsley NHS Foundation Trust* [2013] UKUT 365 AAC

4    S118 (1) (b).

5    'Monitoring the Mental Health Act 2013/4' (page 47), available at **www.cqc.org.uk/content/mental-health-act-annual-report-201314**.

6    The CQC has noted an increase in the use of locked wards, finding that 86% of the wards visited in 2013/14 were locked: see page 47 of its report: *Monitoring the Mental Health Act in 2013/4*.

7    Seclusion is defined in the 2015 MHA Code of Practice (available at **www.gov.uk/government/publications/code-of-practice-mental-health-act-1983**) at 26.103 as 'the supervised confinement and isolation of a patient, away from other patients, in an area from which the patient is prevented from leaving, where it is of immediate necessity for the purpose of the containment of severe behavioural disturbance which is likely to cause harm to others'.

8    See generally Chapter 19 of the Mental Health Act 1983 Code of Practice (2015), available at **www.gov.uk/government/uploads/system/uploads/attachment-data/file/395494/mh-code.pdf**), due to come into force in April 2015 subject to Parliamentary approval.

9    [2011] EWCA Civ 1305.

10   [1989] 11 EHRR 175.

11   **www.cqc.org.uk/content/cqc's-symposium-restrictive-practices**.

## 6    THE CARE HOME SETTING

## A    Introduction

**6.1**    By far the highest number of applications for authorisations under the Deprivation of Liberty Safeguards ('DOLS') are made by care homes.[1] Care homes are defined by s.3 Care Standards Act 2000 as follows:

Care homes.

(1)    For the purposes of this Act, an establishment is a care home if it provides accommodation, together with nursing or personal care, for any of the following persons.

(2)    They are –

    (a)    persons who are or have been ill;
    (b)    persons who have or have had a mental disorder;
    (c)    persons who are disabled or infirm;
    (d)    persons who are or have been dependent on alcohol or drugs.

**6.2**    All care homes in England must be registered with and inspected by the Care Quality Commission ('CQC'). Care homes in Wales are inspected by the Care and Social Services Inspectorate Wales (CSSIW). There are two types of care home:

residential care homes and care homes with nursing, but there is of course a wide variety within these types.

6.3    The CQC explains on its website[2] that residential care homes range in size from very small homes with few beds to large-scale facilities. They offer care and support throughout the day and night. Staff may help with washing, dressing, at meal times and with using the toilet. Care homes with nursing will normally offer the same type of care but with the addition of 24-hour medical care from a qualified nurse. Within these two however there will be a wide variety of provision, because care homes may have different specialisms. These will include dementia, alcohol or drug dependency, mental health or learning disability. This chapter looks at the type of liberty-restricting measures which could be present in the following settings which come within the definition of a care home:

6.3.1    a residential care home for older adults;
6.3.2    a care home with nursing;
6.3.3    a care home for people with severe and enduring mental health problems, including mentally disordered offenders;
6.3.4    a care home for adults with physical and learning disabilities; and
6.3.5    an arrangement for respite.

6.4    This chapter will summarise the legal frameworks which may apply to care home residents. It will then consider the settings listed above and provide scenarios which describe a regime in each setting which amounts to a deprivation of liberty; and, where appropriate, regimes which may be a deprivation of liberty or which we do not consider will amount to a deprivation of liberty. Following the scenarios we set out are questions which can usefully be asked by frontline staff attempting to ascertain where on the spectrum a particular care arrangement may fall. An appendix deals with specific issues that arise in relation to the use of care homes for respite.

## B    The legal framework

6.5    In very general terms, people live in care homes so that their care and support needs can be met. This may be on a short term basis, such as for respite, or for long periods, in some cases for the rest of the resident's life. Residents may or may not contribute financially to the costs of their care. Statutory bodies have various duties under legislation such as the Care Act 2014 (in force as of 1 April 2015) to provide care and support. It is important to keep in mind that the provision of care and support does not, itself, compel the adult concerned to accept it or provide authority to deprive the adult of their liberty in order to receive it. As Munby LJ noted in *Re A* and *Re C*[3] (in relation to the various community care obligations then imposed upon local authorities):

> [t]he essential point for present purposes is that none of these sources of local authority engagement with someone like C confers on the local authority any power

to regulate, control, compel, restrain, confine or coerce. They are concerned with the provision of services and support.

6.6    Some care home residents will have full capacity to consent to their care and support arrangements, including restrictions that follow on from these arrangements, and will have consented to them. As explained at paragraph 2.12, case law provides that the question of whether a person is deprived of their liberty requiring an authorisation only arises in the case of those who have not consented or cannot consent to such restrictions.

6.7    Some care home residents may be subject to one or more of a range of legal measures which have different effects. These are summarised briefly below:

6.7.1    A DOLS authorisation under Schedule A1 to the MCA 2005. If the requirements are met, an authorisation granted by the relevant supervisory body permits the care home ('the managing authority') to deprive the resident of his or her liberty in the care home for the purpose of being given care or treatment.[4] This framework cannot be used to resolve a dispute about whether the resident should be in the care home in the first place. One reason for this is that decisions about where a person should live will engage their right under Article 8 of the European Convention on Human Rights to respect for private and family life. See *London Borough of Hillingdon* v. *Neary*,[5] and also *Re AJ (Deprivation of Liberty Safeguards)*.[6] If in fact it becomes clear that Schedule A1 has been used in this way, legal advice should be sought as soon as possible as to whether an application to the Court of Protection is required.

6.7.2    A welfare order made by the Court of Protection under s.16(2)(a) MCA 2005. Such an order can only be made where: (1) a Court of Protection judge has concluded that the resident lacks capacity to decide where to live and to make decisions in relation to their care arrangements; (2) that the resident is of 'unsound mind' for purposes of Article 5(1)(e);[7] (3) that it is in the resident's best interests to live and receive care at the care home; and (4) that deprivation of the person's liberty is necessary and proportionate to the risk that they would face otherwise. The order may include other provisions, for example, limits on contact with family members. When such orders are made the court nearly always directs that a copy is retained on the resident's file at the care home. The order may, itself, authorise deprivation of liberty or the court may direct that a DOLS authorisation should be used in addition to the welfare order.

6.7.3    Leave granted to a mental health patient under s.17 MHA 1983, probably for a limited trial period to see how he or she settles into the home. The resident is liable to recall back to hospital whilst on leave. A DOLS authorisation can be used alongside s.17 leave if certain conditions are met: see Schedule 1A to the MCA 2005. Section 17 MHA 1983 does not, itself, give authority to deprive the patient of their liberty at the care home.

6.7.4    A guardianship order under s.7 MHA 1983. This gives the guardian (usually an Approved Mental Health Professional ('AMHP') acting on behalf of the local authority) the following powers:[8]

(i)    the power to require the patient to reside at a place specified by the guardian;

(ii)   the power to require the patient to attend at specified places and times for medical treatment, occupation, education or training;

(iii)  the power to require access to the patient to be given, at any place where they are residing, to any registered medical practitioner, AMHP or any other specified person;

(iv)   if certain conditions are met, guardianship can be used alongside DOLS: see Schedule 1A to the MCA 2005. Our view, based on case law, is that guardianship alone does not authorise deprivation of liberty, but also that the mere exercise of the power of the guardian to require a patient to live at a specific place does not itself give rise to a deprivation of liberty.[9]

6.7.5    A Community Treatment Order ('CTO') under s.17A MHA 1983. This will only arise in the cases of residents who have previously been detained in hospital under ss.3 or 37 MHA 1983. A CTO must always contain conditions which require the resident to make themselves available for examination to the patient's Responsible Clinician ('RC') to assess if the order should be renewed and to a doctor appointed by the CQC to give a second opinion on treatment. If the resident does not comply with either of these conditions, the RC may recall the resident. Other conditions may be imposed by the RC but a resident on a CTO cannot be recalled simply because they have breached one of these conditions so this does not itself mean that the person is not free to leave.[10] A CTO does not provide authority to deprive people of their liberty but a DOLS authorisation may be used together with a CTO: see Schedule 1A to the MCA 2005.

6.7.6    A Conditional Discharge. Offender patients who have been detained under 'restricted' sections of the MHA 1983 (for example ss.37 and 41) may be discharged by the Secretary of State for Justice or the Mental Health Tribunal subject to conditions with which they must comply. Such patients will remain liable to recall by their RC or the Secretary of State. A conditional discharge does not authorise deprivation of liberty (see *Secretary of State for Justice* v. *RB*)[11] but where the person lacks capacity to consent to admission to a care home, a conditional discharge order can be used together with a DOLS authorisation when certain conditions are met: see Schedule 1A to the MCA 2005.

6.7.7    An order made under the inherent jurisdiction of the High Court. These cases are so rare that they are not discussed further in this chapter.

## C    A residential care home for older adults: liberty restricting measures

6.8    As with all care settings, there is a huge variety in the way in which each establishment will seek to provide safe and appropriate care for its residents. What follows is not an attempt to stereotype this kind of provision, but recognition of the challenges that can arise in providing such care in the least restrictive environment. These challenges include:

6.8.1    How to promote choice: for example if a resident does not want to eat the meal offered on a particular day how easy is it for them to go out to eat?

6.8.2    The physical environment and the impact of a structured timetable: in many care homes of this type residents may be expected to spend at least part of the day seated in a lounge, perhaps with a television or music. How can residents be given as much autonomy as possible in how they spend their time and where?

6.8.3    Promoting family and private life: how can care settings promote important intimate (which may include sexual) relations between residents?

6.9    The following are examples of potentially liberty-restricting measures that apply in a residential care home for older adults:

- a keypad entry system;
- assistive technology such as sensors or surveillance;[12]
- observation and monitoring;
- an expectation that all residents will spend most of their days in the same way and in the same place;
- a care plan providing that the person will only access the community with an escort;
- restricted opportunities for access to fresh air and activities (including as a result of staff shortages);
- set times for access to refreshment or activities;
- limited choice of meals and where to eat them (including restrictions on residents' ability to go out for meals);
- set times for visits;
- use of restraint in the event of objections or resistance to personal care (in Re AJ,[13] Baker J agreed that in any case where physical restraint is used in the care of an incapacitated adult, all physical intervention should be recorded in the care plan and documented in any DOLS process);
- mechanical restraints such as lapstraps on wheelchairs;
- restricted ability to form or express intimate relationships;
- assessments of risk that are not based on the specific individual; for example, assumptions that all elderly residents are at a high risk of falls, leading to restrictions in their access to the community

## Care home for older adults: a deprivation of liberty

6.10    The measures in the following scenario are likely to amount to a deprivation of liberty:

Peter is 78. He had a stroke last year, which left him blind and with significant short-term memory impairment. He can get disorientated needs assistance with all the activities of daily living. He needs a guide when walking. He is married but his wife Jackie has struggled to care for Peter and with her agreement Peter has been admitted into a residential care home. Peter has his own room at the home. He can summon staff by bell if he needs help. He tends to prefer to spend time in his room rather than with other residents in the communal areas. He can leave his room unaccompanied at any time he wishes. Due to his visual and cognitive impairments, he does not feel safe doing this. He has access to the communal garden, the dining room, the lounge area and any other resident's room. He is able to use the telephone when he wants. It is in a communal area of the home. He is unable to remember a number and dial it himself. He rarely asks to make phone calls. He is visited regularly by Jackie. She has asked to be allowed to stay overnight with Peter in his room but this request has been refused. The home has a keypad entry system, so service users would need to be able to use the keypad to open the doors to get out into the local area. Peter has been taken out by staff after prompting and does not ask to go out. He would not be allowed to go out unaccompanied. Most of the time Peter is content but on occasions he becomes distressed saying that he wishes to leave. Members of staff reassure and distract Peter when this happens.

---

Key factors pointing to a deprivation of liberty:

- the extent to which Peter requires assistance with all activities of daily living and the consequent degree of supervision and control this entails; and
- that Peter is not free to leave either permanently or temporarily.

---

## Care home for older adults: potential deprivation of liberty

6.11    The measures in the following scenario may give rise to a deprivation of liberty:

Mr Ghauri is 88. His wife of 60 years died last year and he has lived alone since then. He has no children. He is generally in good physical health but is in the early stages of dementia. After a fall he decided to move into a local residential care home. At the time he had capacity to make the decision to move. However, his dementia has progressed, and staff consider he may be less able to make more complex decisions. He has his own room. He enjoys the meals at the home in the dining room but otherwise spends most of his time in his room where he listens to music and reads. He has a regular routine whereby he leaves the home for a walk after breakfast. He normally buys a paper and returns before lunch but sometimes eats in a local café and returns in the early afternoon. If he did not return from the café the staff would contact the police to take steps to locate and return him.

---

Key factors pointing towards a potential deprivation of liberty:

- the potential degree of supervision and control within the home – although more information would be required in order to assess whether this satisfied the acid test; and
- that Mr Ghauri is not free to leave the home. However, it is not clear from

> the information available whether he has or lacks the capacity to consent to these care arrangements, which would have to be examined carefully.

## *Care home for older adults: not a deprivation of liberty*

**6.12**   The following scenario is unlikely to amount to a deprivation of liberty:

Mrs Banotti is a widow and is also an alcoholic. She does not have the capacity to decide where to live. She lives in rented social housing unit for older adults, which has a warden. She was found collapsed on the street a few weeks ago and was admitted to hospital. She was persuaded to go into respite from hospital to give Environmental Health staff from the local District Council time to clean up and renovate her flat. She leaves the respite residential care unit every day after breakfast to see friends. In fact she sees a male friend who also has a drink problem. Staff report to the social worker that they are worried whether her male friend is financially exploiting her and whether she is having a proper lunch or whether she is drinking. She comes back every evening about 7pm when meals are finished for the evening and does not have a smell of drink on her. Mrs Banotti has made clear that once her flat is fixed up, she will return to live there but that she is willing to stay in respite in the interim provided that she is allowed to continue to stay out all day every day. Staff are unhappy about the risks to her of her drinking. However, their policies do not allow for physical restraint so the staff have not attempted to stop her leaving and have not followed her or asked her to return. Mrs Banotti has made clear that if staff try to insist on her staying in all day, or only going out with staff, she will stop the respite and go and stay with her male friend. The staff would not take any steps to prevent her doing so if she did do so.

> Key factors pointing away from a deprivation of liberty:
>
> ■   Mrs Banotti is free to leave, whatever the level of supervision and control to which she may be subjected.

## D   A care home with nursing

**6.13**   The challenges to providing care in the least restrictive way identified in paragraph 6.8 will be present here. The liberty-restricting measures described in paragraph 6.9 above are also likely to be present in a care home with nursing: the following features may also be present:

■   use of medication for mental health problems;
■   the need for restraint in the event of objections to personal care (which must be recorded in the resident's care plan: see note in 6.9);
■   the need for interventions to protect staff: for example, removal of residents' false teeth to prevent biting.

It is difficult to identify scenarios in this setting that would not give rise to a real risk of deprivation of liberty (where the individual in question lacks the material capacity to consent to the restrictions imposed upon them).

## Care home with nursing: a deprivation of liberty

**6.14**    The measures in the following scenarios are likely to amount to a deprivation of liberty:

Mr Lopez is an older man with dementia, who lacks capacity to take decisions relating to his residence and care arrangements. He had previously been estranged from his older son as he had disliked his son's wife. The son is now divorced and has visited Mr Lopez once a week at the care home where he resides for the last month. Due to Mr Lopez co-existing physical and other mental health difficulties, including schizoaffective disorder, he has a fully funded continuing healthcare package. Mr Lopez has been quite paranoid and threatening and abusive to staff, and very demanding and engaged in what they call challenging behaviours. There are not enough staff to take Mr Lopez out every day as he has requested and the care package does not include any one-to-one care. Mr Lopez used to be a long distance walker and loses his temper and expresses frustration at not being allowed out on his own. As the home is near a main road, the manager has taken the view that concern for his health and safety demand that he should not be allowed out without one-to-one care.

> Key factors pointing to a deprivation of liberty:
>
> ■    the extent to which staff are required to monitor, control and supervise Mr Lopez to control his 'challenging behaviour';
> ■    his lack of freedom to leave the care home whenever he wishes.

Mrs Neville is 85. She lives in a care home with nursing and has Alzheimer's dementia which is now advanced. She is very confused and disorientated, and can now only manage very simple conversations. She is physically fit and mobile. She spends much of the day wandering in the corridors of the nursing home. The doors are locked and there is a sensor on the doormat at each entry to the home. On one occasion Mrs Neville found her way out of the back door of the home, which had been left open in warm weather. She was spotted walking towards the main road and immediately escorted back. Mrs Neville frequently shouts and screams and is gently escorted from the communal areas when she is making a noise, to reduce disturbance to other residents. Mrs Neville is resistant to personal care and can lash out at staff. All her personal care is delivered by two members of staff.

> Key factors pointing towards a deprivation of liberty:
>
> ■    Mrs Neville is plainly not free to leave; and
> ■    the nature of her care needs and the interventions required make it clear that she is under continuous supervision and control.

## Care home with nursing: potential deprivation of liberty

**6.15**    We suggest that the measures in the following scenario may give rise to a deprivation of liberty:

Mr Alexander is in his 70s and has a long history of mental health problems going back to his 20s. He has lived for the last 30 years in a housing association flat where he has a tenancy support worker. He is subject to a guardianship order and the local authority is his guardian. He also has a CPN. Last year he began to disengage from his CPN and tenancy support worker. He started to neglect himself and would not allow the district nurses to visit to dress an ulcer on his leg. Eventually he allowed access to the district nurses who were concerned about his physical health and he was admitted to the general hospital where he spent a few days. Professionals at the hospital considered he needed a period of convalescence and the guardianship order was then varied to require him to reside at a local nursing home. He has been assessed as lacking capacity to decide where to live, but he has expressed willing-ness to remain in the nursing home for a few weeks until he feels stronger. In the meantime plans are being made to reinstate a home care package. Mr Alexander is not allowed to visit his home during this period as there is concern that he may not return to the nursing home.

> Key factors pointing to a potential deprivation of liberty:
>
> ■   that Mr Alexander is not free to leave (N.B. this lack of freedom to leave does not derive from the guardianship order per se – see paragraph 6.7.4). Whether he will be deprived of his liberty will depend upon the extent to which he is under a sufficient degree of supervision and control at the care home, which requires more investigation on the facts available, but which would appear likely given the nature of the placement.

## E   Care homes for those with severe and enduring mental health problems

**6.16**   Residents in care homes with this specialism may have lower needs for personal care but there will be restrictions in place, some of which may be geared towards managing risk to the public. These will need to be factored into the consideration of whether a resident is deprived of his liberty or not. In addition to some of the measures set out at paragraph 6.9 above, specific liberty-restricting measures may include:

■   having to take part in specified programmes (e.g. sex offender treatments) as a condition of a conditional discharge or CTO;

■   being required to comply with medication as a term of a conditional discharge or CTO;

■   having to avoid certain settings (such as playgrounds);

■   being required to live in the care home as a term of a conditional discharge;

■   a requirement to be escorted when going out (whatever the risk being guarded against);

■   a curfew;

■   having to observe an exclusion zone;

■   restrictions on contact with victims or other persons.

## Care home for those with mental health problems: a deprivation of liberty

**6.17**    The measures in the following scenario are likely to amount to a deprivation of liberty:

Mr Harry Hall is subject to a conditional discharge order made under ss.37/41 MHA 1983 made five years ago for sex offences against female children. He has a delusional disorder and more recently has been diagnosed with vascular dementia. He has lived in a care home since his conditional discharge with conditions which include:

(i)    to reside at the care home;
(ii)   to take treatment as prescribed by his RC;
(iii)  to maintain contact with his social supervisor.

Harry's dementia is getting worse and he is now talking about returning home to London. He has no home in London and last lived there five years ago. He has left the care home several times recently heading for the train station but was brought back by staff. The care plan provides for monitoring within the home so that he does not place vulnerable women at risk. He is only allowed community contact accompanied by a worker which includes going to the local pub two nights a week.

> Key factors pointing to a deprivation of liberty:
>
> ■ the specific monitoring of Harry required within the home;
> ■ the controls placed upon his ability to leave the home when he wishes.

## Care home for those with mental health problems: potential deprivation of liberty

**6.18**    We suggest that measures in the following scenario may give rise to a deprivation of liberty:

Milon is twenty-five years old. He has a diagnosis of schizophrenia which is complicated by his use of illicit drugs. He has accumulated a number of criminal convictions, mainly for shoplifting. He has become estranged from his parents and does not have his own accommodation. He has been detained under the MHA 1983 twice in the past. His most recent admission under s.3 MHA 1983 has been the longest lasting and for the first time he was able to remain abstinent from drugs throughout the admission. Staff attribute this to careful and structured use of leave. Milon made good progress and was placed onto a CTO, with a requirement that he live at a care home for those with mental health problems. All went well for the first month but Milon has been showing signs of relapse and staff believe he has started to use drugs again and have noted that his dosset box suggests that he has not been complying with medication. He appears thought-disordered but is generally cooperative. In an attempt to avoid recall to hospital and with the agreement of Milon's responsible clinician, staff ask Milon to agree to an arrangement where he does not leave the care home unescorted for a few days and where he is supervised when taking medication. If there is no improvement the responsible clinician intends to recall Milon.

> Key factors pointing to a potential deprivation of liberty:
>
> ■ The provisions made in Milon's care arrangements to secure his return to the care home in the event that he leaves it (NB, that the CTO contains a residence condition does not, itself, mean that he lacks the freedom to leave: see paragraph 6.7.5).
> ■ Any assessment of whether Milon is deprived of his liberty would also have to consider whether he can consent to the arrangements and whether that consent is freely given.

## Care home for those with mental health problems: not a deprivation of liberty

**6.19**   The following scenario is unlikely to amount to a deprivation of liberty:

Jim is 60. He has a longstanding diagnosis of schizophrenia. In his 20s he committed two serious assaults against women. He was sentenced to ten years' imprisonment. Both offences were pre-planned and had similarities. During the course of serving his sentence he was transferred to hospital and responded to treatment and was returned to prison where he completed his sentence. Since then he has continued to receive anti-psychotic medication by means of a depot. He is in regular contact with his CPN and Consultant who have known him for many years. He shares a flat with his parents who are elderly and rely on him to a significant degree. Last year he appeared to be showing signs of relapse. He was arrested on suspicion of a high-profile offence which had some similarities to the offences he committed in his youth but no charges are brought. At the request of his psychiatrist and CPN, Jim agreed to a voluntary admission to hospital but was detained under the MHA 1983 when he sought to discharge himself. He was then placed on a CTO. The conditions are:

(i)   to reside in a care home for people with mental health problems;
(ii)  to attend a day centre three times a week;
(iii) attendance at the depot clinic for medication.

Jim is able to spend time with his family during the day (although it is quite a long journey to reach them) but has to tell staff where he is going before leaving. There is a curfew of 11pm. Jim would like to move back in with his parents and has asked his psychiatrist to vary the conditions of the CTO. The psychiatrist has refused to do so. Jim is unhappy but fearful of the consequences if he moves without the approval of the clinical team.

> Key factors pointing away from a deprivation of liberty:
>
> ■    Jim is, in fact, free to leave the home because the CTO does not itself prevent him from doing so: see paragraph 6.7.5.

## F    Care homes for adults with learning disabilities: liberty restricting measures

**6.20**    These homes may involve a range of restrictive measures, especially those catering for residents who present challenging behaviour. This can include hitting out, destructive behaviour, eating inedible objects ('PICA'), and self-injurious behaviour such as head-banging, hand-biting or scratching. A structure may be an important part of a behaviour support plan for residents and may be an important tool in helping a resident to feel safe but entails taking a degree of control over the resident. Liberty-restricting measures may include:

■    a perimeter fence with a locked gate;
■    keypads on doors which residents cannot unlock;
■    a structured routine;
■    monitoring and observation;
■    use of medication, including PRN;
■    use of physical interventions of any type in response to challenging behaviours (see note at 6.9);
■    use of sanctions such as 'time out';
■    residents being told to spend time in a 'quiet room' as part of de-escalation;
■    a care plan which provides that a resident must be escorted outside the care home (including where this results from physical needs e.g. a resident who needs someone to push their wheelchair);
■    restrictions on developing sexual relations;
■    mechanical restraints, e.g. lapstraps;
■    decisions about contact with friends and family taken by others.

### Care home for adults with learning disabilities: a deprivation of liberty

**6.21**    The measures in the following scenario are likely to amount to a deprivation of liberty:

John Jones is 18. He was the subject of a care order six years ago on the grounds of severe neglect. John has a learning disability, a diagnosis of ADHD, and presents with challenging behaviour. He had been in foster care but that broke down when the foster parents' son returned home from boarding school. John was placed by the local authority in a specialist learning disability residential care home. This home is regulated by the Care Quality Commission to take young people below 18, and they can stay on there after 18. John's medication for ADHD seems to wear off in the evenings and he is harder to manage then, but there are fewer staff on at night. The staff have frequently restrained him due to his behaviour towards staff and residents. Contact with parents is once a week in the communal lounge but there has been no contact with siblings who are in care out of county. John's parents' request to take him back home for afternoon tea has been refused. The social worker has been told that when there are incidents, John is told to go to the quiet room, not his bedroom, and if he tries to leave, he is told to go back into that room. Staff remain outside the door and every 15 minutes check on him.

> Key factors pointing to a deprivation of liberty:
>
> - the extent of the restriction on John's movements within the home and his contact with his parents;
> - the use of restraint within the home; and
> - the controls on his ability to leave the home temporarily or permanently.

## Care home for adults with learning disabilities: potential deprivation of liberty

6.22   We suggest that the measures in the following scenario may give rise to a deprivation of liberty:

Max Herner has a learning disability. He is 19. He had been placed in a specialist learning disability care home when he was 16 as his mother could no longer cope with his challenging behaviours. His mother, Greta, is divorced and cares for her younger son Trutz and has remarried. The brothers do not get along. Max has weekend contact from Saturday morning to Sunday afternoon at his mother's home. Max would like to live with his mother full-time, although Greta will not admit to Max that she is quite afraid of him when he gets very agitated. Max has low impulse control and needs constant supervision to ensure that he does not assault other male residents and he is diverted when he shows signs of getting agitated. He is on medication to try to calm down his agitation. Max works five days a week in a local gardening project. Occasionally when he has had an argument with care staff, he has threatened that when he stays with his mother, he may not return to the placement on Sunday afternoons. When Max is with his mother, she allows him to go out and meet with his male cousins at the local pub.

> Key factors pointing to a potential deprivation of liberty:
>
> - the extent of the supervision and control maintained over Max within the home and the use of medication.
> - The key question for the assessment of whether this is a deprivation of liberty will be the extent to which Max is free to leave the home: this will require assessment of what exactly the care home staff will do if he carries through his threat not to return to the home.

## Care home for adults with learning disabilities: not a deprivation of liberty

6.23   The following scenario is unlikely to amount to a deprivation of liberty:

Rina is 35 and has a mild learning disability consequent to Down's syndrome. Both her parents are dead and she has no other family. For the last 15 years she has lived in a small group home with four other women of similar age, one of whom she has known since childhood when they attended the same school. Staff are present twenty four hours a day. Rina's capacity to make decisions about where she lives and about her care needs has not been formally assessed since she moved into the care home on the death of her mother, at which time she was considered to lack capacity to make these decisions. Rina has her own room. She goes to college three days a week. She is able to travel independently. She has a key worker with whom she plans her week. When she is not at college she may visit friends from college. She sometimes socialises with her housemates in the evening but sometimes prefers to stay in her room where she enjoys watching television and knitting. Recently there has been some concern about her relationship with Dan, a man she has met at college. He has a learning disability as well and lives with his father who has a known alcohol and drug problem. At Rina's last annual review her care manager assessed Rina's capacity to make decisions about contact with her friend and his father and also her capacity to consent to sexual relations. Rina had capacity to make decisions in all these areas. She told her care manager she never wanted to move away from her friends and she wanted to go on seeing Dan but preferred not to visit him at home as she did not like his father. Rina's care manager did not consider any intervention was needed.

> Key factors pointing away from a deprivation of liberty:
>
> ■ Rina may now have capacity to decide whether to reside at the care home;
> ■ there is nothing in the scenario to suggest that Rina is not free to leave the care home permanently or temporarily;
> ■ she is not under continuous supervision and control and is able to exercise her autonomy.

## G    Questions for frontline staff

6.24    These questions may help establish whether an individual is deprived of their liberty in this context:

■ Are any of the liberty-restricting measures described above applied to the resident concerned? If so which and for what reason?
■ Are there any restrictions on the person's contact with others? If so do they restrict contact beyond the home's usual visiting arrangements?
■ Is the person's access to the community restricted in anyway? For example must they be escorted? What would staff do if they left the home alone or sought to do so?
■ Is the person required to be at the care home at specified times?
■ Must the person be escorted either within or outside the care home?
■ Is the person required to say where they are going when leaving the care home?
■ Is the person required to take part in a programme of treatment? What happens if they do not?

- Is the person required to take medication? What are the arrangements for this? What happens if they do not take it?
- Is the person required to remain abstinent from alcohol or drugs?
- Are there drugs tests?
- Is any legal framework currently being used e.g. conditional discharge, CTO or guardianship? If so, what are the precise terms?
- Is the person required to observe an exclusion zone? If so how large is it and what implications does it have for (e.g.) visits to family members?
- Is the person required to avoid specific settings?
- Are decisions about contact with friends and family taken by others?
- Is choice extremely limited even in terms of everyday activities?
- Is restraint used to deliver personal care?
- Are the person's wishes often overridden, in their best interests?
- Could any of the liberty-restricting measures be dispensed with?

## Appendix: Respite placements

**6.25**  Care homes can provide places of respite which can be invaluable in allowing a carer to take a break from their role. Respite plays a vital role in promoting the sustainability of arrangements where a vulnerable adult is supported at home by a carer. All the liberty-restricting measures which may apply to a permanent resident of a care home may equally apply to a resident who moves to a care home for the purpose of respite for a short period. In addition, the resident may be unfamiliar with the setting, and where the purpose of the respite is to allow a carer to go on holiday, the lack of contact with a family member will be a further liberty-restricting factor.

**6.26**  In Chapter 3 we discuss the question of how long an arrangement must be in place before it is likely to be considered a 'non-negligible period of time' and may require authorisation. Paragraphs 3.29-3.32 deal with this important point.

**6.27**  In particular you should note paragraph 3.32, which is repeated here:

> Because the period will vary from setting to setting, we have deliberately avoided giving a period of time that can be considered 'safe.' Our clear view is that it is unlikely under any circumstances to extend beyond a few (2-3) days and is likely to be substantially less in settings in which particularly intense measures of control are imposed. We would **strongly** suggest that it is not safe to use the rule of thumb that some public bodies have adopted that a deprivation of liberty is unlikely to arise where a person is confined for less than 7 days. We understand that this may have been taken from a reading of certain paragraphs of the DOLS Code as to the circumstances under which it is appropriate to grant an urgent authorisation.[14] However, this is to conflate the question of **whether** there is a deprivation of liberty with the quite separate question of **how** such deprivation of liberty may be authorised.

**6.28**  Attention is also drawn to the comments of Baker J in Re AJ[15] when he commented that:

professionals need to be on their guard to look out for cases where vulnerable people are admitted to residential care ostensibly for respite when the underlying plan is for a permanent placement without proper consideration as to their Article 5 rights.

**6.29**    This suggests that exactly the same questions would need to be asked by frontline staff considering whether a respite placement might constitute a deprivation of liberty. In addition staff should consider:

■    the impact of being in an unfamiliar setting on the resident and how his or her care plan provides for a response to unsettled behaviour;

■    the impact of reduced contact with a primary carer;

■    the underlying intention of the placement: is there any prospect that it will be extended or made permanent?

**6.30**    To highlight the specific factors relating to respite, we revisit below some of the scenarios described above and change some of the facts to indicate how the considerations may apply in the context of respite. Note that the scenarios below do not consider the question of whether any of the individuals may in fact also be deprived of their liberty while receiving care in their own home. Questions of when such a deprivation of liberty may arise are considered in detail in Chapter 8. However, we would suggest that in reality the care arrangements at home for 'Peter' and 'Max' in particular would require scrutiny, addressing the factors in Chapter 8.

Peter, the care home resident with dementia described in paragraph 6.10, normally lives with his wife Jackie who provides the majority of his care with some help from her daughter. They are both going on holiday for a week, for a break. During this time Peter will be admitted to a care home for respite. Everyone who knows him considers he is unlikely to remember that this is a temporary arrangement and that he will be quite disorientated. His son who lives 300 miles away has agreed to stay locally while Jackie and her daughter are away. He will visit Peter daily. Peter is still likely to be deprived of his liberty.

---

Key factors pointing to a deprivation of liberty:

■    Peter will not be free to leave; and
■    Peter's needs are such that he will be under continuous supervision and control.

---

Max, who is described in paragraph 6.22, in fact lives with Greta full-time, with some help from the local authority. Greta wants to go away for a long weekend. She arranges for Max to spend from Thursday evening to Sunday evening in a care home. He has not stayed there before. Greta takes him to visit before her break so that he can meet staff and residents. Max is excited about staying at the placement because he knows that the residents go out for a meal together every Friday evening. However, the care home staff and Greta think it is likely that at some point over the weekend Max will become anxious and agitated. He will need to be supervised closely and may need physical intervention. It would not be safe for him to be at home on his own. Max will be deprived of his liberty over the weekend.

> Key factors pointing towards a deprivation of liberty:
>
> ■ Max will not be free to leave the home temporarily or permanently; and
> ■ although the period of time at the care home will be short, Max will be under continuous supervision and control and may require intrusive intervention.

Rina, who is described at paragraph 6.23, has exactly the same needs but is in fact living with her sister and brother-in-law in their home where she has her own room. They want to go on holiday together for a fortnight. Rina, and her sister and her care manager have arranged that Rina will stay in a care home while they are away. Rina has been there before and is familiar with the staff and residents there. Rina's routine of going to college will be no different as the care home is very close to her home. If she wishes to go home during this period she has keys to the family home and can return there, although she has never chosen to do this. Rina will not be deprived of her liberty.

> Key factors pointing away from deprivation of liberty:
>
> ■ Rina may have capacity to consent to this arrangement;
> ■ if Rina lacks such capacity, she will be free to leave the care home temporarily while her family are away; and
> ■ she is not under continuous supervision and control.

## Endnotes

1 Around 70% of all applications in 2013-14: see Care Quality Commission's report 'Monitoring the Use of the Mental Capacity Act 2005 Deprivation of Liberty Safeguards' at **www.cqc.org.uk/content/deprivation-liberty-safeguards-201314**.
2 **www.cqc.org.uk/content/care-homes**.
3 [2010] EWHC 978 (Fam).
4 Schedule A1 to the MCA 2005, Paragaphs 1(2) and 2.
5 [2011] EWCOP 1377.
6 [2015] EWCOP 5.
7 This is clear, we suggest, from *Re X (No 1)* [2014] EWCOP 25 at paragraph 14. In *G v. E* [2010] EWCA Civ 822, the Court of Appeal suggested that medical evidence would not always be required. However, we suggest that – as with applications for authorisations under Schedule A1 – medical evidence of unsoundness of mind must always be obtained. It may be that there are cases where the person is unsound in mind but does not have a mental disorder for purposes of the Mental Health Act 1983 (the requirement under Schedule A1), in which case the Court of Protection would be able to make an order even if an authorisation under Schedule A1 cannot be granted.
8 Section 8(1)(a) MHA 1983.
9 See *NL v. Hampshire County Council* [2014] UKUT 475 (AAC).
10 By analogy also with the *NL* case discussed immediately above.
11 [2011] EWCA Civ 1608.
12 The CQC consider this to be a relevant factor in their document 'Using Surveillance,' December 2014, **www.cqc.org.uk/content/using-surveillance-information-service-providers**.
13 [2015] EWCOP 5.
14 Most obviously paragraphs 6.3 and 6.4.
15 [2015] EWCOP 5.

## 7    SUPPORTED LIVING

## A    Introduction

7.1    This chapter focuses upon the intensity of care regimes provided to those lacking the capacity to consent to care arrangements in supported living services, shared lives schemes (formerly known as adult placements) and extra care housing. The deprivation of liberty safeguards are not available, therefore any deprivation of liberty will require authorisation by the Court of Protection.

## B    What is a supported living service?

7.2    The generic term, 'supported living', describes a form of domiciliary care whereby a local authority arranges a package of care and accommodation to be provided to a disabled, elderly or ill person. The individual lives in their own (often rented) home and typically receives social care and/or support to enable them to be as autonomous and independent as possible. The provision of accommodation is thereby separated from the delivery of care at an organisational level. There is usually some form of tenancy or licence arrangement with a landlord attracting housing benefit, with means-tested tailored support being provided by a distinct care provider with activities of daily living, education, training, employment and social interaction. The care setting is therefore *not* likely to constitute a 'care home' for registration purposes.

7.3    Supported living services need only be registered with the Care Quality Commission ('CQC') if they carry on a regulated activity, that is nursing or personal care. If, for example, the individual is supported with cleaning, cooking and shopping, or is supervised to take prescribed medicine, the service does not require registration. If personal care is being provided but not in the place where they are living, for example at day services, registration of the service is not required. However, where nursing or personal care is provided to those, for example, with more complex needs, such care will be a regulated activity requiring CQC registration. The Care Act 2014 adopts the definition of nursing and personal care presently provided for in the Health and Social Care Act 2008 (Regulated Activities) Regulations 2010:

> 'nursing care' means any services provided by a nurse and involving –
>
> (a)    the provision of care; or
> (b)    the planning, supervision or delegation of the provision of care, other than any services which, having regard to their nature and the circumstances in which they are provided, do not need to be provided by a nurse;
>
> 'personal care' means –
> (a)    physical assistance given to a person in connection with –
>
>> (i)     eating or drinking (including the administration of parenteral nutrition),
>> (ii)    toileting (including in relation to the process of menstruation),

     (iii)    washing or bathing,
     (iv)    dressing,
     (v)     oral care, or
     (vi)    the care of skin, hair and nails (with the exception of nail care provided by a chiropodist or podiatrist); or

  (b)  the prompting, together with supervision, of a person, in relation to the performance of any of the activities listed in paragraph (a), where that person is unable to make a decision for themselves in relation to performing such an activity without such prompting and supervision.'

**7.4**    Such regulated activities do not apply to the provision of accommodation to someone by a carer under a shared lives scheme (see below), school, or a further education institution.

## Supported living: liberty-restricting measures

**7.5**    The following are measures which may be found in the specific features of this care setting:

- decision on where to live being taken by others;
- decision on contact with others not being taken by the individual;
- doors of the property locked, and/or chained, and/or bolted for security reasons or to prevent residents leaving;
- access to the community being limited by staff availability;
- a member or members of staff accompanying a resident to access the community to support and meet their care needs;
- mechanical restraint, such as wheelchairs with a lapstrap or harness (e.g. Crelling), reinforced glass in mobility vehicles, protective helmets;
- varying levels of staffing and frequency of observation by staff;
- restricted access to finances, with money being controlled by staff or welfare benefits appointee;
- restricted access to personal items to prevent harm;
- restricted access to parts of the property, such as the kitchen or certain cupboards therein, to minimise health and safety risks;
- chemical restraint, such as medication with a sedative or tranquilising effect;
- physical restraint/intervention, such as with personal care tasks, breakaway or block techniques, distraction methods, staff withdrawing, physical touches or holds;
- restricted access to modes of social communication, such as internet, landline or mobile telephone, correspondence;
- positive behavioural reward systems, to reward 'good' behaviour;
- restricted access to family, depending on level of risk and availability of staff and resources;
- lack of flexibility, in terms of having activities timetabled, set meal times, expected sleep times.

## Supported living: a deprivation of liberty

7.6    The measures in the following scenario are likely to amount to a deprivation of liberty:

Gordon is 30 years old and has autism, cerebral palsy, hearing and visual impairments and a learning disability. He resides in a one-bedroom flat with 1:1 staffing at all times. He requires a second member of staff to access the community who is available 35 hours per week. The front door is locked for his safety. He cannot weight bear and pulls himself around inside, and requires a wheelchair outside. Due to a history of attempting to grab members of the public, a harness is used to strap his torso to the wheelchair, allowing free movement of his arms.

> Key factors pointing to a deprivation of liberty:
>
> ■    Gordon is under continuous supervision and control on a 1:1 basis at all times.

## Supported living: potential deprivation of liberty

7.7    We suggest that the measures in the following scenario may give rise to a deprivation of liberty:

Max is 24 years old, has a mild learning disability and lives with two other residents who receive 24-hour shared staff support. Owing to his agitation and anxiety, Max is prescribed medication with a calming effect. He is employed from 9am to 4pm, five days per week in the local garden centre which he is able to get to and from independently. He has a tenancy for his bedroom and can call upon staff members for assistance in the morning and evening if he requires it. If he wishes to see his family at weekends, a member of staff will take him and be there throughout the contact session owing to previous incidents of aggression from his brother.

> Key factors pointing to a potential deprivation of liberty:
>
> ■    the extent of the supervision and control inherent in the support provided to Max at the placement. A careful assessment will be required of whether he is free to leave in circumstances where he can come and go to the garden centre;
> ■    focus will also be required upon the steps that would be taken if he did not return.

## Supported living: not a deprivation of liberty

7.8    The following scenario is unlikely to amount to a deprivation of liberty:

John, aged 42, was badly assaulted during a night out and sustained an acquired brain injury. The frontal lobe damage makes processing information difficult and he has some left sided weakness and mobility issues. He lives in a flat and, twice a day, receives two-hour visits from support workers. He can dress and wash himself. But they prompt him with medication, take him shopping, and support him to pay his bills. He chooses how to spend the remainder of the day. Often he attends day services without the need for support. Sometimes he meets with friends in the local pub.

> Key factors pointing away from deprivation of liberty:
>
> - the limited nature of the control and supervision to which John is subject;
> - the limited nature of the restrictions placed upon John's ability to come and go from his flat as he pleases.

## C    What are Shared Lives schemes?

7.9    These schemes, formerly known as adult placements, differ from supported living arrangements as they involve the individual being placed in a family setting. They are likened to adult fostering arrangements and are available to those aged 16 and over. Usually a local authority arranges for the person to receive day support, short breaks or respite, or long term care in the family home of a Shared Lives carer so as to enable them to share the family life, social life and community activities. The schemes are designed for those wanting to live independently but not on their own.

7.10    The majority of those receiving such care have learning disabilities, although the scheme extends to those with physical disabilities, mental health issues or drug or alcohol problems. Shared Lives carers are self-employed, with rates of payment set by the local authority or the scheme itself according to the location and the person's level of need. Carers receive payments to cover some of their time, rent and a contribution towards the household running costs.

7.11    In 2012-13 in England there were 121 schemes with 6720 carers supporting over 9660 people, around half of which on a long term basis. In Wales that year there were 1420 people in Shared Lives arrangements.

7.12    Although accommodation is provided often together with personal care, it is not required to be registered as a 'care home'. But Shared Lives schemes are regulated under the Health and Social Care Act 2008. The schemes approve and train the carer, receive referrals (typically from the local authority), match the needs of the person with the carer, and monitor the arrangements. A maximum of three people (two in Wales) can be supported by the carer at any one time and carers do not employ staff.

### Shared Lives schemes: liberty-restricting measures

7.13    The following are measures which may be found in the specific features of this care setting:

- varying levels of supervision and guidance with activities of daily living;
- encouraging participation in family and community activities;
- preventing the person from leaving unaccompanied for their immediate safety;
- ensuring behavioural boundaries;
- conveying the person to health and other appointments;
- addressing challenging behaviour;
- assist with medication, including sedative effect.

## Shared Lives schemes: a deprivation of liberty

7.14    The measures in the following scenario are likely to amount to a deprivation of liberty:

Nora is 18 years old with moderate to severe learning disability. She lives in a stable and secure foster placement in which she is dependent on others as she cannot live independently. She cannot go out on her own and shows no wish to do so. She can communicate her wants and wishes in a limited manner. She lives in an ordinary domestic environment which she regards as home. She is not restrained or not locked in the house. If she tries to leave she would be prevented for her immediate safety. Continuous supervision and control is exercised over her to meet her care needs. Her limitations on movement are generally dictated by her inability and lack of awareness of danger. There are no restrictions on social contacts except by court declaration. She goes to college where she is not under the control of her carer or the local authority. Her mother accepts that Nora should remain where she is and has no objections to the care provided. Nor does she regard Nora as being confined or retained. Nora's sister supports the shared lives placement.

> Key factors pointing to a deprivation of liberty:
>
> - the continuous and complete nature of the control and supervision exercised over her (for beneficent reasons); and
> - the steps that would be taken to prevent her leaving.[1]

## Shared Lives schemes: potential deprivation of liberty

7.15    We suggest that the measures in the following scenario may give rise to a deprivation of liberty:

Matthew is 33 years old and has autism, a moderate learning disability, and little communication skills. He has lived with Mr and Mrs Morgan for four years with their daughter. He requires frequent daily support and someone with or near him all day. For example, he cannot judge water temperature so his carers run him a bath or shower. He cannot dress according to weather conditions so his carers choose his clothing and dress him. He cannot attend to personal care so his carers clean him and brush his teeth and hair. He is able to walk independently but gets anxious with loud noises so one of the family will accompany him outside, when he wears head phones to muffle the noise. The family do the weekly shop and he will only eat a limited range of food. He is able to make a simple sandwich with verbal prompts.

Key factors pointing to a deprivation of liberty:

■ Matthew requires a significant and continuous degree of support throughout the day, and the limitations upon his freedom to leave.

■ A careful assessment would be required as to the extent to which he is under continuous/complete supervision and control, and what would happen were he to try to leave without a family member accompanying him.

## Shared Lives schemes: no deprivation of liberty

7.16    The following scenario is unlikely to amount to a deprivation of liberty:

Jane is 38 years old and resides with Mr and Mrs Baker in their four bedroomed home. One day per week she mucks out the local farm with a job coach. She has no health concerns and she sleeps well. It is not safe for Jane to go out alone as she has no sense of road danger so every Sunday she goes to church and every Tuesday goes shopping with Mrs Baker. The family go out together on regular excursions and holiday twice a year.

Key factors pointing to a deprivation of liberty:

■ there is no evidence that Jane is under any form of continuous/complete supervision and control.

## D    What is extra care housing?

7.17    Extra care housing represents a hybrid between living at home and living in residential care. Usually purpose built, self-contained properties on a single site, schemes provide access to 24-hour domiciliary care and support and community resources. Their models differ from assistive technology in someone's own home to retirement and care villages to, for example, specialist dedicated schemes for those with dementia. Unlike residential care, those in extra care housing usually rent, purchase, or share ownership of typically a one- or two-bedroomed apartment or bungalow in the housing scheme or care village and do not receive one-to-one care. Unlike living in one's own home, those in extra care housing will have 24-hour access to personal care with progressive degrees of privacy, dependent upon their level of need.

7.18    Some individuals will have a domiciliary carer. A warden is also usually on site to check on the welfare of residents. For the larger schemes, there are also on-site facilities and social care services usually available for those requiring daily support. These can include on-site care teams, rehabilitation services, day centre activities, restaurants, laundrettes, hairdressing and beauty suites, and possibly shops, cinemas, gyms, even the garden shed.

**7.19**    Moving into extra care housing may be a lifestyle choice. Or it may be necessary due to an individual's level of social and/or health care need. The decision to move in may or may not be made at a time when the individual had mental capacity, or their mental functioning may deteriorate subsequently, with it no longer being safe for them to go out unaccompanied. It is therefore a common occurrence for those in extra care housing to not be free to access the community but the intensity of care measures varies enormously.

## Extra care housing: liberty-restricting measures

**7.20**    The following are measures which may be found in the specific features of this care setting:

- location devices;
- door sensors to raise to alert staff to the person's exit from their property;
- movement sensors to raise alert staff to the person's movements within their property;
- verbal or physical distraction techniques used, for example, to dissuade the person from going out unaccompanied;
- fobs to go in and out of the scheme which the person may not know how to use;
- doors within the property with handles at the top to prevent the individual leaving;
- prior consent of the resident may enable staff to access their property;
- physical intervention/restraint, such as with personal care tasks;
- access to the community restricted due to staff levels, with residents able to go out in groups only with staff with little or no choice regarding where and when to do so;
- CCTV in entrance areas to schemes; or
- aspects of the property restricted due to safety concerns, such as disabling a cooker.

## Extra care housing: deprivation of liberty

**7.21**    The measures in the following scenario are likely to amount to a deprivation of liberty:

Cyril is 70 years old with Alzheimer's dementia and severe mobility difficulties. He was assessed by a social worker as lacking capacity to decide where to live in order to receive care. In consultation with Cyril and family members, it was considered to be in his best interests to move out of his home into a housing with care setting. He now resides in a one-bed apartment as part of a specialist dementia scheme of extra care housing which was purchased by his financial deputy. From 9am to 8pm he has a carer with him to assist him into and out of bed as well as to attend to his everyday needs. During the night he has pressure sensors around the bed to alert staff to a fall. Occasionally he is aggressive to staff which requires them to withdraw. Staff have unrestricted access to the apartment by means of a safe key. Cyril is able to leave the property but only with the carer.

> Key factors pointing to a deprivation of liberty:
>
> ■ the extent of the supervision and control exercised over Cyril whilst he is awake (and at night);
> ■ Cyril is not free to leave save with a carer.

## Extra care housing: potential deprivation of liberty

**7.22** We suggest that the measures in the following scenario may give rise to a deprivation of liberty:

Charles is 80 years old with early onset dementia. He has been residing in a rented one-bedroomed bungalow in a care village for three years and is believed to have now lost the mental capacity to make decisions as to residence and care. Four hours per day he is helped by a member of staff with personal care, cooking and cleaning tasks. He has door sensors to alert staff to when he leaves the property and is required to wear an alarm device at all times for his safety. He is not allowed to leave the complex without a staff member.

> Key factors pointing to potential deprivation of liberty:
>
> ■ Charles is not free to leave unaccompanied.
> ■ Careful examination will be required as to extent to which the remote monitoring, together with the direct support of staff four hours a day, cumulatively amounts to sufficiently continuous/complete supervision and control to satisfy the acid test.

## Extra care housing: not a deprivation of liberty

**7.23** We suggest that the following scenario is unlikely to amount to a deprivation of liberty:

Mabel is 75 years old and decided with capacity to sell her home and to purchase an apartment in a local housing with care scheme as she was becoming forgetful and worried about her own safety. There are 35 apartments on the site which is accessed with a key fob or code. A warden is available 24 hours a day. She is advised not to go out without a friend, family member or staff member. If she wished to go out alone, she must ensure that a member of staff knows so that if she does not return they can follow the missing persons protocol. Mabel is otherwise left to her own devices without interference from the housing scheme.

> Key factors pointing to potential deprivation of liberty:
>
> ■ Mabel is not under continuous or complete supervision or control.

## E    Questions for frontline practitioners

**7.24**    These questions may help establish whether an individual is deprived of their liberty in this context:

■    To what extent is the person's ability to access the community by themselves limited by others and in what circumstances?

■    Within their place of residence, to what extent is the person (a) actively supervised, (b) liable to be supervised, (c) not even liable to be supervised by others when risks may arise?

■    Is physical intervention used? If so, how often? What type? For how long? And what effect does it have on the person?

■    Do others control their finances?

■    How would the care regime respond to the corresponding risks if the person attempted to leave either to access the community or to simply not return?

■    Are there regular private times, where the person has no direct carer supervision?

■    Is their contact with the outside world restricted? If so, how often? How? For how long? And what effect does this have on the person?

■    To what extent is the person able to decline assistance when it is available?

### Endnotes
1    Based upon the case of MIG in the Supreme Court.

## 8    DEPRIVATION OF LIBERTY AT HOME

### A    Introduction

**8.1**    This chapter considers how to identify deprivation of liberty in an individual's home. For the purposes of this chapter, we use 'home' to mean an individual's own home. This could be a home that they own or rent themselves, or a home owned or rented by a family member or members with whom they live. 'Home-like' arrangements made by the State to place individuals requiring accommodation because of their particular needs, which are usually referred to as 'supported living', are addressed in Chapter 6.[1] The position of children is considered in Chapter 9.

**8.2**    This chapter comes with two 'health warnings,' one relating to the question of State responsibility, and the second stemming from the decision in *Rochdale MBC* v. *KW*.[2] Both of these matters are discussed below.

### B    Health Warning 1: State responsibility

**8.3**    The first health warning is highlighted in Chapter 2 at paragraphs 2.50-2.55. It is not easy to identify a precise point at which the State ceases to be directly responsible for care or health packages delivered in the home environment and, instead, is required to take the (rather vaguer) steps which are required by Article 5 ECHR to provide effective protection to the individual concerned.

8.4    Until there is clarification from the courts, we suggest that there is likely to be sufficient State involvement to make the situation a 'State' deprivation of liberty falling within the scope of Article 5(1) ECHR – and therefore requiring steps to be taken by the relevant State body involved to seek authorisation from the Court of Protection – if:

8.4.1    arrangements are made, whether by a local authority or NHS body, to commission and provide care in the individual's own home;

8.4.2    direct payments (including personal health budgets) are made (whether for social or health care) to a family member or professional carers to arrange and provide care to the individual in the individual's own home;

8.4.3    the decision that the individual should remain in their own home and be cared for there has been taken on their behalf by the Court of Protection. In such a situation, one would expect that questions of deprivation of liberty would be considered by the judge making the decision, but the order may have been made before the *Cheshire West* judgment or arrangements may have changed since the order.

8.5    Where the decision that the individual should remain in their own home and be cared for there has been taken on their behalf by a best interests decision-making process involving the relevant local authority or NHS body, we suggest that the State will then be 'on notice' of any deprivation of liberty that may arise in consequence of that decision. The relevant local authority or NHS body may therefore have an obligation under the positive limb of Article 5 ECHR (discussed at paragraphs 2.50–2.55) to take steps to ensure that there is authority for that deprivation of liberty.

8.6    We also note that a situation may arise where a health and welfare deputy or a financial deputy is making private arrangements for the care of an individual in their own home (e.g. through administering a damages award received following a personal injury claim) and considers that those arrangements amount to an objective deprivation of the individual's liberty to which they cannot consent. We suggest that the deputy should seek their own legal advice as to the steps that they should take. There are arguments to suggest that, as a minimum, a deputy in such a case should notify the relevant local authority for the area in which the individual lives. The deputy may invite the local authority to consider whether any steps need to be taken under the positive limb of Article 5(1) EHCR and in the meantime to consider whether the restrictions on the individual's liberty which may amount to a deprivation of liberty can be reasonably reduced.

## C    Health Warning 2: Can a person be deprived of liberty at home at all?

8.7    In a case decided in November 2014, *Rochdale MBC* v. *KW*,[3] Mostyn J cast doubt as to whether it is possible for a person to be deprived of their liberty at home at all, at least where their own physical disabilities were such that they were house-bound. The case concerned a woman cared for in her own home[4] with a substantial package of care arranged jointly by the relevant local authority and CCG. Contrary to the agreed position of both the local authority and KW (acting by her litigation friend) – Mostyn J held that the woman was not deprived of her liberty. In doing so, he made a number of observations about the approach adopted by the Supreme Court in *Cheshire West*, and the proper construction of the acid test.[5] On the facts of the case, Mostyn J then accepted (it appears) that every element required to bring KW's situation within the scope of Article 5 was satisfied[6] except for the requirement that she was constrained from exercising freedom to leave.[7]

**8.8**    KW's appeal was allowed by consent in February 2015. In endorsing the consent order allowing the appeal, the Court of Appeal did not give a judgment explaining its reasons.[8] However, it seems to us clear that:

**8.8.1**    The conclusions that Mostyn J reached both upon the facts of KW's case and upon the broader position of those cared for in their own homes are clearly incompatible with the decision of the majority in *Cheshire West*. We consider that Mostyn J's approach conflates freedom to leave with ability to leave. This gives rise to a different concept of physical liberty for those who are unable to take advantage of it – contrary to the clear holding of Lady Hale (with whom the other members of the majority agreed) that 'the concept of physical liberty protected by article 5 is the same for everyone, regardless of whether or not they are mentally or physically disabled',[9] and also Lord Kerr's observation that '[liberty] does not depend on one's disposition to exploit one's freedom';[10] such that

**8.8.2**    Mostyn J's judgment did not provide a sound basis upon which to conclude that individuals with severe disabilities cared for at home with a package of care arranged by public authorities *cannot* be deprived of their liberty.

**8.9**    Bearing in mind Lady Hale's warning in *Cheshire West* that we should in the case of the vulnerable err on the side of caution as regards deciding what constitutes a deprivation of liberty,[11] we consider that it is possible for an individual to be deprived of their liberty in their own home in the context of the delivery of care and treatment and for such deprivation of liberty to be imputable to the State.

**8.10**    We should note that, as this guidance was being finalised, we were notified of a decision in which a judge of the High Court (Mr Justice Bodey) held that a woman cared for in her own home, predominantly by her own family, was not deprived of their liberty. The transcript of the judgment was not available at the time of finalising the guidance but we understand that Bodey J placed significant weight both upon the limited nature of the involvement of the local authority and that the woman continued to reside in her own home, in which she had lived for many years before losing capacity. Those who are concerned with deprivations of liberty in the home environment should make sure that they keep abreast of developments, including the full report of this judgment, by making use of the resources identified in Chapter 11.

## D     The home environment: liberty restricting measures

8.11    Almost by definition, arrangements made at home will be more varied and more flexible than arrangements made in any institutional or quasi-institutional setting. It is also more likely that, because the arrangements are likely to be more tailored to the individual, they will less obviously be directed to the control of that individual in the interests of others within a placement (whether other service users or the staff).

8.12    However, it is important to remember that MIG was found to be deprived of her liberty in an adult foster placement – i.e. a home-like environment – in circumstances where the supervision and control to which she was subject was 'intensive support in most aspects of daily living',[12] even though she attended a further education college daily during term time and was taken on trips and holidays by her foster mother.

8.13    We therefore suggest that the following features may constitute liberty-restricting measures in the home environment:

■    the prescription and administration of medication to control the individual's behaviour, including on a PRN basis;
■    the provision of physical support with the majority of aspects of daily living, especially where that support is provided according to a timetable set not by the individual but by others;
■    the use of real-time monitoring within the home environment (for instance by use of CCTV or other assistive technology);[13]
■    the regular use of restraint by family members or professional carers which should always be recorded in the individual's care plan;
■    the door being locked, and where the individual does not have the key (or the number to a keypad) and is unable to come and go as they please, strongly suggests that they are not free to leave;
■    the individual regularly being locked in their room (or in an area of the house) or otherwise prevented from moving freely about the house;[14]
■    use of medication to sedate or manage behaviour, including PRN.

## E     Care arrangements in the home that are imputable to the State

8.14    The scenarios below all describe arrangements made to provide care to a person lacking capacity to consent to them in their own home. In all the cases the State has been involved in some way in making the arrangements and so in the question of whether these are 'imputable' to the State does not arise. This issue is likely to be considered by the courts however, and therefore it will be important to keep up to date on this issue, using the resources which we set out in Chapter 11.

## Care arrangements in the home: a deprivation of liberty

**8.15**    The measures in the following scenario are likely to amount to a deprivation of liberty:

Veronica is a widow of 75. She has a history of mental illness going back to her 30s. Her current diagnosis is of schizoaffective disorder. She has had a number of admissions to hospital under the MHA 1983. She has not been in hospital for some years but sees her psychiatrist fairly regularly and attends regular s.117 MHA 1983 after-care reviews. More recently Veronica has been showing signs of short term memory loss. Veronica lives alone in the home that she shared with her husband. She is very independent but recently her daughter Susan has become concerned that Veronica is leaving pans on the stove unattended, is becoming erratic in compliance with her medication and has visibly lost weight. Veronica's psychiatrist is also concerned and Veronica agrees to an informal admission to hospital to allow her psychiatrist to assess her. During her stay Veronica has an Activities of Daily Living assessment and is noted to be unsafe in the kitchen. An MRI scan suggests some damage. Veronica's psychiatrist assesses her capacity and reaches the conclusion that Veronica lacks capacity to make decisions about her care needs, mainly because she is unable to recognise that her ability to look after herself is impaired. The clinical team consider that Veronica needs 24-hour care. The question is where it should be provided.

A s.117 MHA 1983 meeting takes place. Veronica attends the meeting and pleads not to go to a care home. The CCG and local authority agree to fund 24-hour care in Veronica's home for a trial period. A care provider is sourced and Veronica goes home.

Veronica's care plan is that she will have one carer at home all the time. A spare room is made available for the carer, as it is not considered that waking nights are required. The carer agency will have access to a key safe and will be able to enter Veronica's home even if she does not want them to come in. Veronica will be supervised in the kitchen. She will be supported by the carer in arranging to go out when she wants to, which will include family visits, shopping and visits to galleries and museums which she likes, but the carer will dissuade her from leaving unaccompanied (and has a protocol to follow in the event that Veronica manages to leave whilst the carer is otherwise occupied). The psychiatrist specifies that Veronica must attend a day centre where she is well known at least once a week to facilitate ongoing monitoring of her mental state.

> Key factors pointing to a deprivation:
>
> - the continuous presence of the carer in the home;
> - the supervision of activities whilst in the home; and
> - that Veronica is not able to come and go unaccompanied.

## Care arrangements in the home: potential deprivation of liberty

**8.16**    We suggest that the measures in the following scenario may give rise to a deprivation of liberty:

Gordon is 80 years old with early onset dementia. He lives in his own home, and is believed to have now lost the mental capacity to make decisions as to residence and care. His care package provides for carers to attend four hours a day with personal care, cooking and cleaning tasks. He has door sensors to alert his family when he leaves the property (both and day and at night) and is required to wear an alarm device at all times for his safety. Carers check after each visit that he is wearing the pendant and put it on if he has taken it off. Once he left the home at midnight and his daughter who lives nearby was alerted by the sensor. She immediately went to look for her father and guided him back home.

---

Key factors pointing to potential deprivation of liberty:

■ The restrictions upon his freedom to leave his own home.
■ Careful examination will be required as to extent to which the remote monitoring, together with the direct support of local authority arranged carers four hours a day, cumulatively amounts to sufficiently continuous/complete supervision and control to satisfy the acid test. The fact that, for example, carers gently enforce the requirement to wear the pendant is we suggest a relevant factor.

---

## Care arrangements in the home: not a deprivation of liberty

**8.17** The measures in the following scenario are unlikely to amount to a deprivation of liberty:

Susan and Jim are married. Both have significant histories of alcohol abuse and they met when they were both receiving treatment at a hostel. Although they have been together for a long time the relationship between them can be volatile. They have been homeless in the past but now have a joint tenancy of a housing association flat. Two years ago Susan walked in front of a car and was knocked over. She suffered a brain injury. She has made a reasonable recovery but has impaired cognitive abilities and clinical professionals consider that further improvement is unlikely. Susan's neuro-psychiatrist assesses her capacity. She is able to make decisions about whom she should see but not about her residence and care arrangements.

Jim and Susan were very keen for her to return home. Susan will need some support; for example it would not be safe for her to prepare a meal unsupervised. She is able to go out alone for short periods of time in the local area but she gets anxious about being alone and encourages Jim to accompany her as much as possible. Jim is willing to take on the majority of Susan's care. Staff feel that he will need some respite, and his own lifestyle can sometimes be chaotic. Susan's care plan provides for carers to visit for two hours daily, to supervise and support her in cooking and to ensure she maintains reasonable nutrition. The rest of the time, there is no involvement by local authority funded carers.

> Factors pointing away from a deprivation of liberty:
>
> ■    the limited nature of the supervision and control exercised by the local authority arranged care as compared to the informal care delivered by Jim.

## F    Considerations for frontline practitioners

**8.18**    These questions may help establish whether an individual is deprived of their liberty in this context:

■    Is the person prescribed or administered medication to control their behaviour, including on a PRN basis?

■    What level of support is provided with aspects of daily living? And is that support provided to a timetable set by the individual or by others?

■    Is technology used to monitor the individual's location within the home or to monitor when they leave?

■    Does the individual's care plan provide for the regular use of restraint? If so, under what circumstances and for how long?

■    Is the door to the individual's home locked? If so, do they have the key (or the code to a keypad)?

■    Are they free to come and go from their own home unaccompanied as they please?

■    Are they regularly locked in their room (or an area of their home) or otherwise prevented from moving freely about their home?

■    Are restrictions placed upon them by professionals as to who they can and cannot see?

## Endnotes

1    We recognise that many of those in supported living are likely to consider the place that they are living to be their home. However, we draw the distinction here in particular so as to focus on situations where an individual is not placed by the State so as to meet their care needs, but arrangements are made for them in the place that they were living prior to those needs arising (or being identified).

2    [2014] EWCOP 45.

3    [2014] EWCOP 45.

4    Rented from a Housing Association.

5    Some of which are discussed at paragraphs 3.4-3.22, in particular those relating to the question of when a person may be considered to be free to leave.

6    I.e. that she was under continuous/complete supervision and control (she required the presence of carers 24/7 (paragraph 6), that she lacked the capacity to consent to any deprivation of liberty (paragraph 4), and that any deprivation of liberty would be imputable to the State (paragraph 7).

7    At paragraph 25, he held that KW was 'not in any realistic way being constrained from exercising the freedom to leave, in the required sense, for the essential reason that she does not have the physical or mental ability to exercise that freedom'.

8    A matter addressed by Mostyn J at [2015] EWCOP 13.

9    Paragraphs 33 and 36. We also note that the logic of Mostyn J's conclusion would extend to any other setting in which the person could have been placed by their family and which the individual regards as a home. This would mean, therefore, that many in care homes would not

– on Mostyn J's analysis – be considered to be deprived of their liberty if they were unable to leave the home because of their physical or mental disabilities: this would drive a coach and horses through Schedule A1 to the MCA 2005 and further indicates, we suggest, that the approach adopted by Mostyn J was incorrect.

10 Paragraph 76.
11 Paragraph 57.
12 *Cheshire West* at paragraph 13.
13 Information for family members or carers considering use of surveillance has recently been provided by the Care Quality Commission (CQC): see **www.cqc.org.uk/content/using-hidden-cameras-monitor-care**.
14 Munby LJ in *Re A and Re C* [2010] EWHC 978 (Fam) held that those two individuals (one a child, and one an adult) who were locked in their rooms overnight were not deprived of their liberty. Munby LJ expressly based much of his reasoning upon the judgment of Parker J in the first instance judgment in MIG and MEG; we therefore respectfully suggest that this aspect of his judgment is incorrect in light of the decision of the Supreme Court in *Cheshire West*.

# 9 UNDER 18S

## A Introduction

**9.1** In this chapter, the term 'child' is used to refer to someone under the age of 16. A 'young person' refers to a 16- or 17-year-old. 'Adult' refers to a person aged 18 or over. We do not venture into the circumstances in which those under 16 might be deprived of liberty: the focus on this chapter is exclusively on young persons. This is **not** because Article 5 ECHR is irrelevant to children; far from it. Indeed, as at the time this guidance is produced (March 2015), we understand there will be case law forthcoming that specifically addresses the impact of the Supreme Court's decision for those **under** 16.[1] Rather, it is because the jurisdiction of the Court of Protection to authorise deprivation of liberty is available only from the age of 16. For the same reason, this chapter only addresses the relevance of Article 5 ECHR to young persons who **lack** capacity to decide where to reside in order to receive care and treatment.

**9.2** Care and support is provided to young persons in a very broad range of living arrangements. These include (but are not limited to) the family home, foster homes, adoptive homes, children's homes (secure, non-secure, and certain special schools), care homes, residential special schools, boarding schools, further education colleges with residential accommodation, and hospitals. Many of these care settings are considered in separate chapters to which reference should be made. Thus, where there is an issue regarding deprivation of liberty occurring in the family home, private fostering[2] home, or adoptive home, reference should be made to Chapter 8. This is because parental responsibility rests solely with the parent(s) rather than the State and so is analogous to the family home. For respite in care homes, please see the appendix to Chapter 6; for hospitals, Chapters 4-5; and supported living (available from the age of 16) is considered in Chapter 7.

**9.3** When considering those other chapters please bear in mind the following important provisos. First, the acid test for 'deprivation of liberty' appears to be more nuanced for those under 18 (as explained below). So what may constitute a deprivation of liberty of an adult may not necessarily be so for a young person. The relevant extracts of the Supreme Court's judgment that are unique to those under 18 are set out below to complement Chapter 2. Second, where a young person's inability to consent to their care arrangements results from immaturity, rather than impaired mental functioning, the MCA 2005 is not applicable. So recourse may be needed to alternatives, such as parental responsibility, the family courts or the inherent jurisdiction of the High Court.[3] Finally, a whole raft of legislation, statutory guidance and minimum standards apply to those under 18 and may bear upon the young person's deprivation of liberty.

9.4    This chapter is necessarily modest given the dearth of analogous case law and focuses on those care settings relating to 16- and 17-year-olds which are most likely to raise potential deprivation of liberty issues. They are foster homes (in the absence of a residence order), children's homes, and residential educational establishments.[4] Neither DOLS nor the MHA 1983 are available to authorise deprivations of liberty here, so judicial authorisation will be required. The Court of Protection can authorise the deprivation of liberty of young persons lacking the relevant mental capacity: *Barnsley MBC* v. *GS & Ors*.[5] The inherent jurisdiction of the High Court is also available, regardless of the person's age.[6] The chapter is therefore divided into the following areas:

- Parental responsibility and the nuanced acid test
- Universal constraints
- Liberty-restricting measures
- Foster homes
- Children's homes (non-secure)
- Educational establishments (residential special schools, further education colleges)
- Considerations for frontline practitioners

## B    Parental responsibility and the nuanced acid test

9.5    In *RK* v. *BCC, YB and AK*[7] it was decided that '[d]*etention engages the Article 5 rights of the child and a parent may not lawfully detain or authorise the detention of a child.*' Although cited to the Supreme Court in the *Cheshire West* case, this decision was not referred to in any of the judgments. However, in our opinion, the principle remains good law. It follows that if a young person is deprived of their liberty, the consent of those with parental responsibility cannot be relied upon to authorise it: the decision falls outside the scope of parental responsibility. Logically this would apply as equally to local authorities sharing parental responsibility under a care order as it does to parents.

9.6    One of the individuals before the Supreme Court was 17 years of age and some of the judges considered the application of Article 5 to children and young persons. Our impression is that the test for deprivation of liberty is more nuanced when it comes to this age group because children and young persons are compared with those of the same age and maturity. This tends to reflect aspects of the European jurisprudence as identified in *Nielsen* v. *Denmark*:[8]

> It should be observed at the outset that family life in the Contracting States encompasses a broad range of parental rights and responsibilities in regard to care and custody of minor children. The care and upbringing of children normally and necessarily require that the parents or an only parent decide where the child must reside and also impose, or authorise others to impose, various **restrictions** on the child's liberty. Thus the children in a school or other educational or recreational institution must abide by certain rules which limit their freedom of movement and their liberty in other respects. Likewise a child may have to be hospitalised for medical treatment. Family life in this sense, and especially the rights of parents to exercise parental authority over their children, having due regard to their corresponding parental responsibilities, is recognised and protected by the Convention, in particular by Article 8. Indeed the exercise of parental rights constitutes a fundamental element of family life. [Emphasis added.]
>
> para.61

9.7    With regard to the situation of MIG and MEG, Lady Hale held at paragraph 54:

> If the acid test is whether a person is under the complete supervision and control of those caring for her and is not free to leave the place where she lives, then the truth is that both MIG and MEG are being deprived of their liberty. Furthermore, that deprivation is the responsibility of the State. Similar constraints would not necessarily amount to a deprivation of liberty for the purpose of article 5 if imposed by parents in the exercise of their ordinary parental responsibilities and outside the legal framework governing State intervention in the lives of children or people who lack the capacity to make their own decisions.

9.8    The other critical paragraphs applicable to those aged under 18 are:

> 72. In the case of children living at home, what might otherwise be a deprivation of liberty would normally not give rise to an infringement of article 5 because it will have been imposed not by the State, but by virtue of what the Strasbourg court has called 'the rights of the holder of parental authority', which are extensive albeit that they 'cannot be unlimited' (see *Nielsen* v. *Denmark* (1988) 11 EHRR 175, para.72, a decision which, at least on its facts, is controversial, as evidenced by the strength of the dissenting opinions). However, it is fair to say that, while this point would apply to adoptive parents, I doubt that it would include foster parents (unless, perhaps, they had the benefit of a residence order). But in the great majority of cases of people other than young children living in ordinary domestic circumstances, the degree of supervision and control and the freedom to leave would take the situation out of article 5.4. And, where article 5.4 did apply, no doubt the benignly intimate circumstances of a domestic home would frequently help to render any deprivation of liberty easier to justify.[9]
>
> 77. **The question whether one is restricted (as a matter of actuality) is determined by comparing the extent of your actual freedom with someone of your age and station whose freedom is not limited. Thus a teenager of the same age and familial background as MIG and MEG is the relevant comparator for them.** If one compares their state with a person of similar age and full capacity it is clear that their liberty is in fact circumscribed. They may not be conscious, much less resentful, of the constraint but, objectively, limitations on their freedom are in place.
>
> 78. All children are (or should be) subject to some **level of restraint**. This **adjusts**

with their maturation and change in circumstances. If MIG and MEG had the same freedom from constraint as would any child or young person of similar age, their liberty would not be restricted, whatever their level of disability. As a matter of objective fact, however, **constraints beyond those which apply to young people of full ability are and have to be applied to them. There is therefore a restriction of liberty in their cases. Because the restriction of liberty is and must remain a constant feature of their lives, the restriction amounts to a deprivation of liberty.**

79.  Very young children, of course, because of their youth and dependence on others, have an objectively ascertainable curtailment of their liberty but this is a condition common to all children of tender age. There is no question, therefore, of suggesting that infant children are deprived of their liberty in the normal family setting. A comparator for a young child is not a fully matured adult, or even a partly mature adolescent. While they were very young, therefore, MIG and MEG s liberty was not restricted. **It is because they can and must now be compared to children of their own age and relative maturity who are free from disability and who have access (whether they have recourse to that or not) to a range of freedoms which MIG and MEG cannot have resort to that MIG and MEG are deprived of liberty.**[10] [Emphasis added.]

**9.9**   It appears to follow that for young persons, the acid test should be considered in the context of the liberty-restricting measures that are universally applied to those of the same age and maturity who are free from disability. As a general rule, the younger the person is, the greater the level of constraint to which they would typically be subject. A 5-year-old, for example, regardless of their disability, would be under continuous or complete supervision and control wherever they are and not free to leave. The fact that they are under such control, whether in the care of their family or the State, does not mean they are deprived of liberty. However, if the level of constraint typically afforded to a non-disabled 5-year-old is provided to a disabled 16-year-old, then those constraints must be taken into account in determining whether the acid test is satisfied.

**9.10**   In deciding whether someone aged 16 or 17 is deprived of their liberty, in addition to the content discussed in Chapters 2 and 3, it is therefore necessary to consider the extent to which the care arrangements differ to those typically made for someone of the same age and relative maturity who is free from disability. Universal disability-free measures constraining the liberty of all those of that age and maturity who are not physically or mentally disabled should not be taken into account. We also note that the duration of the constraints were a key feature, at least for one of the judges.

## C   Universal constraints

**9.11**   It is not altogether easy to gauge what amounts to a universal degree of age-appropriate constraint in a multicultural society. What level of constraint is universally applied to all non-disabled 16-year-olds, for example? Moreover, it is important to bear in mind the importance of Article 8 in this context because the exercise of parental rights constitutes a fundamental element of family life. So what follows are merely general comments to provide some context to illustrate the universal constraints required of all young persons by those with parental responsibility.[11] Crucially, what is clear is that, as young people approach adulthood, the intensity or degree of such constraint is expected to lessen as they mature and gain independence.

**9.12**    The living arrangements for young persons should provide a positive, supportive and caring environment. Their welfare must be safeguarded and promoted. But, equally, they must have the physical and emotional freedom to develop and make, and learn from, their own mistakes. Strategies for coping with challenges and stress factors need to be nurtured. How to approach relationships with learning and respect for others needs to be taught. Privacy and dignity must be respected. Responsible parenting, whether in the care of the family or of the State, is therefore a social norm for those under 18.

**9.13**    Responsible parenting provides a homely environment with a certain degree of freedom exercisable alongside sensible precautions. It protects against avoidable risks but avoids excessive caution. It meets the person's needs, especially their disabled needs, and reasonable preferences for clothing, footwear, personal necessities, and perhaps an age appropriate personal allowance. It facilitates religious observance if the individual belongs to a religious persuasion. Subject to restrictions necessary to safeguard and promote welfare, responsible parenting promotes contact with family and friends, and provides access to the world outside.

**9.14**    Responsible parenting promotes and protects physical, emotional and mental health. It provides the person with some private space. After compulsory school age, it assists with arrangements for further education, training and employment opportunities. It encourages the pursuit of age appropriate leisure interests. It grants permission to engage in normal and acceptable age appropriate activities at home and in the community. It aims to develop important life skills, personal responsibility, and the ability to choose and to be independent. This cannot be imposed from upon high: it is nurtured through explanation, discussion, and negotiation within positive, constructive relationships between those parenting and the parented.

**9.15**    As in every family, we cannot always get what we want. The young person's expressed views or wishes may not accord with those with parental responsibility or, of course, the law. For example, those under 18 cannot buy alcohol, cigarettes, fireworks, vote, watch adult movies, or get tattoos. Responsible parenting therefore takes a reasonable, reasoned view as to the best way forward in the interests of all concerned. It provides safety, with rules that are sensibly implemented, taking into account the person's age, without unnecessarily preventing them from taking part in everyday activities. Indeed, those aged 16 or 17 can drink alcohol in a restaurant if having a meal and accompanied by an adult. They can permanently leave home without their parents' consent, secure full-time employment, claim certain welfare benefits, have sexual intercourse, get married (with parental permission), buy National Lottery tickets, drive mopeds (from 16) or cars (from 17), and travel abroad.

## D    Liberty-restricting measures

**9.16**    Mere placement in foster care, a children's home or residential special school of someone lacking the capacity to consent will not in itself constitute a deprivation of liberty. However, the combined effect of more specific measures may do. As explained above, constraints may be universal to a 5-year-old but liberty-restricting when applied to a 16-year-old. Thus, continual supervision would be universally expected of the former but not of the latter.

**9.17**    The following list of measures might be identified in foster care arrangements, children's homes or residential special schools. Some are more relevant to one care setting than another. The list also comes with an important health warning: if the measure would be universal for someone of that age and maturity who is disability-free, it should **not** be taken into account in determining whether the nuanced acid test is met.

- decision on where to reside being taken by others;
- decision on contact with others not being taken by the individual;
- restrictions on developing sexual relations;
- doors of the property locked, and/or chained, and/or bolted for security reasons or to prevent the children or young persons leaving;
- a member or members of staff accompanying the person to access the community to support and meet their care needs;
- access to the community being limited by staff availability;
- mechanical restraint, such as wheelchairs with a lapstrap or specialist harness;
- varying levels of staffing and frequency of observation by staff;
- provision of 'safe spaces' or 'chill out' rooms or spaces during the day or night from which the person cannot leave of their own free will (eg padded tent to sleep in);
- restricted access to personal allowances;
- searching of the person and/or their belongings;[12]
- restricted access to personal belongings to prevent harm;
- medication with a sedative or tranquilising effect;
- physical restraint/intervention, such as with personal care tasks, breakaway or block techniques, distraction methods, staff withdrawing, physical touches or holds (e.g. 'Team-Teach' methods);[13]
- restricted access to modes of social communication, such as internet, landline or mobile telephone or correspondence;
- positive behavioural reward systems to reward 'good' behaviour which might thereby involve restrictions on favoured activities or aspects of the curriculum to improve behaviour;
- disciplinary penalties for poor behaviour;[14]
- restricting excessive pursuance of activities;
- lack of flexibility, in terms of having activities timetabled, set meal times, expected sleep times;
- managing food intake and access to it;
- police called to return the person if they go missing;

■  restricted access to parts of the property, such as the kitchen or certain cupboards therein, to minimise health and safety risks.

## E    Foster homes for looked after persons[15]

**9.18**  Foster care arrangements range from emergency provision to long-term placements with varying aims. Short breaks[16] also form part of a continuum of services to support young persons in need and their families. Their Foster Care Agreement requires carers to care for any young person placed with them as if that person was a member of the foster carer's own family. Accordingly, they should have delegated to them the maximum appropriate flexibility to make day-to-day caring decisions within the framework of an agreed placement plan and parental responsibility.

### Foster home: a deprivation of liberty

**9.19**  The measures in the following scenario are likely to amount to a deprivation of liberty:

David is 16 years old and has Smith Magenis syndrome. His condition is characterised by self-injurious and destructive behaviour, aggression, hyperactivity, and severe sleep disturbances including frequent and prolonged night waking. He also destroys furniture, eats copious amounts of, sometimes uncooked, food. In accordance with the assessments and care plan prepared by the local authority, his foster parents lock him in his bedroom from 7pm until 7am every night to keep David safe. Doors and windows around the house are also kept locked at all times with keys hidden. During the day he receives intensive support from his foster parents with all aspects of daily living, and at least one of them is with him at all times.

> Factors pointing to a deprivation of liberty:
>
> ■  David is regularly locked in his room for 12 hours of each 24, and the doors to the house are locked;
> ■  David is supervised and accompanied by a foster parent on a 1:1 basis throughout the day.

### Foster home: potential deprivation of liberty

**9.20**  We suggest that the measures in the following scenario may give rise to a deprivation of liberty:

Michaela is a 16-year-old girl with severe learning disability and hearing, visual and speech impediments and is largely dependent on others. She does not communicate very readily, hardly at all in sentences, and lives most of her time in her own world, typically listening to music. She can read familiar words and, with support, is able to give a basic account of her living arrangements and to describe her feelings in often monosyllabic speech. She is emotionally attached to her foster mother in a good loving home with the person she regards as 'mummy'. She is supported with basic life skills and personal care with clear boundaries and routines. She attends a school every day during term time and her foster mother provides her with educational input. Continual support is available to meet her care needs and she is taken on exciting holidays and trips. She shows no wish to go out on her own. She is not physically restrained or locked in the home in any way. But if she wished to leave the home by herself she would be prevented from doing so for her own immediate safety as she has no sense of safety, in particular road safety. Some of the parenting provided is in line with that usually provided to a much younger child.

---

Key factors pointing to potential deprivation of liberty:

■    These facts are similar to those of MIG, who was found by the Supreme Court to be deprived of her liberty.

■    However, as Michaela is two years younger, the key question for professionals is the extent to which the measures applied to her are comparable to those which would be applied to a non-disabled young person of comparable age and maturity.

---

*Foster home: not a deprivation of liberty*

**9.21**    The following scenario is unlikely to amount to a deprivation of liberty:

Nathan is 16 years old with mild learning disability. His foster parents prepare his meals, wash his clothes, and are available around the house if he needs them. They do not otherwise support him with activities of daily living any more than they do the activities of Carole, the 16-year-old daughter of his foster parents. He attends a mainstream school with pre-arranged transport. At weekends the family go shopping and on trips. Once his foster parents have helped Nathan to familiarise himself with the route, he is able to go out with his friends and has a mobile phone to call them if he needs help.

---

Key factors pointing away from deprivation of liberty:

■    Nathan's age and the extent to which the measures applied to him are comparable to those which would be applied to a 16-year-old without disabilities, a direct comparison being Carole.

---

## F    Children's homes

**9.22**    A children's home (defined in s.1 Care Standards Act 2000) is generally an establishment providing care and accommodation wholly or mainly for children. Since 1 April 2015 it is subject to the Children's Homes (England) Regulations 2015 and the quality standards therein. Care models differ from the larger children's homes designed with routines to meet the needs of teenagers, to homes providing therapeutic input for young persons with complex needs, to one-bedded homes.

## Children's home: a deprivation of liberty

**9.23**  We suggest that the measures in the following scenario are likely to amount to a deprivation of liberty:

Ahmed, a 16 year-old-boy with autism and learning disability resides in a children's home and attends specialist school. On a daily basis he screams, kicks, bites, and hits out at staff and his peers. He receives two-to-one support throughout the day. Once or twice per week he goes into a soft play area, or 'safe space', in order to calm down, during which the door is closed, not locked, and a teaching assistant watches him through the door window. At many other times he is physically restrained using Team-Teach methods to prevent him assaulting others. He receives visits from his grandparents and mother; his father decides not to visit but could do so if he wished.

> Key factors pointing to deprivation of liberty:
>
> - the intensive and continuous nature of the control and supervision exercised over him;
> - the use of the 'safe space' on a regular basis; and
> - the use of physical restraint – Ahmed would not be free to leave the children's home.

## Children's home: potential deprivation of liberty

**9.24**  We suggest that the measures in the following scenario may give rise to a deprivation of liberty:

Joanna, aged 16, has autism, severe learning disability and epilepsy, and aggressive and self-harming behaviours. She resides in a children's home from Monday to Friday, which her parents can visit at any time, and spends the weekends at her parents' home. During term time she attends school. Both at school and in the children's home she is supervised most of the daytime to prevent her harming herself or others. She compliantly takes her prescribed medicines. She is not physically restrained other than on a few occasions to prevent her attacking others. Her behaviour has led to minor sanctions being imposed on a few occasions, such as not allowing her to eat a takeaway meal or stopping her listening to music when in a car. The front door to the children's home is not locked but, were she to run out of it, she would be brought back.

> Key factors pointing to potential deprivation of liberty:
>
> - similar circumstances were held in *RK v. BCC, YB and AK*[17] not to amount to a deprivation of liberty;
> - however, in light of the decision in *Cheshire West*, we suggest that this conclusion would have to be revisited, in particular, given her age, the continuous nature of the supervision to which she is subjected, and the fact that she is not free to leave.

## Children's home: not a deprivation of liberty

**9.25**    The following scenario is unlikely to amount to a deprivation of liberty:

Connie is 16 years old and has a mild learning disability. After breakfast she is transported to school for 9am and brought back at 3.20pm. From then until 5pm she is supported to do her homework, attend any health or social care appointments, and is able to go out the home to see her friends. Along with the other young persons, Connie helps to prepare the dinner. After eating together, staff spend time with them pursuing their hobbies and interests, watching television and socialising.

> Key factors pointing away from deprivation of liberty:
>
> ■    the extent to which the measures applied to Connie are comparable to those which would be applied to a young person of comparable age and maturity.

## G    Educational establishments

**9.26**    Educational establishments come in many guises: from nurseries and child minders, to schools maintained by the local authority, independent schools, academies and free schools, through to special schools and further education colleges. Those most relevant to this guidance are establishments providing care and accommodation alongside special education: that is, residential special schools.[18]

**9.27**    Proportionate restraint is permitted.[19] In particular, school staff may use reasonable force to prevent a pupil committing an offence, causing personal injury or damage to property, or behaving in a manner prejudicial to the maintenance of good order or discipline.[20]

## Residential special school: a deprivation of liberty

**9.28**    The measures in the following scenario are likely to amount to a deprivation of liberty:

David, aged 17, has been resident in a school for some years. He has autism and severe learning disability with extremely challenging behaviour. His behaviour is managed in large part by the use of a padded blue room in which he was secluded when he exhibited challenging behaviour. He has developed a number of behaviours that are particularly prevalent when in the 'blue room' including defecating, smearing and eating his own urine and faeces, and stripping naked. He is prevented from leaving the blue room for reasons of aggression and nakedness. The blue room is also used as a room to which David had been encouraged to withdraw as a safe place.

Key factors pointing to a deprivation of liberty:

- the particular techniques used to manage his behaviour; and
- the use of seclusion in a blue room from which he was prevented from leaving.[21]

## Residential special school: potential deprivation of liberty

**9.29**    The measures in the following scenario may give rise to a deprivation of liberty:

Gary is 17 years old and has severe learning disability. He is non-weight bearing. Throughout the year he lives in a special school which is in 10 acres of land and surrounded by a high perimeter fence. There are three houses, each with their own care team, in which 2 to 5 children and young persons reside. Entry is via keypad which he cannot use. Gary needs two members of staff to assist him with all personal care interventions and to hoist him from bed to his electric wheelchair. From 9am to 3pm at school, and from 3pm to 9pm in the house, he is supported by one staff member. Waking staff check on him every hour during the night. After a number of incidents when Gary drove his wheelchair into his peers and staff causing injury, staff decided to replace the arm to a slow speed version so as to minimise the risk.

Key factors pointing to a potential deprivation of liberty:

- Gary is not free to leave.
- Whether or not he is deprived of his liberty will depend crucially on the extent to which to the support provided by staff can properly be described as support or whether it is to be considered supervision and control. In light of MIG's case (discussed further at paragraph 2.26), we suggest that caution would need to be exercised before such a conclusion is reached.

## Residential special school: not a deprivation of liberty

**9.30**    The following scenario is unlikely to amount to a deprivation of liberty:

Vanessa is 16 years old and has autism. For 38 weeks per year she lives in a school set in 25 acres which has 11 house groups, each accommodating between 4 and 8 students. It has high fences to prevent students reaching the road and to deter intruders and access to buildings and accommodation is via keypads or double-handled doors. Each house has a care team and each student has a key worker. Throughout the day there is usually one staff member for four students, although some activities like swimming require a higher ratio. All students have a structured, predictable daily routine of activities. During the week they wake at 7am, get washed and dressed, have breakfast, with school starting at 9.15am and finishing at 3.40pm. She has some down-time until 5pm when she eats with the others in her house. Evening activities with staff include art, cookery and sometimes outings. Vanessa is helped to go to bed in her personalised room at 9pm, with waking staff available during the night. Her door is always slightly ajar so staff can check on her. Timings are more flexible at weekends. Staff are trained in positive physical intervention techniques and follow her education and health care plan which does not envisage its use. Paediatricians and psychiatrists visit the school monthly and weekly respectively. Her videos, DVDs and CDs are checked to ensure they are age appropriate. She is encouraged to phone her parents every week and they are encouraged to visit at weekends.

> Key factors pointing away from a deprivation of liberty:
>
> ■ the extent to which the measures applied to Vanessa are comparable to those which would be applied to a child of comparable age and maturity in an educational establishment.

## H    Considerations for frontline practitioners

**9.31**    These questions may help establish whether an individual is deprived of their liberty in this context:

■ Compared to another person of the same age and relative maturity who is not disabled, how much greater is the intensity of the supervision, support, and restrictions?

■ Can the person go out of the establishment without the carer's permission? Can they spend nights away? How do the arrangements differ to the norm for someone of their age who is not disabled?

■ To what extent is the person able to control his or her own finances? How does this differ to the norm for someone of the same age who is not disabled?

■ Can the person choose what to wear outside school hours and buy his or her own clothes?

■ To what extent do the rules and sanctions differ from non-disabled age appropriate settings?

■ Are there regular private times, where the person has no direct carer supervision?

■ What is the carer to person ratio and how different is this to what would usually be expected of someone of that age who is not disabled?

■ Is physical intervention used? If so, what type? How long for? And what effect does it have on the person?

■ Is medication with a sedative effect used? If so, what type? How often? And what effect does it have on the person?

■ How structured is the person's routine compared with someone of the same age and relative maturity who is not disabled?

■ To what extent is contact with the outside world restricted?

# Endnotes

1   See Chapter 11 for details of how to stay abreast of developments.
2   Private fostering is governed by Part 9 of, and Schedule 8 to, the Children Act 1989, and the associated Children (Private Arrangements for Fostering) Regulations 2005. See also the 'Replacement Children Act 1989 guidance on Private Fostering: Every Child Matters' (2005). Whilst a private foster carer becomes responsible for providing the day-to-day care, the overarching responsibility for safeguarding and promoting the child (under 16, or 18 if disabled) remains with those with parental responsibility. Although they do not formally approve or register private foster carers, local authorities are duty bound to satisfy themselves that the welfare of privately fostered children within their area is satisfactorily safeguarded and promoted.
3   For guidance on the relevant provisions of the Children Act 1989, see generally Department of Education, 'Court orders and pre-proceedings: For local authorities' (2014).
4   Other forms of deprivation of liberty, for example under s.23 Children and Young Persons Act 1969 and secure accommodation orders under s.25 Children Act 1989, fall outside the scope of this chapter.
5   [2014] EWCOP 46, paragraphs 23-24. See also regulation 20(3) of the Children's Homes (England) Regulations 2015 which confirms that the Regulations 'do not prevent a child from being deprived of liberty where that deprivation is authorised in accordance with a court order'.
6   With regard to those under 18, see also *Re C (Detention: Medical Treatment)* [1997] 2 FLR 180.
7   [2011] EWCA Civ 1305 at paragraph 14.
8   See also *M and RT and F v. Austria* (Application no. 14013/88) and *Canepa v. Italy* (Application no. 43572/98).
9   Lord Neuberger.
10  Lord Kerr.
11  For those cared for in children's homes, see Department of Education, *'Guide to the Children's Homes Regulations including the quality standards'* (2015).
12  For example, see ss.550ZA to 550ZD of the Education and Inspections Act 1996.
13  Increasing guidance on the use of restrictive practices is becoming available: see, for example, Department of Health *'Positive and Proactive Care: reducing the need for restrictive interventions'* (2014); Skills for Care and Skills for Health, *'A positive and proactive workforce. A guide to workforce development for commissioners and employers seeking to minimize the use of restrictive practices in social care and health'* (2014). For restraint in children's homes, see Department of Education, *'Guide to the Children's Homes Regulations including the quality standards'* (2015), paras 9.48-9.63.
14  See Department of Education, 'Behaviour and discipline in schools: Advice for headteachers and school staff ' (February 2014).
15  See, in particular, Parts 3, 7 and 8 of the Children Act 1989, Care Standards Act 2000, Fostering Services (England) Regulations 2011, the National Minimum Standards for Fostering Services (2011) and *'The Children Act 1989 Guidance and Regulations Volume 4: Fostering Services'* (revised 2011).
16  Pursuant to ss. 17(6) or 20(4) of the Children Act 1989.
17  [2011] EWCA Civ 1305.
18  See the *National Minimum Standards for Residential Special Schools* (2013). Where a school provides, or intends to provide, accommodation to children for more than 295 days a year, it must be registered as a children's home and becomes subject to the Children's Homes (England) Regulations 2015 and the quality standards therein.
19  See s.550A Education Act 1996. In relation to young persons lacking the material capacity, ss.5-6 MCA 2005 will also be relevant.
20  See s.93 of the Education and Inspections Act 2006.
21  See *R (C) v. A Local Authority and others* [2011] EWHC 1539 (Admin) where it was held that similar circumstances were unlawful in the absence of judicial authorisation.

# III FURTHER INFORMATION

## 10   DEPRIVATION OF LIBERTY: KEY CASES

### Introduction

The cases summarised here represent the key English cases relating to deprivation of liberty since 2009,[1] together with (at the end) a list of cases that we consider should not be followed in light of the decision of the Supreme Court in *Cheshire West*. We attach what we call 'health warnings' to those cases.

The chapter includes not just the cases relating to what constitutes a deprivation of liberty but also the most important cases relating to *how* deprivations of liberty in this context can be authorised.

Not all the issues in each case are summarised; rather, the focus is on questions relating to deprivation of liberty.

The cases are set out in chronological order. There are hyperlinks to publicly available transcripts. In the majority of cases, more detailed discussions can be found on the (free) 39 Essex Chambers case summaries database, available at **www.copcasesonline.com**.

References to paragraphs are to paragraphs in the main body of the guidance unless the context makes clear.

### 1   *A Primary Care Trust* v. *P and Ors* [2009] EW Misc 10 (EWCOP) (Hedley J)

**Facts**: P was 24 years old at the time of the hearing. P had lived with his adoptive mother AH for a period of 18 and a half years. He suffered from a severe form of uncontrolled epilepsy and a mild learning disability. There was also a dispute as to whether P suffered from ME. The PCT and the local authority were concerned that both P and his adoptive mother AH were not complying with the medication regime set out by the doctors. P had been admitted as an emergency to hospital with life-threatening epileptic seizures in circumstances where AH had without medical advice withdrawn anti-epileptic medication a few days before. The matter had been before the court on a number of occasions and at the time of the hearing P was accommodated on a hospital ward.

**Issues to be decided**: 1) issues relating to his capacity to make decisions in respect of his medical treatment, residence, care and contact and ability to conduct litigation and, in the event that he lacked capacity; 2) his best interests in particular in relation to where he should live and the extent and frequency of contact with AH. In considering best interests, there were two conflicting proposals before the court. The PCT supported by the local authority concerned wished to provide P with independent living accommodation with limited contact with his mother. AH wished to resume the care of P on a full-time basis. P wished to return to live with AH.

**Decision**: Hedley J found that P lacked capacity in all regards. He concluded that it was in P's best interests to live in independent living accommodation and for his contact with his mother to be restricted and that these arrangements amounted to a deprivation of P's liberty within the meaning of Article 5(1) of the ECHR. In reaching the conclusion that the arrangements in this case amounted to a deprivation of liberty Hedley J took the following 5 factors into account:

1) The degree of control to be exercised by the staff.
2) The constraint on P leaving if it was his intention to go back to AH.
3) The power of the staff to refuse a request from AH for the discharge of P to her care.
4) Necessary restraints on contact between P and AH.
5) It involved a fairly high degree of supervision and control within the placement. Hedley J made orders under s.16 (2)(a) MCA 2005 accordingly.

## 2   Re P (Scope of Schedule A1) (30 June 2010) (Unreported) (Mostyn J)

This case concerns the scope of the powers that are granted by a standard authorisation under Schedule A1 to the MCA 2005. In it, Mostyn J was considering the extent of the powers granted to a local authority and a care home under existing (and any renewed) standard authorisations. He noted that it was common cause that these powers extended to a power to restrain P if he tried to leave the care home. The question for him was whether within those powers there was a power to coerce P to return if he refused to return to the care home from a period of leave. Mostyn J noted that it was understandably in P's interests that he should have access to society in the community and 'escape' the confines of the care home, and that the relevant PCT had agreed to fund 'befrienders' to encourage access to the community.

Mostyn J therefore asked himself whether the powers under the existing standard authorisation extend to coercing P back to the nursing home if P refused to return. He noted that it would be little short of absurd if the local authority and care home had powers to restrain P from leaving but not to compel him to return, and that the greater power must include the lesser. Mostyn J therefore declared that the power was implicit in the current and any future standard authorisation.

**Note**: this case does not, we suggest, provide authority for the proposition that a standard authorisation can be used to authorise a deprivation of liberty in relation to the transfer in or the transfer out of a placement (for instance the initial move into a hospital, or the permanent transfer from one hospital to another). See further in this regard the discussion at paragraph 4.15.

## 3    *BB* v. *AM* [2010] EWHC 1916 (COP) (Baker J)

**Facts**: P was a 31-year-old Bangladeshi woman, known as BB. She was said to have complex needs, being profoundly deaf with a diagnosis of schizoaffective disorder and probable learning difficulties. She lacked capacity to decide where she should live. In April 2010 BB was removed from home by support workers employed by the Community Mental Health Team, following reports that her parents had assaulted her. After a series of moves she was finally transferred to a hospital managed by a Mental Health NHS Trust in May 2010. BB's deprivation of liberty was authorised by that Trust under an urgent authorisation under the MCA 2005 in June 2010. The authorisation lapsed. The medical evidence was that BB was not detainable under the MHA 1983 because she was happy to stay in hospital and take medication. She had made no attempts to leave and she reported being happy. She changed the subject when asked about her home and family but she did so without showing any negative emotion or particular interest. It was contended by the Official Solicitor on behalf of BB that the arrangements amounted to a deprivation of her liberty and that there was no longer any lawful authorisation for BB's deprivation of liberty.

**Issues to be decided**: Issues relating to residence and contact were resolved by consent. However, the issue of whether or not BB was (1) ineligible to be deprived of her liberty within the meaning of the eligibility requirements in Schedule 1A MCA 2005 and (2) deprived of her liberty, were unresolved. A declaration was sought by the Official Solicitor acting for BB that the circumstances amounted to a deprivation of liberty.

**Decision**: Baker J found that BB was not ineligible to be deprived of her liberty within the meaning of the eligibility requirements in Schedule 1A. Accordingly the court was empowered to make an order in relation to her deprivation of liberty under s.16(2)(a) MCA 2005. In the circumstances of the case he found that BB was deprived of her liberty. In reaching this conclusion he took the following 'cumulative' factors into account: (1) BB was away from her family; (2) she was in an institution under sedation; (3) she was in circumstances where her contact with the outside world was strictly controlled; (4) her capacity to have free access to her family was limited by court order; and (5) her movements were under strict control and supervision of hospital staff. Baker J made the declaration sought and made an order authorising her deprivation of liberty under s.16 (2)(a) MCA 2005.

## 4    *A County Council* v. *MB, JB and a Residential Home* [2010] EWHC 2508 (COP) (Charles J)

**Facts**: Mrs B had been admitted to a care home following concerns about her being physically assaulted by her husband. An urgent authorisation was granted and then a standard authorisation lasting for one month. Prior to the expiry of the standard authorisation, a further standard authorisation was sought, but the best interests assessor concluded that the best interests requirement was no longer met. This was because Mrs B had displayed emotional and physical signs of distress at having been removed from her home. The local authority supervisory body sought advice as to what they should do, and following some confusion due to difficulty in contacting the Court of Protection urgently, they requested the care home to issue a second urgent authorisation.

**Issues to be decided**: The question of her best interests in respect of where she should live was no longer an issue at the time of the hearing. The issue before the court was whether the issuing of the second urgent authorisation was lawful.

**Decision**: Charles J found that the second urgent authorisation could not lawfully be issued. Once an urgent authorisation has been given, detention can only lawfully be extended by a standard authorisation or by court order. The court granted a declaration that Mrs B had been unlawfully deprived of her liberty from the expiry of the standard authorisation until the court declared the deprivation of liberty lawful at a subsequent hearing. Charles J did not, however, make any award of damages under the Human Rights Act 1998, noting that – in his view correctly – no such award had been sought. See further in this regard the discussion at paragraphs 2.44-2.48.

Charles J went on to give useful guidance about the duties of managing and supervisory authorities; a full discussion can be found at: **www.39essex.com/court–of–protection/search.php?id=2825**.

## 5   R (C) v. A Local Authority and others [2011] EWHC 1539 (Admin) (Ryder J)

**Facts**: C was an 18-year-old boy who had been resident in a school for some years. He had autism and severe learning disability with extremely challenging behaviour. His behaviour was managed in large part by the use of a padded blue room in which he was secluded when he exhibited challenging behaviour. He had developed a number of behaviours that were particularly prevalent when in the 'blue room' including defecating, smearing and eating his own urine and faeces, and stripping naked. He was prevented from leaving the blue room for reasons of aggression and nakedness. The blue room was also used as a room to which C had been encouraged to withdraw as a safe place and was said to have a calming influence on him. C had brought judicial review proceedings against the local authority, through his mother as his litigation friend. The local authority made an application to the Court of Protection and the two cases were heard together. The Official Solicitor replaced C's mother as his litigation friend.

In the judicial review proceedings the Official Solicitor sought declarations that C's rights under Articles 3, 5 and 8 ECHR had been violated, and damages for C as a result. The Official Solicitor sought orders compelling the local authority to provide an appropriate care plan, and make appropriate transitional arrangements.

It was accepted that C had been deprived of his liberty when he was secluded in the blue room. The DOLS procedure could not be used as the school was not a care home or hospital.

**Issues to be decided**: Whether C's rights under Articles 3, 5 and 8 ECHR had been violated; whether the Code of Practice to the MHA 1983 should apply to C when the provisions of the MHA 1983 were not being used and he was not in hospital.

**Decision**: Ryder J made the following findings: (1) since at least C's 16th birthday the approach of the MCA 2005 was more relevant to his situation than the Children Act 1989, but this approach was not applied to C; (2) as the DOLS Code of Practice and Schedule A1 of the MCA did not apply to C, an application should have been made to the COP before any deprivation of liberty occurred. In this case the application should have been made on C's 16th birthday; (3) since at least C's 16th birthday there had been no lawful authority to deprive C of his liberty; (4) the court could not make even interim declarations as to whether the conditions in which C was being deprived of his liberty were in his best interests until it had heard oral evidence from a number of those caring for C and from instructed experts; (5) the application of good practice in the COP in any determination of best interests must have regard to the same material as that contained in the DOLS Code of Practice; (6) the MHA 1983 Code of Practice reflects best practice in relation to seclusion. It applies to the care, treatment, and in particular seclusion and restraint of those with mental disorder, whether they are being treated in hospital or in the community, and whether the MHA is being used. As such, the provisions applied to C whose condition fell within the definition of mental disorder in the MHA. Moreover the Code should be applied as a matter of good practice to the seclusion of children and young people in children's homes whose disability does not fall within the definition of a mental disorder.

The court considered the limited number of situations in which secluding C could be lawful and in his best interests. Ryder J considered that seclusion could be used to control aggressive behaviour, but only so long as it was necessary and proportionate and it had to be the least restrictive option. It had to be exercised in accordance with an intervention and prevention plan designed to safeguard C's psychological and physical health. However, Ryder J held that it would be not lawful to seclude C used solely for nakedness, such seclusion being little more than 'an amateur attempt at behaviour modification which is not proportionate to any risk or the least restrictive option.' Nor would it be lawful to seclude C as a punishment as part of a behaviour management plan, or solely for reasons of him self-harming.

## 6  *London Borough of Hillingdon* v. *Neary* [2011] EWHC 1377 (COP) (Peter Jackson J)

**Facts**: Steven Neary had autism and a severe learning disability and could become very anxious at unexpected changes. Sometimes this would be manifested through lashing out at others. Steven had grown up with his parents Mark and Julie Neary and had lived with his father Mark after his parents separated, remaining in regular contact with Julie. Between January and May 2008 Steven had lived in a support Unit but then returned home. In December 2009 Mr Neary was unwell and agreed to Steven being placed in respite in a Unit. Staff found his behaviour difficult to manage and it was accepted that Steven wanted to go home. Mr Neary sought Steven's return home. Hillingdon had decided that Steven should not return home but did not tell Mr Neary its position until April 2010. Following an incident in April 2010 when Steven wandered off, an urgent authorisation was granted under DOLS, followed by a series of standard authorisations. Mr Neary was appointed as Steven's representative ('relevant person's representative' or RPR. He made it clear that he wanted to challenge the authorisation insofar as it was being used to enforce Steven's stay at the Unit. He had great difficulty in obtaining legal advice. In October 2010 the local authority applied to the Court of Protection seeking declarations which would allow it to make decisions as to Steven's residence and care. In November 2010 an IMCA's report raised serious questions about Hillingdon's refusal to allow Steven to return home and suggested a trial return home. In December 2010 Mr Neary appealed against the current authorisation to the Court of Protection. The Official Solicitor was appointed to represent Steven. On 23 December 2010 Mr Justice Mostyn terminated the standard authorisation and Steven returned home. An independent psychiatrist and social worker were instructed and both concluded it was in Steven's best interests to remain at home with a package of care. This was agreed between the parties. In the meantime the Official Solicitor sought findings that Steven's human rights had been violated in a number of ways.

**Relevant issues to be decided**: the nature of, and the extent of, the breaches of Steven's rights under Articles 5(1) and (4) and 8 ECHR.

**Decision**: Peter Jackson held that Article 8 was the 'nub' of the matter in the case before the court, and fell to be considered first. He held that Steven's Article 8 ECHR rights had been breached throughout the relevant period. He emphasised that the fact that a court disagrees with a local authority's beliefs as to an individual's best interests does not necessarily imply a breach of Article 8. However, in this case the following factors led the judge to conclude the local authority had not respected Steven's Article 8 rights: the lack of any attempt to weigh up the advantages and disadvantages of care at home or in the Unit; the local authority's unwillingness to listen to Mr Neary or accept the validity of his concerns which persisted to the final hearing; its pursuit of a double agenda and its delay in applying to the Court of Protection.

As regards Article 5, Peter Jackson J held that there had been no lawful authority to deprive Steven of his liberty between January and April 2010 (as no DOLS authorisation had been place). Although a DOLS authorisation was in place between April and December 2010, the deprivation of his liberty was unlawful because the best interests assessments were flawed. Peter Jackson J emphasised that, where best interests assessments are inadequate and the supervisory body knows or ought to know this, the supervisory body is not bound to follow the recommendations. Peter Jackson J also found that Steven's rights under Article 5(4)

ECHR were also breached by the failure to appoint an IMCA under s.39D MCA 2005; the failure to hold an effective review; and the delay in applying to the court. It was not enough, he found, to suggest that Mr Neary should have taken the case to court. The fact that he did not do so did not excuse the local authority of the obligation to act – it redoubled it.

In a subsequent settlement approved by the High Court, Steven Neary was awarded £35,000 in damages (together with costs).

## 7    *A Local Authority* v. *PB and P* [2011] EWHC 2675 (COP) (Charles J)

**Facts**: P was a 49-year-old man, who had a lifelong learning disability. He had been cared for by his mother for the majority of his life, but had been removed from his mother's care in 2008 to be cared for by the local authority. P suffered from glaucoma and at the time of the hearing was effectively blind, with little chance of regaining his eyesight. P had also had significant difficulties with his teeth and all his upper teeth had been removed, as had a number of his lower teeth. On the first occasion that the matter had been before the court, Charles J had found that P lacked capacity to make decisions about where he should live and arrangements with regards to contact. P's mother wished P to return to her care. The evidence showed that P's current placement was 'exceptional' and that he required one-to-one support throughout the day and support that was quickly available during the night because of his multiple needs.

**Issues to be decided**: (1) where it was in P's best interests to live. The local authority was not prepared to offer a supported placement at home that would provide one-to-one support during the day. The choice was therefore between the present placement and regime and a return home on the basis that his mother would shoulder the day-to-day care of P with some respite care provided by the local authority; (2) whether the proposed care regime amounted to a deprivation of P's liberty.

**Decision**: It was in P's short, medium and long-term best interests to continue at his present placement, and not to return to live at his mother's home. In the circumstances, Charles J chose not to come to a concluded view as to whether P was deprived of his liberty. He was satisfied that the proposed care plan and regime for P promoted his best interests and that such aspects of it, if any, that meant that he was being deprived of his liberty by its implementation should be authorised by the court. He made orders under s.16(2)(a) MCA 2005 accordingly.

In the course of his judgment Charles J commented that:

1.  In the exercise by the court of the welfare jurisdiction and the approach under the MCA 2005 more generally the most important issue is whether consent or authorisation should be given to a care regime on behalf of a person who does not have the capacity to give consent himself. That question is not determined by whether or not the person is being deprived of his liberty but by an

assessment of whether the care regime is in his best interests. This will include a determination of whether a less restrictive regime would promote P's best interests and when reviews should take place.

2.   In borderline cases where there is a question whether a person is being deprived of his liberty, and cases in which there will be a deprivation of liberty if identified contingency planning is implemented (involving say restraint), care providers should ensure that there is no breach of Article 5 ECHR and review the regime to ensure it remains in P's best interests. This may involve applying the DOLS regime, or, at the very least considering the qualifying requirements identified in Schedule A1 to the MCA 2005.

3.   If the DOLS regime under Schedule A1 applies, it should be used in preference to authorisation and review by the court.

Note: this judgment pre-dates that of the Supreme Court in *Cheshire West* but we suggest that the approach outlined above remains equally applicable.

## 8   *RK v. (1) BCC(2) YB (3) AK* [2011] EWCA Civ 1305 (Court of Appeal (Thorpe LJJ and Gross LJJ and Baron J))

**Facts**: This was an appeal by RK against a decision by Mostyn J, who had decided that: (1) the provision of accommodation to a child (of any age) under s.20 Children Act 1989 was not capable – in principle – of ever giving rise to a deprivation of liberty within the terms of Article 5 ECHR; and (2) the factual circumstances of the case did not amount to a deprivation of RK's liberty. The parents had consented to the arrangements by which their child was placed in accommodation under s.20 Children Act 1989.

**Issues to be decided**: (1) Whether the provision of accommodation to a child (of any age) under s.20 Children Act 1989 is ever capable – in principle – of giving rise to a deprivation of liberty within the terms of Article 5 ECHR; (2) whether the restrictions authorised by the parent(s) individually or cumulatively amount to detention.

**Decision**: An adult in the exercise of parental responsibility may impose, or authorise others to impose, restrictions upon the liberty of a child but such restrictions may not in their totality amount to a deprivation of liberty. Detention engages the Article 5 rights of the child and a parent may not lawfully detain or authorise the detention of a child. The provision of accommodation to a child under arrangements made between a local authority and the child's parent(s) may therefore give rise to a deprivation of liberty within the terms of Article 5(1) ECHR.

RK's appeal was therefore dismissed.

**Note**: the Court of Appeal agreed with Mostyn J's conclusion that RK was, on the facts, not deprived of her liberty. Key to the Court of Appeal's decision appears to have been the purpose of the restrictions imposed. We therefore suggest that this aspect of their decision needs to be approached with caution in light of the decision of the Supreme Court in *Cheshire West*.

## 9    *J Council* v. *GU (1), J Partnership NHS Foundation Trust (2), CQC (3) and X Limited (4)* [2012] EWHC 3531 COP (Mostyn J)

**Facts**: This case concerned a man known as 'George.' Mostyn J described him as 'very seriously challenged,' with a history which told a very sad story. George had childhood autism, OCD, personality disorder and paedophilia. He lived at Y Care Home, under the terms of a standard authorisation. As a result of George's paedophilia he would write letters about his fantasies and leave them in public places, and would try to leave messages for children. Therefore, George's placement regime involved rigorous restrictions on his contact with others including strip searching, monitoring correspondence and telephone calls to protect the public. It was common ground that George's placement constituted a deprivation of his liberty but also curtailed his rights to respect for private and family life under Article 8 ECHR.

**Issues to be decided**: The question was whether the restrictions impacting on George's private life – and therefore his rights under Article 8 ECHR – were lawful. This was a separate question to consideration of his rights under Article 5 ECHR and therefore had to be considered, even though a standard authorisation was in force.

**Decision**: Although the parties reached agreement in this case, and the judge approved of the order they all sought, Mostyn J gave a written judgment. He noted that the simple fact that George was lawfully deprived of his liberty did not itself authorise restrictions on his right to a private life. But his right to a private life could not be allowed to destroy the purpose of his detention. The example that the judge gave was that of prisoners whose Article 8 rights extend to allowing them to use payphones or write letters but not enjoy conjugal visits. For the restrictions to be 'in accordance with the law' the measures had to (1) have a basis in national law (which could include statutory guidance such as the Code of Practice to the MHA 1983); (2) be accessible to the person concerned (i.e. to George); and (3) compatible with the rule of law. Mostyn J noted that, for a person in George's situation, and by contrast with those detained in high security under the MHA 1983, there were no nationally required procedures or safeguards. He endorsed as necessary to secure George's rights under Article 8 ECHR detailed written policies setting out when George's correspondence could be monitored, when his telephone calls could be monitored and when he could be searched. These included oversight by the CQC. Mostyn J stated that in many cases involving deprivation of liberty where there was also an interference with P's Article 8 rights, a one-off order of the court would be sufficient. But where there is going to be a long-term restrictive regime accompanied by invasive monitoring of the kind to which George was subject, then Mostyn J indicated that policies overseen by the applicable NHS Trust and the CQC are likely to be necessary if serious doubts as to Article 8 compliance are to be avoided.

## 10    DM v. *Doncaster MBC and Secretary of State for Health* [2011] EWHC 3652 (Admin) (Langstaff J)

**Facts**: Both husband (FM) and wife (DM) were in their 80s and had been married for 63 years. He had dementia and was being detained in a care home pursuant to a DOLS authorisation; she wanted him back home. The care home fees were being paid out of his limited income and their joint savings. His wife brought a claim to recover the fees.

**Issues to be decided**: Whether by virtue of the DOLS authorisation, the local authority was under a duty to accommodate FM under the MCA 2005 (no power to charge) rather than under s.21 of the National Assistance Act 1948 (duty to charge in s.22, subject to means testing).

**Decision**: The MCA 2005 did not impose a duty or power on local authorities to accommodate detained care home residents. As the DOLS supervisory body, they were obliged to ensure that the DOLS assessments were carried out, to check whether the six qualifying requirements were made out and, if they were, to grant the requested standard authorisation. They were not obliged to accommodate the person, to arrange for their accommodation, or to pay for it.

**Note**: this decision is also important for making clear that an authorisation under Schedule A1 does not **require** detention; rather its effect is to authorise a public body to deprive a person of their liberty if the relevant conditions are met.

## 11    *Secretary of State for Justice v. (1) RB (2) Lancashire Care NHS Foundation Trust* [2011] EWCA Civ 1608 (Court of Appeal (Kay, Arden and Moses LJJ))

**Facts**: RB was 75. He had a persistent delusional disorder. He was detained under ss. 37/41 MHA 1983. RB wanted to be discharged from hospital. There was general agreement that he could be managed in the community, but that he would need to be subject to conditions for the protection of the public. These conditions included residence in a care home, and a condition that he was escorted at all times in the community. There was no dispute that this proposed care regime amounted to a deprivation of his liberty. Despite the diagnosis of mental illness RB had capacity to decide about residence and treatment, and the question of capacity did not arise in this case. The Upper Tribunal granted RB a conditional discharge, setting conditions which had the effect of depriving RB of his liberty in the care home. RB was content with this arrangement but the Secretary of State appealed to the Court of Appeal.

**Issues to be decided**: The question for the Court of Appeal was whether s.73 MHA 1983 allowed a Mental Health Tribunal to discharge a patient and set conditions which amounted to a deprivation of his or her liberty. The Upper Tribunal had concluded that such a power existed and that the word 'discharge' in s.73 does not automatically imply 'release from detention to a state of liberty'. The Secretary of State disagreed. His argument was that the effect of the Upper Tribunal's decision was to create a new category of patients detained under the MHA 1983, but where there was no obligation to provide treatment and where the patient had reduced rights to apply to the Tribunal.

**Decision**: The Court of Appeal noted that any deprivation of liberty must be 'in accordance with a procedure prescribed by law' to comply with Article 5(1) ECHR. The original order made under ss.37/41 MHA 1983 authorised detention in hospital only, not detention in another setting. Furthermore a patient who was deprived of his liberty following a conditional discharge could apply to a Tribunal but would not know what test he had to satisfy. The detention would not be in accordance with a procedure prescribed by law. The Court of Appeal held that detention in a care home other than for the purpose of treatment and without appropriate medical treatment being available would be counter to the whole scheme of the MHA 1983. It held that a Tribunal could not rely on the best interests of the patient to order conditional discharge on terms that inevitably amount to deprivation of liberty.

(Note that DOLS could not be used in this case as RB had capacity to consent to being accommodated in the care home, and the restrictions proposed were to protect the public, not RB).

## 12   Y *County Council* v. *ZZ (by his litigation friend the Official Solicitor)* [2012] EWCOP B34 (Moor J)

**Facts**: Mr ZZ was a man of young middle age who had a mild learning disability with some autistic traits. From his 20s onwards he had a history of sexualised behaviour towards children and appeared to be sexually aroused by creating emergency situations (for example fire-setting and criminal damage). In 1999 he was placed under a hospital order (s.37 MHA 1983) following charges of arson. After 18 months he moved into residential care and was placed under guardianship. During his period Mr ZZ met and married another service user at the home where he lived. Between 2006 and 2010 concerns about Mr ZZ's behaviour escalated. He carried out a serious assault against a member of staff and was moved to another placement in 2006. His wife remained at the original home and subsequently the relationship between her and Mr ZZ broke down and she moved into independent living. At the new placement Mr ZZ continued to be involved in low level assaults. However, his sexualized behaviour towards children caused even greater concern. He began dropping notes for children with his phone number asking them to contact him, offering money for sexual activity. He would ask to be allowed to go to places where there were likely to be children, such as corner shops. He was noted to be masturbating over children's television programmes. He applied to adopt a child with his wife. At one point ZZ was confronted by the relative of a child who had received a note from ZZ. In September 2010 the situation deteriorated and Mr ZZ was given notice. He was moved to the J. Although it is clear that Mr ZZ was subject to a high level of supervision in his previous placements the J is a locked environment and Mr ZZ was not free to leave and was closely supervised and monitored inside and outside. In summer 2010 Mr ZZ underwent the first sexual offenders treatment plan. He engaged with this but there were concerns he was 'going through the motions.' The forensic psychologist considered ZZ still had a strong desire for deviant activity with children. After his move to the J home, Mr ZZ was placed under guardianship and a standard authorisation and the local authority made an application to the Court of Protection asking the court to determine whether the deprivation of Mr ZZ's liberty was lawful.

**Issues to be decided**: whether ZZ was deprived of his liberty and, if he was, whether this was in ZZ's best interests.

**Decision**: Moor J reminded himself that a standard authorisation under DOLS can run alongside a guardianship order. Whilst the guardianship order was in force, which specified that ZZ should reside at the J home, he did not, as a Court of Protection judge, have jurisdiction to make decisions about ZZ's place of residence. Moor J found that ZZ was deprived of his liberty at the J home. He found that complete and effective control was being exercised over ZZ. The restrictions included being checked hourly, not leaving the J unescorted, using his mobile phone for only one hour a day; and that ZZ was not allowed unsupervised access to the garden as there were children living next door.

Moor J held that he had no doubt that the restrictions upon ZZ were in his best interests. He said:

> They are designed to keep him out of mischief, to keep him safe and healthy, to keep others safe, to prevent the sort of situation where the relative of a child wanted to do him serious harm, which I have no doubt was very frightening for him and they are there to prevent him getting into trouble with the police.

## 13   *Commissioner of Police for the Metropolis* v. *ZH* [2013] EWCA Civ 69 (Court of Appeal (Dyson MR, Richards LJ, Black LJ))

This was an appeal by the Metropolitan Police against the decision of Sir Robert Nelson awarding substantial damages to reflect their breaches of common law and the Disability Discrimination Act 1995. Sir Robert Nelson had found ([2012] EWHC 604 (Admin)) that the police had not only committed the torts of trespass and false imprisonment, but had also breached ZH's rights under Articles 3, 5 and 8 ECHR and also the DDA 1995

**Facts**: ZH was a severely autistic, epileptic 16-year-old young man who suffered from learning disabilities and could not communicate by speech. In September 2008 he was taken by the specialist school he attended to a swimming pool for a familiarisation visit. During the visit he became fixated by the water and could not be persuaded to move from the side of the pool. After 30 minutes a decision was taken by the manager of the pool to ring the police. The arrival of the police gave rise to an escalating series of events which culminated in ZH jumping into the pool, being forcibly removed from it, being handcuffed, put in leg restraints and placed in a cage in the back of a police van, while still wet, for a period of around 40 minutes.

His carers were not permitted to get into the cage to comfort him. ZH suffered consequential psychological trauma and an exacerbation of his epileptic seizures.

**Issues to be determined**: Whether the circumstances amounted to a deprivation of liberty, as found by Sir Robert Nelson, or merely a restriction on movement.

**Decision**: The Court of Appeal upheld Sir Robert's decision that ZH had been deprived of his liberty. Lord Dyson noted that the restraint of ZH was

> closely analogous to the classic or paradigm case of detention in a prison or police cell. In particular, it is difficult to see any difference in kind between being detained in the caged area at the back of a police van and being detained in a police cell. In fact, ZH was deprived of movement throughout the entire period of the restraint. The restraint was intense in nature and lasted for approximately 40 minutes and its effects on ZH were serious.

**Note**: In light of the decision in ZH it is clear that a person can be subjected to a deprivation of liberty which may only last a relatively short period of time (the restraint whilst he was at the poolside lasted about 15 minutes and the restraint in the police van lasted about 25 minutes). The decision also makes clear the extent to which the intensity of the restrictions is of significance in determining how long a period of time is 'non-negligible'. See further the discussion at paragraphs 3.29-3.32.


## 14    *A PCT v. LDV, CC and B Healthcare Group* [2013] EWHC 272 (Fam) (Baker J)

**Facts**: LDV was a former Winterbourne View patient. She was 33 years old and suffered from a mild learning disability and emotionally unstable personality disorder. On 25 May 2012, a tribunal had ordered her discharge from detention under s.3 of the MHA 1983 ('MHA') to take effect on 28 September 2012. It decided that she needed a residential establishment in the community rather than the medium-secure unit. Identifying a suitable community placement was underway and, as a preliminary step, LDV was moved to a hospital closer to home ('WH') in early September 2012.

At around the same time, doctors from the medium-secure unit provided two medical recommendations that she be re-detained under s.3 MHA 1983. However, with no material change in circumstances since the tribunal's decision in May, the Approved Mental Health Professional ('AMHP') concluded that such re-detention would be unlawful and declined to make the s.3 application. As a result, the deferred discharge took effect on 28 September 2012. But LDV remained in WH; now on an informal basis.

During her assessment, the AMHP identified that the restrictions in LDV's care plan seemed to constitute a deprivation of liberty and advised the Primary Care Trust ('PCT') and the hospital trust that an authorisation should be sought through a court order.

LDV was subject to a significant number of restrictions, including as to her ability to leave unaccompanied and to move within the unit. She was also subject to continuous observation (the precise time-frame varying depending upon the level of risk), restraint, searches of her property and person, administration of sedative medication and control over contact with her mother.

On 12 October 2012 an urgent authorisation under Schedule A1 MCA 2005 was granted, and a request for a standard authorisation was made. The best interests assessor concluded that there was indeed a deprivation of liberty but LDV was ineligible to be deprived of her liberty because she was within the scope of the MHA. On 23 October 2012, the PCT therefore made an urgent application to the Court of Protection.

**Issue to be determined**: (1) Whether LDV's circumstances amounted to a deprivation of liberty; (2) what salient details are relevant to the decision whether to be accommodated in hospital for the purpose of being given relevant care or treatment (i.e. the details that the individual must be able to understand, retain and use/ weigh).

**Decision**: (1) The restrictions included in the care plan objectively amounted to a deprivation of LDV's liberty; (2) On the facts of LDV's case, the salient details were that she was in hospital to receive care and treatment for a mental disorder, and the material liberty-restricting features of that care and treatment plan.

**Note**: this decision is important not only in the psychiatric context, because in determining the question of whether LDV had the material capacity, Baker J proceeded as if he were considering the capacity requirement in paragraph 15 of Schedule A1 (although he was not, strictly, bound to do so). See further in this regard the discussion at paragraphs 2.17-2.20.

## 15   *Re M (Best Interests: Deprivation of Liberty)* [2013] EWHC 3456 (COP) (Peter Jackson J)

**Facts**: This s.21A MCA 2005 application was brought by M, a 67-year-old woman, through her IMCA as her litigation friend, who had been resident in a care home since June 2012. M suffered from diabetes which was poorly controlled and lacked capacity to make decisions about her diabetes management due to her 'inflexible but mistaken belief that she [could] manage her own diabetes' which resulted in her being unable to weigh up the serious risks to her health that would be posed by returning home, with an inevitable reduction in the level of supervision.

The two options for M's care were continued residence in the care home, or a return home with a 'standard care package' which involved twice daily visits from district nurses to supervise M's insulin regime, and regular visits each day from carers. Since being at the care home, M's physical condition had improved, but her mental health had worsened. She was being treated for mild depression with antidepressants. She repeatedly and consistently said that she wanted to return home and had said that she would take her own life if that were not allowed to happen. She was still only partially compliant with her insulin regime and refused to eat any food provided by the home.

A psychiatrist commissioned to provide a report to the court under s.49 MCA 2005 took the view that it was in M's best interests to return home despite the risks to her health, and that all options to achieve this had not been fully explored.

**The issue to be decided**: M's best interests. A return home carried with it a real risk of death as a result of M's diabetes and her non-compliance. Remaining at the care home carried a real risk that M would self-harm because of her strongly held wish to return home.

**Decision**: it was in M's best interests for the standard authorisation to be terminated. The judge stated that considerable weight had to be attached to M's wishes, bearing in mind that her incapacity extended only to one area of her life – her diabetes management – and that she was otherwise very aware of her circumstances. He summed up the position as follows:

> 38.    In the end, if M remains confined in a home she is entitled to ask 'What for?' The only answer that could be provided at the moment is 'To keep you alive as long as possible'. In my view that is not a sufficient answer. The right to life and the State's obligation to protect it is not absolute and the court must surely have regard to the person's own assessment of her quality of life. In M's case there is little to be said for a solution that attempts, without any guarantee of success, to preserve for her a daily life without meaning or happiness and which she, with some justification, regards as insupportable.

The judge emphasised that the Court of Protection is the place to make the difficult decisions about whether risks are justified.

> 41.    [ . . .] my decision implies no criticism whatever of any of the witnesses from the local authority or by the CCG. I understand the position taken and the reasons for it; indeed it would be difficult for them to have taken a different view on the facts of the case. There are risks either way and it is perfectly appropriate that responsibility for the outcome should fall on the shoulders of the court and not on the shoulders of the parties.

## 16    AM v. (1) *South London and Maudsley NHS Foundation Trust* (2) *Secretary of State for Health* [2013] UKUT 0365 AAC (Charles J)

**Facts**: AM was detained under s.2 MHA 1983. She was 78 years old. She applied to the First Tier Tribunal to be discharged. She argued at the hearing that she would remain in hospital informally. The Tribunal did not discharge her from detention, considering that if it did AM's daughter would take her home and would not prevent AM's ongoing treatment, even though AM was content on the ward. AM appealed to the Upper Tribunal and argued that she should be discharged from detention under s.2 by a Tribunal and her treatment in hospital could be continued using the Deprivation of Liberty Safeguards.

**Issues to be decided**: What approach should be taken by decision-makers (either AMHPs or the First Tier Tribunal) when considering the admission for assessment and/or treatment of a mentally-disordered patient who lacked capacity to consent to admission to hospital.

**Decision**: Charles J said that, in introducing DOLS, Parliament must have intended to provide an alternative to the MHA 1983 to authorise the detention of an incapacitated person, and that this must have been intended to include occasions where such a person would be detained using DOLS in hospital for mental disorder. Decision-makers under the MHA 1983 (which would include AMHPs and also Tribunals) therefore needed to consider the availability of treatment when a patient's deprivation of liberty was authorised under the DOLS regime.

In such cases, Charles J held, decision-makers should go through the following questions and take into account the following considerations:

- Is admission to hospital required?
- Will P be a mental health patient and if so does he object to all or part of the relevant treatment? If so, he is ineligible for DOLS and the MHA 1983 must be used.
- Does the relevant person have capacity to consent to admission to hospital?
- Can the hospital rely on the provisions of the MCA 2005 to assess and treat the person lawfully? This requires consideration of the likelihood of the person remaining compliant with their treatment (and therefore remain eligible to be deprived of their liberty using DOLS); and also whether there is a risk that cannot sensibly be ignored that the treatment regime will amount to a deprivation of liberty.
- How should the existence of a choice between reliance on the MHA 1983 and the MCA 2005 be taken into account? This involves the FTT (or earlier decision-maker, for example, an AMHP) taking a fact-sensitive approach to try to identify the least restrictive way of best achieving the proposed assessment or treatment. DOLS will not always be less restrictive than detention under the MHA, but may carry less stigma in the eyes of some.
- An AMHP or a Tribunal cannot compel a managing authority to apply for an authorisation or a supervisory body to grant one, so the AMHP or Tribunal needs to know whether those who could implement the MCA/DOLS will do so.

**Note**: in his judgment, Charles J expressly made clear that his reference in *GJ* v. *The Foundation Trust* [2009] EWHC 2972 (Fam) to the MHA 1983 having 'primacy' was not intended to be a general statement.

## 17   *An NHS Trust* v. *Dr A* [2013] EWHC 2442 (COP) (Baker J)

**Facts**: Dr A was a 50-year-old Iranian whose application for asylum in the UK had been refused. He was detained under s.3 MHA 1983, and was receiving treatment for delusional disorder. But he was also on hunger strike, as part of an attempt to compel the UK Border Agency to return his passport. He was being fed through a nasogastric tube. Dr A's mental state improved and the section was rescinded and he remained in hospital informally. A few weeks after this, he removed the nasogastric tube. His physical health deteriorated and reached a life-threatening state. The Trust considered that Dr A lacked capacity to refuse nutrition and hydration and issued an application to the court. Interim declarations were made allowing him to be fed via the tube. Dr A continued to resist this and was detained under s.3 MHA.

**Issues to be decided**: (1) Whether Dr A lacked capacity to make decisions about nutrition and hydration; (2) If he lacked capacity to make such decisions, where did his best interests lie; (3) What powers did the court have to direct provision of nutrition and hydration as this would mean depriving Dr A of his liberty?

**Decision**: Baker J found that Dr A lacked capacity to make decisions about hydration and nutrition and associated treatment, and that it was in his best interests for the court to make an order permitting forcible feeding. Baker J concluded this treatment could not be carried out under s.63 MHA 1983, which permits treatment under the supervision of the patient's approved clinician for the mental disorder from which the patient is suffering, without the patient's consent This was because the judge was not satisfied that the force-feeding was treatment for the mental disorder from which Dr A was suffering. Instead it was for a physical disorder which resulted from his decision to refuse food.

Because he was detained under s.3 MHA 1983, Dr A was ineligible to be deprived of his liberty either through DOLS or through an order of the court by operation of Schedule 1A to the MCA 2005. So, if in order to receive the force-feeding it was necessary to deprive Dr A of his liberty, this could not be lawfully authorised and a new 'Bournewood Gap' appeared to be opening. Referring to the 'ambiguity, obscurity and possible absurdity' of the legislation surrounding DOLS, the judge found himself able to use the inherent jurisdiction to make orders authorising Dr A to be deprived of his liberty in order to receive force-feeding, whilst remaining on s.3 MHA 1983.

**Note**: the effect of this judgment is to make clear that where a patient is detained under the MHA 1983, requires treatment for a physical disorder which cannot be administered under the provisions of s.63 MHA 1983, and that treatment itself will involve a deprivation of their liberty, an application to the High Court will be required because the fact of the detention under the MHA 1983 means the patient will be ineligible for an authorisation under Schedule A1 or an order of the Court of Protection under s.16(2)(a) MCA 2005.

## 18    *Re P* [2014] EWHC 1650 (Fam) (Baker J)

**Facts**: An NHS Trust made an extremely urgent application in the middle of the night for a declaration that it was lawful for its doctors to treat a 17-year-old girl following a drug overdose notwithstanding her refusal to consent to that treatment.

**Issue to be decided**: Whether P had the capacity to make decisions concerning her medical treatment, whether treatment should be administered against her consent, and whether the circumstances of that treatment would amount to a deprivation of her liberty.

**Decision**: The Court was not satisfied that P lacked capacity to make decisions concerning her medical treatment, but was satisfied that – P being a minor – it could authorise treatment to be administered against her consent. Baker J accepted that it might be necessary in the course of administering life-sustaining treatment – which would have to be administered continuously over a 21-hour period – to sedate or restrain P. He declared that such steps would be lawful notwithstanding the fact that they amounted to a deprivation of liberty.

## 19    *Liverpool City Council* v. *SG & Ors* [2014] EWCOP 10 (Holman J)

**Facts**: SG was aged 19, and, whilst arrangements were made to move her into supported living, she continued to be resident in the same children's home as she was in prior to the age of 18, subject to a regime that indisputably amounted to a deprivation of her liberty. She was the subject of very considerable staffing on a 3:1 basis. The staffing includes monitoring her while she was in the bathroom (ensuring her dignity was maintained at all times), locking the front door as a preventative measure, following, observing and monitoring her on visits into the community, and if she 'attempted to leave the staff supporting her, they would follow several paces behind her and attempt to maintain conversation'. Items which could be used for self-harm were removed, and she remained supported 3:1 during the day and 2:1 during the night. She lacked capacity to decide as to her residence and care arrangements.

**Issue to be decided**: Whether the Court of Protection in light of Guidance issued jointly by the President of the Court of Protection and OFSTED on 12 February 2014 entitled *'Deprivation of Liberty – Guidance for Providers of Children's Homes and Residential Special Schools'*, had power to make an order which authorised a deprivation of her liberty at the children's home.

**Decision**: The Court of Protection has the power to make an order which authorises that a person who is not a child (i.e. who has attained the age of 18) may be deprived of his liberty in premises which are a children's home as defined in section 1(2) of the Care Standards Act 2000 and are subject to the Children's Homes Regulations 2001 (as amended). Further, it is the duty of the person or body, in this case the local authority, who is or are depriving the patient of his liberty, to apply to the court for an authorisation; and, indeed, the duty of the court to make such authorisation as in its discretion and on the facts and in the circumstances of the case it considers appropriate.

**Note**: See also *Barnsley MBC* v. *GS & Ors* [2014] EWCOP 46, in which Holman J held that the Guidance was wrong in suggesting that a non-secure children's home or a residential school was unable to deprive a child of their liberty; he further held that, in principle, the Court of Protection could authorise the deprivation of liberty of a 16- or 17-year-old lacking the material capacity in such a place.

## 20    *The Mental Health Trust/The Acute Trust & the Council* v. *DD (by her litigation friend the Official Solicitor), BC* (Number 1 and Number 2) [2014] EWCOP 11 and [2014] EWCOP 13 (Cobb J)

**Facts**: Both these cases concern DD, a 36-year-old woman with a mild to borderline learning disability and autism spectrum disorder. At the time of the hearings she was at an advanced stage of pregnancy. She had what the judge described as 'an extraordinary and complex obstetric history' and was expecting her sixth baby. DD and BC's wishes were for a home birth without social or health care assistance; DD's five children were all cared for by permanent substitute carers and four of the children had been adopted. DD and BC had completely failed to engage with the authorities.

**Issues to be decided**: The applicants sought declarations and orders in relation to DD's capacity; the care and health of DD during the final stage of her pregnancy, and in the safe delivery of the unborn baby; *authorisation for the deprivation of DD's liberty; the use of restraint (even for a short time) and permission to intrude, by force if necessary, into the privacy and sanctity of her home.*

**Decision**: (I) she lacked capacity to litigate the application in so far as it relates to the delivery of her baby; and that (ii) she lacked the capacity to make a decision about the mode of delivery of her unborn baby. (2) It was in DD's best interests to authorise the caesarean and associated actions (which included forced entry into her home, restraint and sedation).

The judge authorised the necessary steps to deprive DD of her liberty but set out in his judgment a number of restrictions:

> Any physical restraint or deprivation of liberty is a significant interference with DD's rights under Articles 5 and Article 8 of the ECHR and, in my judgment, as such should only be carried out:
>
> (i)   by professionals who have received training in the relevant techniques and who have reviewed the individual plan for DD;
> (ii)  as a last resort and where less restrictive alternatives, such as verbal de-escalation and distraction techniques, have failed and only when it is necessary to do so;
> (iii) in the least restrictive manner, proportionate to achieving the aim, for the shortest period possible;
> (iv)  in accordance with any agreed Care Plans, Risk Assessments and Court Orders.

## 21    *NHS Trust & Ors* v. *FG* [2014] EWCOP 30 (Keehan J)

**Facts**: At the time of the application FG was 24 years old and she was in the late stages of her first pregnancy. She had been diagnosed with a schizoaffective disorder and was detained at Hospital under s 3 MHA 1983. FG suffered from persecutory delusions that included a belief that the mental health services were 'murderers' and would murder her and her unborn child. The plans for the delivery of the child included plans for FG's transfer from Trust 1 to the maternity unit in Trust 2, plans for her to receive obstetric, midwifery and anaesthetic care and for her to be returned to Trust 1.

**Issues to be decided**: Whether the proposed plan for FG's transfer and obstetric care was in her best interests. In the event that the court decided that the proposed plan for her transfer and care was in her best interests, the Trusts sought authorisation for the proposed transfer and orders that it was lawful for their staff to use reasonable and proportionate measures to carry out the plans including those which involved physical or medical restraint and a deprivation of liberty.

**Decision**: (1) Keehan J was satisfied that the orders sought by the Trusts in respect of her medical treatment were in her best interests and (2) he made orders accordingly, including orders in relation to physical or medical restraint and deprivation of FG's liberty. In the course of his judgment Keehan J gave detailed guidance, attached as an annex to the judgment, on the steps to be taken when a local authority and/or medical professionals are concerned about and dealing with a pregnant woman who has mental health problems and, potentially lacks capacity to litigate and to make decisions about her welfare or medical treatment.

**Note**: This judgment is important because Keehan J confirmed that the acid test applies in the acute setting. Keehan J observed at paragraph 96 that:

> It will commonly be the case that when at the acute hospital P:
>
> (i)   will have obstetric and midwifery staff constantly present throughout her labour and delivery;
> (ii)  will be under the continuous control of obstetric and midwifery staff who, because she lacks capacity to make decisions about her medical case, will take decisions on her behalf in her best interests;
> (iii) will often not be permitted to leave the delivery suite.
>
> Those factors may, when applying the acid test, lead to a conclusion that P is or will suffer a deprivation of her liberty when at the acute hospital. If the Trusts are to deprive P of her liberty, they have a duty not to do so unlawfully.

## 22    Re AJ (Deprivation of Liberty Safeguards) [2015] EWCOP 5 (Baker J)

**Facts**: An elderly lady, AJ, had lived for a considerable period of time in an annexe of the home of her niece and her husband ('Mr and Mrs C'). She developed vascular dementia and became increasingly dependent on others, in particular Mrs C. In agreement with the relevant local authority, she was taken to a care home by Mr and Mrs C purportedly for respite but, in fact, on the basis that she was to be permanently cared for there if she settled. Mr C was appointed as her unpaid RPR, and a s.39D IMCA was appointed. AJ was objecting to her presence at the care home she was initially placed at, and then the care home she was moved to shortly thereafter, for several months before her RPR ultimately brought proceedings on her behalf in the Court of Protection under s.21A MCA 2005.

**Issues to be decided**: Whether the local authority had breached AJ's rights under Articles 5(1), 5(4) and 8 ECHR in failing to take appropriate steps to ensure that the deprivation of her liberty had been suitably authorised in advance and she had been supported to bring a challenge to that authorisation.

**Decision**: In concluding that AJ's ECHR rights had been breached, Baker J gave wider guidance, which can be summarised thus. (1) In the vast majority of cases, it should be possible to plan in advance so that a standard authorisation can be obtained before the deprivation of liberty begins. It is only in exceptional cases, where the need for the deprivation of liberty is so urgent that it is in the best interests of the person for it to begin while the application is being considered, that a standard authorisation need not be sought before the deprivation begins. (2) Professionals need to be on their guard to look out for cases where vulnerable people are admitted to residential care ostensibly for respite when the underlying plan is for a permanent placement without proper consideration as to their Article 5 rights. (3) It is likely to be difficult for a close relative or friend who believes that it is in P's best interests to move into residential care, and has been actively involved in arranging such a move, into a placement that involves a deprivation of liberty, to fulfil the functions of RPR, which involve making a challenge to any authorisation of that deprivation. (4) The appointment of a RPR and IMCA does not absolve the local authority from responsibility for ensuring that P's Article 5 rights are respected. The local authority must monitor whether the RPR is representing and supporting P in accordance with his statutory duty. (5) The local authority must make sufficient resources available to assist an IMCA and keep in touch with the IMCA to ensure that all reasonable steps are being taken to pursue P's Article 5 rights. (6) In circumstances where a RPR and an IMCA have failed to take sufficient steps to challenge the authorisation, the local authority should consider bringing the matter before the court itself. This is likely, however, to be a last resort since in most cases P's Article 5 rights should be protected by the combined efforts of a properly selected and appointed RPR and an IMCA carrying out their duties with appropriate expedition.

**Note** also that Baker J emphasised the importance of properly recording of the use of physical restraint of incapacitated adults in their care plans and documenting such use in the assessment of whether an authorisation under Schedule A1 should be granted.

## CASES WITH HEALTH WARNINGS

## 1   *DH NHS Foundation Trust* v. *PS* [2010] EWHC 1217 (Fam) (Sir Nicholas Wall P)

**Facts**: PS was 55. Evidence was accepted that she lacked the capacity to make decisions about her healthcare and treatment. She also lacked the capacity to conduct or defend proceedings. PS had cancer of the uterus. The treating doctors were of the opinion that she required a hysterectomy and removal of the fallopian tube and ovaries. PS also suffered from needle phobia. The clinical team treating her came to the conclusion that special arrangements would need to be put in place both to ensure that she had the operation and that she remained in hospital for her post-operative recovery. Such arrangements included sedation if necessary in order to convey her to hospital, the administration of anaesthetic during the operation, and post operatively analgesic with a sedative effect, close supervision and the use of force (as a last resort) to stop her absconding.

**Issues to be decided**: (1) whether it was in her best interests to undergo the proposed operation; and (2) whether it was in her best interests to sedate PS and if necessary for force to be used in order to convey her to hospital, to administer the anaesthetic (because of her needle phobia) and to detain PS in hospital during the period of post-operative recovery.

**Decision**: (1) It was in PS's best interest to undergo a hysterectomy and removal of the fallopian tubes and ovaries. (2) It was necessary and in PS's best interests to use sedation and force, if required, to convey PS to hospital, during the operation and to detain her in hospital post operatively.

**Health Warning**: Sir Nicholas Wall P appeared on the face of the judgment to have come to the view that it was not necessary to invoke the provisions of Schedule A1 to the MCA 2005 because it was necessary for P to have the operation and therefore there was no deprivation of liberty. It is our view following on from the decision in *Cheshire West* that the planned sedation and restraint during the transfer to hospital, and during the administration of the anaesthetic for the operation itself, and the arrangements post operatively, would now be likely to be held to meet the acid test and to be a deprivation of PS's liberty requiring authorisation.

## 2   *Re A and Re C* [2010] EWHC 978 (Fam) (Munby J)

**Facts**: A and C were both female. A was born in 2001 (and therefore a child), and C was born in 1987 (and was an adult). Both suffered from a rare genetic disorder called Smith Magenis Syndrome, characterised by 'self-injurious behaviour, physical and verbal aggression, temper tantrums, destructive behaviour, hyperactivity, restlessness, excitability, distractibility and severe sleep disturbances, which include frequent and prolonged night waking and early morning waking'. Both lived at home 'in the exemplary and devoted care of their parents' in the area of the same local authority. The only way that their parents could keep them safe at night was by locking their bedroom doors.

**Issues to be decided**: Whether the circumstances amounted to a deprivation of liberty, engaging Article 5 of the ECHR and, if so, what (if any) role the local authority had in such cases.

**Decision**: (1) The State was not directly involved in either of the cases. The local authority was providing support services only. It was not directly involved in what happened in the home of either person. It was not the decision-maker. Mere knowledge was not enough, although this might trigger a duty to investigate and seek judicial assistance. Accordingly, the local authority could not be in breach of Article 5 ECHR in these cases even if a deprivation of liberty had occurred. (2)

Neither A nor C were deprived of their liberty. Following the reasoning of Parker J at first instance in *MIG and MEG,* Munby J decided that a loving, caring, proportionate and appropriate regime by devoted parents in a loving family relationship whose objective was solely 'the welfare, happiness and best interests of A and C respectively – fell significantly short of anything that would engage Art 5'. He decided that the restrictions imposed were not to restrict their liberty but to maximise their opportunities and help them to lead their lives to the full. This amounted to an appropriate and proportionate restriction upon liberty, not a deprivation of liberty.

Accordingly as there was no deprivation of liberty, there was no need to decide whether it could be justified as an Article 5 compliant exercise of parental responsibility in respect of A.

**Health Warning**: We consider that it is unlikely that the approach adopted to the question of whether A and C were deprived of their liberty would be the same now, post *Cheshire West*. However, the outcome could well be the same since it seems unlikely on the facts that any such deprivation of liberty would be imputable to the State (or, if it was, that the State could have been required to do anything more than it did by way of bringing the matter to court).

## 3   R (Sessay) v. South London and the Maudsley NHS Foundation Trust [2011] EWHC 2617 (QB) (Divisional Court (Pitchford LJ and Supperstone J))

**Facts**: Ms Sessay was removed from her home by the police following concerns about her welfare and ability to care for her child. She was taken to the s.136 MHA 1983 suite at SLAM's hospital where she was held for 13 hours before a decision was made to admit her under s.2 MHA 1983. At least some of the Trust staff at the s.136 suite were under the impression that she had been brought to the suite under s.136 but this was incorrect. The Trust policy was that the maximum time any patient should be held in the s.136 suite should not exceed eight hours and the aim was for the patient to remain there not more than four hours. Had the Trust been aware that Ms Sessay was not detained under s.135 or s.136 her admission might have been progressed more quickly.

**Issues to be decided**: (1) whether Ms Sessay was deprived of her liberty pending the decision to admit her under s.2 MHA 1983; (2) whether there was any authority for detention during this period; (3) whether the Trust could rely on the common law doctrine of necessity.

**Decision**: Ms Sessay had been detained under the common law, without lawful authority during the 13-hour period. The court held that not all cases of false imprisonment would also involve a deprivation of liberty for the purpose of Article 5 because of the requirement that the detention had been for 'a not negligible length of time': but in the circumstances of this case the cumulative effect of the Trust's actions had been to deprive Ms Sessay of her liberty under Article 5 ECHR as well. The MHA 1983 provided a complete statutory framework for the detention of incapacitated people in hospital for care and treatment and its powers could have been used in this case. The Trust could not rely on the common law doctrine of necessity to detain her.

The court observed that in the normal course of events Article 5 would not have been engaged (nor would she have been imprisoned for purposes of the common law) had Ms Sessay's admission been dealt with within the four to eight hours specified by the Trust's policy.

**Health warning**: Whilst we are of the view (see paragraph 3.27) that regard will be had to the context in which measures are imposed when determining whether the length over which they are imposed will be considered 'non-negligible,' the observation made by the Divisional Court in relation to the Trust's policy was made on the basis of authority from the European Court of Human rights relating to purpose that the ECtHR has now said should not be followed. It may very well be that a court considering the question now would still reach the same conclusion, but may do on the basis of slightly different reasoning.

## 4  C v. Blackburn with Darwen Borough Council and others [2011] EWHC 3321 (COP) (Peter Jackson J)

**Facts**: C was 45 at the time of the judgment. He had a learning disability and lacked capacity to make decisions about where to live. He had a history of aggression, self-harm, and impulsive behaviour such as running into traffic. After a period of time detained under the MHA he went abroad and on return he was admitted to a care home. He was then received into guardianship and, following an incident when he kicked down a door, a standard authorisation under DOLS was granted. C appealed against the authorisation to the Court of Protection. The First Tier Tribunal refused his application to be discharged from guardianship. During the hearing in the Court of Protection, C told the judge that he wanted to go somewhere else and that being in the care home caused him a lot of stress.

**Issues to be decided**: (1) whether C was ineligible for DOLS; (2) whether C was deprived of his liberty; (3) whether the regime at the care home was necessary; (4) the relationship between the guardianship order and DOLS.

**Decision**: C was not ineligible for the use of DOLS; however, the judge found that he was not deprived of his liberty and the standard authorisation was set aside. In coming to this conclusion the judge relied on the decision of the Court of Appeal in *Cheshire West*. A particular feature in this case was that although C was unhappy at the care home and wanted to live somewhere else, there was no alternative available. The restrictions on his liberty were necessary for his safety and that of others.

Peter Jackson J held that the Court of Protection does not have the power to determine C's place of residence while the guardianship order was in effect. However, he held, genuinely disputed issues about the residence of an incapacitated adult should be determined by the Court of Protection. In this case there was a question about whether the use of guardianship was the right vehicle to determine where C should live. The judge invited the local authority, who was the guardian, to consider renouncing its role so the court could make decisions about C's welfare.

**Health warning**: We consider that a court considering these facts now would most probably conclude that C was deprived of his liberty following the decision of the Supreme Court in *Cheshire West*. Importantly, that C had nowhere else to go is not relevant (see paragraph 3.21.3). However the judge's comments about the use of guardianship hold good and should be followed (they are also consistent with the approach taken by the Upper Tribunal in *NL* v. *Hampshire County Council* ([2014] UKUT 475 (AAC)), a decision expressly considering the effect of the Supreme Court decision on guardianship, in which Upper Tribunal Judge Jacobs held that the operation of guardianship does not, itself give rise to ad deprivation of liberty).

## 5    *CC* v. *KK* [2012] EWHC 2136 (COP) (Baker J)

**Facts**: KK was an 82-year-old woman with Parkinson's Disease, vascular dementia, and paralysis down her left side. Following the death of her husband, she moved and settled in a rented bungalow. However, incapacity and best interests determinations had resulted in her being placed in a nursing home between July and October 2010 and from July 2011. Her deprivation of liberty was authorised under Schedule A1 of the MCA from 12 August 2011 which she challenged under s.21 MCA on 2 September 2011. Trial home visits commenced in November 2011 and subsequent requests for DOLS authorisations under Schedule A1 were refused on the basis that there was no deprivation of liberty. The s.21A challenge was dismissed and interim declarations granted as to her incapacity and best interests. By the time of the final hearing in May 2012, she was having daily home visits.

**Issues to be decided**: (1) whether KK had capacity to make decisions about her residence and care, and (2) whether she had been, and or was being, deprived of her liberty.

**Decision**: (1) KK had capacity to make decisions about her residence; and (2) she had not been, and was not being, deprived of her liberty because despite the staff exercising a large measure of control over KK's care and movements and KK objecting strongly to her residence, the arrangements for her care could not be described as one of 'continuous control'.

**Health Warning**: This decision was arrived at while the Supreme Court's decision in *Cheshire West* was awaited. Baker J was therefore bound by the decision of the Court of Appeal, but we consider it clear from the facts that KK was under complete/ continuous supervision control and was not free to leave, such that she would be found (applying the approach in *Cheshire West*) objectively to be deprived of her liberty.

## 6    *Rochdale MBC* v. *KW* [2014] EWCOP 45 (Mostyn J)

**Facts**: A 52-year-old woman, KW, was cared for in her own home. As a result of a subarachnoid haemorrhage sustained during a medical operation many years previously, she had cognitive and mental health problems, epilepsy and physical disability. She was cared for in her own home with a package of 24/7 care funded jointly by Rochdale MBC and the local CCG.

**Issue to be decided**: Whether KW was deprived of her liberty.

**Decision**: Mostyn J held that she was not deprived of her liberty because she was

> not in any realistic way being constrained from exercising the freedom to leave, in the required sense, for the essential reason that she does not have the physical or mental ability to exercise that freedom.

Mostyn J made it very clear that he considered that the Supreme Court had adopted the wrong approach in *Cheshire West* and that the issue of deprivation of liberty should be revisited by that Court.

**Health warning**: KW's appeal against the decision was allowed by consent by the Court of Appeal in February 2015 (without any judgment). As discussed in Chapter 3, the conclusions reached by Mostyn J in this judgment are not compatible with the reasoning of the majority in *Cheshire West* and should not be followed.

## 7    The decisions of the lower courts in the *Cheshire West* cases (apart from the decision of Baker J in Mr P's case)

The judgment of Baker J in Mr P's case ([2011] EWHC 1330 (COP)) was held by the Supreme Court to have been correct on the law and on the facts.[2] However, the decision of the Court of Appeal ([2011] EWCA Civ 1257) was overturned by the Supreme Court and should not be followed. The facts of Mr P's case are given at paragraphs 2.24-2.25.

The decisions of Parker J in P and Q ([2010] EWHC 785 (COP)) and of the Court of Appeal in the same case (known as MIG and MEG) ([2011] EWCA Civ 190) should not be followed as they were overturned by the Supreme Court. The facts of P and Q are given at paragraphs 2.26-2.28.

### Endnotes
1    A date that we have picked since the 'DOLS regime' came into force in April 2009.
2    Although the minority made clear that they might have reached a different conclusion if they had been considering his situation for themselves.

## 11    FURTHER RESOURCES

## A    *Cheshire West* and its implications

■    *Cheshire West* judgment, available on **Bailii**.[i]

### *Official guidance*

■    Department of Health Guidance[ii] on the obligations of local authorities following the decision in *Cheshire West* (28 March 2014).

- Department of Health Guidance[iii] on reducing the use of restrictive practices, inter alia in health care settings, issued by Department of Health (April 2014).
- Care Quality Commission briefing[iv] for providers in health and social care settings (updated April 2014).
- The letter[v] from Niall Fry of the Department of Health to MCA DOLS leads addressing the initiatives that are in place to address the impact of the Supreme Court decision (September 2014).
- ADASS Advice Note[vi]: 'Guidance for Local Authorities in the light of the Supreme Court decisions on deprivation of liberty' (November 2014).
- The letter[vii] from Niall Fry of the Department of Health to MCA DOLS leads addressing, amongst other things, palliative care and unconsciousness (January 2015).
- The letter[viii] from the Chief Social Worker, Lyn Romeo, on the MCA 2005 and the vital role of social workers (January 2015).

## Commentary

- *P, P and Q: The key to the gilded cage*[ix] – a video featuring Jenni Richards QC, Fenella Morris QC, Nicola Greaney and Ben Tankel, all of Thirty Nine Essex Street (March 2014).
- *P v Cheshire West and Chester Council – Supreme Court decision – March 2014*[x] – a webinar produced by Ben Troke of Browne Jacobson (March 2014).
- 'Psychiatry and the Law: An enduring interest for Lord Rodger': The Lord Rodger Memorial Lecture 2014, a speech[xi] given by Lady Hale in October 2014, which includes a very interesting discussion of the judgment.

## Particular practice areas

- *Deprivation of liberty in the hospital setting:*[xii] a paper written by Alex Ruck Keene and Catherine Dobson of 39 Essex Chambers, which considers the law relating to deprivation of liberty in the hospital setting, including what it takes to have capacity to consent to such a deprivation of liberty, and whether the MCA 2005 or the MHA 1983 will apply (March 2015).
- *Mental Capacity Act – Update following P v Cheshire West and P & Q v Surrey County Council cases*[xiii]: a paper focusing on the impact of the decision for psychiatrists and AMHPs by Julie Chalmers, Specialist Advisor in Mental Health Law to the Royal College of Psychiatrists (April 2014).
- Guidance[xiv] from the Intensive Care Society as to the implications of the decision in the intensive care setting (October 2014).

## B    Changes to the procedures for the authorisation of deprivation of liberty

## DOLS

- ADASS's new forms[xv] for applications for DOLS authorisations (January 2015).

These also include a new form (28) for notifying a coroner of a death of a person subject to an authorisation.

## Re X

- The first[xvi] and second[xvii] judgments of the President of the Court of Protection setting out the outlines of the 'streamlined' court authorised DOL process, in particular for supported living and DOL in a person's own home. NB, these are under appeal to the Court of Appeal, the hearing being in February 2015, and judgment being awaited at the time of writing.

## Re X process

- *Practice Direction: 10AA: Deprivation of Liberty applications*[xviii] (note, the material paragraphs for these purposes are paragraphs 27 and onwards). Even though this is still called Practice Direction 10AA, it now contains both the procedures for an appeal against a DOLS authorisation as well as the procedures for the court's handling of applications under the Re X cases.
- COP DOL10 form[xix] and unofficial Word version.[xx]
- Model order[xxi] (in Word).
- A guide[xxii] to *Re X* applications written by members of the 39 Essex Chambers Court of Protection team.

## C    Other resources relating to deprivation of liberty

- DOLS Code of Practice[xxiii] (though Chapter 2 must now be read subject to the cases decided since the Guide was written – see paragraphs 2.59-2.61 of the main body of this guidance).
- For procedures to resolve issues between local authorities as to which local authority is responsible for a DOLS authorisation, see ADASS *Protocol for inter authority management of DOLS applications*[xxiv] (November 2009). Note this that does not reflect the changes that came into force in April 2013 in England with the abolition of PCTs.
- The Chief Coroner's Guidance[xxv] on Deprivation of Liberty safeguards.

## D    Other free legal resources[xxvi]

| Website | Contents |
|---|---|
| www.bailii.org | British and Irish Legal Information Institute: transcripts of judgments including increasing numbers of decisions of the Court of Protection and older judgments accessible in the Family Division area. |

| Website | Contents |
|---|---|
| www.copcasesonline.com | Site maintained by 39 Essex Chambers with searchable database of cases relating to mental capacity law, as well as back issues of newsletter (available for free on a monthly basis. To be added to the mailing list email: **marketing@39essex.com**). |
| www.courtofprotectionhandbook.com | A free site accompanying the Court of Protection Handbook (Legal Action 2014) with links to relevant statutory material and updates on practice and procedure cross-referenced to the book. |
| www.gardensocial.co.uk | Garden Court Chambers has a website and newsletter dedicated to social welfare, including community care, mental health and incapacity issues. |
| www.gov.uk/apply-to-the-court-of-protection<br><br>hmctsformfinder.justice.gov.uk/HMCTS/GetForms.do?court–forms–category=court–of–protection | Contains all the Court of Protection forms and current details as to fees. |
| www.judiciary.gov.uk/publication-type/practice-directions<br><br>www.justice.gov.uk/courts/rcj-rolls-building/court-of-protection | Contains Practice Directions and Court of Protection Rules. |
| hmctsformfinder.justice.gov.uk/courtfinder/forms/cop042-eng.pdf | A booklet giving guidance on applying to the Court of Protection. |
| www.justice.gov.uk/about/opg | A useful guide to LPAs and deputyship which can be of assistance when trying to assess what powers (if any) an attorney or deputy has in relation to deprivation of liberty. |

| Website | Contents |
|---|---|
| www.law.manchester.ac.uk/ medialibrary/Main%20 site/LAC/Acting-as-a-Litigation-Friend-in-the-Court-of-Protection-October-2014.pdf | Guidance commissioned by the Department of Health for IMCAs, RPRs and others considering acting as a litigation friend in the Court of Protection; includes a guide to welfare proceedings in the Court of Protection written for the benefit of non-lawyers. |
| www.mentalhealthlawonline.co.uk | Extensive site containing legislation, case transcripts and other useful material relating to both the Mental Capacity Act 2005 and Mental Health Act 1983. It has transcripts for more Court of Protection cases than any other site (including subscription-only sites). |

## E    Other useful free resources related to mental capacity law

| Website | Contents |
|---|---|
| www.scie.org.uk | The Social Care Institute for Excellence website includes good practice guidance in a number of areas relating to mental capacity and related law. It also includes a directory of mental capacity resources. |
| www.mclap.org.uk | A website maintained by Alex Ruck Keene dedicated to improving understanding of the law and practice in the field of mental capacity law, including articles, papers and other resources on the MCA 2005 and discussion forums. |
| thesmallplaces.wordpress.com | Blog site maintained by Lucy Series, socio-legal researcher and expert commentator upon the Court of Protection. |

| Website | Contents |
| --- | --- |
| www.communitycare.co.uk | Online magazine dedicated to community care matters, which frequently includes useful stories relating to the MCA 2005. |

## Endnotes

i     www.bailii.org/uk/cases/UKSC/2014/19.html
ii    www.39essex.com/docs/newsletters/dh-letter-re-supreme-court-dols-judgment-final-28-march-2014.pdf
iii   www.gov.uk/government/uploads/system/uploads/attachment-data/file/300293/JRA-DoH-Guidance-on-RP-web-accessible.pdf
iv    www.cqc.org.uk/sites/default/files/20140416-supreme-court-judgment-on-deprivation-of-liberty-briefing-v2.pdf
v     www.mentalcapacitylawandpolicy.org.uk/wp-content/uploads/2014/09/DH-Letter-to-MCA-DoLS-Leads-September-2014.pdf
vi    adass.org.uk/uploadedFiles/adass-content/policy-networks/mental-health/key-documents/DoLS%20Guidance%20note%20November%202014.pdf
vii   www.mentalcapacitylawandpolicy.org.uk/wp-content/uploads/2014/04/DH-Letter-to-MCA-DoLS-Leads-14-January-2015-FINAL.pdf
viii  www.adass.org.uk/uploadedFiles/adass-content/news/press-2015/Letter%20-%20MCA%20-%20%20social%20workers%2014%20Jan%202015%20 FINAL.pdf
ix    www.39essex.com/a-deprivation-of-liberty-post-cheshire-west-and-p-q-2
x     www.bjhealthlawyers.com/resource/p-v-cheshire-west-and-chester-council-supreme-court-decision-march-2014
xi    www.supremecourt.uk/docs/speech-141031.pdf
xii   www.39essex.com/docs/articles/deprivation-of-liberty-in-the-hospital-settingv3.pdf
xiii  www.rcpsych.ac.uk/policyandparliamentary/mentalhealthlaw/mentalcapacityact.aspx
xiv   www.mentalcapacitylawandpolicy.org.uk/wp-content/uploads/2014/04/1504320.pdf
xv    www.adass.org.uk/mental-health-Drugs-and-Alcohol/key-documents/New-DoLS-Forms
xvi   www.bailii.org/ew/cases/EWCOP/2014/25.html
xvii  www.bailii.org/ew/cases/EWCOP/2014/37.html
xviii www.judiciary.gov.uk/publications/10aa-deprivation-of-liberty
xix   hmctsformfinder.justice.gov.uk/courtfinder/forms/cop-dol10-eng.pdf
xx    courtofprotectionhandbook.files.wordpress.com/2014/07/copdol10-word-form.doc
xxi   courtofprotectionhandbook.files.wordpress.com/2014/07/copdol10-word-form.doc
xxii  www.39essex.com/content/wp-content/uploads/2014/11/judicial-deprivation-of-liberty-authorisations-guide.pdf
xxiii webarchive.nationalarchives.gov.uk/20130107105354/http://www.dh.gov.uk/prod-consum-dh/groups/dh-digitalassets/@dh/@en/documents/digitalasset/dh-087309.pdf
xxiv  www.mentalcapacitylawandpolicy.org.uk/wp-content/uploads/2014/04/DOLS-9.11.9.doc
xxv   www.judiciary.gov.uk/wp-content/uploads/2013/10/guidance-no16-dols.pdf
xxvi  Reproduced in part from the Court of Protection Handbook (Legal Action Group 2014), with the permission of the publishers.

# APPENDIX

## Notes on authors and the practitioner group and acknowledgments

### *Authors*

This guidance was written by the following specialist lawyers.

ALEX RUCK KEENE (EDITOR)

Alex is a barrister practising at 39 Essex Chambers, specialising in mental capacity law. He is instructed by a wide range of individuals and public bodies in cases involving the MCA 2005, and has appeared in cases involving the Act at all levels up to and including the Supreme Court.

Alex is also an honorary research lecturer at the University of Manchester School of Law and a visiting lecturer at Queen Mary University of London and Keele University.

Alex is an experienced trainer of both social work and health care staff in health and welfare aspects of the MCA 2005, the founder of the website **www.mentalcapacitylandpolicy.org.uk**, and writes extensively in the area. The most recent books to which he has contributed are the *Court of Protection Handbook* (Legal Action Group, 2014) and *The International Protection of Adults* (OUP). Alex is a member of the Mental Health and Disability Committees of the Law Societies of both England and Wales and Scotland, and of the Legal and Ethical Policy Unit of the Faculty of Intensive Care Medicine and Intensive Care Society.

NEIL ALLEN

Neil is a barrister practising at 39 Essex Chambers and a lecturer specialising in mental health and capacity law at Manchester University (where he is also Deputy Director of the Legal Advice Centre). His practice covers all aspects of personal welfare, property and financial affairs as they affect those without mental capacity.

Neil has published widely in mental health and capacity law, teaches at undergraduate and postgraduate level and regularly delivers training for a variety of audiences including health and local authorities, s12 doctors, GPs, AMHPs, the Royal College of Psychiatrists, and law firms. With regard to his Court of Protection practice, he has represented parties in a number of significant cases including *P v Cheshire West* and *Re X*.

In addition to adjudicating fitness to practise hearings, Neil is trustee of the mental health charity, Making Space, and specialist advisor to various research panels and organisations.

SOPHY MILES

Sophy is a solicitor and Chair of the Law Society's Mental Health & Disability Committee. She has been working in the field of mental health and capacity law for over 20 years and represents users of mental health services and their families and carers about detention in hospital, treatment and after care.

Sophy sits as a part-time Legal Member of the Mental Health Review Tribunal and, in 2010, won the Legal Aid Practitioner's Group Legal Aid Lawyer of the Year award in the Mental Health category.

She is the co-author of Legal Action Group's *Court of Protection Handbook* (2014).

After 16 years as founding Partner at Miles and Partners, Sophy became a Consultant in 2012. Her work at Miles and Partners involves acting as advocate in the Court of Protection and Mental Health Tribunal. She is also an accredited mediator.

PAULA SCULLY

Paula is a solicitor at Derbyshire County Council specialising in deprivation of liberty, safeguarding, mental health and community care law. Paula's legal practice began in the Republic of Ireland where she specialised in criminal and family law before moving to Hong Kong where she specialised in health, family and public law litigation for the Hong Kong Department of Justice. Paula also worked for the Hong Kong Law Commission and held the position of Chair of the Hong Kong Guardianship Board. Paula has also worked in Australia as a Public Guardian making complex welfare decisions for adults without capacity.

Paula has been a member of the Law Society's Mental Health and Disability Committee since 2009. She represents the Committee on the CQC's DOLS Advisory Group and was a member of the ADASS Task Force established to consider the practical outcomes and challenges arising from the *Cheshire West* case.

BEVERLEY TAYLOR

Beverley was until recently the Deputy Official Solicitor and head of the property and affairs team at the Office of the Official Solicitor and Public Trustee. Prior to this appointment, Beverley was a senior lawyer at the Office specialising in family and medical law and head of the healthcare and welfare team. She has also held positions in private practice and in academia at Middlesex University as a Principal Lecturer in Law

Beverley co-authored the Law Society publication, '*Mental Capacity Act 2005 – Guide to the New Law*' with Fenella Morris QC and Nicola Greaney. Beverley was also a long time Trustee of Norwood a charity which specialises in supporting adults with learning disabilities and their families and continues to be involved in its important work. Beverley has been a member of the Law Society Mental Health and Disability Committee since 2013.

## Practitioner Group

The authors would like to express their gratitude to the Practitioner Group, whose advice and oversight throughout the production of this guidance was invaluable:

■   Sue Adams, Conwy County Council

Further information    147

- Dr Julie Chalmers, Royal College of Psychiatrists (Dr Chalmers also coordinated input from the following psychiatrists: Dr Rajnish Attavar, Dr Gwen Adshead, Dr Mayura Deshpande, Dr Marinos Kriakopoulos, Dr Hetal Mehta, Dr Richard Latham, Dr Mark Scheepers and Dr Adran Treloar)
- Lorraine Currie, Shropshire County Council
- Dr Chris Danbury, Intensive Care Society and Royal Berkshire Hospital
- Julian Sheather, British Medical Association

## Acknowledgements

The authors would also like to thank the following individuals for their invaluable comments upon chapters in drafts of the Guidance and/or other practical input:

- Dr Dominic Bell, Consultant in Intensive Care, Leeds General Infirmary
- Dr Tim Exworthy, Member of the Law Society's Mental Health and Disability Committee and Clinical Director & Consultant Forensic Psychiatrist, St Andrew's Healthcare
- Sue Garwood, Independent Consultant and Extra Care Specialist
- Camilla Parker, Member of the Law Society's Mental Health and Disability Committee and director, Just Equality
- Ben Troke, Partner, Browne Jacobson Solicitors

# [B]   CASE LAW UPDATES

# Appendix B1
# Summaries of recent key cases

*Beverley Taylor*

## Introduction

The following chapter is a supplementary update to the case summaries in Chapter 10 of this Guidance, giving summaries of an additional seven cases whose judgments were published in 2015. Some cases are included because they provide further examples of the application of the 'acid test' to particular factual situations. Others have been included because they provide helpful guidance (for example, on the level of damages to be awarded for unlawful deprivation of liberty), or illustrate the extremities of power of the Court of Protection. A couple of cases have been included because they provide helpful clarification of the relationship between deprivation of liberty under the Mental Capacity Act 2005 and guardianship under the Mental Health Act 1983.

## 1   Essex County Council v. RF & Ors [2015] EWCOP 1 (DJ Mort)

**Facts**: P was a 91-year-old man who, since the death of his sister in 1998, had lived alone in his own house with his cat. He had dementia and other health problems, including difficulty in mobilising, delirium and kidney injury caused by dehydration. Following concerns regarding P's finances, his vulnerability to exploitation and issues regarding to his self-care, P was removed from his home by Essex County Council (ECC) and placed in a locked dementia unit. P was 'very reluctant' to leave his home and was very distressed. It is not clear if P lacked capacity at the time of his removal and he was removed without any authorisation. Throughout the whole of the period of P's placement he expressed a consistent wish to return to his home. Yet despite assessments concluding that P did have capacity to make decisions regarding his residence, and the recommendations that it was in his best interests to return home, P was detained against his wishes for a period of 17 months. The proceedings were triggered by a concern raised by P's friend RF during the course of ECC's application to become P's financial deputy.

**Issues to be decided**: The matter had been set down for a final hearing to make declarations as to P's capacity and orders as to costs and financial compensation. The local authority, having eventually accepted that P had been unlawfully deprived of his liberty for a period of approximately 13 months, reached agreement with the other parties just before the final hearing. The parties agreed that:

- a declaration be made that P had been unlawfully deprived of his liberty for approximately 13 months;
- ECC would pay P £60,000 damages arising from P's unlawful detention;
- ECC would waive any fees payable by P to the care home in which he was detained (a sum between £23,000 and £25,000);
- ECC would exclude P's damages award from means testing in relation to P being required to pay a contribution to his community care costs; and
- the payment of all P's costs was to be assessed on the standard basis.

At the time of the final hearing P had already returned home with a care package in place and was reported to be happy and content.

**Decision**: The matter came before District Judge Mort to make declarations as to P's capacity, and to approve the compromise agreement. He made declarations that P lacked capacity to make decisions about his residence and care but had capacity to make decisions about contact. He considered and approved the terms of the compromise agreement and made a declaration and orders giving effect to the agreement.

Note: There are very few judgments on the level of damages to be awarded by the Court of Protection for unlawful detention (see paragraphs 2.44–2.48 of this Guidance). This judgment provides some useful guidance. The judge gave a guideline of £3,000 to £4,000 per month as the quantum of damages likely to be recovered for an unlawful deprivation of liberty (taking *Hillingdon LBC* v. *Neary* [2011] EWHC 1377 (COP) as the benchmark). In this case, the approved award lies at the higher end of the spectrum at between £3,500 and £4,600 per month – the judge described ECC's conduct as 'totally inadequate' and their failings as 'significant'.

## 2    The Mental Health Trust v. DD and BC *[2015] EWCOP 4 (Cobb J)*

Facts: This is the sixth decision concerning DD, a 36-year-old woman with a mild to borderline learning disability and autism spectrum disorder (see Case Summary 20 of Chapter 10). DD lived with BC, her long-term partner who has a significant learning difficulty. DD's home was forcibly entered on 16 July 2014 pursuant to the judge's order of 4 July 2014, in order to convey DD to hospital for a caesarean section. After the forced entry to the home, DD and BC became distressed for a short time. DD was helped to leave the flat, and by that time was calm, entering the ambulance independently and without restraint. She was calm on the ambulance journey, and exited the ambulance independently. On 17 July 2014, a sixth child (Child 6) was delivered to DD by caesarean section. Final care and placement orders were made in relation to Child 6, who has been placed for adoption with one of her older siblings.

Following the safe delivery of the child, the applicants wished to ensure that DD did not become pregnant again, because of the risk to DD's life if she did so. Unsuccessful attempts were made to educate DD about different forms of contraception. DD's home was also forcibly entered on three separate occasions, pursuant to court orders; on the last of these occasions in order to administer a Depo-Provera injection. DD and BC were angry at the intrusion. The professionals had to use full seat restraint, during which DD had become angry, upset and aggressive towards staff. It was said that:

> The level of distress however was of a greater level than any other previous visit… I can only assume that any future visits like this are going to increase her resentment towards professional interference in her life and she is going to become more obstructive towards the professionals involved, both verbally and physically.

The applicants formed the view that it was in DD's best interests to undergo a sterilisation.

Issues to be decided: Cobb J was asked to determine DD's capacity to litigate, and her capacity to consider and make decisions concerning long-term contraception and/or therapeutic sterilisation, and, if lacking such capacity, to determine what was in her best interests.

Decision: The judge held that she lacked the relevant capacity and that it was in her best interests to be sterilised, as the 'less restrictive option in its widest application'. With regards to the need to force entry to DD's home in order to convey her to hospital Cobb J noted his concern that each forced entry to the home had been followed by escalating levels of distress experienced and displayed by DD and BC. He repeated at paragraph 136 what he had said prior to the forced entry authorised by him on 4 July 2014:

> Any physical restraint or deprivation of liberty is a significant interference with DD's rights under Articles 5 and Article 8 of the ECHR and, in my judgment, as such should only be carried out:
>
> (i)     by professionals who have received training in the relevant techniques and who have reviewed the individual plan for DD;

(ii)    as a last resort and where less restrictive alternatives, such as verbal de-escalation and distraction techniques, have failed and only when it is necessary to do so;

(iii)    in the least restrictive manner, proportionate to achieving the aim, for the shortest period possible;

(iv)    in accordance with any agreed Care Plans, Risk Assessments and Court Orders.

para.131 [2014] EWCOP 11

He also accepted that the presence of the police at the time of the forced entry and removal was 'on the whole' beneficial.

**Note**: This case illustrates the extremities of the powers available to the Court of Protection, providing for forcible entry, authorisation of physical restraint and deprivation of liberty and the removal and sterilisation of a vulnerable adult.

## 3    W City Council v. Mrs L *[2015] EWCOP 20 (Bodey J)*

**Facts**: Mrs L, a 93-year-old woman with severe Alzheimer's disease, received care at home as a result of an arrangement set up by her two adult daughters and the local authority. She was widowed in 1976 and had lived in her home for the past 39 years. Since her diagnosis in 2004, various family members had looked after her. Mrs L fell twice in 2013. The first time she injured her hip, the second time she was not hurt but became disorientated and walked 'away from her home very unsuitably clothed into the local town'.

In response, her family installed a fence around her previously open garden with a latched gate. Door sensors were fitted so that Mrs L's daughters or the emergency services would be alerted if Mrs L left the property, Mrs L would then be safely guided back into the property. Mrs L received three visits a day from specialist dementia carers and was said to be happy where she was.

The local authority considered that Mrs L was deprived of her liberty, her family did not.

**Issues to be decided**:

(a)    whether the care arrangements for Mrs L constituted a deprivation of her liberty;

(b)    if so, then whether the State was responsible for such deprivation of liberty; and

(c)    if so, then whether such deprivation of liberty should be authorised by the court and what the arrangements for continuing authorisation should be.

**Decision**: Bodey J concluded that Mrs L was not deprived of her liberty in her own home as, while the care arrangements constituted restrictions on her liberty, they did not quite cross the line to being a deprivation of it.

At paragraph 26, Bodey J observed:

Article 5 refers to everyone having a right to 'liberty *and security* of person' [emphasis added]. Mrs L's 'security' is being achieved by the arrangements put into place as being in her best interests, even though involving restrictions. Such restrictions are not continuous or complete. Mrs L has ample time to spend as she wishes, and the carer's visits are the minimum necessary for her safety and wellbeing, being largely concerned to ensure that she is eating, taking liquids and coping generally in other respects.

He further concluded that even if Mrs L were deprived of her liberty, it would not be imputable to the State:

[I]f there is a deprivation of Mrs L's liberty, is it to be imputed to the State? On the facts, I find not. This is a shared arrangement set up by agreement with a caring and pro-active family: and the responsibility of the State is, it seems to me, diluted by the strong role which the family has played and continues to play. I do not consider in such circum-stances that the mischief of the State interference at which Article 5 was and is directed, sufficiently exists.

para.27

**Note**: This is the second case since *Rochdale MBC v. KW* which seeks to distance itself from the factual situation in *Cheshire West*. At the time of going to print, this case has not been appealed and continues to be an unusual example of someone not free to leave but not under continuous supervision.

## 4    NM v. Kent County Council *(Mental health: All)* [2015] UKUT 125 (AAC) *(Upper Tribunal Judge Jacobs)*

**Facts**: Mr M was born in 1972. He had diagnoses of mild learning disability with behavioural difficulties and paedophilic sexual interest. In 2000, he was transferred to a residential placement. He was received into guardianship first in 2005 and, as it was thought that the procedure had been flawed, again in 2013. The county council, as guardian, required Mr M to live in a particular home and to meet with clinicians and therapists for treatment. He was subject to DOLS from 2011, which was confirmed by the Court of Protection in 2012 (see Case Summary 12 in Chapter 10). Mr M applied to the First Tier Tribunal (FTT) in 2014 for the guardianship to be discharged on the basis that guardianship was no longer necessary, as the interests of Mr M and of the public were sufficiently protected by the DOLS. The tribunal rejected this argument, deciding that guardianship was necessary in the interests of Mr M's own welfare and of children whom he wished to contact. M appealed the decision.

**Issues to be decided**: M argued that:

(a)   Guardianship was not necessary because the DOLS authorised the home in which Mr M was living to deprive him of his liberty and he would be prevented if he tried to leave the home without permission, so he could not abscond.

(b)   There was a conflict between the findings of Mr Justice Moore and the FTT judge on the issue of M's capacity to make decisions about where he should live.

**Decision**: Dismissing the appeal, the judge found that there were no errors in law in the decision of the FTT or the reasons given by it for the decision. The FTT's analysis correctly identified the conditions that had to be satisfied if Mr M were to remain subject to guardianship and also justified the need for guardianship despite the DOLS. Furthermore, there was no error in respect of the tribunal's finding on Mr M's capacity. Moor J was not considering issues of enforced residence in the sense allowed by guardianship:

> The key to the case was where Mr M would live. It found that he would not remain in the home without being subject to the guardianship. For practical purposes, he might not be able to abscond from the home itself, but he had opportunities to do so when he was on escorted leave. He needed to be in the home, or in a similar environment, if he were to preserve the continuity of his treatment. That treatment was not complete to the point where he was able to control his behaviour towards children. Without that treatment, children would be at risk if he were able to make contact with them. And that would expose him to the risk of retaliation; he had been frightened when a relative had remonstrated with him in the past. Each of those steps is soundly based in the evidence before the tribunal.

para.23

Judge Jacobs found that while the DOLS would allow the home to prevent Mr M leaving, it would not deal with the possibility that he may abscond, especially given his wish to live elsewhere and the tribunal's findings that he is devious in the pursuit of his own objectives. It was therefore necessary for both the guardianship and DOLS to remain in place:

> Standing back from the detail of the arguments and the complexity of the legislation, the two Acts deal with different issues. The Mental Capacity Act deals with the person's best

interests, whereas the Mental Health Act deals with protection of the patient and the public. Each is subject to different adjudication procedures before different judicial bodies.

para.29

Note: This decision confirms again that guardianship can be used together with DOLS. The judge endorsed the list (set out at para.16 of the judgment) of differences between the two regimes:

- DOLS assumes that the person lacks capacity to make the relevant decisions in their best interests. Guardianship is not based on an assessment of the person's best interests.
- DOLS cannot impose a requirement that the person reside at a particular address, whereas a guardian can. And, (added by the judge), section 18(3) allows this to be enforced by taking the person into custody and returning them to their required residence.
- DOLS cannot authorise anyone to give, or consent to, treatment for someone with a mental disorder.

The judge observed that the list is not necessarily comprehensive.

For full discussion of the legal complexities of the use of DOLS and guardianship see www.39essex.com/content/wp-content/uploads/2015/05/MC-Newsletter-May-2015-HWDOL.pdf.

## CASES WITH HEALTH WARNINGS

### 1    A Local Health Board v. AB [2015] EWCOP 31 (HHJ Parry)

Facts: AB was a 34-year-old woman. She had a mild/borderline learning disability, a working diagnosis of autism and a schizophrenic illness with prominent persecutory thinking. She also had a serious and life-threatening cardiac condition, which required surgery. Prior to having surgery it would be necessary for AB to have her bottom teeth extracted to prevent infection. AB was an in-patient at a low secure private hospital under s.3 MHA 1983.

It was the intention of the local health board for AB to be granted leave under s.17 MHA 1983 by her responsible clinician to attend the general hospital for the purposes of undergoing both treatments.

Issues to be decided:
(a) Did AB lack litigation capacity and capacity to make decisions about her medical treatment?
(b) Was it in her best interests to have cardiac surgery and, prior to that, to have dental surgery to remove her lower teeth?
(c) Did the Court of Protection have power to make an order depriving AB of her liberty?

Decision: HHJ Parry decided that AB lacked litigation capacity and lacked capacity to make decisions with regards to her medical treatment. The judge made orders under the inherent jurisdiction of the High Court that it was in AB's best interests to undergo both medical procedures.

HHJ Parry concluded, on the basis of an agreed statement of the law, that:
1. Both before and during the procedures, AB would be subject to restraints amounting to a deprivation of her liberty. This would be a deprivation of liberty further to that which she was already subjected to as a result of her detention under MHA 1983, for which a separate authority was required (applying Munjaz v. United Kingdom [2012] ECHR 1704).
2. AB was either within Case A or Case B of Schedule 1A to MCA 2005.
3. In either case the Court of Protection could not exercise its powers to authorise the

deprivation of her liberty. It was therefore necessary for relief to be granted under the inherent jurisdiction of the High Court.

Note: As far as the authors are aware, this case is the first discussion (at least in a reported case) of the Strasbourg court's identification in *Munjaz* of the concept of 'residual liberty'.

Health warning: The decision comes with a decided health warning, regarding the correctness of the legal analysis adopted to reach the conclusion that AB would be ineligible to be deprived of her liberty at the general hospital.

In *NHS Trust* v. *FG* [2014] EWCOP 30, Keehan J exercised the jurisdiction of the Court of Protection so as to provide for the lawful deprivation of liberty of a woman detained under s.3 MHA 1983, who was to be granted leave under s.17 MHA 1983 to a general hospital for the purpose of undergoing a Caesarian section. For a full discussion see **www.39essex.com/content/wp-content/uploads/2015/06/MC-Newsletter-June-2015-HWDOL.pdf**.

## 2    KD v. A Borough Council *[2015] UKUT 251 (AAC) (Charles J)*

Summary: KD had Korsakov's Syndrome and, following his detention under MHA 1983, had been subject to guardianship since 2012. He was required to reside in a care home with 24-hour supervision and support where he was not free to leave and not permitted to go out unless accompanied by a member of the care staff. He sought to be discharged from the guardianship order on the basis that it was not necessary because DOLS was less restrictive and guardianship could not authorise his deprivation of liberty. The FTT concluded that it was necessary in the interests of the welfare of KD, and for the protection of other persons, that he should remain under guardianship. KD appealed to the Upper Tribunal (AAC).

Issues to be decided: Permission to bring this appeal was granted by the FTT because in the view of the judge it raises points upon which guidance is needed. Those points concern the relationship between the functions and powers of the FTT under MHA 1983 and those of the Court of Protection, managing authorities and supervisory bodies under MCA 2005 and its Deprivation of Liberty Safeguards. The most relevant provisions of MHA 1983 are those relating to guardianship

Decision: Although the Upper Tribunal found that the FTT had erred in law, Charles J exercised his discretion under s.12 of the Tribunals, Courts and Enforcement Act 2007 not to set aside the decision of the FTT.

Note: This case is important because many of the comments made by Charles J during the course of his judgment apply to DOLS cases, whether or not the person is under guardianship. The following points are of particular note:

(i) The concept of 'deprivation of liberty' in breach of Article 5 is wider or arguably wider that that of 'detention' under MHA 1983 (see para.29).

(ii) The guardian's power to return the person to his place of residence has the effect of a requirement or an injunction preventing him from leaving (see para.30). And such a power is a more readily available, effective and sensible means of enforcing the result that the person lives there than an injunction against that person from the Court of Protection (see para.31).

(iii) A deprivation of liberty during guardianship should be authorised under the MCA (where applicable).

(iv) A standard authorisation under DOLS can provide for it to come into force at a time after the time at which it is given. And the Court of Protection can authorise any deprivation from a date in the future (para.43).

(v) A useful checklist was set out at paragraphs 67–73 for tribunals to approach similar guardianship/MCA cases.

### 3   Bournemouth Borough Council v. PS and DS *[2015] EWCOP 39* *(Mostyn J)*

**Facts**: Ben was 28 years old. He was on the autistic spectrum, had mild learning disabilities and needed continuous care. Since 2011 he had been living in a two-bedroom bungalow with staff, 24 hours a day. There was constant observation and monitoring. He was assisted with personal care and encouraged to engage in a timetable of daily tasks. Ben was not allowed to access the kitchen when staff were cooking. He had free unsupervised access to all parts of the bungalow and garden. All kitchen utensils and medication were locked away.

Ben was given complete privacy in his bedroom when he wished. Ben had no sense of traffic awareness and therefore one-to-one staff support was required at all times in the community. Sensors would alert staff if Ben sought to leave the bungalow by himself, although he had never tried. But if he did leave, staff would follow him, attempt to engage with him and monitor him in the community. If he did not want to return home, an escalation of measures would be used, which if unsuccessful ultimately would lead to consideration being given to calling the police to exercise their powers under s.136, MHA 1983.

Ben's wishes fluctuated between wishing to return to hospital and wishing to live with his mother. Neither option was possible. Indeed, contact with his mother only took place on a monthly, supervised basis, although this was subject to review.

At the time of the hearing Ben had been discharged as a party. But his wishes and feelings were made known by a court-appointed independent mental capacity advocate.

**Issues for the court**:

(a)   Whether Ben was deprived of his liberty;
(b)   whether the proposed care plan was in his best interests; and
(c)   to review contact arrangements with his mother.

**Decision**: Mostyn J concluded that Ben was not deprived of his liberty by virtue of the care package, which he approved as being in Ben's best interests:

> I cannot say that I know that Ben is being detained by the State when I look at his position. Far from it. I agree with Mr Mullins that he is not. First, he is not under continuous supervision. He is afforded appreciable privacy. Second, he is free to leave. Were he to do so his carers would seek to persuade him to return but such persuasion would not cross the line into coercion. The deprivation of liberty line would only be crossed if and when the police exercised powers under the Mental Health Act. Were that to happen then a range of reviews and safeguards would become operative. But up to that point Ben is a free man. In my judgment, on the specific facts in play here, the acid test is not met. Ben is not living in a cage, gilded or otherwise.
>
> para.34

**Note**:

(i)   The judge once again used the 'know it when I see it' legal technique for deciding whether the factual situation met the 'acid test'. However, it is difficult to reconcile this decision with the decision in *Cheshire West*, since the intensity of Ben's care regime appears to be far greater than that of MIG in *Cheshire West*.

It is also worth noting that Ben was not represented, although his wishes and feelings were made known by a court-appointed advocate.

(ii)   On 20 October 2015 the Court of Appeal allowed by consent an appeal against the decision of Mostyn J in this case (*KW v. Rochdale Borough Council* [2015] EWCA Civ 1054).

## 4    R (LF) v. HM Senior Coroner for Inner South London [2015] EWHC 2990 (Admin) (Gross LJ and Charles J)

**Facts**: A patient, MF, with Down's syndrome, severe learning disability and limited mobility died in an intensive care unit (ICU). An inquest into MF's death was held and the senior coroner rejected the argument put forward by her mother, LF, that MF was in 'state detention' at the time of her death, within the meaning of ss.7(2)(a) and 48(1) and (2) of the Coroners and Justice Act (CJA) 2009, and therefore that the inquest must be held with a jury. The claimant challenged the decision by way of judicial review.

**Issues before the court**: The claimant challenged the senior coroner's conclusion on the basis that MF was deprived of her liberty in terms of Article 5 ECHR and was therefore in state detention for the purposes of s.7 CJA 2009 at the time of her death. The coroner contended that the requirement that MF had been in 'state detention' and therefore 'compulsorily detained' under CJA 2009 had not been met because there had been no decision to detain MF, or to confine MF to a place or places from which she was not free to leave.

**Decision**: The claimant's claim for judicial review of the coroner's decision was dismissed. Both judges agreed that the coroner's decision was not '*Wednesbury* unreasonable' and that he had not misdirected himself in law. The judges did not agree, however, as to the basis upon which the coroner was correct to hold that MF was not compulsorily detained. Gross LJ considered that MF was not deprived of her liberty for purposes of Article 5(1) ECHR, and therefore was not compulsorily detained for purposes of the CJA 2009; Charles J dismissed the claim on the basis that 'compulsory detention' in the CJA was a narrower concept that 'deprivation of liberty' for purposes of Article 5.

Both judges considered, for slightly different reasons, that the principles set down by the Supreme Court in *Cheshire West* should not be routinely extended to cover the position of patients in ICUs so as to find that they are deprived of their liberty. On the facts, both judges took the view that MF remained in the ICU, not because she had been detained or deprived of her liberty, but because for pressing medical reasons and treatment she was unable to be elsewhere. In other words, there were no realistic choices open to her, upon which she could have exercised her autonomy, whether or not she had capacity at that time.

Both judges also considered that the approach of asking what would happen if a person sought to remove the patient from the hospital, as suggested in **Chapter 4**, should not be adopted in every case, in part because they considered that its introduction had the potential for promoting and introducing controversy where none exists and could be damaging to the therapeutic relationships involved. In this case the judges agreed that such a question should not sensibly have been asked on the facts of the case.

**Health warning**: This judgment should be treated with some caution because an application for leave to appeal the decision has been made. However, until and unless the decision is overturned upon appeal, it makes clear that patients in ICUs who are present for purposes of receiving treatment for a physical disorder should not routinely be considered to be deprived of their liberty.

# [C] FURTHER GUIDANCE

# Appendix C1
# MCA 2005 Code of Practice: Chapters 1–6

## 1  WHAT IS THE MENTAL CAPACITY ACT 2005?

**1.1**  The Mental Capacity Act 2005 (the Act) provides the legal framework for acting and making decisions on behalf of individuals who lack the mental capacity to make particular decisions for themselves. Everyone working with and/or caring for an adult who may lack capacity to make specific decisions must comply with this Act when making decisions or acting for that person, when the person lacks the capacity to make a particular decision for themselves. The same rules apply whether the decisions are life-changing events or everyday matters.

**1.2**  The Act's starting point is to confirm in legislation that it should be assumed that an adult (aged 16 or over) has full legal capacity to make decisions for themselves (the right to autonomy) unless it can be shown that they lack capacity to make a decision for themselves at the time the decision needs to be made. This is known as the presumption of capacity. The Act also states that people must be given all appropriate help and support to enable them to make their own decisions or to maximise their participation in any decision-making process.

**1.3**  The underlying philosophy of the Act is to ensure that any decision made, or action taken, on behalf of someone who lacks the capacity to make the decision or act for themselves is made in their best interests.

**1.4**  The Act is intended to assist and support people who may lack capacity and to discourage anyone who is involved in caring for someone who lacks capacity from being overly restrictive or controlling. But the Act also aims to balance an individual's right to make decisions for themselves with their right to be protected from harm if they lack capacity to make decisions to protect themselves.

**1.5**  The Act sets out a legal framework of how to act and make decisions on behalf of people who lack capacity to make specific decisions for themselves. It sets out some core principles and methods for making decisions and carrying out actions in relation to personal welfare, healthcare and financial matters affecting people who may lack capacity to make specific decisions about these issues for themselves.

**1.6**  Many of the provisions in the Act are based upon existing common law principles (i.e. principles that have been established through decisions made by courts in individual cases). The Act clarifies and improves upon these principles and builds on current good practice which is based on the principles.

**1.7**  The Act introduces several new roles, bodies and powers, all of which will support the Act's provisions. These include:

- Attorneys appointed under Lasting Powers of Attorney (see chapter 7)
- The new Court of Protection, and court-appointed deputies (see chapter 8)
- Independent Mental Capacity Advocates (see chapter 10).

The roles, bodies and powers are all explained in more depth in the specific chapters of the Code highlighted above.

## What decisions are covered by the Act, and what decisions are excluded?

**1.8**   The Act covers a wide range of decisions made, or actions taken, on behalf of people who may lack capacity to make specific decisions for themselves. These can be decisions about day-to-day matters – like what to wear, or what to buy when doing the weekly shopping – or decisions about major life-changing events, such as whether the person should move into a care home or undergo a major surgical operation.

**1.9**   There are certain decisions which can never be made on behalf of a person who lacks capacity to make those specific decisions. This is because they are either so personal to the individual concerned, or governed by other legislation.

**1.10**   Sections 27–29 and 62 of the Act set out the specific decisions which can never be made or actions which can never be carried out under the Act, whether by family members, carers, professionals, attorneys or the Court of Protection. These are summarised below.

### DECISIONS CONCERNING FAMILY RELATIONSHIPS (SECTION 27)

Nothing in the Act permits a decision to be made on someone else's behalf on any of the following matters:

- consenting to marriage or a civil partnership
- consenting to have sexual relations
- consenting to a decree of divorce on the basis of two years' separation
- consenting to the dissolution of a civil partnership
- consenting to a child being placed for adoption or the making of an adoption order
- discharging parental responsibility for a child in matters not relating to the child's property, or
- giving consent under the Human Fertilisation and Embryology Act 1990.

### MENTAL HEALTH ACT MATTERS (SECTION 28)

Where a person who lacks capacity to consent is currently detained and being treated under Part 4 of the Mental Health Act 1983, nothing in the Act authorises anyone to:

- give the person treatment for mental disorder, or
- consent to the person being given treatment for mental disorder.

Further guidance is given in chapter 13 of the Code.

### VOTING RIGHTS (SECTION 29)

Nothing in the Act permits a decision on voting, at an election for any public office or at a referendum, to be made on behalf of a person who lacks capacity to vote.

### UNLAWFUL KILLING OR ASSISTING SUICIDE (SECTION 62)

For the avoidance of doubt, nothing in the Act is to be taken to affect the law relating to murder, manslaughter or assisting suicide.

**1.11**   Although the Act does not allow anyone to make a decision about these matters on behalf of someone who lacks capacity to make such a decision for themselves (for example, consenting to have sexual relations), this does not prevent action being taken to protect a vulnerable person from abuse or exploitation.

## How does the Act relate to other legislation?

**1.12**    The Mental Capacity Act 2005 will apply in conjunction with other legislation affecting people who may lack capacity in relation to specific matters. This means that healthcare and social care staff acting under the Act should also be aware of their obligations under other legislation, including (but not limited to) the:

- Care Standards Act 2000
- Data Protection Act 1998
- Disability Discrimination Act 1995
- Human Rights Act 1998
- Mental Health Act 1983
- National Health Service and Community Care Act 1990
- Human Tissue Act 2004.

## What does the Act say about the Code of Practice?

**1.13**    Section 42 of the Act sets out the purpose of the Code of Practice, which is to provide guidance for specific people in specific circumstances. Section 43 explains the procedures that had to be followed in preparing the Code and consulting on its contents, and for its consideration by Parliament.

Section 42, subsections (4) and (5), set out the categories of people who are placed under a legal duty to 'have regard to' the Code and gives further information about the status of the Code. More details can be found in the Introduction, which explains the legal status of the Code.

## 2    WHAT ARE THE STATUTORY PRINCIPLES AND HOW SHOULD THEY BE APPLIED?

Section 1 of the Act sets out the five 'statutory principles' – the values that underpin the legal requirements in the Act. The Act is intended to be enabling and supportive of people who lack capacity, not restricting or controlling of their lives. It aims to protect people who lack capacity to make particular decisions, but also to maximise their ability to make decisions, or to participate in decision-making, as far as they are able to do so.

The five statutory principles are:

1. A person must be assumed to have capacity unless it is established that they lack capacity.
2. A person is not to be treated as unable to make a decision unless all practicable steps to help him to do so have been taken without success.
3. A person is not to be treated as unable to make a decision merely because he makes an unwise decision.
4. An act done, or decision made, under this Act for or on behalf of a person who lacks capacity must be done, or made, in his best interests.
5. Before the act is done, or the decision is made, regard must be had to whether the purpose for which it is needed can be as effectively achieved in a way that is less restrictive of the person's rights and freedom of action.

This chapter provides guidance on how people should interpret and apply the statutory principles when using the Act. Following the principles and applying them to the Act's framework for decision-making will help to ensure not only that appropriate action is taken in individual cases, but also to point the way to solutions in difficult or uncertain situations.

> In this chapter, as throughout the Code, a person's capacity (or lack of capacity) refers specifically to their capacity to make a particular decision at the time it needs to be made.

## Quick summary

- Every adult has the right to make their own decisions if they have the capacity to do so. Family carers and healthcare or social care staff must assume that a person has the capacity to make decisions, unless it can be established that the person does not have capacity.
- People should receive support to help them make their own decisions. Before concluding that individuals lack capacity to make a particular decision, it is important to take all possible steps to try to help them reach a decision themselves.
- People have the right to make decisions that others might think are unwise. A person who makes a decision that others think is unwise should not automatically be labelled as lacking the capacity to make a decision.
- Any act done for, or any decision made on behalf of, someone who lacks capacity must be in their best interests.
- Any act done for, or any decision made on behalf of, someone who lacks capacity should be an option that is less restrictive of their basic rights and freedoms – as long as it is still in their best interests.

## What is the role of the statutory principles?

2.1    The statutory principles aim to:

- protect people who lack capacity and
- help them take part, as much as possible, in decisions that affect them.

They aim to assist and support people who may lack capacity to make particular decisions, not to restrict or control their lives.

2.2    The statutory principles apply to any act done or decision made under the Act. When followed and applied to the Act's decision-making framework, they will help people take appropriate action in individual cases. They will also help people find solutions in difficult or uncertain situations.

## How should the statutory principles be applied?

**Principle 1**: 'A person must be assumed to have capacity unless it is established that he lacks capacity.' (section1(2))

2.3    This principle states that every adult has the right to make their own decisions – unless there is proof that they lack the capacity to make a particular decision when it needs to be made. This has been a fundamental principle of the common law for many years and it is now set out in the Act.

2.4    It is important to balance people's right to make a decision with their right to safety and protection when they can't make decisions to protect themselves. But the starting assumption must always be that an individual has the capacity, until there is proof that they do not. Chapter 4 explains the Act's definition of 'lack of capacity' and the processes involved in assessing capacity.

---

**Scenario: Assessing a person's capacity to make decisions**

When planning for her retirement, Mrs Arnold made and registered a Lasting Power of Attorney (LPA) – a legal process that would allow her son to manage her property and financial affairs if she ever lacked capacity to manage them herself. She has now been diagnosed with dementia, and her son is worried that she is becoming confused about money.

Her son must assume that his mother has capacity to manage her affairs. Then he must consider each of Mrs Arnold's financial decisions as she makes them, giving her any help and support she needs to make these decisions herself.

Mrs Arnold's son goes shopping with her, and he sees she is quite capable of finding goods and making sure she gets the correct change. But when she needs to make decisions about her investments, Mrs Arnold gets confused – even though she has made such decisions in the past. She still doesn't understand after her son explains the different options.

Her son concludes that she has capacity to deal with everyday financial matters but not more difficult affairs at this time. Therefore, he is able to use the LPA for the difficult financial decisions his mother can't make. But Mrs Arnold can continue to deal with her other affairs for as long as she has capacity to do so.

---

2.5    Some people may need help to be able to make a decision or to communicate their decision. However, this does not necessarily mean that they cannot make that decision – unless there is proof that they do lack capacity to do so. Anyone who believes that a person lacks capacity should be able to prove their case. Chapter 4 explains the standard of proof required.

**Principle 2**: '*A person is not to be treated as unable to make a decision unless all practicable steps to help him to do so have been taken without success.*' *(section1 (3))*

2.6    It is important to do everything practical (the Act uses the term 'practicable') to help a person make a decision for themselves before concluding that they lack capacity to do so. People with an illness or disability affecting their ability to make a decision should receive support to help them make as many decisions as they can. This principle aims to stop people being automatically labelled as lacking capacity to make particular decisions. Because it encourages individuals to play as big a role as possible in decision-making, it also helps prevent unnecessary interventions in their lives.

2.7    The kind of support people might need to help them make a decision varies. It depends on personal circumstances, the kind of decision that has to be made and the time available to make the decision. It might include:

- using a different form of communication (for example, non-verbal communication)
- providing information in a more accessible form (for example, photographs, drawings, or tapes)
- treating a medical condition which may be affecting the person's capacity or
- having a structured programme to improve a person's capacity to make particular decisions (for example, helping a person with learning disabilities to learn new skills).

Chapter 3 gives more information on ways to help people make decisions for themselves.

---

**Scenario: Taking steps to help people make decisions for themselves**

Mr Jackson is brought into hospital following a traffic accident. He is conscious but in shock. He cannot speak and is clearly in distress, making noises and gestures.

From his behaviour, hospital staff conclude that Mr Jackson currently lacks the capacity to make decisions about treatment for his injuries, and they give him urgent treatment. They hope that after he has recovered from the shock they can use an advocate to help explain things to him.

However, one of the nurses thinks she recognises some of his gestures as sign language, and tries signing to him. Mr Jackson immediately becomes calmer, and the doctors realise that he can communicate in sign language. He can also answer some written questions about his injuries.

The hospital brings in a qualified sign-language interpreter and concludes that Mr Jackson has the capacity to make decisions about any further treatment.

---

**2.8**    Anyone supporting a person who may lack capacity should not use excessive persuasion or 'undue pressure'.[1] This might include behaving in a manner which is overbearing or dominating, or seeking to influence the person's decision, and could push a person into making a decision they might not otherwise have made. However, it is important to provide appropriate advice and information.

---

**Scenario: Giving appropriate advice and support**

Sara, a young woman with severe depression, is getting treatment from mental health services. Her psychiatrist determines that she has capacity to make decisions about treatment, if she gets advice and support.

Her mother is trying to persuade Sara to agree to electro-convulsive therapy (ECT), which helped her mother when she had clinical depression in the past. However, a friend has told Sara that ECT is 'barbaric'.

The psychiatrist provides factual information about the different types of treatment available and explains their advantages and disadvantages. She also describes how different people experience different reactions or side effects. Sara is then able to consider what treatment is right for her, based on factual information rather than the personal opinions of her mother and friend.

---

**2.9**    In some situations treatment cannot be delayed while a person gets support to make a decision. This can happen in emergency situations or when an urgent decision is required (for example, immediate medical treatment). In these situations, the only practical and appropriate steps might be to keep a person informed of what is happening and why.

**Principle 3**: *'A person is not to be treated as unable to make a decision merely because he makes an unwise decision.' (section 1(4))*

**2.10**    Everybody has their own values, beliefs, preferences and attitudes. A person should not be assumed to lack the capacity to make a decision just because other people think their

---

[1]    Undue influence in relation to consent to medical treatment was considered in Re T (Adult: Refusal of Treatment) [1992] 4 All E R 649, 662 and in financial matters in *Royal Bank of Scotland v. Etridge* [2001] UKHL 44.

decision is unwise. This applies even if family members, friends or healthcare or social care staff are unhappy with a decision.

---

**Scenario: Allowing people to make decisions that others think are unwise**

Mr Garvey is a 40-year-old man with a history of mental health problems. He sees a Community Psychiatric Nurse (CPN) regularly. Mr Garvey decides to spend £2,000 of his savings on a camper van to travel around Scotland for six months. His CPN is concerned that it will be difficult to give Mr Garvey continuous support and treatment while travelling, and that his mental health might deteriorate as a result.

However, having talked it through with his CPN, it is clear that Mr Garvey is fully aware of these concerns and has the capacity to make this particular decision. He has decided he would like to have a break and thinks this will be good for him.

Just because, in the CPN's opinion, continuity of care might be a wiser option, it should not be assumed that Mr Garvey lacks the capacity to make this decision for himself.

---

**2.11**    There may be cause for concern if somebody:

- repeatedly makes unwise decisions that put them at significant risk of harm or exploitation or
- makes a particular unwise decision that is obviously irrational or out of character.

These things do not necessarily mean that somebody lacks capacity. But there might be need for further investigation, taking into account the person's past decisions and choices. For example, have they developed a medical condition or disorder that is affecting their capacity to make particular decisions? Are they easily influenced by undue pressure? Or do they need more information to help them understand the consequences of the decision they are making?

---

**Scenario: Decisions that cause concern**

Cyril, an elderly man with early signs of dementia, spends nearly £300 on fresh fish from a door-to-door salesman. He has always been fond of fish and has previously bought small amounts in this way. Before his dementia, Cyril was always very careful with his money and would never have spent so much on fish in one go.

This decision alone may not automatically mean Cyril now lacks capacity to manage all aspects of his property and affairs. But his daughter makes further enquiries and discovers Cyril has overpaid his cleaner on several occasions – something he has never done in the past. He has also made payments from his savings that he cannot

account for.

His daughter decides it is time to use the registered Lasting Power of Attorney her father made in the past. This gives her the authority to manage Cyril's property and affairs whenever he lacks the capacity to manage them himself. She takes control of Cyril's chequebook to protect him from possible exploitation, but she can still ensure he has enough money to spend on his everyday needs.

---

**Principle 4:** '*An act done, or decision made, under this Act for or on behalf of a person who lacks capacity must be done, or made, in his best interests.*' (*section 1 (5)*)

**2.12**    The principle of acting or making a decision in the best interests of a person who lacks capacity to make the decision in question is a well-established principle in the common law.[2] This principle is now set out in the Act, so that a person's best interests must be the basis for all decisions made and actions carried out on their behalf in situations where they lack capacity to make those particular decisions for themselves. The only exceptions to this are around research (see chapter 11) and advance decisions to refuse treatment (see chapter 9) where other safeguards apply.

2.13  It is impossible to give a single description of what 'best interests' are, because they depend on individual circumstances. However, section 4 of the Act sets out a checklist of steps to follow in order to determine what is in the best interests of a person who lacks capacity to make the decision in question each time someone acts or makes a decision on that person's behalf. See chapter 5 for detailed guidance and examples.

**Principle 5**: *'Before the act is done, or the decision is made, regard must be had to whether the purpose for which it is needed can be as effectively achieved in a way that is less restrictive of the person's rights and freedom of action.' (section 1(6))*

**2.14**    Before somebody makes a decision or acts on behalf of a person who lacks capacity to make that decision or consent to the act, they must always question if they can do something else that would interfere less with the person's basic rights and freedoms. This is called finding the 'less restrictive alternative'. It includes considering whether there is a need to act or make a decision at all.

**2.15**    Where there is more than one option, it is important to explore ways that would be less restrictive or allow the most freedom for a person who lacks capacity to make the decision in question. However, the final decision must always allow the original purpose of the decision or act to be achieved.

**2.16**    Any decision or action must still be in the best interests of the person who lacks capacity. So sometimes it may be necessary to choose an option that is not the least restrictive alternative if that option is in the person's best interests. In practice, the process of choosing a less restrictive option and deciding what is in the person's best interests will be combined. But both principles must be applied each time a decision or action may be taken on behalf of a person who lacks capacity to make the relevant decision.

---

**Scenario: Finding a less restrictive option**

Sunil, a young man with severe learning disabilities, also has a very severe and unpredictable form of epilepsy that is associated with drop attacks. These can result in serious injury. A neurologist has advised that, to limit the harm that might come from these attacks, Sunil should either be under constant close observation, or wear a protective helmet.

After assessment, it is decided that Sunil lacks capacity to decide on the most appropriate course of action for himself. But through his actions and behaviour, Sunil makes it clear he doesn't like to be too closely observed – even though he likes having company.

The staff of the home where he lives consider various options, such as providing a special room for him with soft furnishings, finding ways to keep him under close observation or getting him to wear a helmet. In discussion with Sunil's parents, they

---

[2]    See for example *Re MB (Medical Treatment)* [1997] 2 FLR 426, CA; *Re A (Male Sterilisation)* [2000] 1 FLR 549; *Re S (Sterilisation: Patient's Best Interests)* [2000] 2 FLR 389; *Re F (Adult Patient: Sterilisation)* [2001] Fam 15

agree that the option that is in his best interests, and is less restrictive, will be the helmet – as it will enable him to go out, and prevent further harm.

## 3   HOW SHOULD PEOPLE BE HELPED TO MAKE THEIR OWN DECISIONS?

Before deciding that someone lacks capacity to make a particular decision, it is important to take all practical and appropriate steps to enable them to make that decision themselves (statutory principle 2, see chapter 2). In addition, as section 3(2) of the Act underlines, these steps (such as helping individuals to communicate) must be taken in a way which reflects the person's individual circumstances and meets their particular needs. This chapter provides practical guidance on how to support people to make decisions for themselves, or play as big a role as possible in decision-making.

In this chapter, as throughout the Code, a person's capacity (or lack of capacity) refers specifically to their capacity to make a particular decision at the time it needs to be made.

### Quick summary

To help someone make a decision for themselves, check the following points:

#### PROVIDING RELEVANT INFORMATION

- Does the person have all the relevant information they need to make a particular decision?
- If they have a choice, have they been given information on all the alternatives?

#### COMMUNICATING IN AN APPROPRIATE WAY

- Could information be explained or presented in a way that is easier for the person to understand (for example, by using simple language or visual aids)?
- Have different methods of communication been explored if required, including non-verbal communication?
- Could anyone else help with communication (for example, a family member, support worker, interpreter, speech and language therapist or advocate)?

#### MAKING THE PERSON FEEL AT EASE

- Are there particular times of day when the person's understanding is better?
- Are there particular locations where they may feel more at ease?
- Could the decision be put off to see whether the person can make the decision at a later time when circumstances are right for them?

#### SUPPORTING THE PERSON

- Can anyone else help or support the person to make choices or express a view?

### How can someone be helped to make a decision?

3.1     There are several ways in which people can be helped and supported to enable them to make a decision for themselves. These will vary depending on the decision to be made, the time-scale for making the decision and the individual circumstances of the person making it.

**3.2**    The Act applies to a wide range of people with different conditions that may affect their capacity to make particular decisions. So, the appropriate steps to take will depend on:

■    a person's individual circumstances (for example, somebody with learning difficulties may need a different approach to somebody with dementia)
■    the decision the person has to make and
■    the length of time they have to make it.

**3.3**    Significant, one-off decisions (such as moving house) will require different considerations from day-to-day decisions about a person's care and welfare. However, the same general processes should apply to each decision.

**3.4**    In most cases, only some of the steps described in this chapter will be relevant or appropriate, and the list included here is not exhaustive. It is up to the people (whether family carers, paid carers, healthcare staff or anyone else) caring for or supporting an individual to consider what is possible and appropriate in individual cases. In all cases it is extremely important to find the most effective way of communicating with the person concerned. Good communication is essential for explaining relevant information in an appropriate way and for ensuring that the steps being taken meet an individual's needs.

**3.5**    Providing appropriate help with decision-making should form part of care planning processes for people receiving health or social care services. Examples include:

■    Person Centred Planning for people with learning disabilities
■    the Care Programme Approach for people with mental disorders
■    the Single Assessment Process for older people in England, and
■    the Unified Assessment Process in Wales.

## What happens in emergency situations?

**3.6**    Clearly, in emergency medical situations (for example, where a person collapses with a heart attack or for some unknown reason and is brought unconscious into a hospital), urgent decisions will have to be made and immediate action taken in the person's best interests. In these situations, it may not be practical or appropriate to delay the treatment while trying to help the person make their own decisions, or to consult with any known attorneys or deputies. However, even in emergency situations, healthcare staff should try to communicate with the person and keep them informed of what is happening.

## What information should be provided to people and how should it be provided?

**3.7**    Providing relevant information is essential in all decision-making. For example, to make a choice about what they want for breakfast, people need to know what food is available. If the decision concerns medical treatment, the doctor must explain the purpose and effect of the course of treatment and the likely consequences of accepting or refusing treatment.

**3.8**    All practical and appropriate steps must be taken to help people to make a decision for themselves. Information must be tailored to an individual's needs and abilities. It must also be in the easiest and most appropriate form of communication for the person concerned.

### WHAT INFORMATION IS RELEVANT?

**3.9**    The Act cannot state exactly what information will be relevant in each case. Anyone helping someone to make a decision for themselves should therefore follow these steps.

- Take time to explain anything that might help the person make a decision. It is important that they have access to all the information they need to make an informed decision.
- Try not to give more detail than the person needs – this might confuse them. In some cases, a simple, broad explanation will be enough. But it must not miss out important information.
- What are the risks and benefits? Describe any foreseeable consequences of making the decision, and of not making any decision at all.
- Explain the effects the decision might have on the person and those close to them – including the people involved in their care.
- If they have a choice, give them the same information in a balanced way for all the options.
- For some types of decisions, it may be important to give access to advice from elsewhere. This may be independent or specialist advice (for example, from a medical practitioner or a financial or legal adviser). But it might simply be advice from trusted friends or relatives.

## COMMUNICATION – GENERAL GUIDANCE

**3.10**    To help someone make a decision for themselves, all possible and appropriate means of communication should be tried.

- Ask people who know the person well about the best form of communication (try speaking to family members, carers, day centre staff or support workers). They may also know somebody the person can communicate with easily, or the time when it is best to communicate with them.
- Use simple language. Where appropriate, use pictures, objects or illustrations to demonstrate ideas.
- Speak at the right volume and speed, with appropriate words and sentence structure. It may be helpful to pause to check understanding or show that a choice is available.
- Break down difficult information into smaller points that are easy to understand. Allow the person time to consider and understand each point before continuing.
- It may be necessary to repeat information or go back over a point several times.
- Is help available from people the person trusts (relatives, friends, GP, social worker, religious or community leaders)? If so, make sure the person's right to confidentiality is respected.
- Be aware of cultural, ethnic or religious factors that shape a person's way of thinking, behaviour or communication. For example, in some cultures it is important to involve the community in decision-making. Some religious beliefs (for example, those of Jehovah's Witnesses or Christian Scientists) may influence the person's approach to medical treatment and information about treatment decisions.
- If necessary, consider using a professional language interpreter. Even if a person communicated in English or Welsh in the past, they may have lost some verbal skills (for example, because of dementia). They may now prefer to communicate in their first language. It is often more appropriate to use a professional interpreter rather than to use family members.
- If using pictures to help communication, make sure they are relevant and the person can understand them easily. For example, a red bus may represent a form of transport to one person but a day trip to another.
- Would an advocate (someone who can support and represent the person) improve communication in the current situation? (See chapters 10 and 15 for more information about advocates.)

Scenario: Providing relevant information

Mrs Thomas has Alzheimer's disease and lives in a care home. She enjoys taking part in the activities provided at the home. Today there is a choice between going to a flower show, attending her usual pottery class or watching a DVD. Although she has the capacity to choose, having to decide is making her anxious.

The care assistant carefully explains the different options. She tells Mrs Thomas about the DVD she could watch, but Mrs Thomas doesn't like the sound of it. The care assistant shows her a leaflet about the flower show. She explains the plans for the day, where the show is being held and how long it will take to get there in the mini-van. She has to repeat this information several times, as Mrs Thomas keeps asking whether they will be back in time for supper. She also tells Mrs Thomas that one of her friends is going on the trip.

At first, Mrs Thomas is reluctant to disturb her usual routine. But the care assistant reassures her she will not lose her place at pottery if she misses a class. With this information, Mrs Thomas can therefore choose whether or not to go on the day trip.

## HELPING PEOPLE WITH SPECIFIC COMMUNICATION OR COGNITIVE PROBLEMS

**3.11**    Where people have specific communication or cognitive problems, the following steps can help:

- Find out how the person is used to communicating. Do they use picture boards or Makaton (signs and symbols for people with communication or learning difficulties)? Or do they have a way of communicating that is only known to those close to them?
- If the person has hearing difficulties, use their preferred method of communication (for example, visual aids, written messages or sign language). Where possible, use a qualified interpreter.
- Are mechanical devices such as voice synthesisers, keyboards or other computer equipment available to help?
- If the person does not use verbal communication skills, allow more time to learn how to communicate effectively.
- For people who use non-verbal methods of communication, their behaviour (in particular, changes in behaviour) can provide indications of their feelings.
- Some people may prefer to use non-verbal means of communication and can communicate most effectively in written form using computers or other communication technologies. This is particularly true for those with autistic spectrum disorders.
- For people with specific communication difficulties, consider other types of professional help (for example, a speech and language therapist or an expert in clinical neuropsychology).

Scenario: Helping people with specific communication difficulties

David is a deafblind man with learning disabilities who has no formal communication. He lives in a specialist home. He begins to bang his head against the wall and repeats this behaviour throughout the day. He has not done this before.

The staff in the home are worried and discuss ways to reduce the risk of injury. They come up with a range of possible interventions, aimed at engaging him with activities and keeping him away from objects that could injure him. They assess these as less restrictive ways to ensure he is safe. But David lacks the capacity to make a decision about which would the best option.

The staff call in a specialist in challenging behaviour, who says that David's behaviour is communicative. After investigating this further, staff discover he is in pain because of tooth decay. They consult a dentist about how to resolve this, and the dentist decides it is in David's best interests to get treatment for the tooth decay. After treatment, David's head-banging stops.

## What steps should be taken to put a person at ease?

**3.12** To help put someone at ease and so improve their ability to make a decision, careful consideration should be given to both location and timing.

### LOCATION

**3.13** In terms of location, consider the following:

- Where possible, choose a location where the person feels most at ease. For example, people are usually more comfortable in their own home than at a doctor's surgery.
- Would the person find it easier to make their decision in a relevant location? For example, could you help them decide about medical treatment by taking them to hospital to see what is involved?
- Choose a quiet location where the discussion can't be easily interrupted.
- Try to eliminate any background noise or distractions (for example, the television or radio, or people talking).
- Choose a location where the person's privacy and dignity can be properly respected.

### TIMING

**3.14** In terms of timing, consider the following:

- Try to choose the time of day when the person is most alert – some people are better in the mornings, others are more lively in the afternoon or early evening. It may be necessary to try several times before a decision can be made.
- If the person's capacity is likely to improve in the foreseeable future, wait until it has done so – if practical and appropriate. For example, this might be the case after treatment for depression or a psychotic episode. Obviously, this may not be practical and appropriate if the decision is urgent.
- Some medication could affect a person's capacity (for example, medication which causes drowsiness or affects memory). Can the decision be delayed until side effects have subsided?
- Take one decision at a time – be careful to avoid making the person tired or confused.
- Don't rush – allow the person time to think things over or ask for clarification, where that is possible and appropriate.
- Avoid or challenge time limits that are unnecessary if the decision is not urgent. Delaying the decision may enable further steps to be taken to assist people to make the decision for themselves.

---

**Scenario: Getting the location and timing right**

Luke, a young man, was seriously injured in a road traffic accident and suffered permanent brain damage. He has been in hospital several months, and has made good progress, but he gets very frustrated at his inability to concentrate or do things for himself.

Luke now needs surgical treatment on his leg. During the early morning ward round, the surgeon tries to explain what is involved in the operation. She asks Luke to sign a consent form, but he gets angry and says he doesn't want to talk about it.

His key nurse knows that Luke becomes more alert and capable later in the day. After lunch, she asks him if he would like to discuss the operation again. She also knows that he responds better one-to-one than in a group. So she takes Luke into a private room and repeats the information that the surgeon gave him earlier. He understands why the treatment is needed, what is involved and the likely consequences. Therefore, Luke has the capacity to make a decision about the operation.

## SUPPORT FROM OTHER PEOPLE

**3.15**  In some circumstances, individuals will be more comfortable making decisions when someone else is there to support them.

■ Might the person benefit from having another person present? Sometimes having a relative or friend nearby can provide helpful support and reduce anxiety. However, some people might find this intrusive, and it could increase their anxiety or affect their ability to make a free choice. Find ways of getting the person's views on this, for example, by watching their behaviour towards other people.
■ Always respect a person's right to confidentiality.

---

**Scenario: Getting help from other people**

Jane has a learning disability. She expresses herself using some words, facial expressions and body language. She has lived in her current community home all her life, but now needs to move to a new group home. She finds it difficult to discuss abstract ideas or things she hasn't experienced. Staff conclude that she lacks the capacity to decide for herself which new group home she should move to.

The staff involve an advocate to help Jane express her views. Jane's advocate spends time with her in different environments. The advocate uses pictures, symbols and Makaton to find out the things that are important to Jane, and speaks to people who know Jane to find out what they think she likes. She then supports Jane to show their work to her care manager, and checks that the new homes suggested for her are able to meet Jane's needs and preferences.

When the care manager has found some suitable places, Jane's advocate visits the homes with Jane. They take photos of the houses to help her distinguish between them. The advocate then uses the photos to help Jane work out which home she prefers. Jane's own feelings can now play an important part in deciding what is in her best interests – and so in the final decision about where she will live.

---

## What other ways are there to enable decision-making?

**3.16**  There are other ways to help someone make a decision for themselves.

■ Many people find it helpful to talk things over with people they trust – or people who have been in a similar situation or faced similar dilemmas. For example, people with learning difficulties may benefit from the help of a designated support worker or being part of a support network.
■ If someone is very distressed (for example, following a death of someone close) or where

there are long-standing problems that affect someone's ability to understand an issue, it may be possible to delay a decision so that the person can have psychological therapy, if needed.

■ Some organisations have produced materials to help people who need support to make decisions and for those who support them. Some of this material is designed to help people with specific conditions, such as Alzheimer's disease or profound learning disability.

■ It may be important to provide access to technology. For example, some people who appear not to communicate well verbally can do so very well using computers.

---

**Scenario: Making the most of technology**

Ms Patel has an autistic spectrum disorder. Her family and care staff find it difficult to communicate with her. She refuses to make eye contact, and gets very upset and angry when her carers try to encourage her to speak.

One member of staff notices that Ms Patel is interested in the computer equipment. He shows her how to use the keyboard, and they are able to have a conversation using the computer. An IT specialist works with her to make sure she can make the most of her computing skills to communicate her feelings and decisions.

---

## 4   HOW DOES THE ACT DEFINE A PERSON'S CAPACITY TO MAKE A DECISION AND HOW SHOULD CAPACITY BE ASSESSED?

This chapter explains what the Act means by 'capacity' and 'lack of capacity'. It provides guidance on how to assess whether someone has the capacity to make a decision, and suggests when professionals should be involved in the assessment.

---

In this chapter, as throughout the Code, a person's capacity (or lack of capacity) refers specifically to their capacity to make a particular decision at the time it needs to be made.

---

### Quick summary

This checklist is a summary of points to consider when assessing a person's capacity to make a specific decision. Readers should also refer to the more detailed guidance in this chapter and chapters 2 and 3.

#### PRESUMING SOMEONE HAS CAPACITY

■ The starting assumption must always be that a person has the capacity to make a decision, unless it can be established that they lack capacity.

#### UNDERSTANDING WHAT IS MEANT BY CAPACITY AND LACK OF CAPACITY

■ A person's capacity must be assessed specifically in terms of their capacity to make a particular decision at the time it needs to be made.

#### TREATING EVERYONE EQUALLY

■ A person's capacity must not be judged simply on the basis of their age, appearance, condition or an aspect of their behaviour.

SUPPORTING THE PERSON TO MAKE THE DECISION FOR THEMSELVES

■  It is important to take all possible steps to try to help people make a decision for themselves (see chapter 2, principle 2, and chapter 3).

ASSESSING CAPACITY

Anyone assessing someone's capacity to make a decision for themselves should use the two-stage test of capacity.

■  Does the person have an impairment of the mind or brain, or is there some sort of disturbance affecting the way their mind or brain works? (It doesn't matter whether the impairment or disturbance is temporary or permanent.)
■  If so, does that impairment or disturbance mean that the person is unable to make the decision in question at the time it needs to be made?

ASSESSING ABILITY TO MAKE A DECISION

■  Does the person have a general understanding of what decision they need to make and why they need to make it?
■  Does the person have a general understanding of the likely consequences of making, or not making, this decision?
■  Is the person able to understand, retain, use and weigh up the information relevant to this decision?
■  Can the person communicate their decision (by talking, using sign language or any other means)? Would the services of a professional (such as a speech and language therapist) be helpful?

ASSESSING CAPACITY TO MAKE MORE COMPLEX OR SERIOUS DECISIONS

■  Is there a need for a more thorough assessment (perhaps by involving a doctor or other professional expert)?

## What is mental capacity?

4.1  Mental capacity is the ability to make a decision.

■  This includes the ability to make a decision that affects daily life – such as when to get up, what to wear or whether to go to the doctor when feeling ill – as well as more serious or significant decisions.
■  It also refers to a person's ability to make a decision that may have legal consequences – for them or others. Examples include agreeing to have medical treatment, buying goods or making a will.

4.2  The starting point must always be to assume that a person has the capacity to make a specific decision (see chapter 2, principle 1). Some people may need help to be able to make or communicate a decision (see chapter 3). But this does not necessarily mean that they lack capacity to do so. What matters is their ability to carry out the processes involved in making the decision – and not the outcome.

## What does the Act mean by 'lack of capacity'?

4.3  Section 2(1) of the Act states:

For the purposes of this Act, a person lacks capacity in relation to a matter if at the material time he is unable to make a decision for himself in relation to the matter because of an impairment of, or a disturbance in the functioning of, the mind or brain.

This means that a person lacks capacity if:

- they have an impairment or disturbance (for example, a disability, condition or trauma) that affects the way their mind or brain works, and
- the impairment or disturbance means that they are unable to make a specific decision at the time it needs to be made.

**4.4**    An assessment of a person's capacity must be based on their ability to make a specific decision at the time it needs to be made, and not their ability to make decisions in general. Section 3 of the Act defines what it means to be unable to make a decision (this is explained in paragraph 4.14 below).

**4.5**    Section 2(2) states that the impairment or disturbance does not have to be permanent. A person can lack capacity to make a decision at the time it needs to be made even if:

- the loss of capacity is partial
- the loss of capacity is temporary
- their capacity changes over time.

A person may also lack capacity to make a decision about one issue but not about others.

**4.6**    The Act generally applies to people who are aged 16 or older. Chapter 12 explains how the Act affects children and young people – in particular those aged 16 and 17 years.

## *What safeguards does the Act provide around assessing someone's capacity?*

**4.7**    An assessment that a person lacks capacity to make a decision must never be based simply on:

- their age
- their appearance
- assumptions about their condition, or
- any aspect of their behaviour. (section 2(3))

**4.8**    The Act deliberately uses the word 'appearance', because it covers all aspects of the way people look. So for example, it includes the physical characteristics of certain conditions (for example, scars, features linked to Down's syndrome or muscle spasms caused by cerebral palsy) as well as aspects of appearance like skin colour, tattoos and body piercings, or the way people dress (including religious dress).

**4.9**    The word 'condition' is also wide-ranging. It includes physical disabilities, learning difficulties and disabilities, illness related to age, and temporary conditions (for example, drunkenness or unconsciousness). Aspects of behaviour might include extrovert (for example, shouting or gesticulating) and withdrawn behaviour (for example, talking to yourself or avoiding eye contact).

---

**Scenario: Treating everybody equally**

Tom, a man with cerebral palsy, has slurred speech. Sometimes he also falls over for no obvious reason.

One day Tom falls in the supermarket. Staff call an ambulance, even though he says he is fine. They think he may need treatment after his fall.

When the ambulance comes, the ambulance crew know they must not make assumptions about Tom's capacity to decide about treatment, based simply on his condition and the effects of his disability. They talk to him and find that he is capable of making healthcare decisions for himself.

## What proof of lack of capacity does the Act require?

**4.10**    Anybody who claims that an individual lacks capacity should be able to provide proof. They need to be able to show, on the balance of probabilities, that the individual lacks capacity to make a particular decision, at the time it needs to be made (section 2(4)). This means being able to show that it is more likely than not that the person lacks capacity to make the decision in question.

## What is the test of capacity?

To help determine if a person lacks capacity to make particular decisions, the Act sets out a two-stage test of capacity.

### STAGE 1: DOES THE PERSON HAVE AN IMPAIRMENT OF, OR A DISTURBANCE IN THE FUNCTIONING OF, THEIR MIND OR BRAIN?

**4.11**    Stage 1 requires proof that the person has an impairment of the mind or brain, or some sort of or disturbance that affects the way their mind or brain works. If a person does not have such an impairment or disturbance of the mind or brain, they will not lack capacity under the Act.

**4.12**    Examples of an impairment or disturbance in the functioning of the mind or brain may include the following:

- conditions associated with some forms of mental illness
- dementia
- significant learning disabilities
- the long-term effects of brain damage
- physical or medical conditions that cause confusion, drowsiness or loss of consciousness
- delirium
- concussion following a head injury, and
- the symptoms of alcohol or drug use.

---

**Scenario: Assessing whether an impairment or disturbance is affecting someone's ability to make a decision**

Mrs Collins is 82 and has had a stroke. This has weakened the left-hand side of her body. She is living in a house that has been the family home for years. Her son wants her to sell her house and live with him.

Mrs Collins likes the idea, but her daughter does not. She thinks her mother will lose independence and her condition will get worse. She talks to her mother's consultant to get information that will help stop the sale. But he says that although Mrs Collins is anxious about the physical effects the stroke has had on her body, it has not caused any mental impairment or affected her brain, so she still has capacity to make her own decision about selling her house.

---

**STAGE 2: DOES THE IMPAIRMENT OR DISTURBANCE MEAN THAT THE PERSON IS UNABLE TO MAKE A SPECIFIC DECISION WHEN THEY NEED TO?**

**4.13**    For a person to lack capacity to make a decision, the Act says their impairment or disturbance must affect their ability to make the specific decision when they need to. But first people must be given all practical and appropriate support to help them make the decision for themselves (see chapter 2, principle 2). Stage 2 can only apply if all practical and appropriate support to help the person make the decision has failed. See chapter 3 for guidance on ways of helping people to make their own decisions.

## What does the Act mean by 'inability to make a decision'?

**4.14**    A person is unable to make a decision if they cannot:

1.    understand information about the decision to be made (the Act calls this 'relevant information')
2.    retain that information in their mind
3.    use or weigh that information as part of the decision-making process, or
4.    communicate their decision (by talking, using sign language or any other means). See section 3(1).

**4.15**    These four points are explained in more detail below. The first three should be applied together. If a person cannot do any of these three things, they will be treated as unable to make the decision. The fourth only applies in situations where people cannot communicate their decision in any way.

**UNDERSTANDING INFORMATION ABOUT THE DECISION TO BE MADE**

**4.16**    It is important not to assess someone's understanding before they have been given relevant information about a decision. Every effort must be made to provide information in a way that is most appropriate to help the person to understand. Quick or inadequate explanations are not acceptable unless the situation is urgent (see chapter 3 for some practical steps). Relevant information includes:

■    the nature of the decision
■    the reason why the decision is needed, and
■    the likely effects of deciding one way or another, or making no decision at all.

**4.17**    Section 3(2) outlines the need to present information in a way that is appropriate to meet the individual's needs and circumstances. It also stresses the importance of explaining information using the most effective form of communication for that person (such as simple language, sign language, visual representations, computer support or any other means).

**4.18**    For example:

■    a person with a learning disability may need somebody to read information to them. They might also need illustrations to help them to understand what is happening. Or they might stop the reader to ask what things mean. It might also be helpful for them to discuss information with an advocate.
■    a person with anxiety or depression may find it difficult to reach a decision about treatment in a group meeting with professionals. They may prefer to read the relevant documents in private. This way they can come to a conclusion alone, and ask for help if necessary.
■    someone who has a brain injury might need to be given information several times. It will be necessary to check that the person understands the information. If they have difficulty understanding, it might be useful to present information in a different way (for

example, different forms of words, pictures or diagrams). Written information, audio-tapes, videos and posters can help people remember important facts.

**4.19** Relevant information must include what the likely consequences of a decision would be (the possible effects of deciding one way or another) – and also the likely consequences of making no decision at all (section 3(4)). In some cases, it may be enough to give a broad explanation using simple language. But a person might need more detailed information or access to advice, depending on the decision that needs to be made. If a decision could have serious or grave consequences, it is even more important that a person understands the information relevant to that decision.

---

**Scenario: Providing relevant information in an appropriate format**

Mr Leslie has learning disabilities and has developed an irregular heartbeat. He has been prescribed medication for this, but is anxious about having regular blood tests to check his medication levels. His doctor gives him a leaflet to explain:

- the reason for the tests
- what a blood test involves
- the risks in having or not having the tests, and
- that he has the right to decide whether or not to have the test.

The leaflet uses simple language and photographs to explain these things. Mr Leslie's carer helps him read the leaflet over the next few days, and checks that he understands it.

Mr Leslie goes back to tell the doctor that, even though he is scared of needles, he will agree to the blood tests so that he can get the right medication. He is able to pick out the equipment needed to do the blood test. So the doctor concludes that Mr Leslie can understand, retain and use the relevant information and therefore has the capacity to make the decision to have the test.

---

RETAINING INFORMATION

**4.20** The person must be able to hold the information in their mind long enough to use it to make an effective decision. But section 3(3) states that people who can only retain information for a short while must not automatically be assumed to lack the capacity to decide – it depends on what is necessary for the decision in question. Items such as notebooks, photographs, posters, videos and voice recorders can help people record and retain information.

---

**Scenario: Assessing a person's ability to retain information**

Walter, an elderly man, is diagnosed with dementia and has problems remembering things in the short term. He can't always remember his great-grandchildren's names, but he recognises them when they come to visit. He can also pick them out on photographs.

Walter would like to buy premium bonds (a type of financial investment) for each of his great-grandchildren. He asks his solicitor to make the arrangements. After assessing his capacity to make financial decisions, the solicitor is satisfied that Walter has capacity to make this decision, despite his short-term memory problems.

**USING OR WEIGHING INFORMATION AS PART OF THE DECISION-MAKING PROCESS**

**4.21**    For someone to have capacity, they must have the ability to weigh up information and use it to arrive at a decision. Sometimes people can understand information but an impairment or disturbance stops them using it. In other cases, the impairment or disturbance leads to a person making a specific decision without understanding or using the information they have been given.[3]

**4.22**    For example, a person with the eating disorder anorexia nervosa may understand information about the consequences of not eating. But their compulsion not to eat might be too strong for them to ignore. Some people who have serious brain damage might make impulsive decisions regardless of information they have been given or their understanding of it.

**INABILITY TO COMMUNICATE A DECISION IN ANY WAY**

**4.23**    Sometimes there is no way for a person to communicate. This will apply to very few people, but it does include:

- people who are unconscious or in a coma, or
- those with the very rare condition sometimes known as 'locked-in syndrome', who are conscious but cannot speak or move at all.

If a person cannot communicate their decision in any way at all, the Act says they should be treated as if they are unable to make that decision.

**4.24**    Before deciding that someone falls into this category, it is important to make all practical and appropriate efforts to help them communicate. This might call for the involvement of speech and language therapists, specialists in non-verbal communication or other professionals. Chapter 3 gives advice for communicating with people who have specific disabilities or cognitive problems.

**4.25**    Communication by simple muscle movements can show that somebody can communicate and may have capacity to make a decision.[4] For example, a person might blink an eye or squeeze a hand to say 'yes' or 'no'. In these cases, assessment must use the first three points listed in paragraph 4.14, which are explained in more depth in paragraphs 4.16–4.22.

## What other issues might affect capacity?

**PEOPLE WITH FLUCTUATING OR TEMPORARY CAPACITY**

**4.26**    Some people have fluctuating capacity – they have a problem or condition that gets worse occasionally and affects their ability to make decisions. For example, someone who has manic depression may have a temporary manic phase which causes them to lack capacity to make financial decisions, leading them to get into debt even though at other times they are perfectly able to manage their money. A person with a psychotic illness may have delusions that affect their capacity to make decisions at certain times but disappear at others. Temporary factors may also affect someone's ability to make decisions. Examples include acute illness, severe pain, the effect of medication, or distress after a death or shock. More guidance on how to support someone with fluctuating or temporary capacity to make a

---

[3]    This issue has been considered in a number of court cases, including *Re MB* [1997] 2 FLR 426; *R v. Collins and Ashworth Hospital Authority ex parte Brady* [2001] 58 BMLR 173

[4]    This was demonstrated in the case *Re AK (Adult Patient) (Medical Treatment: Consent)* [2001] 1 FLR 129

decision can be found in chapter 3, particularly paragraphs 3.12–3.16. More information about factors that may indicate that a person may regain or develop capacity in the future can be found at paragraph 5.28.

**4.27**    As in any other situation, an assessment must only examine a person's capacity to make a particular decision when it needs to be made. It may be possible to put off the decision until the person has the capacity to make it (see also guidance on best interests in chapter 5).

## ONGOING CONDITIONS THAT MAY AFFECT CAPACITY

**4.28**    Generally, capacity assessments should be related to a specific decision. But there may be people with an ongoing condition that affects their ability to make certain decisions or that may affect other decisions in their life. One decision on its own may make sense, but may give cause for concern when considered alongside others.

**4.29**    Again, it is important to review capacity from time to time, as people can improve their decision-making capabilities. In particular, someone with an ongoing condition may become able to make some, if not all, decisions. Some people (for example, people with learning disabilities) will learn new skills throughout their life, improving their capacity to make certain decisions. So assessments should be reviewed from time to time. Capacity should always be reviewed:

- whenever a care plan is being developed or reviewed
- at other relevant stages of the care planning process, and
- as particular decisions need to be made.

**4.30**    It is important to acknowledge the difference between:

- unwise decisions, which a person has the right to make (chapter 2, principle 3), and
- decisions based on a lack of understanding of risks or inability to weigh up the information about a decision.

Information about decisions the person has made based on a lack of understanding of risks or inability to weigh up the information can form part of a capacity assessment – particularly if someone repeatedly makes decisions that put them at risk or result in harm to them or someone else.

---

**Scenario: Ongoing conditions**

Paul had an accident at work and suffered severe head injuries. He was awarded compensation to pay for care he will need throughout his life as a result of his head injury. An application was made to the Court of Protection to consider how the award of compensation should be managed, including whether to appoint a deputy to manage Paul's financial affairs. Paul objected as he believed he could manage his life and should be able to spend his money however he liked.

He wrote a list of what he intended to spend his money on. This included fully-staffed luxury properties and holiday villas, cars with chauffeurs, jewellery and various other items for himself and his family. But spending money on all these luxury items would not leave enough money to cover the costs of his care in future years.

The court judged that Paul had capacity to make day-to-day financial decisions, but he did not understand why he had received compensation and what the money was supposed to be used for. Nor did he understand how buying luxuries now could affect his future care. The court therefore decided Paul lacked capacity to manage large amounts of money and appointed a deputy to make ongoing financial decisions relating to his care. But it gave him access to enough funds to cover everyday needs and occasional treats.

## WHAT OTHER LEGAL TESTS OF CAPACITY ARE THERE?

**4.31**    The Act makes clear that the definition of 'lack of capacity' and the two-stage test for capacity set out in the Act are 'for the purposes of this Act'. This means that the definition and test are to be used in situations covered by this Act. Schedule 6 of the Act also amends existing laws to ensure that the definition and test are used in other areas of law not covered directly by this Act.

For example, Schedule 6, paragraph 20 allows a person to be disqualified from jury service if they lack the capacity (using this Act's definition) to carry out a juror's tasks.

**4.32**    There are several tests of capacity that have been produced following judgments in court cases (known as common law tests).[5] These cover:

- capacity to make a will[6]
- capacity to make a gift[7]
- capacity to enter into a contract[8]
- capacity to litigate (take part in legal cases),[9] and
- capacity to enter into marriage.[10]

**4.33**    The Act's new definition of capacity is in line with the existing common law tests, and the Act does not replace them. When cases come before the court on the above issues, judges can adopt the new definition if they think it is appropriate. The Act will apply to all other cases relating to financial, healthcare or welfare decisions.

## When should capacity be assessed?

**4.34**    Assessing capacity correctly is vitally important to everyone affected by the Act. Someone who is assessed as lacking capacity may be denied their right to make a specific decision – particularly if others think that the decision would not be in their best interests or could cause harm. Also, if a person lacks capacity to make specific decisions, that person might make decisions they do not really understand. Again, this could cause harm or put the person at risk. So it is important to carry out an assessment when a person's capacity is in doubt. It is also important that the person who does an assessment can justify their conclusions. Many organisations will provide specific professional guidance for members of their profession.[11]

---

[5]    For details, see British Medical Association & Law Society, *Assessment of Mental Capacity: Guidance for Doctors and Lawyers* (Second edition) (London: BMJ Books, 2004)
[6]    *Banks v. Goodfellow* (1870) LR 5 QB 549
[7]    *Re Beaney (deceased)* [1978] 2 All ER 595
[8]    *Boughton v. Knight* (1873) LR 3 PD 64
[9]    *Masterman-Lister v. Brutton & Co and Jewell & Home Counties Dairies* [2003] 3 All ER 162 (CA)
[10]    *Sheffield City Council v. E & S* [2005] 1 FLR 965
[11]    See for example, British Medical Association & Law Society, *Assessment of Mental Capacity: Guidance for Doctors and Lawyers* (Second edition) (London: BMJ Books, 2004); the Joint Royal Colleges Ambulance Service Liaison Committee Clinical Practice Guidelines (JRCALC, available online at **www2.warwick.ac.uk/fac/med/research/hsri/emergencycare/jrcalc–2006/clinical-guidelines–2006.pdf**) and British Psychological Society, *Guidelines on assessing capacity* (BPS, 2006 available online at **www.bps.org.uk**)

**4.35**    There are a number of reasons why people may question a person's capacity to make a specific decision:

■    the person's behaviour or circumstances cause doubt as to whether they have the capacity to make a decision
■    somebody else says they are concerned about the person's capacity, or
■    the person has previously been diagnosed with an impairment or disturbance that affects the way their mind or brain works (see paragraphs 4.11–4.12 above), and it has already been shown they lack capacity to make other decisions in their life.

**4.36**    The starting assumption must be that the person has the capacity to make the specific decision. If, however, anyone thinks a person lacks capacity, it is important to then ask the following questions:

■    Does the person have all the relevant information they need to make the decision?
■    If they are making a decision that involves choosing between alternatives, do they have information on all the different options?
■    Would the person have a better understanding if information was explained or presented in another way?
■    Are there times of day when the person's understanding is better?
■    Are there locations where they may feel more at ease?
■    Can the decision be put off until the circumstances are different and the person concerned may be able to make the decision?
■    Can anyone else help the person to make choices or express a view (for example, a family member or carer, an advocate or someone to help with communication)?

**4.37**    Chapter 3 describes ways to deal with these questions and suggest steps which may help people make their own decisions. If all practical and appropriate steps fail, an assessment will then be needed of the person's capacity to make the decision that now needs to be made.

## Who should assess capacity?

**4.38**    The person who assesses an individual's capacity to make a decision will usually be the person who is directly concerned with the individual at the time the decision needs to be made. This means that different people will be involved in assessing someone's capacity to make different decisions at different times.

For most day-to-day decisions, this will be the person caring for them at the time a decision must be made. For example, a care worker might need to assess if the person can agree to being bathed. Then a district nurse might assess if the person can consent to have a dressing changed.

**4.39**    For acts of care or treatment (see chapter 6), the assessor must have a 'reasonable belief' that the person lacks capacity to agree to the action or decision to be taken (see paragraphs 4.44–4.45 for a description of reasonable belief).

**4.40**    If a doctor or healthcare professional proposes treatment or an examination, they must assess the person's capacity to consent. In settings such as a hospital, this can involve the multi-disciplinary team (a team of people from different professional backgrounds who share responsibility for a patient). But ultimately, it is up to the professional responsible for the person's treatment to make sure that capacity has been assessed.

**4.41**    For a legal transaction (for example, making a will), a solicitor or legal practitioner must assess the client's capacity to instruct them. They must assess whether the client has the capacity to satisfy any relevant legal test. In cases of doubt, they should get an opinion from a doctor or other professional expert.

**4.42**    More complex decisions are likely to need more formal assessments (see paragraph 4.54 below). A professional opinion on the person's capacity might be necessary. This could be, for example, from a psychiatrist, psychologist, a speech and language therapist, occupational therapist or social worker. But the final decision about a person's capacity must be made by the person intending to make the decision or carry out the action on behalf of the person who lacks capacity – not the professional, who is there to advise.

**4.43**    Any assessor should have the skills and ability to communicate effectively with the person (see chapter 3). If necessary, they should get professional help to communicate with the person.

---

**Scenario: Getting help with assessing capacity**

Ms Dodd suffered brain damage in a road accident and is unable to speak. At first, her family thought she was not able to make decisions. But they soon discovered that she could choose by pointing at things, such as the clothes she wants to wear or the food she prefers. Her behaviour also indicates that she enjoys attending a day centre, but she refuses to go swimming. Her carers have assessed her as having capacity to make these decisions.

Ms Dodd needs hospital treatment but she gets distressed when away from home. Her mother feels that Ms Dodd is refusing treatment by her behaviour, but her father thinks she lacks capacity to say no to treatment that could improve her condition.

The clinician who is proposing the treatment will have to assess Ms Dodd's capacity to consent. He gets help from a member of staff at the day centre who knows Ms Dodd's communication well and also discusses things with her parents. Over several meetings the clinician explains the treatment options to Ms Dodd with the help of the staff member. The final decision about Ms Dodd's capacity rests with the clinician, but he will need to use information from the staff member and others who know Ms Dodd well to make this assessment.

---

## What is 'reasonable belief' of lack of capacity?

**4.44**    Carers (whether family carers or other carers) and care workers do not have to be experts in assessing capacity. But to have protection from liability when providing care or treatment (see chapter 6), they must have a 'reasonable belief' that the person they care for lacks capacity to make relevant decisions about their care or treatment (section 5 (1)). To have this reasonable belief, they must have taken 'reasonable' steps to establish that that the person lacks capacity to make a decision or consent to an act at the time the decision or consent is needed. They must also establish that the act or decision is in the person's best interests (see chapter 5).

They do not usually need to follow formal processes, such as involving a professional to make an assessment. However, if somebody challenges their assessment (see paragraph 4.63 below), they must be able to describe the steps they have taken. They must also have objective reasons for believing the person lacks capacity to make the decision in question.

**4.45**    The steps that are accepted as 'reasonable' will depend on individual circumstances and the urgency of the decision. Professionals, who are qualified in their particular field, are normally expected to undertake a fuller assessment, reflecting their higher degree of knowledge and experience, than family members or other carers who have no formal qualifications. See paragraph 4.36 for a list of points to consider when assessing someone's capacity. The following may also be helpful:

- Start by assuming the person has capacity to make the specific decision. Is there anything to prove otherwise?
- Does the person have a previous diagnosis of disability or mental disorder? Does that condition now affect their capacity to make this decision? If there has been no previous diagnosis, it may be best to get a medical opinion.
- Make every effort to communicate with the person to explain what is happening.
- Make every effort to try to help the person make the decision in question.
- See if there is a way to explain or present information about the decision in a way that makes it easier to understand. If the person has a choice, do they have information about all the options?
- Can the decision be delayed to take time to help the person make the decision, or to give the person time to regain the capacity to make the decision for themselves?
- Does the person understand what decision they need to make and why they need to make it?
- Can they understand information about the decision? Can they retain it, use it and weigh it to make the decision?
- Be aware that the fact that a person agrees with you or assents to what is proposed does not necessarily mean that they have capacity to make the decision.

## What other factors might affect an assessment of capacity?

**4.46**    It is important to assess people when they are in the best state to make the decision, if possible. Whether this is possible will depend on the nature and urgency of the decision to be made. Many of the practical steps suggested in chapter 3 will help to create the best environment for assessing capacity. The assessor must then carry out the two stages of the test of capacity (see paragraphs 4.11–4.25 above).

**4.47**    In many cases, it may be clear that the person has an impairment or disturbance in the functioning of their mind or brain which could affect their ability to make a decision. For example, there might be a past diagnosis of a disability or mental disorder, or there may be signs that an illness is returning. Old assumptions about an illness or condition should be reviewed. Sometimes an illness develops gradually (for example, dementia), and it is hard to know when it starts to affect capacity. Anyone assessing someone's capacity may need to ask for a medical opinion as to whether a person has an illness or condition that could affect their capacity to make a decision in this specific case.

---

**Scenario: Getting a professional opinion**

Mr Elliott is 87 years old and lives alone. He has poor short-term memory, and he often forgets to eat. He also sometimes neglects his personal hygiene. His daughter talks to him about the possibility of moving into residential care. She decides that he understands the reasons for her concerns as well as the risks of continuing to live alone and, having weighed these up, he has the capacity to decide to stay at home and accept the consequences.

Two months later, Mr Elliott has a fall and breaks his leg. While being treated in hospital, he becomes confused and depressed. He says he wants to go home, but the staff think that the deterioration in his mental health has affected his capacity to make this decision at this time. They think he cannot understand the consequences or weigh up the risks he faces if he goes home. They refer him to a specialist in old age psychiatry, who assesses whether his mental health is affecting his capacity to make this decision. The staff will then use the specialist's opinion to help their assessment of Mr Elliott's capacity.

**4.48**    Anyone assessing someone's capacity must not assume that a person lacks capacity simply because they have a particular diagnosis or condition. There must be proof that the diagnosed illness or condition affects the ability to make a decision when it needs to be made. The person assessing capacity should ask the following questions:

- Does the person have a general understanding of what decision they need to make and why they need to make it?
- Do they understand the likely consequences of making, or not making, this decision?
- Can they understand and process information about the decision? And can they use it to help them make a decision?

In borderline cases, or where there is doubt, the assessor must be able to show that it is more likely than not that the answer to these questions is 'no'.

## What practical steps should be taken when assessing capacity?

**4.49**    Anyone assessing someone's capacity will need to decide which of these steps are relevant to their situation.

- They should make sure that they understand the nature and effect of the decision to be made themselves. They may need access to relevant documents and background information (for example, details of the person's finances if assessing capacity to manage affairs). See chapter 16 for details on access to information.
- They may need other relevant information to support the assessment (for example, healthcare records or the views of staff involved in the person's care).
- Family members and close friends may be able to provide valuable background information (for example, the person's past behaviour and abilities and the types of decisions they can currently make). But their personal views and wishes about what they would want for the person must not influence the assessment.
- They should again explain to the person all the information relevant to the decision. The explanation must be in the most appropriate and effective form of communication for that person.
- Check the person's understanding after a few minutes. The person should be able to give a rough explanation of the information that was explained. There are different methods for people who use nonverbal means of communication (for example, observing behaviour or their ability to recognise objects or pictures).
- Avoid questions that need only a 'yes' or 'no' answer (for example, did you understand what I just said?). They are not enough to assess the person's capacity to make a decision. But there may be no alternative in cases where there are major communication difficulties. In these cases, check the response by asking questions again in a different way.
- Skills and behaviour do not necessarily reflect the person's capacity to make specific decisions. The fact that someone has good social or language skills, polite behaviour or good manners doesn't necessarily mean they understand the information or are able to weigh it up.
- Repeating these steps can help confirm the result.

**4.50**    For certain kinds of complex decisions (for example, making a will), there are specific legal tests (see paragraph 4.32 above) in addition to the two-stage test for capacity. In some cases, medical or psychometric tests may also be helpful tools (for example, for assessing cognitive skills) in assessing a person's capacity to make particular decisions, but the relevant legal test of capacity must still be fulfilled.

## When should professionals be involved?

**4.51**   Anyone assessing someone's capacity may need to get a professional opinion when assessing a person's capacity to make complex or major decisions. In some cases this will simply involve contacting the person's general practitioner (GP) or family doctor. If the person has a particular condition or disorder, it may be appropriate to contact a specialist (for example, consultant psychiatrist, psychologist or other professional with experience of caring for patients with that condition). A speech and language therapist might be able to help if there are communication difficulties. In some cases, a multi-disciplinary approach is best. This means combining the skills and expertise of different professionals.

**4.52**   Professionals should never express an opinion without carrying out a proper examination and assessment of the person's capacity to make the decision. They must apply the appropriate test of capacity. In some cases, they will need to meet the person more than once – particularly if the person has communication difficulties. Professionals can get background information from a person's family and carers. But the personal views of these people about what they want for the person who lacks capacity must not influence the outcome of that assessment.

**4.53**   Professional involvement might be needed if:

- the decision that needs to be made is complicated or has serious consequences
- an assessor concludes a person lacks capacity, and the person challenges the finding
- family members, carers and/or professionals disagree about a person's capacity
- there is a conflict of interest between the assessor and the person being assessed
- the person being assessed is expressing different views to different people – they may be trying to please everyone or telling people what they think they want to hear
- somebody might challenge the person's capacity to make the decision – either at the time of the decision or later (for example, a family member might challenge a will after a person has died on the basis that the person lacked capacity when they made the will)
- somebody has been accused of abusing a vulnerable adult who may lack capacity to make decisions that protect them
- a person repeatedly makes decisions that put them at risk or could result in suffering or damage.

---

**Scenario: Involving professional opinion**

Ms Ledger is a young woman with learning disabilities and some autistic spectrum disorders. Recently she began a sexual relationship with a much older man, who is trying to persuade her to move in with him and come off the pill. There are rumours that he has been violent towards her and has taken her bankbook.

Ms Ledger boasts about the relationship to her friends. But she has admitted to her key worker that she is sometimes afraid of the man. Staff at her sheltered accommodation decide to make a referral under the local adult protection procedures. They arrange for a clinical psychologist to assess Ms Ledger's understanding of the relationship and her capacity to consent to it.

---

**4.54**   In some cases, it may be a legal requirement, or good professional practice, to undertake a formal assessment of capacity. These cases include:

- where a person's capacity to sign a legal document (for example, a will), could later be challenged, in which case an expert should be asked for an opinion[12]
- to establish whether a person who might be involved in a legal case needs the assistance of the Official Solicitor or other litigation friend (somebody to represent their views to a court and give instructions to their legal representative) and there is doubt about the person's capacity to instruct a solicitor or take part in the case[13]
- whenever the Court of Protection has to decide if a person lacks capacity in a certain matter
- if the courts are required to make a decision about a person's capacity in other legal proceedings[14]
- if there may be legal consequences of a finding of capacity (for example, deciding on financial compensation following a claim for personal injury).

## Are assessment processes confidential?

**4.55**   People involved in assessing capacity will need to share information about a person's circumstances. But there are ethical codes and laws that require professionals to keep personal information confidential. As a general rule, professionals must ask their patients or clients if they can reveal information to somebody else – even close relatives. But sometimes information may be disclosed without the consent of the person who the information concerns (for example, to protect the person or prevent harm to other people).[15]

**4.56**   Anyone assessing someone's capacity needs accurate information concerning the person being assessed that is relevant to the decision the person has to make. So professionals should, where possible, make relevant information available. They should make every effort to get the person's permission to reveal relevant information. They should give a full explanation of why this is necessary, and they should tell the person about the risks and consequences of revealing, and not revealing information. If the person is unable to give permission, the professional might still be allowed to provide information that will help make an accurate assessment of the person's capacity to make the specific decision. Chapter 16 has more detail on how to access information.

## What if someone refuses to be assessed?

**4.57**   There may be circumstances in which a person whose capacity is in doubt refuses to undergo an assessment of capacity or refuses to be examined by a doctor or other professional. In these circumstances, it might help to explain to someone refusing an assessment why it is needed and what the consequences of refusal are. But threats or attempts to force the person to agree to an assessment are not acceptable.

**4.58**   If the person lacks capacity to agree or refuse, the assessment can normally go ahead, as long as the person does not object to the assessment, and it is in their best interests (see chapter 5).

**4.59**   Nobody can be forced to undergo an assessment of capacity. If someone refuses to open the door to their home, it cannot be forced. If there are serious worries about the person's mental health, it may be possible to get a warrant to force entry and assess the person for treatment in hospital – but the situation must meet the requirements of the Mental Health

---

[12]   *Kenward* v. *Adams*, The Times, 29 November 1975
[13]   Civil Procedure Rules 1998, r 21.1
[14]   *Masterman-Lister* v. *Brutton & Co and Jewell & Home Counties Dairies* [2002] EWCA Civ 1889, CA at 54
[15]   For example, in the circumstances discussed in *W* v. *Egdell and others* [1990] 1 All ER 835 at 848; *S* v. *Plymouth City Council and C*, [2002] EWCA Civ 388) at 49

Act 1983 (section 135). But simply refusing an assessment of capacity is in no way sufficient grounds for an assessment under the Mental Health Act 1983 (see chapter 13).

## Who should keep a record of assessments?

**4.60**   Assessments of capacity to take day-to-day decisions or consent to care require no formal assessment procedures or recorded documentation. Paragraphs 4.44–4.45 above explain the steps to take to reach a 'reasonable belief' that someone lacks capacity to make a particular decision. It is good practice for paid care workers to keep a record of the steps they take when caring for the person concerned.

### PROFESSIONAL RECORDS

**4.61**   It is good practice for professionals to carry out a proper assessment of a person's capacity to make particular decisions and to record the findings in the relevant professional records.

- A doctor or healthcare professional proposing treatment should carry out an assessment of the person's capacity to consent (with a multi-disciplinary team, if appropriate) and record it in the patient's clinical notes.
- Solicitors should assess a client's capacity to give instructions or carry out a legal transaction (obtaining a medical or other professional opinion, if necessary) and record it on the client's file.
- An assessment of a person's capacity to consent or agree to the provision of services will be part of the care planning processes for health and social care needs, and should be recorded in the relevant documentation. This includes:
  - Person Centred Planning for people with learning disabilities
  - the Care Programme Approach for people with mental illness
  - the Single Assessment Process for older people in England, and
  - the Unified Assessment Process in Wales.

### FORMAL REPORTS OR CERTIFICATES OF CAPACITY

**4.62**   In some cases, a more detailed report or certificate of capacity may be required, for example,

- for use in court or other legal processes
- as required by Regulations, Rules or Orders made under the Act.

## How can someone challenge a finding of lack of capacity?

**4.63**   There are likely to be occasions when someone may wish to challenge the results of an assessment of capacity. The first step is to raise the matter with the person who carried out the assessment. If the challenge comes from the individual who is said to lack capacity, they might need support from family, friends or an advocate. Ask the assessor to:

- give reasons why they believe the person lacks capacity to make the decision, and
- provide objective evidence to support that belief.

**4.64**   The assessor must show they have applied the principles of the Mental Capacity Act (see chapter 2). Attorneys, deputies and professionals will need to show that they have also followed guidance in this chapter.

**4.65**   It might be possible to get a second opinion from an independent professional or another expert in assessing capacity. Chapter 15 has other suggestions for dealing with disagreements. But if a disagreement cannot be resolved, the person who is challenging the assessment may be able to apply to the Court of Protection. The Court of Protection can rule on whether a person has capacity to make the decision covered by the assessment (see chapter 8).

## 5   WHAT DOES THE ACT MEAN WHEN IT TALKS ABOUT 'BEST INTERESTS'

One of the key principles of the Act is that any act done for, or any decision made on behalf of a person who lacks capacity must be done, or made, in that person's best interests. That is the same whether the person making the decision or acting is a family carer, a paid care worker, an attorney, a court-appointed deputy, or a healthcare professional, and whether the decision is a minor issue – like what to wear – or a major issue, like whether to provide particular healthcare.

As long as these acts or decisions are in the best interests of the person who lacks capacity to make the decision for themselves, or to consent to acts concerned with their care or treatment, then the decision-maker or carer will be protected from liability.

There are exceptions to this, including circumstances where a person has made an advance decision to refuse treatment (see chapter 9) and, in specific circumstances, the involvement of a person who lacks capacity in research (see chapter 11). But otherwise the underpinning principle of the Act is that all acts and decisions should be made in the best interests of the person without capacity.

Working out what is in someone else's best interests may be difficult, and the Act requires people to follow certain steps to help them work out whether a particular act or decision is in a person's best interests. In some cases, there may be disagreement about what someone's best interests really are. As long as the person who acts or makes the decision has followed the steps to establish whether a person has capacity, and done everything they reasonably can to work out what someone's best interests are, the law should protect them.

This chapter explains what the Act means by 'best interests' and what things should be considered when trying to work out what is in someone's best interests. It also highlights some of the difficulties that might come up in working out what the best interests of a person who lacks capacity to make the decision actually are.

> In this chapter, as throughout the Code, a person's capacity (or lack of capacity) refers specifically to their capacity to make a particular decision at the time it needs to be made.

### Quick summary

A person trying to work out the best interests of a person who lacks capacity to make a particular decision ('lacks capacity') should:

#### ENCOURAGE PARTICIPATION

- do whatever is possible to permit and encourage the person to take part, or to improve their ability to take part, in making the decision

#### IDENTIFY ALL RELEVANT CIRCUMSTANCES

- try to identify all the things that the person who lacks capacity would take into account if they were making the decision or acting for themselves

## FIND OUT THE PERSON'S VIEWS

■    try to find out the views of the person who lacks capacity, including:

–    the person's past and present wishes and feelings – these may have been expressed verbally, in writing or through behaviour or habits.
–    any beliefs and values (e.g. religious, cultural, moral or political) that would be likely to influence the decision in question.
–    any other factors the person themselves would be likely to consider if they were making the decision or acting for themselves.

## AVOID DISCRIMINATION

■    not make assumptions about someone's best interests simply on the basis of the person's age, appearance, condition or behaviour.

## ASSESS WHETHER THE PERSON MIGHT REGAIN CAPACITY

■    consider whether the person is likely to regain capacity (e.g. after receiving medical treatment). If so, can the decision wait until then?

## IF THE DECISION CONCERNS LIFE-SUSTAINING TREATMENT

■    not be motivated in any way by a desire to bring about the person's death. They should not make assumptions about the person's quality of life.

## CONSULT OTHERS

■    if it is practical and appropriate to do so, consult other people for their views about the person's best interests and to see if they have any information about the person's wishes and feelings, beliefs and values. In particular, try to consult:

–    anyone previously named by the person as someone to be consulted on either the decision in question or on similar issues
–    anyone engaged in caring for the person
–    close relatives, friends or others who take an interest in the person's welfare
–    any attorney appointed under a Lasting Power of Attorney or Enduring Power of Attorney made by the person
–    any deputy appointed by the Court of Protection to make decisions for the person.

■    For decisions about major medical treatment or where the person should live and where there is no-one who fits into any of the above categories, an Independent Mental Capacity Advocate (IMCA) must be consulted. (See chapter 10 for more information about IMCAs.)
■    When consulting, remember that the person who lacks the capacity to make the decision or act for themselves still has a right to keep their affairs private – so it would not be right to share every piece of information with everyone.

## AVOID RESTRICTING THE PERSON'S RIGHTS

■    see if there are other options that may be less restrictive of the person's rights.

## TAKE ALL OF THIS INTO ACCOUNT

■    weigh up all of these factors in order to work out what is in the person's best interests.

## *What is the best interests principle and who does it apply to?*

**5.1**    The best interests principle underpins the Mental Capacity Act. It is set out in section 1(5) of the Act.

> An act done, or decision made, under this Act for or on behalf of a person who lacks capacity must be done, or made, in his best interests.

The concept has been developed by the courts in cases relating to people who lack capacity to make specific decisions for themselves, mainly decisions concerned with the provision of medical treatment or social care.

**5.2**    This principle covers all aspects of financial, personal welfare and healthcare decision-making and actions. It applies to anyone making decisions or acting under the provisions of the Act, including:

- family carers, other carers and care workers
- healthcare and social care staff
- attorneys appointed under a Lasting Power of Attorney or registered Enduring Power of Attorney
- deputies appointed by the court to make decisions on behalf of someone who lacks capacity, and
- the Court of Protection.

**5.3**    However, as chapter 2 explained, the Act's first key principle is that people must be assumed to have capacity to make a decision or act for themselves unless it is established that they lack it. That means that working out a person's best interests is only relevant when that person has been assessed as lacking, or is reasonably believed to lack, capacity to make the decision in question or give consent to an act being done.

People with capacity are able to decide for themselves what they want to do. When they do this, they might choose an option that other people don't think is in their best interests. That is their choice and does not, in itself, mean that they lack capacity to make those decisions.

### EXCEPTIONS TO THE BEST INTERESTS PRINCIPLE

**5.4**    There are two circumstances when the best interests principle will not apply. The first is where someone has previously made an advance decision to refuse medical treatment while they had the capacity to do so. Their advance decision should be respected when they lack capacity, even if others think that the decision to refuse treatment is not in their best interests (guidance on advance decisions is given in chapter 9).

The second concerns the involvement in research, in certain circumstances, of someone lacking capacity to consent (see chapter 11).

## *What does the Act mean by best interests?*

**5.5**    The term 'best interests' is not actually defined in the Act. This is because so many different types of decisions and actions are covered by the Act, and so many different people and circumstances are affected by it.

**5.6**    Section 4 of the Act explains how to work out the best interests of a person who lacks capacity to make a decision at the time it needs to be made. This section sets out a checklist of common factors that must always be considered by anyone who needs to decide what is in the best interests of a person who lacks capacity in any particular situation. This checklist is only the starting point: in many cases, extra factors will need to be considered.

5.7    When working out what is in the best interests of the person who lacks capacity to make a decision or act for themselves, decision-makers must take into account all relevant factors that it would be reasonable to consider, not just those that they think are important. They must not act or make a decision based on what they would want to do if they were the person who lacked capacity.

---

**Scenario: Whose best interests?**

Pedro, a young man with a severe learning disability, lives in a care home. He has dental problems which cause him a lot of pain, but refuses to open his mouth for his teeth to be cleaned.

The staff suggest that it would be a good idea to give Pedro an occasional general anaesthetic so that a dentist can clean his teeth and fill any cavities. His mother is worried about the effects of an anaesthetic, but she hates to see him distressed and suggests instead that he should be given strong painkillers when needed.

While the views of Pedro's mother and carers are important in working out what course of action would be in his best interests, the decision must *not* be based on what would be less stressful for them. Instead, it must focus on Pedro's best interests.

Having talked to others, the dentist tries to find ways of involving Pedro in the decision, with the help of his key worker and an advocate, to try to find out the cause and location of the problem and to explain to him that they are trying to stop the pain. The dentist tries to find out if any other forms of dental care would be better, such as a mouthwash or dental gum.

The dentist concludes that it would be in Pedro's best interests for:

- a proper investigation to be carried out under anaesthetic so that immediate treatment can be provided
- options for his future dental care to be reviewed by the care team, involving Pedro as far as possible.

---

## Who can be a decision-maker?

5.8    Under the Act, many different people may be required to make decisions or act on behalf of someone who lacks capacity to make decisions for themselves. The person making the decision is referred to throughout this chapter, and in other parts of the Code, as the 'decision-maker', and it is the decision-maker's responsibility to work out what would be in the best interests of the person who lacks capacity.

- For most day-to-day actions or decisions, the decision-maker will be the carer most directly involved with the person at the time.
- Where the decision involves the provision of medical treatment, the doctor or other member of healthcare staff responsible for carrying out the particular treatment or procedure is the decision-maker.
- Where nursing or paid care is provided, the nurse or paid carer will be the decision-maker.
- If a Lasting Power of Attorney (or Enduring Power of Attorney) has been made and registered, or a deputy has been appointed under a court order, the attorney or deputy will be the decision-maker, for decisions within the scope of their authority.

5.9    What this means is that a range of different decision-makers may be involved with a person who lacks capacity to make different decisions.

**5.10**   In some cases, the same person may make different types of decision for someone who lacks capacity to make decisions for themselves. For instance, a family carer may carry out certain acts in caring for the person on a day-to-day basis, but if they are also an attorney, appointed under a Lasting Power of Attorney (LPA), they may also make specific decisions concerning the person's property and affairs or their personal welfare (depending on what decisions the LPA has been set up to cover).

**5.11**   There are also times when a joint decision might be made by a number of people. For example, when a care plan for a person who lacks capacity to make relevant decisions is being put together, different healthcare or social care staff might be involved in making decisions or recommendations about the person's care package. Sometimes these decisions will be made by a team of healthcare or social care staff as a whole. At other times, the decision will be made by a specific individual within the team. A different member of the team may then implement that decision, based on what the team has worked out to be the person's best interests.

**5.12**   No matter who is making the decision, the most important thing is that the decision-maker tries to work out what would be in the best interests of the person who lacks capacity.

---

**Scenario: Coming to a joint decision**

Jack, a young man with a brain injury, lacks capacity to agree to a rehabilitation programme designed to improve his condition. But the healthcare and social care staff who are looking after him believe that he clearly needs the programme, and have obtained the necessary funding from the Primary Care Trust.

However, Jack's family want to take him home from hospital as they believe they can provide better care for him at home.

A 'best interests' case conference is held, involving Jack, his parents and other family members and the relevant professionals, in order to decide what course of action would be in the Jack's best interests.

A plan is developed to enable Jack to live at home, but attend the day hospital every weekday. Jack seems happy with the proposals and both the family carers and the healthcare and social care staff are satisfied that the plan is in his best interests.

---

### What must be taken into account when trying to work out someone's best interests?

**5.13**   Because every case – and every decision – is different, the law can't set out all the factors that will need to be taken into account in working out someone's best interests. But section 4 of the Act sets out some common factors that must always be considered when trying to work out someone's best interests. These factors are summarised in the checklist here:

- Working out what is in someone's best interests cannot be based simply on someone's age, appearance, condition or behaviour. (see paragraphs 5.16–5.17).
- All relevant circumstances should be considered when working out someone's best interests (paragraphs 5.18–5.20).
- Every effort should be made to encourage and enable the person who lacks capacity to take part in making the decision (paragraphs 5.21–5.24).
- If there is a chance that the person will regain the capacity to make a particular decision, then it may be possible to put off the decision until later if it is not urgent (paragraphs 5.25–5.28).

- Special considerations apply to decisions about life-sustaining treatment (paragraphs 5.29–5.36).
- The person's past and present wishes and feelings, beliefs and values should be taken into account (paragraphs 5.37–5.48).
- The views of other people who are close to the person who lacks capacity should be considered, as well as the views of an attorney or deputy (paragraphs 5.49–5.55).

It's important not to take shortcuts in working out best interests, and a proper and objective assessment must be carried out on every occasion. If the decision is urgent, there may not be time to examine all possible factors, but the decision must still be made in the best interests of the person who lacks capacity. Not all the factors in the checklist will be relevant to all types of decisions or actions, and in many cases other factors will have to be considered as well, even though some of them may then not be found to be relevant.

**5.14**    What is in a person's best interests may well change over time. This means that even where similar actions need to be taken repeatedly in connection with the person's care or treatment, the person's best interests should be regularly reviewed.

**5.15**    Any staff involved in the care of a person who lacks capacity should make sure a record is kept of the process of working out the best interests of that person for each relevant decision, setting out:

- how the decision about the person's best interests was reached
- what the reasons for reaching the decision were
- who was consulted to help work out best interests, and
- what particular factors were taken into account.

This record should remain on the person's file.

For major decisions based on the best interests of a person who lacks capacity, it may also be useful for family and other carers to keep a similar kind of record.

## What safeguards does the Act provide around working out someone's best interests?

**5.16**    Section 4(1) states that anyone working out someone's best interests must not make unjustified assumptions about what their best interests might be simply on the basis of the person's age, appearance, condition or any aspect of their behaviour. In this way, the Act ensures that people who lack capacity to make decisions for themselves are not subject to discrimination or treated any less favourably than anyone else.

**5.17**    'Appearance' is a broad term and refers to all aspects of physical appearance, including skin colour, mode of dress and any visible medical problems, disfiguring scars or other disabilities. A person's 'condition' also covers a range of factors including physical disabilities, learning difficulties or disabilities, age-related illness or temporary conditions (such as drunkenness or unconsciousness). 'Behaviour' refers to behaviour that might seem unusual to others, such as talking too loudly or laughing inappropriately.

---

**Scenario: Following the checklist**

Martina, an elderly woman with dementia, is beginning to neglect her appearance and personal hygiene and has several times been found wandering in the street unable to find her way home. Her care workers are concerned that Martina no longer has capacity to make appropriate decisions relating to her daily care. Her daughter is her personal welfare attorney and believes the time has come to act under the Lasting Power of Attorney (LPA).

She assumes it would be best for Martina to move into a care home, since the staff would be able to help her wash and dress smartly and prevent her from wandering.

However, it cannot be assumed *simply on the basis of her age, condition, appearance or behaviour* either that Martina lacks capacity to make such a decision or that such a move would be in her best interests.

Instead, steps must be taken to assess her capacity. If it is then agreed that Martina lacks the capacity to make this decision, all the relevant factors in the best interests' checklist must be considered to try to work out what her best interests would be.

Her daughter must therefore consider:

- Martina's past and present wishes and feelings
- the views of the people involved in her care
- any alternative ways of meeting her care needs effectively which might be less restrictive of Martina's rights and freedoms, such as increased provision of home care or attendance at a day centre.

By following this process, Martina's daughter can then take decisions on behalf of her mother and in her best interests, when her mother lacks the capacity to make them herself, on any matters that fall under the authority of the LPA.

## How does a decision-maker work out what 'all relevant circumstances' are?

5.18   When trying to work out someone's best interests, the decision-maker should try to identify all the issues that would be most relevant to the individual who lacks capacity and to the particular decision, as well as those in the 'checklist'. Clearly, it is not always possible or practical to investigate in depth every issue which may have some relevance to the person who lacks capacity or the decision in question. So relevant circumstances are defined in section 4(11) of the Act as those:

(a)    of which the person making the determination is aware, and
(b)    which it would be reasonable to regard as relevant.

5.19   The relevant circumstances will of course vary from case to case. For example, when making a decision about major medical treatment, a doctor would need to consider the clinical needs of the patient, the potential benefits and burdens of the treatment on the person's health and life expectancy and any other factors relevant to making a professional judgement.[16] But it would not be reasonable to consider issues such as life expectancy when working out whether it would be in someone's best interests to be given medication for a minor problem.

5.20   Financial decisions are another area where the relevant circumstances will vary. For example, if a person had received a substantial sum of money as compensation for an accident resulting in brain injury, the decision-maker would have to consider a wide range of circumstances when making decisions about how the money is spent or invested, such as:

- whether the person's condition is likely to change
- whether the person needs professional care, and
- whether the person needs to live somewhere else to make it easier for them.

These kinds of issues can only be decided on a case-by-case basis.

---

[16] *An Hospital NHS Trust v. S* [2003] EWHC 365 (Fam), paragraph 47

## How should the person who lacks capacity be involved in working out their best interests?

**5.21**   Wherever possible, the person who lacks capacity to make a decision should still be involved in the decision-making process (section 4(4)).

**5.22**   Even if the person lacks capacity to make the decision, they may have views on matters affecting the decision, and on what outcome would be preferred. Their involvement can help work out what would be in their best interests.

**5.23**   The decision-maker should make sure that all practical means are used to enable and encourage the person to participate as fully as possible in the decision-making process and any action taken as a result, or to help the person improve their ability to participate.

**5.24**   Consulting the person who lacks capacity will involve taking time to explain what is happening and why a decision needs to be made. Chapter 3 includes a number of practical steps to assist and enable decision-making which may be also be helpful in encouraging greater participation. These include:

■   using simple language and/or illustrations or photographs to help the person understand the options
■   asking them about the decision at a time and location where the person feels most relaxed and at ease
■   breaking the information down into easy-to-understand points
■   using specialist interpreters or signers to communicate with the person.

This may mean that other people are required to communicate with the person to establish their views. For example, a trusted relative or friend, a full-time carer or an advocate may be able to help the person to express wishes or aspirations or to indicate a preference between different options.

More information on all of these steps can be found in chapter 3.

---

**Scenario: Involving someone in working out their best interests**

The parents of Amy, a young woman with learning difficulties, are going through a divorce and are arguing about who should continue to care for their daughter. Though she cannot understand what is happening, attempts are made to see if Amy can give some indication of where she would prefer to live.

An advocate is appointed to work with Amy to help her understand the situation and to find out her likes and dislikes and matters which are important to her. With the advocate's help, Amy is able to participate in decisions about her future care.

---

## How do the chances of someone regaining and developing capacity affect working out what is in their best interests?

**5.25**   There are some situations where decisions may be deferred, if someone who currently lacks capacity may regain the capacity to make the decision for themselves. Section 4(3) of the Act requires the decision-maker to consider:

■   whether the individual concerned is likely to regain the capacity to make that particular decision in the future, and
■   if so, when that is likely to be.

It may then be possible to put off the decision until the person can make it for themselves.

**5.26**   In emergency situations – such as when urgent medical treatment is needed – it may *not* be possible to wait to see if the person may regain capacity so they can decide for themselves whether or not to have the urgent treatment.

**5.27**   Where a person currently lacks capacity to make a decision relating to their day-to-day care, the person may – over time and with the right support – be able to develop the skills to do so. Though others may need to make the decision on the person's behalf at the moment, all possible support should be given to that person to enable them to develop the skills so that they can make the decision for themselves in the future.

---

**Scenario: Taking a short-term decision for someone who may regain capacity**

Mr Fowler has suffered a stroke leaving him severely disabled and unable to speak. Within days, he has shown signs of improvement, so with intensive treatment there is hope he will recover over time. But at present both his wife and the hospital staff find it difficult to communicate with him and have been unable to find out his wishes.

He has always looked after the family finances, so Mrs Fowler suddenly discovers she has no access to his personal bank account to provide the family with money to live on or pay the bills. Because the decision can't be put off while efforts are made to find effective means of communicating with Mr Fowler, an application is made to the Court of Protection for an order that allows Mrs Fowler to access Mr Fowler's money.

The decision about longer-term arrangements, on the other hand, can be delayed until alternative methods of communication have been tried and the extent of Mr Fowler's recovery is known.

---

**5.28**   Some factors which may indicate that a person may regain or develop capacity in the future are:

- the cause of the lack of capacity can be treated, either by medication or some other form of treatment or therapy
- the lack of capacity is likely to decrease in time (for example, where it is caused by the effects of medication or alcohol, or following a sudden shock)
- a person with learning disabilities may learn new skills or be subject to new experiences which increase their understanding and ability to make certain decisions
- the person may have a condition which causes capacity to come and go at various times (such as some forms of mental illness) so it may be possible to arrange for the decision to be made during a time when they do have capacity
- a person previously unable to communicate may learn a new form of communication (see chapter 3).

## How should someone's best interests be worked out when making decisions about life-sustaining treatment?

**5.29**   A special factor in the checklist applies to decisions about treatment which is necessary to keep the person alive ('life-sustaining treatment') and this is set out in section 4(5) of the Act. The fundamental rule is that anyone who is deciding whether or not life-sustaining treatment is in the best interests of someone who lacks capacity to consent to or refuse such treatment must not be motivated by a desire to bring about the person's death.

**5.30**   Whether a treatment is 'life-sustaining' depends not only on the type of treatment, but also on the particular circumstances in which it may be prescribed. For example, in some situations giving antibiotics may be life-sustaining, whereas in other circumstances antibiotics are used to treat a non-life-threatening condition. It is up to the doctor or healthcare professional providing treatment to assess whether the treatment is life-sustaining in each particular situation.

**5.31** All reasonable steps which are in the person's best interests should be taken to prolong their life. There will be a limited number of cases where treatment is futile, overly burdensome to the patient or where there is no prospect of recovery. In circumstances such as these, it may be that an assessment of best interests leads to the conclusion that it would be in the best interests of the patient to withdraw or withhold life-sustaining treatment, even if this may result in the person's death. The decision-maker must make a decision based on the best interests of the person who lacks capacity. They must not be motivated by a desire to bring about the person's death for whatever reason, even if this is from a sense of compassion. Healthcare and social care staff should also refer to relevant professional guidance when making decisions regarding life-sustaining treatment.

**5.32** As with all decisions, before deciding to withdraw or withhold life-sustaining treatment, the decision-maker must consider the range of treatment options available to work out what would be in the person's best interests. All the factors in the best interests checklist should be considered, and in particular, the decision-maker should consider any statements that the person has previously made about their wishes and feelings about life-sustaining treatment.

**5.33** Importantly, section 4(5) cannot be interpreted to mean that doctors are under an obligation to provide, or to continue to provide, life-sustaining treatment where that treatment is not in the best interests of the person, even where the person's death is foreseen. Doctors must apply the best interests' checklist and use their professional skills to decide whether life-sustaining treatment is in the person's best interests. If the doctor's assessment is disputed, and there is no other way of resolving the dispute, ultimately the Court of Protection may be asked to decide what is in the person's best interests.

**5.34** Where a person has made a written statement in advance that requests particular medical treatments, such as artificial nutrition and hydration (ANH), these requests should be taken into account by the treating doctor in the same way as requests made by a patient who has the capacity to make such decisions. Like anyone else involved in making this decision, the doctor must weigh written statements alongside all other relevant factors to decide whether it is in the best interests of the patient to provide or continue life-sustaining treatment.

**5.35** If someone has made an advance decision to refuse life-sustaining treatment, specific rules apply. More information about these can be found in chapter 9 and in paragraph 5.45 below.

**5.36** As mentioned in paragraph 5.33 above, where there is any doubt about the patient's best interests, an application should be made to the Court of Protection for a decision as to whether withholding or withdrawing life-sustaining treatment is in the patient's best interests.

## *How do a person's wishes and feelings, beliefs and values affect working out what is in their best interests?*

**5.37** Section 4(6) of the Act requires the decision-maker to consider, as far as they are 'reasonably ascertainable':

(a)    the person's past and present wishes and feelings (and in particular, any relevant written statements made by him when he had capacity),

(b)    the beliefs and values that would be likely to influence his decision if he had capacity, and

(c)    the other factors that he would be likely to consider if he were able to do so.

Paragraphs 5.38–5.48 below give further guidance on each of these factors.

**5.38**    In setting out the requirements for working out a person's 'best interests', section 4 of the Act puts the person who lacks capacity at the centre of the decision to be made. Even if they cannot make the decision, their wishes and feelings, beliefs and values should be taken fully into account – whether expressed in the past or now. But their wishes and feelings, beliefs and values will not necessarily be the deciding factor in working out their best interests. Any such assessment must consider past and current wishes and feelings, beliefs and values alongside all other factors, but the final decision must be based entirely on what is in the person's best interests.

---

**Scenario: Considering wishes and feelings as part of best interests**

Andre, a young man with severe learning disabilities who does not use any formal system of communication, cuts his leg while outdoors. There is some earth in the wound. A doctor wants to give him a tetanus jab, but Andre appears scared of the needle and pushes it away. Assessments have shown that he is unable to understand the risk of infection following his injury, or the consequences of rejecting the injection.

The doctor decides that it is in the Andre's best interests to give the vaccination. She asks a nurse to comfort Andre, and if necessary, restrain him while she gives the injection. She has objective reasons for believing she is acting in Andre's best interests, and for believing that Andre lacks capacity to make the decision for himself. So she should be protected from liability under section 5 of the Act (see chapter 6).

---

**WHAT IS 'REASONABLY ASCERTAINABLE'?**

**5.39**    How much someone can learn about a person's past and present views will depend on circumstances and the time available. 'Reasonably ascertainable' means considering all possible information in the time available. What is available in an emergency will be different to what is available in a non-emergency. But even in an emergency, there may still be an opportunity to try to communicate with the person or his friends, family or carers (see chapter 3 for guidance on helping communication).

**WHAT ROLE DO A PERSON'S PAST AND PRESENT WISHES AND FEELINGS PLAY?**

**5.40**    People who cannot express their current wishes and feelings in words may express themselves through their behaviour. Expressions of pleasure or distress and emotional responses will also be relevant in working out what is in their best interests. It is also important to be sure that other people have not influenced a person's views. An advocate could help the person make choices and express their views.

**5.41**    The person may have held strong views in the past which could have a bearing on the decision now to be made. All reasonable efforts must be made to find out whether the person has expressed views in the past that will shape the decision to be made. This could have been through verbal communication, writing, behaviour or habits, or recorded in any other way (for example, home videos or audiotapes).

**5.42**    Section 4(6)(a) places special emphasis on written statements the person might have made before losing capacity. These could provide a lot of information about a person's wishes. For example, these statements could include information about the type of medical treatment they would want in the case of future illness, where they would prefer to live, or how they wish to be cared for.

**5.43**    The decision-maker should consider written statements carefully. If their decision does not follow something a person has put in writing, they must record the reasons why. They should be able to justify their reasons if someone challenges their decision.

**5.44**    A doctor should take written statements made by a person before losing capacity which request specific treatments as seriously as those made by people who currently have capacity to make treatment decisions. But they would not have to follow a written request if they think the specific treatment would be clinically unnecessary or not appropriate for the person's condition, so not in the person's best interests.

**5.45**    It is important to note the distinction between a written statement expressing treatment preferences and a statement which constitutes an advance decision to refuse treatment. This is covered by section 24 of the Act, and it has a different status in law. Doctors cannot ignore a written statement that is a valid advance decision to refuse treatment. An advance decision to refuse treatment must be followed if it meets the Act's requirements and applies to the person's circumstances. In these cases, the treatment must not be given (see chapter 9 for more information). If there is not a valid and applicable advance decision, treatment should be provided based on the person's best interests.

### WHAT ROLE DO BELIEFS AND VALUES PLAY?

5.46  Everybody's values and beliefs influence the decisions they make. They may become especially important for someone who lacks capacity to make a decision because of a progressive illness such as dementia, for example. Evidence of a person's beliefs and values can be found in things like their:

- cultural background
- religious beliefs
- political convictions, or
- past behaviour or habits.

Some people set out their values and beliefs in a written statement while they still have capacity.

---

Scenario: Considering beliefs and values

Anita, a young woman, suffers serious brain damage during a car accident. The court appoints her father as deputy to invest the compensation she received. As the decision-maker he must think about her wishes, beliefs and values before deciding how to invest the money.

Anita had worked for an overseas charity. Her father talks to her former colleagues. They tell him how Anita's political beliefs shaped her work and personal beliefs, so he decides not to invest in the bonds that a financial adviser had recommended, because they are from companies Anita would not have approved of. Instead, he employs an ethical investment adviser to choose appropriate companies in line with her beliefs.

**WHAT OTHER FACTORS SHOULD A DECISION-MAKER CONSIDER?**

**5.47**    Section 4(6)(c) of the Act requires decision-makers to consider any other factors the person who lacks capacity would consider if they were able to do so. This might include the effect of the decision on other people, obligations to dependants or the duties of a responsible citizen.

**5.48**    The Act allows actions that benefit other people, as long as they are in the best interests of the person who lacks capacity to make the decision. For example, having considered all the circumstances of the particular case, a decision might be made to take a blood sample from a person who lacks capacity to consent, to check for a genetic link to cancer within the family, because this might benefit someone else in the family. But it might still be in the best interests of the person who lacks capacity. 'Best interests' goes beyond the person's medical interests.

For example, courts have previously ruled that possible wider benefits to a person who lacks capacity to consent, such as providing or gaining emotional support from close relationships, are important factors in working out the person's own best interests.[17] If it is likely that the person who lacks capacity would have considered these factors themselves, they can be seen as part of the person's best interests.

## Who should be consulted when working out someone's best interests?

**5.49**    The Act places a duty on the decision-maker to consult other people close to a person who lacks capacity, where practical and appropriate, on decisions affecting the person and what might be in the person's best interests. This also applies to those involved in caring for the person and interested in the person's welfare. Under section 4(7), the decision-maker has a duty to take into account the views of the following people, where it is practical and appropriate to do so:

- anyone the person has previously named as someone they want to be consulted
- anyone involved in caring for the person
- anyone interested in their welfare (for example, family carers, other close relatives, or an advocate already working with the person)
- an attorney appointed by the person under a Lasting Power of Attorney, and
- a deputy appointed for that person by the Court of Protection.

**5.50**    If there is no-one to speak to about the person's best interests, in some circumstances the person may qualify for an Independent Mental Capacity Advocate (IMCA). For more information on IMCAs, see chapter 10.

**5.51**    Decision-makers must show they have thought carefully about who to speak to. If it is practical and appropriate to speak to the above people, they must do so and must take their views into account. They must be able to explain why they did not speak to a particular person – it is good practice to have a clear record of their reasons. It is also good practice to give careful consideration to the views of family carers, if it is possible to do so.

**5.52**    It is also good practice for healthcare and social care staff to record at the end of the process why they think a specific decision is in the person's best interests. This is particularly important if healthcare and social care staff go against the views of somebody who has been consulted while working out the person's best interests.

**5.53**    The decision-maker should try to find out:

---

[17]    See for example *Re Y (Mental Incapacity: Bone marrow transplant)* [1996] 2 FLR 787; *Re A (Male Sterilisation)* [2000] 1 FLR 549

- what the people consulted think is in the person's best interests in this matter, and
- if they can give information on the person's wishes and feelings, beliefs and values.

**5.54**    This information may be available from somebody the person named before they lost capacity as someone they wish to be consulted. People who are close to the person who lacks capacity, such as close family members, are likely to know them best. They may also be able to help with communication or interpret signs that show the person's present wishes and feelings. Everybody's views are equally important – even if they do not agree with each other. They must be considered alongside the views of the person who lacks capacity and other factors. See paragraphs 5.62–5.69 below for guidance on dealing with conflicting views.

---

**Scenario: Considering other people's views**

Lucia, a young woman with severe brain damage, is cared for at home by her parents and attends a day centre a couple of days each week. The day centre staff would like to take some of the service users on holiday. They speak to Lucia's parents as part of the process of assessing whether the holiday would be in her best interests.

The parents think that the holiday would be good for her, but they are worried that Lucia gets very anxious if she is surrounded by strangers who don't know how to communicate with her. Having tried to seek Lucia's views and involve her in the decision, the staff and parents agree that a holiday would be in her best interests, as long as her care assistant can go with her to help with communication.

---

**5.55**    Where an attorney has been appointed under a Lasting Power of Attorney or Enduring Power of Attorney, or a deputy has been appointed by a court, they must make the decisions on any matters they have been appointed to deal with. Attorneys and deputies should also be consulted, if practical and appropriate, on other issues affecting the person who lacks capacity.

For instance, an attorney who is appointed only to look after the person's property and affairs may have information about the person's beliefs and values, wishes and feelings, that could help work out what would be in the person's best interests regarding healthcare or treatment decisions. (See chapters 7 and 8 for more information about the roles of attorneys and deputies.)

## How can decision-makers respect confidentiality?

**5.56**    Decision-makers must balance the duty to consult other people with the right to confidentiality of the person who lacks capacity. So if confidential information is to be discussed, they should only seek the views of people who it is appropriate to consult, where their views are relevant to the decision to be made and the particular circumstances.

**5.57**    There may be occasions where it is in the person's best interests for personal information (for example, about their medical condition, if the decision concerns the provision of medical treatment) to be revealed to the people consulted as part of the process of working out their best interests (further guidance on this is given in chapter 16). Healthcare and social care staff who are trying to determine a person's best interests must follow their professional guidance, as well as other relevant guidance, about confidentiality.

## When does the best interests principle apply?

**5.58**    Section 1(5) of the Act confirms that the principle applies to any act done, or any decision made, on behalf of someone where there is reasonable belief that the person lacks capacity under the Act. This covers informal day-to-day decisions and actions as well as decisions made by the courts.

## REASONABLE BELIEF ABOUT A PERSON'S BEST INTERESTS

**5.59**    Section 4(9) confirms that if someone acts or makes a decision in the reasonable belief that what they are doing is in the best interests of the person who lacks capacity, then – provided they have followed the checklist in section 4 – they will have complied with the best interests principle set out in the Act. Coming to an incorrect conclusion about a person's capacity or best interests does not necessarily mean that the decision-maker would not get protection from liability (this is explained in chapter 6). But they must be able to show that it was reasonable for them to think that the person lacked capacity and that they were acting in the person's best interests at the time they made their decision or took action.

**5.60**    Where there is a need for a court decision, the court is likely to require formal evidence of what might be in the person's best interests. This will include evidence from relevant professionals (for example, psychiatrists or social workers). But in most day-to-day situations, there is no need for such formality. In emergency situations, it may not be practical or possible to gather formal evidence.

**5.61**    Where the court is not involved, people are still expected to have reasonable grounds for believing that they are acting in somebody's best interests. This does not mean that decision-makers can simply impose their own views. They must have objective reasons for their decisions – and they must be able to demonstrate them. They must be able to show they have considered all relevant circumstances and applied all elements of the best interests checklist.

---

**Scenario: Demonstrating reasonable belief**

Mrs Prior is mugged and knocked unconscious. She is brought to hospital without any means of identification. She has head injuries and a stab wound, and has lost a lot of blood. In casualty, a doctor arranges an urgent blood transfusion. Because this is necessary to save her life, the doctor believes this is in her best interests.

When her relatives are contacted, they say that Mrs Prior's beliefs meant that she would have refused all blood products. But since Mrs Prior's handbag had been stolen, the doctor had no idea who the woman was nor what her beliefs her. He needed to make an immediate decision and Mrs Prior lacked capacity to make the decision for herself. Therefore he had reasonable grounds for believing that his action was in his patient's best interests – and so was protected from liability.

Now that the doctor knows Mrs Prior's beliefs, he can take them into account in future decisions about her medical treatment if she lacks capacity to make them for herself. He can also consult her family, now that he knows where they are.

---

## What problems could arise when working out someone's best interests?

**5.62**    It is important that the best interests principle and the statutory checklist are flexible. Without flexibility, it would be impossible to prioritise factors in different cases – and it would be difficult to ensure that the outcome is the best possible for the person who lacks capacity to make the particular decision. Some cases will be straightforward. Others will require decision-makers to balance the pros and cons of all relevant factors.[18] But this flexibility could lead to problems in reaching a conclusion about a person's best interests.

## WHAT HAPPENS WHEN THERE ARE CONFLICTING CONCERNS?

**5.63**    A decision-maker may be faced with people who disagree about a person's best interests. Family members, partners and carers may disagree between themselves. Or they might have different memories about what views the person expressed in the past. Carers and family might disagree with a professional's view about the person's care or treatment needs.

**5.64**    The decision-maker will need to find a way of balancing these concerns or deciding between them. The first approach should be to review all elements of the best interests checklist with everyone involved. They should include the person who lacks capacity (as much as they are able to take part) and anyone who has been involved in earlier discussions. It may be possible to reach an agreement at a meeting to air everyone's concerns. But an agreement in itself might not be in the person's best interests. Ultimate responsibility for working out best interests lies with the decision-maker.

---

**Scenario: Dealing with disagreement**

Some time ago, Mr Graham made a Lasting Power of Attorney (LPA) appointing his son and daughter as joint attorneys to manage his finances and property. He now has Alzheimer's disease and has moved into private residential care. The son and daughter have to decide what to do with Mr Graham's house.

His son thinks it is in their father's best interests to sell it and invest the money for Mr Graham's future care. But his daughter thinks it is in Mr Graham's best interests to keep the property, because he enjoys visiting and spending time in his old home.

After making every effort to get Mr Graham's views, the family meets to discuss all the issues involved. After hearing other family views, the attorneys agree that it would be in their father's best interests to keep the property for so long as he is able to enjoy visiting it.

---

## FAMILY, PARTNERS AND CARERS WHO ARE CONSULTED

**5.65**    If disagreement continues, the decision-maker will need to weigh up the views of different parties. This will depend entirely upon the circumstances of each case, the people involved and their relationship with the person who lacks capacity. Sometimes the decision-maker will find that carers have an insight into how to interpret a person's wishes and feelings that can help them reach a decision.

**5.66**    At the same time, paid care workers and voluntary sector support workers may have specialist knowledge about up-to-date care options or treatments. Some may also have known the person for many years.

**5.67**    People with conflicting interests should not be cut out of the process (for example, those who stand to inherit from the person's will may still have a right to be consulted about the person's care or medical treatment). But decision-makers must always ensure that the interests of those consulted do not overly influence the process of working out a person's best interests. In weighing up different contributions, the decision-maker should consider:

- how long an individual has known the person who lacks capacity, and
- what their relationship is.

---

[18]   *Re A (Male Sterilisation)* [2000] 1 FLR 549

---

**Scenario: Settling disagreements**

Robert is 19 and has learning disabilities and autism. He is about to leave his residential special school. His parents want Robert to go to a specialist unit run by a charitable organisation, but he has been offered a place in a local supported living scheme. The parents don't think Robert will get appropriate care there.

The school sets up a 'best interests' meeting. People who attend include Robert, his parents, teachers from his school and professionals involved in preparing Robert's care plan. Robert's parents and teachers know him best. They set out their views and help Robert to communicate where he would like to live.

Social care staff identify some different placements within the county. Robert visits these with his parents. After further discussion, everyone agrees that a community placement near his family home would be in Robert's best interests.

---

### SETTLING DISPUTES ABOUT BEST INTERESTS

**5.68**   If someone wants to challenge a decision-maker's conclusions, there are several options:

- Involve an advocate to act on behalf of the person who lacks capacity to make the decision (see paragraph 5.69 below).
- Get a second opinion.
- Hold a formal or informal 'best interests' case conference.
- Attempt some form of mediation (see chapter 15).
- Pursue a complaint through the organisation's formal procedures.

Ultimately, if all other attempts to resolve the dispute have failed, the court might need to decide what is in the person's best interests. Chapter 8 provides more information about the Court of Protection.

### ADVOCACY

**5.69**   An advocate might be useful in providing support for the person who lacks capacity to make a decision in the process of working out their best interests, if:

- the person who lacks capacity has no close family or friends to take an interest in their welfare, and they do not qualify for an Independent Mental Capacity Advocate (see chapter 10)
- family members disagree about the person's best interests
- family members and professionals disagree about the person's best interests
- there is a conflict of interest for people who have been consulted in the best interests assessment (for example, the sale of a family property where the person lives)
- the person who lacks capacity is already in contact with an advocate
- the proposed course of action may lead to the use of restraint or other restrictions on the person who lacks capacity
- there is a concern about the protection of a vulnerable adult.

## 6    WHAT PROTECTION DOES THE ACT OFFER FOR PEOPLE PROVIDING CARE OR TREATMENT?

Section 5 of the Act allows carers, healthcare and social care staff to carry out certain tasks without fear of liability. These tasks involve the personal care, healthcare or treatment of people who lack capacity to consent to them. The aim is to give legal backing for acts that need to be carried out in the best interests of the person who lacks capacity to consent.[19]

This chapter explains:

- how the Act provides protection from liability
- how that protection works in practice
- where protection is restricted or limited, and
- when a carer can use a person's money to buy goods or services without formal permission.

> In this chapter, as throughout the Code, a person's capacity (or lack of capacity) refers specifically to their capacity to make a particular decision at the time it needs to be made.

## Quick summary

The following steps list all the things that people providing care or treatment should bear in mind to ensure they are protected by the Act.

### ACTING IN CONNECTION WITH THE CARE OR TREATMENT OF SOMEONE WHO LACKS CAPACITY TO CONSENT

- Is the action to be carried out in connection with the care or treatment of a person who lacks capacity to give consent to that act?
- Does it involve major life changes for the person concerned? If so, it will need special consideration.
- Who is carrying out the action? Is it appropriate for that person to do so at the relevant time?

### CHECKING WHETHER THE PERSON HAS CAPACITY TO CONSENT

- Have all possible steps been taken to try to help the person make a decision for themselves about the action?
- Has the two-stage test of capacity been applied?
- Are there reasonable grounds for believing the person lacks capacity to give permission?

### ACTING IN THE PERSON'S BEST INTERESTS

- Has the best interests checklist been applied and all relevant circumstances considered?
- Is a less restrictive option available?
- Is it reasonable to believe that the proposed act is in the person's best interests?

### UNDERSTANDING POSSIBLE LIMITATIONS ON PROTECTION FROM LIABILITY

- If restraint is being considered, is it necessary to prevent harm to the person who lacks capacity, and is it a proportionate response to the likelihood of the person suffering harm – and to the seriousness of that harm?
- Could the restraint be classed as a 'deprivation of the person's liberty'?
- Does the action conflict with a decision that has been made by an attorney or deputy under their powers?

---

[19] The provisions of section 5 are based on the common law 'doctrine of necessity' as set out in *Re F (Mental Patient: Sterilisation)* [1990] 2 AC 1

PAYING FOR NECESSARY GOODS AND SERVICES

- If someone wishes to use the person's money to buy goods or pay for services for someone who lacks capacity to do so themselves, are those goods or services necessary and in the person's best interests?
- Is it necessary to take money from the person's bank or building society account or to sell the person's property to pay for goods or services? If so, formal authority will be required.

## What protection do people have when caring for those who lack capacity to consent?

6.1    Every day, millions of acts are done to and for people who lack capacity either to:

- take decisions about their own care or treatment, or
- consent to someone else caring for them.

Such acts range from everyday tasks of caring (for example, helping someone to wash) to life-changing events (for example, serious medical treatment or arranging for someone to go into a care home).

In theory, many of these actions could be against the law. Legally, people have the right to stop others from interfering with their body or property unless they give permission. But what happens if someone lacks capacity to give permission? Carers who dress people who cannot dress themselves are potentially interfering with someone's body without their consent, so could theoretically be prosecuted for assault. A neighbour who enters and cleans the house of a person who lacks capacity could be trespassing on the person's property.

6.2    Section 5 of the Act provides 'protection from liability'. In other words, it protects people who carry out these actions. It stops them being prosecuted for acts that could otherwise be classed as civil wrongs or crimes. By protecting family and other carers from liability, the Act allows necessary caring acts or treatment to take place as if a person who lacks capacity to consent had consented to them. People providing care of this sort do not therefore need to get formal authority to act.

6.3    Importantly, section 5 does not give people caring for or treating someone the power to make any other decisions on behalf of those who lack capacity to make their own decisions. Instead, it offers protection from liability so that they can act in connection with the person's care or treatment. The power to make decisions on behalf of someone who lacks capacity can be granted through other parts of the Act (such as the powers granted to attorneys and deputies, which are explained in chapters 7 and 8).

## What type of actions might have protection from liability?

6.4    Section 5(1) provides possible protection for actions carried out *in connection with care or treatment*. The action may be carried out on behalf of someone who is believed to lack capacity to give permission for the action, so long as it is in that person's best interests (see chapter 5). The Act does not define 'care' or 'treatment'. They should be given their normal meaning. However, section 64(1) makes clear that treatment includes diagnostic or other procedures.

6.5    Actions that might be covered by section 5 include:

PERSONAL CARE

- helping with washing, dressing or personal hygiene
- helping with eating and drinking

- helping with communication
- helping with mobility (moving around)
- helping someone take part in education, social or leisure activities
- going into a person's home to drop off shopping or to see if they are alright
- doing the shopping or buying necessary goods with the person's money
- arranging household services (for example, arranging repairs or maintenance for gas and electricity supplies)
- providing services that help around the home (such as homecare or meals on wheels)
- undertaking actions related to community care services (for example, day care, residential accommodation or nursing care) – but see also paragraphs 6.7–6.14 below
- helping someone to move home (including moving property and clearing the former home).

## HEALTHCARE AND TREATMENT

- carrying out diagnostic examinations and tests (to identify an illness, condition or other problem)
- providing professional medical, dental and similar treatment
- giving medication
- taking someone to hospital for assessment or treatment
- providing nursing care (whether in hospital or in the community)
- carrying out any other necessary medical procedures (for example, taking a blood sample) or therapies (for example, physiotherapy or chiropody)
- providing care in an emergency.

**6.6**    These actions only receive protection from liability if the person is reasonably believed to lack capacity to give permission for the action. The action must also be in the person's best interests and follow the Act's principles (see paragraph 6.26 onwards).

**6.7**    Some acts in connection with care or treatment may cause major life changes with significant consequences for the person concerned. Those requiring particularly careful consideration include a change of residence, perhaps into a care home or nursing home, or major decisions about healthcare and medical treatment. These are described in the following paragraphs.

## A CHANGE OF RESIDENCE

**6.8**    Sometimes a person cannot get sufficient or appropriate care in their own home, and they may have to move – perhaps to live with relatives or to go into a care home or nursing home. If the person lacks capacity to consent to a move, the decision-maker(s) must consider whether the move is in the person's best interests (by referring to the best interests checklist in chapter 5 and in particular the person's past and present wishes and feelings, as well as the views of other relevant people). The decision-maker(s) must also consider whether there is a less restrictive option (see chapter 2, principle 5).

This may involve speaking to:

- anyone currently involved in the person's care
- family carers and other family members close to the person and interested in their welfare
- others who have an interest in the person's welfare
- anyone the person has previously named as someone to be consulted, and
- an attorney or deputy who has been legally appointed to make particular decisions on their behalf.

**6.9**    Some cases will require an Independent Mental Capacity Advocate (IMCA). The IMCA represents and supports the person who lacks capacity and they will provide information to make sure the final decision is in the person's best interests (see chapter 10). An IMCA is needed when there is no-one close to the person who lacks capacity to give an opinion about what is best for them, and:

- an NHS body is proposing to provide serious medical treatment or
- an NHS body or local authority is proposing to arrange accommodation in hospital or a care home or other longer-term accommodation and

  – the person will stay in hospital longer than 28 days, or
  – they will stay in a care home for more than eight weeks.

There are also some circumstances where an IMCA may be appointed on a discretionary basis. More guidance is available in chapter 10.

**6.10**    Sometimes the final outcome may not be what the person who lacks capacity wanted. For example, they might want to stay at home, but those caring for them might decide a move is in their best interests. In all cases, those making the decision must first consider other options that might restrict the person's rights and freedom of action less (see chapter 2, principle 5).

**6.11**    In some cases, there may be no alternative but to move the person. Such a move would normally require the person's formal consent if they had capacity to give, or refuse, it. In cases where a person lacks capacity to consent, section 5 of the Act allows carers to carry out actions relating to the move – as long as the Act's principles and the requirements for working out best interests have been followed. This applies even if the person continues to object to the move.

However, section 6 places clear limits on the use of force or restraint by only permitting restraint to be used (for example, to transport the person to their new home) where this is necessary to protect the person from harm and is a proportionate response to the risk of harm (see paragraphs 6.40–6.53). Any action taken to move the person concerned or their property could incur liability unless protected under section 5.

**6.12**    If there is a serious disagreement about the need to move the person that cannot be settled in any other way, the Court of Protection can be asked to decide what the person's best interests are and where they should live. For example, this could happen if members of a family disagree over what is best for a relative who lacks capacity to give or deny permission for a move.

**6.13**    In some circumstances, being placed in a hospital or care home may deprive the person of their liberty (see paragraphs 6.49–6.53). If this is the case, there is no protection from liability – even if the placement was considered to be in the best interests of the person (section 6(5)). It is up to the decision-maker to first look at a range of alternative and less restrictive options to see if there is any way of avoiding taking away the person's liberty.

**6.14**    If there is no alternative way of caring for the person, specific authority will be required to keep the person in a situation which deprives them of their liberty. For instance, sometimes the Court of Protection might be prepared to grant an order of which a consequence is the deprivation of a person's liberty – if it is satisfied that this is in the person's best interests. In other cases, if the person needs treatment for a mental disorder and meets the criteria for detention under the Mental Health Act 1983, this may be used to admit or keep the person in hospital (see chapter 13).

## HEALTHCARE AND TREATMENT DECISIONS

**6.15**   Section 5 also allows actions to be taken to ensure a person who lacks capacity to consent receives necessary medical treatment. This could involve taking the person to hospital for out-patient treatment or arranging for admission to hospital. Even if a person who lacks capacity to consent objects to the proposed treatment or admission to hospital, the action might still be allowed under section 5 (but see paragraphs 6.20 and 6.22 below). But there are limits about whether force or restraint can be used to impose treatment (see paragraphs 6.40–6.53).

**6.16**   Major healthcare and treatment decisions – for example, major surgery or a decision that no attempt is to be made to resuscitate the patient (known as 'DNR' decisions) – will also need special consideration. Unless there is a valid and applicable advance decision to refuse the specific treatment, healthcare staff must carefully work out what would be in the person's best interests (see chapter 5). As part of the process of working this out, they will need to consider (where practical and appropriate):

- the past and present wishes and feelings, beliefs and values of the person who lacks capacity to make the treatment decision, including any advance statement the person wrote setting out their wishes when they had capacity
- the views of anyone previously named by the person as someone to be consulted
- the views of anyone engaged in caring for the person
- the views of anyone interested in their welfare, and
- the views of any attorney or deputy appointed for the person.

In specific cases where there is no-one else available to consult about the person's best interests, an IMCA must be appointed to support and represent the person (see paragraph 6.9 above and chapter 10).

Healthcare staff must also consider whether there are alternative treatment options that might be less intrusive or restrictive (see chapter 2, principle 5). When deciding about the provision or withdrawal of life-sustaining treatment, anyone working out what is in the best interests of a person who lacks capacity must not be motivated by a desire to bring about the person's death (see chapter 5).

**6.17**   Multi-disciplinary meetings are often the best way to decide on a person's best interests. They bring together healthcare and social care staff with different skills to discuss the person's options and may involve those who are closest to the person concerned. But final responsibility for deciding what is in a person's best interest lies with the member of healthcare staff responsible for the person's treatment. They should record their decision, how they reached it and the reasons for it in the person's clinical notes. As long as they have recorded objective reasons to show that the decision is in the person's best interests, and the other requirements of section 5 of the Act are met, all healthcare staff taking actions in connection with the particular treatment will be protected from liability.

**6.18**   Some treatment decisions are so serious that the court has to make them – unless the person has previously made a Lasting Power of Attorney appointing an attorney to make such healthcare decisions for them (see chapter 7) or they have made a valid advance decision to refuse the proposed treatment (see chapter 9). The Court of Protection must be asked to make decisions relating to:[20]

- the proposed withholding or withdrawal of artificial nutrition and hydration (ANH) from a patient in a permanent vegetative state (PVS)

---

[20]   The procedures resulting from those court judgements are set out in a Practice Note from the Official Solicitor (available at **www.officialsolicitor.gov.uk**) and will be set out in a Practice Direction from the new Court of Protection.

- cases where it is proposed that a person who lacks capacity to consent should donate an organ or bone marrow to another person
- the proposed non-therapeutic sterilisation of a person who lacks capacity to consent (for example, for contraceptive purposes)
- cases where there is a dispute about whether a particular treatment will be in a person's best interests.

See paragraphs 8.18–8.24 for more details on these types of cases.

**6.19**    This last category may include cases that introduce ethical dilemmas concerning untested or innovative treatments (for example, new treatments for variant Creutzfeldt-Jakob Disease (CDJ)) where it is not known if the treatment will be effective, or certain cases involving a termination of pregnancy. It may also include cases where there is conflict between professionals or between professionals and family members which cannot be resolved in any other way.

Where there is conflict, it is advisable for parties to get legal advice, though they may not necessarily be able to get legal aid to pay for this advice. Chapter 8 gives more information about the need to refer cases to court for a decision.

## Who is protected from liability by section 5?

**6.20**    Section 5 of the Act is most likely to affect:

- family carers and other kinds of carers
- care workers
- healthcare and social care staff, and
- others who may occasionally be involved in the care or treatment of a person who lacks capacity to consent (for example, ambulance staff, housing workers, police officers and volunteer support workers).

**6.21**    At any time, it is likely that several people will be carrying out tasks that are covered by section 5 of the Act. Section 5 does not:

- give one person more rights than another to carry out tasks
- specify who has the authority to act in a specific instance
- allow somebody to make decisions relating to subjects other than the care or treatment of the person who lacks capacity, or
- allow somebody to give consent on behalf of a person who lacks capacity to do so.

**6.22**    To receive protection from liability under section 5, all actions must be related to the care or treatment of the person who lacks capacity to consent. Before taking action, carers must first reasonably believe that:

- the person lacks the capacity to make that particular decision at the time it needs to be made, and
- the action is in the person's best interests.

This is explained further in paragraphs 6.26–6.34 below.

---

**Scenario: Protecting multiple carers**

Mr Rose, an older man with dementia, gets help from several people. His sister sometimes cooks meals for him. A district nurse visits him to change the dressing on a pressure sore, and a friend often takes Mr Rose to the park, guiding him when they cross the road. Each of these individuals would be protected from liability under section 5 of the Act – but only if they take reasonable steps to check that he lacks

> capacity to consent to the actions they take and hold a reasonable belief that the
> actions are in Mr Rose's best interests.

**6.23** Section 5 may also protect carers who need to use the person's money to pay for goods or services that the person needs but lacks the capacity to purchase for themselves. However, there are strict controls over who may have access to another person's money. See paragraphs 6.56–6.66 for more information.

**6.24** Carers who provide personal care services must not carry out specialist procedures that are normally done by trained healthcare staff. If the action involves medical treatment, the doctor or other member of healthcare staff with responsibility for the patient will be the decision-maker who has to decide whether the proposed treatment is in the person's best interests (see chapter 5). A doctor can delegate responsibility for giving the treatment to other people in the clinical team who have the appropriate skills or expertise. People who do more than their experience or qualifications allow may not be protected from liability.

### CARE PLANNING

**6.25** Decisions about a person's care or treatment are often made by a multi-disciplinary team (a team of professionals with different skills that contribute to a person's care), by drawing up a care plan for the person. The preparation of a care plan should always include an assessment of the person's capacity to consent to the actions covered by the care plan, and confirm that those actions are agreed to be in the person's best interests. Healthcare and social care staff may then be able to assume that any actions they take under the care plan are in the person's best interests, and therefore receive protection from liability under section 5. But a person's capacity and best interests must still be reviewed regularly.

## What steps should people take to be protected from liability?

**6.26** As well as taking the following steps, somebody who wants to be protected from liability should bear in mind the statutory principles set out in section 1 of the Act (see chapter 2).

**6.27** First, reasonable steps must be taken to find out whether a person has the capacity to make a decision about the proposed action (section 5(1)(a)). If the person has capacity, they must give their consent for anyone to take an action on their behalf, so that the person taking the action is protected from liability. For guidance on what is classed as 'reasonable steps', see paragraphs 6.29–6.34. But reasonable steps must always include:

- taking all practical and appropriate steps to help people to make a decision about an action themselves, and
- applying the two-stage test of capacity (see chapter 4).

The person who is going to take the action must have a 'reasonable belief' that the individual lacks capacity to give consent for the action at the time it needs to be taken.

**6.28** Secondly, the person proposing to take action must have reasonable grounds for believing that the action is in the best interests of the person who lacks capacity. They should apply all elements of the best interests checklist (see chapter 5), and in particular

- consider whether the person is likely to regain capacity to make this decision in the future. Can the action wait until then?
- consider whether a less restrictive option is available (chapter 2, principle 5), and
- have objective reasons for thinking an action is in the best interests of the person who lacks capacity to consent to it.

## WHAT IS 'REASONABLE'?

**6.29**    As explained in chapter 4, anyone assessing a person's capacity to make decisions for themselves or give consent must focus wholly on whether the person has capacity to make a specific decision at the time it needs to be made and not the person's capacity to make decisions generally. For example, a carer helping a person to dress can assess a person's capacity to agree to their help by explaining the different options (getting dressed or staying in nightclothes), and the consequences (being able to go out, or staying in all day).

**6.30**    Carers do not have to be experts in assessing capacity. But they must be able to show that they have taken *reasonable steps* to find out if the person has the capacity to make the specific decision. Only then will they have *reasonable grounds for believing* the person lacks capacity in relation to that particular matter. See paragraphs 4.44–4.45 for guidance on what is classed as 'reasonable' – although this will vary, depending on circumstances.

**6.31**    For the majority of decisions, formal assessment processes are unlikely to be required. But in some circumstances, professional practice requires some formal procedures to be carried out (for example, where consent to medical treatment is required, the doctor will need to assess – and record the person's capacity to consent). Under section 5, carers and professionals will be protected from liability as long as they are able to provide some objective reasons that explain why they believe that the person lacks capacity to consent to the action. If somebody challenges their belief, both carers and professionals will be protected from liability as long as they can show that they took steps to find out whether the person has capacity and that they have a reasonable belief that the person lacks capacity.

**6.32**    Similarly, carers, relatives and others involved in caring for someone who lacks capacity must have *reasonable grounds for believing* that their action is in the person's best interests. They must not simply impose their own views. They must be able to show that they considered all relevant circumstances and applied the best interests checklist. This includes showing that they have tried to involve the person who lacks capacity, and find out their wishes and feelings, beliefs and values. They must also have asked other people's opinions, where practical and appropriate. If somebody challenges their decision, they will be protected from liability if they can show that it was reasonable for them to believe that their action was in the person's best interests – in all the circumstances of that particular case.

**6.33**    If healthcare and social care staff are involved, their skills and knowledge will affect what is classed as 'reasonable'. For example, a doctor assessing somebody's capacity to consent to treatment must demonstrate more skill than someone without medical training. They should also record in the person's healthcare record the steps they took and the reasons for the finding. Healthcare and social care staff should apply normal clinical and professional standards when deciding what treatments to offer. They must then decide whether the proposed treatment is in the best interests of the person who lacks capacity to consent. This includes considering all relevant circumstances and applying the best interests checklist (see chapter 5).

**6.34**    Healthcare and social care staff can be said to have 'reasonable grounds for believing' that a person lacks capacity if:

■    they are working to a person's care plan, and
■    the care planning process involved an assessment of the person's capacity to make a decision about actions in the care plan.

It is also reasonable for them to assume that the care planning process assessed a person's best interests. But they should still make every effort to communicate with the person to find out if they still lack capacity and the action is still in their best interests.

> **Scenario: Working with a care plan**
>
> Margaret, an elderly woman, has serious mental health and physical problems. She lives in a nursing home and a care plan has been prepared by the multi-disciplinary team, in consultation with her relatives in deciding what course of action would be in Margaret's best interests. The care plan covers the medication she has been prescribed, the physiotherapy she needs, help with her personal care and other therapeutic activities such as art therapy.
>
> Although attempts were made to involve Margaret in the care planning process, she has been assessed by the doctor responsible for her care as lacking capacity to consent to most aspects of her care plan. The care plan can be relied on by the nurse or care assistant who administers the medication, by the physiotherapist and art therapist, and also by the care assistant who helps with Margaret's personal care, providing them with reasonable grounds for believing that they are acting in her best interests.
>
> However, as each act is performed, they must all take reasonable steps to communicate with Margaret to explain what they are doing and to ascertain whether she has the capacity to consent to the act in question. If they think she does, they must stop the treatment unless or until Margaret agrees that it should continue.

## What happens in emergency situations?

**6.35**  Sometimes people who lack capacity to consent will require emergency medical treatment to save their life or prevent them from serious harm. In these situations, what steps are 'reasonable' will differ to those in non-urgent cases. In emergencies, it will almost always be in the person's best interests to give urgent treatment without delay. One exception to this is when the healthcare staff giving treatment are satisfied that an advance decision to refuse treatment exists (see paragraph 6.37).

## What happens in cases of negligence?

**6.36**  Section 5 does not provide a defence in cases of negligence – either in carrying out a particular act or by failing to act where necessary. For example, a doctor may be protected against a claim of battery for carrying out an operation that is in a person's best interests. But if they perform the operation negligently, they are not protected from a charge of negligence. So the person who lacks capacity has the same rights in cases of negligence as someone who has consented to the operation.

## What is the effect of an advance decision to refuse treatment?

**6.37**  Sometimes people will make an advance decision to refuse treatment while they still have capacity to do so and before they need that particular treatment. Healthcare staff must respect this decision if it is valid and applies to the proposed treatment.

**6.38**  If healthcare staff are satisfied that an advance decision is valid and applies to the proposed treatment, they are not protected from liability if they give any treatment that goes against it. But they are protected from liability if they did not know about an advance decision or they are not satisfied that the advance decision is valid and applies in the current circumstances (section 26(2)). See chapter 9 for further guidance.

## What limits are there on protection from liability?

**6.39**  Section 6 imposes some important limitations on acts which can be carried out with protection from liability under section 5 (as described in the first part of this chapter). The key areas where acts might not be protected from liability are where there is inappropriate use of restraint or where a person who lacks capacity is deprived of their liberty.

## USING RESTRAINT

**6.40**    Section 6(4) of the Act states that someone is using restraint if they:

- use force – or threaten to use force – to make someone do something that they are resisting, or
- restrict a person's freedom of movement, whether they are resisting or not.

**6.41**    Any action intended to restrain a person who lacks capacity will not attract protection from liability unless the following two conditions are met:

- the person taking action must reasonably believe that restraint is *necessary* to prevent *harm* to the person who lacks capacity, and
- the amount or type of restraint used and the amount of time it lasts must be a *proportionate response* to the likelihood and seriousness of harm.

See paragraphs 6.44–6.48 for more explanation of the terms *necessary*, *harm* and a *proportionate response*.

**6.42**    Healthcare and social care staff should also refer to:

- professional and other guidance on restraint or physical intervention, such as that issued by the Department of Health[21] or Welsh Assembly Government,[22] and
- limitations imposed by regulations and standards, such as the national minimum standards for care services (see chapter 14).

**6.43**    In addition to the requirements of the Act, the common law imposes a duty of care on healthcare and social care staff in respect of all people to whom they provide services. Therefore if a person who lacks capacity to consent has challenging behaviour, or is in the acute stages of illness causing them to act in way which may cause harm to others, staff may, under the common law, take appropriate and necessary action to restrain or remove the person, in order to prevent harm, both to the person concerned and to anyone else.

However, within this context, the common law would not provide sufficient grounds for an action that would have the effect of depriving someone of their liberty (see paragraphs 6.49–6.53).

## WHEN MIGHT RESTRAINT BE 'NECESSARY'?

**6.44**    Anybody considering using restraint must have objective reasons to justify that restraint is necessary. They must be able to show that the person being cared for is likely to suffer harm unless proportionate restraint is used. A carer or professional must not use restraint just so that they can do something more easily. If restraint is necessary to prevent harm to the person who lacks capacity, it must be the minimum amount of force for the shortest time possible.

---

[21]  For guidance on using restraint with people with learning disabilities and autistic spectrum disorder, see *Guidance for restrictive physical interventions* (published by the Department of Health and Department for Education and Skills and available at **www.dh.gov.uk/assetRoot/04/06/84/61/04068461.pdf**).

[22]  In Wales, the relevant guidance is the Welsh Assembly Government's *Framework for restrictive physical intervention policy and practice* (available at **www.childrenfirst.wales.gov.uk/content/framework/phys-int-e.pdf**).

---

**Scenario: Appropriate use of restraint**

Derek, a man with learning disabilities, has begun to behave in a challenging way. Staff at his care home think he might have a medical condition that is causing him distress. They take him to the doctor, who thinks that Derek might have a hormone imbalance. But the doctor needs to take a blood test to confirm this, and when he tries to take the test Derek attempts to fight him off.

The results might be negative – so the test might not be necessary. But the doctor decides that a test is in Derek's best interests, because failing to treat a problem like a hormone imbalance might make it worse. It is therefore in Derek's best interests to restrain him to take the blood test. The temporary restraint is in proportion to the likely harm caused by failing to treat a possible medical condition.

---

## WHAT IS 'HARM'?

**6.45**    The Act does not define 'harm', because it will vary depending on the situation. For example,

- a person with learning disabilities might run into a busy road without warning, if they do not understand the dangers of cars
- a person with dementia may wander away from home and get lost, if they cannot remember where they live
- a person with manic depression might engage in excessive spending during a manic phase, causing them to get into debt
- a person may also be at risk of harm if they behave in a way that encourages others to assault or exploit them (for example, by behaving in a dangerously provocative way).

6.46 Common sense measures can often help remove the risk of harm (for example, by locking away poisonous chemicals or removing obstacles). Also, care planning should include risk assessments and set out appropriate actions to try to prevent possible risks. But it is impossible to remove all risk, and a proportionate response is needed when the risk of harm does arise.

## WHAT IS A 'PROPORTIONATE RESPONSE'?

**6.47**    A 'proportionate response' means using the least intrusive type and minimum amount of restraint to achieve a specific outcome in the best interests of the person who lacks capacity. On occasions when the use of force may be necessary, carers and healthcare and social care staff should use the minimum amount of force for the shortest possible time.

For example, a carer may need to hold a person's arm while they cross the road, if the person does not understand the dangers of roads. But it would not be a proportionate response to stop the person going outdoors at all. It may be appropriate to have a secure lock on a door that faces a busy road, but it would not be a proportionate response to lock someone in a bedroom all the time to prevent them from attempting to cross the road.

**6.48**    Carers and healthcare and social care staff should consider less restrictive options before using restraint. Where possible, they should ask other people involved in the person's care what action they think is necessary to protect the person from harm. For example, it may be appropriate to get an advocate to work with the person to see if they can avoid or minimise the need for restraint to be used.

> **Scenario: Avoiding restraint**
>
> Oscar has learning disabilities. People at the college he attends sometimes cannot understand him, and he gets frustrated. Sometimes he hits the wall and hurts himself.
>
> Staff don't want to take Oscar out of class, because he says he enjoys college and is learning new skills. They have allowed his support worker to sit with him, but he still gets upset. The support worker could try to hold Oscar back. But she thinks this is too forceful, even though it would stop him hurting himself.
>
> Instead, she gets expert advice from members of the local community team. Observation helps them understand Oscar's behaviour better. They come up with a support strategy that reduces the risk of harmful behaviour and is less restrictive of his freedom.

## WHEN ARE ACTS SEEN AS DEPRIVING A PERSON OF THEIR LIBERTY?

**6.49**    Although section 5 of the Act permits the use of restraint where it is necessary under the above conditions, section 6(5) confirms that there is no protection under the Act for actions that result in someone being deprived of their liberty (as defined by Article 5(1) of the European Convention on Human Rights). This applies not only to public authorities covered by the Human Rights Act 1998 but to everyone who might otherwise get protection under section 5 of the Act. It also applies to attorneys or deputies – they cannot give permission for an action that takes away a person's liberty.

**6.50**    Sometimes there is no alternative way to provide care or treatment other than depriving the person of their liberty. In this situation, some people may be detained in hospital under the Mental Health Act 1983 – but this only applies to people who require hospital treatment for a mental disorder (see chapter 13). Otherwise, actions that amount to a deprivation of liberty will not be lawful unless formal authorisation is obtained.

**6.51**    In some cases, the Court of Protection might grant an order that permits the deprivation of a person's liberty, if it is satisfied that this is in a person's best interests.

**6.52**    It is difficult to define the difference between actions that amount to a restriction of someone's liberty and those that result in a deprivation of liberty. In recent legal cases, the European Court of Human Rights said that the difference was 'one of degree or intensity, not one of nature or substance'.[23] There must therefore be particular factors in the specific situation of the person concerned which provide the 'degree' or 'intensity' to result in a deprivation of liberty. In practice, this can relate to:

■   the type of care being provided
■   how long the situation lasts
■   its effects, or
■   the way in a particular situation came about.[24]

The European Court of Human Rights has identified the following as factors contributing to deprivation of liberty in its judgments on cases to date:

---

[23]  *HL v. The United Kingdom* (Application no, 45508/99). Judgement 5 October 2004, paragraph 89
[24]  In *HL v. UK* (also known as the 'Bournewood' case), the European Court said that 'the key factor in the present case [is] that the health care professionals treating and managing the applicant exercised complete and effective control over his care and movements'. They found 'the concrete situation was that the applicant was under continuous supervision and control and was not free to leave.'

- restraint was used, including sedation, to admit a person who is resisting
- professionals exercised complete and effective control over care and movement for a significant period
- professionals exercised control over assessments, treatment, contacts and residence
- the person would be prevented from leaving if they made a meaningful attempt to do so
- a request by carers for the person to be discharged to their care was refused
- the person was unable to maintain social contacts because of restrictions placed on access to other people
- the person lost autonomy because they were under continuous supervision and control.[25]

**6.53**    The Government has announced that it intends to amend the Act to introduce new procedures and provisions for people who lack capacity to make relevant decisions but who need to be deprived of their liberty, in their best interests, otherwise than under the Mental Health Act 1983 (the so-called 'Bournewood provisions'). This chapter will be fully revised in due course to reflect those changes. Information about the Government's current proposals in respect of the Bournewood safeguards is available on the Department of Health website. This information includes draft illustrative Code of Practice guidance about the proposed safeguards. See paragraphs 13.52–13.55 for more details.

## How does section 5 apply to attorneys and deputies?

**6.54**    Section 5 does not provide protection for actions that go against the decision of someone who has been authorised to make decisions for a person who lacks capacity to make such decision for themselves. For instance, if someone goes against the decision of an attorney acting under a Lasting Power of Attorney (LPA) (see chapter 7) or a deputy appointed by the Court of Protection (see chapter 8), they will not be protected under section 5.

**6.55**    Attorneys and deputies must only make decisions within the scope of the authority of the LPA or court order. Sometimes carers or healthcare and social care staff might feel that an attorney or deputy is making decisions they should not be making, or that are not in a person's best interests. If this is the case, and the disagreement cannot be settled any other way, either the carers, the staff or the attorney or deputy can apply to the Court of Protection. If the dispute concerns the provision of medical treatment, medical staff can still give life-sustaining treatment, or treatment which stops a person's condition getting seriously worse, while the court is coming to a decision (section 6(6)).

## Who can pay for goods or services?

**6.56**    Carers may have to spend money on behalf of someone who lacks capacity to purchase necessary goods or services. For example, they may need to pay for a milk delivery or for a chiropodist to provide a service at the person's home. In some cases, they might have to pay for more costly arrangements such as house repairs or organising a holiday. Carers are likely to be protected from liability if their actions are properly taken under section 5, and in the best interests of the person who lacks capacity.

**6.57**    In general, a contract entered into by a person who lacks capacity to make the contract cannot be enforced if the other person knows, or must be taken to have known, of the lack of capacity. Section 7 of the Act modifies this rule and states that where the contract is

---

[25]   These are listed in the Department of Health's draft illustrative Code of Practice guidance about the proposed safeguards. **www.dh.gov.uk/assetRoot/04/14/17/64/04141764.pdf**.

for 'necessary' goods or services for a person who lacks capacity to make the arrangements for themselves, that person must pay a reasonable price for them.

## WHAT ARE NECESSARY GOODS AND SERVICES?

**6.58**   'Necessary' means something that is suitable to the person's condition in life (their place in society, rather than any mental or physical condition) and their actual requirements when the goods or services are provided (section 7(2)). The aim is to make sure that people can enjoy a similar standard of living and way of life to those they had before lacking capacity. For example, if a person who now lacks capacity previously chose to buy expensive designer clothes, these are still necessary goods – as long as they can still afford them. But they would not be necessary for a person who always wore cheap clothes, no matter how wealthy they were.

**6.59**   Goods are not necessary if the person already has a sufficient supply of them. For example, buying one or two new pairs of shoes for a person who lacks capacity could be necessary. But a dozen pairs would probably not be necessary.

## HOW SHOULD PAYMENTS BE ARRANGED?

**6.60**   If a person lacks capacity to arrange for payment for necessary goods and services, sections 5 and 8 allow a carer to arrange payment on their behalf.

**6.61**   The carer must first take reasonable steps to check whether a person can arrange for payment themselves, or has the capacity to consent to the carer doing it for them. If the person lacks the capacity to consent or pay themselves, the carer must decide what goods or services would be necessary for the person and in their best interests. The carer can then lawfully deal with payment for those goods and services in one of three ways:

- If neither the carer nor the person who lacks capacity can produce the necessary funds, the carer may promise that the person who lacks capacity will pay. A supplier may not be happy with this, or the carer may be worried that they will be held responsible for any debt. In such cases, the carer must follow the formal steps in paragraphs 6.62–6.66 below.
- If the person who lacks capacity has cash, the carer may use that money to pay for goods or services (for example, to pay the milkman or the hairdresser).
- The carer may choose to pay for the goods or services with their own money. The person who lacks capacity must pay them back. This may involve using cash in the person's possession or running up an IOU. (This is not appropriate for paid care workers, whose contracts might stop them handling their clients' money.) The carer must follow formal steps to get money held in a bank or building society account (see paragraphs 6.63–6.66 below).

**6.62**   Carers should keep bills, receipts and other proof of payment when paying for goods and services. They will need these documents when asking to get money back. Keeping appropriate financial records and documentation is a requirement of the national minimum standards for care homes or domiciliary care agencies.

## ACCESS TO A PERSON'S ASSETS

**6.63**   The Act does not give a carer or care worker access to a person's income or assets. Nor does it allow them to sell the person's property.

**6.64**   Anyone wanting access to money in a person's bank or building society will need formal legal authority. They will also need legal authority to sell a person's property. Such authority could be given in a Lasting Power of Attorney (LPA) appointing an attorney to deal with property and affairs, or in an order of the Court of Protection (either a single decision of the court or an order appointing a deputy to make financial decisions for the person who lacks capacity to make such decisions).

---

**Scenario: Being granted access to a person's assets**

A storm blew some tiles off the roof of a house owned by Gordon, a man with Alzheimer's disease. He lacks capacity to arrange for repairs and claim on his insurance. The repairs are likely to be costly.

Gordon's son decides to organise the repairs, and he agrees to pay because his father doesn't have enough cash available. The son could then apply to the Court of Protection for authority to claim insurance on his father's behalf and for him to be reimbursed from his father's bank account to cover the cost of the repairs once the insurance payment had been received.

---

**6.65**    Sometimes another person will already have legal control of the finances and property of a person who lacks capacity to manage their own affairs. This could be an attorney acting under a registered EPA or an appropriate LPA (see chapter 7) or a deputy appointed by the Court of Protection (see chapter 8). Or it could be someone (usually a carer) that has the right to act as an 'appointee' (under Social Security Regulations) and claim benefits for a person who lacks capacity to make their own claim and use the money on the person's behalf. But an appointee cannot deal with other assets or savings from sources other than benefits.

**6.66**    Section 6(6) makes clear that a family carer or other carer cannot make arrangements for goods or services to be supplied to a person who lacks capacity if this conflicts with a decision made by someone who has formal powers over the person's money and property, such as an attorney or deputy acting within the scope of their authority. Where there is no conflict and the carer has paid for necessary goods and services the carer may ask for money back from an attorney, a deputy or where relevant, an appointee.

# Appendix C2
# MCA 2005 Deprivation of Liberty Safeguards: Code of Practice

## INTRODUCTION

The Mental Capacity Act 2005 ('the Act'), covering England and Wales, provides a statutory framework for acting and making decisions on behalf of people who lack the capacity to make those decisions for themselves. These can be small decisions – such as what clothes to wear – or major decisions, such as where to live.

In some cases, people lack the capacity to consent to particular treatment or care that is recognised by others as being in their best interests, or which will protect them from harm. Where this care might involve depriving vulnerable people of their liberty in either a hospital or a care home, extra safeguards have been introduced, in law, to protect their rights and ensure that the care or treatment they receive is in their best interests.

This Code of Practice helps explain how to identify when a person is, or is at risk of, being deprived of their liberty and how deprivation of liberty may be avoided. It also explains the safeguards that have been put in place to ensure that deprivation of liberty, where it does need to occur, has a lawful basis. In addition, it provides guidance on what someone should do if they suspect that a person who lacks capacity is being deprived of their liberty unlawfully.

These safeguards are an important way of protecting the rights of many vulnerable people and should not be viewed negatively. Depriving someone of their liberty can be a necessary requirement in order to provide effective care or treatment. By following the criteria set out in the safeguards, and explained in this Code of Practice, the decision to deprive someone of their liberty can be made lawfully and properly.

### How does this Code of Practice relate to the main Mental Capacity Act 2005 Code of Practice?

This document adds to the guidance in the main Mental Capacity Act 2005 Code of Practice ('the main Code'), which was issued in April 2007, and should be used in conjunction with the main Code. It focuses specifically on the deprivation of liberty safeguards added to the Act. These can be found in sections 4A and 4B of, and Schedules A1 and 1A to, the Act.

Though these safeguards were mentioned in the main Code (particularly in chapters 6 and 13), they were not covered in any detail. That was because, at the time the main Code was published, the deprivation of liberty safeguards were still going through the Parliamentary process as part of the Mental Health Bill.[1]

Although the main Code does not cover the deprivation of liberty safeguards, the principles of that Code, and much of its content, are directly relevant to the deprivation of liberty safeguards. It is important that both the Act and the main Code are adhered to whenever capacity and best interests issues, and the deprivation of liberty safeguards, are being considered. The deprivation of liberty safeguards are in addition to, and do not replace, other safeguards in the Act.

---

[1] The Mental Health Bill was used as a vehicle to amend the Mental Capacity Act 2005 in order to introduce the deprivation of liberty safeguards. The Bill became the Mental Health Act 2007 following completion of its Parliamentary passage.

## How should this Code of Practice be used?

This Code of Practice provides guidance to anyone working with and/or caring for adults who lack capacity, but it particularly focuses on those who have a 'duty of care' to a person who lacks the capacity to consent to the care or treatment that is being provided, where that care or treatment may include the need to deprive the person of their liberty. This Code of Practice is also intended to provide information for people who are, or could become, subject to the deprivation of liberty safeguards, and for their families, friends and carers, as well as for anyone who believes that someone is being deprived of their liberty unlawfully.

In this Code of Practice, as throughout the main Code, references to 'lack of capacity' refer to the capacity to make a particular decision at the time it needs to be made. In the context of the deprivation of liberty safeguards, the capacity is specifically the capacity to decide whether or not to consent to care or treatment which involves being kept in a hospital or care home in circumstances that amount to a deprivation of liberty, at the time that decision needs to be made.

## What is the legal status of this Code of Practice?

As with the main Code, this Code of Practice is published by the Lord Chancellor, under sections 42 and 43 of the Mental Capacity Act 2005. The purpose of the main Code is to provide guidance and information about how the Act works in practice.

Both this Code and the main Code have statutory force, which means that certain people are under a legal duty to have regard to them. More details can be found in the Introduction to the main Code, which explains the legal status of the Code and who should have regard to it.

In addition to those for whom the main Code is intended, this Code of Practice specifically focuses on providing guidance for:

- people exercising functions relating to the deprivation of liberty safeguards, and
- people acting as a relevant person's representative[2] under the deprivation of liberty safeguards (see chapter 7).

## Scenarios used in this Code of Practice

This Code of Practice includes boxes within the main text containing scenarios, using imaginary characters and situations. These are intended to help illustrate what is meant in the main text. They should not in any way be taken as templates for decisions that need to be made in similar situations. Decisions must always be made on the facts of each individual case.

## Alternative formats and further information

This Code of Practice is also available in Welsh and can be made available in other formats on request.

## 1   WHAT ARE THE DEPRIVATION OF LIBERTY SAFEGUARDS AND WHY WERE THEY INTRODUCED?

The deprivation of liberty safeguards were introduced to provide a legal framework around the deprivation of liberty. Specifically, they were introduced to prevent breaches of the European Convention on Human Rights (ECHR) such as the one identified by the judgment of the European Court of Human Rights (ECtHR) in the case of *HL* v. *the United Kingdom*[3]

---

[2]   A 'relevant person' is a person who is, or may become, deprived of their liberty in accordance with the deprivation of liberty safeguards.

[3]   (2004) Application No: 00045508/99

(commonly referred to as the 'Bournewood' judgment). The case concerned an autistic man (HL) with a learning disability, who lacked the capacity to decide whether he should be admitted to hospital for specific treatment. He was admitted on an informal basis under common law in his best interests, but this decision was challenged by HL's carers. In its judgment, the ECtHR held that this admission constituted a deprivation of HL's liberty and, further, that:

■    the deprivation of liberty had not been in accordance with 'a procedure prescribed by law' and was, therefore, in breach of Article 5(1) of the ECHR, and

■    there had been a contravention of Article 5(4) of the ECHR because HL had no means of applying quickly to a court to see if the deprivation of liberty was lawful.

To prevent further similar breaches of the ECHR, the Mental Capacity Act 2005 has been amended to provide safeguards for people who lack capacity specifically to consent to treatment or care in either a hospital or a care home[4] that, in their own best interests, can only be provided in circumstances that amount to a deprivation of liberty, and where detention under the Mental Health Act 1983 is not appropriate for the person at that time. These safeguards are referred to in this Code of Practice as 'deprivation of liberty safeguards'.

## What are the deprivation of liberty safeguards

**1.1**    The deprivation of liberty safeguards provide legal protection for those vulnerable people who are, or may become, deprived of their liberty within the meaning of Article 5 of the ECHR in a hospital or care home, whether placed under public or private arrangements. They do not apply to people detained under the Mental Health Act 1983. The safeguards exist to provide a proper legal process and suitable protection in those circumstances where deprivation of liberty appears to be unavoidable, in a person's own best interests.

**1.2**    Every effort should be made, in both commissioning and providing care or treatment, to prevent deprivation of liberty. If deprivation of liberty cannot be avoided, it should be for no longer than is necessary.

**1.3**    The safeguards provide for deprivation of liberty to be made lawful through 'standard' or 'urgent' authorisation processes. These processes are designed to prevent arbitrary decisions to deprive a person of liberty and give a right to challenge deprivation of liberty authorisations.

**1.4**    The deprivation of liberty safeguards mean that a 'managing authority' (i.e. the relevant hospital or care home – see paragraph 3.1) must seek authorisation from a 'supervisory body' in order to be able lawfully to deprive someone of their liberty. Before giving such an authorisation, the supervisory body must be satisfied that the person has a mental disorder[5] and lacks capacity to decide about their residence or treatment. The supervisory body could be a primary care trust, a local authority, Welsh Ministers or a local health board (LHB) (see paragraph 3.3).

**1.5**    A decision as to whether or not deprivation of liberty arises will depend on all the circumstances of the case (as explained more fully in chapter 2). It is neither necessary nor appropriate to apply for a deprivation of liberty authorisation for everyone who is in hospital

---

[4]    Throughout this document, the term 'care home' means a care home registered under the Care Standards Act 2000.

[5]    As defined in section 1 of the Mental Health Act 1983, a mental disorder is any disorder or disability of the mind, apart from dependence on alcohol and drugs. This includes all learning disabilities. The distinction in the Mental Health Act 1983 between learning disabilities depending on whether or not they are associated with abnormally aggressive or seriously irresponsible behaviour is not relevant.

or a care home simply because the person concerned lacks capacity to decide whether or not they should be there. In deciding whether or not an application is necessary, a managing authority should carefully consider whether any restrictions that are, or will be, needed to provide ongoing care or treatment amount to a deprivation of liberty when looked at together.

1.6    The deprivation of liberty safeguards cover:

- how an application for authorisation should be applied for
- how an application for authorisation should be assessed
- the requirements that must be fulfilled for an authorisation to be given
- how an authorisation should be reviewed
- what support and representation must be provided for people who are subject to an authorisation, and
- how people can challenge authorisations.

## Who is covered by these safeguards

1.7    The safeguards apply to people in England and Wales who have a mental disorder and lack capacity to consent to the arrangements made for their care or treatment, but for whom receiving care or treatment in circumstances that amount to a deprivation of liberty may be necessary to protect them from harm and appears to be in their best interests. A large number of these people will be those with significant learning disabilities, or older people who have dementia or some similar disability, but they can also include those who have certain other neurological conditions (for example as a result of a brain injury).

1.8    In order to come within the scope of a deprivation of liberty authorisation, a person must be detained in a hospital or care home, for the purpose of being given care or treatment in circumstances that amount to a deprivation of liberty. The authorisation must relate to the individual concerned and to the hospital or care home in which they are detained.

1.9    For the purposes of Article 5 of the ECHR, there is no distinction in principle between depriving a person who lacks capacity of their liberty for the purpose of treating them for a physical condition, and depriving them of their liberty for treatment of a mental disorder. There will therefore be occasions when people who lack capacity to consent to admission are taken to hospital for treatment of physical illnesses or injuries, and then need to be cared for in circumstances that amount to a deprivation of liberty. In these circumstances, a deprivation of liberty authorisation must be applied for. Consequently, this Code of Practice must be followed and applied in acute hospital settings as well as care homes and mental health units.

1.10    It is important to bear in mind that, while the deprivation of liberty might be for the purpose of giving a person treatment, a deprivation of liberty authorisation does not itself authorise treatment. Treatment that is proposed following authorisation of deprivation of liberty may only be given with the person's consent (if they have capacity to make the decision) or in accordance with the wider provisions of the Mental Capacity Act 2005. More details of this are contained in paragraphs 5.10 to 5.13 of this Code.

1.11    The safeguards cannot apply to people while they are detained in hospital under the Mental Health Act 1983. The safeguards can, however, apply to a person who has previously been detained in hospital under the Mental Health Act 1983. There are other cases in which people who are – or could be – subject to the Mental Health Act 1983 will not meet the eligibility requirement for the safeguards. Chapter 13 of the main Code contains guidance on the relationship between the Mental Capacity Act 2005 and the Mental Health Act 1983 generally, as does the Code of Practice to the Mental Health Act 1983 itself. Paragraphs 4.40 to 4.57 of the present Code explain the relationship of the deprivation of liberty safeguards to the Mental Health Act 1983, and in particular how to assess if a person is eligible to be deprived of their liberty under the safeguards.

**1.12**    The safeguards relate only to people aged 18 and over. If the issue of depriving a person under the age of 18 of their liberty arises, other safeguards must be considered – such as the existing powers of the court, particularly those under section 25 of the Children Act 1989, or use of the Mental Health Act 1983.

## When can someone be deprived of their liberty?

**1.13**    Depriving someone who lacks the capacity to consent to the arrangements made for their care or treatment of their liberty is a serious matter, and the decision to do so should not be taken lightly. The deprivation of liberty safeguards make it clear that a person may only be deprived of their liberty:

- in their own best interests to protect them from harm
- if it is a proportionate response to the likelihood and seriousness of the harm, and
- if there is no less restrictive alternative.

**1.14**    Under no circumstances must deprivation of liberty be used as a form of punishment, or for the convenience of professionals, carers or anyone else. Deprivation of liberty should not be extended due to delays in moving people between care or treatment settings, for example when somebody awaits discharge after completing a period of hospital treatment.

## Are there any cultural considerations in implementing the safeguards?

**1.15**    The deprivation of liberty safeguards should not impact in any different way on different racial or ethnic groups, and care should be taken to ensure that the provisions are not operated in a manner that discriminates against particular racial or ethnic groups. It is up to managing authorities and supervisory bodies to ensure that their staff are aware of their responsibilities in this regard and of the need to ensure that the safeguards are operated fairly and equitably.

**1.16**    Assessors who carry out deprivation of liberty assessments to help decide whether a person should be deprived of their liberty (see chapter 4) should have the necessary skills and experience to take account of people's diverse backgrounds. Accordingly, they will need to have an understanding of, and respect for, the background of the relevant person. Supervisory bodies must take these factors into account when appointing assessors and must seek to appoint the most suitable available person for each case.

**1.17**    Interpreters should be available, where necessary, to help assessors to communicate not only with the relevant person but also with people with an interest in their care and treatment. An interpreter should be suitably qualified and experienced to enable them to provide effective language and communication support in the particular case concerned, and to offer appropriate assistance to the assessors involved. Information should be made available in other languages where relevant.

**1.18**    Any decision about the instruction of Independent Mental Capacity Advocates (see paragraphs 3.22 to 3.28) or relevant person's representatives (see chapter 7) should take account of the cultural, national, racial or ethnic background of the relevant person.

## Where do the safeguards apply?

**1.19**    Although the Bournewood judgment was specifically about a patient who lacked capacity to consent to admission to hospital for mental health treatment, the judgment has wider implications that extend to people who lack capacity and who might be deprived of their liberty either in a hospital or in a care home.

**1.20** It will only be lawful to deprive somebody of their liberty elsewhere (for example, in their own home, in supported living arrangements other than in a care home, or in a day centre) when following an order of the Court of Protection on a personal welfare matter. In such a case, the Court of Protection order itself provides a legal basis for the deprivation of liberty. This means that a separate deprivation of liberty authorisation under the processes set out in this Code of Practice is not required. More information about applying to the Court of Protection regarding personal welfare matters is given in chapter 10.

#### HOW DO THE SAFEGUARDS APPLY TO PRIVATELY ARRANGED CARE OR TREATMENT?

**1.21** Under the Human Rights Act 1998, the duty to act in accordance with the ECHR applies only to public authorities. However, all states that have signed up to the ECHR are obliged to make sure that the rights set out in the ECHR apply to all of their citizens. The Mental Capacity Act 2005 therefore makes it clear that the deprivation of liberty safeguards apply to both publicly and privately arranged care or treatment.

### How do the safeguards relate to the rest of the Mental Capacity Act 2005?

**1.22** The deprivation of liberty safeguards are in addition to, and do not replace, other safeguards in the Mental Capacity Act 2005. This means that decisions made, and actions taken, for a person who is subject to a deprivation of liberty authorisation must fulfil the requirements of the Act in the same way as for any other person. In particular, any action taken under the deprivation of liberty safeguards must be in line with the principles of the Act:

■ A person must be assumed to have capacity to make a decision unless it is established that they lack the capacity to make that decision.
■ A person is not to be treated as unable to make a decision unless all practicable steps to help them to do so have been taken without success.
■ A person is not to be treated as unable to make a decision merely because they make an unwise decision.
■ An act done, or decision made, under the Act for or on behalf of a person who lacks capacity must be done, or made, in their best interests.
■ Before the act is done, or the decision is made, regard must be had to whether the purpose for which it is needed can be as effectively achieved in a way that is less restrictive of the person's rights and freedom of action.

These principles are set out in chapter 2 of the main Code and explained in more detail in chapters 3 to 6 of the same document. Paragraph 5.13 of the main Code contains a checklist of factors that need to be taken into account in determining a person's best interests.

## 2  WHAT IS DEPRIVATION OF LIBERTY?

There is no simple definition of deprivation of liberty. The question of whether the steps taken by staff or institutions in relation to a person amount to a deprivation of that person's liberty is ultimately a legal question, and only the courts can determine the law. This guidance seeks to assist staff and institutions in considering whether or not the steps they are taking, or proposing to take, amount to a deprivation of a person's liberty. The deprivation of liberty safeguards give best interests assessors the authority to make recommendations about proposed deprivations of liberty, and supervisory bodies the power to give authorisations that deprive people of their liberty.

This chapter provides guidance for staff and institutions on how to assess whether particular steps they are taking, or proposing to take, might amount to a deprivation of liberty, based on existing case law. It also considers what other factors may be taken into account when considering the issue of deprivation of liberty, including, importantly, what is permissible under the Mental Capacity Act 2005 in relation to restraint or restriction. Finally, it provides a summary of some of the most important cases to date.

Further legal developments may occur after this guidance has been issued, and healthcare and social care staff need to keep themselves informed of legal developments that may have a bearing on their practice.

## What does case law say to date?

**2.1**    The European Court of Human Rights (ECtHR) has drawn a distinction between the deprivation of liberty of an individual (which is unlawful, unless authorised) and restrictions on the liberty of movement of an individual.

**2.2**    The ECtHR made it clear that the question of whether someone has been deprived of liberty depends on the particular circumstances of the case. Specifically, the ECtHR said in its October 2004 judgment in *HL v. the United Kingdom*:

> to determine whether there has been a deprivation of liberty, the starting-point must be the specific situation of the individual concerned and account must be taken of a whole range of factors arising in a particular case such as the type, duration, effects and manner of implementation of the measure in question. The distinction between a deprivation of, and restriction upon, liberty is merely one of degree or intensity and not one of nature or substance.

**2.3**    The difference between deprivation of liberty and restriction upon liberty is one of degree or intensity. It may therefore be helpful to envisage a scale, which moves from 'restraint' or 'restriction' to 'deprivation of liberty'. Where an individual is on the scale will depend on the concrete circumstances of the individual and may change over time. For more information on how the Act defines restraint, see paragraphs 2.8–2.12.

**2.4**    Although the guidance in this chapter includes descriptions of past decisions of the courts, which should be used to help evaluate whether deprivation of liberty may be occurring, each individual case must be assessed on its own circumstances. No two cases are likely to be identical, so it is important to be aware of previous court judgments and the factors that the courts have identified as important.

**2.5**    The ECtHR and UK courts have determined a number of cases about deprivation of liberty. Their judgments indicate that the following factors can be relevant to identifying whether steps taken involve more than restraint and amount to a deprivation of liberty. It is important to remember that this list is not exclusive; other factors may arise in future in particular cases.

- Restraint is used, including sedation, to admit a person to an institution where that person is resisting admission.
- Staff exercise complete and effective control over the care and movement of a person for a significant period.
- Staff exercise control over assessments, treatment, contacts and residence.
- A decision has been taken by the institution that the person will not be released into the care of others, or permitted to live elsewhere, unless the staff in the institution consider it appropriate.

- A request by carers for a person to be discharged to their care is refused.
- The person is unable to maintain social contacts because of restrictions placed on their access to other people.
- The person loses autonomy because they are under continuous supervision and control.

There is more information on some relevant cases at the end of this chapter (paragraphs 2.17–2.23).

## How can deprivation of liberty be identified

2.6    In determining whether deprivation of liberty has occurred, or is likely to occur, decision-makers need to consider all the facts in a particular case. There is unlikely to be any simple definition that can be applied in every case, and it is probable that no single factor will, in itself, determine whether the overall set of steps being taken in relation to the relevant person amount to a deprivation of liberty. In general, the decision-maker should always consider the following:

- All the circumstances of each and every case
- What measures are being taken in relation to the individual? When are they required? For what period do they endure? What are the effects of any restraints or restrictions on the individual? Why are they necessary? What aim do they seek to meet?
- What are the views of the relevant person, their family or carers? Do any of them object to the measures?
- How are any restraints or restrictions implemented? Do any of the constraints on the individual's personal freedom go beyond 'restraint' or 'restriction' to the extent that they constitute a deprivation of liberty?
- Are there any less restrictive options for delivering care or treatment that avoid deprivation of liberty altogether?
- Does the cumulative effect of all the restrictions imposed on the person amount to a deprivation of liberty, even if individually they would not?

## What practical steps can be taken to reduce the risk of deprivation of liberty occurring?

2.7    There are many ways in which providers and commissioners of care can reduce the risk of taking steps that amount to a deprivation of liberty, by minimising the restrictions imposed and ensuring that decisions are taken with the involvement of the relevant person and their family, friends and carers. The processes for staff to follow are:

- Make sure that all decisions are taken (and reviewed) in a structured way, and reasons for decisions recorded.
- Follow established good practice for care planning.
- Make a proper assessment of whether the person lacks capacity to decide whether or not to accept the care or treatment proposed, in line with the principles of the Act (see chapter 3 of the main Code for further guidance).
- Before admitting a person to hospital or residential care in circumstances that may amount to a deprivation of liberty, consider whether the person's needs could be met in a less restrictive way. Any restrictions placed on the person while in hospital or in a care home must be kept to the minimum necessary, and should be in place for the shortest possible period.
- Take proper steps to help the relevant person retain contact with family, friends and carers. Where local advocacy services are available, their involvement should be encouraged to support the person and their family, friends and carers.
- Review the care plan on an ongoing basis. It may well be helpful to include an independent element, possibly via an advocacy service, in the review.

## What does the Act mean by 'restraint'?

**2.8**    Section 6(4) of the Act states that someone is using restraint if they:

- use force – or threaten to use force – to make someone do something that they are resisting, or
- restrict a person's freedom of movement, whether they are resisting or not.

**2.9**    Paragraphs 6.40 to 6.48 of the main Code contain guidance about the appropriate use of restraint. Restraint is appropriate when it is used to prevent harm to the person who lacks capacity and it is a proportionate response to the likelihood and seriousness of harm. Appropriate use of restraint falls short of deprivation of liberty.

**2.10**    Preventing a person from leaving a care home or hospital unaccompanied because there is a risk that they would try to cross a road in a dangerous way, for example, is likely to be seen as a proportionate restriction or restraint to prevent the person from coming to harm. That would be unlikely, in itself, to constitute a deprivation of liberty. Similarly, locking a door to guard against immediate harm is unlikely, in itself, to amount to a deprivation of liberty.

**2.11**    The ECtHR has also indicated that the duration of any restrictions is a relevant factor when considering whether or not a person is deprived of their liberty. This suggests that actions that are immediately necessary to prevent harm may not, in themselves, constitute a deprivation of liberty.

**2.12**    However, where the restriction or restraint is frequent, cumulative and ongoing, or if there are other factors present, then care providers should consider whether this has gone beyond permissible restraint, as defined in the Act. If so, then they must either apply for authorisation under the deprivation of liberty safeguards (as explained in chapter 3) or change their care provision to reduce the level of restraint.

## How does the use of restraint apply within a hospital or when taking someone to a hospital or a care home?

### WITHIN A HOSPITAL

**2.13**    If a person in hospital for mental health treatment, or being considered for admission to a hospital for mental health treatment, needs to be restrained, this is likely to indicate that they are objecting to treatment or to being in hospital. The care providers should consider whether the need for restraint means the person is objecting (see paragraph 4.46 of this Code for guidance on how to decide whether a person is objecting for this purpose). A person who objects to mental health treatment, and who meets the criteria for detention under the Mental Health Act 1983, is normally ineligible for an authorisation under the deprivation of liberty safeguards. If the care providers believe it is necessary to detain the person, they may wish to consider use of the Mental Health Act 1983.

### TAKING SOMEONE TO A HOSPITAL OR A CARE HOME

**2.14**    Transporting a person who lacks capacity from their home, or another location, to a hospital or care home will not usually amount to a deprivation of liberty (for example, to take them to hospital by ambulance in an emergency.) Even where there is an expectation that the person will be deprived of liberty within the care home or hospital, it is unlikely that the journey itself will constitute a deprivation of liberty so that an authorisation is needed before the journey commences. In almost all cases, it is likely that a person can be lawfully taken to a hospital or a care home under the wider provisions of the Act, as long as it is considered that being in the hospital or care home will be in their best interests.

**2.15**   In a very few cases, there may be exceptional circumstances where taking a person to a hospital or a care home amounts to a deprivation of liberty, for example where it is necessary to do more than persuade or restrain the person for the purpose of transportation, or where the journey is exceptionally long. In such cases, it may be necessary to seek an order from the Court of Protection to ensure that the journey is taken on a lawful basis.

### HOW SHOULD MANAGING AUTHORITIES AVOID UNNECESSARY APPLICATIONS FOR STANDARD AUTHORISATIONS?

**2.16**   While it is unlawful to deprive a person of their liberty without authorisation, managing authorities should take into consideration that unnecessary applications for standard authorisations in cases that do not in fact involve depriving a person of liberty may place undue stress upon the person being assessed and on their families or carers. Moreover, consideration must always be given to the possibility of less restrictive options for delivering care or treatment that avoid deprivation of liberty altogether.

## Examples of case law

**2.17**   To provide further guidance, the following paragraphs contain short descriptions of what appear to be the significant features of recent or important cases in England and Wales and the ECtHR dealing with deprivation of liberty. Remember that:

- these descriptions are for guidance only
- only the courts can authoritatively determine the law; and
- the courts are likely to give judgments in cases after this guidance is issued. Staff will need to keep up to date and take account of further relevant legal developments.

### CASES WHERE THE COURTS FOUND THAT THE STEPS TAKEN DID NOT INVOLVE A DEPRIVATION OF LIBERTY

**2.18**   *LLBC* v. *TG* (judgment of High Court of 14 November 2007)

TG was a 78-year-old man with dementia and cognitive impairment. TG was resident in a care home, but was admitted to hospital with pneumonia and septicaemia. While he was in hospital, there was a dispute between the local authority and TG's daughter and granddaughter about TG's future. The daughter and granddaughter wanted TG to live with them, but the local authority believed that TG needed 24-hour care in a residential care home.

The council obtained an order from the court, directing that TG be delivered to the care home identified as appropriate by the council. Neither the daughter nor granddaughter was informed that a court hearing was taking place. That order was subsequently changed and TG was able to live with his daughter and granddaughter.

TG's daughter and granddaughter claimed that the period of time he had spent at the care home amounted to a deprivation of his liberty.

The judge considered that there was no deprivation of liberty, but the case was borderline. The key factors in his decision included:

- The care home was an ordinary care home where only ordinary restrictions of liberty applied.
- The family were able to visit TG on a largely unrestricted basis and were entitled to take him out from the home for outings.

- TG was personally compliant and expressed himself as happy in the care home. He had lived in a local authority care home for over three years and was objectively content with his situation there.
- There was no occasion where TG was objectively deprived of his liberty.

The judge said:

> Whilst I agree that the circumstances of the present case may be near the borderline between mere restrictions of liberty and Article 5 detention, I have come to the conclusion that, looked at as a whole and having regard to all the relevant circumstances, the placement of TG in Towerbridge falls short of engaging Article 5.

### 2.19    Nielsen v. Denmark (ECtHR; (1988) 11 EHRR 175)

The mother of a 12-year-old boy arranged for his admission to the state hospital's psychiatric ward. The boy had a nervous disorder and required treatment in the form of regular talks and environmental therapy. The treatment given, and the conditions under which it was administered, was appropriate. The duration of treatment was 5½ months. The boy, however, applied to the ECtHR, feeling that he had been deprived of his liberty.

The restrictions placed on the applicant's freedom of movement and contacts with the outside world were not much different from restrictions that might be imposed on a child in an ordinary hospital. The door of the ward was locked to prevent children exposing themselves to danger or running around disturbing other patients. The applicant was free to leave the ward with permission and to go out if accompanied by a member of staff. He was able to visit his family and friends, and towards the end of his stay to go to school.

The Court held:

> The restrictions imposed on the applicant were not of a nature or degree similar to the cases of deprivation of liberty specified in paragraph (1) of Article 5. In particular, he was not detained as a person of unsound mind. ..... Indeed, the restrictions to which the applicant was subject were no more than the normal requirements for the care of a child of 12 years of age receiving treatment in hospital. The conditions in which the applicant stayed thus did not, in principle, differ from those obtaining in many hospital wards where children with physical disorders are treated.

It concluded:

> the hospitalisation of the applicant did not amount to a deprivation of liberty within the meaning of Article 5, but was a responsible exercise by his mother of her custodial rights in the interests of the child.

### 2.20    HM v. Switzerland (ECtHR; (2002) 38 EHRR 314)

An 84-year-old woman was placed indefinitely in a nursing home by state authorities. She had had the possibility of staying at home and being cared for there, but she and her son had refused to co-operate with the relevant care association, and her living conditions had subsequently deteriorated. The state authorities placed her in the home in order to provide her with necessary medical care and satisfactory living conditions and hygiene.

The woman was not placed in the secure ward of the home but was free to move within the home and to have social contacts with the outside world. She was initially undecided as to what solution she preferred and, after moving into the home, the applicant had agreed to stay there. However, she subsequently applied to the courts saying that she had been deprived of her liberty.

The Court held that she had not been deprived of her liberty:

> Bearing these elements in mind, in particular the fact that [the authorities] had ordered the applicant's placement in the nursing home in her own interests in order to provide

her with the necessary medical care and satisfactory living conditions and standards of hygiene, and also taking into consideration the comparable circumstances of *Nielsen* v. *Denmark* [see case summary above], the Court concludes that in the circumstances of the present case the applicant's placement in the nursing home did not amount to a deprivation of liberty within the meaning of Article 5(1), but was a responsible measure taken by the competent authorities in the applicant's best interests.

## CASES WHERE THE COURTS HAVE FOUND THAT THE STEPS TAKEN INVOLVE A DEPRIVATION OF LIBERTY

**2.21** *DE and JE v. Surrey County Council (SCC) (High Court judgment of 29 December 2006)*

DE was a 76-year-old man who, following a major stroke, had become blind and had significant short-term memory impairment. He also had dementia and lacked capacity to decide where he should live, but was still often able to express his wishes with some clarity and force.

DE was married to JE. In August 2003, DE was living at home with JE. There was an occasion when JE felt that she could not care for DE, and placed him on a chair on the pavement in front of the house and called the police. The local authority then placed him in two care homes, referred to in the judgment of the court as the X home and the Y home.

Within the care homes, DE had a very substantial degree of freedom and lots of contact with the outside world. He was never subject to physical or chemical restraint.

DE repeatedly expressed the wish to live with JE, and JE also wanted DE to live with her. SCC would not agree to DE returning to live with, or visit, JE and made it clear that if JE were to persist in an attempt to remove DE, SCC would contact the police. DE and JE applied to the courts that this was a deprivation of his liberty.

In his judgment, Justice Munby said:

> The fundamental issue in this case … is whether DE has been and is deprived of his liberty to leave the X home and whether DE has been and is deprived of his liberty to leave the Y home. And when I refer to leaving the X home and the Y home, I do not mean leaving for the purpose of some trip or outing approved by SCC or by those managing the institution; I mean leaving in the sense of removing himself permanently in order to live where and with whom he chooses, specifically removing himself to live at home with JE.

He then said:

> DE was not and is not 'free to leave', and was and is, in that sense, completely under the control of [the local authority], because, as [counsel for DE] put it, it was and is [the local authority] who decides the essential matters of where DE can live, whether he can leave and whether he can be with JE.

He concluded:

> The simple reality is that DE will be permitted to leave the institution in which [the local authority] has placed him and be released to the care of JE only as and when, – if ever; probably never, – [the local authority] considers it appropriate. [The local authority's] motives may be the purest, but in my judgment, [it] has been and is continuing to deprive DE of his liberty.

**2.22** *HL v. United Kingdom (ECtHR; (2004) 40 EHRR 761)*

A 48-year-old man who had had autism since birth was unable to speak and his level of understanding was limited. He was frequently agitated and had a history of self-harming behaviour. He lacked the capacity to consent to treatment.

For over 30 years, he was cared for in Bournewood Hospital. In 1994, he was entrusted to carers and for three years he lived successfully with his carers. Following an incident of self-harm at a day centre on 22 July 1997, the applicant was taken to Bournewood Hospital where he was re-admitted informally (not under the Mental Health Act 1983).

The carers wished to have the applicant released to their care, which the hospital refused. The carers were unable to visit him.

In its judgment in *HL v. the United Kingdom*, the ECtHR said that:

> the key factor in the present case [is] that the health care professionals treating and managing the applicant exercised complete and effective control over his care and movements from the moment he presented acute behavioural problems on July 22, 1997 to the date when he was compulsorily detained on October 29, 1997.

> His responsible medical officer (Dr M) was clear that, had the applicant resisted admission or tried to leave thereafter, she would have prevented him from doing so and would have considered his involuntary committal under s. 3 of the 1983 Act; indeed, as soon as the Court of Appeal indicated that his appeal would be allowed, he was compulsorily detained under the 1983 Act. The correspondence between the applicant's carers and Dr M reflects both the carer's wish to have the applicant immediately released to their care and, equally, the clear intention of Dr M and the other relevant health care professionals to exercise strict control over his assessment, treatment, contacts and, notably, movement and residence; the applicant would only be released from hospital to the care of Mr and Mrs E as and when those professionals considered it appropriate. ... it was clear from the above noted correspondence that the applicant's contact with his carers was directed and controlled by the hospital, his carers visiting him for the first time after his admission on 2 November 1997.

> Accordingly, the concrete situation was that the applicant was under continuous supervision and control and was not free to leave.

### 2.23    *Storck v. Germany (ECtHR; (2005) 43 EHRR 96)*

A young woman was placed by her father in a psychiatric institution on occasions in 1974 and 1975. In July 1977, at the age of 18, she was placed again in a psychiatric institution. She was kept in a locked ward and was under the continuous supervision and control of the clinic personnel and was not free to leave the clinic during her entire stay of 20 months. When she attempted to flee, she was shackled. When she succeeded one time, she was brought back by the police. She was unable to maintain regular contact with the outside world.

She applied to the courts on the basis that she had been deprived of her liberty. There was a dispute about whether she consented to her confinement.

The Court noted:

> the applicant, on several occasions, had tried to flee from the clinic. She had to be shackled in order to prevent her from absconding and had to be brought back to the clinic by the police when she managed to escape on one occasion. Under these circumstances, the Court is unable to discern any factual basis for the assumption that the applicant – presuming that she had the capacity to consent – agreed to her continued stay in the clinic. In the alternative, assuming that the applicant was no longer capable of consenting following her treatment with strong medication, she cannot, in any event, be considered to have validly agreed to her stay in the clinic.

**2.24**    These cases reinforce the need to carefully consider all the specific circumstances of the relevant individual before deciding whether or not a person is being deprived of their liberty. They also underline the vital importance of involving family, friends and carers in this decision-making process: a significant feature of a number of the cases that have come before the courts is a difference of opinion or communication issue between the commissioners or providers of care and family members and carers.

## 3   HOW AND WHEN CAN DEPRIVATION OF LIBERTY BE APPLIED FOR AND AUTHORISED?

There are some circumstances in which depriving a person, who lacks capacity to consent to the arrangements made for their care or treatment, of their liberty is necessary to protect them from harm, and is in their best interests.

Deprivation of liberty can be authorised by supervisory bodies (primary care trusts (PCTs), local authorities, Welsh Ministers or local health boards (LHBs). To obtain authorisation to deprive someone of their liberty, managing authorities have to apply for an authorisation following the processes set out in this chapter.[6] Once an application has been received, the supervisory body must then follow the assessment processes set out in chapter 4 before it can authorise deprivation of liberty. It should be borne in mind that a deprivation of liberty authorisation does not, in itself, give authority to treat someone. This issue is covered in paragraphs 5.10 to 5.13.

In the vast majority of cases, it should be possible to plan in advance so that a standard authorisation can be obtained before the deprivation of liberty begins. There may, however, be some exceptional cases where the need for the deprivation of liberty is so urgent that it is in the best interests of the person for it to begin while the application is being considered. In that case, the care home or hospital may give an urgent authorisation for up to seven days (see chapter 6).

### How, in summary, can deprivation of liberty be authorised?

**3.1**   A **managing authority** has responsibility for applying for authorisation of deprivation of liberty for any person who may come within the scope of the deprivation of liberty safeguards:

- In the case of an NHS hospital, the managing authority is the NHS body responsible for the running of the hospital in which the relevant person is, or is to be, a resident.
- In the case of a care home or a private hospital, the managing authority will be the person registered, or required to be registered, under part 2 of the Care Standards Act 2000 in respect of the hospital or care home.

**3.2**   If a healthcare or social care professional thinks that an authorisation is needed, they should inform the managing authority. This might be as a result of a care review or needs assessment but could happen at any other time too. (See chapter 9 for guidance on action to take if there is a concern that a person is already being deprived of their liberty, without authorisation.)

**3.3**   A **supervisory body** is responsible for considering requests for authorisations, commissioning the required assessments (see chapter 4) and, where all the assessments agree, authorising the deprivation of liberty:

- Where the deprivation of liberty safeguards are applied to a person in a hospital situated in England, the supervisory body will be:

---

[6]   If a person is lawfully deprived of liberty in a care home or hospital as **a consequence of an order of the Court of Protection**, there is no need to apply for an authorisation. However, once the order of the Court of Protection has expired, for lawful deprivation of liberty to continue authorisation must be obtained by following the processes set out in this chapter.

- – if a PCT commissions[7] the relevant care or treatment (or it is commissioned on the PCT's behalf), that PCT
- – if the Welsh Ministers or an LHB commissions the relevant care and treatment in England, the Welsh Ministers, or
- – in any other case, the PCT for the area in which the hospital is situated.

■ Where the deprivation of liberty safeguards are applied to a person in a hospital situated in Wales, the supervisory body will be the Welsh Ministers or an LHB **unless** a PCT commissions the relevant care and treatment in Wales, in which case the PCT will be the supervisory body.

■ Where the deprivation of liberty safeguards are applied to a person in a care home, whether situated in England or Wales, the supervisory body will be the local authority for the area in which the person is ordinarily resident. However, if the person is not ordinarily resident in the area of any local authority (for example a person of no fixed abode), the supervisory body will be the local authority for the area in which the care home is situated.[8]

3.4    There are two types of authorisation: standard and urgent. A managing authority must request a standard authorisation when it appears likely that, at some time during the next 28 days, someone will be accommodated in its hospital or care home in circumstances that amount to a deprivation of liberty within the meaning of Article 5 of the European Convention on Human Rights. The request must be made to the supervisory body. Whenever possible, authorisation should be obtained in advance. Where this is not possible, and the managing authority believes it is necessary to deprive someone of their liberty in their best interests **before** the standard authorisation process can be completed, the managing authority must itself give an urgent authorisation and then obtain standard authorisation within seven calendar days (see chapter 6).

3.5    The flowchart at Annex 1 gives an overview of how the deprivation of liberty safeguards process should operate.

## How should managing authorities decide whether to apply for an authorisation?

3.6    Managing authorities should have a procedure in place that identifies:

■ whether deprivation of liberty is or may be necessary in a particular case
■ what steps they should take to assess whether to seek authorisation
■ whether they have taken all practical and reasonable steps to avoid a deprivation of liberty
■ what action they should take if they do need to request an authorisation
■ how they should review cases where authorisation is or may be necessary, and
■ who should take the necessary action.

---

[7]    Guidance on establishing the responsible commissioner can be found at www.dh.gov.uk/en/Publicationsandstatistics/Publications/PublicationsPolicyAndGuidance/DH-078466.

[8]    To work out the place of ordinary residence, the usual mechanisms under the National Assistance Act 1948 apply (see www.dh.gov.uk/en/SocialCare/Deliveringadultsocialcare/Ordinaryresidence/DH-079346). Any unresolved questions about the ordinary residence of a person will be handled by the Secretary of State or by the Welsh Ministers. Until a decision is made, the local authority that received the application must act as the supervisory body. After the decision is made, the local authority of ordinary residence must become the supervisory body. Regulations 17 to 19 of the Mental Capacity (Deprivation of Liberty: Standard Authorisations, Assessments and Ordinary Residence) Regulations 2008 set out, for England, arrangements that are to have effect while any question as to the ordinary residence of a person is determined in a case in which a local authority has received a request for a standard authorisation or a request to decide whether there is an unauthorised deprivation of liberty.

A flowchart that can be used to help develop such a procedure is at Annex 2.

## What is the application process?

**3.7**    A managing authority must apply for a standard authorisation. The application should be made in writing to the supervisory body. A standard form is available for this purpose.

**3.8**    In England, the request from a managing authority for a standard authorisation must include:

- the name and gender of the relevant person
- the age of the relevant person or, where this is not known, whether the managing authority reasonably believes that the relevant person is aged 18 years or older
- the address at which the relevant person is currently located, and the telephone number at the address
- the name, address and telephone number of the managing authority and the name of the person within the managing authority who is dealing with the request
- the purpose for which the authorisation is requested
- the date from which the authorisation is sought, and
- whether the managing authority has given an urgent authorisation and, if so, the date on which it expires.

**3.9**    A request for a standard authorisation must also include, if it is available or could reasonably be obtained by the managing authority:

- any medical information relating to the relevant person's health that the managing authority reasonably considers to be relevant to the proposed restrictions to their liberty
- the diagnosis of the mental disorder (within the meaning of the Mental Health Act 1983 but disregarding any exclusion for persons with learning disability) from which the relevant person is suffering
- any relevant care plans and needs assessments
- the racial, ethnic or national origins of the relevant person
- whether the relevant person has any special communication needs
- details of the proposed restrictions on the relevant person's liberty
- whether it is necessary for an Independent Mental Capacity Advocate (IMCA) to be instructed
- where the purpose of the proposed restrictions to the relevant person's liberty is to give treatment, whether the relevant person has made an advance decision that may be valid and applicable to some or all of that treatment
- whether there is an existing standard authorisation in relation to the detention of the relevant person and, if so, the date of the expiry of that authorisation
- whether the relevant person is subject to any requirements of the Mental Health Act 1983, and
- the name, address and telephone number of:
    - anyone named by the relevant person as someone to be consulted about their welfare
    - anyone engaged in caring for the person or interested in their welfare
    - any donee of a Lasting Power of Attorney ('donee') granted by the person
    - any deputy appointed for the person by the court, and
    - any IMCA who has already been instructed.

If there is an existing authorisation, information that has not changed does not have to be resupplied.

**3.10**    In Wales, the request from a managing authority for a standard authorisation must include:

- the name of the relevant person
- the name, address and telephone number of the managing authority
- the reasons why the managing authority considers that the relevant person is being or will be detained in circumstances which amount to a deprivation of liberty
- the reasons why the managing authority considers that the relevant person satisfies the qualifying requirements
- details of any urgent authorisation
- information or documents in support of why the relevant person satisfies the qualifying requirements
- the name, address and telephone number of any person who has an interest in the welfare of the relevant person, and
- details of any relevant valid and applicable advance decision.

## WHERE SHOULD APPLICATIONS BE SENT?

3.11    If the application is being made by a care home, the application must be sent to the local authority for the area in which the relevant person is ordinarily resident. If the relevant person is not ordinarily resident in the area of any local authority (for example, is of no fixed abode), if the care home does not know where the person currently lives, or if the person does not live in England or Wales, the application should be sent to the local authority in whose area the care home is located.

3.12    When the application is being made by a hospital:

- if the care is commissioned by a PCT, the application should be sent to that PCT
- if the care is commissioned by the Welsh Ministers, the application should be sent to the LHB for the area in which the relevant person is ordinarily resident
- if the care is commissioned by an LHB, the application should be sent to that LHB, and
- in any other case (for example, care that is commissioned privately), the application should be sent to the PCT for the area in which the relevant hospital is situated.

3.13    An application sent to the wrong supervisory body can be passed on to the correct supervisory body without the managing authority needing to reapply. But the managing authority should make every effort to establish which is the correct supervisory body to minimise delays in handling the application. (Footnote 8 explains how place of ordinary residence is determined and how disputes about the place of ordinary residence will be resolved.)

3.14    The managing authority must keep a written record of each request made for a standard authorisation and the reasons for making the request.

## Who should be informed that an application has been made?

3.15    The managing authority should tell the relevant person's family, friends and carers, and any IMCA already involved in the relevant person's case, that it has applied for an authorisation of deprivation of liberty, unless it is impractical or impossible to do so, or undesirable in terms of the interests of the relevant person's health or safety. Anyone who is engaged in caring for the relevant person or interested in their welfare, or who has been named by them as a person to consult, must be given the opportunity to input their views on whether deprivation of liberty is in the best interests of the relevant person, as part of the best interests assessment (see paragraphs 4.58 to 4.76), as far as is practical and appropriate. The views of the relevant person about who to inform and consult should be taken into account.

3.16    The managing authority must notify the supervisory body if it is satisfied that there is no one who should be consulted in determining the relevant person's best interests, except those providing care and treatment for the relevant person in a professional capacity or for remuneration. In such a case, the supervisory body must instruct an IMCA to represent and support the relevant person before any assessments take place (see paragraphs 3.22 to 3.27 regarding the rights and role of an IMCA instructed in these circumstances).

### What action does the supervisory body need to take when it receives an application for authorisation?

**3.17**    When it receives an application for authorisation of deprivation of liberty, the supervisory body must, as soon as is practical and possible:

- consider whether the request is appropriate and should be pursued, and
- seek any further information that it requires from the managing authority to help it with the decision.

If the supervisory body has any doubts about proceeding with the request, it should seek to resolve them with the managing authority.

**3.18**    Supervisory bodies should have a procedure in place that identifies the action they should take, who should take it and within what timescale. As far as practical and possible, they should communicate the procedure to managing authorities and give them the relevant contact details for making an application. The flowchart at Annex 3 summarises the process that a supervisory body should follow on receipt of a request from a managing authority for a standard deprivation of liberty authorisation.

### Can an application for authorisation be made in advance?

**3.19**    A standard authorisation comes into force when it is given, or at any later time specified in the authorisation. Paragraph 3.4 refers to the timescales for initially applying for authorisations: 28 days are allowed so that authorisations can usually be sought as part of care planning (such as planning of discharge from hospital). There is no statutory limit on how far in advance of the expiry of one authorisation a fresh authorisation can be sought. Clearly, however, an authorisation should not be applied for too far in advance as this may prevent an assessor from making an accurate assessment of what the person's circumstances will be at the time the authorisation will come into force.

**3.20**    If a supervisory body considers that an application for an authorisation has been made too far in advance, it should raise the matter with the managing authority. The outcome may be an agreement with the managing authority that the application should be withdrawn, to be resubmitted at a more appropriate time.

### What happens when the managing authority and the supervisory body are the same organisation?

**3.21**    In some cases, a single organisation will be both supervisory body and managing authority – for example, where a local authority itself provides a residential care home, rather than purchasing the service from another organisation. This does not prevent it from acting in both capacities. However, in England the regulations specify that in such a situation the best interests assessor cannot be an employee of the supervisory body/managing authority, or providing services to it. For example, in a case involving a local authority care home, the best interests assessor could be an NHS employee or an independent practitioner. (See paragraphs 4.13 and 4.60 for full details of who can be a best interests assessor.) There are similar provisions for Wales.

## When should an IMCA be instructed?

**3.22**   If there is nobody appropriate to consult, other than people engaged in providing care or treatment for the relevant person in a professional capacity[9] or for remuneration, the managing authority must notify the supervisory body when it submits the application for the deprivation of liberty authorisation. The supervisory body must then instruct an IMCA straight away to represent the person. It is particularly important that the IMCA is instructed quickly if an urgent authorisation has been given, so that they can make a meaningful input at a very early stage in the process. (See paragraph 3.28 for other stages in the deprivation of liberty safeguards process when an IMCA must or may be instructed.)

**3.23**   Chapter 10 of the main Code ('What is the new Independent Mental Capacity Advocate service and how does it work?') describes the wider rights and role of an IMCA. Supervisory bodies should follow the guidance in that chapter in identifying an IMCA who is suitably qualified to represent the relevant person. However, it is also important to note that an IMCA instructed at this initial stage of the deprivation of liberty safeguards process has additional rights and responsibilities compared to an IMCA more generally instructed under the Mental Capacity Act 2005. IMCAs in this context have the right to:

- as they consider appropriate, give information or make submissions to assessors, which assessors must take into account in carrying out their assessments
- receive copies of any assessments from the supervisory body
- receive a copy of any standard authorisation given by the supervisory body
- be notified by the supervisory body if they are unable to give a standard authorisation because one or more of the deprivation of liberty assessments did not meet the qualifying requirements
- receive a copy of any urgent authorisation from the managing authority
- receive from the managing authority a copy of any notice declining to extend the duration of an urgent authorisation
- receive from the supervisory body a copy of any notice that an urgent authorisation has ceased to be in force, and
- apply to the Court of Protection for permission to take the relevant person's case to the Court in connection with a matter relating to the giving or refusal of a standard or urgent authorisation (in the same way as any other third party can).

The assessment and authorisation processes are described in chapters 4 and 5.

**3.24**   IMCAs will need to familiarise themselves with the relevant person's circumstances and to consider what they may need to tell any of the assessors during the course of the assessment process. They will also need to consider whether they have any concerns about the outcome of the assessment process.

**3.25**   Differences of opinion between an IMCA and an assessor should ideally be resolved while the assessment is still in progress. Where there are significant disagreements between an IMCA and one or more of the assessors that cannot be resolved between them, the supervisory body should be informed before the assessment is finalised. The supervisory body should then consider what action might be appropriate, including perhaps convening a meeting to discuss the matter. Wherever possible, differences of opinion should be resolved informally in order to minimise the need for an IMCA to make an application to the Court of Protection. However, an IMCA should not be discouraged from making an application to the Court of Protection should they consider it necessary. (Chapter 15 of the main Code ('What are the best ways to settle disagreements and disputes about issues covered in the Act?') contains general guidance about the resolution of disputes arising under the Act.)

---

[9]   A friend or family member is **not** considered to be acting in a professional capacity simply because they have been appointed as the person's representative for a previous authorisation.

**3.26**    An IMCA will also need to consider whether they have any concerns about the giving of an urgent authorisation (see chapter 6), and whether it would be appropriate to challenge the giving of such an authorisation via the Court of Protection.

**3.27**    Once a relevant person's representative is appointed (see chapter 7), the duties imposed on the IMCA cease to apply. The IMCA may, however, still apply to the Court of Protection for permission to take the relevant person's case to the Court in connection with the giving of a standard authorisation; but, in doing so, the IMCA must take account of the views of the relevant person's representative.

### OTHER CIRCUMSTANCES IN WHICH AN IMCA MUST OR MAY BE INSTRUCTED

**3.28**    An IMCA must also be instructed during gaps in the appointment of a relevant person's representative (for instance, if a new representative is being sought – see paragraphs 7.34 to 7.36). In addition, an IMCA may be instructed at any time where:

■    the relevant person does not have a paid 'professional' representative
■    the relevant person or their representative requests that an IMCA is instructed to help them, or
■    a supervisory body believes that instructing an IMCA will help to ensure that the person's rights are protected (see paragraphs 7.37 to 7.41).

## 4    WHAT IS THE ASSESSMENT PROCESS FOR A STANDARD AUTHORISATION OF DEPRIVATION OF LIBERTY?

When a supervisory body gives a standard authorisation of deprivation of liberty, the managing authority may lawfully deprive the relevant person of their liberty in the hospital or care home named in the authorisation.

This chapter describes the assessments that have to be undertaken in order for a standard authorisation to be given. It also sets out who is eligible to undertake the assessments.

### *What assessments are required before giving a standard authorisation?*

**4.1**    As soon as the supervisory body has confirmed that the request for a standard authorisation should be pursued, it must obtain the relevant assessments to ascertain whether the qualifying requirements of the deprivation of liberty safeguards are met. The supervisory body has a legal responsibility to select assessors who are both suitable and eligible. Assessments must be completed within 21 days for a standard deprivation of liberty authorisation, or, where an urgent authorisation has been given, before the urgent authorisation expires.

**4.2**    The assessments (described in paragraphs 4.23 to 4.76) are:

■    age assessment (paragraphs 4.23 and 4.24)
■    no refusals assessment (paragraphs 4.25 to 4.28)
■    mental capacity assessment (paragraphs 4.29 to 4.32)
■    mental health assessment (paragraphs 4.33 to 4.39) eligibility assessment (paragraphs 4.40 to 4.57), and
■    best interests assessment (paragraphs 4.58 to 4.76).

Standard forms are available for completion by each of the assessors.

**4.3**    If the person being assessed is not currently in the supervisory body's area, the supervisory body should seek, as far as is practical and possible, to arrange to use assessors based near where the person currently is.

USING EQUIVALENT ASSESSMENTS

**4.4**    The Act states that where an 'equivalent assessment' to any of these assessments has already been obtained, it may be relied upon instead of obtaining a fresh assessment.

**4.5**    An equivalent assessment is an assessment:

■    that has been carried out in the last 12 months, not necessarily for the purpose of a deprivation of liberty authorisation (where the required assessment is an age assessment, there is no time limit on the use of an equivalent assessment)

■    that meets all the requirements of the deprivation of liberty assessment,

■    of which the supervisory body is satisfied that there is no reason to believe that it is no longer accurate, and

■    of which the supervisory body has a written copy.

An example would be a recent assessment carried out for the purposes of the Mental Health Act 1983, which could serve as an equivalent to a mental health assessment.

**4.6**    Great care should be taken in deciding to use an equivalent assessment and this should not be done routinely. The older the assessment is, even if it took place within the last 12 months, the less likely it is to represent a valid equivalent assessment (unless it is an age assessment). For example, only a very recent mental capacity assessment would be appropriate where capacity is known to fluctuate, since one of the principles of the Act is that a person must be assumed to have capacity unless it is established that they lack capacity.

**4.7**    If an equivalent best interests assessment is used, the supervisory body must also take into account any information given, or submissions made, by the relevant person's representative or an Independent Mental Capacity Advocate (IMCA) instructed under the deprivation of liberty safeguards.

**4.8**    Supervisory bodies should record the reasons why they have used any equivalent assessment. A standard form is available for this purpose.

## When must assessments take place?

**4.9**    The regulations for England[10] specify that all assessments required for a standard authorisation must be completed within 21 calendar days from the date on which the supervisory body receives a request from a managing authority. The regulations for Wales specify that all assessments required for a standard authorisation must be completed within 21 days from the date the assessors were instructed by the supervisory body.

**4.10**    However, if an urgent authorisation is already in force, the assessments must be completed before the urgent authorisation expires. The regulations for Wales specify that, where the managing authority has given itself an urgent authorisation and applies for a standard authorisation, the assessors must complete the assessments within five days of the date of instruction.

**4.11**    Urgent authorisations may be given by managing authorities for an initial period not exceeding seven days. If there are exceptional reasons why it has not been possible to deal with the request for a standard authorisation within the period of the urgent authorisation, they may be extended **by the supervisory body** for up to a further seven days. It is for the supervisory body to decide what constitutes an 'exceptional reason', taking into account all the circumstances of an individual case.

---

[10]    The Mental Capacity (Deprivation of Liberty: Standard Authorisations, Assessments and Ordinary Residence) Regulations 2008.

**4.12**    Supervisory bodies must keep a record of all requests for standard authorisations that they receive and should acknowledge the receipt of requests from managing authorities for standard authorisations.

## How should assessors be selected?

**4.13**    The six assessments do not have to be completed by different assessors. In fact, it is highly unlikely that there will be six separate assessors – not least because it is desirable to minimise the burden on the person being assessed. However, each assessor must make their own decisions, and to ensure that an appropriate degree of objectivity is brought to the assessment process:

- there **must** be a minimum of two assessors
- the mental health and best interests assessors **must** be different people
- the best interests assessor can be an employee of the supervisory body or managing authority, but **must not** be involved in the care or treatment of the person they are assessing nor in decisions about their care
- a potential best interests assessor should not be used if they are in a line management relationship with the professional proposing the deprivation of liberty or the mental health assessor
- none of the assessors may have a financial interest in the case of the person they are assessing (a person is considered to have a financial interest in a case where that person is a partner, director, other office-holder or major shareholder of the managing authority that has made the application for a standard authorisation)
- an assessor **must not** be a relative of the person being assessed, nor of a person with a financial interest in the person's care. For this purpose, a 'relative' is:

  a.    a spouse, ex-spouse, civil partner or ex-civil partner
  b.    a person living with the relevant person as if they were a spouse or a civil partner
  c.    a parent or child
  d.    a brother or sister
  e.    a child of a person falling within definitions a, b or d
  f.    a grandparent or grandchild
  g.    a grandparent-in-law or grandchild-in-law
  h.    an aunt or uncle
  i.    a sister-in-law or brother-in-law
  j.    a son-in-law or daughter-in-law
  k.    a first cousin, or
  l.    a half-brother or half-sister.

  These relationships include step-relationships
- where the managing authority and supervisory body are both the same body (see paragraph 3.21), the supervisory body may not select to carry out a best interests assessment a person who is employed by the body, or providing services to it, and
- the supervisory body should seek to avoid appointing assessors in any other possible conflict of interests situations that might bring into question the objectivity of an assessment.

**4.14**    Other relevant factors for supervisory bodies to consider when appointing assessors include:

- the reason for the proposed deprivation of liberty
- whether the potential assessor has experience of working with the service user group from which the person being assessed comes (for example, older people, people with learning disabilities, people with autism, or people with brain injury)
- whether the potential assessor has experience of working with people from the cultural background of the person being assessed, and

■    any other specific needs of the person being assessed, for example communication needs.

**4.15**    Supervisory bodies should ensure that sufficient assessors are available to meet their needs, and must be satisfied in each case that the assessors have the skills, experience, qualifications and training required by regulations to perform the function effectively. The regulations also require supervisory bodies to be satisfied that there is an appropriate criminal record certificate issued in respect of an assessor. It will be useful to keep a record of qualified assessors and their experience and availability. Supervisory bodies should consider making arrangements to ensure that assessors have the necessary opportunities to maintain their skills and knowledge (of legal developments, for example) and share, audit and review their practice.

**4.16**    Assessors act as individual professionals and are personally accountable for their decisions. Managing authorities and supervisory bodies must not dictate or seek to influence their decisions.

**4.17**    There is no reason in principle why interviews, examinations and fact-finding required as part of any deprivation of liberty safeguards assessment cannot serve more than one purpose, in order to avoid unnecessary burdens both on the person being assessed and on staff. However, if this does happen, all purposes of the interview or examination should be made clear to the relevant person, and to any family members, friends, carers or advocates supporting them.

### PROTECTION AGAINST LIABILITY

**4.18**    Nobody can or should carry out an assessment unless they are protected against any liabilities that might arise in connection with carrying out the assessment. Individual assessors will need to satisfy themselves, and any supervisory body that selects them as an assessor, that they are appropriately covered by either employers' or personal insurance.

## What is the assessment process?

**4.19**    As indicated in paragraph 4.2, there are six assessments that must be conducted before a supervisory body can give an authorisation.

**4.20**    The assessments are set out in the order in which it will normally be most appropriate to complete them. In particular, it is recommended that the best interests assessment, which is likely to be the most time-consuming, is not started until there is a reasonable expectation that the other five qualifying requirements will be met.

**4.21**    But, ultimately, it is for the supervisory body to decide on the order in which the assessments should be undertaken and, in the light of the time available to complete the overall assessment process, the extent to which they should be undertaken to separate or simultaneous timescales. The supervisory body's decision about how many assessors will undertake the assessments (see paragraph 4.13) will also be a relevant factor.

**4.22**    The following paragraphs explain the assessment process.

### AGE ASSESSMENT

**4.23**    The purpose of the age assessment is simply to confirm whether the relevant person is aged 18 or over. This is because, as paragraph 1.12 explains, the deprivation of liberty safeguards apply only to people aged 18 or over. For people under the age of 18, a different safeguards process applies. In most cases, this is likely to be a fairly straightforward assessment. If there is any doubt, age should be established by a birth certificate or other evidence that the assessor considers reliable. Where it is not possible to verify with any certainty whether a person is aged 18 or over, the assessor should base the assessment on the best of their knowledge and belief.

**4.24**    This assessment can be undertaken by anybody whom the supervisory body is satisfied is eligible to be a best interests assessor.

## NO REFUSALS ASSESSMENT

**4.25**    The purpose of the no refusals assessment is to establish whether an authorisation to deprive the relevant person of their liberty would conflict with other existing authority for decision-making for that person.

**4.26**    The following are instances of a conflict that would mean that a standard authorisation could not be given:

■    If the relevant person has made **an advance decision to refuse treatment** that remains valid and is applicable to some or all of the treatment that is the purpose for which the authorisation is requested, then a standard authorisation cannot be given. See sections 24 to 26 of the Mental Capacity Act 2005 and chapter 9 of the main Code ('What does the Act say about advance decisions to refuse treatment?') for more information about advance decisions and when they are valid and applicable. Remember too that the deprivation of liberty authorisation does not, in itself, provide authority to treat the person (see paragraphs 5.10 to 5.13 of this Code).

■    If any part of the proposal to deprive the person of their liberty (including any element of the care plan) would be in conflict with a **valid decision of a donee or a deputy** made within the scope of their authority, then a standard authorisation cannot be given. For example, if a donee or deputy decides that it would not be in the best interests of the relevant person to be in a particular care home, and that decision is within the scope of their authority, then the care plan will need to be reviewed with the donee or deputy.

**4.27**    If there is any such conflict, the no refusals assessment qualifying requirement will not be met and a standard authorisation for deprivation of liberty cannot be given.

**4.28**    The no refusals assessment can be undertaken by anybody that the supervisory body is satisfied is eligible to be a best interests assessor.

## MENTAL CAPACITY ASSESSMENT

**4.29**    The purpose of the mental capacity assessment is to establish whether the relevant person lacks capacity to decide whether or not they should be accommodated in the relevant hospital or care home to be given care or treatment. The assessment refers specifically to the relevant person's capacity to make this decision at the time it needs to be made. The starting assumption should always be that a person has the capacity to make the decision.

**4.30**    Sections 1 to 3 of the Act set out how a person's capacity to make decisions should be determined. Chapter 4 of the main Code ('How does the Act define a person's capacity to make a decision and how should capacity be assessed?') gives further guidance on ways to assess capacity. When assessing the capacity of a person being considered for the deprivation of liberty safeguards, these guidelines should be followed.

**4.31**    The regulations for England specify that the mental capacity assessment can be undertaken by anyone who is eligible to act as a mental health or best interests assessor. In deciding who to appoint for this assessment, the supervisory body should take account of the need for understanding and practical experience of the nature of the person's condition and its impact on decision-making.

**4.32**    Supervisory bodies may wish to consider using an eligible assessor who already knows the relevant person to undertake this assessment, if they think it would be of benefit. This will primarily arise if somebody involved in the person's care is considered best placed to carry out a reliable assessment, using their knowledge of the person over a period of time. It may also help in reducing any distress that might be caused to the person if they were assessed by somebody they did not know.

## MENTAL HEALTH ASSESSMENT

**4.33**    The purpose of the mental health assessment is to establish whether the relevant person has a mental disorder within the meaning of the Mental Health Act 1983. That means any disorder or disability of mind, apart from dependence on alcohol or drugs. It includes all learning disabilities. This is not an assessment to determine whether the person requires mental health treatment.

**4.34**    A distinction can be drawn between the mental health assessment and the mental capacity assessment:

- Although a person must have an impairment or disturbance of the functioning of the mind or brain in order to lack capacity, it does not follow that they automatically have a mental disorder within the meaning of the Mental Health Act 1983.
- The objective of the mental health assessment is to ensure that the person is medically diagnosed as being of 'unsound mind' and so comes within the scope of Article 5 of the European Convention on Human Rights.

**4.35**    In both England and Wales, the regulations specify that:

- the mental health assessment must be carried out by a doctor, and
- the assessing doctor has to either be approved under section 12 of the Mental Health Act 1983, or be a registered medical practitioner with at least three years' post-registration experience in the diagnosis or treatment of mental disorder, such as a GP with a special interest. This includes doctors who are automatically treated as being section 12 approved because they are approved clinicians under the Mental Health Act 1983.

**4.36**    To be eligible to undertake assessments, in England a doctor will need to have completed the standard training for deprivation of liberty mental health assessors. Except in the 12 month period beginning with the date the doctor has successfully completed the standard training, the regulations for England also require the supervisory body to be satisfied that the doctor has, in the 12 months prior to selection, completed further training relevant to their role as a mental health assessor. In Wales, a doctor will need to have completed appropriate training and have appropriate skills and experience.

**4.37**    Supervisory bodies must consider the suitability of the assessor for the particular case (for example, whether they have experience relevant to the person's condition).

**4.38**    As with the mental capacity assessment, supervisory bodies may wish to consider using an eligible assessor who already knows the relevant person to undertake this assessment, if they think it would be of benefit.

**4.39**    The mental health assessor is required to consider how the mental health of the person being assessed is likely to be affected by being deprived of their liberty, and to report their conclusions to the best interests assessor. The mental health and best interests assessments cannot be carried out by the same person.

## ELIGIBILITY ASSESSMENT

**4.40**   This assessment relates specifically to the relevant person's status, or potential status, under the Mental Health Act 1983.

**4.41**   A person is not eligible for a deprivation of liberty authorisation if:

■   they are detained as a hospital in-patient under the Mental Health Act 1983, or
■   the authorisation, if given, would be inconsistent with an obligation placed on them under the Mental Health Act 1983, such as a requirement to live somewhere else. This will only affect people who are on leave of absence from detention under the Mental Health Act 1983 or who are subject to guardianship, supervised community treatment or conditional discharge.

**4.42**   Where the proposed authorisation relates to a care home, or to deprivation of liberty in a hospital for non-mental health treatment, the eligibility assessment will simply be a matter of checking that authorisation would not be inconsistent with an obligation placed on the person under the Mental Health Act 1983.

**4.43**   When a person is subject to guardianship under the Mental Health Act 1983, their guardian can decide where they are to live, but cannot authorise deprivation of liberty and cannot require them to live somewhere where they are deprived of liberty unless that deprivation of liberty is authorised.

**4.44**   Occasionally, a person who is subject to guardianship and who lacks capacity to make the relevant decisions may need specific care or treatment in a care home or hospital that cannot be delivered without deprivation of liberty. This may be in a care home in which they are already living or in which the guardian thinks they ought to live, or it may be in a hospital where they need to be for physical health care. It may also apply if they need to be in hospital for mental health care. The process for obtaining a deprivation of liberty authorisation and the criteria to be applied are the same as for any other person.

**4.45**   If the proposed authorisation relates to deprivation of liberty in a hospital **wholly or partly for the purpose of treatment of mental disorder**, then the relevant person will not be eligible if:

■   they object to being admitted to hospital, or to some or all the treatment they will receive there for mental disorder, **and**
■   they meet the criteria for an application for admission under section 2 or section 3 of the Mental Health Act 1983 (unless an attorney or deputy, acting within their powers, had consented to the things to which the person is objecting).

**4.46**   In many cases, the relevant person will be able to state an objection. However, where the person is unable to communicate, or can only communicate to a limited extent, assessors will need to consider the person's behaviour, wishes, feelings, views, beliefs and values, both present and past, so far as they can be ascertained (see paragraphs 5.37 to 5.48 of the main Code for guidance on how to do this). If there is reason to think that a person would object if able to do so, then the person should be assumed to be objecting. Occasionally, it may be that the person's behaviour initially suggests an objection, but that this objection is in fact not directed at the treatment at all. In that case, the person should **not** be taken to be objecting.

**4.47**   Assessors should always bear in mind that their job is simply to establish whether the person objects to treatment or to being in hospital: whether that objection is reasonable or not is not the issue.

**4.48**    Even where a person does not object and a deprivation of liberty authorisation is possible, it should not be assumed that such an authorisation is invariably the correct course. There may be other factors that suggest that the Mental Health Act 1983 should be used (for example, where it is thought likely that the person will recover relevant capacity and will then refuse to consent to treatment, or where it is important for the hospital managers to have a formal power to retake a person who goes absent without leave). Further guidance on this is given in the Mental Health Act 1983 Code of Practice.

**4.49**    The eligibility assessor is not required to decide (or even consider) whether an application under the Mental Health Act 1983 would be in the person's best interests.

**4.50**    If the proposed authorisation relates to deprivation of liberty in a hospital **wholly or partly for the purpose of treatment of mental disorder**, then the person will also not be eligible if they are:

- currently on leave of absence from detention under the Mental Health Act 1983
- subject to supervised community treatment, or
- subject to conditional discharge, in which case powers of recall under the Mental Health Act 1983 should be used.

**4.51**    People on leave of absence from detention under the Mental Health Act 1983 or subject to supervised community treatment or conditional discharge are, however, eligible for the deprivation of liberty safeguards if they require treatment in hospital for a physical disorder.

## WHO CAN CONDUCT AN ELIGIBILITY ASSESSMENT?

**4.52**    The regulations for England specify that the eligibility assessment must be completed by:

- a mental health assessor who is also a section 12 doctor, or
- a best interests assessor who is also an approved mental health professional (AMHP).

**4.53**    The assessment cannot be carried out by a non-section 12 doctor, even if they are qualified to be a mental health assessor, nor by a non-AMHP, even if they are qualified to be a best interests assessor. This will ensure that the eligibility assessor is sufficiently familiar with the Mental Health Act 1983, which will be particularly important in cases in which it appears that the powers available under the Mental Health Act 1983 may be more appropriate than the deprivation of liberty safeguards.

**4.54**    The eligibility assessment will often be carried out by the best interests assessor but, where this is not the case, the eligibility assessor must request the best interests assessor to provide any relevant eligibility information that the best interests assessor may have, and the best interests assessor must comply with this request.

## WHAT HAPPENS WHEN PEOPLE ARE ASSESSED AS INELIGIBLE?

**4.55**    If the eligibility assessor believes that the relevant person is not eligible, but (on the basis of the report of the best interests assessor) that they should nevertheless be deprived of liberty in their best interests, the eligibility assessor should immediately inform the supervisory body.

**4.56**    In the case of someone already subject to the Mental Health Act 1983, the eligibility assessor should inform the supervisory body with a view to contact being made with the relevant responsible clinician (i.e. the clinician in overall charge of the person's treatment) or, if the person is subject to guardianship, the relevant local social services authority. Otherwise, the assessor or supervisory body should take steps to arrange for the person to be assessed further with a view to an application being made for admission to hospital under the Mental Health Act 1983. Assessors will need to be familiar with local arrangements for doing this.

**4.57**   In some cases, even before the eligibility assessment is undertaken, it may be known that there is a chance that the person will have to be assessed with a view to an application under the Mental Health Act 1983 because the eligibility assessment might conclude that they are ineligible for a deprivation of liberty authorisation. In such cases, steps should be taken, where practical and possible, to arrange assessments in a way that minimises the number of separate interviews or examinations the person has to undergo.

## BEST INTERESTS ASSESSMENT

**4.58**   The purpose of the best interests assessment is to establish, firstly, whether deprivation of liberty is occurring or is going to occur and, if so, whether:

- it is in the best interests of the relevant person to be deprived of liberty
- it is necessary for them to be deprived of liberty in order to prevent harm to themselves, and
- deprivation of liberty is a proportionate response to the likelihood of the relevant person suffering harm and the seriousness of that harm.

**4.59**   The best interests assessor is the person who is responsible for assessing what is in the best interests of a relevant person.

**4.60**   In both England and Wales, the best interests assessment must be undertaken by an AMHP, social worker, nurse, occupational therapist or chartered psychologist with the skills and experience specified in the regulations. In England, this includes at least two years' post-registration experience. In England, the supervisory body must also be satisfied that the assessor:

- is not suspended from the register or list relevant to the person's profession
- has successfully completed training that has been approved[11] by the Secretary of State to be a best interests assessor
- except in the 12 month period beginning with the date the person has successfully completed the approved training, has, in the 12 months prior to selection, completed further training relevant to their role as a best interests assessor, and
- has the skills necessary to obtain, evaluate and analyse complex evidence and differing views and to weigh them appropriately in decision-making.

**4.61**   Section 4 of the Mental Capacity Act 2005 sets out the best interests principles that apply for the purpose of the Act. Chapter 5 of the main Code ('What does the Act mean when it talks about 'best interests'?') explains this in more detail, and, in particular, paragraph 5.13 of the main Code includes a checklist of factors that need to be taken into account in working out what is in a person's best interests. These principles and guidance apply equally to working out a person's best interests for the purpose of the deprivation of liberty safeguards. However, when it comes to best interests around deprivation of liberty, additional factors apply, including:

- whether any harm to the person could arise if the deprivation of liberty does not take place

---

[11] Approved courses can be found at: www.dh.gov.uk/en/SocialCare/Deliveringadultsocialcare/MentalCapacity/MentalCapacityActDeprivationofLibertySafeguards/index.htm.

- what that harm would be
- how likely that harm is to arise (i.e. is the level of risk sufficient to justify a step as serious as depriving a person of liberty?)
- what other care options there are which could avoid deprivation of liberty, and
- if deprivation of liberty is currently unavoidable, what action could be taken to avoid it in future.

## ESTABLISHING WHETHER DEPRIVATION OF LIBERTY IS OCCURRING

**4.62**   The first task of a best interests assessor is to establish whether deprivation of liberty is occurring, or is likely to occur, since there is no point in the assessment process proceeding further if deprivation of liberty is not at issue. If the best interests assessor concludes that deprivation of liberty is **not** occurring and is not likely to occur, they should state in their assessment report to the supervisory body that deprivation of liberty is not in the person's best interests because there is obviously a less restrictive option available. The best interests requirement will therefore not be met in such a case.

**4.63**   To establish whether deprivation of liberty is occurring, or is likely to occur, the best interests assessor must consult the managing authority of the hospital or care home where the person is, or will be, accommodated and examine any relevant needs assessments and care plans prepared for the person. The best interests assessor must consider whether the care plan and the manner in which it is being, or will be, implemented constitutes a deprivation of liberty. If not, then no deprivation of liberty authorisation is required for that care plan.

**4.64**   The managing authority and supervisory body must provide the best interests assessor with any needs assessments or care plans that they have undertaken or which have been undertaken on their behalf.

## THE BEST INTERESTS ASSESSMENT PROCESS

**4.65**   If the best interests assessor considers that deprivation of liberty is occurring, or is likely to occur, they should start a full best interests assessment. In line with section 4(7) of the Act this involves seeking the views of a range of people connected to the relevant person to find out whether they believe that depriving the relevant person of their liberty is, or would be, in the person's best interests to protect them from harm or to enable them to follow the care plan proposed. The best interests assessor should, as far as is practical and possible, seek the views of:

- anyone the person has previously named as someone they want to be consulted
- anyone involved in caring for the person
- anyone interested in the person's welfare (for example, family carers, other close relatives, or an advocate already working with the person), and
- any donee or deputy who represents the person.

**4.66**   This may mean that the best interests assessor needs to explain key aspects of the care plan and what it aims to do to the people being consulted. The best interests assessor should then take the views received into account as far as is practical and appropriate. It is essential that the best interests assessor provides an independent and objective view of whether or not there is a genuine justification for deprivation of liberty, taking account of all the relevant views and factors.

**4.67**   The best interests assessor must state in their assessment the name and address of every interested person whom they have consulted in carrying out the assessment.

**4.68**   Family and friends may not be confident about expressing their views: it is the responsibility of the best interests assessor to enable them to do so – using support to meet communication or language needs as necessary.

---

**Scenario: Consulting around best interests**

Mr Simpson is 60 and has dementia with particularly poor short-term memory, which clinicians agree is most likely to be related to chronic excessive alcohol intake. After initial treatment in hospital, he has been admitted to a care home – a decision which he consented to.

However, though he had the mental capacity to consent to hospital admission, he has no insight into his dementia. He is unable to understand the health and safety implications of continuing to drink, and will do so heavily whenever he has access to alcohol and the money to buy it.

Although Mr Simpson had no access to alcohol in hospital, there is a pub within walking distance of the care home, which he visits and drinks in. When he returns to the home intoxicated, his behaviour can be very distressing and potentially dangerous to other residents. The care home staff believe that if this continues, there may be no other option than to return him to hospital under the Mental Health Act 1983.

The care home staff have asked Mr Simpson to drink only in moderation, but this has not proved successful; and the landlord has been asked not to serve him more than one drink but has refused to do so. The manager of the home is now considering a care plan to prevent Mr Simpson from leaving the home without an escort, and to prevent visits from friends who bring alcohol. He believes this would be in Mr Simpson's best interests.

As the pub is open all day, if this new care plan was adopted, Mr Simpson would be stopped from going out at all without an escort, even though he often goes to the shops and the park as well as the pub. Staffing levels are such that an escort would only be available on some days and for limited periods.

Mr Simpson's daughter, his closest relative, is concerned that these restrictions are excessive and would amount to a deprivation of liberty. She believes that having a drink and socialising in the pub is her father's 'only remaining pleasure', and is sure that, if he still had capacity, he would choose to carry on drinking, regardless of the health risks.

She requests a best interests meeting to consider whether a less restrictive care plan could still meet his needs.

At this meeting, Mr Simpson's community mental health nurse confirms that Mr Simpson is likely to lack capacity in relation to this particular issue, and advises that if he continues to drink to excess his dementia is likely to advance rapidly and his life expectancy will be reduced. However, small amounts of alcohol will not be significantly harmful.

The consensus is that the proposed restrictions would severely limit Mr Simpson's ability to maintain social contact and to carry on the life he has been used to, and that this would amount to deprivation of liberty. Bearing in mind his daughter's view, it is felt that it would not be in Mr Simpson's best interests to prevent him from having any alcohol at all. However, in view of the health risks and the likelihood that he would otherwise have to be detained in hospital, it would be in Mr Simpson's best interests to ensure that he does not get intoxicated. (The possibility of limiting his access to his money would be unacceptable since he retains the capacity to decide how to spend it in other ways.)

> Discussion then focuses on ways of minimising restrictions so that he is still able to visit the pub, but drinks in moderation. The care home key worker says that when she has gone to the pub with Mr Simpson he has been fully co-operative and has had just one drink before coming back with her. It is therefore agreed that the home will provide an escort for him to visit the pub at least three times a week, and the shops and the park at other times, and that his daughter will be able to take him out at any time.
>
> It is agreed that care home staff (in consultation with his daughter) will review Mr Simpson's care plan in two months' time and, if it is felt that increased restrictions are required, consider whether it is then necessary to request an authorisation for deprivation of liberty.

4.69    The best interests assessor must involve the relevant person in the assessment process as much as is possible and practical, and help them to participate in decision-making. The relevant person should be given the support needed to participate, using non-verbal means of communication where needed (see paragraphs 3.10 and 3.11 of the main Code) or the support of speech and language therapists. It may also help to involve others whom the relevant person already trusts and who are used to communicating with the relevant person.

4.70    The best interests assessor will need to consider the conclusions of the mental health assessor about how the person being assessed is likely to be affected by being deprived of their liberty. If the proposed care would involve the person being moved, then the assessor should consider the impact of the upheaval and of the journey itself on the person.

4.71    If the best interests assessment supports deprivation of liberty in the care home or hospital in question, the assessor must state what the maximum authorisation period should be in the case concerned. This must not exceed 12 months. The assessor should set out the reasons for selecting the period stated. This decision will be based on the information obtained during the consultation process – but should also reflect information from the person's care plan about how long any treatment or care will be required in circumstances that amount to a deprivation of liberty. It should also take into account any available indication of how likely it is that the relevant person's circumstances will change, including the expected progression of the illness or disability. The underlying principle is that deprivation of liberty should be for the minimum period necessary so, for the maximum 12-month period to apply, the assessor will need to be confident that there is unlikely to be a change in the person's circumstances that would affect the authorisation within that timescale.

## THE REPORT OF THE BEST INTERESTS ASSESSOR

4.72    The best interests assessor must provide a report that explains their conclusion and their reasons for it. If they do not support deprivation of liberty, then their report should aim to be as useful as possible to the commissioners and providers of care in deciding on future action (for example, recommending an alternative approach to treatment or care in which deprivation of liberty could be avoided). It may be helpful for the best interests assessor to discuss the possibility of any such alternatives with the providers of care **during the assessment process**.

4.73    If the best interests assessor does not support deprivation of liberty, it would be good practice for their report to be included in the relevant person's care plan or case notes, to ensure that any views about how deprivation of liberty can be avoided are made clear to the providers of care and all relevant staff on an ongoing basis.

4.74    The best interests assessor may recommend that conditions should be attached to the authorisation. For example, they may make recommendations around contact issues, issues relevant to the person's culture or other major issues related to the deprivation of liberty, which – if not dealt with – would mean that the deprivation of liberty would cease to be in the person's best interests. The best interests assessor may also recommend conditions in order to work towards avoiding deprivation of liberty in future. But it is not the best interests assessor's role to specify conditions that do not directly relate to the issue of deprivation of liberty.

**4.75**   Conditions should not be a substitute for a properly constructed care plan (see paragraph 2.7 on good practice for care planning). In recommending conditions, best interests assessors should aim to impose the minimum necessary constraints, so that they do not unnecessarily prevent or inhibit the staff of the hospital or care home from responding appropriately to the person's needs, whether they remain the same or vary over time. It would be good practice for the best interests assessor to discuss any proposed conditions with the relevant personnel at the home or hospital before finalising the assessment, and to make clear in their report whether the rejection or variation of recommended conditions by the supervisory body would significantly affect the other conclusions they have reached.

**4.76**   Where possible, the best interests assessor should recommend someone to be appointed as the relevant person's representative (see chapter 7). The assessor should be well placed, as a result of the consultation process, to identify whether there is anybody suitable to take on this role. The appointment of the relevant person's representative cannot take place unless and until an authorisation is given. However, by identifying someone to take on this role at an early stage, the best interests assessor can help to ensure that a representative is appointed as soon as possible.

---

Mrs Jackson is 87 years old and lives by herself in an isolated bungalow in a rural area. Over the past few years, staff at her local health centre have become increasingly concerned about her wellbeing and ability to look after herself. Her appearance has become unkempt, she does not appear to be eating properly and her house is dirty.

The community mental health team have attempted to gain her trust, but she is unwilling to engage with them. She has refused care workers entry to her home and declined their help with personal hygiene and household chores.

Because it is believed that she is a potential risk to herself, she is admitted to psychiatric hospital under section 2 of the Mental Health Act 1983 for assessment of her mental disorder.

Following the assessment, it is felt that Mrs Jackson requires further treatment for mental disorder. An application is made for her detention to be continued under section 3 of the Mental Health Act 1983. She is prescribed antipsychotic medication, but this seems to have little effect on her behaviour. She remains extremely suspicious of people to the point of being delusional. She is assessed as potentially having mild dementia, most probably of the Alzheimer type, but because there is no obvious benefit from anti-dementia medication, further treatment for mental disorder is felt unnecessary.

Mrs Jackson insists that she wishes to return to her own home, but given past failed attempts to gain her acceptance of support at home and her likely future mental deterioration, transfer to a care home is believed to be most appropriate.

A best interests meeting is held by the mental health team to consider her future care and placement, and the team's approved social worker and the instructed IMCA are invited. The meeting concludes that Mrs Jackson does not have sufficient mental capacity to make an informed decision on her stated wish to return home. There is no advance decision in existence, no Lasting Power of Attorney or court deputy appointed and no practical way of contacting her immediate family.

An appropriate care home is identified. A care plan is developed to give Mrs Jackson as much choice and control over her daily living as possible. However, it is felt that the restrictions still necessary to ensure Mrs Jackson's wellbeing will be so intense and of such duration that a request for a standard deprivation of liberty authorisation should be made by the care home manager (the relevant managing authority).

The best interests assessor agrees that the proposed course of action is in Mrs Jackson's best interests and recommends a standard authorisation for six months in the first instance.

## What guidelines are there relating to the work of assessors?

### ACCESS TO RECORDS

**4.77**    All assessors may, at any reasonable time, examine and take copies of:

- any health record
- any record of, or held by, a local authority that was compiled in accordance with a social services function, and
- any record held by a care home

which they consider may be relevant to their assessment. Assessors should list in their assessment report what records they examined.

### RECORDING AND REPORTING ASSESSMENTS

**4.78**    As soon as possible after carrying out their assessments, assessors must keep a written record of the assessment and must give copies of their assessment report(s) to the supervisory body. The supervisory body must in turn give copies of the assessment report(s) to:

- the managing authority
- the relevant person and their representative, and
- any IMCA instructed

at the same time that it gives them copies of the deprivation of liberty authorisation or notification that an authorisation is not to be given (see paragraphs 5.7 and 5.18 respectively).

## 5    WHAT SHOULD HAPPEN ONCE THE ASSESSMENTS ARE COMPLETE?

If all the assessments in the standard authorisation assessment process indicate that the relevant person meets all the qualifying requirements, then the supervisory body will give a deprivation of liberty authorisation. If any of the qualifying requirements are not met, however, different actions will need to be taken, depending on the circumstances of the individual case.

This chapter identifies potential outcomes of the assessment process and offers guidance on what should happen next.

## What action should the supervisory body take if the assessments conclude that the person meets the requirements for authorisation?

5.1    If all the assessments conclude that the relevant person meets the requirements for authorisation, and the supervisory body has written copies of all the assessments, it must give a standard authorisation. A standard form is available for this purpose.

5.2    The supervisory body cannot give a standard authorisation if any of the requirements are not fulfilled.

5.3    The supervisory body must set the period of the authorisation, which may not be longer than that recommended by the best interests assessor (see paragraph 4.71). 5.4  When the supervisory body gives a standard authorisation, it must do so in writing and must state the following:

- the name of the relevant person
- the name of the relevant hospital or care home
- the period during which the authorisation is to be in force (which may not exceed the period recommended by the best interests assessor)
- the purpose for which the authorisation is given (i.e. why the person needs to be deprived of their liberty)
- any conditions subject to which the authorisation is given (see paragraph 5.5), and
- the reason why each qualifying requirement is met.

5.5    The supervisory body may attach conditions to the authorisation. Before deciding whether to give the authorisation subject to conditions, the supervisory body must consider any recommendations made by the best interests assessor (see paragraph 4.74). Where the supervisory body does not attach conditions as recommended by the best interests assessor, it should discuss the matter with the best interests assessor in case the rejection or variation of the conditions would significantly affect the other conclusions the best interests assessor reached in their report.

5.6    It is the responsibility of the supervisory body to appoint a representative for the relevant person (see chapter 7).

5.7    As soon as possible after giving the authorisation, the supervisory body must give a copy of the authorisation to:

- the managing authority
- the relevant person
- the relevant person's representative
- any Independent Mental Capacity Advocate (IMCA) involved, and
- every interested person named by the best interests assessor in their report as somebody they have consulted in carrying out their assessment.

The supervisory body must also keep a written record of any standard authorisation that it gives and of the matters referred to in paragraph 5.4.

5.8    The managing authority must take all practical and possible steps to ensure that the relevant person understands the effect of the authorisation and their rights around it. These include their right to challenge the authorisation via the Court of Protection, their right to request a review, and their right to have an IMCA instructed, along with the process for doing so (see paragraphs 7.37 to 7.41). Appropriate information must be given to the relevant person both orally and in writing. Any written information must also be given to the relevant person's representative. This must happen as soon as possible and practical after the authorisation is given.

## How long can an authorisation last?

**5.9**   A deprivation of liberty should last for the shortest period possible. The best interests assessor should only recommend authorisation for as long as the relevant person is likely to meet all the qualifying requirements. The authorisation may be for quite a short period. A short period may, for example, be appropriate if:

■   the reason that the deprivation of liberty is in the person's best interests is because their usual care arrangements have temporarily broken down, or

■   there are likely to be changes in the person's mental disorder in the relatively near future (for example, if the person is in rehabilitation following brain injury).

## What restrictions exist on authorisations?

**5.10**   A deprivation of liberty authorisation – whether urgent or standard – relates solely to the issue of deprivation of liberty. It does not give authority to treat people, nor to do anything else that would normally require their consent. The arrangements for providing care and treatment to people in respect of whom a deprivation of liberty authorisation is in force are subject to the wider provisions of the Mental Capacity Act 2005.

**5.11**   This means that any treatment can only be given to a person who has not given their consent if:

■   it is established that the person lacks capacity to make the decision concerned

■   it is agreed that the treatment will be in their best interests, having taken account of the views of the person and of people close to them, and, where relevant in the case of serious medical treatment, of any IMCA involved

■   the treatment does not conflict with a valid and applicable advance decision to refuse treatment, and

■   the treatment does not conflict with a decision made by a donee of Lasting Power of Attorney or a deputy acting within the scope of their powers.

**5.12**   In deciding what is in a person's best interests, section 4 of the Act applies in the same way as it would if the person was not deprived of liberty. The guidance in chapter 5 of the main Code on assessing best interests is also relevant.

**5.13**   Life-sustaining treatment, or treatment to prevent a serious deterioration in the person's condition, may be provided while a decision in respect of any relevant issue is sought from the Court of Protection. The need to act in the best interests of the person concerned will continue to apply in the meantime.

## Can a person be moved to a different location under a standard authorisation?

**5.14**   If a person who is subject to a standard authorisation moves to a different hospital or care home, the managing authority of the new hospital or care home must request a new standard authorisation. The application should be made **before** the move takes place.

**5.15**   If the move has to take place so urgently that this is impossible, the managing authority of the new hospital or care home will need to give an urgent authorisation (see chapter 6).

**5.16**   The only exception is if the care regime in the new facility will not involve deprivation of liberty.

**5.17**   These arrangements are not an alternative to applying the provisions of sections 38 and 39 of the Act regarding change of residence.

## What happens if an assessment concludes that one of the requirements is not met?

**5.18**   If any of the assessments conclude that one of the requirements is not met, then the assessment process should stop immediately and authorisation may not be given. The supervisory body should:

- inform anyone still engaged in carrying out an assessment that they are not required to complete it
- notify the managing authority, the relevant person, any IMCA involved and every interested person consulted by the best interests assessor that authorisation has not been given (a standard form is available for this purpose), and
- provide the managing authority, the relevant person and any IMCA involved with copies of those assessments that have been carried out. This must be done as soon as possible, because in some cases different arrangements will need to be made for the person's care.

**5.19**   If the reason the standard authorisation cannot be given is because the eligibility requirement is not met, it may be necessary to consider making the person subject to the Mental Health Act 1983. If this is the case, it may be possible to use the same assessors to make that decision, thereby minimising the assessment processes.

## What are the responsibilities of the managing authority and the commissioners of care if a request for an authorisation is turned down?

**5.20**   The managing authority is responsible for ensuring that it does not deprive a person of their liberty without an authorisation. The managing authority must comply with the law in this respect: where a request for an authorisation is turned down, it will need to review the relevant person's actual or proposed care arrangements to ensure that a deprivation of liberty is not allowed to either continue or commence.

**5.21**   Supervisory bodies and other commissioners of care will need to purchase care packages in a way that makes it possible for managing authorities to comply with the outcome of the deprivation of liberty safeguards assessment process when a request for a standard authorisation is turned down.

**5.22**   The actions that both managing authorities and commissioners of care should consider if a request for an authorisation is turned down will depend on the reason why the authorisation has not been given:

- If the best interests assessor concluded that the relevant person was not in fact being, or likely to be, deprived of liberty, no action is likely to be necessary.
- If the best interests assessor concluded that the proposed or actual deprivation of liberty was not in the relevant person's best interests, the managing authority, in conjunction with the commissioner of the care, will need to consider how the care plan could be changed to avoid deprivation of liberty. (See, for example, the guidance on practical ways to reduce the risk of deprivation of liberty in paragraph 2.7.) They should examine carefully the reasons given in the best interests assessor's report, and may find it helpful to discuss the matter with the best interests assessor. Where appropriate, they should also discuss the matter with family and carers. If the person is not yet a resident in the care home or hospital, the revised care plan may not involve admission to that facility unless the conditions of care are adapted to be less restrictive and deprivation of liberty will not occur.

- If the mental capacity assessor concluded that the relevant person **has** capacity to make decisions about their care, the care home or hospital will need to consider, in conjunction with the commissioner of the care, how to support the person to make such decisions.
- If the relevant person was identified as not eligible to be subject to a deprivation of liberty authorisation, it may be appropriate to assess whether an application should be made to detain the person under the Mental Health Act 1983.
- If the relevant person does not have a mental disorder as defined in the Mental Health Act 1983, the care plan will need to be modified to avoid a deprivation of liberty, since there would be no lawful basis for depriving a person of liberty in those circumstances.
- Where there is a valid refusal by a donee or deputy, or an applicable and valid advance decision (see paragraphs 4.25 to 4.28), alternative care arrangements will need to be made. If there is a question about the refusal, a decision may be sought from the Court of Protection.
- If the person is under 18, use of the Children Act 1989 may be considered.

5.23    Working out what action should be taken where a request for a standard deprivation of liberty authorisation is turned down in respect of a 'self-funder' may present particular problems, because the managing authority may not be able to make alternative care arrangements without discussing them with those controlling the funding, whether relatives of the person concerned or others. The desired outcome should be the provision of a care regime that does not constitute deprivation of liberty.

5.24    Where the best interests assessor comes to the conclusion that the best interests requirement is not met, but it appears to the assessor that the person being assessed is already being deprived of their liberty, the assessor must inform the supervisory body and explain in their report why they have reached that conclusion. The supervisory body must then inform the managing authority to review the relevant person's care plan immediately so that unauthorised deprivation of liberty does not continue. Any necessary changes must be made urgently to stop what would be an unlawful deprivation of liberty. The steps taken to stop the deprivation of liberty should be recorded in the care plan. Where possible, family, friends and carers should be involved in deciding how to prevent the unauthorised deprivation of liberty from continuing. If the supervisory body has any doubts about whether the matter is being satisfactorily resolved within an appropriately urgent timescale, it should alert the inspection body (see chapter 11).

## 6    WHEN CAN URGENT AUTHORISATIONS OF DEPRIVATION OF LIBERTY BE GIVEN?

Wherever possible, applications for deprivation of liberty authorisations should be made before the deprivation of liberty commences. However, where deprivation of liberty unavoidably needs to commence before a standard authorisation can be obtained, an urgent authorisation can be given which will make the deprivation of liberty lawful for a short period of time.

This chapter contains guidance on the rules around urgent authorisations.

### When can an urgent authorisation be given?

6.1    A managing authority can itself give an urgent authorisation for deprivation of liberty where:

- it is required to make a request to the supervisory body for a standard authorisation, but believes that the need for the person to be deprived of their liberty is so urgent that deprivation needs to begin before the request is made, or

■    it has made a request for a standard authorisation, but believes that the need for a person to be deprived of liberty has now become so urgent that deprivation of liberty needs to begin before the request is dealt with by the supervisory body.

This means that an urgent authorisation can never be given without a request for a standard authorisation being made simultaneously. Therefore, before giving an urgent authorisation, a managing authority will need to have a reasonable expectation that the six qualifying requirements for a standard authorisation are likely to be met.

6.2    Urgent authorisations should normally only be used in response to sudden unforeseen needs. However, they can also be used in care planning (for example, to avoid delays in transfer for rehabilitation, where delay would reduce the likely benefit of the rehabilitation).

6.3    However, an urgent authorisation should not be used where there is no expectation that a standard deprivation of liberty authorisation will be needed. Where, for example:

■    a person who lacks capacity to make decisions about their care and treatment has developed a mental disorder as a result of a physical illness, and
■    the physical illness requires treatment in hospital in circumstances that amount to a deprivation of liberty, and
■    the treatment of that physical illness is expected to lead to rapid resolution of the mental disorder such that a standard deprivation of liberty authorisation would not be required,

it would not be appropriate to give an urgent authorisation simply to legitimise the short-term deprivation of liberty.

6.4    Similarly, an urgent deprivation of liberty authorisation should not be given when a person is, for example, in an accident and emergency unit or a care home, and it is anticipated that within a matter of a few hours or a few days the person will no longer be in that environment.

6.5    Any decision to give an urgent authorisation and take action that deprives a person of liberty must be in the person's best interests, as set out in section 4 of the Mental Capacity Act 2005. Where restraint is involved, all actions must comply with the additional conditions in section 6 of the Act (see chapter 6 of the main Code).

6.6    The managing authority must decide the period for which the urgent authorisation is given, but this must not exceed seven days (see paragraphs 6.20 to 6.28 regarding the possible extension of the seven-day period). The authorisation must be in writing and must state:
■    the name of the relevant person
■    the name of the relevant hospital or care home
■    the period for which the authorisation is to be in force, and
■    the purpose for which the authorisation is given.

A standard form is available for a managing authority to use to notify a supervisory body that it has given an urgent authorisation.

6.7    Supervisory bodies and managing authorities should have a procedure in place that identifies:

■    what actions should be taken when an urgent authorisation needs to be made
■    who should take each action, and
■    within what timescale.

## What records should be kept about urgent authorisations?

**6.8**    The managing authority must keep a written record of any urgent authorisations given, including details of why it decided to give an urgent authorisation. They must give a copy of the authorisation to the relevant person and any IMCA instructed, and place a copy in the relevant person's records. The managing authority must also seek to ensure that, as far as possible, the relevant person understands the effect of the authorisation and the right to challenge the authorisation via the Court of Protection. Appropriate information must be given both orally and in writing.

**6.9**    The managing authority should, as far as possible and appropriate, notify the relevant person's family, friends and carers when an urgent authorisation is given in order to enable them to offer informed support to the person.

**6.10**    The processes surrounding the giving and receiving of urgent authorisations should be clearly recorded, and regularly monitored and audited, as part of a managing authority's or supervisory body's governance structure.

## Who should be consulted before giving an urgent authorisation?

**6.11**    If the managing authority is considering depriving a person of liberty in an emergency and giving an urgent authorisation, they must, as far as is practical and possible, take account of the views of anyone engaged in caring for the relevant person or interested in their welfare. The aim should be to consult carers and family members at as early a stage as possible so that their views can be properly taken into account before a decision to give an urgent authorisation is taken.

**6.12**    The steps taken to involve family, friends or carers should be recorded in the relevant person's records, along with their views. The views of the carers will be important because their knowledge of the person will put them in a good position to gauge how the person will react to the deprivation of their liberty, and the effect it will have on their mental state. It may also be appropriate to consult any staff who may have some involvement in the person's case.

**6.13**    The ultimate decision, though, will need to be based on a judgement of what is in the relevant person's best interests. The decision-maker from the managing authority will need to be able to show that they have made a reasonable decision based on their professional judgement and taking account of all the relevant factors. This is an important decision, because it could mean the deprivation of a person's liberty without, at this stage, the full deprivation of liberty safeguards assessment process having taken place. The decision should therefore be taken at a senior level within the managing authority.

---

**Scenario: Urgent authorisation followed by short-term standard authorisation**

Mr Baker is 75, widowed and lives near his only family – his daughter. He is admitted to hospital having been found by his daughter on his kitchen floor. He is uncharacteristically confused and is not able to give a reliable history of what has happened. He has a routine physical examination, as well as blood and urine investigations, and is diagnosed as having a urinary tract infection. He is given antibiotics, but his nursing care is complicated by his fluctuating confusion. Once or twice he removes his clothes and walks through the ward naked, and at times he tries to leave the ward, unaware that he is in hospital, and believing that he is late for an important work meeting. During more lucid moments, however, he knows where he is and accepts the need for investigation and treatment in hospital.

The responsible consultant, in consultation with ward nursing staff and Mr Baker's daughter, feels that it would be in his best interests to place him in a side room to protect his dignity, and restrict his movements to ensure he remains on the ward.

However, after two days, his confusion appears to worsen: he starts having hallucinations and has to be restrained more often by staff to prevent him leaving the ward. After assessment by a doctor from the liaison psychiatry team, Mr Baker is prescribed antipsychotic medication for his own and other patients' safety. He does not resist taking this medication. The likely benefits and possible side effects are discussed with his daughter and, on balance, the medication is felt to be in his best interests in order to continue his medical investigations.

Staff become concerned about the level of restriction of liberty Mr Baker is now subject to. In particular, they are concerned about the duration of the restrictions; the fact that Mr Baker no longer has lucid intervals when he can give his consent to ongoing care and treatment in hospital; and the physical restraint that is still being required on occasion.

After discussion between the ward manager and Mr Baker's daughter, the managing authority gives an urgent authorisation and submits a request for a standard authorisation to the supervisory body (PCT). A best interests assessor is appointed, and the liaison psychiatrist provides the mental health and mental capacity assessments. In making all the deprivation of liberty safeguards assessments to see whether the qualifying requirements are met, it is considered that although restraint is being used, this does not mean he is objecting having regard to all the circumstances, so he is not ineligible and a standard authorisation is given.

## Can a person be moved into care under an urgent authorisation?

**6.14**    There may be cases in which managing authorities are considering giving an urgent authorisation to enable them to move the relevant person to a new type of care. This may occur, for example, when considering whether to admit a person living at home or with relatives into a hospital care regime that would deprive them of their liberty, and when the need for admission appears to be so urgent that there would not be enough time to follow the standard authorisation process.

**6.15**    For some people, such a change of location may have a detrimental effect on their mental health, which might significantly distort the way they come across during any assessment process. In such a case, managing authorities should consider whether giving the urgent authorisation and admitting the person to hospital would outweigh the benefits of leaving the person in their existing location, where any assessment of their needs might be more accurate. This will involve looking carefully at the existing care arrangements and consulting with any carers involved, to establish whether or not the person could safely and beneficially be cared for in their home environment while the assessment process takes place. Where the relevant person is already known to statutory care providers, for example the community mental health team or social services, it will be important to involve them in this decision-making process. The relevant person's GP may also be an important source of knowledge about the person's situation, and may be able to offer a valuable opinion when the appropriateness of moving the person into a different care setting is under consideration.

## What happens at the end of an urgent authorisation period?

**6.16**    An urgent authorisation will terminate at the end of the period for which it is given. As noted above, this is normally a maximum of seven days, but in exceptional circumstances an urgent authorisation can be extended to a maximum of 14 days **by the supervisory body**, as explained in paragraphs 6.20 to 6.28.

**6.17**   An urgent authorisation will terminate before this time if the standard authorisation applied for is given.

**6.18**   An urgent authorisation will also terminate if a managing authority receives notice from the supervisory body that the standard authorisation will not be given. It will not then be lawful to continue to deprive the relevant person of their liberty.

**6.19**   The supervisory body must inform the relevant person and any IMCA instructed that the urgent authorisation has ended. This notification can be combined with the notification to them of the outcome of the application for standard authorisation.

---

**Scenario: Considering an urgent authorisation**

Mr Watson is 35. He has autism and learning disabilities. He lives in the family home with his parents. Although he is well settled and generally calm at home, Mr Watson sometimes becomes disturbed when in an unfamiliar and crowded environment.

While his parents are away for a couple of days, and Mr Watson is in the care of a paid carer, he has an accident at home. His carer is concerned that he may have broken his arm and takes him to the A&E department at the local hospital, where it is decided that his arm needs to be X-rayed to check for a break. The outcome is that there is no break, just bad bruising, so there is no medical need to admit him.

However, because of the pain he is in and the crowded environment, Mr Watson has become very agitated to the extent that hospital security personnel feel a need to control him physically. The carer tries to restrain him and lead him outside where she says he is likely to be more settled and calm down.

Because restraint is being used, the A&E doctor wonders whether it his duty to use an urgent authorisation or other measure to detain Mr Watson in hospital if he believes it is in his best interests.

He consults a liaison psychiatry nurse, who reassures him that such restraint is permitted under the Mental Capacity Act 2005 where it is necessary to prevent harm to the person himself and so long as it is a proportionate response. The nurse assists the carer with gentle restraint to take Mr Watson to a quieter area. She suggests the doctor phone Mr Watson's parents for further information, and obtains painkillers for Mr Watson.

The doctor speaks to Mr Watson's parents, who believe that Mr Watson does not have the mental capacity to decide on his care and treatment in the current circumstances. They have experienced similar situations many times, and are confident that Mr Watson will calm down once he is back in his home environment. They state that if any more detailed assessment of his mental state is required it should take place there, in the company of the carer whom they know and trust. They reassure the doctor that Mr Watson is highly unlikely to present a danger to himself, his carer or the general public.

The doctor decides that it will be in Mr Watson's best interests to return home with his carer.

## How and when can an urgent authorisation be extended?

**6.20** If there are exceptional reasons why the request for a standard authorisation cannot be dealt with within the period of the original urgent authorisation, the managing authority may ask the supervisory body to extend the duration of the urgent authorisation for a maximum of a further seven days. The managing authority must keep a written record of the reason for making the request and must notify the relevant person, in writing, that they have made the request. Standard forms are available for managing authorities to request the extension of an urgent authorisation from a supervisory body and for supervisory bodies to record their decision in response to such a request.

**6.21** Unless the duration of the urgent authorisation is extended by the supervisory body, or a standard authorisation is given before the urgent authorisation expires, the authority to deprive the person of liberty will cease once the urgent authorisation period has expired. It is therefore essential that any request for an extension of an urgent authorisation is made promptly. This will necessitate good communication between the managing authority and the supervisory body regarding the progress of the standard authorisation assessment process. Particular care may need to be taken where an urgent authorisation is due to expire over the weekend or on a bank holiday, when appropriate people at the managing authority and supervisory body may not be immediately available.

**6.22** The supervisory body may only extend the duration of the urgent authorisation if:

- the managing authority has made a request for a standard authorisation
- there are exceptional reasons why it has not yet been possible to make a standard authorisation, and
- it is essential for the deprivation of liberty to continue while the supervisory body makes its decision.

**6.23** Extensions can only be granted for exceptional reasons. An example of when an extension would be justified might be where:

- it was not possible to contact a person whom the best interests assessor needed to contact
- the assessment could not be relied upon without their input, and
- extension for the specified period would enable them to be contacted.

**6.24** It is for the supervisory body to decide what constitutes an 'exceptional reason', but because of the seriousness of the issues involved, the supervisory body's decision must be soundly based and defensible. It would not, for example, be appropriate to use staffing shortages as a reason to extend an urgent authorisation.

**6.25** An urgent authorisation can only be extended once.

**6.26** The supervisory body must notify the managing authority of the length of any extension granted and must vary the original urgent authorisation so that it states the extended duration. The supervisory body must also keep a written record of the outcome of the request and the period of the extension.

**6.27** The managing authority must give a copy of the varied urgent authorisation to the relevant person and any IMCA instructed, and must seek to ensure that, as far as possible, the relevant person understands the effect of the varied authorisation and the right to challenge the authorisation via the Court of Protection. The appropriate information must be given both orally and in writing.

**6.28**    If the supervisory body decides not to extend the urgent authorisation, it must inform the managing authority of its decision and the reasons for it. The managing authority must give a copy of the notice to the relevant person and any IMCA involved.

## 7    WHAT IS THE ROLE OF THE RELEVANT PERSON'S REPRESENTATIVE?

Once a standard deprivation of liberty authorisation has been given, supervisory bodies must appoint the relevant person's representative as soon as possible and practical to represent the person who has been deprived of their liberty.

This chapter explains the role of the relevant person's representative and gives guidance on their selection and appointment.

### What is the role of the relevant person's representative?

**7.1**    The supervisory body must appoint a relevant person's representative for every person to whom they give a standard authorisation for deprivation of liberty. It is important that the representative is appointed at the time the authorisation is given or as soon as possible and practical thereafter.

**7.2**    The role of the relevant person's representative, once appointed, is:

■    to maintain contact with the relevant person, and
■    to represent and support the relevant person in all matters relating to the deprivation of liberty safeguards, including, if appropriate, triggering a review, using an organisation's complaints procedure on the person's behalf or making an application to the Court of Protection.

This is a crucial role in the deprivation of liberty process, providing the relevant person with representation and support that is independent of the commissioners and providers of the services they are receiving.

**7.3**    The best interests principle of the Act applies to the relevant person's representative in the same way that it applies to other people acting or making decisions for people who lack capacity.

### How should managing authorities work with the relevant person's representative?

**7.4**    As soon as possible and practical after a standard deprivation of liberty authorisation is given, the managing authority must seek to ensure that the relevant person and their representative understand:

■    the effect of the authorisation
■    their right to request a review (see chapter 8)
■    the formal and informal complaints procedures that are available to them
■    their right to make an application to the Court of Protection to seek variation or termination of the authorisation (see chapter 10), and
■    their right, where the relevant person does not have a paid 'professional' representative, to request the support of an Independent Mental Capacity Advocate (IMCA) (see paragraphs 7.37 to 7.41).

**7.5**    When providing information to the person and their representative, the managing authority should take account of the communication and language needs of both the person and their representative. Provision of information should be seen as an ongoing responsibility, rather than a one-off activity.

## Who can be the relevant person's representative?[12]

7.6    To be eligible to be the relevant person's representative, a person must be:

- 18 years of age or over
- able to keep in contact with the relevant person, and
- willing to be appointed.

The person must not be:

- financially interested in the relevant person's managing authority (a person is considered to be financially interested where that person is a partner, director, other officeholder or major shareholder of the managing authority)
- a relative of a person who has a financial interest in the relevant person's managing authority (paragraph 4.13 explains what is meant by 'relative')
- employed by, or providing services to, the care home in which the person relevant person is residing
- employed by the hospital in a role that is, or could be, related to the treatment or care of the relevant person, or
- employed to work in the relevant person's supervisory body in a role that is, or could be, related to the relevant person's case.

7.7    The appointment of the relevant person's representative is in addition to, and does not affect, any appointment of a donee or deputy. Similarly, the functions of the representative are in addition to, and do not affect, the authority of any donee, the powers of any deputy or any powers of the court. A donee or deputy may themselves be appointed as the relevant person's representative if they meet the eligibility criteria set out in paragraph 7.6.

7.8    There is no presumption that the relevant person's representative should be the same as the person who is their nearest relative for the purposes of the Mental Health Act 1983, even where the relevant person is likely to be subject simultaneously to an authorisation under these safeguards and a provision of the Mental Health Act 1983. This is because the relevant person's representative is not selected in the same way as the nearest relative under the Mental Health Act 1983, nor do they perform the same role. However, there is nothing to stop the relevant person's representative being the same as their nearest relative under the Mental Health Act 1983.

## When should the relevant person's representative be identified?

7.9    The process of identifying a representative must begin as soon as possible.

7.10    Normally, this should be when the best interests assessor is appointed – even if one or more of the other assessments has not yet been completed. This is because the best interests assessor must, as part of the assessment process, identify if there is anyone they would recommend to become the relevant person's representative. The best interests assessor should discuss the representative role with the people interviewed as part of the assessment.

---

[12]    Requirements relating to the eligibility, selection and appointment of relevant person's representatives are covered in regulations. The regulations for England are The Mental Capacity (Deprivation of Liberty: Appointment of Relevant Person's Representative) Regulations 2008. The regulations for Wales are The Mental Capacity (Deprivation of Liberty: Appointment of Relevant Person's Representative) (Wales) Regulations 2008.

**7.11**    This does leave a risk that the process to identify a representative might begin in cases where authorisation is not given. Nevertheless, it is important that the process begins, so that the representative can be appointed immediately the authorisation is given or as soon as possible and practical thereafter.

## How should the relevant person's representative be selected?

**7.12**    The best interests assessor should first establish whether the relevant person has the capacity to select their own representative and, if so, invite them to do so. If the relevant person has capacity and selects an eligible person (according to the criteria set out in paragraph 7.6), the best interests assessor must recommend that person to the supervisory body for appointment.

**7.13**    Alternatively, if the relevant person lacks capacity and there is a donee or deputy with the appropriate authority, the donee or deputy may select the person to be recommended as the relevant person's representative, again subject to the criteria set out in paragraph 7.6. If a donee or deputy selects an eligible person, then the best interests assessor must recommend that person to the supervisory body for appointment.

**7.14**    It is up to the best interests assessor to confirm whether any representative proposed by the relevant person, a donee or a deputy is eligible. If the best interests assessor decides that a proposed representative is not eligible, they must advise the person who made the selection and invite them to make a further selection.

**7.15**    If neither the relevant person, nor a donee or deputy, selects an eligible person, then the best interests assessor must consider whether they are able to identify someone eligible who could act as the relevant person's representative.

**7.16**    In making a recommendation, the assessor should consider, and balance, factors such as:

■    Does the relevant person have a preference?
■    If they do not have the capacity to express a preference now, is there any written statement made by the relevant person when they had capacity that indicates who they may now want to be their representative?
■    Will the proposed representative be able to keep in contact with the relevant person?
■    Does the relevant person appear to trust and feel comfortable with the proposed representative?
■    Would the proposed representative be able to represent the relevant person effectively?
■    Is the proposed representative likely to represent the relevant person's best interests?

In most cases, the best interests assessor will be able to check at the same time that the proposed representative is willing to take on the role.

**7.17**    It should not be assumed that the representative needs to be someone who supports the deprivation of liberty.

**7.18**    The best interests assessor must not select a representative where the relevant person, if they have the capacity to do so, or a donee or a deputy acting within the scope of their authority, states they are not content with that selection.

**7.19**    If the best interests assessor is unable to recommend anybody to be the relevant person's representative, they must notify the supervisory body accordingly. The supervisory body must then itself identify an eligible person to be appointed as the representative. In doing so, the supervisory body may select a person who:

- would be performing the role in a professional capacity
- has satisfactory skills and experience to perform the role
- is not a family member, friend or carer of the relevant person
- is not employed by, or providing services to, the relevant person's managing authority, where the relevant person's managing authority is a care home
- is not employed to work in the relevant person's managing authority in a role that is, or could be, related to the relevant person's case, where the relevant person's managing authority is a hospital
- is not employed to work in the supervisory body that is appointing the representative in a role that is, or could be, related to the relevant person's case, and
- the supervisory body is satisfied that an appropriate criminal record certificate has been issued in respect of.

**7.20**   The supervisory body may pay a person they select to be the relevant person's representative in the circumstances set out in paragraph 7.19. This service could be commissioned, for example, through an advocacy services provider, ensuring that the service provides effective independent representation for the relevant person.

**7.21**   When selecting a suitable representative for the relevant person, the best interests assessor or supervisory body should pay particular attention to the communication and cultural needs of the relevant person.

## How should the relevant person's representative be appointed?

**7.22**   The supervisory body must invite, in writing, the person recommended by the best interests assessor to become the relevant person's representative. If the best interests assessor does not recommend anyone, then the supervisory body should identify and appoint someone to undertake the role. If the person is willing to become the representative, the supervisory body must formally appoint them. If the person refuses, a further eligible person must be identified and invited to become the representative. This process must continue until an eligible person is appointed.

**7.23**   The appointment of the relevant person's representative by the supervisory body must be in writing and set out the role and responsibilities of the relevant person's representative. The letter of appointment should also state the name of the appointed person and the date of expiry of the appointment, which must be for the period of the standard authorisation that has been given. The supervisory body must send copies of the written appointment to:

- the appointed person
- the relevant person
- Sany donee or deputy of the relevant person
- any IMCA involved
- every interested person named by the best interests assessor in their report as somebody they have consulted in carrying out their assessment, and
- the managing authority of the relevant hospital or care home.

**7.24**   The relevant person's representative must confirm to the supervisory body in writing that they are willing to accept the appointment and have understood their roles and responsibilities in respect of the relevant person.

## How should the work of the relevant person's representative be supported and monitored?

**7.25**   It is important that the representative has sufficient contact with the relevant person to ensure that the relevant person's best interests are being safeguarded. In order to fulfil their role, therefore, the representative will need to be able to have face-to-face contact with the relevant person. That means that the care home or hospital should accommodate visits by the representative at reasonable times. The name of the person's representative should be recorded in the person's health and social care records.

**7.26** Managing authorities and supervisory bodies should inform the relevant person's representative about sources of support and information available to help them in the role, including how to access the support of an IMCA (see paragraphs 7.37 to 7.41).

**7.27** If the representative has insufficient contact with the relevant person, for whatever reason, the person may effectively be unable to access important review and appeal rights. For this reason, if the representative does not maintain an appropriate level of contact with the person, the managing authority will need to consider informing the supervisory body. When the managing authority is reviewing the person's care plan, it should consider whether the representative is in sufficient contact with the relevant person to offer effective support. Records kept by managing authorities about frequency of contact will support this consideration.

**7.28** Because the appropriate levels and methods of contact between a relevant person and their representative will vary from case to case, this is a matter about which the managing authority will need to exercise discretion. If the managing authority has any concerns, it may be best to raise the matter with the representative initially to see whether any perceived problems can be resolved informally. If after this the representative still does not maintain what the managing authority considers to be an appropriate level of contact with the relevant person, then the managing authority should notify the supervisory body.

## When can the appointment of the relevant person's representative be terminated?

**7.29** The appointment of the relevant person's representative will be terminated in any of the following circumstances:

- The standard authorisation comes to an end and a new authorisation is not applied for or, if applied for, is not given.
- The relevant person, if they have capacity to do so, objects to the representative continuing in their role and a different person is selected to be their representative instead.
- A donee or deputy, if it is within their authority to do so and the relevant person lacks the capacity to decide, objects to the representative continuing in their role and a different person is selected to be the representative instead.
- The supervisory body becomes aware that the representative is no longer willing or eligible to continue in the role.
- The supervisory body becomes aware that the relevant person's representative is not keeping in touch with the person, is not representing and supporting them effectively or is not acting in the person's best interests.
- The relevant person's representative dies.

**7.30** If the supervisory body becomes aware that the representative may not be keeping in touch with the person, is not acting in the relevant person's best interests, or is no longer eligible, it should contact the representative to clarify the position before deciding whether to terminate the appointment.

**7.31** When the appointment of the relevant person's representative ends, the supervisory body must give notice to all those listed in paragraph 7.23. This notice should be given as soon as possible, stating when the appointment ended and the reason why.

**7.32**    When the appointment of a relevant person's representative ends but the lawful deprivation of liberty continues, the supervisory body must appoint a suitable replacement to be the relevant person's representative as soon as possible and practical after they become aware of the vacancy. As before, a person qualified to be a best interests assessor should make a recommendation to the supervisory body and the supervisory body should take account of any such recommendations.

**7.33**    If the reason for the termination of the former representative's appointment is that they are no longer eligible, the views of the former representative on who might replace them should be sought. The person identified as most suitable should then be invited to accept the appointment. This process should continue until an eligible person is willing to accept appointment.

## What happens when there is no relevant person's representative available?

**7.34**    A person who is being deprived of their liberty will be in a particularly vulnerable position during any gaps in the appointment of the relevant person's representative, since there may be nobody to represent their interests or to apply for a review on their behalf. In these circumstances, if there is nobody who can support and represent the person (other than a person engaged in providing care and treatment for the relevant person in a professional capacity or for remuneration), the managing authority must notify the supervisory body, who must instruct an IMCA to represent the relevant person until a new representative is appointed.

**7.35**    The role of an IMCA instructed in these circumstances is essentially the same as that of the relevant person's representative. The role of the IMCA in this situation ends when the new relevant person's representative is appointed.

**7.36**    At any time when the relevant person does not have a representative, it will be particularly important for supervisory bodies to consider exercising their discretion to carry out a review if there is any significant change in the person's circumstances.

## When should an IMCA be instructed?

**7.37**    Both the person who is deprived of liberty under a standard authorisation and their representative have a statutory right of access to an IMCA. It is the responsibility of the supervisory body to instruct an IMCA if the relevant person or their representative requests one. The intention is to provide extra support to the relevant person or a family member or friend acting as their representative if they need it, and to help them make use of the review process or access the Court of Protection safeguards. Where the relevant person has a paid 'professional' representative (see paragraphs 7.19 and 7.20), the need for additional advocacy support should not arise and so there is no requirement for an IMCA to be provided in those circumstances.

**7.38**    The role of the IMCA is to help represent the relevant person and, in particular, to assist the relevant person and their representative to understand the effect of the authorisation, what it means, why it has been given, why the relevant person meets the criteria for authorisation, how long it will last, any conditions to which the authorisation is subject and how to trigger a review or challenge in the Court of Protection. The IMCA can also provide support with a review (see chapter 8) or with an application to the Court of Protection (see chapter 10), for example to help the person to communicate their views.

**7.39**    The IMCA will have the right to make submissions to the supervisory body on the question of whether a qualifying requirement should be reviewed, or to give information, or make submissions, to any assessor carrying out a review assessment. Both the person and their representative must be told about the IMCA service and how to request an IMCA.

**7.40**    An IMCA must be instructed whenever requested by the relevant person or their representative. A request may be made more than once during the period of the authorisation. For example, help may be sought at the start of the authorisation and then again later in order to request a review.

**7.41**    In addition, if the supervisory body has reason to believe that the review and Court of Protection safeguards might not be used without the support of an IMCA, then they must instruct an IMCA. For example, if the supervisory body is aware that the person has selected a representative who needs support with communication, it should consider whether an IMCA is needed.

## 8    WHEN SHOULD AN AUTHORISATION BE REVIEWED AND WHAT HAPPENS WHEN IT ENDS?

When a person is deprived of their liberty, the managing authority has a duty to monitor the case on an ongoing basis to see if the person's circumstances change – which may mean they no longer need to be deprived of their liberty.

The managing authority must set out in the care plan clear roles and responsibilities for monitoring and confirm under what circumstances a review is necessary. For example, if a person's condition is changing frequently, then their situation should be reviewed more frequently.

This chapter explains the duties of managing authorities and supervisory bodies in relation to reviewing cases, and what happens when an authorisation ends. The review process is set out in flowchart form at Annex 4.

### When should a standard authorisation be reviewed?

**8.1**    A standard authorisation can be reviewed at any time. The review is carried out by the supervisory body.

**8.2**    There are certain statutory grounds for carrying out a review. If the statutory grounds for a review are met, the supervisory body must carry out a review. If a review is requested by the relevant person, their representative or the managing authority, the supervisory body must carry out a review. Standard letters are available for the relevant person or their representative to request a review. There is also a standard form available for the managing authority to request a review. A supervisory body can also decide to carry out a review at its own discretion.

**8.3**    The statutory grounds for a review are:

- The relevant person no longer meets the age, no refusals, mental capacity, mental health or best interests requirements.
- The relevant person no longer meets the eligibility requirement because they now object to receiving mental health treatment in hospital and they meet the criteria for an application for admission under section 2 or section 3 of the Mental Health Act 1983 (see paragraphs 4.45 to 4.48).
- There has been a change in the relevant person's situation and, because of the change, it would be appropriate to amend an existing condition to which the authorisation is subject, delete an existing condition or add a new condition.

■     The reason(s) the person now meets the qualifying requirement(s) is(are) different from the reason(s) given at the time the standard authorisation was given.

**8.4**     Different arrangements apply if the person no longer meets the eligibility requirement because they have been detained under the Mental Health Act, or become subject to a requirement under that Act that conflicts with the authorisation. (See paragraphs 8.19 to 8.21 regarding the short-term suspension of a standard authorisation.)

**8.5**     A managing authority must request a review if it appears to it that one or more of the qualifying requirements is no longer met, or may no longer be met.

## What happens when a review is going to take place?

**8.6**     The supervisory body must tell the relevant person, their representative and the managing authority if they are going to carry out a review. This must be done either before the review begins or as soon as possible and practical after it has begun. A standard form is available for this purpose.

**8.7**     The relevant person's records must include information about any formal reviews that have been requested, when they were considered, and the outcome. These records must be retained by the supervisory body.

**8.8**     Deprivation of liberty can be ended before a formal review. An authorisation only **permits** deprivation of liberty: it does not mean that a person **must be** deprived of liberty where circumstances no longer necessitate it. If a care home or hospital decides that deprivation of liberty is no longer necessary then they must end it immediately, by adjusting the care regime or implementing whatever other change is appropriate. The managing authority should then apply to the supervisory body to review and, if appropriate, formally terminate the authorisation.

## How should standard authorisations be reviewed?

**8.9**     When a supervisory body receives a request for a review, it must first decide which, if any, of the qualifying requirements need to be reviewed. A standard form is available for recording this decision.

**8.10**     If the supervisory body concludes that none of the qualifying requirements need to be reviewed, no further action is necessary. For example, if there has been a very recent assessment or review and no new evidence has been submitted to show that the relevant person does not meet the criteria, or that circumstances have changed, no review is required.

**8.11**     If it appears that one or more of the qualifying requirements should be reviewed, the supervisory body must arrange for a separate review assessment to be carried out for each of these requirements.

**8.12**     The supervisory body must record when a review is requested, what it decides to do (whether it decides to carry out a review or not) and the reasons for its decision.

**8.13**     In general, review processes should follow the standard authorisation processes – so supervisory bodies should conduct the assessments outlined in chapter 4 of this Code of Practice for each of the qualifying requirements that need to be reviewed.

**8.14**     Where the supervisory body decides that the best interests requirement should be reviewed solely because details of the **conditions** attached to the authorisation need to be changed, and the review request does not include evidence that there is a significant change in the relevant person's overall circumstances, there is no need for a full reassessment of best interests. The supervisory body can simply vary the conditions attached to the authorisation as appropriate. In deciding whether a full reassessment is necessary, the supervisory body should consider whether the grounds for the authorisation, or the nature of the conditions, are being contested by anyone as part of the review request.

**8.15**    If the review relates to any of the other requirements, or to a significant change in the person's situation under the best interests requirement, the supervisory body must obtain a new assessment.

**8.16**    If the assessment shows that the requirement is still met, the supervisory body must check whether the reason that it is met has changed from the reason originally stated on the authorisation. If it has, the supervisory body should make any appropriate amendments to the authorisation. In addition, if the review relates to the best interests requirement, the supervisory body must consider whether any conditions should be changed following the new assessment.

---

**Scenario: The review process**

Jo is 29 and sustained severe brain damage in a road traffic collision that killed her parents. She has great difficulty in verbal and written communication. Jo can get very frustrated and has been known to lash out at other people in the nursing care home where she now lives. At first, she regularly attempted to leave the home, but the view of the organisation providing Jo's care was that such a move would place her at serious risk, so she should be prevented from leaving.

Jo was assessed under the deprivation of liberty safeguards and an authorisation was made for six months. That authorisation is not due to end for another three months. However, Jo has made huge progress at the home and her representative is no longer sure that the restrictions are necessary. Care home staff, however, do not think that her improvement reduces the best interests requirement of the deprivation of liberty authorisation.

Jo is assisted by her representative to request a review, in the form of a letter with pictures. The pictures appear to describe Jo's frustration with the legal processes that she perceives are preventing her from moving into her own accommodation.

The supervisory body appoints a best interests assessor to coordinate the review. The best interests assessor considers which of the qualifying requirements needs to be reviewed and by whom. It appears that the best interests assessment, as well as possibly the mental health and mental capacity assessments, should be reviewed.

To assess Jo's mental capacity and her own wishes for the best interests assessment, the best interests assessor feels that specialist help would be beneficial. A speech and language therapist meets with Jo and uses a visual communication system with her. Using this system, the therapist is able to say that in her view Jo is unlikely to have capacity to make the decision to leave the care home. The mental health assessment also confirmed that Jo was still considered to have a mental disorder.

The best interests assessor was uncertain, however, whether it was still in Jo's best interests to remain under the deprivation of liberty authorisation. It was not possible to coordinate full updated assessments from the rehabilitation team, who knew her well, in the time limits required. So, because the care home believed that the standard authorisation was still required, and it was a complex case, the best interests assessor recommended to the supervisory body that two conditions should be applied to the standard authorisation:

- assessments must be carried out by rehabilitation specialists on Jo's clinical progress, and
- a full case review should be held within one month.

At this review meeting, to which Jo's representative and the best interests assessor were invited, it was agreed that Jo had made such good progress that deprivation of liberty was no longer necessary, because the risks of her having increased freedom had reduced. The standard authorisation was therefore terminated, and a new care plan was prepared which focused on working towards more independent living.

## What happens if any of the requirements are not met?

8.17    If any of the requirements are not met, then the authorisation must be terminated immediately.

8.18    The supervisory body must give written notice of the outcome of a review and any changes that have been made to the deprivation of liberty authorisation to:

- the managing authority and the care home or hospital itself
- the relevant person
- the relevant person's representative, and
- any Independent Mental Capacity Advocate (IMCA) involved.

### SHORT-TERM SUSPENSION OF AUTHORISATION

8.19    There are separate review arrangements for cases in which the eligibility requirement ceases to be met for a short period of time for reasons other than that the person is objecting to receiving mental health treatment in hospital. For example, if the relevant person is detained as a hospital in-patient under the Mental Health Act 1983, the managing authority must notify the supervisory body, who will suspend the authorisation.

8.20    If the relevant person then becomes eligible again within 28 days, the managing authority must notify the supervisory body who will remove the suspension. If no such notice is given within 28 days, then the authorisation will be terminated. Standard forms are available for managing authorities to notify supervisory bodies about the need for suspension of an authorisation, or that a suspension should be lifted.

8.21    If the person ceases to meet the eligibility requirement because they begin to object to receiving mental health treatment in hospital and they meet the criteria for an application for admission under section 2 or section 3 of the Mental Health Act 1983, a review should be started immediately (see paragraph 8.3).

## Is a review necessary when the relevant person's capacity fluctuates?

8.22    Guidance about people with fluctuating or temporary capacity is contained in paragraphs 4.26 and 4.27 of the main Code. In the context of deprivation of liberty safeguards, where a relevant person's capacity to make decisions about the arrangements made for their care and treatment fluctuates on a short-term basis, a balance needs to be struck between:

- the need to review and terminate an authorisation if a person regains capacity, and
- spending time and resources constantly reviewing, terminating and then seeking fresh deprivation of liberty authorisations as the relevant person's capacity changes.

**8.23**   Each case must be treated on its merits. Managing authorities should keep all cases under review: where a person subject to an authorisation is deemed to have regained the capacity to decide about the arrangements made for their care and treatment, the managing authority must assess whether there is consistent evidence of the regaining of capacity on a longer-term basis. This is a clinical judgement that will need to be made by a suitably qualified person.

**8.24**   Where there is consistent evidence of regaining capacity on this longer-term basis, deprivation of liberty should be lifted immediately, and a formal review and termination of the authorisation sought. However, it should be borne in mind that a deprivation of liberty authorisation carries with it certain safeguards that the relevant person will lose if the authorisation is terminated. Where the regaining of capacity is likely to be temporary, and the authorisation will be required again within a short period of time, the authorisation should be left in place, but with the situation kept under ongoing review.

---

**Scenario: Fluctuating capacity**

Walter, an older man with severe depression, is admitted to hospital from a care home. He seems confused and bewildered, but does not object. His family are unable to look after him at home, but they would prefer him to go into a different care home rather than stay in hospital. However, there is no alternative placement available, so when the assessment concludes that Walter lacks capacity to make decisions about his care and treatment, the only option seems to be that he should stay on the ward.

Because the care regime in the ward is extremely restrictive – Walter is not allowed to leave the hospital and his movement within the hospital is restricted for his own safety – ward staff think that they need to apply for a deprivation of liberty authorisation which is subsequently given.

However, over time Walter starts to experience lucid passages, during which he expresses relief at being on the ward rather than in the care home. A review meeting is convened and the participants agree that Walter now sometimes has capacity to make decisions about the arrangements made for his care and treatment. As this capacity fluctuates, it is decided, in consultation with his family, that the deprivation of liberty authorisation should remain in place for the time being.

Walter remains on the ward and his progress is such that his family feel they could look after him at home. Walter seems happy with this proposal and the consultant psychiatrist with responsibility for his care agrees to this. The deprivation of liberty authorisation is reviewed and terminated.

---

## What happens when an authorisation ends?

**8.25**   When an authorisation ends, the managing authority cannot lawfully continue to deprive a person of their liberty.

**8.26**   If the managing authority considers that a person will still need to be deprived of liberty after the authorisation ends, they need to request a further standard authorisation to begin immediately after the expiry of the existing authorisation.

**8.27**   There is no statutory time limit on how far in advance of the expiry of one authorisation the managing authority can apply for a renewal authorisation. It will need to be far enough in advance for the renewal authorisation to be given before the existing authorisation ends (but see paragraphs 3.19 and 3.20 about not applying for authorisations too far in advance).

**8.28**     Once underway, the process for renewing a standard authorisation is the same as that for obtaining an original authorisation, and the same assessment processes must take place. However, the need to instruct an IMCA will not usually arise because the relevant person should at this stage have a representative appointed.

**8.29**     When the standard authorisation ends, the supervisory body must inform in writing:

- the relevant person
- the relevant person's representative
- the managing authority, and
- every interested person named by the best interests assessor in their report as somebody they have consulted in carrying out their assessment.

## 9     WHAT HAPPENS IF SOMEONE THINKS A PERSON IS BEING DEPRIVED OF THEIR LIBERTY WITHOUT AUTHORISATION

It is a serious issue to deprive someone of their liberty without authorisation if they lack the capacity to consent. If anyone believes that a person is being deprived of their liberty without authorisation, they should raise this with the relevant authorities.

If the conclusion is that the person is being deprived of their liberty unlawfully, this will normally result in a change in their care arrangements, or in an application for a deprivation of liberty authorisation being made.

This chapter explains the process for reporting concerns and for assessing whether unauthorised deprivation of liberty is occurring. The flowchart at Annex 3 summarises the process that a supervisory body should follow when it receives a request from somebody other than the managing authority to examine whether or not there is a current unauthorised deprivation of liberty.

## What action should someone take if they think a person is being deprived of their liberty without authorisation?

**9.1**     If the relevant person themselves, any relative, friend or carer or any other third party (such as a person carrying out an inspection visit or a member of an advocacy organisation) believes that a person is being deprived of liberty without the managing authority having applied for an authorisation, they should draw this to the attention of the managing authority. A standard letter is available for this purpose. In the first instance, they should ask the managing authority to apply for an authorisation if it wants to continue with the care regime, or to change the care regime immediately. Given the seriousness of deprivation of liberty, a managing authority must respond within a reasonable time to the request. This would normally mean within 24 hours.

**9.2**     It may be possible for the managing authority to resolve the matter informally with the concerned person. For example, the managing authority could discuss the case with the concerned person, and perhaps make some adjustment to the care arrangements so that concerns that a deprivation of liberty may be occurring are removed. However, if the managing authority is unable to resolve the issue with the concerned person quickly, they should submit a request for a standard authorisation to the supervisory body.

**9.3**     If the concerned person has raised the matter with the managing authority, and the managing authority does not apply for an authorisation within a reasonable period, the concerned person can ask the supervisory body to decide whether there is an unauthorised deprivation of liberty. They should:

- tell the supervisory body the name of the person they are concerned about and the name of the hospital or care home, and
- as far as they are able, explain why they think that the person is deprived of their liberty.

A standard letter is available for this purpose.

**9.4**    In such circumstances, the supervisory body must select and appoint a person who is suitable and eligible to carry out a best interests assessment to consider whether the person is deprived of liberty.

**9.5**    The supervisory body does not, however, need to arrange such an assessment where it appears to the supervisory body that:

- the request they have received is frivolous or vexatious (for example, where the person is very obviously not deprived of their liberty) or where a very recent assessment has been carried out and repeated requests are received, or
- the question of whether or not there is an unauthorised deprivation of liberty has already been decided, and since that decision, there has been no change of circumstances that would merit the question being considered again.

The supervisory body should record the reasons for their decisions. A standard form is available for this purpose.

**9.6**    The supervisory body must notify the person who raised the concern, the relevant person, the managing authority of the relevant hospital or care home and any IMCA involved:

- that it has been to asked to assess whether or not there is an unauthorised deprivation of liberty
- whether or not it has decided to commission an assessment, and
- where relevant, who has been appointed as assessor.

## What happens if somebody informs the supervisory body directly that they think a person is being deprived of their liberty without authorisation?

**9.7**    If a person raises concerns about a potential unauthorised deprivation of liberty directly with the supervisory body, the supervisory body should immediately arrange a preliminary assessment to determine whether a deprivation of liberty is occurring. The supervisory body should then immediately notify the managing authority, rather than asking the concerned person to contact the managing authority themselves, to ask them to request a standard authorisation in respect of the person who is possibly deprived of liberty. The supervisory body should agree with the managing authority what is a reasonable period within which a standard authorisation should be requested (unless the managing authority is able to resolve the matter informally with the concerned person as described in paragraph 9.2). If the managing authority does not submit an application within the agreed period, and the matter has not been resolved informally, the supervisory body should follow the process set out in paragraphs 9.3 to 9.6 to assess whether unlawful deprivation of liberty is occurring. Even if the concerned person prefers to deal directly with the managing authority, the supervisory body should monitor what happens very closely to ensure that no unlawful deprivation of liberty may be occurring without proper action being taken.

## How will the assessment of unlawful deprivation of liberty be conducted?

**9.8**    An assessment of whether an unlawful deprivation of liberty is occurring must be carried out within seven calendar days. Although the assessment must be completed by somebody who is suitable and eligible to carry out a best interests assessment, it is not a best interests assessment as such. The purpose of the assessment is simply to establish whether unlawful deprivation of liberty is occurring.

**9.9**    The person nominated to undertake the assessment must consult the managing authority of the relevant hospital or care home, and examine any relevant needs assessments and care plans to consider whether they constitute a deprivation of liberty. They should also speak to the person who raised the concern about why they believe that the relevant person is being deprived of their liberty and consult, as far as is possible, with the relevant person's family and friends. If there is nobody appropriate to consult among family and friends, they should inform the supervisory body who must arrange for an IMCA to be instructed to support and represent the person. A standard form is available for the assessor to record the outcome of their assessment.

## What happens once the assessment has been conducted?

**9.10**    There are three possible outcomes of this assessment. The assessor may conclude that:

- the person is not being deprived of their liberty
- the person is being lawfully deprived of their liberty because authorisation exists (this, though, is an unlikely outcome since the supervisory body should already be aware if any authorisation exists, thus rendering any assessment in response to a third party request unnecessary), or
- the person is being deprived of their liberty unlawfully.

**9.11**    The supervisory body must notify the following people of the outcome of the assessment:

- the concerned third party who made the request
- the relevant person
- the managing authority of the relevant hospital or care home, and
- any IMCA involved.

A standard form is available for this purpose.

**9.12**    If the outcome of the assessment is that there is an unauthorised deprivation of liberty, then the full assessment process should be completed as if a standard authorisation for deprivation of liberty had been applied for – unless the managing authority changes the care arrangements so that it is clear that there is no longer any deprivation of liberty.

**9.13**    If, having considered what could be done to avoid deprivation of liberty, the managing authority decides that the need to continue the deprivation of liberty is so urgent that the care regime should continue while the assessments are carried out, it must give an urgent authorisation and seek a standard authorisation within seven days. The managing authority must supply the supervisory body with the same information it would have had to include in a request for a standard authorisation.

**9.14**    If the concerned person does not accept the outcome of their request for assessment, they can apply to the Court of Protection to hear their case. See chapter 10 for more details of the role of the Court of Protection.

## 10    WHAT IS THE COURT OF PROTECTION AND WHEN CAN PEOPLE APPLY TO IT?

To comply with Article 5(4) of the European Convention on Human Rights, anybody deprived of their liberty in accordance with the safeguards described in this Code of Practice is entitled to the right of speedy access to a court that can review the lawfulness of their deprivation of liberty. The Court of Protection, established by the Mental Capacity Act 2005, is the court for this purpose. Chapter 8 of the main Code provides more details on its role, powers and responsibilities.

## When can people apply to the Court of Protection about the deprivation of liberty safeguards and who can apply?

### APPLYING BEFORE AN AUTHORISATION IS GIVEN

**10.1**    The relevant person, or someone acting on their behalf, may make an application to the Court of Protection **before** a decision has been reached on an application for authorisation to deprive a person of their liberty. This might be to ask the court to declare whether the relevant person has capacity, or whether an act done or proposed to be done in relation to that person is lawful (this may include whether or not the act is or would be in the best interests of the relevant person). It is up to the Court of Protection to decide whether or not to consider such an application in advance of the decision on authorisation.

### APPLYING AFTER AN AUTHORISATION HAS BEEN GIVEN

**10.2**    Once a standard authorisation has been given, the relevant person or their representative has the right to apply to the Court of Protection to determine any question relating to the following matters:

- whether the relevant person meets one or more of the qualifying requirements for deprivation of liberty
- the period for which the standard authorisation is to be in force
- the purpose for which the standard authorisation is given, or
- the conditions subject to which the standard authorisation is given.

**10.3**    Where an urgent authorisation has been given, the relevant person or certain persons acting on their behalf, such as a donee or deputy, has the right to apply to the Court of Protection to determine any question relating to the following matters:

- whether the urgent authorisation should have been given
- the period for which the urgent authorisation is to be in force, or
- the purpose for which the urgent authorisation has been given.

**10.4**    Where a standard or urgent authorisation has been given, any other person may also apply to the Court of Protection for permission to take the relevant person's case to court to determine whether an authorisation should have been given. However, the Court of Protection has discretion to decide whether or not to consider an application from these people.

**10.5**    Wherever possible, concerns about the deprivation of liberty should be resolved informally or through the relevant supervisory body's or managing authority's complaints procedure, rather than through the Court of Protection. Chapter 15 of the main Code ('What are the best ways to settle disagreements and disputes about issues covered in the Act?') contains general guidance on how to settle disputes about issues covered in the Mental Capacity Act 2005. The review processes covered in chapter 8 of this Code also provide a way of resolving disputes or concerns, as explained in that chapter.

**10.6**    The aim should be to limit applications to the Court of Protection to cases that genuinely need to be referred to the court. However, with deprivation of liberty at stake, people should not be discouraged from making an application to the Court of Protection if it proves impossible to resolve concerns satisfactorily through other routes in a timely manner.

## How should people apply to the Court of Protection?

**10.7**    Guidance on the court's procedures, including how to make an application, is given in the Court of Protection Rules and Practice Directions issued by the court.[13]

**10.8**    The following people have an automatic right of access to the Court of Protection and do not have to obtain permission from the court to make an application:

- a person who lacks, or is alleged to lack, capacity in relation to a specific decision or action
- the donor of a Lasting Power of Attorney to whom an application relates, or their donee
- a deputy who has been appointed by the court to act for the person concerned
- a person named in an existing court order[14] to which the application relates, and
- the person appointed by the supervisory body as the relevant person's representative.

**10.9**    All other applicants must obtain the permission of the court before making an application. (See section 50 of the Mental Capacity Act 2005, as amended.) This can be done by completing the appropriate application form.

## What orders can the Court of Protection make?

**10.10**    The court may make an order:

- varying or terminating a standard or urgent authorisation, or
- directing the supervisory body (in the case of a standard authorisation) or the managing authority (in the case of an urgent authorisation) to vary or terminate the authorisation.

## What is the role of the Court of Protection in respect of people lacking capacity who are deprived of their liberty in settings other than hospitals or care homes?

**10.11**    The deprivation of liberty safeguards relate only to circumstances where a person is deprived of their liberty in a hospital or care home. Depriving a person who lacks capacity to consent to the arrangements made for their care or treatment of their liberty in other settings (for example in a person's own home, in supported living arrangements other than in care homes or in a day centre) will only be lawful following an order of the Court of Protection on a best interests personal welfare matter (see paragraph 6.51 of the main Code).

**10.12**    In such a case, application to the Court of Protection should be made before deprivation of liberty begins. A Court of Protection order will then itself provide a legal basis for the deprivation of liberty. A separate deprivation of liberty authorisation under the processes set out in this Code will not be required.

---

[13]  There will usually be a fee for applications to the court. Details of the fees charged by the court and the circumstances in which fees may be waived or remitted are available from the Office of the Public Guardian (**www.publicguardian.gov.uk**).

[14]  Examples of existing court orders include orders appointing a deputy or declarations made by the court in relation to treatment issues.

## Is legal aid available to support applications to the Court of Protection in deprivation of liberty safeguards cases?

**10.13**    Legal aid will be available both for advice and representation before the Court of Protection.

## 11   HOW WILL THE SAFEGUARDS BE MONITORED?

The deprivation of a person's liberty is a significant issue. The deprivation of liberty safeguards are designed to ensure that a person who lacks capacity to consent to the arrangements made for their care or treatment is suitably protected against arbitrary detention. In order to provide reassurance that the safeguards processes are being correctly operated, it is important for there to be an effective mechanism for monitoring the implementation of the safeguards.

## Who will monitor the safeguards?

**11.1**    Regulations[15] will confer the responsibility for the inspection process of the operation of the deprivation of liberty safeguards in England on a new regulator, the Care Quality Commission, bringing together functions from the existing Commission for Social Care Inspection, the Healthcare Commission and the Mental Health Act Commission. The new body will be established during 2008, subject to the passage of the relevant legislation through Parliament, and is expected to be fully operational by 2009/10 in line with the deprivation of liberty safeguards coming into force.

**11.2**    In Wales, the functions of monitoring the operation of the deprivation of liberty safeguards will fall to Welsh Ministers. These functions will be performed on their behalf by Healthcare Inspectorate Wales and the Care and Social Services Inspectorate Wales.

## What will the inspection bodies do and what powers will they have?

**11.3**    The inspection bodies for care homes and hospitals will be expected to:

- monitor the manner in which the deprivation of liberty safeguards are being operated by:
  - visiting hospitals and care homes in accordance with their existing visiting programme
  - interviewing people accommodated in hospitals and care homes to the extent that they consider it necessary to do so, and
  - requiring the production of, and inspecting, relevant records relating to the care or treatment of people accommodated in hospitals and care homes

- report annually, summarising their activity and their findings about the operation of the deprivation of liberty safeguards. In England this report will be made to the Secretary of State for Health, and in Wales the report will be made to the Welsh Ministers. It will be for each monitoring body to decide whether there should be a deprivation of liberty safeguards specific report or whether the report should form part of a wider report on the monitoring body's activities.

**11.4**    The inspection bodies will have the power to require supervisory bodies and managing authorities of hospitals or care homes to disclose information to them.

---

[15]   Draft regulations for England will be consulted upon later. Welsh Ministers are currently considering how they will use their regulation-making powers for Wales.

**11.5**    The inspection process will not cover the revisiting of individual assessments (other than by way of a limited amount of sampling).

**11.6**    The inspection process will not constitute an alternative review or appeal process. However, if the inspection body comes across a case where they believe deprivation of liberty may be occurring without an authorisation, they should inform the supervisory body in the same way as any other third party may do.

**11.7**    The inspection bodies will look at the deprivation of liberty protocols and procedures in place within managing authorities and supervisory bodies. The aim is to use a small amount of sampling to evaluate the effect of these protocols and procedures on individual cases. Monitoring should take place at a time when the monitoring body is visiting the care home or in-patient setting as part of routine operations, not as an exception.

**11.8**    Supervisory bodies and managing authorities should keep their protocols and procedures under review and supervisory bodies should assess the nature of the authorisations they are giving in light of their local population. This information may be relevant to policy decisions about commissioning care and support services.

## CHECKLISTS

### Key points for care homes and hospitals (managing authorities)

- Managing authorities need to adapt their care planning processes to incorporate consideration of whether a person has capacity to consent to the services which are to be provided and whether their actions are likely to result in a deprivation of liberty.
- A managing authority must not, except in an urgent situation, deprive a person of liberty unless a standard authorisation has been given by the supervisory body for that specific situation, and remains in force.
- It is up to the managing authority to request such authorisation and implement the outcomes.
- Authorisation should be obtained from the supervisory body in advance of the deprivation of liberty, except in circumstances considered to be so urgent that the deprivation of liberty needs to begin immediately. In such cases, authorisation must be obtained within seven calendar days of the start of the deprivation of liberty.
- A managing authority must ensure that they comply with any conditions attached to the authorisation.
- A managing authority should monitor whether the relevant person's representative maintains regular contact with the person.
- Authorisation of deprivation of liberty should only be sought if it is genuinely necessary for a person to be deprived of liberty in their best interests in order to keep them safe. It is not necessary to apply for authorisations for all admissions to hospitals and care homes simply because the person concerned lacks capacity to decide whether to be admitted.

### Key points for local authorities and NHS bodies (supervisory bodies)

- Supervisory bodies will receive applications from managing authorities for standard authorisations of deprivation of liberty. Deprivation of liberty cannot lawfully begin until the supervisory body has given authorisation, or the managing authority has itself given an urgent authorisation.
- Before an authorisation for deprivation of liberty may be given, the supervisory body must have obtained written assessments of the relevant person in order to ensure that they meet the qualifying requirements (including that the deprivation of liberty is necessary to protect them from harm and will be in their best interests).
- Supervisory bodies will need to ensure that sufficient assessors are available to meet the

needs of their area and that these assessors have the skills, qualifications, experience and training to perform the function.

■ Authorisation may not be given unless all the qualifying requirements are met.

■ In giving authorisation, the supervisory body must specify its duration, which may not exceed 12 months and may not be for longer than recommended by the best interests assessor. Deprivation of liberty should not continue for longer than is necessary.

■ The supervisory body may attach conditions to the authorisation if it considers it appropriate to do so.

■ The supervisory body must give notice of its decision in writing to specified people, and notify others.

■ The supervisory body must appoint a relevant person's representative to represent the interests of every person for whom they give a standard authorisation for deprivation of liberty.

■ When an authorisation is in force, the relevant person, the relevant person's representative and any IMCA representing the individual have a right at any time to request that the supervisory body reviews the authorisation.

## Key points for managing authorities and supervisory bodies

In addition to the above, both managing authorities and supervisory bodies should be aware of the following key points:

■ An authorisation may last for a maximum period of 12 months.

■ Anyone engaged in caring for the person, anyone named by them as a person to consult, and anyone with an interest in the person's welfare must be consulted in decision-making.

■ Before the current authorisation expires, the managing authority may seek a fresh authorisation for up to another 12 months, provided it is established, on the basis of further assessment, that the requirements continue to be met.

■ The authorisation should be reviewed, and if appropriate revoked, before it expires if there has been a significant change in the person's circumstances. To this end, the managing authority will be required to ensure that the continued deprivation of liberty of a person remains necessary in the best interests of the person.

■ A decision to deprive a person of liberty may be challenged by the relevant person, or by the relevant person's representative, by an application to the Court of Protection. However, managing authorities and supervisory bodies should always be prepared to try to resolve disputes locally and informally. No one should be forced to apply to the court because of failure or unwillingness on the part of a managing authority or supervisory body to engage in constructive discussion.

■ If the court is asked to decide on a case where there is a question about whether deprivation of liberty is lawful or should continue to be authorised, the managing authority can continue with its current care regime where it is necessary:

–    for the purpose of giving the person life-sustaining treatment, or
–    to prevent a serious deterioration in their condition while the court makes its decision.

■ The complete process of assessing and authorising deprivation of liberty should be clearly recorded, and regularly monitored and audited, as part of an organisation's governance structure.

■ Management information should be recorded and retained, and used to measure the effectiveness of the deprivation of liberty processes. This information will also need to be shared with the inspection bodies.

# ANNEX 1 – OVERVIEW OF THE DEPRIVATION OF LIBERTY SAFEGUARDS PROCESS

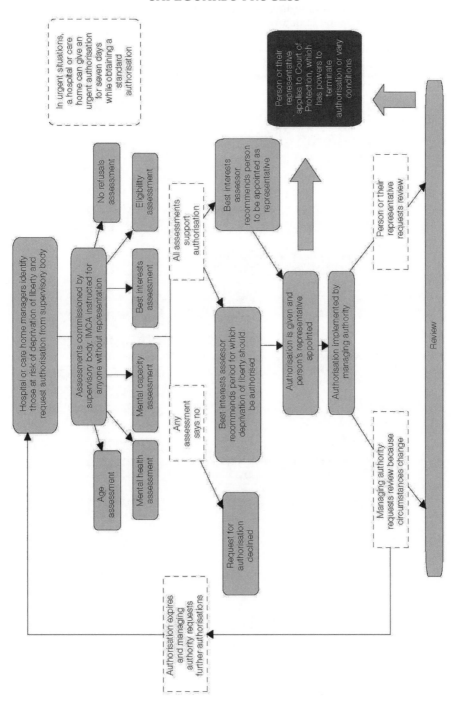

## ANNEX 2 – CONSIDERATIONS FOR A MANAGING AUTHORITY

### What should a managing authority consider before applying for authorisation of deprivation of liberty?

These questions are relevant **both** at admission **and** when reviewing the care of patients and residents. By considering the following questions in the following or der, a managing authority will be helped to know whether an application for authorisation is required.

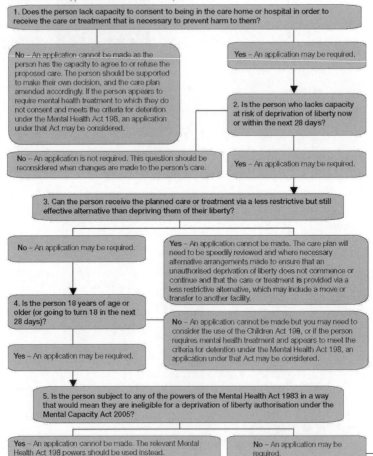

1. Does the person lack capacity to consent to being in the care home or hospital in order to receive the care or treatment that is necessary to prevent harm to them?

No – An application cannot be made as the person has the capacity to agree to or refuse the proposed care. The person should be supported to make their own decision, and the care plan amended accordingly. If the person appears to require mental health treatment to which they do not consent and meets the criteria for detention under the Mental Health Act 198, an application under that Act may be considered.

Yes – An application may be required.

2. Is the person who lacks capacity at risk of deprivation of liberty now or within the next 28 days?

No – An application is not required. This question should be reconsidered when changes are made to the person's care.

Yes – An application may be required.

3. Can the person receive the planned care or treatment via a less restrictive but still effective alternative than depriving them of their liberty?

No – An application may be required.

Yes – An application cannot be made. The care plan will need to be speedily reviewed and where necessary alternative arrangements made to ensure that an unauthorised deprivation of liberty does not commence or continue and that the care or treatment is provided via a less restrictive alternative, which may include a move or transfer to another facility.

4. Is the person 18 years of age or older (or going to turn 18 in the next 28 days)?

No – An application cannot be made but you may need to consider the use of the Children Act 198, or if the person requires mental health treatment and appears to meet the criteria for detention under the Mental Health Act 198, an application under that Act may be considered.

Yes – An application may be required.

5. Is the person subject to any of the powers of the Mental Health Act 1983 in a way that would mean they are ineligible for a deprivation of liberty authorisation under the Mental Capacity Act 2005?

Yes – An application cannot be made. The relevant Mental Health Act 198 powers should be used instead.

No – An application may be required.

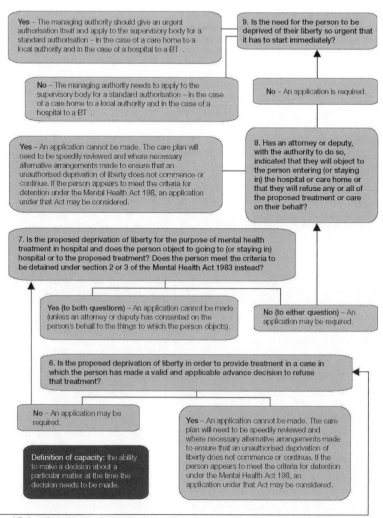

Yes – The managing authority should give an urgent authorisation itself and apply to the supervisory body for a standard authorisation – in the case of a care home to a local authority and in the case of a hospital to a PCT .

9. Is the need for the person to be deprived of their liberty so urgent that it has to start immediately?

No – The managing authority needs to apply to the supervisory body for a standard authorisation – in the case of a care home to a local authority and in the case of a hospital to a PCT .

No – An application is required.

Yes – An application cannot be made. The care plan will need to be speedily reviewed and where necessary alternative arrangements made to ensure that an unauthorised deprivation of liberty does not commence or continue. If the person appears to meet the criteria for detention under the Mental Health Act 198, an application under that Act may be considered.

8. Has an attorney or deputy, with the authority to do so, indicated that they will object to the person entering (or staying in) the hospital or care home or that they will refuse any or all of the proposed treatment or care on their behalf?

7. Is the proposed deprivation of liberty for the purpose of mental health treatment in hospital and does the person object to going to (or staying in) hospital or to the proposed treatment? Does the person meet the criteria to be detained under section 2 or 3 of the Mental Health Act 1983 instead?

Yes (to both questions) – An application cannot be made (unless an attorney or deputy has consented on the person's behalf to the things to which the person objects).

No (to either question) – An application may be required.

6. Is the proposed deprivation of liberty in order to provide treatment in a case in which the person has made a valid and applicable advance decision to refuse that treatment?

No – An application may be required.

Yes – An application cannot be made. The care plan will need to be speedily reviewed and where necessary alternative arrangements made to ensure that an unauthorised deprivation of liberty does not commence or continue. If the person appears to meet the criteria for detention under the Mental Health Act 198, an application under that Act may be considered.

Definition of capacity: the ability to make a decision about a particular matter at the time the decision needs to be made.

NB: An authorisation only relates to deprivation of liberty and does not give authority for any course of treatment.

## ANNEX 3 – PROCESS FOR SUPERVISORY BODIES

**Supervisory body action on receipt of a request from:**
a)  **a managing authority for a standard deprivation of liberty authorisation**
b)  **somebody other than a managing authority (an eligible person) to determine whether or not there is a current unauthorised deprivation of liberty**

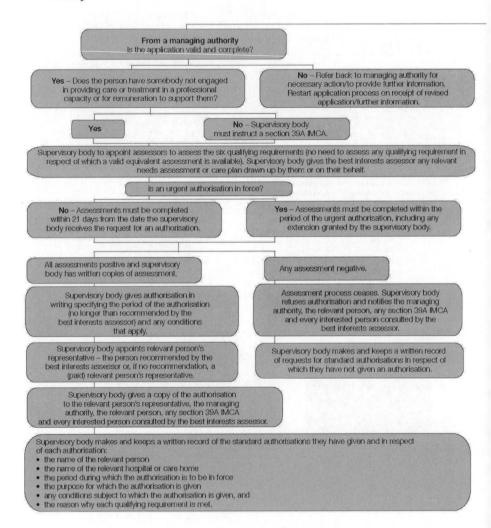

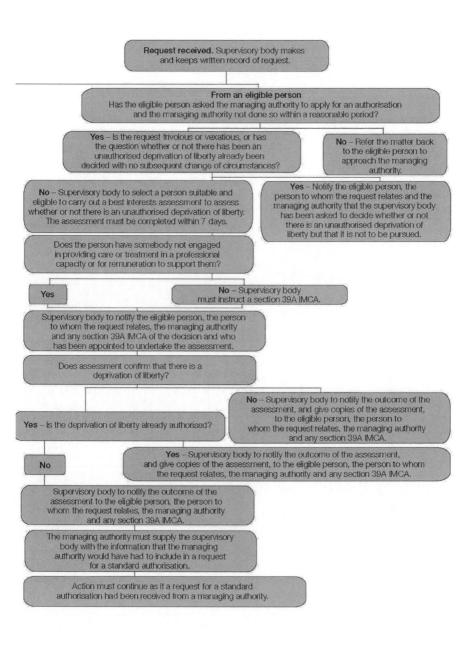

**ANNEX 4** – STANDARD AUTHORISATION REVIEW PROCESS

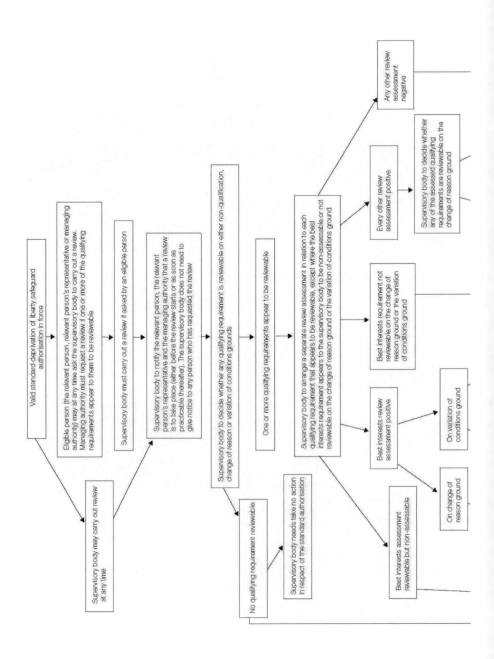

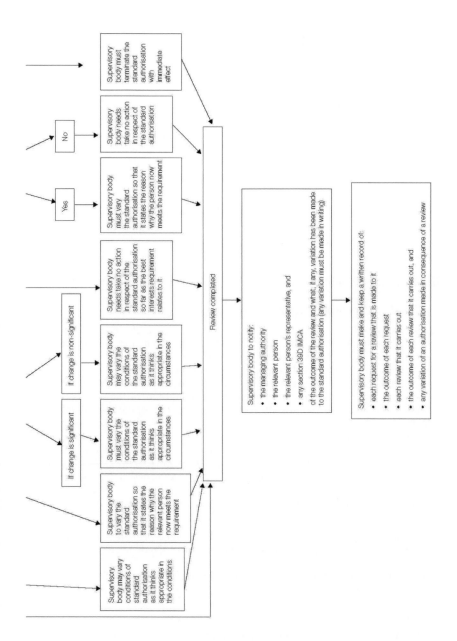

# MHA 1983 Code of Practice 2015: Chapter 13

## Why read this chapter?

**13.1**   A sound understanding and application of the principles and provisions of the Mental Capacity Act (MCA) and the Deprivation of Liberty Safeguards (DoLS) and of the common law relating to consent, is essential to enable decision-makers to fulfil their legal responsibilities and to safeguard their patients' rights under the European Convention on Human Rights (ECHR).

**13.2**   Practitioners should be able to identify the legal framework that governs a patient's assessment and treatment and authorise any appropriate deprivation of a patient's liberty whether the MCA or Metal Health Act (the Act). The legal framework is not static and may change as the patient's circumstances and needs change.

## Definitions and principles

**13.3**   Definitions for the purposes of this chapter:

- **Deprivation of liberty safeguards (DoLS)** – the framework of safeguards under the Mental Capacity Act 2005 (MCA), as amended by the Mental Health Act 2007, for people who need to be deprived of their liberty in their best interests for care or treatment to which they lack the capacity to consent themselves
- **DoLS authorisation** – an authorisation under Schedule A1 to the MCA given by a 'supervisory body' (a local authority or, in certain circumstances, the Welsh Ministers) which authorises a deprivation of liberty in a care home or hospital after completion of the statutory assessment process, which includes an assessment that the detention is in the best interests of the person, and
- **Court of Protection order** – a welfare order made by the Court of Protection that authorises a deprivation of liberty for an individual who lacks the capacity to decide whether or not to be accommodated in the relevant location, in their best interests.

**13.4**   Age and applicability of the MCA and DoLS:

- the MCA, in general, applies to individuals aged 16 years and over
- however, a DoLS authorisation can only be made in respect of an individual aged 18 or over. A Court of Protection order can be made in respect of individuals aged 16 or over, and
- a person must be 18 to make an advance decision to refuse treatment or create a lasting power of attorney (LPA) under the MCA.

**13.5**   This chapter describes:

- the MCA, including the definition of 'lack of capacity'
- the importance of the MCA in care planning
- acts that can be performed by professionals under the MCA on behalf of individuals who lack capacity
- treatment of individuals who lack capacity for physical conditions who are liable to be detained under the Act

■ the authorisation of a deprivation of liberty by a DoLS authorisation or a Court of Protection order
■ considerations when determining whether an individual is to be detained under the Act or deprived of their liberty under a DoLS authorisation or Court of Protection order (including a flowchart to aid decision-making)
■ matters relevant to the MCA and Electro-Convulsive Therapy (ECT), and
■ a case study that demonstrates decision making in relation to detention under the Act and deprivation of liberty under DoLS.

**13.6**  This chapter should be read in close reference to other chapters in this Code, particularly:

■ Children and young people under the age of 18 (chapter 19)
■ Applications for detention in hospital (chapter 14)
■ Guardianship (chapter 30), and
■ Wishes expressed in advance (chapter 9).

**13.7**  Further detailed information can be found in the:

■ Mental Capacity Act 2005 Code of Practice (MCA Code of Practice)
■ Deprivation of Liberty Safeguards: Code of Practice (DoLS Code of Practice), and
■ Department of Health Guidance on Consent.[1]

**13.8**  In this chapter, references to 'the Act' refer to the Mental Health Act and MCA to the Mental Capacity Act.

## What is the MCA?

**13.9**  The MCA empowers individuals to make their own decisions where possible and protects the rights of those who lack capacity. Where an individual lacks capacity to make a specific decision at a particular time, the MCA provides a legal framework for others to act and make that decision on their behalf, in their best interests, including where the decision is about care and/or treatment.

**13.10**  The MCA applies to hundreds of thousands of people at any one time, and potentially to all adults at some point in their lives. The MCA places a strong emphasis on the need to support individuals to make their own decisions. Information should be explained in a manner best suited to the individual to aid the individual's understanding. All individuals should be encouraged to participate in decision making and professionals should carefully consider the individual's wishes at all times.

**13.11**  The MCA should be central to the approach professionals take to patients who lack capacity in all health and care settings (including psychiatric and general hospitals). The starting point should always be that the MCA should be applied wherever possible to individuals who lack capacity and are detained under the Act.

**13.12**  In some situations, the provision of treatment under the Act will limit the operation of aspects of the MCA. For example, if a patient's treatment is being regulated by part 4 of the Act, then the MCA cannot in general be used to authorise medical treatment for mental disorder. For such a patient, any advance decision by them under the MCA to refuse proposed medical treatment for mental disorder or any decision taken by their attorney

---

[1]  Reference Guide to Consent for Examination or Treatment. Department of Health. 2009. www.gov.uk/government/uploads/system/uploads/attachment–data/file/138296/ dh-103653--1-.pdf.

under the MCA to refuse consent to proposed medical treatment, cannot prevent medical treatment for mental disorder being given under sections 58 and 63 of the Act.

**13.13**    An exception to this is electro-convulsive therapy (ECT). A person who has made a valid and applicable advance decision under the MCA, or for whom a decision has been taken by their attorney, to refuse ECT, cannot be given that treatment under section 58A of the Act although treatment can be given in specific emergency situations under section 62(1A).

**13.14**    At the heart of the MCA are five statutory principles.

## Five statutory principles of the MCA

**Principle one**: A person must be assumed to have capacity unless it is established that they lack capacity.

**Principle two**: A person is not to be treated as unable to make a decision unless all practicable steps to help them to do so have been taken without success.

**Principle three**: A person is not to be treated as unable to make a decision merely because they make an unwise decision.

**Principle four**: An act done, or decision made, on behalf of a person who lacks capacity, must be done, or made, in their best interests.

**Principle five**: Before the act is done, or the decision is made, regard must be had to whether the purpose of the act or the decision can be as effectively achieved in a way that is less restrictive of the person's rights and freedom of action.

**13.15**    It is important for professionals to be aware that individuals with a mental disorder, including those liable to be detained under the Act, do not necessarily lack capacity. The assumption should always be that a patient subject to the Act has capacity, unless it is established otherwise in accordance with the MCA.

**13.16**    Healthcare providers have a legal duty to care for and treat patients who lack capacity in accordance with the MCA, when it applies. Failure to do so could result in enforcement action being taken by the Care Quality Commission (CQC).

## How does the MCA define 'lack of capacity'?

**13.17**    A person lacks capacity in relation to a matter if, at the material time, the person is unable to make a decision for themselves in relation to the matter because of an impairment of, or a disturbance in the functioning of, the mind or brain.

**13.18**    The above definition contains both a 'diagnostic test' and a 'functional test'. The diagnostic test determines whether the individual has an impairment of, or a disturbance in the functioning of, the mind or brain. The impairment or disturbance can be temporary or permanent, but if it is temporary, the decision-maker should justify why the decision cannot wait until the circumstances change.

**13.19**    The functional test determines whether the individual is unable to make the specific decision in question themselves because of the impairment or disturbance. The elements of the functional test are set out in section 3(1) of the MCA. The inability to make the decision must be because of the impairment or disturbance, as opposed to some other cause. Both tests must be satisfied for an individual to be deemed to lack capacity to make the specific decision in question at the material time.

**13.20**    A person is 'unable to make a decision' for themselves if they are unable to do any one of the following:

- understand information which is relevant to the decision to be made
- retain that information in their mind
- use or weigh that information as part of the decision-making process, or
- communicate their decision (whether by talking, sign language or any other means).

**13.21**    As capacity relates to specific matters and can change over time, capacity should be reassessed as appropriate over time and in respect of specific treatment decisions. Decision-makers should note that the MCA test of capacity should be used whenever assessing a patient's capacity to consent for the purposes of the Act (including, for instance, under section 58 of the Act).

**13.22**    Decision-makers should ensure that where a capacity assessment is undertaken, this is recorded in the individual's care and treatment record. As well as the outcome of the test, the following should be recorded:

- the specific decision for which capacity was assessed
- the salient points that the individual needs to understand and comprehend and the information that was presented to the individual in relation to the decision
- the steps taken to promote the individual's ability to decide themselves. How the information was given in the most effective way to communicate with the individual
- how the diagnostic test was assessed, and how the assessor reached their conclusions, and
- how the functional test was undertaken, and how the assessor reached their conclusions.

## Care planning

**13.23**    The five statutory principles of the MCA form a vital part of developing a patient's care plan and should be integral to this process.

**13.24**    Professionals should seek to involve those who lack capacity in decisions about their care as much as they would involve those who have capacity. Care plans should be developed in collaboration with the patient as much as possible. Where professionals and patients disagree over elements of the care plan the emphasis should be on discussion and compromise where possible. Restrictions (including restraint) and the deprivation of liberty should only be considered when absolutely necessary and when all appropriate efforts at building consensus and agreement have failed.

**13.25**    Care planning, including planning for discharge, must adhere to the steps for determining what is in the person's best interests set out in section 4 of the MCA. This ensures participation by the person and consideration of their wishes, feelings, beliefs and values and consultation with specified others (eg carers, attorneys and people nominated by the person) about the person's best interests.

## The Court of Protection

**13.26**    The Court of Protection is a specialist court set up by the MCA to deal with cases involving individuals lacking capacity. It operates on a 24-hour basis.

**13.27**    A Court of Protection order may be made under the MCA to authorise a deprivation of liberty. Such orders may also authorise care or treatment.

**13.28**    In certain cases, a Court of Protection order is the only way to authorise a deprivation of liberty under the MCA. This includes where:

■    the deprivation of liberty is to occur in a place other than a hospital or care home (DoLS authorisations can only be given in respect of a care home or hospital), or
■    the person is aged 16 or 17 (DoLS authorisations can only be given in relation to persons aged 18 or over).

**13.29**    An application to the Court of Protection should also be made if decision-makers have not found it possible to determine the capacity or best interests of a person in relation to a particular decision.

## Acts that can be performed under the MCA

**13.30**    The MCA recognises that situations will occur when carers, healthcare and social care staff will need to make decisions on behalf of individuals who lack capacity to make particular decisions themselves (including decisions that relate to care and/or treatment for mental and/or physical conditions).

**13.31**    The MCA can be relied upon to treat mental disorder where the patient lacks capacity to make the decision in question and such treatment is in the patient's best interests, provided that the treatment is not regulated by Part 4 of the Act.

**13.32**    The Act does not regulate the treatment of physical conditions that are unrelated to mental disorders.

**13.33**    Sections 5 and 6 of the MCA offer protection from legal liability for certain acts of restraint – provided those acts are reasonably believed to be in the best interests of the individual. In this context restraint means using or threatening to use force to make a person do something they are resisting, or may resist, or restricting the person's liberty of movement, whether or not the person resists.

**13.34**    In considering the use of restraint, decision-makers should carefully take into account the need to respect an individual's liberty and autonomy.[2] Section 6 of the MCA states that, in addition to needing to be in the best interests of the person who lacks capacity in respect of the relevant decision, acts of restraint will only be permitted if:

■    the person taking action reasonably believes that restraint is necessary to prevent harm to the person who lacks capacity, and
■    the amount or type of restraint used and the amount of time it lasts is a proportionate response to the likelihood and seriousness of that harm.

   (More information on restraint and the MCA can be found from paragraph 6.40 onwards of the MCA Code of Practice.)

**13.35**    However, sections 5 and 6 of the MCA cannot be relied on if the overall care package, including any proposed measures of restraint and/or proposed restrictions on movement, will give rise to a 'deprivation of liberty'. A deprivation of liberty will engage article 5 of the ECHR and must be specifically authorised under the MCA by a DoLS authorisation or a Court of Protection order, or otherwise made lawful by way of detention under the Act.

---

[2]    If a person is, or is likely to be, restrained within the meaning of section 6(4), of the MCA, the guidance on 'restrictive intervention' given in chapter 26 may apply.

**13.36**    It is important to note that if a potential deprivation of liberty is identified, the first step should always be to review the care plan to see if a less restrictive approach could be taken that would prevent that deprivation of liberty from arising.

## Treatment for physical conditions (where the individual is liable to be detained under the Act)

**13.37**    The Act regulates medical treatment of mental disorder for individuals who are liable to be detained under the Act. This may include treatment of physical conditions that is intended to alleviate or prevent a worsening of symptoms or a manifestation of the mental disorder (eg a clozapine blood test) or where the treatment is otherwise part of, or ancillary to, treatment for mental disorder.

**13.38**    Where individuals liable to be detained under the Act have a physical condition unrelated to their mental disorder, consent to treat this physical condition must be sought from the individual. If the individual does not have the capacity to consent, treatment can be provided under the MCA as long as it is in their best interests.

**13.39**    If the individual is deprived of their liberty and the need for physical treatment is the only reason why the person needs to be detained in hospital, then the patient is not within the scope of the Mental Health Act (as the purpose of the deprivation of liberty is not to treat mental disorder) and a DoLS authorisation or a Court of Protection order should be sought.

## Authorising deprivations of liberty under the MCA and the DoLS

**13.40**    The DoLS are part of the MCA and as such are rooted in the MCA's five statutory principles. The DoLS only apply to individuals who lack the capacity to consent to accommodation in a care home or hospital where care and/or treatment provided in that accommodation amounts (or is likely to amount) to a deprivation of liberty.

**13.41**    A DoLS authorisation does not in itself authorise care or treatment, only the deprivation of liberty that results from the implementation of the proposed care plan. Any necessary care or treatment should be provided in accordance with the MCA.

**13.42**    When considering whether to apply for a DoLS authorisation, decision-makers should first assess the capacity of the person to consent to the arrangements for their care or treatment, in accordance with the MCA.

**13.43**    Next, decision-makers should consider whether the circumstances of the proposed accommodation and treatment amount (or are likely to amount) to a deprivation of liberty. Consideration must also be given at this stage to whether the patient's care plan can be amended to avoid any potential deprivation of liberty.

**13.44**    The precise scope of the term 'deprivation of liberty' is not fixed. In its 19 March judgment *P v Cheshire West and Chester Council and another and P and Q v Surrey County Council* ('Cheshire West'),[3] the Supreme Court clarified that there is a deprivation of liberty in circumstances where a person is under continuous control and supervision, is not free to leave and lacks capacity to consent to these arrangements.

**13.45**    The Supreme Court also noted that factors which are not relevant in determining whether there is a deprivation of liberty include the person's compliance or lack of objection

---

[3]    *P v Cheshire West and Chester Council and another and P and Q v Surrey County Council*, 2014 WLR 2. www.supremecourt.uk/decided-cases/docs/UKSC-2012-0068-Judgment.pdf.

and the reason or purpose behind a particular placement. The relative normality of the placement (whatever the comparison made) is also not relevant.

**13.46**    A deprivation of liberty can occur in domestic settings where the state is responsible for such arrangements. In such cases, an order should be sought from the Court of Protection.

**13.47**    The definition of a deprivation of liberty develops over time in accordance with the case law of the European Court of Human Rights and UK courts on article 5 of the ECHR. In order for decision-makers to be able to assess whether the situation they are faced with constitutes (or is likely to constitute) a deprivation of liberty, they should keep abreast of the latest case law developments.

**13.48**    The criteria that must be satisfied to obtain a DoLS authorisation is detailed in the box below.

---

### DoLS authorisations

In general, a DoLS authorisation under Schedule A1 to the MCA is given by a 'supervisory body' (a local authority or, in certain circumstances, the Welsh Ministers), following a request from a 'managing authority' (the hospital or care home at which the individual is placed or is likely to be placed). Best practice would be for an authorisation to be in place at the time the deprivation of liberty occurs.

An authorisation will only be given if the individual concerned is assessed to meet all six of the qualifying requirements, on which detailed guidance is given in the DoLS Code of Practice. The six qualifying requirements are summarised below.

a.    Age – is the individual aged 18 or over?

b.    Mental health – does the individual have a mental disorder as defined by the Act? (It should be noted that the exclusion in the Act in respect of a learning disability is not relevant for the purposes of DoLS)

c.    Mental capacity – does the individual lack capacity to decide whether or not they should be accommodated in the care home or hospital specified at the material time (ie the time of the assessment)?

d.    Best interests:

   (i)    Is it in the best interest of the individual for them to be deprived of their liberty?

   (ii)   Is it necessary for them to be deprived of their liberty in order to prevent harm to themselves?

   (iii)  Is the deprivation of liberty a proportionate response to the likelihood of the individual suffering harm and the seriousness of that harm?

e.    Eligibility – this qualifying requirement is met unless the person is ineligible to be deprived of their liberty by the MCA (Schedule 1A to the MCA sets out who is ineligible for this purpose)

f.    No refusals – has the person made a valid and applicable advance decision to refuse some or all of the treatment in question or is there is a valid and conflicting decision by a donee or deputy? If so, they may not meet the qualifying criteria for DoLS.

Note 1: there is a different procedure in Schedule A1 of the MCA for an urgent DoLS authorisation. However, an urgent authorisation is generally only given if a request for a standard DoLS authorisation has been made, and therefore, there must be a

> reasonable expectation that the six qualifying requirements for a standard authorisation are likely to be met (For further information, see paragraph 6.1 of the DoLS Code of Practice).
>
> **Note 2**: DoLS authorisations should be notified to the CQC.

## Detention under the Act or deprivation of liberty under a DoLS authorisation?

**13.49**    If an individual:

a.    is suffering from a mental disorder (within the meaning of the Act)

b.    needs to be assessed and/or treated in a hospital[4] setting for that disorder or for physical conditions related to that disorder (and meets the criteria for an application for admission under sections 2 or 3 of the Act)

c.    has a care treatment package that may or will amount to a deprivation of liberty

d.    lacks capacity to consent to being accommodated in the relevant hospital for the purpose of treatment, and

e.    does not object to being admitted to hospital, or to some or all the treatment they will receive there for mental disorder.

Then in principle a DoLS authorisation (or potentially a Court of Protection order) and detention under the Act would both be available (subject to the assessments required for a DoLS authorisation, including the eligibility assessment). This is the one situation where the option of using either the Act or DoLS exists. It is important to note that a person cannot be detained under the Act at the same time as being subject to a DoLS authorisation or a Court of Protection order.

**13.50**    Below is an options grid summarising the availability of the Act and of DoLS where a deprivation of liberty has been identified for a mental health patient, accommodated in hospital for the purpose of treatment for a mental disorder.

**13.51**    Whether a patient is objecting has to be considered in the round, taking into account all the circumstances, so far as they are reasonably ascertainable. The decision to be made is whether the patient objects, the reasonableness of that objection is not the issue. In many cases the patient will be perfectly able to state their objection. In other cases the relevant person will need to consider the patient's behaviour, wishes, feelings, views, beliefs and values, both present and past, so far as they can be ascertained. In deciding whether a patient objects to being admitted to hospital, or to some or all of the treatment they will receive there for mental disorder, decision-makers should err on the side of caution and, where in doubt, take the position that a patient is objecting.

---

[4]    Detention under the Act can only occur in a hospital (as defined in section 145(2) of the Act) or a registered establishment (as defined in section 34(2) of the Act). Therefore if a person is to be accommodated and treated elsewhere then no question arises of detaining that person under the Act.

## FIGURE 5 – OPTIONS GRID SUMMARISING THE AVAILABILITY OF THE ACT AND OF DOLS

|  | Individual **objects** to the proposed accommodation in a hospital for care and/ or treatment; or to any of the treatment they will receive there for mental disorder | Individual **does not object** to the proposed accommodation in a hospital for care and/or treatment; or to any of the treatment they will receive there for mental disorder |
|---|---|---|
| Individual has the capacity to consent to being accommodated in a hospital for care and/or treatment | Only the Act is available | The Act is available. Informal admission might also be appropriate. Neither DoLS authorisation nor Court of Protection order available |
| Individual lacks the capacity to consent to being accommodated in a hospital for care and/or treatment | Only the Act is available | The Act is available. DoLS authorisation is available, or potentially a Court of Protection order |

## *Important points for consideration*

**13.52**    Figure 5 above reveals a number of important points in addition to those discussed earlier in this chapter.

**13.53**    First, a person who lacks capacity to consent to being accommodated in a hospital for care and/or treatment for mental disorder and who is likely to be deprived of their liberty should never be informally admitted to hospital (whether they are content to be admitted or not.[5]

**13.54**    Decision-makers should also consider whether an individual deprived of their liberty may regain capacity or may have fluctuating capacity. Such a situation is likely to indicate use of the Act to authorise a deprivation of liberty should be preferred over use of a DoLS authorisation or Court of Protection order.

**13.55**    An individual will be ineligible for a DoLS authorisation or a Court of Protection order if they fall within Schedule 1A to the MCA, which should be considered carefully.

**13.56**    Individuals who are ineligible include the following:

- those persons detained in a hospital under sections 2, 3, 4, 35 – 38, 44, 45A, 47, 48 or 51 of the Act
- those persons liable to be detained under one of the above mentioned sections of the Act but who are not detained in a hospital under that regime; AND (i) proposed care and treatment in a hospital or care home would conflict with a requirement imposed on them in connection with their liability to detention under the Act (eg as a condition of a leave of absence) OR (ii) the relevant care and treatment consists in whole or in part of treatment for mental disorder in a hospital
- those persons on a community treatment order (CTO) under the Act AND (i) proposed care and treatment in a hospital or care home would conflict with a condition of their

---

[5]    In an emergency situation, it should be noted that section 4B of the MCA allows for the deprivation of an individual's liberty for the purpose of life-sustaining treatment or doing any vital act while a decision is sought from the court. This section is not available in certain circumstances, for example, if the person is ineligible under Schedule 1A to the MCA. Section 4 of the Act also makes provision for admission in cases of emergency.

CTO OR (ii) the relevant care and treatment consists in whole or in part of treatment for mental disorder in a hospital

■ those persons subject to guardianship under the Act AND (i) proposed detention or care and treatment would conflict with a requirement imposed on them by the guardianship regime (eg a requirement that they should reside elsewhere) OR (ii) it is proposed that the person will be detained in a hospital for treatment for mental disorder and they object, or are likely to object (and the person's attorney or deputy has not consented), and

■ those persons who would meet the criteria for being detained under section 2 or 3 of the Act, but who is not liable to be detained under sections 4, 35–38, 44, 45A, 47, 48 or 51 or subject to a CTO or guardianship, AND it is proposed that the person will be detained in a hospital for treatment for mental disorder, AND the person objects to being accommodated in hospital for that treatment, or to being given some or all of that treatment (and the person's attorney or deputy has not consented where the person objects)

**13.57**    For those individuals detailed in paragraph 13.49 where both detention under the Act and a DoLS authorisation or a Court of Protection order are available, decision-makers should determine which regime is the more appropriate. The following paragraphs detail factors that should feature in this decision-making process.

**13.58**    The choice of legal regime should never be based on a general preference for one regime or the other, or because one regime is more familiar to the decision-maker than the other. Such considerations are not legally relevant and lead to arbitrary decision-making. In addition decision-makers should not proceed on the basis that one regime is generally less restrictive than the other. Both regimes are based on the need to impose as few restrictions on the liberty and autonomy of patients as possible. In the particular circumstances of an individual case, it may be apparent that one regime is likely to prove less restrictive. If so, this should be balanced against any potential benefits associated with the other regime.

**13.59**    Both regimes provide appropriate procedural safeguards to ensure the rights of the person concerned are protected during their detention. Decision-makers should not therefore proceed on the basis that one regime generally provides greater safeguards than the other. However, the nature of the safeguards provided under the two regimes are different and decision-makers will wish to exercise their professional judgement in determining which safeguards are more likely to best protect the interests of the patient in the particular circumstances of each individual case.

**13.60**    In the relatively small number of cases where detention under the Act and a DoLS authorisation or Court of Protection order are available, this Code of Practice does not seek to preferentially orientate the decision-maker in any given direction. Such a decision should always be made depending on the unique circumstances of each case. Clearly recording the reasons for the final decision made will be important. The most pressing concern should always be that if an individual lacks capacity to consent to the matter in question and is deprived of their liberty they should receive the safeguards afforded under either the Act or through a DoLS authorisation or a Court of Protection order.

**13.61**    Part 9 of the DoLS Code of Practice details steps to be taken if someone thinks a person is being deprived of their liberty without authorisation. These steps include raising the matter with the responsible person at the managing authority (the provider) and if necessary with the supervisory body (the local authority). Hospitals should have policies in place to deal with circumstances where disagreement results in an inability to take a decision as to whether the Act or DoLS should be used to give legal authorisation to a deprivation of liberty – to ensure that one is selected.

## *Deciding whether the Act and/or MCA will be available to be used*

**13.62**   The flowchart opposite describes the key decision-making steps when determining whether the Act and/or the MCA including the DoLS will be available to be used. The flowchart does not replace careful consideration by decision-makers of all relevant circumstances in individual cases. Decision-makers should use their professional judgment within the framework of the legislation. Annex D provides a written description of Figure 6.

### FIGURE 6 – DECIDING WHETHER THE ACT AND/OR MCA WILL BE AVAILABLE TO BE USED

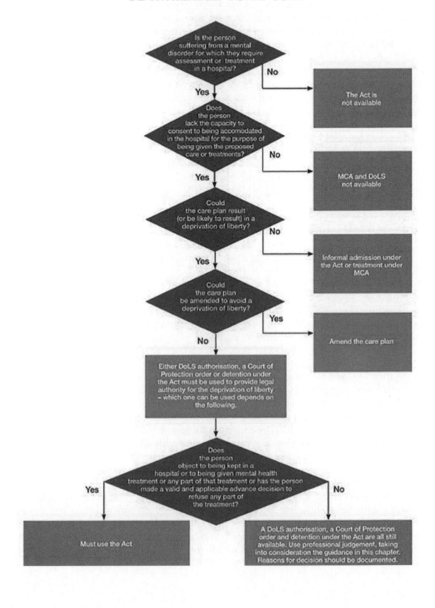

## Electro-convulsive therapy (ECT)

**13.63**   ECT cannot be given to an individual who has the capacity to consent to that treatment but refuses to do so unless it is immediately necessary to save the patient's life or to prevent a serious deterioration in the patient's condition.[6]

**13.64**   Under the Act, ECT can only be given to individuals who lack capacity if approved by a second opinion appointed doctor (SOAD). See paragraphs 25.19 – 25.25 for further information on ECT.

**13.65**   If ECT is to be given to an individual who lacks capacity and is under a DoLS authorisation or Court of Protection order, consideration should be given to seeking an independent second medical opinion before treatment which could, in principle, be given under the MCA (remembering that a DoLS authorisation only authorises the deprivation of liberty, not the treatment).

**13.66**   It is worth noting that ECT is likely to be considered under the MCA to be 'serious medical treatment' and that as such, if appropriate, an independent mental capacity advocate (IMCA) may need to be appointed.

## Complex cases

**13.67**   This guidance does not seek to provide definitive answers in complex cases. Every individual case is unique with a complex mix of factors that need to be considered. A patient's eligibility for detention under the Act or for a deprivation of liberty under a DoL authorisation or a Court of Protection order should always be considered.

**13.68**   In most cases, only one of the regimes will be available. However, in some cases, both will be available and must be considered. Decision-makers should exercise their professional judgement, taking legal advice where necessary, within the framework of the relevant legislation and guidance.

**13.69**   In the rare cases where neither the Act nor a DoLS authorisation nor a Court of Protection order is appropriate, then to avoid an unlawful deprivation of liberty it may be necessary to make an application to the High Court to use its inherent jurisdiction to authorise the deprivation of liberty.

**13.70**   A hypothetical case is considered below. This case is illustrative only and is not intended to provide a template for decision-making. The case does not form part of the Code.

CASE EXAMPLE

a.   P is a 72 year old woman suffering from dementia. Following a sudden deterioration in the community it is proposed that P be taken to hospital to be assessed for her future care and treatment needs. P is assessed as lacking the capacity to decide whether or not to be taken to hospital to be assessed, so she is taken and admitted to hospital in her best interests under the protection of the MCA.

On arrival, the clinical team decide that P will need to be kept in hospital under continuous control and supervision to be assessed, and would not be free to leave. This would amount to a deprivation of liberty. An application to detain P for assessment is therefore made under section 2 of the Act to authorise the deprivation of liberty during the assessment.

---

[6]   Sections 58A(1)(a) and (2) and 62(1)(a) and (b) and (1A) of the Act.

b.    The period of section 2 detention is reaching an end. During her assessment, P is given treatment for mental disorder. The clinical team decide that P will continue to need to be detained to receive treatment for mental disorder. P objects to staying in hospital to receive treatment and often says she will leave the hospital. In such an event, P would be prevented from leaving and the clinical team judge that a deprivation of liberty would arise. The clinical team determine that the criteria for detention under section 3 of the Act are satisfied and detain P under section 3. Treatment for mental disorder is provided.

c.    When the course of treatment is finished, the clinical team decide that P no longer needs to be kept in a hospital for on-going treatment.

d.    The clinical team considers (in consultation with P's family and other relevant individuals and with respect to P's previously stated views and beliefs) that it would not be in P's best interests to discharge her back into the community immediately because she lives alone and the clinical team does not believe she would be able to look after herself. The clinical team assess that P lacks capacity to decide whether to live in a care home (and lacks capacity to decide whether to remain in hospital).

e.    The hospital contacts the local authority to arrange a place at a residential care home. The care home states that a place will not be available for two weeks. The hospital believes it is in P's best interests to remain in hospital until the care home is ready to receive her (again, consulting with family and relevant individuals and taking P's likely views and beliefs into consideration).

f.    P's assigned mental health professional asks the clinical team where P will stay until she can be moved to the care home. The clinical team say P will remain on the ward with patients who, unlike P, are still detained under the Act. If P attempts to leave the ward, the clinical team say that she will be prevented from doing so – and so a deprivation of liberty could potentially occur. The clinical team assesses that P does not and is not likely to object to remaining on the ward.

g.    The DoL best interests assessor (BIA) concludes that P meets the qualifying requirements for a DoL authorisation. The hospital applies to the local authority and receives a standard DoL authorisation covering P's remaining stay in hospital.

h.    When P is moved to the care home, the care home reassesses P's situation and decides that P does not have capacity to decide whether to remain in the care home. The care home believes that it is in P's best interests to remain at the care home (she would not be allowed to go home if she requested to do so, as the care home still believes she would be unable to look after herself adequately). Therefore the care home (assessing that the situation represents a deprivation of liberty) requests a DoL authorisation from the local authority.

### EXPLANATION OF IMPORTANT POINTS IN (A) TO (H) ABOVE:

a.    P lacks capacity and so the protection of section 5 and 6 of the MCA is available for P to be conveyed to hospital. P is detained under the Act when it is clear that that is required to authorise the deprivation of liberty required for P's assessment.

b.    The proposed care plan involves a potential deprivation of liberty. Treatment is for a mental disorder. The DoLS and the Act are both potentially available at this point. However, P objects to the proposed stay in hospital so she is ineligible to be deprived of liberty by a DoL authorisation or Court of Protection order. As such she can only be detained under the Act.

c.    P no longer needs to be detained in hospital for care and treatment for the mental disorder. As such, the Act is no longer available.

d.    The clinical team reaches a best interests decision and correctly reassesses capacity for a significant new care decision.

e.    It becomes clear that it will be in P's best interests to remain in hospital, pending the availability of an appropriate care home place.

f.    A potential deprivation of liberty is identified – a legal regime must therefore be found to authorise that deprivation. The Act cannot be used as P does not meet the criteria for detention. The DoLS need to be used.

g.   A standard DoL authorisation is received. (The clinical team might have felt it necessary to apply for an urgent authorisation together with the standard authorisation if the team determined that, after P's detention under the Act had finished, the need for P to be deprived of her liberty was so urgent that deprivation of liberty needed to begin before the request for a standard authorisation could be considered or granted by the local authority.)

h.   P moves to a care home. The care home rightly re-assesses P's capacity and whether a deprivation of liberty could potentially occur. The care home applies for a DoL authorisation to authorise the detention. P cannot be detained under the Act at this stage because the Act does not apply to care homes. Care and treatment can be provided under the MCA.

## Related material

■   Mental Capacity Act 2005: Code of Practice. Department for Constitutional Affairs (now Ministry of Justice). 2007.
    www.gov.uk/government/publications/mental-capacity-act-code-of-practice

■   Mental Capacity Act 2005: Deprivation of Liberty Safeguards – Code of Practice to supplement the main Mental Capacity Act 2005 Code of Practice. 2008.
    webarchive.nationalarchives.gov.uk/20130107105354/http:/www.dh.gov.uk/en/
    Publicationsandstatistics/Publications/PublicationsPolicyAndGuidance/DH–
    085476

■   Reference Guide to Consent for Examination or Treatment. Department of Health. 2009.
    www.gov.uk/government/uploads/system/uploads/attachment–data/file/138296/
    dh–103653––1–.pdf

This material does not form part of the Code. It is provided for assistance only.

Appendix C4
# Office of the Public Guardian and Department of Health: Deprivation of Liberty Safeguards – A guide for hospitals and care homes

## 1   ABOUT THIS BOOKLET

The purpose of this booklet is to tell you about the Mental Capacity Act 2005 Deprivation of Liberty Safeguards (MCA DOLS). This is a new system that helps to protect people who are not capable of making care and treatment decisions for themselves. It comes into force on 1 April 2009.

The MCA DOLS apply to people in hospitals and care homes registered under the Care Standards Act 2000, whether they have been placed there by a primary care trust (PCT), a local authority or through private arrangements.

The guidance in this booklet is mainly for hospital and care home managers. It aims to help them understand their roles and responsibilities under the MCA DOLS. Other people who work in hospitals and care homes will also be affected by the MCA DOLS and will need to know about the new system.

This booklet should be used alongside the MCA DOLS Code of Practice, which explains in detail how MCA DOLS' processes and procedures work. This can be downloaded at: **www.dh.gov.uk/en/Publicationsandstatistics/Publications/ PublicationsPolicyAndGuidance/DH–085476**.

Key terms used in the MCA DOLS legislation include:

- **supervisory body**: this refers to PCTs and local authorities
- **managing authority**: this is the person or body with management responsibility for the hospital or care home in which a person is being, or may be, deprived of liberty
- **standard authorisation**: this permits lawful deprivation of liberty and is issued by a supervisory body (see page 13)
- **urgent authorisation**: this permits lawful deprivation of liberty and is issued by a managing authority (see page 13)
- **relevant person**: this is the person who needs to be deprived of liberty
- **relevant person's representative**: this is the person who represents the relevant person (see page 25)
- **best interests assessor**: this is the person who assesses whether or not deprivation of liberty is in the person's best interests, is necessary to prevent harm to the person and is a proportionate response to the likelihood and seriousness of that harm (see page 15)
- **advance decision**: this is a decision to refuse specified treatment made in advance by a person who has capacity to do so. The decision will then apply at a future time when that person lacks capacity to consent to, or refuse, the specified treatment. Specific rules apply to advance decisions to refuse life sustaining treatment (see page 15)
- **donee of lasting power of attorney**: this is the person appointed under a lasting power of attorney who has the legal right to make decisions within the scope of their authority on behalf of the person (the donor) who made the lasting power of attorney (see page 15)

■   **Independent Mental Capacity Advocate (IMCA):** this is a person who provides support and representation for a person who lacks capacity to make specific decisions in certain defi ned circumstances. The IMCA was established by the Mental Capacity Act and is not the same as an ordinary advocacy service (see page 16).

## Record-keeping requirements

Hospitals and care homes must keep detailed records as part of the MCA DOLS process. To help meet this requirement, and to make sure the administration of the MCA DOLS systems is as simple as possible, the Department of Health has developed a number of standard forms. If used without alteration, these ensure that hospitals and care homes comply with the required standards.

Altogether there are six forms that hospitals and care homes may need. These are available to download, together with accompanying guidance, at: **www.dh.gov.uk/en/Publicationsand statistics/Publications/ PublicationsPolicyAndGuidance/DH-089772**.

Standard forms for primary care trusts and local authorities are also available through the same link.

An overview of the MCA DOLS process can be found [at Annex 1 of Appendix C2 of this Guidance].

## 2   ABOUT THE MCA DOLS

Some people living in hospitals and care homes cannot make their own decisions about their care or treatment because they do not have the 'mental capacity' to do so. These people need additional protection to ensure they do not suffer harm, especially in situations where delivering the necessary care requires their personal freedoms to be restricted to the point of actually depriving them of their liberty. People who need this additional protection may include those with severe learning disabilities, older people with the range of dementias or people with neurological conditions such as brain injuries.

The European Court of Human Rights (ECtHR) has ruled that the rights of people who are unable to make their own decisions, especially where they need to be deprived of liberty in their own best interests, need to be protected.

While we must deliver care without restricting people's personal freedoms wherever possible, health and social care staff may believe that it is necessary to deprive someone of their liberty, in certain circumstances, in order to give them care or treatment that is in the person's best interests and protects them from harm.

The Mental Capacity Act 2005 Deprivation of Liberty Safeguards (MCA DOLS) exist to protect people who cannot make decisions about their care and treatment when they need to be cared for in a particularly restrictive way. They set out a standard process that hospitals and care homes should follow if they think it will be necessary to deprive a person of their liberty to deliver a particular care plan that is in the person's best interests.

By following the MCA DOLS, hospital and care home staff can ensure that people are deprived of liberty only when necessary and within the law.

## What is deprivation of liberty?

The ECtHR has said deprivation of liberty depends on the specific circumstances of each individual case. As a result, there is no single definition or a standard checklist that can be used to identify where people are being deprived of their liberty. However, a number of cases concerning deprivation of liberty have come before the ECtHR and the UK courts. The following list is based on the judgments in several of these cases and indicates what circumstances have led to the courts deciding that patients may have been deprived of their liberty:

■ restraint was used to admit a person to a hospital or care home when the person is resisting admission
■ medication was given forcibly, against a patient's will
■ staff exercised complete control over the care and movements of a person for a long period of time
■ staff took all decisions on a person's behalf, including choices relating to assessments, treatments, visitors and where they can live
■ hospital or care home staff took responsibility for deciding if a person can be released into the care of others or allowed to live elsewhere
■ when carers requested that a person be discharged to their care, hospital or care home staff refused
■ the person was prevented from seeing friends or family because the hospital or care home has restricted access to them
■ the person was unable to make choices about what they wanted to do and how they wanted to live, because hospital or care home staff exercised continuous supervision and control over them.

People are entitled to be cared for in the least restrictive way possible and care planning should always consider if there are other, less restrictive options available to avoid unnecessary deprivation of liberty. However, if all alternatives have been explored and the hospital or care home believes that it is necessary to deprive a person of their liberty to deliver the care or treatment they need, then there is a standard process they must follow to ensure that the deprivation of liberty is lawful and that they are protected.

## How do the MCA DOLS protect people?

The MCA DOLS introduce a standard process that hospitals and care homes must follow before they deprive a person of their liberty.

If people do need to be deprived of their liberty in their own best interests, the MCA DOLS protect them by providing:

■ a representative to act for them and protect their interests
■ rights of challenge to the Court of Protection against unlawful deprivation of liberty
■ rights for their deprivation of liberty to be reviewed and monitored on a regular basis.

## Who is covered by the MCA DOLS?

The MCA DOLS apply to people in hospitals and care homes who meet all of the following criteria. A person must:

■ be aged 18 or over
■ have a mental disorder such as dementia or a learning disability
■ lack the capacity to consent to where their treatment and/or care is given
■ need to have their liberty taken away in their own best interests to protect them from harm.

## When should the MCA DOLS be used?

The MCA DOLS should be used for all people in hospitals or care homes who lack the capacity to make their own decisions and where personal freedoms need to be restricted in the patient's best interests, to the extent that they amount to a deprivation of liberty. The MCA DOLS should not, however, be used if a person meets the criteria for detention under the Mental Health Act 1983 and either is, or should be, detained under the terms of that Act.

The managing authority (the hospital or care home) must apply to the supervisory body (the PCT in the case of hospitals or local authority in the case of care homes) for authorisation of deprivation of liberty if a person who lacks capacity is:

■    about to be admitted to the hospital or care home and the managing authority believes the person risks being deprived of their liberty
■    already in the hospital or care home and is being cared for or treated in a way which deprives them of their liberty.

The supervisory body must first decide if the application is appropriate. If it is, the supervisory body will commission a series of assessments and either grant or refuse authorisation for deprivation of liberty as appropriate.

It is important to remember that depriving someone of their liberty in a hospital or care home should be a relatively rare occurrence. Therefore, only a small number of people should need MCA DOLS authorisation. **Before applying for an authorisation, the managing authority should ALWAYS think about providing care or treatment in ways which avoid depriving someone of their liberty.**

## How do the MCA DOLS relate to the Mental Capacity Act 2005 (MCA)?

The MCA DOLS do not replace other safeguards in the MCA. Instead, any action taken under the MCA DOLS must be in line with the five key principles of the MCA:

1    A person must be assumed to have capacity unless it is established that he lacks capacity.
2    A person is not to be treated as unable to make a decision unless all practicable steps to help him to do so have been taken without success.
3    A person is not to be treated as unable to make a decision merely because he makes an unwise decision.
4    An act done, or decision made, under this Act for or on behalf of a person who lacks capacity must be done, or made, in his best interests.
5    Before the act is done, or the decision is made, regard must be had to whether the purpose for which it is needed can be as effectively achieved in a way that is less restrictive of the person's rights and freedom of action.

The MCA DOLS permit the hospital or care home to detain the person only in a specific hospital or care home. It is important to understand that an MCA DOLS authorisation does not, in itself, authorise care or treatment. Any care or treatment still needs to be carried out under the wider 'best interests' provisions of the MCA and follow the five key principles of the Act listed above.

---

Amelia didn't have a formal assessment before entering the care home. Her son says her level of confusion isn't bad, but from the beginning she is very distressed and difficult to calm and repeatedly tries to leave.

The matron wonders whether it is necessary to use the MCA DOLS to keep her safe.

Prior to requesting an assessment for an MCA DOLS authorisation, the matron asks for a comprehensive assessment of her needs, including exploring Amelia's previous interests and preferences with her son. It appears that Amelia has a urinary tract infection and so has been more confused than usual. The GP prescribes antibiotics. Amelia's son spends some time with her every day for the rest of the week to help her settle in. She is shown the greenhouse as she has been a keen gardener; they discover that she still plays the piano and enjoys jigsaws. Over the course of the next two weeks she settles in and becomes quite content with the freedom she is able to maintain; therefore the matron takes the view that a request for a standard authorisation is not currently necessary.

## 3    WHAT DOES A MANAGING AUTHORITY NEED TO DO?

For everybody in a hospital or care home who lacks capacity, the following questions should be asked:

- Does the care or treatment being provided take away the person's freedom to do what they want to do to such an extent that it amounts to a deprivation of their liberty?
- Do you believe that the care or treatment being provided is in the person's best interests?

If the answer to these questions is 'yes', you need to ask yourself whether the care or treatment could be given in a way which does not deprive the person of their liberty.

If the answer to this question is 'no', and the person cannot be cared for or treated any other way, the managing authority must apply to the supervisory body for authorisation to continue with the care programme and deprive the person of their liberty. The supervisory body will then carry out a series of assessments to decide if it is right to deprive the person of their liberty.

There are two kinds of authorisations: standard authorisations and urgent authorisations.

- **Standard authorisations** follow the process outlined above. Managing authorities should apply for a standard authorisation before a deprivation of liberty occurs – for example, when a new care plan is agreed that would mean depriving a person of their liberty.
- **Urgent authorisations** can be made by managing authorities themselves – such as where a standard authorisation has been applied for, but not yet granted, and the need to deprive a person of their liberty is now urgent. Urgent authorisations can never be made without a simultaneous application for a standard authorisation to the supervisory body.

### Applying for standard authorisations

Managing authorities should apply to the supervisory body for a standard authorisation using the form available at: **www.dh.gov.uk/en/Publicationsandstatistics/Publications/PublicationsPolicyAndGuidance/DH–089772.**

The supervisory body will then begin the assessment process (see below) which must be completed within 21 calendar days.

A managing authority cannot apply for a standard authorisation more than 28 days before a deprivation of liberty is due to take place.

### Applying for urgent authorisations

Any decision to issue an urgent authorisation must be taken in the best interests of the patient in accordance with section 4 of the MCA. Where restraint is involved, the decision must comply with section 6 of the MCA.

There is a standard form available for managing authorities that require an urgent authorisation.

Urgent authorisations last for a maximum of seven calendar days. During that period, the necessary assessment process must be completed. Also, the managing authority must request a standard authorisation if it has not already done so.

In exceptional circumstances, an urgent authorisation can be extended by a supervisory body for an additional seven calendar days. The managing authority must inform the supervisory body when an extension is needed and only one such extension can be granted. There is a standard form for this purpose.

## How does the assessment process work?

The supervisory body commissions the assessments which are used to authorise a deprivation of liberty. The assessments are then carried out by a minimum of two trained assessors: the mental health assessor and the best interests assessor. There are six assessments in all, which are:

- age assessment, which determines if the person is 18 years old or over
- mental health assessment, which decides whether the person is suffering from a mental disorder
- mental capacity assessment, which determines if a person lacks the capacity to consent to receive care or treatment in the particular hospital or care home making the application for deprivation of liberty
- eligibility assessment, which determines whether the person is, or should be, subject to a requirement under the Mental Health Act 1983 (in which case they are not eligible for this process)
- no refusals assessment, which determines if the person has refused treatment or made decisions in advance about the treatment they wish to receive; this assessment also determines if the authorisation conflicts with valid decisions made on the person's behalf by a donee of a lasting power of attorney or a deputy appointed for the person by the court
- best interests assessment, which determines if there is a deprivation of liberty and whether this is:
    - in the person's best interests
    - necessary in order to keep the person from harm
    - a reasonable response to the likelihood of the person suffering harm and the likely seriousness of that harm.

An authorisation will be granted only if all six assessments support the authorisation.

## Providing support throughout the assessment process

The managing authority must tell the supervisory body if the person involved has no family member or non-professional carer to support them through the assessment process. The supervisory body must then appoint an Independent Mental Capacity Advocate (IMCA), under section 39A of the Act, to support them. (This is often known as a section 39A IMCA.)

The supervisory body and the managing authority must work together to make sure the person and their representative:

- understand the MCA DOLS process
- know their rights and entitlements
- receive the right support once the authorisation process begins and after the authorisation has been granted or denied.

## What happens when a MCA DOLS authorisation is granted?

Not every assessment process will result in an authorisation. However, once a person in a hospital or care home has an MCA DOLS authorisation, a relevant person's representative (RPR) must be appointed to support them and look after their interests.

The managing authority (together with its supervisory body) must:

- make regular checks to see if the authorisation is still necessary
- remove the authorisation when it is no longer necessary
- provide the person's RPR with information about the care and treatment of the person who has an MCA DOLS authorisation.

Erik's care home is granted a standard authorisation to help meet his care needs legitimately.

His brother is appointed as his relevant person's representative for the standard authorisation. The staff tell Erik as clearly as possible what the authorisation means and explain his brother's role as his representative. They give him simple written information about it and provide copies for his brother. A copy of the authorisation is placed in Erik's file and his care plans are amended, making it clear that Erik's brother should now be involved in any major care decisions and care reviews.

There are conditions attached to the authorisation which relate to visits by Erik's other family members and these are incorporated into his care plans. The expiry date of the standard authorisation is noted in the diary so that the home can apply for a new authorisation before the current term expires.

The manager of the care home meets Erik's brother to check that he understands the nature and effect of the authorisation. The manager explains the complaints and appeals procedure in detail and tells him about the right to request a review or apply for termination of the standard authorisation.

## What happens if a request for an authorisation is turned down?

If an authorisation request is turned down, the managing authority must not deprive the person of their liberty and will need to take alternative steps. The steps will depend on the reason the authorisation was turned down.

- It may be appropriate for the person to be detained under the Mental Health Act 1983.
- If the person is under 18, the Children Act 1989 may be used for meeting their care requirements.
- There may be ways to support the person in a less restrictive manner that avoids a deprivation of liberty.
- Often, people make valid decisions about refusing care or treatment when they are still capable of doing so or there are valid refusals by attorneys or deputies appointed on their behalf. If the managing authority wishes to challenge these decisions, it can apply to the Court of Protection.
- If the deprivation of liberty is not in the person's best interests, the managing authority (together with the commissioner of care) needs to make sure that the person is supported in a way that avoids deprivation of liberty.
- If the person has the capacity to make decisions about their own care, the managing authority must help them to make their own decisions.
- If the relevant person is not being deprived of liberty, the managing authority should continue to support them without taking further action.

Jean has moved into a local care home because of her mild Alzheimer's disease. Her care is complicated by regular visits to her local pub, and on one occasion she returns home drunk.

After speaking with Jean's daughter, who lives at some distance, the care home manager decides that the only way to stop the drinking is to keep Jean from leaving the care home at any time.

The care home manager completes an urgent authorisation and requests a standard authorisation. Jean passes the age, no refusals, mental capacity, mental health and eligibility assessments, but the best interests assessor considers that the restrictions used to limit the alcohol misuse are disproportionate to the risk, and are not in Jean's best interests.

The best interests assessor asks the care home to immediately stop depriving Jean of her liberty, and suggests they urgently draw up a new care plan to manage the risk of excess alcohol use without being so restrictive. In his report, the best interests assessor suggests involving Jean's care manager in this process.

A new package of care is arranged which includes trips out and accompanied visits to the pub.

## When should a standard authorisation be reviewed?

The authorisation review is a formal process that takes a fresh look at the person who has been deprived of their liberty. A standard authorisation can be reviewed at any time.

The managing authority must make regular checks to see if the deprivation of liberty is still needed. A review must be triggered if there has been a change in the relevant person's situation that requires the deprivation of liberty authorisation to be altered, temporarily suspended or terminated altogether.

The supervisory body has to carry out a review if asked to by any of the following people:

- the relevant person
- the relevant person's representative
- any section 39A IMCA representing the individual.

The managing authority must also inform the supervisory body if there has been a change in the situation of a person who has been deprived of their liberty. This is especially important if the change in circumstances means that the person no longer meets one or more of the six qualifying requirements.

There is a standard form that a managing authority can use to request a review.

The reasons for a review may include:

- evidence that the person no longer meets either the age, no refusals, mental capacity, mental health or best interests authorisation requirements
- the fact that the person no longer meets the eligibility requirement because they are subject to detention or treatment under the terms of the Mental Health Act 1983 instead of the MCA DOLS
- changes in the person's situation
- the fact that the person still meets all six qualifying requirements, but for different reasons than those set out in the original authorisation.

The supervisory body makes the arrangements necessary to review any or all of the six qualifying requirements as required. The supervisory body must also inform the managing authority, the relevant person, the RPR and any section 39A IMCA involved about the outcome of the review.

The outcome of a review may bring an authorisation to an early conclusion. If the relevant person does not meet any one of the six requirements, the authorisation must be ended immediately.

## Short-term suspensions of standard authorisations

It may be necessary to suspend an authorisation for a short period of time. This could happen, for example, if the relevant person fails to meet the eligibility requirement because they are temporarily subject to provisions under the Mental Health Act 1983. In such cases, the managing authority must tell the supervisory body, which will suspend the MCA DOLS authorisation. There is a standard form for the managing authority to use for this purpose.

If the relevant person becomes eligible for an MCA DOLS authorisation again within 28 days, the managing authority must tell the supervisory body, which will reinstate the authorisation. Again, there is a standard form for the managing authority to use for this purpose.

If the managing authority does not let the supervisory body know that the person is eligible again within the 28 days, then the authorisation will cease automatically at the end of this period. The managing authority would then need to seek a new authorisation if deprivation of liberty was to continue.

A person may no longer meet the eligibility requirement if they begin to object to their treatment. In such cases, they may be more appropriately detained under section 2 or 3 of the Mental Health Act 1983 and the managing authority should request a review immediately.

---

Samir was only 45 when he had a stroke, leaving him with considerable nursing needs, cognitive impairment, and impulsive and sometimes violent behaviour. He was detained using a standard authorisation as he met all the criteria for authorisation.

Over the course of a year, Samir improves considerably. He stops hitting out at staff, and his awareness and judgement become better. As a result, his wife is confident that she can look after him and the care home (the managing authority) works with her to organise trips out.

At a regular care review, Samir's keyworker asks whether it is still necessary or in his interests to have the standard authorisation in place, and queries whether he even still meets the mental capacity or mental health criteria for the authorisation.

The care home manager writes to the supervisory body to request a review. The review finds that although Samir still meets the mental capacity criteria, he no longer meets the mental health or best interests criteria. The standard authorisation is terminated. The supervisory body compliments the care home staff on the way they are working with Samir and his wife to free up the restrictions on his liberty.

---

## What happens when an authorisation ends?

Deprivation of liberty authorisations should last for the shortest time possible and are valid for a maximum of 12 months. The duration of an authorisation will vary from person to person depending on their individual circumstances. Typically, the best interests assessor will recommend the period of time required for a specific authorisation.

When an authorisation comes to an end, the managing authority cannot lawfully continue to deprive someone of their liberty. However, if the managing authority thinks that the person involved still needs to be deprived of their liberty for their own protection, they can request a new standard authorisation.

A new authorisation process will then be triggered. However, the relevant person may not need an IMCA at the time of assessment as they will already have an RPR in place.

## Unauthorised deprivation of liberty

The managing authority must make every effort to decide if a person in a hospital or care home is being deprived of their liberty. However, if a member of staff, family member, carer, or any other third party suspects unauthorised deprivation of liberty, the law entitles them to tell the managing authority. If the managing authority fails to satisfy their concerns, the person can ask the supervisory body to investigate. Standard letters are available for this purpose.

Margaret suffers from a chronic psychotic mental illness; she is suspicious of others, reclusive, and severely neglects herself. She is living in squalor, having refused all care.

After assessment and treatment in hospital under the Mental Health Act 1983, doctors feel that she is likely to remain unwell in the long term. Margaret still lacks insight into her mental illness and its effects, and insists on leaving hospital in order to return home. The doctors feel that she needs to move to a care home, so she has trial leave there but repeatedly requests permission to leave.

The hospital team discusses a standard authorisation with staff from the care home at a Care Programme Approach meeting. They agree that Margaret will stay in hospital under the Mental Health Act, while the care home (the managing authority for Margaret's placement) requests a standard authorisation from the local authority to commence on the day she is discharged from the Mental Health Act. The standard forms are completed, copied for Margaret's records, and sent with all relevant background paperwork to assist the best interests assessor. As there is no obvious next of kin or other person to consult, the care home notify the local authority that an IMCA will be required to represent Margaret's interests.

## 4   ROLES AND RESPONSIBILITIES

### What is the role of the relevant person's representative?

As soon as a standard authorisation has been granted, the supervisory body must appoint a relevant person's representative (RPR) to represent the person who has been deprived of their liberty. The RPR provides independent support, acting only in the best interests of the person involved, rather than in the interests of commissioners or service providers.

The RPR is usually a family member or someone known to the person deprived of liberty. If the person has no family member, friend or carer, the supervisory body has to appoint a representative, who can be paid as appropriate.

The managing authority has a responsibility to ensure that both the RPR and the relevant person:

- understand what the deprivation of liberty authorisation means
- are aware of their right to request a review at any time
- have information about the formal and informal complaints procedures
- understand that they have the right to challenge the deprivation of liberty through the Court of Protection
- understand that they are entitled to the support of an Independent Mental Capacity Advocate (IMCA), unless they are a paid representative.

The RPR must stay in touch with the person deprived of their liberty in order to fulfil their statutory role. If the RPR does not keep in regular contact, then the rights of the relevant person to review or appeal their deprivation of liberty may not be sufficiently protected.

The managing authority should monitor this closely. If there is any doubt that the RPR is supporting the person effectively, the authority must:

- talk to the RPR about these concerns and attempt to resolve issues informally
- if an informal resolution is unsuccessful, raise the issues with the supervisory body.

William is sad to see his wife Elaine leave their home and move into the nursing home. He agrees with the use of the standard authorisation, though, as she would have been a risk to herself and others if she had been allowed more freedom. He is pleased to be appointed as her RPR by the supervisory body. This allows him to carry on caring for Elaine and to ensure that the restrictions used to keep her safe are really in her best interests.

Unfortunately, William then has a stroke himself, and is only rarely able to visit, having moved to live near his daughter. John, the care home manager, considers that William's lack of regular contact means that he is unable to carry on representing his wife's interests. John talks to William about this, but William says that his ill-health prevents him from visiting.

John informs the supervisory body about his concerns. William agrees that he should be kept up to date by copies of the care plans. The supervisory body appoints an IMCA as an alternative relevant person's representative, as no other suitable person can be immediately identified.

## What is the role of the IMCA?

The relevant person and their representative have the right to be represented by an IMCA as part of the MCA DOLS process.

If the person has no family member or carer to support them through the assessment process, the managing authority must tell the supervisory body and an IMCA must be appointed at once, under section 39A of the Act.

The person and the RPR also have a statutory right of access to an IMCA once a deprivation of liberty has been authorised, under section 39D of the Act (this is known as a section 39D IMCA). A relevant person with a 'paid' representative has no such right since it is assumed that the 'paid' representative would meet their advocacy support needs.

Once a RPR has been appointed, there may be less for the IMCA to do. However, the IMCA can still:

- apply to take the person's case to the Court of Protection
- be retained by the supervisory body if it believes the relevant person's rights would be better protected.

## What is the role of the Care Quality Commission?

The Care Quality Commission (CQC) will monitor MCA DOLS operations. The CQC will have the power to visit hospitals and care homes and interview the people involved in each case. They will also be able to access and view all relevant records to ensure that people are being adequately protected.

## What is the role of the Court of Protection?

If a person, or their representative, does not agree with the decision to deprive them of their liberty, the new system gives them the right to appeal against the decision in the Court of Protection. This provides a forum for solving problems related to the Mental Capacity Act in general and gives people the right of appeal in MCA DOLS cases to ensure compliance with the rulings of the ECtHR.

The person who is likely to be deprived of their liberty, or somebody acting on their behalf, can appeal to the Court of Protection before the authorisation process is completed. The Court of Protection will decide whether to proceed before an authorisation decision has been made.

If an urgent authorisation has been granted, the Court of Protection can:

- determine if the urgent authorisation should have been granted
- determine how long the authorisation should be in place
- examine the reasons why the urgent authorisation has been granted.

After a standard authorisation has been granted, the Court of Protection has powers similar to those listed above. However, it can also determine whether the person meets one or more of the MCA DOLS qualifying requirements or if the standard authorisation should be subject to any specific conditions.

The following people have an automatic right of access to the Court of Protection once an urgent or standard authorisation has been granted:

- the person deprived of their liberty
- their representative
- the donee of a relevant lasting power of attorney
- a deputy appointed by the Court of Protection to act for the person concerned.

## 5    FURTHER SOURCES OF INFORMATION AND GUIDANCE

If you want to find out more about what MCA DOLS means for you or your organisation, visit our website at: **www.dh.gov.uk/en/SocialCare/Deliveringadultsocialcare/ MentalCapacity/ MentalCapacityActDeprivationofLibertySafeguards/ index.htm**.

You can contact the team in writing at:

MCA DOLS Implementation Programme
Department of Health
Wellington House, Room 124
133–155 Waterloo Road
London SE1 8UG

Email: **dols@dh.gsi.gov.uk**

Information on the Mental Capacity Act Deprivation of Liberty Safeguards is brought to you by the following organisations:

- Department of Health
- Office of the Public Guardian

## Appendix C5
# ADASS Advice Note: Guidance for local authorities in the light of the Supreme Court decisions on deprivation of liberty safeguards

## Background

On 19 March 2014, the Supreme Court handed down its judgment in the case of 'P v Cheshire West and Chester Council and another' and 'P and Q v Surrey County Council'. The full judgment can be found on the Supreme Court's website at the following link: **supremecourt.uk/decided-cases/docs/UKSC–2012–0068–Judgment.pdf**.

This is the third advice note issued by ADASS in response to the judgement.

ADASS have led a task force to support local Councils following the judgement and the work of the task force is now drawing to a close. ADASS continues to press for increased funding and early amendments to legislation.

## Extent of the increase in applications

The DH requested voluntary data collection in order to monitor demand. This data can be found at **www.hscic.gov.uk/catalogue/PUB15856** and in summary shows

|  | Quarter One 2014 | Quarter Two 2014 | 2013–14 full year |
|---|---|---|---|
| Number of councils responding | 141 | 132 | For the same 132 Councils |
| Number of applications | 23,900 | 31,300 | 12,500 |
| Number granted | 12,000 | 9,400 | 7,100 |
| Nor granted | 3,000 | 2,400 | 5,000 |
| Not yet decided | 8,900 | 19,400 | 400 |

These figures help to illustrate the developing picture for Councils attempting to manage the huge deluge in referrals. The total number of requests so far in 2014/15 is 55,200 which can reasonably be expected to produce a year end figure of approximately 110,000 compared to an annual figure last year of 12,500. This is approaching a tenfold increase and may exceed that. Most striking is the fact that 19,400 applications have not been processed. This means 19,400 people are potentially unlawfully deprived of liberty and not receiving the protection of the safeguards in a timely manner.

ADASS remind its members that compliance with the legislation is not optional. However in recognition of the exceptional challenge facing Councils the ADASS task force has agreed that some form of prioritisation is useful is deciding those situations which have a more urgent need for speedy assessment. A tool has been developed to assist with this which is attached.

Prioritisation of applications is a temporary measure to attempt to manage demand but ADASS advise members that care homes and hospitals should not be prevented from making referrals. Care homes and hospitals are becoming increasingly concerned about their own position in relation to risk and Councils may want to consider offering them some practical tips when assessments are delayed. Remembering that underpinning the safeguards are assessments of capacity and best interests decision making.

## Unintended consequence

Another area of concern to ADASS on behalf of its members is the seemingly unintended consequence of DoLS applications in Intensive care and end of life situations. With the associated need for referrals to the coroner following any death whilst subject to a DoLS authorisation. Further advice may soon be available from the Chief Coroner but in the meantime all deaths must continue to be notified to the relevant coroner.

The Intensive care society have issued guidance to assist clinicians with these decisions. http://journal.ics.ac.uk/pdf/1504320.pdf.

Although in one sense this guidance does not assist Councils as it highlights that intensive care patients do appear to meet the acid test, there are some useful factors which should be drawn out of this guidance, in particular the following examples of exclusions where patients are not considered to be deprived of their liberty:

- those who have the capacity to decide to be admitted to intensive care
- Those who can/do consent to the restrictions applied to them
- Those who gave consent for intensive care admission prior to losing capacity – for instance prior to surgery (though they must have had an understanding that they may be under continuous supervision and control and not free to leave at some time within their stay).

It must also be borne in mind that not every patient in an intensive care setting will have a mental disorder and the DoLS only apply where there is a mental disorder as well as a lack of mental capacity.

The use of DoLS at the end of life involves consideration of issues similar to the above. Many people in hospices will have consented with capacity to their admission. Many will be able to consent to the restrictions applied to them. Many people approach the end of their life and do not have a mental disorder therefore the DoLS do not apply to them. Fundamentally in the current climate the ADASS priority tool would not routinely give high priority to people in intensive care or at the end of life as there would not appear to be any benefit to them of the use of such safeguards. Individual cases may vary of course.

## The Task Force

The task force has continued to focus its work in three areas

1. **Workforce**: A list of BIA courses available around the Country is attached. It is worth noting that a number of Universities are now able to offer Fast track courses or bespoke courses. A list of Independent BIA's is still being finalised and will be available in December.
2. **Process issues**: The review of DoLS forms is now complete up to final draft stage. Forms will be circulated to all DoLS leads week commencing 17th November and final versions are anticipated the first week in December.

   ADASS reviewed its protocol for reciprocal agreements in 2013 this is to be reviewed again the light of the Supreme Court judgement, in December. In the meantime whilst acknowledging the difficulties and challenges being faced in every Council in the Country ADASS would urge co-operation and reciprocation of arrangements where possible. ADASS continues to make representations for changes in legislation to ease the burden on Councils, particularly in terms of unintended consequences such as Intensive Care and end of life situations.

3.  **Finance**: The figures collected by ADASS from its members in June have proven to be very accurate in terms of numbers of applications. ADASS consider that a number of the initial assumptions in the impact assessment have proved to be unsound and better evidence is now available on which to fully assess the financial burden.

ADASS along with the LGA have made a formal approach to government for the burden to be funded. This is an unsustainable burden on Councils who are already experiencing reductions in their budgets. A joint letter was issued on **31 July** requesting an urgent response and follow up sent on **17 October** after the data release from the HSCIC. ADASS is awaiting a face to face meeting with the Minister for Care Services at the time of writing.

## Legislative matters

ADASS will continue to contribute to the Law Society review of DoLS both the Safeguards and the extension to community settings. This review is expected to conclude in 2017 with a consultation document being issued in early 2015.

It remains the view of ADASS that early changes to legislation would both help to ease the burden on Councils and ensure proper application of the safeguards where they were intended to be applied. ADASS would like to see early legislative changes such as;

■   Changes to ease timescales for authorisation requests,
■   Changes which clarify that DoLS are generally not applicable in intensive care and end of life settings
■   Changes which will ensure everyone has the same process and protection whether they are in a community setting or a care home or hospital.

An added benefit of regional DoLS leads meeting together in the Task Force has been the ability to support each other but also to identify anomalies within the scheme and areas of law requiring interpretation and clarity. ADASS is continuing to work with LGA to identify possibilities for sharing legal advice. This will both feed into the work of the Law Commission and help individual Councils act within the law. The Task Force is to make a decision on continuing meetings for Regional Leads and would see this as an ideal means by which issues of concern can be raised, regional and national trends can be identified and legal advice can be shared to ensure consistency of approach. A list of Regional Leads is attached to this guidance note.

## Community DoL's (Deprivation of liberty in 'domestic settings')

The Supreme Court also held that a deprivation of liberty can occur in domestic settings where the State is responsible for imposing such arrangements. This includes placements in supported living in the community as well as domiciliary arrangements which may amount to a deprivation of liberty. Such placements must be authorised by the Court of Protection.

The decision from the Court of Protection in Re X was issued in August and ADASS advised its members of the actions which would be needed in response to this.

On 17 November 2014, the Court of Protection will launch a new streamlined process for managing court-authorised deprivations of liberty. The new process implements guidelines set out by the President of the Court of Protection in two recent judgments: *Re X and others (Deprivation of Liberty)* [2014] EWCOP 25, and, *Re X and others* (Deprivation of Liberty) (Number 2) EWCOP 37.

The new Re X procedure is set out in a practice direction issued by the President, and is accompanied by new application forms, designed exclusively for applying for court-authorised deprivations of liberty. You can download a saveable pdf of the form here: **COPDL10 form**. You will find the practice direction and a suggested draft Re X order on the Judiciary website or you can access it from the Court of Protection pages on Direct Gov (**www.gov.uk/court-of-protection**) by clicking on the 'deprivation of liberty' link.

The Re X procedure is designed to enable the court to decide applications for a court-authorised deprivation of liberty on the papers only, without holding a hearing, provided certain safeguards are met: Those safeguards include ensuring that:

- The person who is the subject of the application and all relevant people in their life are consulted about the application and have an opportunity to express their wishes and views to the court.
- The person who is the subject of the application has not expressed a wish to take part in the court proceedings
- The person who is the subject of the application and all relevant people in their life do not object to the application.
- There are no other significant factors that ought to be brought to the attention of the court that would make the application unsuitable for the streamlined procedure.

The process has been designed after informal consultation with the judiciary and court users. The Court of Protection intends to review the process once it has been up and running for a while, and would be grateful for any feedback on how it works in practice. You can email your comments to the DoL Team. **COPDOLS/S16@hmcts.gsi.gov.uk**

The Court of Protection has set up a dedicated team to deal with applications made under the Re X procedure. The contact details are:

Court of Protection
P.O. Box 70185
London
WC1A 9JA
Tel 0207 421 8665

To help prepare for this streamlined process, Councils are advised to

- Scope the likely impact
- Identify those people in a variety of community settings who may be deprived of liberty
- Ensure all those identified have assessments of capacity and best interests in relation to their accommodation for care
- Staff will need to carry out necessary consultation with those named or interested in the persons welfare
- Staff will need to determine if the person meets the acid test requirements
- All those identified will need confirmation of a mental disorder.

Whilst the forms will guide practitioners through the process there is no reason not to be collecting evidence ahead of applications.

## Implications for councils

The implications for councils continue to expand as a result of this judgement. ADASS reiterate its position that this judgement stands as law and cannot be ignored.

ADASS is very grateful to its members for complying with the voluntary data collection which is providing the much needed evidence of the extent of the financial burden.

ADASS are concerned about the personal cost arising from the judgment both to service users who do not have the protection of the safeguards when they are entitled to but also to staff who are battling the sense of futility when attempting to meet impossible time scales.

The number of applications for DoLS Authorisations both Urgent and Standard, are placing enormous pressure on council DoLS Teams and on the capacity of Best Interests Assessors. This is a national challenge and councils have responded in a variety of positive ways to mitigate against the impact on Council resources.

## Recommendations

ADASS reminds councils to –

1.  Remember it is unacceptable to refuse to accept applications for DoLS from Managing Authorities
2.  Continue to risk assess and prioritise using the ADASS tool where appropriate to determine those at highest risk have the earliest protection of the safeguards
3.  Continue to support the supervisory body role by releasing social workers who are trained as BIA's to carry out assessments.
4.  Continue to support and advise Managing Authorities particularly in relation to delays in processing applications.
5.  Keep partners including; elected members, staff, Best Interests Assessors, care home staff, hospital staff, supported living and other care environments briefed with developments. These briefings should disseminate information in a measured and accurate way.
6.  Keep insurers and Local Authority solicitors fully briefed on potential risks
7.  Ensure close working relationships between care management teams and DoLS teams/BIA's in order to facilitate applications to the Court of Protection for community DoL's

## Longer Term ADASS would expect councils to

1.  Train and recruit sufficient additional BIAs to meet the new level of demand
2.  Update training materials in relation to MCA and DoLS to reflect the acid test
3.  Update all relevant policies and procedures in line with the acid test

## Wider MCA issues

ADASS also reminds its members about the request for MCA materials to be submitted to the Social Care Institute for Excellence (SCIE) in order that they can conduct a rapid but comprehensive review of MCA guidance and associated materials for the health and care sector. The aim will be to identify those materials that best provide different MCA audiences (e.g. social workers, nurses, ambulance services) with the information and tools that they require. These materials will then be jointly endorsed by national system partners and their existence advertised. Materials can still be submitted at www.scie.org.uk/opportunities/callsforevidence/mca2005.asp.

## Useful resources

Details of Supreme Court DoLS Judgment: www.gov.uk/government/uploads/system/uploads/attachment–data/file/300106/DH–Note–re–Supreme–Court–DoLS–Judgment.pdf

Further guidance for providers from CQC: www.cqc.org.uk/sites/default/files/media/documents/20140404––dols–briefing–for–health–and–social–care–providers.pdf

A letter from the Department of Health to MCA-DoLS Leads in local authorities and the NHS dated 8th September 2014: www.adass.org.uk/DHletter/MCA-DoLS/Sept14/

Joint ADASS and LGA letters to government: www.local.gov.uk/health-wellbeing-and-adult-social-care/-/journal–content/56/10180/6415062/ARTICLE

## ADASS TASK FORCE

### A screening tool to prioritise the allocation of requests to authorise a deprivation of liberty

Due to the vast increase in demand for assessments under the Deprivation of liberty safeguards the ADASS task force members have shared practice in relation to prioritisation and produced this screening tool. The aim of the tool is to assist Councils to respond in a timely manner to those requests which have the highest priority. The tool sets out the criteria most commonly applied which indicates that an urgent response may be needed so as to safeguard the individuals concerned. The use of this tool must be balanced against the legal criteria for the Deprivation of Liberty Safeguards which remains unchanged. **The criteria should be used as an indicative guide only as it will generally be based on information provided by the Managing Authority in the application and each case must be judged on its own facts.**

| Higher | Medium | Lower |
|---|---|---|
| ■ Psychiatric or Acute Hospital and not free to leave<br>■ Continuous 1:1 care during the day and / or night<br>■ Sedation/medication used frequently to control behaviour<br>■ Physical restraint used regularly – equipment or persons<br>■ Restrictions on family/friend contact (or other Article 8 issue)<br>■ Objections from relevant person (verbal or physical)<br>■ Objections from family/friends<br>■ Attempts to leave<br>■ Confinement to a particular part of the establishment for considerable period of time<br>■ New or unstable placement<br>■ Possible challenge to Court of Protection, or Complaint<br>■ Already subject to DoL about to expire | ■ Asking to leave but not consistently<br>■ **Not making any active attempts to leave**<br>■ **Appears to be unsettled some of the time**<br>■ **Restraint or medication used infrequently.**<br>■ Appears to meet some but not all aspects of the acid test | ■ Minimal evidence of control and supervision<br>■ No specific restraints or restrictions being used. E.g. in a care home not objecting, no additional restrictions in place.<br>■ Have been living in the care home for some time (at least a year)<br>■ Settled placement in care home/hospital placement, no evidence of objection etc. but may meet the requirements of the acid test.<br>■ End of life situations, intensive care situations which may meet the acid test but there will be no benefit to the person from the Safeguards |
| Case No: | Date: | Prioritised by: |
| Summary of criteria | | |
| Allocated priority: | | |

# LETTER REGARDING THE IMPLEMENTATION OF THE RE X PROCEDURE

[06 November 2014]

Dear Court User

I am writing to update you on the arrangements we are putting in place to implement the streamlined process for the Court of Protection (CoP) to manage applications for a court-authorised deprivation of liberty in the light of the Supreme Court decision in *P v Cheshire West and Chester Council and P and Q v Surrey County Council* [2014] UKSC 19:

On 7 August 2014 the President of the CoP handed down his first judgment in *Re X and others (Deprivation of Liberty)* [2014] EWCOP 25. I know that most of you are aware of the content of the judgment, but in summary it:

- Set out a broad framework for a streamlined process for handling the majority of cases on paper without holding a hearing;
- Identified trigger factors that would give rise to an oral hearing, including:
    - Where P does not consent to the DoL o Where P wishes to take part in the proceedings o Where anyone with an interest in P's welfare did not support the DoL
    - Where a previous decision made by P (eg advance directive) or on behalf of P (eg by attorney) conflicts with the proposed DoL
- Identified some issues that would need to be considered by the CoP Rules Group including: the wider question of how P should be involved in proceedings and potential changes to the rules on permission.

The MoJ and HMCTS intend to implement the new process, as set out in the judgment in 2 phases:

- Phase one: a new practice direction and forms to deal with judicial authorisations for a DoL. This will be an interim process and users will be invited to provide feedback on how it works in practice.
- Phase two: revision of the forms, practice direction and process to take into account any further guidance set out in the President's judgment, feedback from users, and any changes that come out of the CoP rules committee.

This letter explains what we are doing to implement phase one.

We have developed a new practice direction which will replace practice direction 10AA which currently deals only with applications relating to urgent and standard authorisations in hospital and care home settings. We have also developed new forms and guidance for applications for a court-authorised deprivation of liberty. As part of this process, we carried out an informal consultation with an ad-hoc group of users in the summer. Given the need to roll the process out as soon as possible, we do not plan to carry out any further consultation but will instead, pilot the process and invite feedback on how it works in practice. We hope to publish the forms and practice direction in the next couple of weeks along with standard draft orders.

To ensure there is sufficient judicial resource to deal with the work, HMCTS have run an expressions of interest to nominate judges working in the Social Entitlement Chamber to deal with applications under the streamlined procedure. The first group of nominees will be trained in mid-November.

We have also set up a dedicated team within the CoP which will deal exclusively with deprivation of liberty work. The new staff are already trained to do the existing CoP work, and have been briefed on the proposed new Re X processes. The intention is to ring fence the Re X work so it does not impact on the other work of the CoP.

We will be in touch shortly when the forms, practice direction and draft orders have been signed off by the President of the CoP, and in relation to the practice direction only, when it has been agreed by the Secretary of State. We will explain how to access the new forms, etc. and provide contact details for the deprivation of liberty team.

Finally, I must thank everyone who has been in touch since March for your patience and understanding while we have been developing these new processes; and a special thank you to all who have contributed to developing the new forms, etc, both as part of the ad-hoc user group and by email.

Yours faithfully,

James Batey

Court of Protection

# Appendix C6
# Intensive Care Society: Deprivation of liberty in intensive care

## INTRODUCTION

Most patients in intensive care units lack mental capacity to inform decision-making, whether because of drugs or disease. The introduction of the Mental Capacity Act in England and Wales in 2005 has changed the way that doctors and institutions deal with patients who lack capacity. This is especially true when physical, mechanical or pharmacological restraints are used to allow the patient's treatment. Recently, the Supreme Court has ruled that if a person is under continuous supervision and control, and is not free to leave the place they are being treated, then they are deprived of their liberty. This article explains the ramification of this ruling for patients in intensive care whose care must now meet Deprivation of Liberties Standards. The procedures both for staff caring for these patients and for the Trusts where they are receiving care are described.

The majority of patients in intensive care units lack the mental capacity to make material decisions during a large proportion of their stay, due to drugs or disease. The use of patient restraints (physical, mechanical or pharmacological) is commonly deployed, under the auspices of relevant legislation, to facilitate safe intensive care. Recent developments have led to uncertainty in many clinical settings including intensive care regarding the lawfulness of these practices. The Law Commission is launching a review of the law relating to the deprivation of liberty of those without capacity, which may in due course shed light upon the area, but not for several years. In the meantime, this document aims to provide guidance until current law is more clearly defined or amended.

## BACKGROUND: THE LEGAL JOURNEY

### 2005 – The Mental Capacity Act

The Mental Capacity Act 2005 (MCA)[1] was enacted in England and Wales to empower adults who lack capacity to make decisions for themselves.[2] It allows medical treatment to be used, including physical or pharmacological restraint, as long as it is judged to be in the patient's best interests and it meets certain additional criteria reflecting the need for proportionality in the extent of the intervention. The MCA stipulates that before any actions or decisions are taken on behalf of a person who lacks capacity, acting in their best interests, consideration should be given to whether there is a less restrictive alternative.[3] The MCA draws a clear line between restraint and deprivation of a person's liberty.

If a person is restrained, again in their best interests, this must be reasonably believed to be necessary to prevent harm to the person and must be proportionate to the likelihood and seriousness of that harm (MCA s5,6).

---

[1]   NB. These factors (compliance/objection and the reason or purpose for the placement) are of course still relevant to assessment of best interests and consideration of Article 8 rights.

[2]   www.gov.uk/government/uploads/system/uploads/attachment–data/file/318730/cm8884-valuing-every-voice.pdf.

[3]   www.gov.uk/government/uploads/system/uploads/attachment–data/file/318730/cm8884-valuing-every-voice.pdf.

If a person who lacks capacity to consent to this is deprived of their liberty, this can only be lawful using the Deprivation of Liberty Safeguards or an Order of the Court of Protection, or where the deprivation of liberty is necessary to give life-sustaining treatment or to do a vital act, while an Order of the Court is sought. (MCA s4A, 4B)

## 2009 – Deprivation of Liberty Safeguards

The Deprivation of Liberty Safeguards (DoLS) were added to the Mental Capacity Act by amendments made by the Mental Health Act (MHA) 2007. The safeguards were introduced in response to a judgment from the European Court of Human Rights (ECtHR) (*HL v. the United Kingdom 2004*), commonly referred to as the Bournewood judgment. The ECtHR ruled that an autistic man with a severe learning disability was unlawfully deprived of his liberty following admission to a psychiatric hospital. HL had initially been admitted informally under common law – ie, without using the MHA – but was then prevented from leaving the hospital. He was sedated in hospital and kept under continuous observation by nursing staff. His foster family was not allowed to see him or to take him home. Although he did not object to being kept in hospital and never tried to leave, the ECtHR found that he was subject to complete and effective control over his care and movements by healthcare professionals and that he was not free to leave. The Court found this to have breached his right to liberty under Article 5(1) of the European Convention on Human Rights (ECHR). Due to the informality of the procedures used to detain HL (especially compared to the procedural safeguards offered by the Mental Health Act 1983), the ECtHR also found that he had no effective right to challenge his detention before a court, and that his rights under Article 5(4) ECHR were therefore also breached.

The DoLS scheme was introduced in response. Its aim was to provide protection for the human rights of vulnerable people who lack capacity to decide about their care and treatment, where the arrangements made for such care or treatment in hospitals or care homes may amount to a deprivation of their liberty. The safeguards came into force in April 2009, and allow, in essence, the 'administrative' authorisation of a deprivation of a person's liberty. They created a framework within which an organisation must work when it is deemed necessary to deprive a person of their liberty. They also provide a number of protections, including independent scrutiny and the appointment of a representative to act on a person's behalf. They also provide the patient or their representative the right to challenge the decision to deprive the patient of their liberty in the Court of Protection and the right for the decision to be reviewed on a regular basis.

If DoLS cannot be used, a deprivation of liberty can only be authorised by the Court of Protection.

In outline, the DoLS scheme is 'administrative' because it provides a system by which a care home or hospital (a 'managing authority') can refer cases of suspected deprivation of liberty to the relevant local authority (as a 'supervisory body') to carry out independent assessments, which may lead to the grant of a DoLS authorisation for a period of up to a year without involvement of the Court.

## 2014 – WHAT HAS CHANGED?

The current uncertainty arises from a Supreme Court ruling on 19 March 2014 usually known as 'Cheshire West' (*P v Cheshire West and Chester Council and P&Q v Surrey County Council 2014*) about the meaning of a 'deprivation of liberty' in the context of the provision of care and treatment to those unable to consent to their accommodation arrangements.

These two cases, heard together by the Supreme Court, involved three people with significant learning disabilities who required varying levels of restraint to facilitate care in a community setting.

P and Q (also known as MIG and MEG) were sisters with learning disabilities who were cared for in foster accommodation and a residential home respectively. MIG never attempted to leave the foster home by herself but would have been prevented from doing so had she tried. MEG had more complex needs and sometimes required physical or chemical restraint. In 2009, a Court of Protection judge found that these living arrangements were in the best interests of MIG and MEG and did not amount to a deprivation of liberty, so the additional independent scrutiny and regular reviews required to authorise such a deprivation were not triggered. The Court of Appeal upheld this conclusion.

The other case was of P, a gentleman with cerebral palsy and Down's syndrome who required intervention on occasion due to his challenging behaviour. A Court of Protection judge found that the interventions used *did* represent a deprivation of liberty but that it was in P's best interests for them to continue. The Court of Appeal overturned the finding that P had been deprived of his liberty, largely based on a comparison between his circumstances and those of another individual of similar age and disability, holding that there would not typically be a deprivation of liberty where the care was relatively normal for someone with those needs.

In 2014, the Supreme Court overturned both Court of Appeal decisions and found that MIG, MEG and P had all been deprived of their liberty. Importantly, the judgment of the majority identified an 'acid test' for deprivation of liberty, namely that if a person is under continuous supervision and control and is not free to leave, then this constitutes an objective deprivation of their liberty. If the person is unable to consent to the deprivation of liberty, then (and if it is also 'imputable to the State' which will be the case in all hospitals), an authorisation will be required under the DoLS regime or from the Court of Protection if the deprivation of liberty is to be lawful.

## DEPRIVATION OF LIBERTY: WHO, WHAT, WHEN AND WHY TO CONSIDER IT IN INTENSIVE CARE

### Who is at risk of being unlawfully deprived of their liberty?

The DoLS regime applies to hospitals, although the conventional understanding of the legislation was that applications for DoLS authorisations should not be made where a patient would cease to be deprived of their liberty within seven days. This meant that applications had not been made routinely in the intensive (as opposed to chronic) care setting.

The acid test framed by the Supreme Court was not decided in the intensive care setting. However, the concept of a deprivation of liberty is not context-specific, so is capable in principle of applying in this setting. Due to their circumstances, most patients in intensive care units would seemingly fit the 'acid test' criteria, and it could therefore be construed that we are depriving them of their liberty. This is supported by a recent case (published 28 August 2014), in which a judge applied the Cheshire West acid test to a maternity unit in a general hospital.

Despite this there are some exclusions where patients are *not* considered to be deprived of their liberty, namely those who:

- have the capacity to decide to be admitted to *intensive* care
- consent to the restrictions applied to them
- gave consent for intensive care admission prior to losing capacity – for instance prior to surgery (though they must have had an understanding that they may be under continuous supervision and control and not free to leave at some time within their stay).

Note also that patients detained under the Mental Health Act 1983 will be considered differently, as detention under that Act constitutes authorisation of any deprivation of liberty to which they are subjected.

Current MCA DoLS legislation refers only to patients in England and Wales. The position in Scotland is different, although it is expected that legislation will be introduced there in due course, equivalent to the DoLS regime.

## Why may it be appropriate to deprive a patient of their liberty?

The MCA DoLS code of practice highlights that deprivation of liberty is justifiable, where the person lacks capacity to consent to this:

- if it is in their best interests to protect them from harm
- if it is a proportional response when compared with the potential harm faced by the person
- if there is no less restrictive alternative.

## What actions constitute deprivation of liberty?

Although the Supreme Court has made the position very much clearer by the framing of the acid test, it is important to note that there is still no statutory definition of a deprivation of liberty.

The Mental Capacity Act simply defines deprivation of liberty' by reference to the ECtHR case law, and it is this case law which is distilled by the Supreme Court in the Cheshire West case. However, other guidance, such as the DoLS Code of Practice is still relevant and helpful, though it must be read in light of the Supreme Court judgment.

It is useful to consider restrictions imposed upon a person's activities as a scale ranging from minimal restriction at one extreme to deprivation of liberty at the other. Furthermore, the ECtHR has stipulated that deprivation of liberty depends on the specifics of each individual case.

In many cases in intensive care, it will be possible to identify relatively easily that the acid test is satisfied. However, it is important to note that other factors may be relevant to the assessment of the extent to which continuous supervision and control is being exercised, including, in particular:

- the use of restraint to bring about admission
- the use of restraint/medication being used forcibly against the patient's will during the course of the admission
- staff taking decisions on a person's behalf regarding treatments and contact with visitors
- duration of the restrictions.

Crucially, the Supreme Court in Cheshire West made it clear that in all cases, the following principles are *not* relevant when considering whether deprivation of liberty is occurring:

- the reason for treatment
- compliance with treatment
- lack of objection
- family/carer's agreement
- appropriateness or 'normality' of the treatment
- lack of an alternative safe place for treatment.

Note that it would appear that focus in deciding whether a patient is 'free to leave' should not be on whether the patient is actually physically capable of leaving, but rather upon what actions hospital staff would take if – for instance – family members sought to remove them.

## At what point does deprivation of liberty begin?

A deprivation of liberty must last more than a 'non-negligible' period of time. There is no fixed definition of how long a period of time is required. However the following principles should be considered:

- Though it has not yet been tested in the Courts, it would appear unlikely that a court would find that the acid test for deprivation of liberty means that someone is unlawfully deprived of their liberty by the provision of life-sustaining treatment in a true emergency situation.
- In all cases, life-sustaining interventions or the provision of emergency care should be given as clinically required and never delayed for prior deprivation of liberty authorisation to be sought (see MCA s4B).
- However, you should bear in mind that MCA s4B allows a deprivation of liberty where necessary to provide life-sustaining treatment or perform a 'vital act' (which is reasonably believed to be necessary to prevent a serious deterioration in the person's condition) 'while a decision as respects any relevant issue is sought from the Court.'
- Although there is no clear period of time after which a patient in intensive care would be considered to be deprived of their liberty, and therefore an application to Court is required if the DoLS cannot be used, the risk of a deprivation of liberty increases with increasing duration of treatment and when initial emergency treatment transitions to ongoing care. Such transition points must be considered on an individual patient basis and will be context dependent.
- Deprivation of liberty exists on a spectrum of levels of intervention and control over someone's life, with the duration of the intervention being only one of many factors. In some cases, very extreme degrees of intervention have been held to be a deprivation of liberty even though they only lasted for a few minutes.
- Deprivation of liberty should be considered separately from medically treating a patient in their best interests. The pre-existing justifications used for treating patients who lack the capacity to consent still apply. Consider this example:

A patient (P) is admitted to the intensive care unit following a cardiac arrest. There is a high clinical index of suspicion of hypoxic brain injury. P should be treated without delay according to clinical needs. After a few days of treatment, it is clear that P has suffered major hypoxic brain injury and is likely to require treatment in hospital for considerable time. He is under continuous supervision and control and is not free to leave and, being unconscious, does not have mental capacity to consent to his care. At this point, it can be argued that P satisfies the criteria set out by the acid test. Treatment must continue in exactly the same way based on P's clinical needs. However, in addition, there would be a request for DoLS authorisation for P to meet the Article 5 rights to due process and independent scrutiny where he is deprived of liberty.

## DEPRIVATION OF LIBERTY AUTHORISATION

### What is a DoLS authorisation?

A DoLS authorisation allows lawful deprivation of liberty. It does not, in itself, authorise specific treatments or procedures. Any treatments required for a patient who lacks capacity must therefore be provided under the 'best interests' provision of the Mental Capacity Act (and with appropriate regard to whether the patient has made any relevant advance decision to refuse such treatment).

There are two forms of DoLS authorisations. Standard authorisations are ideally applied for in advance of a person requiring deprivation of their liberty. They are granted by the supervisory body (usually the local authority where a person resides) within 21 days of application. Urgent authorisations can be made by the managing authority itself (ie, the manager responsible for the hospital/care home within which the deprivation of liberty will occur). Urgent authorisations can only be made where a standard authorisation has been applied for but is not yet granted. As such, an urgent authorisation can never be made without a simultaneous application for a standard authorisation. Urgent authorisations last for a maximum of seven days but in exceptional circumstances the supervisory body can extend this for an additional seven days. If necessary, it can be granted by the on-call manager of a Trust.

Within intensive care it is likely that all DoLS authorisations will be made as urgent authorisations in the first instance.

Once in place, a DoLS authorisation ensures that the supervisory body will appoint a representative for the patient, regularly review whether ongoing deprivation of liberty is required and remove the authorisation when it is no longer necessary.

DoLS authorisations are not transferrable between institutions and are subject to regular review. A review can occur at any time and may be triggered by the patient, their appointed representative or an independent mental capacity advocate (IMCA) for the patient. This usually occurs when a person's circumstances change. The maximum duration a standard authorisation can be in place is 12 months.

## What does the assessment process involve?

There are six assessments made to authorise deprivation of liberty under DoLS:

1.  Age assessment: Is the person over 18 years of age?
2.  Mental health assessment: Is the person suffering from a mental disorder? This can include acute confusion, delirium or drug-induced disorder of cognition.
3.  Mental capacity assessment: Does the person lack capacity to consent to admission for care and treatment?
4.  Eligibility assessment: is (or should) the person be subject to treatment under the MHA 1983? (note that such a patient may still be eligible to be deprived of their liberty under the DoLS regime in a general hospital for purposes of receiving treatment for their physical disorders).
5.  'No refusals' assessment: has the person refused treatment or made a relevant advance decision or will the authorisation conflict with valid decisions made on a person's behalf by a lasting power of attorney *or* a court appointed deputy?
6.  Best interests assessment: is the deprivation of liberty required and is it in the person's best interests?

The person must meet the criteria of all six assessments to allow a DoLS authorisation to occur.

## Why may a DoLS authorisation be refused?

There are multiple reasons why a DoLS authorisation may be rejected by the supervisory body. This will usually be because:

■   there is a less restrictive way to provide safe care for the patient
■   a deprivation of liberty is not deemed to be in the patient's best interests
■   the patient requires detention under the Mental Health Act 1983

*or*

■   the decision to deprive a patient of their liberty is refused or objected to by an attorney appointed by the patient when they had capacity or a deputy appointed by the Court of Protection to act on the patient's behalf.

## SUMMARY OF RECOMMENDATIONS:

## For the lead clinician

1.  Emergency treatment and clinical care should be the first priority. The legal implications

of deprivation of liberty are not optional but should not hinder or delay provision of essential clinical care .
2.  Every patient admitted to intensive care should be considered at risk of deprivation of liberty. All patients should be regularly assessed for mental capacity and whether they are being deprived of their liberty. This assessment should be written in the case notes.
3.  A relevant change in the patient's circumstances, including a material change in their duration of stay, should trigger a repeat assessment of deprivation of liberty. Bear in mind that the duration of the intensive care unit stay should not be seen in isolation from the time that the patient may spend as an inpatient overall.
4.  Patient compliance and/or family agreements are not relevant to whether a situation represents deprivation of liberty.
5.  Every effort should be made to prevent deprivation of liberty where possible and to use the 'least restrictive' alternative available to facilitate safe treatment/care.
6.  Patients whom are deprived of their liberty should be referred for an urgent DOLS authorisation from the managing authority within the hospital Trust at the earliest safe time.
7.  A DoLS authorisation does not, in itself, authorise specific treatments. Treatment provided for patients who lack capacity should be undertaken under the 'best interests' provisions of the Mental Capacity Act (and taking into account whether any relevant advance decisions have been made refusing the proposed treatment).
8.  A DoLS authorisation should be regularly reviewed, and amended (in the case of a change of circumstances) or revoked when required.
9.  Where a DoLS authorisation is refused, the clinicians involved in the patient's care must ensure that deprivation of the patient's liberty does not occur. Unlawful deprivation of liberty exposes the Trust to potential liabilities and is a breach of the patient's human rights.
10. All deaths of patients which occur where a DoLS authorisation is in place should be reported to the coroner.

## For the Trust

1.  Every Trust should have an agreed DoL policy to ensure compliance with the assessment process. Intensive care representation should be sought to achieve this.
2.  All patients who are deprived of their liberty should be assessed for an urgent DoLS authorisation as soon as feasibly possible.
3.  Urgent DoLS authorisations should only be made in parallel with a request for a standard authorisation from the supervisory body.
4.  Ensure that appropriate procedures and support are in place to allow review of DoLS authorisations.
5.  All DoLS notifications and authorisation requests should be appropriately recorded and scrutinised at Trust level.
6.  Legal advice should be sought promptly where there is any doubt as to whether a case falls within the Trust's DoL policy.
7.  Ensure that there is appropriate provision of ongoing training, and regular review of policies and procedures, as the case law in this area is moving fast.

## Declaration

This article is based on the work performed at a colloquium organised jointly by the ICS and FICM

## Conflicts of interest

None declared.

## References

1.  **UK Government Legislation**. *Mental Capacity Act 2005 c.9*. London: The Stationery

Office;  2005.  Available  at:  **www.legislation.gov.uk/ukpga/2005/9/pdfs/ukpga–20050009–en.pdf** Accessed 16th September 2014.

2. **Department of Constitutional Affairs**. *Mental Capacity Act 2005*. Code of Practice. London: The Stationery Office; 2007. Available at: **www.justice.gov.uk/downloads/protecting-the-vulnerable/mca/mca-code-practice-0509.pdf** Accessed 16th September 2014.

3. **Ministry of Justice**. *Mental Capacity Act 2005*: Deprivation of liberty safeguards – Code of Practice to supplement the main Mental Capacity Act 2005 Code of Practice. London: The Stationery Office; 2008. Available at: **webarchive.nationalarchives.gov.uk/20130107105354/http://www.dh.gov.uk/prod–consum–dh/groups/dh–digitalassets/@dh/@en/documents/digitalasset/dh–087309.pdf**. Accessed 16th September 2014.

4. *HL* v. *United Kingdom* ECtHR [2004] 40 EHRR 761

5. **Brindle N, Branton T**. Interface between the Mental Health Act and Mental Capacity Act: deprivation of liberty safeguards. *Adv Psychiatr Treat* 2010;16:430-37.

6. **UK Government Legislation**. *Mental Health Act 1983 c.20 London*: WJ Sharp; 1983. Available at: **www.legislation.gov.uk/ukpga/1983/20/pdfs/ukpga–19830020–en.pdf**. Accessed 16th September 2014.

7. *P v Cheshire West and Chester Council and another. P and Q v Surrey County Council* [2014] UKSC 19. On appeal from: [2011] EWCA Civ 1257; [2011] EWCA Civ 190]

8. *NHS Trust & Ors* v. *FG* [2014] EWCOP 30.

9. Office of the Public Guardian. *Deprivation of Liberty Safeguards: A guide for hospitals and care homes*. London: Department of Health OPG 60; 2009. Available at: **www.scie-socialcareonline.org.uk/deprivation-of-liberty-safeguards-a-guide-for-hospitals-and-care-homes/r/a11G00000018164IAA**. Accessed 16 September 2014.

## Media/other resources

■   House of Lords Select Committee on the Mental Capacity Act 2005, *Mental Capacity Act 2005: post-legislative scrutiny* [HL Paper 139, 13.03.14] Available at: **www.publications.parliament.uk/pa/ld201314/ldselect/ldmentalcap/139/139.pdf** accessed on 16th September 2014.

■   Health and Social Care Information Centre. *Mental Capacity Act 2005, deprivation of liberty safeguards assessments [England]: annual report, 2012/13*. 2013:9. Available at: **www.google.co.uk/url?sa=t&rct=j&q=&esrc=s&source=web&cd=2&ved=0CCwQFjAB&url=http%3A%2F%2Fwww.hscic.gov.uk%2Fcatalogue%2FPUB11379%2Fm-c-a-2005-dep-lib-saf-ass-eng-2012-13-tab-ratesv2.xls&ei=-MgZVKjQK8–maOOfgIAG&usg=AFQjCNFviVUxuIraB8ceB–xc23jJ–Wg–A&sig2=JyyzZqu4Tzjuc5jLWbgecQ&bvm=bv.75097201,d.d2s**.    Accessed    16 September 2014.

■   *MCA and MHA Decision Pathways Support Application*. Imperial College Healthcare NHS Trust. Available at: **www.appannie.com/apps/ios/app/mca-mha-decision-pathways**. Accessed 16th September 2014.

## About the authors

**Maryam Crews:** Specialist Trainee Year 7 in Anaesthesia and Intensive Care Medicine, Critical Care Directorate, Royal Liverpool and Broadgreen University Hospitals Trust

**David Garry:** Specialist Trainee Year 7 in Anaesthetics and Intensive Care, Department of Anaesthetics, John Radcliffe Hospital, Oxford University Hospitals NHS Trust

**Claire Phillips:** Specialist Trainee Year 7, Intensive Care Medicine, Royal Berkshire Hospital, Reading

**Adrian Wong:** Specialist Trainee Year 7, Anaesthetics/Intensive Care Medicine, Deptartment of Critical Care, Queen Alexandra Hospital, Portsmouth

**Ben Troke:** Solicitor, Browne Jacobson LLP

**Alex Ruck Keene:** Barrister and Honorary Research Lecturer, University of Manchester

**Christopher Danbury:** Consultant Intensivist, Visiting Fellow in Health Law, Royal Berkshire Hospital and School of Law, University of Reading chris.danbury@nhs.net

## Appendix C7
# Chief Coroner's Guidance No.16:
# Deprivation of Liberty Safeguards

## Introduction

1. This guidance concerns persons who die at a time when they are deprived of their liberty under the Mental Capacity Act 2005 (MCA 2005). Under the MCA 2005 a person who lacks capacity and is in a hospital or care home for the purpose of being given care or treatment may be detained in circumstances which amount to deprivation of liberty.

2. No detention amounting to deprivation of liberty may be permitted without authorisation under the statutory scheme. It would amount otherwise to false imprisonment. The scheme, set out in Schedule A1 to the MCA 2005, provides safeguards known as Deprivation of Liberty Safeguards (DoLS).

3. The questions which are raised for coroners and must be answered are:

- Are these persons in state detention for the purposes of the Coroners and Justice Act 2009 (the 2009 Act)?
- Should an inquest be held into their death?
- If so, must there be an inquest in all cases, even when they die of natural causes?
- Should there be a jury inquest?
- Will it be an Article 2 inquest?

4. These questions arise urgently since the use of DoLS in hospitals and care homes is now widespread and increasing. The Department of Health (DH) and Care Quality Commission (CQC) expect applications for DoLS to rise from 13,000 a year to over 100,000. Most cases concern vulnerable people with dementia. Others may have a severe learning disability or acquired brain injury.

5. For the future the Law Commission has commenced a fundamental review of DoLS provisions in the MCA 2005. It will report in 2017 with recommendations for reform and a draft Bill.

6. But for now the purpose of this guidance is to give coroners a steer on the application of DoLS in the context of coroner work. It will of course be a matter for coroners in the exercise of their independent judgment, and subject to any subsequent ruling of the High Court, to decide each case for themselves.

7. For the purpose of simplicity, the statutory authorisation for deprivation of liberty of a person in a hospital or care home will be referred to in this guidance as a DoL.

## What are DoLS? How is deprivation of liberty authorised?

8. Following the decision in R v. Bournewood Community and Mental Health NHS Trust, ex p L [1999] 1 AC 458 and its reconsideration at Strasbourg in HLv. UK (2004) 40 EHRR 761, it became necessary for the UK to introduce machinery for the protection of the thousands of mentally incapacitated people who were regularly deprived of their liberty in hospitals and care homes (and elsewhere).

9. Accordingly the MCA 2005 was amended by the Mental Health Act 2007 so as to provide a new statutory scheme for persons in hospitals or care homes who were proved on a balance of probabilities to lack capacity.

## Lack of capacity

10. Under the MCA 2005 lack of capacity is expressed in this way. A person lacks capacity in relation to a matter if he or she is unable to make a decision for himself or herself in relation to the matter because of an impairment (permanent or temporary) of, or a disturbance in the functioning of, the mind or brain: sections 1 and 2, MCA 2005.

11. Persons who lack capacity may be subject to deprivation of liberty, but only by authorisation under Schedule A1 of the MCA 2005 or by order of the Court of Protection (section 4A).

## Meaning of 'deprivation of liberty'

12. Section 64(5) of the MCA 2005, the interpretation section, provides that references in the Act to deprivation of a person's liberty have the same meaning as in Article 5(1) of the European Convention on Human Rights. Article 5(1) of the Convention provides:

> Everyone has the right to liberty and security of person. No one shall be deprived of his liberty save in the following cases and in accordance with a procedure prescribed by law: [ . . .] e) the lawful detention of persons for the prevention of the spreading of infectious diseases, of persons of unsound mind, alcoholics or drug addicts, or vagrants.

13. In P v Cheshire West and Cheshire Council; P and Q v Surrey County Council [2014] UKSC 19 (a DoLS case but not a coroner case) the Supreme Court stated that the purpose of Article 5 was to ensure that people were not deprived of their liberty without proper safeguards.

14. The Supreme Court decided (by a majority), citing HL v. UK (above), that deprivation of liberty arose when the person concerned 'was under continuous supervision control and was not free to leave' [49], [63] and [87]. This should be determined 'primarily on an objective basis' [76] – [87].

15. It did not matter that the patient in hospital or the resident of a care home was content or compliant or voiced no objection. As Lady Hale said at [46], 'A gilded cage is still a cage.'

16. Accordingly, once there is, or is likely to be, deprivation of liberty, the detention must be authorised under the DoLS scheme in the MCA 2005.

## Authorisation

17. An authorisation which deprives a person of his or her liberty is obtained in the following way. The 'managing authority' of the hospital or care home (public or private) may request authorisation from the 'supervisory body'. There must be a request **and** an authorisation before a person is lawfully deprived of his or her liberty.

### THE MANAGING AUTHORITY

18. The managing authority of an NHS hospital is the health trust, board or special health authority. For independent (private) hospitals the managing authority is the person registered or required to be registered by statute. For care homes the managing authority is the person registered or required to be registered by statute. See paragraphs 175-178, Schedule A1.

### THE SUPERVISORY BODY

19. Since 2009 the supervisory body for all hospitals and care homes, both public and private, is the local authority.

### STANDARD AND URGENT AUTHORISATIONS

20. There are two types of authorisation: standard authorisations and urgent authorisations.

21. The DH has issued forms and guidance: see **www.gov.uk/government/collections/dh-mental-capacity-act-2005-deprivation-of-liberty-safeguards**. Form No.1 is for urgent authorisations, Form No.12 for standard authorisations.

22. The *DoLS Code of Practice* issued by the DH can be found at **webarchive.nationalarchives.gov.uk/20130107105354/http://www.dh.gov.uk/prod–consum–dh/groups/dh–digitalassets/@dh/@en/documents/digitalasset/dh– 087309.pdf**

23. *Standard authorisations* are made by the local authority. They must state in writing (amongst other things) the name of the person to be detained, the hospital or care home at which deprivation of liberty is authorised, the duration of the authorisation, the purpose for which it was given, the reason why each qualifying requirement (see below) was met, and 'any conditions' subject to which the authorisation is given. It may be renewed. See paragraphs 21-73, Schedule A1.

24. There is a statutory duty upon the managing authority of a hospital or care home to apply for authorisation where the qualifying requirements are likely to be met within the following 28 days. See paragraphs 24-26, Schedule A1.

25. *Urgent authorisations* are made by the managing authority of the hospital or care home in urgent cases only, for a period of seven days, pending a request for a standard authorisation. They do not involve recourse to the supervisory body. See paragraphs 74-90, Schedule A1.

26. Once the authorisation is given (standard or urgent), the hospital or care home may deprive the person of their liberty by detaining the person for the purpose of their being given care or treatment. See paragraph 1(2), Schedule A1.

## Safeguards

27. Safeguards (as in the phrase Deprivation of Liberty Safeguards) are provided by Schedule A1 of the MCA 2005. They involve a rigorous procedure of assessment and authorisation, independent of the hospital or home.

28. Safeguards are provided by the precondition of six qualifying requirements having to be met. These are the age, mental health, mental capacity, best interests, eligibility and no refusals requirements. See paragraph 12, Schedule A1.

29. Following a request the supervisory body must carry out assessments of all qualifying requirements before granting an authorisation: paragraph 33, Schedule A1. The six assessments must be completed by a minimum of two assessors, usually including a social worker or care worker, sometimes a psychiatrist or other medical person (see *DoLS Code of Practice* 4.13-4.57). If all assessments are in writing and 'positive', ie all qualifying requirements are met, the supervisory body must give a standard authorisation: paragraph 50, Schedule A1. This authorisation may be 'reviewed' by the supervisory body later.

30. As one would expect, where the liberty of the subject is at stake, the provisions are detailed and extensive. There are 188 paragraphs in Schedule A1. It is not the purpose of this guidance to detail all the requirements and conditions.

## Court of Protection

31. The Court of Protection may make a similar order authorising deprivation of liberty in a domestic setting (outside hospitals and care homes) in relation to personal welfare: see sections 4A and 16 of the MCA 2005. This will include a placement in a supported living arrangement.

32. The authorisation of any DoL may be challenged in the Court of Protection: section 21A, MCA 2005. See, for example, *RB (by his Litigation Friend, the Official Solicitor)* v. *Brighton and Hove City Council* [2014] EWCA Civ 561 (unsuccessful application to terminate a standard authorisation).

## No challenge to validity of DoLS before coroner

33.  Where an authorisation to deprive a person of liberty has been given, its validity cannot be challenged by or before a coroner.

## The Coroners and Justice Act 2009: 'in state detention'

34.  In order to decide whether a coroner must investigate the death of a person who was subject to a DoL, it is necessary to consider the relevant provisions of the 2009 Act. Has a person who was subject to a DoL died in state detention for the purposes of the 2009 Act?

35.  A coroner must commence an investigation into a person's death under the relevant wording of section 1 of the 2009 Act where the coroner has reason to suspect that 'the deceased died while in custody **or otherwise in state detention**': section 1(2)(c). The Explanatory Notes to section 1 suggest that state detention includes persons 'held under mental health legislation': paragraph 61.

36.  '**State detention**' is defined in section 48(2). 'A person is in state detention if he or she is compulsorily detained by a public authority within the meaning of section 6 of the Human Rights Act 1998.' Section 6 is headed 'Acts of public authorities'.

37.  If a duty to investigate arises under section 1, the investigation may not be discontinued if the coroner has reason to suspect that the deceased 'died while in custody **or otherwise in state detention**': section 4(2)(b). In those circumstances the coroner must therefore hold an inquest: section 6.

## Two opposing views

38.  Two alternative views have been expressed about DoLS and whether they are included within the phrase 'in state detention'.

39.  *The first view* is that the deprivation of liberty of DoLS extends more widely than cases of ordinary physical detention, for example to cases of persons living in relative normality, not seeking to leave or complaining about being restrained, but would be restrained if they sought to leave. See *Jervis on Coroners* 13th Edn. (2014) at paragraph 5-85.

40.  In addition *Jervis* suggests that the restraint, such as it is, is outside the scope of the definition of state detention in section 48(2) (above) when it is not by a 'public authority' for the purposes of the Human Rights Act 1998, as for example in the case of a private care home.

41.  On this view the death of a person in hospital or a care home who was subject to a DoL would not automatically require a coroner's investigation. Indeed in most cases there would be no need for an investigation, although the coroner would have to decide on a case by case basis whether one was necessary.

42.  *The second and opposing view* is that a person subject to a DoL falls squarely within the 2009 Act's definition of 'in state detention'. However quiet and comfortable the person may be in, say, a care home, the reality of their position is that they have been deprived of their liberty by the authority of the state and are being held in detention under that authority – as in 'the gilded cage' referred to by Lady Hale.

43.  On this view, whether intended by Parliament or not, all persons who die subject to a DoL must be the subject of a coroner investigation, whether the death was from natural causes or not. For the purposes of the 2009 Act they were 'in state detention', therefore section 1 is triggered.

44.  These two competing views are not easily reconciled. They may ultimately be a matter for decision of the High Court. The former view, for example, may require coroners to consider every DoLS death on a case by case basis to see if an investigation is required. Some coroners say that the burden of doing so would be immense. The latter view, for example,

may cause local authorities great concern over additional and unexpected expenditure by the coroner service as a result of many extra inquests.

## The Chief Coroner's view

45. The Chief Coroner favours the second view. It is his opinion that, on the law as it now stands, the death of a person subject to a DoL should be the subject of a coroner investigation because that person was in state detention within the meaning of the Coroners and Justice Act 2009.

46. The Chief Coroner, who sits in the High Court on coroner cases, is not providing a judgment or ruling. This guidance is no more than the expression of an opinion, subject to the ruling of the High Court. Coroners, who are of course entitled to make their own independent judicial decisions, will do as they see fit in any particular case. But they are invited to take this guidance into account.

47. The Chief Coroner's view is the view which was expressed in the Chief Coroners Guide to the Coroners and Justice Act 2009 Act at paragraph 54:

> This [the definition of 'state detention' in section 48(2)], in effect, extends the definition of state detention to institutions such as immigration detention and secure mental health hospitals. It would also appear to extend to deprivation of liberty orders (Schedule A1, Mental Capacity Act 2005).

48. The Ministry of Justice collaborated with the Chief Coroner on the Guide and approved this wording.

49. The Department of Health also shares this view.

50. It was also the view of the Government in 2009 as expressed during the passage of the Coroners and Justice Bill. In response to questions from the Joint Parliamentary Committee on Human Rights, the then Government acknowledged that 'in state detention' would include the following circumstances:

(a)   detention by a constable or other public authority pursuant to statutory or common law powers;

(b)   **detention or deprivation of liberty pursuant to the requirements of mental health legislation, including the Mental Health Act 1983 and the Mental Capacity Act 2005, as amended by the Mental Health Act 2007;**

(c)   the placement of a child in secure accommodation;

(d)   detention pursuant to immigration and asylum legislation; and

(e)   the detention of any person in custody or otherwise detained while he or she is being transported from one place to another.

51. In accepting that the examples in the above list would come under the definition of state detention, the then Government considered that listing them in the Bill was unnecessary. On this basis it could be said that the wording of the 2009 Act, which makes no reference to DoLS, was clearly intended by the drafters of the 2009 Act to include DoLS in the meaning of 'in state detention'.

52. This view appears to accord with the Explanatory Notes to section 1 of the 2009 Act (see paragraph 35 above).

53. It should of course be noted that the High Court may be less willing to resort to some of these extra-statutory materials in interpreting relevant provisions of the 2009 Act.

54. This view may be further supported by the language used in Schedule A1 of the MCA 2005 which refers to a person 'detained in a hospital or care home' and 'place of detention'. In short once the relevant conditions are satisfied, the person is detained by operation of law. This appears to be consistent with 'compulsorily detained' in section 48(2) of the 2009 Act.

55. This view suggests that those subject to DoLS are subject in plain language to the restrictions of state detention. They are detained compulsorily under the statutory framework of the state. There should therefore be a coroner's investigation (including inquest: section 6) in all cases.

## Public authority

56. On the 'public authority' point, it is certainly arguable that all hospitals and care homes are public authorities for the purposes of the Human Rights Act (see section 48(2) above). Those in public ownership clearly are. Those in private ownership will be if they are carrying out 'functions of a public nature', so as to fall within the meaning of 'public authority' in section 6(3)(b) of the Human Rights Act 1998.

57. On this point see, for example, *R (A)* v. *Partnerships in Care Ltd* [2002] 1 WLR 2610, in which a private provider of mental health care was held to be a functional public authority, performing public functions within the meaning of section 6(3)(b) of the Act. By contrast the decision in *YL* v. *Birmingham City Council* [2008] 1 AC 95 decided on its particular facts that the private care home was not a public body, but was providing a service for which it charged the local authority a fee for some of its residents but not all. However, the decision in *YL* has been reversed since by statute. Section 145 of the Health and Social Care Act 2008 states that where accommodation, together with nursing or personal care, is provided by a private care home and the local authority are paying for it, the care home is deemed to be a 'public authority' for the purposes of section 6(3)(b) of the Human Rights Act.

58. There is also an argument that the local authority, which as the supervisory body authorises a person to be deprived of their liberty by a DoL, is the relevant public authority. On the other hand section 64(6) of the MCA 2005 provides that for the purposes of references to deprivation of a person's liberty 'it does not matter whether a person is deprived of his liberty by a public authority or not'. That suggests that the detention is the act of the managing authority, not the supervisory body.

59. The ultimate question might therefore be: Is the detention by the managing authority in the case of a private care home a public function? The answer to that question may well be Yes. The detention is a public function because of the detailed statutory scheme which permits it. The exercise of powers of compulsory detention could therefore be considered a public function for the purposes of section 6 of the Human Rights Act.

## Inquest with jury?

60. In many cases there will be no need for a jury inquest. The mandatory requirement for an inquest to be held with a jury where 'the deceased died in custody or otherwise in state detention' does not apply to deaths from natural causes. It only applies where the death is a violent or unnatural one or the cause of death is unknown: section 7(2)(a) of the 2009 Act.

## Article 2

61. The mere fact that the inquest will be concerned with a death 'in state detention' does not mean that it will necessarily be an Article 2 inquest. In some cases it may be. But in many cases, particularly those where the death is from natural causes, there will be no arguable breach of the state's general duty to protect life. Nor will there be any arguable breach of the *Osman* test that the state knew or ought to have known of a real or immediate risk to the life of the deceased and failed to take measures within the scope of their powers: *Osman* v. *UK* [1998] 29 EHRR 245.

62. Accordingly, in most cases the procedural duty to hold a *Middleton* inquest and ascertain under section 5(2) of the 2009 Act 'in what circumstances' the deceased came by his or her death will not apply.

63. The Article 2 procedural duty may, however, arguably arise where the death is not from natural causes and/or the fact of detention under DoLS may be a relevant factor in the cause of death.

## Conclusions

64. **The Chief Coroner's present view, subject to a decision of the High Court, is that any person subject to a DoL is 'in state detention' for the purposes of the 2009 Act.**

65. When that person dies the death should therefore be reported to the coroner and the coroner should commence an investigation under section 1.

66. The person is not 'in state detention' for these purposes until the DoL is authorised.

67. Where the authorisation relates to a care home and the person is removed to a hospital and dies there (or in transit), coroners should err on the side of caution in deciding that the DoL may extend from the care home to the hospital in cases of medical necessity and therefore an investigation must be commenced. Even if the DoL is strictly place-specific (see paragraphs 25-26, Schedule A1), the law of necessity may allow the hospital to 'detain' the person, therefore an inquest would be necessary.

68. The investigation cannot be discontinued: section 4(2)(b). There must be an inquest.

69. There is no requirement for a jury where the death was from natural causes: section 7(2)(a).

70. In many cases the inquest will not be an Article 2 inquest.

71. In many cases of this kind which are uncontroversial the inquest may be a 'paper' inquest, decided in open court but on the papers without witnesses having to attend. Intelligent analysis of relevant information (without the need for a post-mortem examination) may be the best approach. Bereaved families should have all of this explained to them in advance.

72. Nevertheless, there will always be a public interest in the careful scrutiny of any death in state detention. As in all cases there must be sufficiency of coroner inquiry.

73. Senior coroners should maintain close liaison with the DoLS lead in their local authority, working together to deal with this extra activity.

**HH Judge Peter Thornton QC**
**Chief coroner**
**5 December 2014**

# Appendix C8
# Department of Health: Positive and proactive care – reducing the need for restrictive interventions

## INTRODUCTION

### The need for a guidance framework

1. In recent years a number of reports have focused on the use, or abuse, of restrictive interventions in health and care services. In 2012 the Department of Health published *Transforming Care: A national response to Winterbourne View Hospital*[1] which outlined the actions to be taken to avoid any repeat of the abuse and illegal practices witnessed at Winterbourne View Hospital. A subsequent Care Quality Commission (CQC) inspection of nearly 150 learning disability in-patient services found providers were often uncertain about the use of restrictive interventions, with some services having an over-reliance on the use of 'restraint' rather than on preventative approaches to 'challenging behaviour'.

2. Further impetus to drive forward the use of positive and proactive approaches arose from the publication of *Mental Health Crisis Care: physical restraint in crisis* in June 2013 by Mind.[2] The report found evidence of significant variations in the use of restraint across the country. They raised concerns about the use of face down or 'prone' restraint and the numbers of restraint related injuries that were sustained.

3. In response to these and other concerns about the inappropriate use of restrictive interventions across a wide range of health and care settings the Coalition Government committed the Department of Health to publish guidance on the use of positive and proactive approaches with the aim of developing a culture across health and social care where physical interventions are only ever used as a last resort when all other alternatives have been attempted and only then for the shortest possible time.

4. This guidance forms a key part of the Coalition Government's commitment set out in *Closing the Gap: essential priorities for change in mental health*[3] to end the use of restrictive interventions across all health and adult social care. 'Positive and Safe' is a new initiative to drive this forward. 'Positive and Safe' recognises that therapeutic environments are most effective for promoting both physical and emotional wellness and that restrictive interventions should only be used in modern compassionate health and social care services where there is a real possibility of harm to the person or to staff, the public or others.

5. The purpose of this guidance is to provide a framework to support the development of service cultures and ways of delivering care and support which better meet people's needs and which enhance their quality of life. It provides guidance on the delivery of services together with key actions that will ensure that people's quality of life is enhanced and that their needs are better met, which will reduce the need for restrictive interventions and promote recovery.

## KEY ACTIONS

### Improving care

■    Staff must not deliberately restrain people in a way that impacts on their airway, breathing or circulation, such as face down restraint on any surface, not just on the floor. [Para 70]

■    If restrictive intervention is used it must not include the deliberate application of pain. [Paras 58, 69, 75]

■    If a restrictive intervention has to be used, it must always represent the least restrictive option to meet the immediate need. [Paras 64, 96]

■    Staff must not use seclusion other than for people detained under the Mental Health Act 1983. [Paras 80, 89]

■    People who use services, families and carers must be involved in planning, reviewing and evaluating all aspects of care and support. [Paras 25, 36, 42, 53, 58, 62, 108, 116, 118]

■    Individualised support plans, incorporating behaviour support plans, must be implemented for all people who use services who are known to be at risk of being exposed to restrictive interventions. [Paras 35, 61, 65, 106, 108, 115]

### Leadership, assurance and accountability

■    A board level, or equivalent, lead must be identified for increasing the use of recovery-based approaches including, where appropriate, positive behavioural support planning, and reducing restrictive interventions. [Paras 29-31, 109]

■    Boards must maintain and be accountable for overarching restrictive intervention reduction programmes. [Para 109]

■    Executive boards (or equivalent) must approve the increased behavioural support planning and restrictive intervention reduction to be taught to their staff. [Paras 108, 119, 124, 125]

■    Governance structures and transparent polices around the use of restrictive interventions must be established by provider organisations. [Paras 105-109]

■    Providers must have clear local policy requirements and ensure these are available and accessible to users of services and carers. [Paras 114-118]

■    Providers must report on the use of restrictive interventions to service commissioners, who will monitor and act in the event of concerns. [Paras 109, 128]

■    Boards must receive and develop actions plans in response to an annual audit of behaviour support plans. [Paras 58, 109]

■    Post-incident reviews and debriefs must be planned so that lessons are learned when incidents occur where restrictive interventions have had to be used. [Paras 46-53]

### Transparency

■    Providers must ensure that internal audit programmes include reviews of the quality, design and application of behaviour support plans, or their equivalents. [Paras 58, 109]

■    Accurate internal data must be gathered, aggregated and published by providers including progress against restrictive intervention reduction programmes and details of training and development in annual quality accounts or equivalent. [Paras 111, 118]

■    Service commissioners must be informed by providers about restrictive interventions used for those for whom they have responsibility. [Paras 109-128]

■    Accurate internal data must be gathered, aggregated and reported by providers

> through mandatory reporting mechanisms where these apply, e.g. National
> Reporting and Learning Service (NRLS) and National Mental Health Minimum
> Data Set (NMHMDS). [Paras 110-112]
>
> ## Monitoring and oversight
>
> - Care Quality Commission's (CQC) monitoring and inspection against compli-
>   ance with the regulation on use of restraint and its ratings of providers will be
>   informed by this guidance. [Paras 8-10, 105, 106, 112]
> - CQC will review organisational progress against restrictive intervention reduc-
>   tion programmes. [Para 108]
> - CQC will scrutinise the quality of behaviour support plans which include the use
>   of restrictive interventions. [Para 106]

## The status of the guidance

6. For adult users of health and social care services (18 or over), this new guidance replaces the 2002 non-statutory guidance.[4] *The use of restrictive physical interventions for staff working with children and adults who display extreme behaviour in association with learning disability and/or autistic spectrum disorders* and *The use of restrictive physical interventions for pupils with severe behavioural difficulties.* However these may continue to be useful reference documents for those working with children and young people. Additional guidance is in preparation that will take account of the different legal framework and implications of the UN Convention on the Rights of the Child[5] for children, young people and individuals transitioning to adult services

7. The guidance provides information and good practice guidance to all health and social care for adults delivered or commissioned by the NHS or local authorities in England, including care delivered in an individual's own home or non-care settings such as police cells, immigration removal centres and prisons.

8. The Care Quality Commission (CQC) is responsible for registering and monitoring registered providers, and the quality and safety of the care they provide, under the Health and Social Care Act 2008. This guidance will inform CQC's programme of regular monitoring and inspection against CQC standards, particularly in relation to regulation 11 (safeguarding service users against abuse) of the Health and Social Care Act 2008 (Regulated Activities) Regulations 2010[6]. The Department is currently consulting on new regulations which will introduce new fundamental standards of care, and will replace the regulations referenced above by October 2014 (subject to parliamentary approval). One of these fundamental standards requires that care and treatment must be appropriate and safe, and includes reference to appropriate use of restraint.

9. Subject to parliamentary approval, this new regulation will give CQC the power to take action against providers who use control or restraint that is not provided in accordance with guidance and standards issued by appropriate professional and expert bodies, is unlawful, or is not necessary to prevent, or proportional to the risk posed were restraint not used.

10. This guidance will be one of the sources CQC use when assessing whether a provider is delivering safe and appropriate care, once the fundamental standards come into force. The guidance will also be used by CQC in determining what good looks like in care and treatment in CQC's new ratings system (inadequate/requires improvement/good/ outstanding) for its integrated model of inspection. Where the guidance is not implemented the CQC will consider using its regulatory powers to facilitate change and improvement in local services.

## Who is this guidance for?

11.  This guidance is of particular significance for health and social care services where individuals who are known to be at risk of being exposed to restrictive interventions are cared for. Such settings may provide services to people with mental health conditions, autistic spectrum conditions, learning disability, dementia and/or personality disorder, older people and detained patients. It is more broadly applicable across general health and social care settings where people using services may on occasion present with behaviour that challenges but which cannot reasonably be predicted and planned for on an individual basis. This may include homes where individuals employ their own support staff, and community-based primary and secondary care settings.

12.  The guidance requires that actions are taken by those with responsibility at all levels in health and social care including commissioners of services, executive directors, frontline staff and all those who care for and support people in a variety of settings. This guidance must be considered and acted on by:

- commissioners of health and social care services
- executive directors of health and social care provider organisations
- service managers, governance leads and executive quality leads in health and social care services
- staff of all disciplines and degrees of seniority working in health and social care services
- enforcement and inspection staff
- chairs (and members) of local safeguarding adults boards
- lecturers and others who deliver professional training to health and social care staff
- academic and research staff
- those who provide training in PBS, and
- those who provide training on the use restrictive interventions.

13.  The guidance will also be relevant to:

- people who use services
- family members, carers and parents of people receiving services
- independent advocates and organisations
- the police and people working in criminal justice settings
- professional regulatory bodies
- local authorities
- legal representatives, and
- security staff working in health and social care settings.

14.  This guidance applies equally to health and social care staff working in non-health settings such as police cells, immigration removal centres and prisons. It does not apply to staff from other professions including the police and people working within criminal justice settings (for whom own professional guidance will apply).

15.  It is important to note that healthcare centres in prisons come under their own rules and regulations. The control and order of people in healthcare centres, as well as prisoners in transit to an outside hospital and while they are undergoing medical treatment, which could include overnight in-patient treatment for an extended period, is the responsibility of the governor/director, or person in charge of the establishment.

## Aims of this guidance

16.  This guidance aims to:

- encourage a culture across health and social care organisations that is committed to developing therapeutic environments where physical interventions are only used as a last resort
- provide guidance on the use of effective governance arrangements and models of

restrictive intervention reduction so that lasting reductions in the use of restrictive interventions of all forms can be achieved

- help promote best practice principles across a range of health and social care settings
- ensure that restrictive interventions are used in a transparent, legal and ethical manner.

## Restrictive interventions defined

17. 'Restrictive interventions' are defined in this guidance as:

deliberate acts on the part of other person(s) that restrict an individual's movement, liberty and/or freedom to act independently in order to:

- take immediate control of a dangerous situation where there is a real possibility of harm to the person or others if no action is undertaken; and
- end or reduce significantly the danger to the person or others; and
- contain or limit the person's freedom for no longer than is necessary.

18. Judgements as to the acceptability and legitimacy of restrictive interventions will always be based on all presenting circumstances. Without a clear ethical basis and appropriate safeguards such acts may be unlawful.

19. If carried out for any other purpose than those listed above concerns about the misuse of restrictive interventions should always be escalated through local safeguarding procedures and protocols.

## Related guidance

20. A range of useful guidance documents have recently been published which focus on the care and support of people who present with behaviours that challenge. This document cross references to those sources rather than repeating their content. Together they provide useful additional guidance concerning positive and proactive ways of reducing the need for restrictive interventions as well as providing a template for their safe, ethical and lawful application when used as a last resort. Whilst some documents focus on specific settings, user groups or interventions, they are unified by a set of common principles and by the central aim of providing safe, supportive and compassionate care.

21. A synopsis of the following key documents is provided in Appendix 1.

- *NHS Protect: Meeting needs and educing distress: guidance on the prevention and management of clinically related challenging behaviour in NHS settings*[7]
- *HM Government: The Mental Health Crisis Care Concordat: improving outcomes for people experiencing mental health crisis*[8]
- *NHS England & LGA: A Core Principles Commissioning Tool*[9]
- *NICE: Clinical Guideline 25. Violence: the short-term management of disturbed/violent behaviour in in-patient psychiatric and emergency departments*[10]
- *DH: Mental Health Act Code of Practice*[11]
- *Skills for Health and Skills for Care (2014) A Positive and Proactive Workforce. A guide to workforce development for commissioners and employers seeking to minimise the use of restrictive practices in social care and heal*[12]
- *DH (In preparation) Positive and Proactive: guidance on support and care of children and young people*

## KEY PRINCIPLES UNDERPINNING THE GUIDANCE

## Six key principles

22. This guidance is based on six key principles which underpin the need to deliver positive and proactive care; there are applicable across all service settings. Rigorous governance is

needed to ensure that positive and proactive care is the main approach within services to reduce excessive reliance on restrictive interventions and to ensure that if they are used, it is only ever as a last resort, and they are undertaken in a proportionate and least restrictive way.

23. For people who lack the capacity to consent to the use of a restrictive intervention, services must balance people's right to autonomy with the right to be protected from harm. Any decision to use restrictive interventions for a person who lacks capacity, must be made in the best interests of the person within the framework of the Mental Capacity Act[14](MCA) (sections 4,5 and 6). However, the Mental Health Act 1983 applies to any mental health treatment given to a person being treated under that Act.

---

## Key principles underpinning the guidance

- Compliance with the relevant rights in the **European Convention on Human Rights**[13] at all times
- Understanding people's behaviour allows their unique needs, aspirations, experiences and strengths to be recognised and their **quality of life** to be enhanced
- **Involvement and participation** of people with care and support needs, their families, carers and advocates is essential, wherever practicable and subject to the person's wishes and confidentiality obligations
- People must be treated with **compassion**, dignity and kindness
- Health and social care services must support people to balance safety from harm and freedom of **choice**
- Positive **relationships** between the people who deliver services and the people they support must be protected and preserved

---

## A human rights based approach

24. The Human Rights Act (HRA)[15] imposes a duty on public authorities, (including NHS Trusts, Local Authorities, and police forces) and services exercising functions of a public nature not to act in a manner that is incompatible with the European Convention on Human Rights[13] (ECHR) rights that have been made part of UK law by the HRA.

25. A human rights based approach can be achieved by applying what has been described as the 'PANEL' principles.[16, 17] Table 1 shows the five 'PANEL' principles and how these might be applied when thinking about the care and support of people who present with behaviour that challenges services.

Table 1

| Key principle | What is means | What it looks like in practice |
|---|---|---|
| Participation | Enabling participation of all key people and stakeholders | Consulting with the person, staff and other stakeholders; involving the person, carers and support staff in developing risk assessments and behaviour support plans where possible; using advance statements where appropriate; identifying and reducing barriers to the person exercising their rights. |

| Key principle | What is means | What it looks like in practice |
|---|---|---|
| Accountability | Ensuring clear accountability, identifying who has legal duties and practical responsibilities for a human rights based approach | Clearly outlining responsibilities under the Mental Health Act[18] and the Mental Capacity Act[14] (where relevant); ensuring staff are aware of their obligations to respect human rights and are measuring outcomes, including quality of life, against agreed standards. |
| Non-discriminatory | Avoiding discrimination, paying attention to groups who are vulnerable to rights violations | Using person-centred planning approaches that do not discriminate on the basis of religion or belief, race or culture, gender, sexual preference, disability, mental health; making sure staff are sensitive to culture and diversity and how interventions may affect rights. |
| Empowerment | Empowering staff and people who use services with the knowledge and skills to realise rights | Raising awareness of rights for people who use services, carers and staff through education and use of accessible resources; explaining how human rights are engaged by restrictive interventions; empowering people through appropriate interventions. |
| Legality | Complying with relevant legislation including human rights obligations, particularly the Human Rights Act | Identifying the human rights implications in both the challenges a person presents and responses to those challenges; considering the principles of fairness, respect, equality, dignity and autonomy.[19] |

# THE GUIDANCE FRAMEWORK

26. People might be exposed to restrictive interventions as a response to some form of behaviour that challenges in a wide variety of different settings and situations. They include settings where people are well known and where individualised support can be planned with the aim of reducing the incidence of such behaviours. They also include other settings where it is not possible because the individual may not be known to the service. In both settings robust governance is essential to ensure appropriate practice.

## Individualised approaches

27. Some services support people whose needs and histories mean that individuals can reasonably be predicted to present with behaviours that challenge. Examples of such services might include acute psychiatric settings (including secure services), and residential units specialising in working with people with learning disabilities who present with 'challenging behaviour' or services for people who are elderly and confused who may become agitated.

28. Within such services the use of recovery-based approaches and delivery of care in accordance with the principles of positive behavioural support is essential.

## Recovery-based approaches

29. Recovery means working in partnership with people to improve their clinical and social outcomes. Originating in mental health services, recovery models are consistent with contemporary service philosophies across wider health and social care settings[20] and include the promotion of human rights based approaches, enhancing personal independence, promoting and honouring choices and increasing social inclusion.

30. These models are founded on the principle that recovery is possible for everyone. Each person can achieve a satisfying and fulfilling life, in keeping with their own preferences, goals and aims, through empowerment, self-determination and unconditional engagement within wider communities and society more generally.

31. International literature on seclusion and restraint reduction demonstrates that a recovery-focused model is essential for achieving a reduction in the use of restrictive interventions carried out against a person's wishes.[21, 22]

## Positive behavioural support

32. Positive behavioural support (PBS) provides a framework that seeks to understand the context and meaning of behaviour in order to inform the development of supportive environments and skills that can enhance a person's quality of life. Evidence has shown that PBS-based approaches can enhance quality of life and also reduce behaviours that challenge[23,24] which in turn can lead to a reduction in the use of restrictive interventions. It is founded on principles that have applicability for a much broader range of people and may use different terminology. PBS provides a conceptual framework[25] which recognises that people may engage in behaviours that are challenging because:

- they have challenging or complex needs that are not being met – these could be associated with unusual needs and personal preferences, sensory impairments, or mental or physical health conditions
- they are exposed to challenging environments in which behaviours of concern are likely to develop – examples might include environments which are barren and lack stimulation, where there are high levels of demand placed on people, where there may be institutional blanket rules, restricted or unpredictable access to preferred activities and those things the person values and where there is insufficient availability of positive social interactions, or where personal choices are not offered and/or honoured
- they typically have a generally impoverished quality of life.

33. Within PBS-based approaches these underlying difficulties are seen as the target for therapeutic intervention. The introduction of PBS or similar principles in a systematic, organisation wide context is an important mechanism by which to deliver many of the key elements associated with restrictive intervention reduction programmes[26] (see paragraphs 40-42).

34. PBS approaches comprise a number elements:

- Using **person-centred, values-based approaches** to ensure people are living the best life they possibly can. This involves assisting a person to develop personal relationships, improve their health be more active in their community and to develop personally. When done properly, person centred planning processes make sure that those who support people get to know them as individuals.
- Skilled assessment in order to **understand probable reasons why a person presents behaviours of concern**; what predicts their occurrence and what factors maintain and sustain them (this area of assessment is often referred to as a functional assessment). This requires consideration of a range of contextual factors including personal constitutional factors, mental and physical health, communication skills and the person's ability to influence the world around them. Patterns of behaviour provide important data, skilled analysis of which enables key areas of unmet need to be understood.

- The use of **behaviour support plans** which have been informed by an assessment of these factors in order to ensure that aspects of the person's environment that they find challenging are identified and addressed, that quality of life is enhanced and that wherever possible people are supported to develop alternative strategies by which they can better meet their own needs. These are referred to as **primary preventative strategies**.
- The behaviour support plan must detail the responses such as **de-escalation techniques**, distraction, diversion and sometimes disengagement to be used by carers/staff when a person starts to become anxious, aroused or distressed. These are referred to as **secondary preventative strategies** and aim to promote relaxation and avert any further escalation to a crisis.
- Behaviour support plans include guidance as to how people should react when a person's agitation further escalates to a crisis where they place either themselves or others at significant risk of harm. This may include the use of restrictive interventions. Within behaviour support plans these are as identified as **tertiary strategies**.

35. Any person who can reasonably be predicted to be at risk of being exposed to restrictive interventions must have an individualised behaviour support plan.

36. **Care programme approach care plans, personal recovery plans or other personalised approach planning structures** may also incorporate behaviour support plans. They must always include clear evidence of health and social needs assessment, and be created with input from the person, their carers, relatives or advocates. This should identify:

- the context within which behaviours of concern occur
- clear primary preventative strategies which focus on improvement of quality of life and ensuring that needs are met
- secondary preventative strategies which aim to ensure that early signs of anxiety and agitation are recognised and responded to
- tertiary strategies which may include detail of planned restrictive interventions to be used in the safest possible manner and which should only be used as an absolute last resort.

## Whole service approaches

37. In some services, people's histories and health and social care needs may not be known or well understood and therefore individual planning is not possible. Examples include mental health services that admit patients without much knowledge of their background history; an accident and emergency department where a disagreement develops; a primary healthcare setting where a patient aggressively resists an intervention; or where the police service have contact with someone who may have a mental health problem, learning disability or autism.

38. In such services a range of whole service approaches can promote therapeutic engagement, avoidance of conflict situations and the safe support of people at times of behavioural crisis. These approaches must also be considered across all services of the nature identified in paragraph 27.

39. Oppressive environments and the use of blanket restrictions such as locked doors, lack of access to outdoor space or refreshments can have a negative impact on how people behave, their care and recovery. They are inconsistent with a human rights-based approach. Providers should ensure that they abide by the Human Rights Act[15] and where possible do not have blanket restrictions in place. Where these are considered necessary, providers should have a clear policy in place and ensure that the reasons are communicated and justified to people who use services, family members and carers. Providers may be challenged to justify the use of such restrictions under the Human Rights Act[15].

## Restrictive intervention reduction programmes

40. A number of recent studies have shown that it is possible to achieve significant reductions in the use of restrictive interventions through a determined organisational commitment to changing approaches to aggression/violence management.[22,27,28] A thorough knowledge review conducted by the Irish Mental Health Commission in 2012[29] explored a range of models for restrictive intervention reduction and found nine consistent components to be necessary:

- government level support
- careful attention to policy and regulation
- involvement of people who use services, their family and advocates
- effective leadership
- training and education
- staffing changes
- using data to monitor the use of restrictive intervention
- effective review procedures and debriefing and
- judicious use of medication.

41. All services where restrictive interventions may be used must have in place **restrictive intervention reduction programmes** which can reduce the incidence of violence and aggression and ensure that less detrimental alternatives to restrictive interventions are used. Such programmes should be planned in the context of robust governance arrangements, a clear understanding of the legal context for applying restrictions and effective training and development for staff.

42. Services' restrictive intervention reduction programmes must be based on the principles of:

- providing effective leadership
- involving and empowering of people who use services, their families and advocates
- developing programmes of activities and care pathways for people using services
- using clear crisis management strategies and restrictive intervention reduction tools
- effective models of post-incident review including learning from critical incidents
- data-driven quality assurance.

## Reducing and managing conflict

43. The Safewards[30] model has demonstrated significant effectiveness in achieving reductions in incidents of conflict and the use of physical restraint, seclusion and rapid tranquillisation in acute UK mental health settings. A range of practical approaches can be used which have wide ranging influences on people's behaviour and staff responses so that flashpoints are avoided, de-escalation is more effectively achieved and alternatives to restrictive interventions are consolidated into practice. Many of these highly practical approaches could be replicated across broader service settings and all providers should consider the implications of the Safewards model to their context.

44. The Design Council[31] has recently reported on the use of design solutions and modified signage within A&E departments. They put forward a cost effective model which led to significant reductions in levels of frustration and potential triggers to violence.

45. All health and social care providers need to consider the contribution that environmental design may make to preventing conflict by better meeting people's needs at times of heightened anxiety, the negative impact of oppressive environments and blanket restrictions, and the practical implications of the Safewards model. These approaches can contribute to reducing undue reliance on restrictive interventions.

## Post-incident reviews

46. Service providers must ensure that where appropriate lessons are learned when incidents occur where restrictive interventions have had to be used.

47. The aims of post-incident reviews are to:

- evaluate the physical and emotional impact on all individuals involved (including any witnesses)
- identify if there is a need, and if so, provide counselling or support for any trauma that might have resulted
- help people who use services and staff to identify what led to the incident and what could have been done differently
- determine whether alternatives, including less restrictive interventions, were considered
- determine whether service barriers or constraints make it difficult to avoid the same course of actions in future
- where appropriate recommend changes to the service's philosophy, policies, care environment, treatment approaches, staff education and training
- where appropriate avoid a similar incident happening on another occasion.

48. Whenever a restrictive intervention has been used, staff and people should have separate opportunities to reflect on what happened. People with cognitive and/or communication impairments may need to be helped to engage in this process, for example, by the use of simplified language or visual imagery. Other people may not be able to be involved due to the nature of their impairment.

49. People who use services should not be compelled to take part in post-incident reviews. They should be told of their right to talk about the incident with an independent advocate (which may include an independent mental health advocate or independent mental capacity advocate), family member or another representative.

50. Discussions should only take place when those involved have recovered their composure. Immediate or post-incident reviews should:

- acknowledge the emotional responses to the event
- promote relaxation and feelings of safety
- facilitate a return to normal patterns of activity
- ensure that all appropriate parties have been informed of the event
- ensure that necessary documentation has been completed
- begin to consider whether there is a specific need for emotional support in response to any trauma that has been suffered.

51. Many restrictive intervention reduction models also include the use of a more in-depth review process, typically the next day, in response either to more serious incidents or a person's request. This may take the form of a facilitated staff team discussion to establish the warning signs of an impending crisis, what de-escalation strategies were used, how effective they were, and what could be done differently in future.

52. Someone who was not involved in the incident should be involved in both post-incident and in-depth reviews with people who use services. Reviews should be in a blame free context. The aim should be to understand from the person's point of view how the service failed to understand what they needed, what upset them the most, whether staff did anything that was helpful, what staff did wrong, and how things could be better the next time. It is also important to establish whether anything could be done differently to make a restrictive intervention less traumatic.

53. The care team together with the person, their families and advocates should consider whether behaviour support plans or other aspects of individual care plans need to be revised/updated in response to the post-incident review. Any organisational factors such as

the need for policy reviews, environmental modifications, staffing reviews or training needs must to be formally reported to service managers using robust governance arrangements.

## Managing unforeseen behaviour that challenges

54. The key principles within this guidance must be applied to the management of unforeseen behaviours that challenge, even in contexts where they cannot be anticipated or responses pre-planned such as accident and emergency departments or the ambulance service.

55. NHS Protect provides[7] useful guidance on understanding and responding to behaviour that challenges, whether or not it was anticipated. The Crisis Care Concordat[8] states key principles that will be relevant to many service settings (in particular A&E settings, acute mental health services and the ambulance service). In services where hospital security staff may be needed to respond to emergency situations to assist in the management of violent or aggressive incidents, they should also adhere to the provisions of the Mental Capacity Act 2005 (MCA),[14] as well as to Skills for Security good practice guidance.[32]

56. The Crisis Care Concordat also states that once a person is in a mental health setting, the MHA Code of Practice[11] requires the organisation to make sure staff are properly trained in the restraint of patients. There should be a clear local protocol about the circumstances when, very exceptionally, police may be called to manage patient behaviour within a health or care setting. Health staff should be alert to the risk of any respiratory or cardiac distress and continue to monitor the patient's physical and psychological wellbeing. Further guidance for the police is available in the Association of Chief Police Officers and National Policing Improvement Agency's *Guidance on Responding to People with Mental Ill Health or Learning Disabilities*[33]. The National Police College is working on improving this guidance and the training that police officers receive as their response to the national Crisis Care Concordat.

57. The provisions of the Mental Health Act 1983 (MHA)[18] will only very rarely authorise the application of restrictive interventions in community-based health and social care services and non-mental health hospital settings. The MCA[14] will, if certain conditions are met, provide legal protection for acts performed in the care or treatment of people who lack the capacity to consent to the care or treatment (see paras 93-97). The MCA will be particularly relevant when staff in general hospitals are considering the use of restrictive interventions to protect the person. If the MHA and/or MCA do not apply, the use of force is only justified legally for the purposes of self-defence, the defence of others, prevention of crime, lawful arrest or to protect property and the same statutory and common law provisions apply within health and care services as elsewhere.

## The safe and ethical use of all forms of restrictive interventions

58. The legal and ethical basis for organisations to allow their staff to use restrictive interventions as a last resort is founded on eight overarching principles.

- Restrictive interventions should never be used to punish or for the sole intention of inflicting pain, suffering or humiliation.
- There must be a real possibility of harm to the person or to staff, the public or others if no action is undertaken.
- The nature of techniques used to restrict must be proportionate to the risk of harm and the seriousness of that harm.
- Any action taken to restrict a person's freedom of movement must be the least restrictive option that will meet the need.
- Any restriction should be imposed for no longer than absolutely necessary.
- What is done to people, why and with what consequences must be subject to audit and monitoring and must be open and transparent.

> ■ Restrictive interventions should only ever be used as a last resort.
> ■ People who use services, carers and advocate involvement is essential when reviewing plans for restrictive interventions.

59. If organisations and staff impose restrictive interventions on those in their care they must have a lawful basis for doing so. The law in respect of issues relevant to restrictive interventions, and the degree of restriction that might amount to an unlawful deprivation of liberty, continues to evolve and services should review and update their local policies on an on-going basis in light of legal developments.

60. There is considerable concern and controversy surrounding potential harm to individuals caused by restrictive interventions. In some instances they have caused serious physical and psychological trauma, and even death[34].

61. All restrictive interventions can pose risks. Transparent policies and appropriate governance structures must be established against a context of positive and proactive working and within care pathways which provide behaviour support plans. The risks vary from intervention to intervention; it is important that those who use restrictive interventions understand the risks associated with each intervention. In many instances a rigorous practice of identifying and assessing risks can be an effective safeguard to minimise risks.

62. Effective governance strategies must ensure that there is transparency around the use of restrictive interventions. Wherever possible people should be engaged in all aspects of planning their care including how crisis situations should be responded to. People should be involved in post-incident debriefings, and there should be rigorous reporting arrangements for staff and collation of data regarding the use of restrictive interventions.

63. Restrictive interventions are being used which may amount to assault or battery (if the person has mental capacity to refuse what is proposed), wilful neglect or ill treatment of people lacking mental capacity (an offence under section 44 of the MCA[14]) or unlawful deprivations of liberty.

64. When confronted with acute behavioural disturbance, the choice of restrictive intervention must always represent the least restrictive option to meet the immediate need. It should always be informed by the person's preference (if known), any particular risks associated with their general health and an appraisal of the immediate environment. Individual risk factors which suggest a person is at increased risk of physical and/ or emotional trauma must be taken into account when applying restrictive interventions. For example, this would include recognising that for a person with a history of traumatic sexual/physical abuse, any physical contact may carry an additional risk of causing added emotional trauma. Or for a person known to have muscular-skeletal problems such as a curvature of the spine, some positions may carry a risk of injury.

65. Where there is a known likelihood that restrictive interventions might need to be used, they should, so far as possible be planned in advance and recorded in a behaviour support plan (or equivalent), which includes primary and secondary preventative strategies.

66. Restrictive interventions, as defined in this guidance, can take a number of forms. These are detailed below.

## PHYSICAL RESTRAINT

67. Physical restraint refers to: *'any direct physical contact where the intervener's intention is to prevent, restrict, or subdue movement of the body, or part of the body of another person.'*

68. A member of staff should take responsibility for communicating with the person throughout any period of restraint in order to continually attempt to de-escalate the situation.

69. Staff must not cause deliberate pain to a person in an attempt to force compliance with their instructions. Where there is an immediate risk to life, in accordance with NICE guidelines[10], recognised techniques that cause pain as a stimulus may be used as an intervention to mitigate that risk. These techniques must be used proportionately and only in the most exceptional circumstances and never for longer than is necessary to mitigate that immediate risk to life. These techniques should only be used by trained staff having due regard for the safety and dignity of patients. The use of these techniques must be embedded in local policies.

70. People must not be deliberately restrained in a way that impacts on their airway, breathing or circulation The mouth and/or nose must never be covered and techniques should not incur pressure to the neck region, rib cage and/or abdomen. There must be no planned or intentional restraint of a person in a prone/face down position on any surface, not just the floor.

71. This will best be achieved through the adoption and sustained implementation of restrictive practice reduction programmes and the delivery of care pathways that incorporate PBS.

72. If exceptionally a person is restrained unintentionally in a prone/face down position, staff should either release their holds or reposition into a safer alternative as soon as possible.

73. Where unplanned or unintentional incidents of any restrictive practice occur there should always be recording and debrief to ensure learning and continuous safety improvements.

74. Staff must not deliberately use techniques where a person is allowed to fall, unsupported, other than where there is a need to escape from a life-threatening situation.

75. Staff must not use physical restraint or breakaway techniques that involve the use of pain, including holds where movement by the individual induces pain, other than for the purpose of an immediate rescue in a life-threatening situation.

76. In all circumstances where restraint is used one of the support staff must monitor the person's airway and physical condition throughout the restraint to minimise the potential of harm or injury. Observations that include vital clinical indicators such as pulse, respiration and complexion (with special attention to pallor or discolouration) must be carried out and recorded, and staff should be trained so that they are competent to interpret these vital signs. If the person's physical condition and/ or their expressions of distress give rise to concern, the restraint must stop immediately.

77. Support staff must continue to monitor the individual for signs of emotional or physical distress for a significant period of time following the application of restraint.

## MECHANICAL RESTRAINT

78. Mechanical restraint refers to: '*the use of a device to prevent, restrict or subdue movement of a person's body, or part of the body, for the primary purpose of behavioural control*'.

79. Mechanical restraints should never be a first line means of managing disturbed behaviour. The use of mechanical restraint to manage extreme violence directed towards others should be exceptional, and seldom used in this or other contexts outside of high secure settings.

80. It is recognised that following rigorous assessment there may be exceptional circumstances where mechanical restraints need to be used to limit self-injurious behaviour of extremely high frequency and intensity[35]. This contingency is most notably encountered with small numbers of people who have severe cognitive impairments, where devices such as arm splints or cushioned helmets may be required to safeguard a person from the hazardous consequences of their behaviour. Wherever mechanical restraint is used as a planned

contingency it must be identified within a broad ranging, robust behaviour support plan which aims to bring about the circumstances where continued use of mechanical restraint will no longer be required.

81. There may be occasions when the use of restraint (including handcuffs) is needed for security purposes, for example when transferring prisoners into a healthcare setting. Guidance for prison and NHS staff to develop local procedures was agreed in a concordat[36] between the National Offender Management Service (NOMS) and the NHS Counter Fraud and Security Service (now NHS Protect), which forms part of the National Security Framework. Further guidance of transferring prisoners into a secure mental health setting is provided in the Mental Health Act 1983 Code of Practice.[11]

82. There may be occasions where restraint (including handcuffs) is used for security purposes for transferring restricted patients in secure settings to non-secure settings. The use of restraint in these circumstances should form part of individual risk assessments to take account of dignity and respect and the physical and mental condition of the individual.

83. Medical staff have the right to request the removal of restraints while treatment is carried out. On occasion, in high risk cases, the Secretary of State for Justice will make permission for a restricted patient to leave the hospital conditional on the use of restraint. Hospital staff should discuss any concerns about this with mental health casework section.

## CHEMICAL RESTRAINT

84. Chemical restraint refers to: '*The use of medication which is prescribed, and administered for the purpose of controlling or subduing disturbed/violent behaviour, where it is not prescribed for the treatment of a formally identified physical or mental illness*'.

85. Chemical restraint should be used only for a person who is highly aroused, agitated, overactive, aggressive, is making serious threats or gestures towards others, or is being destructive to their surroundings, when other therapeutic interventions have failed to contain the behaviour. Chemical restraint should only ever be delivered in accordance with acknowledged, evidence-based best practice guidelines.[10,37,38] Prescribers should provide information to those who provide care and support regarding of any physical monitoring that may be required as well as the medication to be used and the route of medication.

86. The use of medication to manage acutely disturbed behaviour must be a very short-term strategy designed solely to reduce immediate risk; this is distinct from treating any underlying mental illness. The associated term 'rapid tranquillisation' refers to intramuscular injections and oral medication. Oral medication should always be considered first. Where rapid tranquillisation in the form of an intramuscular injection is required, the prescriber should indicate the preferred injection site having taken full account of the need to avoid face down restraint.

## SECLUSION

87. Seclusion refers to: '*The supervised confinement and isolation of a person, away from other users of services, in an area from which the person is prevented from leaving. Its sole aim is the containment of severely disturbed behavior which is likely to cause harm to others.*'

88. Only people detained under the MHA[18] should be considered for seclusion. If an emergency situation arises involving an informal patient and, as a last resort, seclusion is necessary to protect others from risk of injury or harm, then it should be used for the shortest possible period to manage the emergency situation and an assessment for detention under the MHA should be undertaken immediately. The MHA Code of Practice[11] lays down clear procedures for the use of seclusion including its initiation, ongoing implementation and review and termination.

89.  The seclusion of a person under the MHA in a community setting (for whom neither a Deprivation of Liberty authorisation nor a Court of Protection order under the MCA to authorise the deprivation of their liberty is in place) is also likely to amount to an unlawful deprivation of liberty. If the circumstances of a person's care resemble seclusion, it is seclusion whatever it is called locally. An assessment should be undertaken promptly to determine whether the person should be detained under the MHA immediately.

### LONG-TERM SEGREGATION

90.  Long-term segregation refers to a situation where a person is prevented from mixing freely with other people who use a service. This form of restrictive intervention should rarely be used and only ever for hospital patients who present an almost continuous risk of serious harm to others and for whom it is agreed that they benefit from a period of intensive care and support in a discrete area that minimises their contact with other users of the service.

91.  Long-term segregation must never take place outside of hospital settings and should never be used with people who are not detained under the MHA. As such it must only ever be undertaken in conjunction with the safeguards for its use in the MHA Code of Practice.[11] The does not apply to the segregation of prisoners within prison establishments.

## Where restrictive interventions are not enough

92.  NHS Protect guidance[7] indicates trigger points for the need to seek further assistance from the police service. If the police are called upon to help manage a dangerous situation they will use techniques and act in accordance with their professional training. Care and support staff have a continuing responsibility to alert police officers to any specific risks or health problems that the person may have as well as to monitor the person's physical and emotional wellbeing and alert police officers to any specific concerns.

## The lawful use of restrictive interventions in respect of people who lack capacity

93.  The MCA[14] presumes that all persons 16 and over have the ability to make their own decisions and protects their right to make and act on their own free and informed decisions. It also provides important safeguards where people lack the capacity to make their own decision. The five principles of the MCA are shown below.

---

### Five statutory principles of the Mental Capacity Act

1.  A person must be assumed to have capacity unless it is proved otherwise.
2.  A person must not be treated as unable to make a decision unless all practicable steps to help have been taken without success.
3.  A person is not to be treated as unable to make a decision merely because an unwise decision is made.
4.  An act done, or decision made under the Act for, or on behalf of a person who lacks capacity, must be done in their best interests.
5.  Before an act is done, or a decision made, consideration must be given to whether the same outcome can be achieved in a less restrictive way.

---

94.  Staff should seek a person's consent if they are proposing to act in connection with the care or treatment of that person. This means that staff must explain any proposed procedure in an accessible and easily understandable way to enable a person to make their own decisions. They should support the person to ask questions and to weigh up information relevant to the decision to be made.

95. If the person is unable to make the decision within the meaning of section 3 of the MCA, staff should carry out a formal assessment of the person's capacity in relation to the proposed specific intervention. Chapter 5 of the MCA Code of Practice[39] provides guidance on how to assess capacity. If the person is found to lack capacity within the meaning of section 2 of the MCA,[14] then a decision about their care and treatment may need to be made on their behalf, in their best interests.

96. The person who does the act should follow section 4 of the MCA and the guidance outlined in chapter 5 of the MCA Code of Practice[39] in determining what is in the person's best interests. The person making the decision will need to:

- consider all relevant circumstances
- consider whether the decision can be delayed until the person regains capacity
- involve the person as fully as possible in making the decision and any act done for them
- consider the person's past and present wishes and feelings
- consider any advance decisions to refuse treatment or statements made about how they should be cared for and supported (including identifying whether the person has a donee of Lasting Power of Attorney or a deputy with the legal authority to make decisions)
- consider the person's beliefs and values that would be likely to influence their decision if they had capacity
- consult the person's family and informal carers
- take account of the views of an independent mental capacity advocate or other key people (such as family members and those who usually provide care and support)
- consider whether it is the least restrictive option, in terms of the person's rights and freedoms, by which to meet the person's need.

97. Section 5 of the MCA[14] (subject to the limits in section 6) will provide legal protection from liability (except for negligence) for acts that involve restrictive interventions if:

- the person applying the intervention has taken reasonable steps to establish that the person lacks capacity to consent to the intervention, and reasonably believes the person lacks capacity at the time it is applied and that it is in the person's best interests
- the person applying the restrictive intervention reasonably believes that it is necessary in order to prevent harm to the person, not others. Interventions for the protection of others would need to be justified by reference to other statutory or common law powers or defences; and
- any use, or threat of force, to implement a restrictive intervention which the person is resisting, or which restricts the person's liberty of movement, whether or not the person resists, is a proportionate response to:
  - the likelihood of the person suffering harm, and
  - the seriousness of that harm.

98. Sections 5 and 6 permit restrictions on liberty in the circumstances outlined above, but do not authorise acts that deprive a person of their liberty. Whether or not an act amounts to a deprivation, rather than a restriction, of liberty depends on the circumstances of the individual case. Factors which may amount to a deprivation of liberty in the circumstances of individual cases include:

- staff having complete control over a person's care or movements for a long period of time
- staff making all decisions about a person, including choices about assessments, treatment and visitors and controlling where they can go and when
- staff refusing to allow a patient to leave, for example, to live with a carer or family member
- staff restricting a person's access to their friends or family.

99. There will be a deprivation of liberty if a person is under continuous supervision and control and is not free to leave, and the person lacks capacity to consent to these arrangements. If a deprivation of liberty is necessary, it can only be authorised by a procedure set out in law, which enables the lawfulness of that deprivation of liberty to be reviewed. Legal authority to deprive the person of their liberty may be obtained under the Deprivation of Liberty Safeguards (DoLS)[40] in the MCA[14] or the MHA[18]. Each regime provides a procedure to authorise deprivation of liberty.

100. The DoLS were incorporated in the MCA[14] to ensure that there is a procedure for authorising deprivation of liberty in hospitals and care homes for adults who lack capacity to consent to admission or treatment for mental disorder. The Court of Protection can authorise deprivation of liberty in other settings. Detailed guidance on DoLS procedures can be found within the Deprivation of Liberty Safeguards Code of Practice[40].

101. Where the person is unable to consent and it is not clear restrictive interventions are in the person's best interest, consideration should be given to approaching the Court of Protection for a best interests decision as to the appropriateness of the proposed intervention.

102. The key safeguards afforded to people deprived of their liberty under the MCA are:

- the right to a representative and/or a independent mental capacity advocate
- the right to challenge a deprivation of liberty
- mechanisms for the deprivation of liberty to be reviewed.

103. The MHA[18] authorises deprivation of liberty if the person meets the criteria for being detained for the purpose of assessment and/or treatment for mental disorder, even in the absence of their consent. Guidance is given on the delivery of safe and therapeutic care and safeguards around the use of restrictive interventions in chapter 15 of the MHA Code of Practice[11].

104. Statutory or common law defences may apply, in the rare circumstances where, neither the MCA[14] nor MHA[18] apply. Reasonable force may be used for the purposes of self-defence, the defence of others, prevention of crime, lawful arrest or to protect property. In order to be 'reasonable', the force involved should be necessary and proportionate in the specific circumstances. Force should only be used as a last resort. These justifications and defences should not be relied on for the recurrent, long-term, and/or planned use of restrictive physical interventions in respect of an individual.

## Good governance

### CORPORATE ACCOUNTABILITY

105. In response to *Transforming Care: a national response to Winterbourne View Hospital*[1] and the *Report of the Mid Staffordshire NHS Foundation Trust Public Inquiry*[41] the CQC has developed a robust system of registration, regulation and inspection which allows corporate and NHS boards to be held to account for failings in care. In extreme circumstances, the CQC will prosecute providers without issuing prior warning notices.

106. During service visits and routine reviews (including regulatory inspections of service quality), the CQC will seek to assure themselves that people who are exposed to restrictive interventions have access to high quality behaviour support plans, designed, implemented and reviewed by staff with the necessary skills and that restrictive interventions are undertaken lawfully.

### PROTECTING EMPLOYEES AND OTHERS IN THE WORKING ENVIRONMENT

107. The use of physical interventions is hazardous and places both staff and people who use services at risk of physical or emotional harm. The Health and Safety at Work Act 1974[42]

(HSWA) places a duty on employers to ensure, so far as is reasonably practicable, that the health, safety and welfare at work of their employees and the health and safety of others who may be affected by the employer's undertaking is safeguarded. Within this Act, and other more specific health and safety legislation, there are requirements that employers need to comply with to protect employees and others. Employers need to:

- Assess the risks to employees and others (including reasonably foreseeable violence), decide on the significance of these risks, how the risks can be prevented or controlled and implement these arrangements to reduce the risks[43].
- Provide adequate information, instruction, training and supervision to ensure the health and safety of the employees. This would include the risks that arise from both violence and aggression, as well as those linked to the use of restrictive interventions and restraint[43].
- Monitor and review the arrangements implemented to reduce the risks to ensure they are effective[43].
- Establish transparent processes to ensure that both the hazardous nature of any foreseeable violence and aggression in the workplace, and of any restrictive interventions that are permitted are acknowledged.

## Key approaches to reducing harm

108.  Key approaches include the following.

- Services must have restrictive intervention reduction programmes based on the principles of effective leadership, data informed practice, workforce development, the use of specific restrictive intervention reduction tools, service user empowerment and a commitment to effective models of post incident review.
- Restrictive intervention reduction programmes must be reviewed on an ongoing basis. As a minimum there must be evidence of at least an annual, full, evidence-based review of control measures leading to revision and update of corporate action plans.

    –    All restrictive intervention reduction programmes and evidence of associated reviews must be made available for inspection by the regulators: CQC and Monitor.

- Where services are delivered to people who are known to present behaviours that challenge, care must be delivered in accordance with the principles of PBS.
- Any service user with a behaviour support plan advocating the use of restrictive interventions should have clear proactive strategies including details of primary and secondary preventative strategies.
- There must be assurance mechanisms which routinely examine the quality of training provided to staff about positive behavioural support, de-escalation and the use of restrictive interventions.
- There must be arrangements for staff with differing degrees of specialism and seniority to maintain the competence associated with their role (i.e. the competencies required to deliver an effective behaviour support plan are qualitatively and quantitatively different than those required by a specialist practitioner who undertakes complex assessments and devises behaviour support plans).
- Service providers must acknowledge and seek to minimise the risks associated with any restrictive interventions taught to staff. Training providers should issue care providers with specific risk profiles for each technique taught.
- There must be details of how board level (or equivalent) authorisation and approval of any restrictive interventions taught to their staff and used in practice.
- Services must maintain accurate information that allows them to readily identify which service users have behaviour support plans that include the use of restrictive interventions as tertiary strategies.

109. Effective governance frameworks are founded on transparency and accountability. Accordingly, all services where restrictive interventions are used must:

■ Have an identified executive director or equivalent who takes a lead responsibility for restrictive intervention reduction programmes. People who use services and families should be informed who this is.
■ Demonstrate a process of board level (or equivalent) reviews of restrictive intervention reduction programmes.
■ Report on progress with restrictive intervention reduction programmes to commissioners of services.
■ Reviews of the quality of design and application of all positive behaviour support plans should be included within a service provider's internal audit and should inform organisational increased behaviour support planning and restrictive intervention reduction strategies.

## Recording and reporting

110. Services must comply with all expected data requirements, including recording and reporting on restraint in the National Reporting Learning Set (NRLS) and for mental health and learning disability providers the requirements in the National Mental Health Minimum Data Set (NMHMDS). NHS England will provide further guidance on NRLS reporting for all NHS-funded care.

111. Services must also publish a public, annually updated, accessible report on their increased behaviour support planning and restrictive intervention reduction, which outlines the training strategy, techniques used (how often) and reasons why, whether any significant injuries resulted, and details of ongoing strategies for bringing about reductions in the use of restrictive interventions. These should be included within annual quality accounts (or equivalent publications).

112. Clear and accurate recording of the use of restrictive interventions is needed to evaluate services' progress against their increase positive behaviour support planning and restrictive intervention reduction programmes. If restrictive interventions are to be used as a last resort, then senior managers must understand the extent of their application and this needs to be founded on accurate and transparent data:

■ Services must monitor the incidence of the restrictive interventions defined in this guidance.
■ If CQC inspectors find restraint used and not recorded or reported this will be construed as indicative of poor quality of practice.
■ Any person with a behaviour support plan advocating the use of restrictive interventions should have clear proactive strategies including details of primary and secondary preventative strategies.
■ Following any occasion where a restrictive intervention is used, whether planned or unplanned, a full record should be made. This should be recorded as soon as practicable (and always within 24 hours of the incident). The record should allow aggregated data to be reviewed and should indicate:
    – the names of the staff and people involved
    – the reason for using the specific type of restrictive intervention (rather than an alternative less restrictive strategy)
    – the type of intervention employed
    – the date and the duration of the intervention
    – whether the person or anyone else experienced injury or distress
    – what action was taken.

113. To help protect the interests of people with whom restrictive interventions are used, it is good practice to involve the person and, wherever possible, family carers, advocates and

other relevant representatives (e.g. the attorney or deputy for a person who lacks capacity) in planning, monitoring and reviewing how and when they are used. This includes ensuring all reasonable adjustments and that documentation is a format the individual understands. If a person is not involved this should be fully documented and justified.

## Local policy frameworks

114.  Organisations that provide care and support to people who are at risk of being exposed to restrictive interventions must have clear organisational policies which reflect professional or clinical guidance, current legislation, case law and evidence of best practice.

115.  Policies should outline the organisational approach to restrictive intervention reduction, including training strategies. Arrangements for the provision of high quality behaviour support plans for people who are likely to present behaviours that may require the use of restrictive interventions must be included. Employers and managers are responsible for ensuring that staff receive training, including updates and refresher courses, appropriate to their role and responsibilities within the service.

116.  All policies must be co-produced with people who use services and carers. They must include guidance to employees on the safe use of restrictive interventions as a demonstrable last resort, either as part of a behaviour support plan or as an emergency measure where behaviours cannot be predicted. There must be guidance on how the hazards associated with restrictive interventions will be minimised, for example, first aid procedures in the event of an injury or distress arising as a result of physical restraint.

117.  Clear recording and reporting arrangements should be explicit along with the mechanism by which this data will inform the on-going review of a restrictive intervention reduction programme.

118.  The policy should explain how people who use services, their carers, families and advocates participate in planning, monitoring and reviewing the use of restrictive interventions and in determining the effectiveness of restrictive intervention reduction programmes. This will include providing accessible updates and publishing key data within quality accounts (or equivalent report).

## Staff training and development

119.  Education and training are central to promoting and supporting change. Staff who may be required to use restrictive interventions must have specialised training. Detailed guidance on staff development and training has been published jointly by Skills for Health and Skills for Care.[12] Corporate training strategies need to be explicit regarding learning outcomes relating to:

■ the experience of people who use services
■ trauma informed care
■ core skills in building therapeutic relationships
■ the principles of positive behavioural support
■ legal and ethical issues
■ risks associated with restrictive interventions
■ staff thoughts and feelings on being exposed to disturbed behaviour
■ the use of safety planning tools and advance decisions
■ alternatives to restrictive interventions
■ effective use of de-escalation techniques
■ the risks associated with restrictive interventions and how these risks can be minimised
■ the use of breakaway techniques by which to disengage from grabs and holds
■ safe implementation of restrictive physical interventions; and
■ post-incident debriefing and support for staff and people who use services.

120.  In accordance with the recommendations of Skills for Care and Skills for Health[12]:

- anyone who may carry out a restrictive intervention or provide training in this area should have completed training in the MCA; and
- learning about a human rights-based, positive and proactive, non-aversive approach must precede any training on application of restrictive interventions.

121. Workforce development must include people who use services and experts by experience to increase awareness of what it feels like to be subject to restrictive interventions.

122. It is highly unlikely that a single training option will fit all health and care settings. NICE guidelines[10] identify potential core components of training in the use of physical interventions, although this guidance is aimed only at psychiatric in-patient services and emergency departments. The forthcoming NICE guidance will explore the evidence base relating to a far broader range of settings.

123. The precise nature and extent of restrictive intervention techniques, as well as the frequency of refresher training will depend upon the characteristics of the people who may require a physical intervention, the behaviours they present, the settings in which they are cared for, and the responsibilities of individual members of staff. As a minimum, staff should receive annual refresher training or professional development in accordance with Skills for Care and Skills for Health recommendations.[12]

124. Frontline staff who are often in the position to decide whether or not to use restrictive interventions, should be the focus of training initiatives[35]. Executive board members who authorise the use of restrictive interventions in their organisations should also undertake appropriate training in the use of PBS and physical interventions to ensure they are fully aware of the techniques their staff are being trained in.

125. Boards need to ensure that training and workforce development reflects the therapeutic nature and purpose of health and care settings and ensure that it has been appropriately developed for use in health and social care settings by health and social care staff rather than for other purposes (e.g. security). For specialist services it should be tailored to meet the needs of particular people (e.g. for those with a learning disability, autism or dementia).

126. Staff should only use methods of restrictive intervention for which they have received and passed professional development and/or training. Training records must record precisely the techniques that a member of staff has been trained to use.

127. There are no universally accepted standards for the use of physical restraint although both the British Institute of Learning Disabilities (BILD)[44] and the Institute of Conflict Management (ICM)[45] offer voluntary quality accreditation schemes. Over the last decade BILD have produced a range of publications and materials in relation to positive behavioural support and physical interventions.

## Responsible commissioning

128. All NHS and local authority commissioners, especially those who fund placements for people who are known to present with behaviours that challenge or regularly experience crisis situations where the risk of using restrictive interventions is increased, must assure themselves that the service has the necessary competencies to provide effective support and is pursuing a policy of reducing restrictive interventions. This must include ensuring that people have access to the specialist skills needed to develop effective behaviour support plans, including specialist skills to support individuals with particular needs. In the case of learning disability services, the Challenging Behaviour National Strategy Group has produced a range of publications to help commissioners know what is required[46].

129. Health and social care service commissioners must:

- Not place people in services which use restrictive interventions unless these services have robust, regularly reviewed, organisational restrictive intervention reduction programmes.

- Ensure that placements are only made and sustained on the basis of a full understanding of a person's needs and any associated risks.
- Ensure through their review processes that commissioned services continue to meet the needs of individuals, their families and carers. This must include a review of all data regarding the application of restrictive interventions.
- Where it is known that people present with behaviours that challenge, special attention should be paid to services' ability to deliver PBS.
- Assure themselves that there are satisfactory arrangements within any commissioned services to maintain appropriate knowledge and skills across the workforce.
- Assure themselves that commissioned services have mechanisms in place to ensure that physical interventions are delivered in as safe a manner as possible.
- Take concerted and timely action as part of contract compliance where this is not the case.

## SUMMARY OF ACTIONS

130. Across the full range of health and social care services delivered or commissioned by the NHS or local authorities in England, people who present with behaviour that challenges are at higher risk of being subjected to restrictive interventions. Many restrictive interventions place people who use services, and to a lesser degree, staff and those who provide support, at risk of physical and/or emotional harm.

---

131. The following actions will ensure that people's quality of life is enhanced and that their needs are better met which will reduce the need for restrictive interventions, and that staff and those who provide support are protected.

- All services where restrictive interventions are used must have an identified **board level**, or equivalent, **lead** for increasing positive behaviour support planning and reducing restrictive interventions.
- All services where restrictive interventions may be used should have **restrictive intervention reduction programmes** in place. Such programmes must be based on the principles of effective leadership, data informed practice, workforce development, the use of specific restrictive intervention reduction tools, service user empowerment and a commitment to effective models of post incident review.
- In those services where people can reasonably be predicted to be at risk of being exposed to restrictive interventions, individualised support plans must incorporate the key elements of **behaviour support plans**. This will include how needs will be met and environments structured to reduce the incidents of behaviours of concern. They must also detail how early warning signs of behaviour escalation can be recognised and responded to together with plans for the safe application of restrictive interventions if a crisis develops.
- Plans for the use of restrictive interventions **must not include the physical restraint of people in a way that impacts on their airways, breathing or circulation**, such as face down restraint.
- Plans for the use of physical or mechanical restraint **must not include the deliberate application of pain** in an attempt to force compliance with instructions. Painful holds or stimuli cannot be justified unless there is an immediate threat to life.
- Where behaviour support plans, or equivalents which incorporate the key components, are used, reviews of their quality of design and application should be included within a service provider's **internal audit** programmes.

- Appropriate governance structures and **transparent policies** around the use of restrictive interventions must be established within a context of positive and proactive working.
- The choice of any restrictive intervention that has to be used must always represent the **least restrictive option** to meet the immediate need.
- Wherever possible, people who use services, family carers, advocates and other relevant representatives should be **engaged in all aspects** of planning their care including how to respond to crisis situations, post-incident debriefings, rigorous reporting arrangements for staff and collation of data regarding the use of restrictive interventions.
- Provider organisations must use a process whereby there is **board level (or equivalent) authorisation** and approval of the restrictive interventions taught to their staff and used in practice.
- Organisations that provide care and support to people who are at risk of being exposed to restrictive interventions **must have clear organisational policies** which reflect current legislation, case law and evidence of best practice. Accessible versions of the policies should be available to those who use the services.
- Services must publish a **public, annually updated, accessible report on the use of restrictive interventions** which outlines the training strategy, techniques used (how often) and reasons why, whether any significant injuries resulted, and details of ongoing strategies for bringing about reductions in the use of restrictive interventions.
- Service **commissioners** must be informed about restrictive interventions used for those for whom they have responsibility.
- There must be **clear and accurate recording** of the use of restrictive interventions to evaluate services' progress against their restrictive intervention reduction programmes.
- Service providers must ensure that **post-incident reviews and debriefs** are planned so that lessons are learned when incidents occur where restrictive interventions have had to be used.
- All staff who may be required to use restrictive interventions must have **high quality, specialised training**.
- Service commissioners must assure themselves that the **service has the necessary competencies** to provide effective support for the people they are funding.

## REFERENCES

1    Department of Health (2012) Transforming care: A National response to Winterbourne View hospital London: DH
2    Mind (2012) Mental health crisis care: physical restraint in crisis London: Mind
3    HM Government (2014) *Closing the Gap: essential priorities for change in mental health*: London: TSO
4    Department of Health (2002) *Guidance for restrictive physical interventions: How to provide safe services for people with learning disabilities and autistic spectrum conditions* London: DH
5    United Nations (1989) *Convention on the Rights of the Child.*
6    Health and Social Care Act 2008 (Regulated Activities) Regulations 2010 London: HMSO
7    NHS Protect (2013) *Meeting Needs and Reducing Distress – Guidance on the prevention and management of clinically related challenging behaviour in NHS Settings* London: DH
8    HM Government (2014) *The Mental Health Crisis Care Concordat: improving outcomes for people experiencing mental health crisis.* London: TSO
9    NHS England & Local Government Association (2014) *Ensuring quality services. Core Principles Commissioning Tool for the development of Local Specifications for services supporting Children, Young People, Adults and Older People with Learning Disabilities and/or Autism who Display or are at Risk of Displaying Behaviour that Challenges* London: NHS England & LGA
10   NICE (2005) *Violence: The short-term management of disturbed/violent behaviour in in-patient psychiatric settings and emergency departments* London: NICE

11    DH (2008) *Code of Practice, Mental Health Act 1983* London: TSO
12    Skills for Care & Skills for Health (2014) *A Positive and Proactive Workforce. A guide to workforce development for commissioners and employers seeking to minimise the use of restrictive practices in social care and health* London: SfH/SfC
13    Council of Europe (1950) *The European Convention of Human Rights*
14    *Mental Capacity Act 2005* London: HMSO
15    *Human Rights Act 1998* HMSO
16    Scottish Human Rights Commission (2009) *Human Rights in a Health Care Setting: Making it Work – An Evaluation of a human rights-based approach at The State Hospital.* Glasgow: SHRC.
17    British Institute of Human Rights. (2013). *The Difference it Makes: Putting Human Rights at the Heart of Health and Social Care.* www.bihr.org.uk. [Accessed 25 January 2014].
18    *Mental Health Act 1984* London: HMSO
19    Curtice, M.J. and Exworthy, T. (2010) FREDA: a human rights-based approach to healthcare. *The Psychiatrist* 34(4): 150-156.
20    South London and Maudsley NHS Foundation Trust and South West London and St George's Mental Health NHS Trust (2010) *Recovery is for All. Hope, Agency and Opportunity in Psychiatry. A Position Statement by Consultant Psychiatrists.* London: SLAM/SWLSTG
21    Smith, G.M., Davis, R.H., Bixler, E.O., Lin, H.M., Altenor, A., Altenor, R.J., Hardenstine, B.D. and Kopchick, G.A. (2005) Pennsylvania State Hospital system's seclusion and restraint reduction program *Psychiatric Services* 56: 1115-1122
22    Huckshorn, K.A. (2004) *Reducing the use of seclusion and restraint@ A national initiative for culture change and transformation* Lincoln, Nebraska: Roman Hruska Law Centre
23    Carr, E.G., Horner, R.H., Turnball, A.P., McLaughlin, D.M., McAtee, M.L., Smith, C.E., Ryan, K., Ruef, M., Doolabh, A. and Braddoch, D. (1999). *Positive behaviour support for people with developmental disabilities: A research synthesis.* American Association of Mental Retardation: Washington, DC.
24    Allen, D., Kaye, N., Horwood, S., Gray, D., Mines, S. (2012) The impact of a whole-organisation approach to positive behavioural support on the use of physical interventions *International Journal of Positive Behavioural Support* 2(1): 26-30
25    McGill, P. (1993) Challenging behaviour, challenging environments and challenging needs. *Clinical Psychology Forum*, 56, 14-18
26    Allen, D. (2011) *Reducing the use of restrictive practices with people who have intellectual disabilities* Kidderminster: British Institute of Learning Disabilities
27    Smith, G.M., Davis, R.H., Bixler, E.O., Lin, H.M., Altenor, A., Altenor, R.J., Hardenstine, B.D. and Kopchick, G.A. (2005) Pennsylvania State Hospital system's seclusion and restraint reduction program *Psychiatric Services* 56: 1115-1122
28    Ashcroft, L., Bloss, M., Anthony, W.A. (2012) Best practices: The development and implementation of 'no force first' as a best practice. *Psychiatric Services* 63(5) 415-417
29    Mental Health Commission (2012) *Seclusion and Physical Restraint Reduction* Dublin: MHC
30    Bowers, L. (2014) *Safewards: a new model of conflict and containment on psychiatric wards* London: Institute of Psychiatry
31    Design Council and Department of Health (2011) *Reducing violence and aggression in A&E* London: Design Council
32    Skills for Security (2010) *Physical Intervention: reducing risk. A guide to good practice for employers of security personnel operating in healthcare settings.* Worcester: Skills for Security
33    Association of Chief Police Officers and National Policing Improvement Agency (2010) *Guidance on Responding to People with Mental Ill Health or Learning Disabilities* London: ACPO/NPIA
34    McVilly (2008) *Physical restraint in disability services: current practices; contemporary concerns and future directions* Victoria, Australia: Department of Human Services
35    Schreiner, G. M., Crafton, C. G. and Sevin, J. A. (2004) Decreasing the use of mechanical restraints and locked seclusion *Administration and Policy in Mental Health* 31: 449– 463
36    Ministry of Justice National Offender Management Service (2010) *Concordat between the National Offender management Service & NHS Counter Fraud and Security Management Service. Prisoner Escort and Bedwatch Function* London: MoJ
37    Taylor, D., Paton, C., Kapur, S. (2012) *The Maudsley Prescribing Guidelines in Psychiatry* London: Wiley-Blackwell
38    Bhaumik, S. and Branford, D. (2005) *The Frith Prescribing Guidelines for Adults with Learning Disability* London: Taylor Francis
39    Department for Constitutional Affairs (2007) *Mental Capacity Act 2005 Code of Practice* London: TSO

40    Ministry of Justice (2008) *Deprivation of Liberty Safeguards Code of Practice to supplement the main Mental Capacity Act 2005 Code of Practice*: London: TSO

41    Francis, R. (2013). *Report of the Mid Staffordshire NHS Foundation Trust Public Inquiry: executive summary*. London: Stationery Office

42    *Health and Safety at Work Act 1974* London: The Stationery Office

43    *Management of Health and Safety at Work Regulations* 1999 SI 1999 No 2051 London: HMSO

44    BILD (2010) *Code of Practice for the use of restrictive physical interventions* Kidderminster: BILD Publications

45    Institute of Conflict Management (2008) *Quality award for training in managing work related violence* Leicester: ICM

46    McGill, P., Cooper, V. and Honeyman, G. (2010) *Developing better commissioning for individuals with behaviour that challenges services – a scoping exercise* Kent: Tizard Centre & The Challenging Behaviour Foundation

## APPENDIX 1: USEFUL DOCUMENTS THAT COMPLEMENT THIS GUIDANCE

■ *NHS Protect (2013): Meeting needs and reducing distress: guidance on the prevention and management of clinically related challenging behaviour in NHS settings*[7]

This guidance was developed by an expert group comprising doctors, security specialists and nurses. It provides important practical strategies, which should be applied across clinical settings, in order to help identify, assess, understand, prevent and manage clinically related 'challenging behaviour', by preventing or minimising a person's distress, meeting their needs, and ensuring that high quality care is delivered within a safe environment.

The principles and approaches outlined apply to any adult patient in an NHS healthcare setting. Although specific techniques and interventions may differ, strategies for delivering high quality personalised care that meets a person's needs remain the same. The importance of positive engagement, communication between staff and de-escalation approaches are strongly emphasised.

■ *HM Government (2014): The Mental Health Crisis Care Concordat: improving outcomes for people experiencing mental health crisis*[8]

This Concordat is a multi-agency agreement between signed by more than 20 organisations including the police, mental health trusts and paramedics that describes what people experiencing a mental health crisis should be able to expect of the public services that respond to their needs.

It is about how these different services can best work together, and it establishes key principles of good practice that local services and partnerships should use to raise standards and strengthen working arrangements. In particular it examines how local authorities, health providers (including A&E departments) and the police service should work effectively.

■ *NHS England & Local Government Association (2014): A Core Principles Commissioning Tool for the development of Local Specifications for services supporting Children, Young People, Adults and Older People with Learning Disabilities and/or Autism who Display or are at Risk of Displaying Behaviour that Challenges*[9]

With the aim of informing decisions concerning the commissioning of services, the document was produced as a direct response to the scandalous events revealed to have occurred at Winterbourne View. It describes the core principles that should be present across all services for people with learning disabilities and/or autism who either display or are at risk of displaying behaviour which challenges.

The document highlights the importance of a relentless person centred focus on outcomes, with all decisions being based on the best interests of the individual and a full recognition that family carers are most often those who know what the 'best interests' are. Rigorous adherence to the core principles will improve individuals' quality of life and reduce the prevalence and incidence of behaviour that challenges as well as inappropriate placements and the use of restrictive interventions

- *NICE (2005): Clinical Guideline 25. Violence: the short-term management of disturbed / violent behaviour in in-patient psychiatric and emergency departments*[10]

This guidance examined and reported on the evidence base for the emergency management of acute behavioural disturbance across a selection of healthcare settings. Interventions and topics that are examined include: the care environment, prediction of violence and aggression, training, service user perspectives, emergency departments and the use of intensive supportive observations and a range of restrictive interventions.

It is currently being updated in light of new and emerging clinical evidence and the new guidance is expected to be published in April 2015. When published, the expanded guidance will have broader applicability across the full range of adult health and social care services.

- *Department of Health (2008): Mental Health Act 1983 Code of Practice*[11]

The Code provides guidance to staff who are involved in the treatment, care and support of people under the Mental Health Act 1983. Chapter 15 of the Code is of particular interest; it provides guidance on a range of interventions which may be considered for the safe and therapeutic management of hospital in-patients (whether or not they are detained under the Mental Health Act 1983) whose behaviour presents a particular risk to themselves or to others.

The Code is currently being revised and is likely to be published late 2014. This will compliment this guidance, including having a stronger focus on positive and proactive care as well as additional safeguards around the application of restrictive interventions.

- *Skills for Care/Skills for Health (2014) A Positive and Proactive Workforce: a guide to workforce development for commissioners and employers seeking to minimise the use of restrictive practices in social care and health*[12]

This important guide is for commissioners and employers who are responsible for the development of a skilled, knowledgeable and competent health and social care. The document provides advice on the development of staff with the aim of ensuring that the use of restrictive interventions is minimised.

The document addresses issues or developing person-centred organisational cultures, staff recruitment and retention, support, supervision, development of skills and knowledge and how to commission high quality training.

- *Department of Health (forthcoming 2014) Positive and Proactive care: reducing the new for restrictive interventions in the support and care of children, young people and individuals transitioning to adulthood*

Children and young people face particular difficulties in relation to positive and proactive care and support. This requires careful consideration of their physical and emotional characteristics as maturing, still developing people with varying needs and capacity to understand their circumstances and who exhibit a very diverse range of behaviours. The care and support of children and young people is provided within different legal and service context and in accordance with the UN Convention on the Rights of the Child.

Additional and separate guidance on reducing reliance on restrictive interventions when delivering services to children, young people and individuals in transition is being developed.

# Appendix C9
# Department of Health letter:
# Deprivation of Liberty Safeguards

Mr Niall Fry
Social Care Quality & Safety Team
Area 313B, Richmond House
79 Whitehall, London SW1A 2NS
E-mail: niall.fry@dh.gsi.gov.uk

28th March 2014

Dear Colleague,

### DEPRIVATION OF LIBERTY SAFEGUARDS (DOLS)
#### Judgment of the Supreme Court
#### P v Cheshire West and Chester Council and another
#### P and Q v Surrey County Council

I am writing to draw your attention to last week's judgment in the Supreme Court to help to ensure that health and social care organisations continue to comply with the law following the revised test now supplied by the Supreme Court about the meaning of a deprivation of liberty.

The contents of this letter are specifically addressed to all those who are

- involved in the assessment and/or authorisation of a deprivation of liberty
- involved in the care of individuals who may lack capacity
- responsible for policies and procedures relating to the care of individuals who may lack capacity.

Mental Capacity Act (MCA) and Deprivation of Liberty Safeguard (DoLS) leads should ensure this letter is cascaded to all relevant staff.

## Background

On 19 March 2014, the Supreme Court handed down its judgment in the case of 'P v Cheshire West and Chester Council and another' and 'P and Q v Surrey County Council'. The full judgment can be found on the Supreme Court's website at the following link:

**supremecourt.uk/decided-cases/docs/UKSC-2012-0068-Judgment.pdf**

The accompanying press release with a short description of the cases under consideration can be found at the following link:

**supremecourt.uk/decided-cases/docs/UKSC-2012-0068-PressSummary.pdf**

The judgment is significant in the determination of whether arrangements made for the care and/or treatment of an individual lacking capacity to consent to those arrangements amount to a deprivation of liberty.

A deprivation of liberty for such a person must be authorised in accordance with one of the following legal regimes: a deprivation of liberty authorisation or Court of Protection order under the Deprivation of Liberty Safeguards (DoLS) in the Mental Capacity Act 2005, or (if applicable) under the Mental Health Act 1983.

## Key points from the Supreme Court judgment

### REVISED TEST FOR DEPRIVATION OF LIBERTY

The Supreme Court has clarified that there is a deprivation of liberty for the purposes of Article 5 of the European Convention on Human Rights in the following circumstances:

> The person is under continuous supervision and control and is not free to leave, and the person lacks capacity to consent to these arrangements.

The Supreme Court held that factors which are NOT relevant to determining whether there is a deprivation of liberty include the person's compliance or lack of objection and the reason or purpose behind a particular placement. It was also held that the relative normality of the placement, given the person's needs, was not relevant. This means that the person should not be compared with anyone else in determining whether there is a deprivation of liberty. However, young persons aged 16 or 17 should be compared to persons of a similar age and maturity without disabilities.

### DEPRIVATION OF LIBERTY IN 'DOMESTIC' SETTINGS

The Supreme Court has held that a deprivation of liberty can occur in domestic settings where the State is responsible for imposing such arrangements. This will include a placement in a supported living arrangement in the community. Hence, where there is, or is likely to be, a deprivation of liberty in such placements that must be authorised by the Court of Protection.

## Suggested actions

### RELEVANT STAFF SHOULD

- Familiarise themselves with the provisions of the Mental Capacity Act, in particular the five principles and specifically the 'least restrictive' principle.
- When designing and implementing new care and treatment plans for individuals lacking capacity, be alert to any restrictions and restraint which may be of a degree or intensity that mean an individual is being, or is likely to be, deprived of their liberty (following the revised test supplied by the Supreme Court)
- Take steps to review existing care and treatment plans for individuals lacking capacity to determine if there is a deprivation of liberty (following the revised test supplied by the Supreme Court)
- Where a potential deprivation of liberty is identified, a full exploration of the alternative ways of providing the care and/ or treatment should be undertaken, in order to identify any less restrictive ways of providing that care which will avoid a deprivation of liberty
- Where the care/ treatment plan for an individual lacking capacity will unavoidably result in a deprivation of liberty judged to be in that person's best interests, this MUST be authorised.

### LOCAL AUTHORITIES SHOULD IN ADDITION

- Review their allocation of resources in light of the revised test given by the Supreme Court to ensure they meet their legal responsibilities.

Although local authorities are the supervisory body for DoLS for both care home and hospital settings, the NHS (commissioners and providers) have a vital role to play in correctly implementing DoLS (and the wider MCA). We expect that the NHS and local authorities will continue to work closely together on this.

## Authorising a deprivation of liberty

The DoLS process for obtaining a standard authorisation or urgent authorisation can be used where individuals lacking capacity are deprived of their liberty in a hospital or care home.

The Court of Protection can also make an order authorising a deprivation of liberty; this is the only route available for authorising deprivation of liberty in domestic settings such as supported living arrangements. This route is also available for complex cases in hospital and/ or care home settings.

Individuals may also be deprived of their liberty under the Mental Health Act if the requirements for detention under that Act are met.

## Further information

In the first instance professionals should contact their organisation's MCA-DoLS lead for further information.

In the meantime the Government is preparing its response to the House of Lords Select Committee report into the MCA and DoLS. We expect to issue this response by the summer.

I also enclose an annex with some additional background.

Yours faithfully,

**Niall Fry**
**Policy Manager – Mental Capacity Act/DoLS**

## ANNEX – FURTHER BACKGROUND AND STEPS FOR CONSIDERATION

It is difficult to predict the number of individuals who lack capacity whose arrangements should be assessed in light of the Supreme Court judgment and the number of additional individuals for whom deprivation of liberty will need to be authorised.

Local authorities submit information on the number of assessments undertaken for deprivation of liberty authorisations under the Mental Capacity Act 2005 and the number of authorisations approved to the Health and Social Care Information Centre. The Department of Health and the Care Quality Commission will explore how best to monitor the evolving situation to assist in determining the practical impact of the Supreme Court's revised test.

Professionals must remember that the deprivation of liberty authorisations and Court of Protection orders under the Deprivation of Liberty Safeguards (DoLS) in the Mental Capacity Act 2005 are rooted in the principles of that Act. DoLS exists to provide protection to individuals – to safeguard these individuals when a deprivation of liberty is an unavoidable part of a best interests care plan. Individuals who are identified as potentially deprived of their liberty must be considered on a case-by-case basis and all appropriate steps taken to remove the risk of a deprivation of liberty where possible. The emphasis should be on empowerment and enablement.

Further steps that Local Authorities could consider taking are:

- Ensuring awareness of the Supreme Court judgment among care providers
- Ensuring awareness of the need to reduce restraint and restrictions and promote liberty in care plans
- Mapping any additional requirements for Best Interest Assessors (BIAs) and working collaboratively with other Local Authorities to reduce training costs
- Reviewing information on the number of individuals in supported living arrangements to identify those individuals whose arrangements should be reviewed.

## Appendix C10
# Department of Health letter: Update following the 19 March 2014 Supreme Court judgment

Mr Niall Fry
Social Care Quality & Safety Team
Area 313B, Richmond House
79 Whitehall, London SW1A 2NS
E-mail: niall.fry@dh.gsi.gov.uk

8 September 2014

## F.A.O: MCA-DOLS LEADS IN LOCAL AUTHORITIES AND THE NHS

Dear Colleagues,

### Update following the 19 March 2014 Supreme Court judgment

I wanted to write to you personally to set out some of the latest developments with respect to the Deprivation of Liberty Safeguards (DoLS) and on-going work in this area.

But first I'd like to take the opportunity to thank you and your teams for the considerable efforts you have made since 19 March 2014. I have managed to discuss the issues with a good number of you since the judgment but I'm aware of how many I have not yet been able to personally speak to. It is clear the judgment sparked a considerable increase in DoLS activity and the commitment of professionals such as yourself in responding to this challenge has been truly impressive.

### Approaches to responding to the 19 March 2014 judgment

There has been a good deal of consensus around how the response should be handled. It was clear to many local authorities that the clarified Supreme Court deprivation of liberty test could not be fully implemented overnight. It is equally clear however that a 'do nothing' approach is not acceptable.

Best practice has been to rapidly identify those individuals who may potentially be subject to a deprivation of liberty and then work through this list, assessing first those individuals who stand to benefit most from the safeguards. Managing authorities and supervisory bodies need to have a plan as to how they will move towards full compliance with the law but it is clear that this action should be undertaken in a proportionate manner that does not for example, result in a decline in the level of care and support provided to service-users.

Particularly impressive is the re-assertion of the wider principles of the Mental Capacity Act 2005 (MCA). As you know, we face a considerable challenge is raising understanding and awareness of the MCA across the health and care system, and it is clear that success in this endeavour will reap benefits for the correct application of DoLS. In particular, the first step in identifying a potential deprivation of liberty should always be to seek to reduce restrictions and restraint where possible to avoid a deprivation of liberty occurring in the first place.

It is important to remember the fundamental purpose of DoLS. It is not, nor should it be, purely a paper-based exercise to provide the legal authority for depriving an individual of their liberty in their best interests. DoLS is about the individual and ensuring that a light is shone on the conditions of their care; maximising their empowerment and human rights. There are countless examples of how DoLS has led to a real improvement in the care individuals receive. The individual must be central to our response to the Supreme Court judgment. Certainly, bulk assessments (for example assessing all individuals in a care home as one rather than considering each individual case-by-case) are clearly not in keeping with the purpose of DoLS.

The Department of Health, ADASS and the Care Quality Commission (CQC) support the type of response to the Supreme Court judgment detailed above.

## ADASS-led DoLS Task Group

The Department is very grateful to ADASS for leading a Task Group these past few months to consider the implications of the Supreme Court judgment and provide some practical tips as to how local authorities might respond. Particular thanks are due to Sarah Norman and Lorraine Currie for leading this Task Group. The Task Group meets next on 18 September 2014 and ADASS will circulate a guidance note thereafter. Annexed to this letter is a list of the members of this Task Group. Should you wish to raise particular issues that require national attention, you may do so via the regional lead for your area.

The Task Group was established on a time-limited basis and together with ADASS we shall review whether there is value in this Task Force continuing after this calendar year.

## Establishing the impact of the Supreme Court judgment

As mentioned earlier, it is clear that the Supreme Court judgment has resulted in significant increased activity on DoLS but the extent of this increase in terms of actual numbers of DoLS applications and authorisations nationally remains to be fully understood. You may be aware that ADASS conducted a survey of local authorities a few months ago. Looking through this survey it is clear that the expected increase in DoLS applications varied considerably across different local authorities; some predicted a 2-fold increase (still of course significant) whereas others predicted a 20-fold increase.

For future planning purposes and to understand the current challenges better, the Department has decided it would not be appropriate to wait for the next annual DoLS collection. The Health and Social Care Information Centre (HSCIC) has therefore agreed to conduct an additional voluntary DoLS data collection. The HSCIC has now circulated a letter in respect of this collection (supplied in annex here also). We anticipate that quarter one data will be published in early October 2014 and quarter two data in early November 2014.

This collection is voluntary and it is understandable that respondents may have concerns about the resource required to provide this data while continuing to manage the response to the Supreme Court judgment. However, we would strongly encourage you to respond to this collection. A truly robust and reliable national picture of the impact will help inform the national response.

## Work due for completion by February 2015

### DOLS STANDARD FORMS

You may be aware that the Government, in its response to the House of Lords Select Committee Inquiry on the MCA, committed to revising the standard DoLS forms and publishing a new set by the end of November 2014. This was a challenging timetable but one that recognised the situation following the Supreme Court judgment.

We are delighted that ADASS and Lorraine Currie (lorraine.currie@shropshire.gov.uk) have agreed to lead this piece of work. Many of you may have made alterations to the DoLS forms over the years to suit your purposes. ADASS will be in touch to inform you how you can submit these forms for consideration in the process of drafting the new forms. The forms will remain non-statutory; local authorities are not obliged to use the new forms. However, there are clear advantages to be had in a shared set of forms and the Department would encourage you to engage with ADASS during this process to feed in your views.

## DOLS CASE LAW GUIDANCE

Another commitment from the Government response to the House of Lords was to produce new case law guidance as to what constitutes a deprivation of liberty in both social care and health care settings.

I am very pleased to say that the Law Society, in particular their Mental Health Committee, have agreed to undertake this work, liaising closely with DoLS practitioners in the process. We expect this guidance to be published in February 2015.

If you would be interested in feeding into this work, please contact Anselm Benedict at the Law Society: **Anselm.Benedict@LawSociety.org.uk**.

## INCREASING THE PROVISION OF BEST INTEREST ASSESSOR TRAINING

Many of you have highlighted that one of the biggest challenges in responding to the Supreme Court judgment is the supply of Best Interest Assessors (BIAs).

To try and provide assistance in this regard, the Department is currently considering providing a small amount of funding for a tender for BIA training. The expectation is that the successful bidder(s) would provide an increased number of training places on condensed BIA courses for a reduced cost over the coming six to twelve months. Local authorities would still need to pay for their staff to attend these courses but the cost would in effect be subsidised by the Department.

The Department will discuss this proposal with the members of the ADASS-led Task Group on 18th September before reaching a final decision. Again, your views would be welcomed and should be directed to the Task Group via your regional lead.

## Long term work

As you know, the Government asked the Law Commission to consult on and review the legislation underpinning deprivation of liberty in community settings, whilst learning lessons for the existing DoLS system.

In response to recent developments and following consultation with stakeholders and the Law Commission, the Department has decided to extend the scope of this work to consider the legislation underpinning DoLS in its entirety (in addition to community settings).

It should be strongly emphasised however, that this should not in any way distract attention from the need for supervisory bodies and managing authorities to implement the current DoLS system fully. The outcome of the Law Commission's work will not be known for at least two years.

The Law Commission's work has already commenced and we would encourage you to engage with this process. Without your engagement our efforts to identify legislative changes that are going to achieve the outcomes for service users we all desire is unlikely to be successful. The initial point of contact at the Law Commission is Tim Spencer-Lane: tim.spencer-lane@lawcommission.gsi.gov.uk.

Some stakeholders have voiced their opinion that legislative change should be considered within a much shorter timeframe. As noted in the Government response to the House of

Lords, we are determined that legislative change should not be rushed and should be developed in a transparent, consultative manner. Changes proposed (for example, extending DoLS now to community settings) may seem like attractive short-term solutions, but the Department's view is that such changes are far from simple, are substantive rather than merely cosmetic, and therefore require full and robust consultation – hence the engagement of the Law Commission.

## Funding

A number of local authorities as well as ADASS and the LGA have expressed their concerns regarding the financial pressures resulting from the Supreme Court judgment. As you know, central government has funded local government to fulfil its statutory responsibilities under DoLS since the regime came into force in 2009. In this financial year alone, central government has provided over £35m for MCA-DoLS activities.

Government policy in respect of DoLS is unchanged but clearly the clarification in the law following the Supreme Court judgment has resulted in a significant increase in applications to local authorities. We will continue to assess the impact over the next few months (and in light of the HSCIC data return) and feed this into our future financial planning as has been the case previously.

## Wider MCA work

As mentioned above, it is important to see the approach to DoLS as part of the wider effort to raise awareness and understanding of the MCA. The Department and our system partners, co-ordinating through our national MCA Steering Group, are working to implement the commitments made in the Government response to the House of Lords Inquiry (*Valuing every voice, respecting every right*).

The Department will write out to you again later this year with an update on progress but I would draw your attention to one major commitment; the Social Care Institute of Excellence (SCIE) review of MCA guidance, toolkits and other materials. SCIE will be launching this month a public call for practitioners to submit MCA materials that they find valuable with a view to identifying the very best in the country and providing these online for national dissemination. This review will only be a success if practitioners like yourself submit all your materials – we would strongly encourage you to do so.

Further information will be provided by SCIE in due course. The SCIE contact is David Cundy: **David.Cundy@scie.org.uk**.

Finally, I would draw your attention to a letter from the Chief Social Worker for Adults, Lyn Romeo, regarding the vital role of social workers in implementing the MCA – see annex.

Thank you once again for all you are doing. Please pass on the Department's thanks to your team. The Supreme Court judgment has clearly resulted in a significant increase in DoLS activity but, handled in a manner that puts individuals first and foremost, it provides a real opportunity to provide real benefits to some of the most vulnerable individuals in our society.

Yours sincerely

Niall Fry
Policy Lead
Mental Capacity Act & Deprivation of Liberty Safeguards
Department of Health

## ANNEX A – REGIONAL MCA-DOLS MEMBERS OF THE ADASS-LED DOLS TASK GROUP

| Region | Name of Lead | Email |
|---|---|---|
| North West | Penny Davidson | pdavidson@warrington.gov.uk |
| North East | | |
| South West | Dennis Little | dennis–little@bathnes.gov.uk |
| South East | Sarah Pady | spady@buckscc.gov.uk |
| East | Joseph Yow | joseph.yow@cambidgeshire.gov.uk |
| West Midlands | Lorraine Currie | Lorraine.currie@shropshire.gov.uk |
| East Midlands | Heather Blow | Heather.bow@lincolnshire.gov.uk |
| London | Liana Kotz | Liana.Kotze@enfield.gov.uk |

Appendix C11

# Department of Health letter: Update on the Mental Capacity Act and following the 19 March 2014 Supreme Court judgment

Mr Niall Fry
Social Care Quality & Safety Team
Area 313B, Richmond House
79 Whitehall, London SW1A 2NS
E-mail: niall.fry@dh.gsi.gov.uk

14 January 2015

## TO: MCA-DOLS LEADS IN LOCAL AUTHORITIES AND THE NHS

Dear Colleague,

### Update on the Mental Capacity Act and following the 19 March 2014 Supreme Court judgment

I wanted to write to you with an update on developments following the 19 March 2014 Supreme Court judgment and also on developments concerning the wider Mental Capacity Act 2005 (MCA) following the House of Lords Select Committee report and subsequent Government response.

### Mental Capacity Act

Following the publication in June 2014 of the Government response to the House of Lords report, the Department and our partners have been focussing on taking forward our commitments. Of particular note for the coming weeks and months:

– The Government has now confirmed its intention to establish a new 'National Mental Capacity Forum'. This Forum will bring stakeholders from health and social care together with those from other sectors (for example, finance, legal, police, housing) to identify complementary actions that member organisations can pursue, especially at a local level, to improve MCA implementation. We shall begin the recruitment of an independent chair for the Forum as soon as possible. Please get in touch with me if you are interested in joining the Forum.
– A new on-line 'MCA Directory' containing MCA tools and guidance for all sectors will be launched on the web-site of the Social Care Institute of Excellence (SCIE) by the end of February. We hope that this resource will provide a spur to local implementation efforts. There is still time to submit your materials to SCIE. Please send them by email to mca@scie.org.uk.
– On 13th March 2015 the 'Chief Social Worker's MCA Seminar' will bring social workers together with other professionals to share learning, best practice, and concerns/ challenges face-to-face. We also hope this event will kick-start local multi-agency collaborations to raise MCA awareness. Further details, including how to express your interest in attending plus a useful summary of social workers thoughts on

how social work can help drive better MCA implementation can be found in the enclosed letter from Lyn Romeo.

The coming year will be a busy one as we seek to build on the opportunity provided by the House of Lords report. I have spoken with a number of you about the benefits of ensuring good communication from the national through the regional and to the local level. As you may be aware, the national organisations with a key role in MCA implementation sit on a DH-led MCA Steering Group that meets every few months.

You may be interested in a few documents this group has produced and which I have enclosed with this letter:

- A '**statement of ambition**' that describes the aims of the MCA Steering Group and which all member organisations have signed up to.
- A description of the **roles and responsibilities** of each member organisation of the MCA Steering Group. We hope this may assist stakeholders in understanding which organisations to look to for specific assistance.
- A document entitled '**MCA expectations**'. This is our attempt at a list of key MCA attributes that stakeholders can consult and consider addressing when preparing guidance, toolkits etc. Any comments welcome.

To help keep you and other colleagues up to-date with developments at the national level I intend to post Twitter updates (@NiallatDH). Please look out for these and feel free to re-tweet to your colleagues.

Of course, communication works both ways, especially as the key driver of better MCA implementation will be local level action. Please do feed your local updates up to your regional leads. I will be meeting with regional leads throughout the year to ensure that what we do nationally is informed by your needs. The list of regional MCA leads is attached at Annex to this letter.

## *Supreme Court judgment*

The official statistics from the Health and Social Care Information Centre (HSCIC) paint a clear picture of the very significant increase in Deprivation of Liberty Safeguard (DoLS) applications since the 19 March 2014 Supreme Court judgment. Over 55,000 applications in the six months following the judgment points to a more than 8 fold-plus increase on 2013-14 figures. (The next data set is due for release on 3 February 2015).

Let me put on record again the Department's thanks for the impressive response you and your teams have made to this challenge. I hope that as you reflect on the last nine months you will take comfort from the knowledge that thousands more individuals have received valuable scrutiny of the conditions of their care.

The Department continues to stress the importance of an MCA-centred approach to the challenge posed by the Supreme Court judgment. The focus should always be on the individual and supporting their well-being. The Department is aware that many local authorities are struggling to meet legal deadlines for processing applications and that local authorities are working hard across a number of different areas and priorities (for example, implementation of the Care Act). We do not expect that local authorities who are following national DH, ADASS and CQC guidance (and who have a plan in place for responding to the Supreme Court judgment in a way that makes clear that paramount importance of the well-being of vulnerable individuals) should be unfairly penalised.

The CQC will be publishing its annual DoLS report shortly and will be reflecting on the Supreme Court judgment and the challenge for the year ahead.

I am pleased to confirm that the new standard forms supporting the DoLS process have now gone live. I hope that the reduction in the number of these forms from 32 to 13 will help your teams negotiate the significant extra number of applications. The forms can be found at the following link and new short guidance on their use will be available shortly. Although these forms are not prescribed by statute I would strongly encourage you to use them. There are clear benefits in all local authorities and managing authorities operating from the same set of forms.

www.adass.org.uk/mental-health-Drugs-and-Alcohol/key-documents/New-DoLS-Forms

I am also happy to say that new guidance from the Law Society to assist practitioners in understanding what may constitute a deprivation of liberty following the Supreme Court judgment is in the final stages of production and will be available by the end of February.

In addition, the revised Code of Practice for the Mental Health Act will be published shortly. The Code includes a new chapter on the interface between the Mental Health Act and MCA-DoLS which you will want to take note of. The new Code will be available online – I will post a twitter message to alert you.

Finally, I am particularly grateful to ADASS for leading the Task Group that has been examining practical solutions and assistance for local authorities. Their most recent guidance note – including a helpful DoLS application prioritisation tool – can be found at the link below.

www.adass.org.uk/uploadedFiles/adass–content/policy–networks/mental–health/key–documents/DoLS%20Guidance%20note%20November%202014.pdf

A good place to find resources to assist your response to the Supreme Court judgment is the Mental Capacity Law and Policy website. It includes further links to CQC briefing, guidance from the Intensive Care Society, and details of the new (and now live) system for Court of Protection applications from community settings.

www.mentalcapacitylawandpolicy.org.uk/resources-2/cheshire-west-resources

## Specific implications

The Supreme Court judgment continues to have a number of knock-on implications in addition to the increase in applications. In all these cases, our priority is to establish a proportionate approach that prioritises the well-being of the individual who may lack capacity; considers closely the wishes and feelings of family, friends and carers; and which ensures the system as a whole focuses on delivering care, support and scrutiny that benefits the individual. In short, we do not wish a system that puts paperwork before people.

### PALLIATIVE CARE

One area that has caused particular concern is that of palliative care. For the purpose of this guidance, we consider palliative care to be concerned with the *last few weeks of life*.

The first thing to say here is that if a person receiving palliative care has the capacity to consent to the arrangements for their care, and does consent, then there is no deprivation of liberty.

Furthermore, if the person has capacity to consent to the arrangements for their care at the time of their admission or at a time before losing capacity, and does consent, the Department considers this consent to cover the period until death and that hence there is no deprivation of liberty. (An important exception would be if the care package to which the individual consented were to change in a manner that imposed significant extra restrictions or which included care contrary to the previously expressed wishes and preferences of the individual. In such circumstances, the individual's consent is unlikely to cover the changed care and an application for a DoLS authorisation or a Court of Protection order may be required if there is or will be a deprivation of liberty.)

Where an individual lacks capacity and there is no valid consent, there will be no deprivation of liberty unless the Supreme Court judgment 'acid test' is met:

–    Are they 'free to leave'? Just because they are physically unable to leave of their own accord does not mean they are not free to leave for the purpose of the test – they may for example be able to leave with family assistance.
–    Are they under 'continuous control and supervision'? If the individual is in a private room and checked only every few hours then they may not necessarily be under continuous control and supervision.

In providing this guidance we would make clear that a person who lacks capacity and is receiving palliative care is entitled to the same rights under the law as every other citizen. Such individuals can indeed have a care and support package that results in a best interests deprivation of liberty. If there is no valid consent, and the acid test is met, such a deprivation of liberty must be authorised. Managing authorities and local authorities must be alert to this.

We must remember that the reality on the ground is, that in the great majority of palliative care cases, the family and loved ones of the individual concerned do not recognise any 'deprivation of liberty' in a conventional sense. Rather they see a normal care situation. Practitioners will be only too aware that an unnecessary DoLS assessment could cause considerable distress to the family with no benefit to the individual.

## MEANING OF 'MENTAL DISORDER'

It is important to remember that standard authorisations can only be given under Schedule A1 of the MCA if the person concerned is suffering from mental disorder within the meaning of the Mental Health Act (but disregarding any exclusion for persons with learning disability), and therefore meets the mental health qualifying requirement to be eligible for an authorisation.

It may be helpful for you to be aware that the Department of Health does not consider a state of unconsciousness *in itself* as being a mental disorder. As such, we would not consider that an individual who is unconscious and who does not have a mental disorder would be eligible for a standard authorisation.

## CORONER'S INVESTIGATIONS

You may be aware that the Chief Coroner recently issued guidance to coroners on the Supreme Court judgment. This can be found at the link below.

**www.judiciary.gov.uk/wp-content/uploads/2013/10/guidance-no16-dols.pdf**

In this guidance, the Chief Coroner notes his view (which is not binding on local coroners) that the death of an individual who is subject to a DoLS authorisation (or a relevant Court of Protection Order) is, under the law, classified as a death in 'state detention' and as such the death should be subject to a coroner's investigation.

The Department of Health recognises the current law and the view of the Chief Coroner regarding state detention. We do wish to note, however, that while the death of an individual who is subject to a DoLS authorisation (or a relevant Court of Protection Order) may in legal terms be a death in 'state detention' – and while we of course would fully support a robust investigation where there may be suspicion of any untoward factors – it is important to recognise that on the ground and for the family, in the great majority of cases, the death has occurred in a 'normal' care environment.

Where it is clear that there is no suspicion of untoward factors contributing to the death, we would hope that any inquest puts the least possible stress on the family and is completed as rapidly as possible. DH and the CQC have heard concerns of bereaved families being visited by uniformed police officers assigned to investigate deaths on behalf of the coroner or of delays in releasing the body of a loved one to their family. We would strongly urge that such situations be avoided wherever possible.

It is likely to be of great benefit for coroners to keep in close communication with the DoLS Lead in their local authority so that they can ensure a consistent message is given to providers and so that they can work together in dealing with the considerable extra activity as a result of the Supreme Court judgment. Part of the challenge in responding to the Supreme Court judgment is in raising awareness with our partners of the true nature of DoLS. For example, that DoLS does not cause a deprivation of liberty, rather it exists to ensure that any deprivation of liberty is in the best interests of the individual concerned.

### DEPRIVATIONS OF LIBERTY IN THE COMMUNITY

I'm sure you will be aware that on 17 November 2014, a new streamlined process went live for applications to the Court of Protection to authorise deprivations of liberty outside of care homes and hospitals. This is known as the 'Re X procedure' and is supported by a new Court of Protection application form and a new practice direction. The following guide produced by 39 Essex Street is a useful reference and contains links to the relevant documents:

www.39essex.com/docs/newsletters/judicial-deprivation-of-liberty-authorisations-guide.pdf

The Court of Protection will be monitoring the number of applications received and clearly the Department will be studying these closely to determine the level of applications made under this new process. As with DoLS applications we urge a proportionate, risk-based approach that seeks to identify individuals who stand to benefit most from this additional scrutiny and ensure these individuals receive timely access to the Court.

It is already clear that local authority MCA-DoLS teams (already processing increased numbers of DoLS applications) and NHS organisations (who may also be making applications to the Court on behalf of service users) will need the assistance and engagement of local partners in identifying these individuals in community settings potentially deprived of their liberty. Implementing the MCA and DoLS is a shared responsibility for all professionals caring for and treating those who may lack capacity.

### BEST INTEREST ASSESSORS OPERATING IN WALES

Finally, a few local authorities have asked me whether Best Interest Assessors (BIAs), trained and registered in England, are able to perform best interest assessments for an English local authority that has placed an individual for whom they have responsibility into accommodation in Wales. The Department believes there is no block to this happening.

## Concluding thoughts

I hope this information is helpful to you. The implications of the Supreme Court judgment continue to emerge and there remain many challenges ahead. However, I hope you will look back on your achievements to-date with considerable pride.

In terms of our long-term plan, the Law Commission's work to fundamentally review DoLS and propose new legislation that covers care homes, hospitals and community settings continues apace and I again would encourage you to engage with this work. The Department believes that it is only through this consultative approach, considering all issues in the round, that we will achieve future legislation that better balances the need to protect the rights of individuals with the need to avoid unnecessary bureaucracy.

Please do keep in touch over the coming year. Thank you again for all you are doing to move this important work forwards.

Yours sincerely

**Niall Fry**
Policy Lead
Mental Capacity Act & Deprivation of Liberty Safeguards
Department of Health

# ANNEX

## *Regional MCA-DoLS Leads*

| Region | Name of Lead | Email |
|---|---|---|
| East of England | Joseph Yow | joseph.yow@cambidgeshire.gov.uk |
| East Midlands | Heather Blow | Heather.blow@lincolnshire.gov.uk |
| London | Liana Kotz | Liana.Kotze@enfield.gov.uk |
| North East | Rachel Abbott | Rachel.Abbott@southtyneside.gov.uk |
| North West | Penny Davidson | pdavidson@warrington.gov.uk |
| South East | Sarah Pady | spady@buckscc.gov.uk |
| South West | Dennis Little | dennis–little@bathnes.gov.uk |
| West Midlands | Lorraine Currie | Lorraine.currie@shropshire.gov.uk |
| Yorkshire and the Humber | Amanda Coyne | Amanda.Coyne@rotherham.gov.uk |

## Appendix C12
# Department of Health letter: MCA 2005 and the vital role of social workers

Office of the Chief Social Worker for Adults (England)
70 Whitehall
London
SW1A 2NS
T: 020 7210 5917
www.dh.gov.uk

### TO: DIRECTORS OF ADULT SOCIAL SERVICES – FOR CIRCULATION TO ADULT SOCIAL SERVICE TEAMS AND APPROPRIATE PARTNERS

14 January 2015

Dear Colleague,

### *Mental Capacity Act 2005 and the vital role of social workers*

In August 2014 I wrote to social workers in England seeking views as to what we as a profession can do to realise improved awareness, understanding and practice of the Mental Capacity Act 2005 ('the MCA'). The many responses received were insightful and greatly appreciated. As promised, I have summarised these in annex to this letter. I am sure you will find it useful (as I have done) to reflect upon these with your teams. I would be grateful if you could forward this letter to your social work managers and teams.

The responses highlight a genuine enthusiasm for the MCA and for a social care culture that reflects MCA values. They highlight the need to communicate the basics about the MCA to service users and their families; to demonstrate the value and use of the MCA in real-life situations; the importance of consultation with the carers and families of those who may lack capacity in producing a care plan; and the importance of practice-based training. The responses suggest that social workers are keen to promote the MCA among other professionals, including in the NHS, but need to be empowered and supported to do so.

2014 was perhaps the most significant year for the MCA since the Act came into force. In March the House of Lords praised the Act as a '*visionary piece of legislation... with the potential to transform the lives of many*' but highlighted that for many individuals who may lack capacity '*the empowering ethos has not been delivered.... The rights conferred by the Act have not been realised*'. In the same month, the Supreme Court (ruling in the case of Cheshire West) provided an 'acid test' for what constitutes a deprivation of liberty. As a result, there has been a more than eight-fold increase in the number of applications under the Deprivation of Liberty Safeguards (DoLS). I know many of you have been closely involved in responding to these developments and I hope you will accept my gratitude for your considerable efforts. I know that there is active consideration of the impact of this additional work, by the Department of Health, the LGA and ADASS

The coming year will be critical if we are to maintain positive momentum and seize the opportunity presented by the House of Lords report and the Supreme Court judgment to realise real benefits for service users.

On the wider MCA, the Department and our system partners will be continuing to push ahead with the programme of work laid out in the Government response to the House of Lords; *Valuing every voice*. This will include forming a new National Mental Capacity Forum. This new Forum will bring together the widest possible stakeholder voice to inform Government policy but vitally, will focus the majority of its efforts on forging new collaborations across different sectors and professional groups, identifying actions that members of the Forum can pursue to improve implementation of the MCA.

At the national level we shall:

– Provide an accessible source of key MCA tools and information materials. This will be made available through a new online 'MCA Directory' to be hosted by the Social Care Institute of Excellence. This will be ready by the end of February 2015.
– Highlight the importance of the MCA in social work training. You will be aware that last year I consulted on a draft 'Knowledge and Skills Statement' (KSS) for social workers who have finished their assessed and supported year in employment (ASYE). We are currently analysing the responses to that consultation, but I can tell you now that a strong MCA element will be included in the final statement, which should be published before the end of February.

I do believe that improved implementation of the MCA will be driven primarily by local, tailored action and by local multi-agency collaboration. I would therefore urge you to ensure that the MCA is a regular agenda item for your team and senior management meetings. Through the new National Mental Capacity Forum we shall be in a position to better circulate national updates and facilitate peer-to-peer learning. I would encourage you to engage with this new forum. Regular updates on all MCA-DoLS matters will be posted on Twitter by the Department's MCA-DoLS Policy Lead, Niall Fry. Follow @NiallatDH.

In terms of the Deprivation of Liberty Safeguards (DoLS), our challenge is to continue to negotiate the very significant number of DoLS applications (and indeed applications from 'community settings' to the Court of Protection) while keeping true to the values of the MCA. In other words, putting the individual first and foremost and resisting any urge to treat DoLS as a bureaucratic 'tick-box' exercise. Applied properly, DoLS can realise real benefits for vulnerable individuals. Niall Fry will be writing out to MCA-DoLS policy leads in local authorities with a detailed update shortly. This will include detail of the revised (and reduced) standard forms for making DoLS applications and also the imminent publication of a new Code of Practice for the Mental Health Act that includes a new chapter on the interface between that Act and MCA-DoLS.

With a view to the MCA-DoLS challenge facing us all in 2015, I wish to invite expressions of interest in attending a '**Chief Social Worker's MCA Seminar**' on Friday 13 March 2015 in London. The purpose of the seminar is two-fold. First, I feel it will be valuable to share learning, best practice, and concerns/ challenges face-to-face. Second, I believe it will be valuable to share directly some of the recent MCA developments (including tools and guidance) and discuss how we can use these to instigate local collaborations and improvements in application of the Act. I would welcome attendance from anyone with an interest in the Act – from all professional groups, especially the NHS.

If you would like to attend this event please email **chiefsocialworkerforadults@dh.gsi.gov.uk**. Depending on demand we may need to randomly select attendees but please do get in touch. It would be very useful if, prior to your attendance at this event, you could consider and reflect upon the points noted in annex to this letter.

Thank you for your continuing engagement and all you are doing in helping lead better implementation of the MCA. It has been heartening to hear from so many colleagues with a clear passion for the values of the MCA. Our challenge now is to reach out to colleagues, and across different organisations to spread understanding and hence realise real benefits for service users.

Yours sincerely,

**Lyn Romeo**
Chief Social Worker for Adults (England)

# ANNEX

## *Common issues and themes raised by respondents*

The Chief Social Worker's letter of 12 August 2014, asked for the views of social workers on the Mental Capacity Act (MCA). Five questions were asked. A non-exhaustive summary of responses is provided below.

1.  **How can professionals best communicate the rights afforded by the MCA? How can professionals use the MCA to guide their interactions with service users?**

    ■   A cultural shift is needed whereby the MCA is used for promoting rights; rather than for defending practice
    ■   We need to communicate the rights afforded by the MCA to service users and their family in simple language. E.g. through a specific information leaflet
    ■   Professionals need to 'sell' the positive aspects of the Act; that the MCA offers protection and transparency, it is not just a bureaucratic procedure
    ■   Don't just give the 'MCA spiel' – use the key principles but relevant to the specific decision and circumstances at hand
    ■   We should encourage forward planning – Lasting Powers of Attorney (LPAs) but also broader early expression of wishes
    ■   MCA information on local authority customer information website, public online access to social work procedures manuals
    ■   Social workers need to promote the use of advocacy
    ■   It is important that professionals communicate to service users and their family about when and why a capacity assessment is taking place – ideally in advance and by letter together with information about what is to expect
    ■   Knowledge of the individual and their circumstances prior to making a capacity assessment is important in making a good assessment. Developing and sustaining relationships is important.
    ■   The biggest hurdle to assessing capacity is staff confidence and the incorrect belief there is someone out there better qualified.

2.  **When a care plan is being developed, what prompts or tips could assist social workers to ensure the principles of the MCA are followed?**

    ■   It would be useful to have a guidance sheet containing prompts about the MCA – for reference when constructing a care plan
    ■   Need a person-centred approach where the 'what's not working question' leads to discussions on rights, choice and control. Having information about the MCA present for the individual and their family makes it clear social workers are working within a legal framework
    ■   It is important to have close cooperation between the social worker putting together the care plan and the carer who has day-to-day knowledge of the individual and as such is well-placed to help communicate their wishes and preferences. The social worker making the care plan is initially unlikely to have a clear understanding of the person

- It is important to keep good records and evidence of the service-users ongoing care, and their values, beliefs, wishes and preferences. This helps to build a better picture when it comes to care planning/ review
- Useful to actively demonstrate when constructing a care plan how the individual has been involved (and supported to be involved) in the creation of their plan
- When signing off a care plan we check that capacity has been considered
- Care plans must ask assessors to record consent and where there is doubt over capacity – should record the nature of the capacity assessment undertaken and outcome

3.    **What forms of MCA training are likely to be attractive to social workers?**

- Social workers need more than a basic competency in the MCA. A greater number should be qualified Best Interest Assessors (BIAs)
- Training needs to be practical and focussed on real life situations. It should not be too theoretical or overly 'legalistic'
- Specialist skills training in how to conduct mental capacity assessments and how to communicate with people to maximise their capacity
- An expectation that career progression is dependent on showing how professionals implement the MCA to a high standard.
- There is a responsibility for Higher Educational Institutions to firmly embed the MCA into their social work degrees. MCA should be included as a core part of the social worker training curriculum (undergraduate and postgraduate).
- Joint training for social workers, medical professionals but also other disciplines (e.g. police) helps to engender a shared understanding and multi-disciplinary working
- Need to incorporate the MCA into continuous professional development (CPD)
- Thoughts on attractive forms of training included:
  - Relevant to client group
  - Interactive
  - Contains time to reflect and try out learning
  - Includes on-going support from an 'MCA Champion' focusing on practice
  - Provides clear guidelines
  - Provided within working environment
  - E-guides, creative tools
  - Competency based 'blended learning approaches'
  - Should be part of induction training for new staff
  - How to be professionally assertive and confident with other professionals
  - Practical role play and job shadowing
  - Initial supervision of capacity assessments by more experienced staff
  - Feedback from audited files to identify good practice
  - For already skilled practitioners – master classes to build on their expertise
  - Case law updates with the expectation that learning is then incorporated into supervision and case discussion within teams
  - 'Social work forums' as CPD opportunities for case discussions on MCA issues
  - Particular lessons could be learned from speech and language therapists around communicating with people who have difficulty articulating their views
  - 'Floorwalker' that works alongside those who have received training

back in their workplace to carry out self-audits and then share learning as part of a wider peer support network

4.  **Would you feel well placed as a social worker to highlight the importance of the MCA to other professionals? What might help?**

    ■   Social workers feel it is their role to be 'trailblazers' for the MCA
    ■   Social workers often have more MCA knowledge than other professionals
    ■   Social workers already go to great lengths to put the individual's perspective at the forefront of decision-making. But a paternalistic approach in the wider system can be hard to shift
    ■   Social workers advice is not always well received by other professionals; including for example in the NHS. Helpful if empowered to do so by senior staff
    ■   If social workers are to play a lead role in highlighting the MCA to others then they need easy-to-access regular updates and core materials
    ■   We must stress that all professionals have an MCA responsibility; this should not be left to social workers alone
    ■   Court of Protection uses psychologists and psychiatrists as expert witnesses. Social workers need to build to that expert witness level because their practice in the field is unique
    ■   We have a Quality Practice Standard specifically related to the MCA which sets out our expectation of social workers
    ■   Part of being an effective social worker is to advocate for our customers and to challenge colleagues where their practice falls outside of thee Act
    ■   You need to be a very strong social worker to challenge on behalf of vulnerable adults when you are surrounded by health professionals

5.  **Are there any other ways by which social workers could encourage a culture that better reflects the principles and values of the MCA?**

    ■   Every local authority should have an 'MCA Board' on a statutory footing. This should not be an add-on to the safeguarding board. It should include service users, professionals, independent community members
    ■   Senior social work managers must lead by example and ensure that better MCA implementation is on the agenda of relevant meetings
    ■   Practice will evolve as social workers begin to practice more bravely under the MCA (and are backed to do so by senior colleagues)
    ■   Confidence is probably an issue for some who may want to 'cover themselves'. So we need to have clear positive risk taking policies. And we need support from managers to ensure professionals do not become too risk averse
    ■   Be clear: we are working for ordinary lives – not super-safe lives or difficulty-free lives
    ■   Could use the multi-agency partnerships at Safeguarding Adult Boards to promote a better culture of understanding of the MCA principles.

# Appendix C13
# Care Quality Commission briefing: Deprivation of liberty in health and social care

## ISSUE

On 19 March 2014, the Supreme Court handed down its judgment in the case of *P v Cheshire West and Chester Council and another* and *P and Q v Surrey County Council*.

Read the full judgment on the Supreme Court's website: **www.supremecourt.uk/decided-cases/docs/UKSC-2012-0068-Judgment.pdf**.

The judgment is important for deciding whether arrangements made for the care and/or treatment of an individual who might lack capacity to consent to those arrangements amount to a deprivation of liberty: it has widened and clarified the definition of deprivation of liberty.

A deprivation of liberty in such a situation must be authorised in accordance with one of the following legal regimes: a deprivation of liberty authorisation or Court of Protection order under the Mental Capacity Act Deprivation of Liberty Safeguards, or (if applicable) under the Mental Health Act 1983, or, in some rare situations, under the inherent jurisdiction of the High Court.

### Information for providers and CQC Inspectors

Following the Supreme Court judgement on 19 March 2014, health and social care staff, and CQC inspectors, must be aware of how they should now judge whether a person might be deprived of their liberty.

It is clear that the intention of the majority of the Supreme Court was to extend the safeguard of independent scrutiny.

They said: 'A gilded cage is still a cage' and that 'we should err on the side of caution in deciding what constitutes a deprivation of liberty.' They also highlighted that a person in supported living might also be deprived of their liberty.

It is certain that, following this judgement, many more requests for authorisations under the deprivation of liberty safeguards will be made for people in hospitals or care homes. Since the deprivation of liberty safeguards apply only in hospitals and care homes, it is also certain that many more applications will be made to the Court of Protection for those in domestic settings with support.

The deprivation of liberty safeguards code of practice lists the factors which may indicate a deprivation of liberty: these are still relevant but must now be read in the light of this decision of the Supreme Court.

Read the deprivation of liberty safeguards code of practice: webarchive.nationalarchives.gov.uk/20130107105354/http:/www.dh.gov.uk/en/Publicationsandstatistics/Publications/PublicationsPolicyAndGuidance/DH-085476.

*The Supreme Court has now confirmed that there are two key questions to ask:*

**Is the person subject to continuous supervision and control?** *It is still not clear what exactly this means: but the three cases in the Annex to this guidance show how wide the definition appears to be.*

AND

**Is the person free to leave?** *The person may seem happy to stay, but the issue is about how staff would react if the person did try to leave or if relatives/friends asked to remove them permanently.*

It is now clear that if a person lacking capacity to consent to the arrangements is subject both to **continuous supervision and control** *and* **not free to leave,** they are deprived of their liberty.

It may not be a deprivation of liberty, although the person is not free to leave, if the person is not supervised or monitored all the time and is able to make decisions about what to do and when, that are not subject to agreement by others.

The Supreme Court ruled that the following factors **are not relevant to whether or not someone is deprived of their liberty**:

1.   the person's compliance or happiness or lack of objection;
2.   the suitability or relative normality of the placement (after comparing the person's circumstances with another person of similar age and condition); or
3.   the reason or purpose leading to a particular placement

though of course all these factors are still relevant to whether or not the situation is in the person's best interests, and should be authorised.

If a provider suspects, from the initial care plan or prior knowledge of the person, that someone coming in to their care may be deprived of liberty, the authorisation should be in place before the person arrives. It protects the person's rights; it does not mean they have to restrict the person's freedoms unless they have to do so in the person's best interests.

Whenever a person might lack the mental capacity to make their own decisions about care or treatment, providers must work within the principles of the Mental Capacity Act, for example by doing everything possible to empower people to make as many decisions for themselves as they can.

Care plans for people lacking mental capacity to agree to arrangements for their care or treatment should show evidence of best interests decision-making in accordance with the Mental Capacity Act, based on decision-specific capacity assessments.

In particular, providers should ensure that restrictions on the freedom of anyone lacking capacity to consent to them are proportionate to the risk and seriousness of harm to that person, and that no less restrictive option can be identified. Useful guidance on care planning within an empowering ethos is available in the Mental Capacity Act main code of practice.

Read the MCA code of practice on the Ministry of Justice website: **www.justice.gov.uk/ protecting-the-vulnerable/mental-capacity-act**.

## POINTS TO NOTE, ARISING FROM THIS JUDGEMENT:

(1) *Widening of scope:* The annex to this guidance gives a short account of the cases that were considered by the Supreme Court. These clarify for providers of care to people with learning disabilities the sort of situations that now may come within the definition of deprivation of liberty, but which might not have been recognised as such before the Supreme Court judgement. It is clear, however, from the way the deprivation of liberty safeguards are used already, that the many of the people who might be deprived of their

liberty in their own best interests are older people, often in care homes (currently about 75% of all authorisation requests). Following this judgement, more older people at risk of deprivation of liberty are likely to be identified in domestic settings such as supported living or extra-care housing. They are living with dementia or with acquired brain injury, for example from a stroke, or with neurological conditions such as Parkinson's disease or Huntington's disease; they often have complex health and care needs.

A typical situation that might now fall within the expanded definition of deprivation of liberty is that of an older person with dementia, living at home with considerable support. Staff monitor her well-being continuously at home because she forgets to eat, is unsafe in her use of appliances, and leaves the bath taps running; she is accompanied whenever she leaves her home because she forgets where she lives and is at risk of road accidents or abuse from others. She shows no sign of being unhappy or wanting to live elsewhere, but, in her best interests, she would not be allowed to leave to go and live somewhere else even if she wanted to.

(2) *What is relevant to identifying a deprivation of liberty:* It is essential to separate the question of whether restrictions amount to a deprivation of liberty, in terms of the new Supreme Court test above, from whether staff actions are necessary, proportionate, and in the person's best interests. The former determines whether the situation must be assessed independently: the latter are crucial to deciding whether it will be authorised as being in the person's best interests. The most important step for providers who suspect that they may be depriving someone of their liberty is to reduce restraint and any restriction on the person's freedoms wherever possible.

(3) *In a hospital or care home:* where it seems likely that a person is being deprived of their liberty, and this seems to be in the person's best interests, a referral to the Local Authority deprivation of liberty safeguards team should be made by the provider. If they have not done so even after prompting, a third party, such as a CQC inspector, can contact the local authority directly. If it is apparent that a person lacking capacity to consent to a forthcoming admission to hospital or a care home might be deprived of their liberty, the provider must seek the authorisation in advance of that admission wherever possible.

(4) *In a psychiatric inpatient setting:* clinical staff may want to review the situation of all informal patients who lack mental capacity to consent to admission, and consider if they are deprived of their liberty. If they are at risk of being deprived of their liberty, the first step is to scrutinise the care plan to see if this could be safely altered to reduce the restrictions so there is no longer a deprivation of liberty. If this is not possible then the provider must decide between using the Mental Health Act and the MCA deprivation of liberty safeguards to protect the person's rights. The criteria for deciding between these have not been changed by this judgement. Professionals should not assume one regime is 'less restrictive' than the other. It is the care plan which imposes the restrictions, not the procedural safeguards that are required if these restrictions amount to a deprivation of liberty.

(5) *For all other settings,* such as supported living, adult placement/shared lives or domiciliary care, the deprivation of liberty safeguards cannot be used, so an application must be made to the Court of Protection.

In these settings, care providers (where appropriate, with local authority care managers) should examine the situation of people who lack the mental capacity to agree to their living arrangements, to see if they appear to be deprived of their liberty in the light of the Supreme Court judgement. They may wish to seek legal advice, and liaise with the commissioners of the service, if they think they might be depriving someone of their liberty and cannot find a less restrictive option for providing care or treatment.

**While this is happening, they must continue to provide care and attention to the person.**

(6) *CQC inspectors* must continue to expect providers to work within the law. Inspectors remain an important safeguard of the rights of vulnerable people who use services, and always have the right and duty to take action as they see fit to ensure this. In the very

short term, however, while waiting for further national guidance, it will in many situations be sufficient evidence of providers' attempts and intention to work within the changes brought in by the Supreme Court judgement if they can demonstrate that they are:

- aware of the outline of the judgement, hence reviewing (where appropriate, with care managers or commissioners of their services) situations that might now be brought into the widened definition of deprivation of liberty. The purpose of this review is to assess if the restrictions can safely be reduced or the person's capacity enhanced so that they can make relevant decisions for themselves; *and*
- in discussion with commissioners of services, and as appropriate either liaising with the local authority supervisory body for the deprivation of liberty safeguards or seeking legal advice, as to how to ensure the protection of the human rights of vulnerable people who use services.

(7)  *Providers must notify CQC* of all applications to deprive someone of their liberty, whether through the deprivation of liberty safeguards or by applying to the Court of Protection, and their outcomes.

Read our guidance on notifying deprivations of liberty: **www.cqc.org.uk/sites/default/files/ media/documents/guidance–on–statutory–notifications–asc–ih–pdc–pa–reg–persons– v5.pdf.**

Providers and Inspectors must remember that authorisations under the Mental Capacity Act are NOT transferrable. Those given under the deprivation of liberty safeguards only cover that particular hospital or care home. Court Orders only cover what they say they cover.

*This is not a full statement of law but is designed to help providers and CQC staff understand the practical implications of the Supreme Court judgement.*

## ANNEX: THE EXAMPLES WHICH THE SUPREME COURT DECIDED WERE DEPRIVATION OF LIBERTY

1.  An adult (P) with a learning disability living in a bungalow with two other residents, with two members of staff on duty during the day and one 'waking' member of staff overnight. He requires prompting and help with all the activities of daily living, getting about, eating, personal hygiene and continence. P requires further intervention including restraint to stop him harming himself, but is not prescribed any tranquilising medication. He is unable to go anywhere or do anything without one to one support; he gets 98 hours a week of personal support to enable him to leave the home frequently for activities and socialising.

2.  A 17 year old (Q, or MEG) with mild learning disabilities living with three others in an NHS residential home for learning disabled adolescents with complex needs. She has occasional outbursts of aggression towards the other three residents and then requires restraint. She is prescribed (and administered) tranquilising medication. She has one to one and sometimes two to one support. Continuous supervision and control is exercised so as to meet her care needs. She is accompanied by staff whenever she leaves. She attends a further education unit daily during term time, and has a full social life. She shows no wish to go out on her own, but she would be prevented from doing so in her best interests.

3.  An 18 year old (P, or MIG) with a moderate to severe learning disability and problems with her sight and hearing, who requires assistance crossing the road because she is unaware of danger. She lives with a 'foster mother' (commonly called adult placement, or shared lives) whom she regards as 'mummy.' Her foster mother provides her with intensive support in most aspects of daily living. She is not on any medication. She has never attempted to leave the home by herself and showed no wish to do so, but if she did,

her foster mother would restrain her in her best interests. She attends a further education unit daily during term time and is taken on trips and holidays by her foster mother.